ACHIEVEMENT, STRESS, AND ANXIETY

THE SERIES IN CLINICAL AND COMMUNITY PSYCHOLOGY

CONSULTING EDITORS

Charles D. Spielberger and Irwin G. Sarason

IN PREPARATION

ACHIEVEMENT, STRESS, AND ANXIETY

Edited by
Heinz W. Krohne
University of Osnabrück, West Germany

and

Lothar Laux
University of Mainz, West Germany

● HEMISPHERE PUBLISHING CORPORATION
Washington   New York   London

Distribution outside the United States
McGRAW-HILL INTERNATIONAL BOOK COMPANY
Auckland   Bogotá   Hamburg   Guatemala   Johannesburg
Lisbon   London   Madrid   Mexico   Montreal
New Delhi   Panama   Paris   San Juan   São Paulo
Singapor   Sydney   Tokyo   Toronto

ACHIEVEMENT, STRESS, AND ANXIETY

1 2 3 4 5 6 7 8 9 0   B C B C   8 9 8 7 6 5 4 3 2 1

Library of Congress Cataloging in Publication Data

Main entry under title:

Achievement, stress, and anxiety.

 (The Series in clinical and community psychology)
 Bibliography: p.
 Includes indexes.
 1. Achievement Motivation.   2. Stress
(Psychology)   3. Anixety.   4. Test anxiety.
I. Krohne, Heinz W.   II. Laux, Lothar, date.
[DNLM: 1. Achievement.   2. Anxiety.   3. Stress,
Psychological.   WM172 A178]
BF503.A24   152.4   79-28840
ISBN 0-89116-187-2 (Hemisphere)
ISBN 0-07-035521-2 (McGraw-Hill)
ISSN 0146-0846

Contents

PART IV
ACHIEVEMENT MOTIVATION, CAUSAL ATTRIBUTION, AND ANXIETY

PART V
METHODS IN STRESS AND ANXIETY RESEARCH

Contributors

PETER BECKER, University of Trier, Trier, FRG
CAROL S. DWECK, University of Illinois, Urbana-Champaign, Illinois, USA
HEINZ HECKHAUSEN, University of Bochum, Bochum, FRG
DARLENE L. HEINRICH, Florida State University, Tallahassee, Florida, USA
DAVID HENSHAW, University of Waterloo, Waterloo, Ontario, Canada
NORMAN HIMEL, University of Waterloo, Waterloo, Ontario, Canada
VOLKER HODAPP, University of Mainz, Mainz, FRG
B. KENT HOUSTON, University of Kansas, Lawrence, Kansas, USA
HEINZ W. KROHNE, University of Osnabrück, Osnabrück, FRG
LOTHAR LAUX, University of Mainz, Mainz, FRG
ULF LUNDBERG, University of Stockholm, Stockholm, Sweden
DAVID MAGNUSSON, University of Stockholm, Stockholm, Sweden
JOSEPH E. McGRATH, University of Illinois, Urbana, Illinois, USA
DONALD MEICHENBAUM, University of Waterloo, Waterloo, Ontario, Canada
JOSEF ROGNER, University of Osnabrück, Osnabrück, FRG
WOLFGANG SCHÖNPFLUG, Free University of Berlin, Berlin, FRG
PETER SCHULZ, Free University of Berlin, Berlin, FRG
CHARLES D. SPIELBERGER, University of South Florida, Tampa, Florida, USA
HÅKAN STATTIN, University of Stockholm, Stockholm, Sweden
MANFRED VELDEN, University of Mainz, Mainz, FRG
GERHARD VOSSEL, University of Mainz, Mainz, FRG
BERNARD WEINER, University of California, Los Angeles, California, USA
GEERD WEYER, University of Frankfurt, Frankfurt, FRG
JERI DAWN WINE, Ontario Institute for Studies in Education, Toronto, Ontario, Canada
CAMILLE B. WORTMAN, University of Michigan, Ann Arbor, Michigan, USA

Preface

In our Western societies, stress and anxiety, especially in achievement situations, have become important issues. There is a general concern about the adverse effects of stress and anxiety on academic achievement and other aspects of human behavior.

The purpose of this volume is to describe recent advances in achievement-related stress and anxiety research. The notion of achievement is broadly conceived and encompasses all activities in which individuals know that their performance is being evaluated (by themselves or by others). During the past three decades performance in achievement contexts has been studied from widely discrepant conceptual positions and methodological approaches, including the broad and difficult to define area of research on stress and coping, as well as the more restricted fields of test anxiety, learned helplessness, and achievement motivation and attribution theory. While each of these fields is characterized by significant advances in theory and research, only rarely have attempts at a theoretical integration been made. Hence the present book not only gathers original contributions from the various research fields in order to encourage future research and theory construction (see Chapter 1 for a detailed discussion). In support of this aim special emphasis is given to methodological advances in achievement-related stress and anxiety research, as illustrated by topics such as the unbiased measurement of achievement under stress and the analysis of causal relationships between anxiety and achievement.

The primary focus is on achievement-related stress and anxiety research. Obviously the advances in this specified field cannot be discussed without addressing general problems of theory, methodology, and applications in stress and anxiety research. For that reason several broadly conceived issues (e.g., current definitions of stress or problems of design and measurement) in stress research have been included.

The volume is divided into five parts. Part I is concerned with theoretical and methodological issues. A thematic overview of central topics in the area of achievement-related stress and anxiety research is provided in the first chapter, which is mainly based on the 17 original contributions for this book. In Part II the authors investigate strategies of coping with stress. The conceptualization of stress as imbalance between perceived demand and perceived response capability provides a broad framework to guide research on behavior in evaluative contexts. Anxiety, as well as other negatively toned emotions such as depression or anger, may be conceived of as an outcome of stressful appraisals and coping processes. Part III deals with anxiety as the central emotion elicited in achievement situations. In addition to the discussion of different types and components of anxiety, the relationships between coping dispositions, actual coping processes, and anxiety are investigated. Part IV considers contributions from the areas of achievement motivation and attribution theory. Attempts are made to build a bridge between these theories and the test-anxiety field. Part V is concerned with recent developments of special methods and techniques in stress and anxiety research.

The book is intended primarily for psychologists and students of psychology but will also be useful to educators and social, behavioral, or medical scientists who are concerned with a more comprehensive understanding of the interrelationships among stress, anxiety, and achievement.

The editors would like to express their appreciation to Irwin G. Sarason, professor of psychology, University of Washington, and to Charles D. Spielberger, professor of psychology, University of South Florida, for their encouragement in the preparation and development of this book.

Heinz W. Krohne
Lothar Laux

I

BASIC PROBLEMS

1

BASIC PROBLEMS

1

Theoretical and Methodological Issues in Achievement-related Stress and Anxiety Research

Lothar Laux and Gerhard Vossel
University of Mainz

The basic aim of this chapter is to provide a thematic overview of central topics in the area of achievement-related stress and anxiety research. Another major goal is to highlight the need for a joint consideration of the divergent theoretical approaches in this field. Such approaches include not only different stress and anxiety models but also contributions from achievement theory and attribution theory.

The last four of the seven sections of this chapter pertain to methodology. Especially mentioned are those methodological approaches that may provide an impetus for improvement of future research and theorizing in the field.

Though we focus on the theoretical advances presented in the following chapters of this book, we also refer to other recent developments. In particular this chapter encompasses the substantive issues of the current transactional theory of stress as formulated by Lazarus and his colleagues (Lazarus & Cohen, 1978; Lazarus & Launier, 1978). Of all the scientific terms used in the subsequent chapters, *stress* is by far the broadest and most ambiguous. We therefore start with a discussion of current definitions of stress.

CONCEPTS OF STRESS

In recent comprehensive reviews of the literature three main usages of the concept of stress have been identified and compared: stimulus-based, response-based, and interactional definitions (see Cox, 1978; Laux, in press; Lazarus & Launier, 1978; Mason, 1975a, 1975b; McGrath, 1970a). Each of these categories encompasses quite different approaches.

Stimulus-based approaches may be subdivided into those that explicitly acknowledge the importance of individual appraisals of events and those that ignore such mediating cognitive processes. In Spielberger's Trait-State Anxiety Theory *stress* is used to denote environmental conditions that are characterized by some degree of objective physical or psychological danger (Spielberger, 1972; Heinrich & Spielberger, chapter 7, this volume). In contrast to simplistic S-R models Spielberger assumes that stressful conditions must be appraised as threatening in order to evoke an anxiety reaction. Following this conception of stress, objectively nonstressful situations may be appraised as threatening if a person for some reason perceives them as harmful. On the other hand, objectively stressful situations may be regarded as nonthreatening by certain persons. The actual appraisal of a situation as physically or psychologically dangerous is determined by individual differences in personality dispositions, aptitudes, and personal experience with similar situations in the past that may lead an individual to develop coping skills.

Instead of making a conceptual distinction between stress as an objective condition and threat as the consequence of the appraisal process, other writers prefer to include the subjective appraisal of a situation in the definition of stress. Chan (1977), who views stress as stimuli or situations that severely tap the coping resources, argues that an event becomes stressful only when it is perceived as such.

A rather influential group of writers proposed situation-based stress models that fail to allow for differences in individual appraisals of events. An example is Holmes and Rahe's (1967) original work on stressful life events. The basic assumption behind their life stress approach has been that the amount of readjustment required to cope with life changes, regardless of the desirability of these changes, is associated with the occurrence of illness. Serious doubts have been raised, however, about equating life changes or readjustment with stress (see Hurst, Jenkins, & Rose, 1978; Lazarus & Cohen, 1978; Lazarus & Launier, 1978; Lundberg & Theorell, 1976; Paykel, 1976; Redfield & Stone, 1979; Vossel & Froehlich, 1979). Assigning group-derived standardized scores (Life Change Units) for life change events ignores differences in the way people are influenced by various events. The salient role played by the individual's own appraisal of life changes has convincingly been demonstrated by Lundberg, Theorell, and Lind (1975). They showed that the difference in the psychological amount of life change between a group of myocardial infarction patients and a control group increased with the weight accorded to the individual's own perception of his life changes (see Lundberg in chapter 4 of this volume).

The most popular *response-based definition* of stress has been developed by Selye. He defines stress as the state manifested by a specific syndrome consisting of all the nonspecifically induced changes within a biological system (Selye, 1976). The validity of this nonspecificity concept of stress has been questioned by Mason (1971, 1975a, 1975b), who argues that the nonspecific physiological responses in Selye's General Adaptation Syndrome may largely be a reflection of the ubiquity of emotional arousal. He contends that the conventional physical stressors Selye used (e.g., heat, cold, exercise, fasting) very often elicit psychological reactions related to pain, discomfort, or emotion. When psychological variables are controlled or minimized in the study of physical stimuli, the pituitary-adrenal cortical system is not activated in the nonspecific manner described by Selye.

This specificity view of stress emphasizes the importance of cognitive processes in determining the evocation of different physiological endocrine reactions in different situations. In line with Mason's approach is Lazarus's notion that "Selye has paid attention to the bodily defense processes *after* they have been aroused neuro-humorally, and not to the physiological and psychological signalling system that 'recognizes' the noxious effects or possibilities and distinguishes them from benign events" (Lazarus, 1974, p. 324).

In a reply to Mason, Selye pointed out that in Mason's experimental work the specific actions of the stressors might have inhibited their nonspecific effects (Selye, 1975; Taché & Selye, 1978). Though Selye in many respects still disagrees with Mason's conception of stress, he tends to consider problems of individual perception and interpretation of stimuli in his most recent writings (Taché & Selye, 1978).

Lundberg's contribution in chapter 4 is especially concerned with the problem of stress-related illness susceptibility. Lazarus, Cohen, Folkman, Kanner, and Schaefer (1980) and Mason (1974), who adhere to a specificity view on illness susceptibility, argue that specific stressors are connected via different physiological and endocrine systems to specific illnesses. According to Lundberg the nonspecificity view of stress and illness susceptibility has been supported mainly by studies of the relationship between life changes and onset of illness, while the results of studies on the etiology of coronary heart disease could be taken as evidence for the specificity view.

In the third general approach stress is conceived of as *interaction* of individual and situation. For example, Cox (1978) concludes that stress arises from the existence of a particular relationship between the person and the environment. Interactional approaches to stress have been proposed to overcome the inadequacies of models that define stress *solely* in terms of stimulus or response parameters (see Cox, 1978; Mason, 1975b; McGrath, 1970a, 1976).

Those stimulus-related and response-related models of stress, however, that refer to some appraising, perceiving, or interpreting processes are also examples of an interactional perspective. According to Spielberger, who adheres to a situation-based definition of stress, persons high in A-Trait have a tendency to perceive situations that involve failure or threats to self-esteem as more threatening than persons who are low in A-Trait, and thus they are expected to respond to such situations with A-State elevations of greater intensity. The interactional nature of this approach has been emphasized by Shedletsky and Endler (1974). Also, response models of stress (as, e.g. the threshold model of Cofer & Appley, 1964) emphasize the importance of threat perception and situation-organism interaction in order to understand why stress arises in some exposed individuals and not in others (see also Appley & Trumbull, 1967; Sells, 1970).

Interactional definitions of stress typically emphasize that "stress occurs when there is a substantial imbalance between environmental demand and the response capability of the focal organism" (McGrath, 1970a, p. 17). In this view stress exists in an imbalance between *perceived* demand and *perceived* response capability (see Cox, 1978, for a similar view). Another example for such an imbalance conception may be found in Sarason's theoretical framework for stress research: "Stress follows a call for action when one's capabilities are perceived as falling short of the needed personal resources" (Sarason, 1979, p. 4). In Sarason's model a call for action is issued when either the environment or personal resources identify the need to do something. For Lazarus psychological stress also refers to demands that tax or exceed available resources as appraised by the person involved (Lazarus & Launier, 1978). Schulz and Schönpflug in chapter 3 propose an experimental paradigm for a stress conception based on such a demand-capability imbalance.

In the anxiety and stress literature Endler and Magnusson (1976a) and Lazarus and Launier (1978), among others, have called attention to at least two major and contradictory usages of the term *interaction*. Following the logic of analysis of variance model, interaction has been defined in terms of the interaction of two independent variables (persons and situations) that influence behavior. In contrast to this first type of interaction, which refers to unidirectional causality, the second one focuses upon reciprocal causation; that is, not only does the situation influence behavior but the behavior of an individual is also an active agent in affecting the environment. Pervin (1968) suggested using the term *interaction* for unidirectional causality only and the term *transaction* for reciprocal causation.

In their most recent writings Lazarus and his colleagues adopt Pervin's distinction and strongly argue against the traditional interactional model in stress and anxiety research:

> ... *most or perhaps even* all *adaptive transactions involve two-way cause-and-effect relationships via a complex set of feedback processes. The environment is perceived and interpreted—or as we would put it, appraised—leading to adaptive or coping processes arising out of the person's own personal agendas; the effects of these processes on the environment are also appraised and reacted to in an interplay whose status is constantly changing in a continuous flow. (Lazarus & Cohen, 1978, p. 114)*

Feedback processes that influence the individual's perception of a situation or alter the actual nature of the demand are also central to McGrath's descriptive model of a "stress cycle" in chapter 2.

ADVANCEMENT IN COPING CONCEPTIONS

The concept of coping has grown to such an extent that it now occupies a central place in current theoretical models of stress and emotion (Coelho, Hamburg & Adams, 1974; Lazarus & Launier, 1978; Meichenbaum, 1977). Lazarus even argues that stress as a concept pales in significance compared with coping: "how people cope with stress is even more important to overall morale, social functioning and somatic health than the frequency and severity of the stress episodes themselves" (Roskies & Lazarus, in press).

A simple but useful classification scheme for coping acts was offered by Lazarus (1966). His distinction of two main modes of coping—direct actions and intrapsychic modes—has been adopted by many authors, including the originators of cognitively oriented treatment programs (Meichenbaum, 1977). In chapter 4 Lundberg proposes to add a third category of coping strategies: the effort invested by the individual in counteracting the detrimental effects of stressful stimulation (e.g., noise) on behavior. In principle, a person exposed to distracting stimuli while engaged in mental work can either maintain performance at a constant level by increasing effort or keep his or her effort constant by decreasing performance level. Lundberg's experimental work shows that the former strategy involves higher subjective and physiological costs (see also Glass & Singer, 1972).

One of the factors that may influence the subject's choice of coping strategy is his or her level of aspiration established by prior experience with the task. In chapter 14 Schönpflug points out that the role of aspiration shifts has not been sufficiently recognized in current stress research. It should be emphasized that performance degradation under stress can be interpreted as due not only to impairment of function but also to lowering of aspiration level as well.

Schönpflug's own experimental work focuses on the role of feedback (success and failure) on aspiration level and causal attribution.

Within the framework of his transactional model of stress, Lazarus has recently reorganized and expanded the former classificatory scheme for coping (see Lazarus & Launier, 1978). Of prime interest is the emphasis on the two main functions of coping: *altering the troubled transaction* (instrumental) and *regulating the emotion* (palliative). The intended effect of the instrumental or problem-solving aspect is the alteration of the stressful person-environment relationship. Palliative coping, on the other hand, consists of efforts to manage the somatic and subjective components of stress emotions (e.g., anxiety, anger, depression) without changing the actual person-environment relationship. Examples of palliative coping include attention deployment, taking tranquilizers, or engaging in relaxation techniques. The new scheme for coping classification also takes into account several other factors and distinctions. The important category of *coping modes* includes information seeking, direct action, inhibition of action, and intrapsychic modes. Each of the four modes of coping may be used either for altering the troubled relationship or for regulating the emotion.

Many convergences can be found between the major tenets of the Lazarus theory and the approaches of the cognitive behavior therapists (Beck, 1976; Goldfried, 1977; Meichenbaum, 1977). Most important is the joint emphasis on the central role of cognitive processes in determining the person's emotional response and the mode of coping strategy that will be used to manage it (see Roskies & Lazarus, in press). Meichenbaum, Henshaw, and Himel in chapter 6 review in detail methods to make inferences about cognitive processes based on the assessment of the subject's internal dialogue (i.e., the thoughts and images that precede, accompany, and follow task performance). Such methods as task interruption protocols, videotape reconstruction, and others may be used to assess facilitative and interfering thoughts in achievement situations. These methods have stimulated intervention programs that modify the client's internal dialogue with resultant stress management. In particular the authors highlight the therapeutic value of teaching clients a problem-solving mental set as a key ingredient of the coping process.

According to Lazarus and Launier (1978) previous research in the area of coping has been dominated by a coping trait orientation, while the description of the actual coping processes has been neglected. In such research it is usually assumed that a certain coping trait will be manifested as process in a given stress situation.

Houston (chapter 9) not only attempts to study (cognitive) coping processes as they actually occur in stressful achievement situations but also calls attention to the relation between such coping processes and trait anxiety conceived as a coping disposition. Especially in Eriksen's (1966) explanatory accounts of defensive behavior, anxiety is treated as a coping disposition related to the way individuals respond to or express their anxiety. He hypothesizes high-anxious subjects as those who preferably employ rationalization and intellectualization and low-anxious subjects as those who use avoidance maneuvers (see also Saltz, 1970). Houston's results for two different achievement situations, however, are contrary to this view since he found that high-anxious subjects tend to lack cognitive strategies for coping with stress and instead tend to be self-preoccupied (see Sarason, 1975).

Krohne and Rogner in chapter 8 also deal with the relationship between coping state and coping trait since they conceive repression-sensitization as a personality dimension that is supposed to predict repressive or sensitive coping styles. Krohne and Rogner propose a model in which coping is related to the possibility of controlling information and/or behavior in threatening performance situations. In particular they investigate the influence of repressive or sensitive coping on the anticipation period and on the task-solution period of the performance situation. Their analysis of studies emphasizes the necessity to use state measures of repression and sensitization since the usual trait measures very often proved to be weak predictors of performance under stress. One may conclude with the suggestion that what is needed is to develop state scales that permit one to study coping processes.

TEST ANXIETY, ACHIEVEMENT MOTIVATION, AND CAUSAL ATTRIBUTION

At least three major research areas have addressed the issue of performance in achievement settings: the test anxiety field, the achievement motivation area, and the area of learned helplessness. As Dweck and Wortman point out in chapter 5 there has been relatively little exchange of ideas among these areas. Their paper provides an overview of the theoretical and empirical work in each field. They then compare and contrast the three major research trends, which leads to a description of the strengths and weaknesses that have characterized research and theoretical issues. Most valuable for subsequent research is the authors' identification of central questions raised by a joint consideration of these fields of research. Likewise, our intention in this part is to demonstrate the necessity of building a bridge between test anxiety theory, achievement theory, and attribution theory.

In examining the effects of *test anxiety* on performance in achievement settings, two separate components, namely worry and emotionality, have been proposed (two-component theory of test anxiety, Liebert & Morris, 1967). While worry is marked by cognitive concern about performance (self-focused task-irrelevant cognitions), the emotionality component refers to self-perceived physiological arousal. Wine in chapter 10 concludes that it is the worry or cognitive component that interferes most directly with performance and triggers physiological arousal. Additionally, research has provided support for viewing worry as a stable disposition. Emotionality, however, has a transient quality and is high only during the test period. These formulations of test anxiety clearly emphasize the cognitive component and not the physiological activity evoked by evaluative situations. In line with these conceptions is Sarason's (1978) definition of test anxiety as a cognitive response marked by self-doubt, feelings of inadequacy, and self-blame.

In other formulations of test anxiety, however, the relationship between the emotional and the cognitive component has been reversed. Spielberger, Anton, and Bedell (1976) assume that high levels of state anxiety, which roughly correspond to Liebert and Morris's (1967) emotionality component, activate "task-irrelevant worry responses that distract the test anxious individual from effective task performance" (p. 324). Additionally, it is assumed that state anxiety may activate task-related error tendencies that compete with correct responses (cf. Spence & Spence, 1966). Heinrich and Spielberger (chapter 7) especially deal with the impact of state anxiety on performance. The conceptual framework for their review is provided by the Spence-Taylor Drive Theory and the Trait-State Anxiety Theory. The theoretical expectations with regard to performance on complex learning tasks refer to stress, state anxiety (or drive level) and trait anxiety, and task difficulty. The difficulty of a learning task is supposed to vary as a function of task complexity, stage of learning, the availability of memory support or conceptual aids to learning, and the intelligence of the subject. The conclusion of Heinrich and Spielberger, namely that anxiety and task difficulty have interactive effects on complex learning that are consistent with predictions derived from Drive Theory, challenges Morris and Liebert's (1969) contention that "It is worry, not 'anxiety' which affects performance on intellectual-cognitive tasks" (pp. 243-244). Hodapp's results (see chapter 18), obtained with different methods of causal analysis, do not support the purely cognitive view that worry alone influences educational achievement, but indicate that the emotional components of anxiety are also related to achievement. Future research and theoretical analysis should be addressed to those factors that determine the relative amount of worry and emotionality components of anxiety in stressful achievement situations (see Deffenbacher, in press; Holroyd & Appel, in press, for a fuller discussion).

Until now test anxiety theorists have not considered the advances of *achievement theory* and *attribution theory* in a systematic way. In utilizing concepts and methods from the achievement motivation area, Becker in chapter 13 and Heckhausen in chapter 12 attempt to advance test anxiety theory.

Heckhausen's empirical work on achievement in stress situations focuses on a joint consideration of test anxiety variables and variables of motivation process (e.g., aspiration level, the grade received, the causal attribution of the grade) and motivation state (e.g., success-oriented or failure-oriented motivation). Especially four results deserve notice: (1) As expected by the two-component theory of test anxiety, the examination grades covary with the cognitive but not with the emotional components of the motivation state. (2) Regardless of their frequency, task-irrelevant cognitions are comparatively more disturbing in a failure-oriented than in a success-oriented state of motivation. (3) A close relation between bias in causal attribution and individual differences in motivation was found: Failure-motivated persons are convinced that luck, but not the amount of preparation, influence their grades. (4) When not becoming two dominant, certain types of task-irrelevant cognitions may even exert a facilitative function. These results strongly demonstrate the necessity of including variables of individual motivation as moderator variables in test anxiety research.

Also in Becker's study on "examination fear" and achievement behavior (see chapter 13) cognitive variables (such as the subjective estimate of competence, the subjective probabilities of failing the examination, and the personal importance of failure) turned out to be of substantial importance for the prediction of individual level of fear and the number of points gained in the examination. In addition, level of achievement motivation contributed to fear as well as grade level. While in many studies on test anxiety and achievement behavior the important variables were measured before the examination only once, in Becker's study some variables (including estimated competence and amount of fear of examination) were administered at five points of time prior to the examination. Based on this process-oriented study, two types of examination fear were discovered: inverted U-shaped curves characterizing fear levels of most of the success-oriented students and the monotonous fear increase of the failure-oriented students. These results may be taken as evidence for the fruitfulness of conceiving of examination fear (or test anxiety) as a time-related process demanding repeated measurements in addition to a single occasion trait-oriented research style.

Though it seems trite to point out that anxiety is not the only emotion produced in stressful achievement situations, test anxiety research has neglected the consideration of important emotional reactions not related to anxiety. Weiner's attributional analysis of affective consequences of success and failure in achievement contexts refers to anxiety as well as to other negatively or positively toned emotions (see chapter 11). According to his most recent theorizing, emotions appear to be either outcome or attributionally generated. Given success one feels "good" (feelings of pleasure, happiness, satisfaction) and given failure one feels "bad" (uncheerful, displeased, upset). These general outcome-linked feelings are accompanied by more specific attributionally generated emotions. If success is due to one's ability, pride is elicited; if success is due to others, gratitude is generated. Failure ascribed to interference from others elicits aggression, whereas causal ascriptions of failure to the internal factors of ability and effort generate anxiety-related affects. Depressive affects arise when causal ascriptions are made to internal and stable factors (lack of ability, lack of typical effort).

Such an attributional analysis of emotion has much in common with the cognitive theory of emotions proposed by Lazarus, Averill, and Opton (1971) and more recently by Lazarus, Kanner, and Folkman (1980). This theory states that each specific emotion is generated and guided by its own particular pattern of appraisal:

> Anger, for example, includes the attribution of blame for a particular kind of injury or threat, and guilt also involves such attribution of blame to oneself, with the further implication that one has not only done harm but has acted badly in accordance with personal standards of behavior. These attributions are forms of cognitive appraisal that are more than initial evaluations; they become an ongoing and critical dynamic in the experience of anger and guilt. (Lazarus et al., 1980)

Though Lazarus puts emphasis on the psychodynamics of stress emotions (negatively toned emotions such as fear, anxiety, guilt, sadness-depression, envy, jealousy, anger, etc.), the concept of mediating cognitive appraisal also has relevance for positively toned emotions such as joy, love, exhilaration (see Lazarus, Kanner, & Folkman, 1980). Lazarus's specificity view of emotion is not limited to cognitive appraisals. In speaking of *patterned somatic reaction* he takes the position that each emotion is characterized by a particular physiological response configuration. Such a view is in sharp contrast to those stress and emotion theories that claim that physiological arousal is the same in any emotion (see Holmes & Masuda, 1974; Schachter & Singer, 1962).

PROBLEMS OF CHOOSING ADEQUATE RESEARCH STRATEGIES

This topic is primarily concerned with the question of choosing appropriate settings for stress and anxiety research. Together with the formulation of a transactional model of stress, Lazarus and Launier (1978) strongly argue against the laboratory experiment as an adequate research strategy for studying stress, coping, and their adaptational outcomes. Their arguments can be summarized as follows: (1) Laboratory experiments do not readily provide information about the sources of stress responses in daily life. (2) Laboratory experiments do not provide information about long-lasting effects of stress and coping, since the laboratory experiment is normally a very time-limited event. (3) Practical as well as ethical considerations make it impossible to generate stress reactions as intense as found in real life. (4) The desired laboratory control can often not be achieved, since uncontrolled effects, such as experimenter effects (Rosenthal, 1976) or demand characteristics (Orne, 1962), may be of greater importance than the manipulated stimulus conditions. From this discussion of the disadvantages of the laboratory experiment in stress research, Lazarus and Launier conclude that the study of stress, coping, and their adaptational outcomes must be performed in real-life settings.

The discussion of Lazarus and Launier, however, seems to underestimate the possibilities of the laboratory experiment. A series of studies stimulated by the Trait-State Anxiety Theory (Spielberger, 1972, 1975) suggests that ego-involving achievement situations that do not differ from real-life achievement situations (e.g., examinations) with regard to the intensity of anxiety reactions can be produced in the laboratory. Also McGrath's discussion (see chapter 2) of the problem of choosing appropriate research settings in stress research indicates that Lazarus and Launier tend to underestimate the possibilities of the laboratory experiment and overestimate the advantages of field studies. Thus McGrath convincingly argues that stress must not necessarily be at maximum strength in real-life settings, since the strength of any stress condition is not under perfect control of the researcher, and since persons in natural stress situations may already have successfully attenuated the effects of stress by coping processes. Furthermore, real-life settings may simply be changed by the use of highly reactive and obtrusive operations in the research process. Finally, even ethical problems may be greater in real-life research, since it may well be that an experimenter is obliged to help attenuate negative effects of stressful situations if there is a possibility of preventing persons from severe harm.

Summarizing the discussion on research strategies, McGrath concludes that both strategies—field research and laboratory experiment—bring with them inevitable costs and potential benefits. This detailed analysis by McGrath indicates that the discussion of Lazarus and Launier on research strategies is rather biased in favor of field studies. Furthermore, it should be mentioned that Lazarus and Launier do not take into account the various possibilities of an *interplay* between laboratory experiment and real-life research. Thus field studies may allow the formulation of hypotheses that can be examined in controlled laboratory experiments; on the other hand, predictions derived from laboratory research can be tested in natural settings (e.g., Glass & Singer, 1972). A good example of such an interplay between naturalistic field investigation and laboratory experiment is given in the work of Schulz and Schönpflug in chapter 3 on regulatory activity during states of stress. In order to investigate the effects of noise, uncertainty, and evaluative feedback on various performance measures, the authors started with a detailed analysis in an industrial setting that led to the construction of experimental tasks simulating the most important features of the field setting. On the basis of the results of the laboratory experiment, another field study was performed leading to a modified experimental approach (Schönpflug, 1979). This alternation between field study and laboratory experiment can be continued until convergence of results allows the formulation of a theory that adequately describes similar paradigms in very different settings, as, for example, in classroom settings.

The work of Houston (chapter 9) also demonstrates the advantages of combining both research strategies. In one of his studies on the relationship between trait anxiety and cognitive behaviors for coping with stress, two different settings (laboratory versus classroom) were selected. This made it possible to evaluate the consistency of results across different situations and to arrive at more confident conclusions about the generalizability of the findings.

DESCRIPTION AND CLASSIFICATION
OF STRESSFUL SITUATIONS

One of the principal problems in stress and anxiety research has been the production of realistic stressful situations. As a survey of the literature shows, a variety of techniques to induce stress has been tried in the past. This variety of methods has probably led to considerable confusion, since it is very likely that each of these techniques has a somewhat different effect upon achievement, physiological, and subjective stress responses (e.g., Lazarus, Deese, & Osler, 1952). In order to classify these divergent stress situations, several broad subdivisions have been proposed: for example, failure-induced versus task-induced stress (Lazarus et al., 1952) or ego threat versus physical threat (Saltz, 1970, 1971; Shedletsky & Endler, 1974; Spielberger, 1972). Classification systems that use more than two categories have been proposed by Cofer and Appley (1964), Janke (1969, 1974), Lazarus and Cohen (1978), and Prystav (1979), among others. McGrath in chapter 2 presents a more elaborated *a priori classification system* of stressful situations. After reviewing about 200 stress studies he identifies the following types of stressor conditions: physical threat, ego threat, and interpersonal threat (cf. McGrath, 1970b). Each of these three stress-inducing conditions can either involve the actual or the anticipated impingement of the threatening event. Furthermore it is possible, as McGrath concludes from his review, that physical threat, ego threat, or interpersonal threat can also be induced by the constriction or the deprivation of certain kinds of stimuli, conditions, or events.

While such a priori classification systems are useful to classify the variety of stressful conditions already studied, it also seems necessary to develop *empirically derived classification systems* in order to clarify the dimensions of situations that produce different stress reactions and thus to improve predictions of behavior in different stressful settings. This need for systematic analyses of situations has been especially emphasized in connection with the growing research on person-by-situation interactions (e.g., Endler & Magnusson, 1976b; Magnusson & Endler, 1977). However, as Magnusson and Stattin note in chapter 15, systematic empirical analyses of stressful situations are rare, although most researchers in the field of stress and anxiety accept an interactional or transactional point of view. In their review of the literature on empirical analyses of stressful situations Magnusson and Stattin—in agreement with most theoretical formulations of stress and anxiety—clearly favor a *subjective situation approach*, that is, an approach that refers to the person's perception and construction of the physical and social environment. Three fundamental methods are proposed to describe situations in this approach: (1) the perceptual approach, which describes and categorizes the subjective situation in terms of the cognitive-perceptual appraisal and construction of the situation; (2) the reaction approach, which is based on the person's spontaneous reactions; and (3) the action approach, which describes the situation in terms of manifest, molar behavior. For each of these three fundamental methods, existing instruments are presented and methodological problems are discussed.

Weyer in chapter 16 describes some examples of situation perception inventories. In particular, Weyer's chapter is concerned with questionnaires designed to measure job stress as a function of person-situation interaction. After discussing theoretical and psychometric properties of several inventories, the validity of the Job-related Subjective Pressure and Dissatisfaction Scales by Weyer, Hodapp, and Neuhäuser (in press) is evaluated in terms of its relationship to other questionnaires designed to measure similar variables, environmental and personality variables, coping variables, and diastolic blood pressure.

CAUSAL ANALYSIS IN STRESS
AND ANXIETY RESEARCH

In chapter 18 Hodapp not only presents a detailed empirical analysis of causal relationships between anxiety and educational achievement but also gives an overview of available causal analytic methods. Among other things, he describes recursive systems and path analysis and their connection with covariance selection; moreover, questions related to panel analyses and nonrecursive systems are raised. The increasing availability of these methods, which allow one to infer causal relationships from nonexperimental data with some justification, also has important implications for theoretical formulations of stress. As already mentioned, Schulz and Schönpflug (chapter 3, of this volume) and Lazarus and Launier (1978) recently presented transactional models of stress. In particular, Lazarus and Launier emphasize in this context the distinction between interactional and transactional models (i.e., models of unidirectional causation versus models of reciprocal causation) and strongly argue against interactional models in stress theory and research. They underline instead the need for transactional formulations, which are—according to their view—more adequate for the study of stress, coping, and their adaptational outcomes. However, as Endler and Magnusson (1976a, p. 13) note, one of the reasons why theories and empirical research based on transactional models have been less advanced in the past is that the methodology and technology to examine reciprocal causation have not yet been fully developed. Hodapp, in connection with his discussion on nonrecursive systems, points to some methods (mainly developed within the field of econometrics) that allow the analysis of reciprocal relationships and feedback loops and thus provide the possibility for examing recent transactional formulations of stress by more adequate means (see also James & Singh, 1978). Moreover, the increasing availability of methods like these should encourage researchers in the field of stress and anxiety to formulate models that are based on the concept of reciprocal causation (see Bandura, 1978).

RESPONSE BIAS IN STRESS
AND ANXIETY RESEARCH

In general terms, response bias or response strategy can be defined as a tendency of a person to favor a particular response regardless of the stimulus characteristics. Examples of response bias would be the tendency to answer "yes" to a questionnaire item regardless of the item content or the tendency to avoid false-positive responses in a vigilance experiment (i.e., saying "yes" when actually no critical signal had been presented). The problem of response bias first arose within the context of classical psychophysics where it was largely resolved by means of signal detection theory (Green & Swets, 1966), which allows the isolation of the effects of response bias from a person's ability to detect signals or to discriminate between stimuli. Velden in chapter 17 starts with a short description of the rationale of signal detection theory before discussing the relevance of this approach in stress and anxiety research. From a review of applications of the signal detection theory approach he distinguishes between (1) measurement of achievement under stress conditions and (2) measurement of stress and anxiety states.

As to the application of signal detection theory to the *measurement of achievement under stress conditions*, it is concluded that this approach offers a useful tool because achievement scores, unaffected by response bias, can be obtained. Thus it is possible to investigate the effects of stress on achievement and response strategy independently. Since most studies designed to examine theoretical formulations about relationships between stress and/or anxiety and achievement did not use unbiased performance measures, the conclusions drawn from these studies must be considered very carefully. This is because the theoretically predicted relationships between stress and/or anxiety and achievement may at least be attributable in part to the effects of stress and/or anxiety on response strategy; Velden illustrates this in connection with the Spence-Taylor theory of anxiety and the results of Clark and Greenberg's (1971) study of the effects of stress and knowledge of results on performance in a recognition memory task, which was analyzed by signal detection theory. This discussion indicates that the application of the signal detection theory approach to the measurement of achievement under stress may well question the adequacy of existing theoretical formulations and may thus contribute to a revision of theories of stress, anxiety, and achievement in future times.

The second application of signal detection theory to stress and anxiety research is concerned with the *measurement of stress and anxiety states*. One of the main goals is to control the effects of response sets, such as acquiescence or social desirability (cf. Wilde, 1977), and thus to obtain unbiased measures of emotional states. Although several methods are already available to measure response sets in order to assess their influence in other tests (e.g., Edwards Social Desirability Scale, Crowne-Marlow Social Desirability Scale, Cough-Keniston Acquiescence Scale), the generality of these methods seems to be rather limited because they are not free of the influence of content (Zuckerman & Lubin, 1965, p. 18). Since most theories of stress and anxiety emphasize the importance of subjective processes (e.g., Cofer & Appley, 1964; Lazarus, 1966; Lazarus & Launier, 1978; McGrath, 1970a, chapter 2 of this volume; Sarason, 1975; Spielberger, 1972; Wine, 1971, chapter 10 of this volume) and, consequently, heavily rely on subjective measurement techniques, a pure measure of response bias, as it is provided by a straight-forward application of signal detection theory, would be very useful. Based on the formal analogy between the ratings commonly used to measure emotional states and the signal detection theory paradigm, therefore, several attempts have been made to apply signal detection theory in order to isolate the effects of response set from measures of emotional states such as depression (Clark, Kurlander, Bieber, & Glassman, 1977), anxiety (Chapman & Feather, 1971), or experienced aversiveness (Neufeld, 1975). For example,. Neufeld examined the effects of an intellectualization-denial passage designed to modify cognitive appraisal of stressor stimuli (gory scenes) on subjective reports of aversiveness. From the results analyzed by signal detection theory Neufeld concludes that the passage led to reduction of "felt stress" for certain stimuli, while there was no rise in criterion for reporting stress. Moreover, the tendency on the part of the repressers to report less stress was related to the amount of "felt stress" rather than to a distortion of the actual amount of stress in the verbal report.

However, as Velden points out, the application of signal detection theory to obtain unbiased measures of stress and anxiety states still holds grave methodological problems because subjects are able to make a *stimulus contingent bias*, a possibility that is not considered within the signal detection theory approach. Velden's discussion of this problem should therefore serve as a warning when interpreting the results of studies that apply signal detection theory to the measurement of emotional states, since the possibility of a contingent choice of criterion can actually lead to wrong conclusions about subjects' mood.

REFERENCES

Appley, M. H., & Trumbull, R. On the concept of psychological stress. In M. H. Appley & R. Trumbull (Eds.), *Psychological stress: Issues in research*. New York: Appleton-Century-Crofts, 1967.

Bandura, A. The self-system in reciprocal determinism. *American Psychologist*, 1978, *33*, 344–358.

Beck, A. T. *Cognitive therapy and the emotional disorders*. New York: International Universities Press, 1976.

Chan, K. B. Individual differences in reactions to stress and their personality and situational determinants: Some implications for community mental health. *Social Science and Medicine*, 1977, *11*, 89–103.

Chapman, C. R., & Feather, B. W. Sensitivity to phobic imagery: A sensory decision theory analysis. *Behavior Research and Therapy*, 1971, *9*, 161–168.

Clark, W. C., & Greenberg, D. B. Effect of stress, knowledge of results, and proactive inhibition on verbal recognition memory (d') and response criterion (L_X). *Journal of Personality and Social Psychology*, 1971, *17*, 42–47.

Clark, W. C., Kurlander, K., Bieber, R., & Glassman, A. H. Signal detection theory treatment of response set in mood questionnaires. In C. D. Spielberger & I. G. Sarason (Eds.), *Stress and anxiety* (Vol. 4). Washington, D.C.: Hemisphere, 1977.

Coelho, G. V., Hamburg, D. A., & Adams, J. E. (Eds.), *Coping and adaptation*. New York: Basic Books, 1974.

Cofer, C. N., & Appley, M. H. *Motivation: Theory and research*. New York: Wiley, 1964.

Cox, T. *Stress*. London: Macmillan, 1978.

Deffenbacher, J. L. Worry and emotionality in test anxiety. In I. G. Sarason (Ed.), *Test anxiety: Theory, research, and applications*. Hillsdale, NJ: Erlbaum, in press.

Endler, N. S., & Magnusson, D. Personality and person by situation interactions. In N. S. Endler & D. Magnusson (Eds.), *Interactional psychology and personality*. Washington, D.C.: Hemisphere, 1976. (a)

Endler, N. S., & Magnusson, D. (Eds.). *Interactional psychology and personality*. Washington, D.C.: Hemisphere, 1976. (b)

Eriksen, C. W. Cognitive responses to internally cued anxiety. In C. D. Spielberger (Ed.), *Anxiety and behavior*. New York: Academic Press, 1966.

Glass, D. C., & Singer, J. E. *Urban stress: Experiments on noise and social stressors*. New York: Academic Press, 1972.

Goldfried, M. R. The use of relaxation and cognitive relabeling as coping skills. In R. B. Stuart (Ed.), *Behavioral self-management: Strategies, techniques, and outcome*. New York: Brunner/Mazel, 1977.

Green, D. M., & Swets, J. A. *Signal detection theory and psychophysics*. New York: Wiley, 1966.

Holmes, T. H., & Masuda, M. Life change and illness susceptibility. In B. S. Dohrenwend & B. P. Dohrenwend (Eds.), *Stressful life events: Their nature and effects*. New York: Wiley, 1974.

Holmes, T. H., & Rahe, R. H. The Social Readjustment Rating Scale. *Journal of Psychosomatic Research*, 1967, *11*, 213–218.

Holroyd, K. A., & Appel, M. A. Test anxiety and physiological responding. In I. G. Sarason (Ed.), *Test anxiety: Theory, research, and applications*. Hillsdale, NJ: Erlbaum, in press.

Hurst, M. W., Jenkins, C. D., & Rose, R. M. The assessment of life change stress: A comparative and methodological inquiry. *Psychosomatic Medicine*, 1978, *40*, 126–141.

James, L. R., & Singh, B. K. An introduction to the logic, assumptions, and basic analytic procedures of the two-stage least squares. *Psychological Bulletin*, 1978, *85*, 1104–1122.

Janke, W. Methoden der Induktion von Aktiviertheit. In W. Schönpflug (Ed.), *Methoden der Aktivierungsforschung*. Bern: Huber, 1969.

Janke, W. Psychophysiologische Grundlagen des Verhaltens. In M. v. Kerekjasto (Ed.), *Medizinische Psychologie*. Berlin: Springer, 1974.

Laux, L. Psychologische Stresskonzeptionen. In H. Thomae (Ed.), *Handbuch der Psychologie. Allgemeine Psychologie* (Vol. 2). *Motivation* (2nd ed.). Göttingen: Hogrefe, in press.

Lazarus, R. S. *Psychological stress and the coping process*. New York: McGraw-Hill, 1966.

Lazarus, R. S. Psychological stress and coping in adaptation and illness. *International Journal of Psychiatry in Medicine*, 1974, *5*, 321–333.

Lazarus, R. S., Averill, J. R., & Opton, E. M. Towards a cognitive theory of emotion. In L. Levi (Ed.), *Society, stress and disease* (Vol. 1). *The psychosocial environment and psychosomatic dieseases*. London: Oxford University Press, 1971.

Lazarus, R. S., & Cohen, J. B. Environmental stress. In J. Altman & J. F. Wohlwill (Eds.), *Human behavior and the environment*. New York: Plenum, 1978.

Lazarus, R. S., Cohen, J. B., Folkman, S., Kanner, A., & Schaefer, C. Psychological stress and adaptation: Some unresolved issues. In H. Selye (Ed.), *Guide to stress research*. New York: Van Nostrand, 1980.

Lazarus, R. S., Deese, J., & Osler, S. F. The effects of psychological stress upon performance. *Psychological Bulletin*, 1952, *49*, 293–317.

Lazarus, R. S., Kanner, A., & Folkman, S. Emotions: A cognitive-phenomenological analysis. In R. Plutchik & H. Kellermann (Eds.), *Theories of emotion*. New York: Academic Press, 1980.

Lazarus, R. S., & Launier, R. Stress-related transactions between person and environment. In L. A. Pervin & M. Lewis (Eds.), *Perspectives in interactional psychology*. New York: Plenum, 1978.

Liebert, R. M., & Morris, L. W. Cognitive and emotional components of test anxiety: A distinction and some initial data. *Psychological Reports*, 1967, *20*, 975–978.

Lundberg, V., & Theorell, T. Scaling of life changes: Differences between three diagnostic groups and between recently experienced and non-experienced events. *Journal of Human Stress*, 1976, *2*(2), 7–17.

Lundberg, V., Theorell, T., & Lind, E. Life changes and myocardial infarction: Individual differences in life change scaling. *Journal of Psychosomatic Research*, 1975, *19*, 27–32.

Magnusson, D., & Endler, N. S. (Eds.). *Personality at the cross-roads: Current issues in interactional psychology*. Hillsdale, NJ: Erlbaum, 1977.

Mason, J. W. A reevaluation of the concept of "non-specificity" in stress theory. *Journal of Psychiatric Research*, 1971, *8*, 323–333.

Mason, J. W. Specificity in the organization of neuroendocrine response profiles. In P. Seeman & G. Brown (Eds.), *Frontiers in neurology and neuroscience research*. Toronto: University of Toronto, 1974.

Mason, J. W. A historical view of the stress field. Part I. *Journal of Human Stress,* 1975, *1*(1), 7–12. (a)

Mason, J. W. A historical view of the stress field. Part II. *Journal of Human Stress,* 1975, *1*(2), 22–36. (b)

McGrath, J. E. A conceptual formulation for research on stress. In J. E. McGrath (Ed.), *Social and psychological factors in stress.* New York: Holt, Rinehart and Winston, 1970. (a)

McGrath, J. E. Settings, measures, and themes: An integrative review of some research on social-psychological factors in stress. In J. E. McGrath (Ed.), *Social and psychological factors in stress.* New York: Holt, Rinehart and Winston, 1970. (b)

McGrath, J. E. Stress and behavior in organizations. In M. D. Dunnette (Ed.), *Handbook of industrial and organizational psychology.* Chicago: Rand McNally, 1976.

Meichenbaum, D. *Cognitive-behavior modification: An integrative approach.* New York: Plenum, 1977.

Morris, L. W., & Liebert, R. M. Effects of anxiety on timed and untimed intelligence tests. *Journal of Consulting and Clinical Psychology,* 1969, *33,* 240–244.

Neufeld, R. W. J. Effect of cognitive appraisal on d' and response bias to experimental stress. *Journal of Personality and Social Psychology,* 1975, *31,* 735–743.

Orne, M. T. On the social psychology of the psychological experiment: With particular reference to demand characteristics and their implications. *American Psychologist,* 1962, *17,* 776–783.

Paykel, E. S. Life stress, depression, and attempted suicide. *Journal of Human Stress,* 1976, *2*(3), 3–12.

Pervin, L. A. Performance and satisfaction as a function of individual-environment fit. *Psychological Bulletin,* 1968, *69,* 56–68.

Prystav, G. Die Bedeutung der Vorhersagbarkeit und Kontrollierbarkeit von Stressoren für Klassifikationen von Belastungssituationen. *Zeitschrift für Klinische Psychologie,* 1979, *8,* 283–301.

Redfield, J., & Stone, A. Individual viewpoints of stressful life events. *Journal of Consulting and Clinical Psychology,* 1979, *47,* 147–154.

Rosenthal, R. *Experimenter effects in behavioral research.* New York: Appleton-Century-Crofts, 1976.

Roskies, E., & Lazarus, R. S. Coping theory and the teaching of coping skills. In P. Davidson (Ed.), *Behavioral medicine: Changing health life styles.* New York: Brunner/Mazel, in press.

Saltz, E. Manifest anxiety: Have we misread the data? *Psychological Review,* 1970, *77,* 568–573.

Saltz, E. *The cognitive bases of human learning.* Homewood, IL: Dorsey, 1971.

Sarason, I. G. Anxiety and self-preoccupation. In I. G. Sarason & C. D. Spielberger (Eds.), *Stress and anxiety* (Vol. 2). Washington, D.C.: Hemisphere, 1975.

Sarason, I. G. The Test Anxiety Scale: Concept and research. In C. D. Spielberger & I. G. Sarason (Eds.), *Stress and anxiety* (Vol. 5). Washington, D.C.: Hemisphere, 1978.

Sarason, I. G. *Life stress, self-preoccupation, and social supports* (Tech. Rep. SCS-LS-008). Arlington, VA, 1979.

Schachter, S., & Singer, J. E. Cognitive, social and physiological determinants of emotional state. *Psychological Review,* 1962, *69,* 379–399.

Schönpflug, W. Regulation und Fehlregulation im Verhalten. *Psychologische Beiträge,* 1979, *21,* 174–202.

Sells, S. B. On the nature of stress. In J. E. McGrath (Ed.), *Social and psychological factors in stress.* New York: Holt, Rinehart and Winston, 1970.

Selye, H. Confusion and controversy in the stress field. *Journal of Human Stress,* 1975, *1*(2), 37–44.

Selye, H. *The stress of life* (rev. ed.). New York: McGraw-Hill, 1976.

Shedletsky, R., & Endler, N. S. Anxiety: The state-trait model and the interaction model. *Journal of Personality,* 1974, *42,* 511–527.

Spence, J. T., & Spence, K. W. The motivational components of manifest anxiety: Drive and drive stimuli. In C. D. Spielberger (Ed.), *Anxiety and behavior.* New York: Academic Press, 1966.

Spielberger, C. D. Anxiety as an emotional state. In C. D. Spielberger (Ed.), *Anxiety: Current trends in theory and research* (Vol. 1). New York: Academic Press, 1972.

Spielberger, C. D. Anxiety: State-Trait-process. In C. D. Spielberger & I. G. Sarason (Eds.), *Stress and anxiety* (Vol. 1). Washington, D.C.: Hemisphere, 1975.

Spielberger, C. D., Anton, W. D., & Bedell, J. The nature and treatment of test anxiety. In M. Zuckerman & C. D. Spielberger (Eds.), *Emotions and anxiety. New concepts, methods, and applications.* Hillsdale, NJ: Erlbaum, 1976.

Taché, J., & Selye, H. On stress and coping mechanisms. In C. D. Spielberger & I. G. Sarason (Eds.), *Stress and anxiety* (Vol. 5). Washington, D.C.: Hemisphere, 1978.

Vossel, G., & Froehlich, W. D. Life stress, job tension, and subjective reports of task performance effectiveness. In I. G. Sarason & C. D. Spielberger (Eds.), *Stress and anxiety* (Vol. 6). Washington, D.C.: Hemisphere, 1979.

Weyer, G., Hodapp, V., & Neuhäuser, S. Weiterentwicklung von Fragebogenskalen zur Erfassung der subjektiven Belastung und Unzufriedenheit im beruflichen Bereich (SBUS-B). *Psychologische Beiträge*, in press.

Wilde, G. J. S. Trait description and measurement by personality questionnaires. In R. B. Cattell & R. M. Dreger (Eds.), *Handbook of modern personality theory.* Washington, D.C.: Hemisphere, 1977.

Wine, J. Test anxiety and direction of attention. *Psychological Bulletin*, 1971, *76*, 92–104.

Zuckerman, M., & Lubin, B. *Manual for the Multiple Affect Adjective Check List.* San Diego: Educational and Industrial Testing Service, 1965.

2

Methodological Problems in Research on Stress

Joseph E. McGrath
University of Illinois, Urbana

Research on stress has available to it the same array of research strategies, data collection methods, and data analysis techniques as does research on any other problem area within the behavioral sciences. It therefore falls heir to the same array of nasty and seemingly intractible methodological problems that beset research throughout the behavioral sciences. It is not so much the case that stress research poses new and different methodological problems as that research on stress makes certain methodological problems even more salient and more difficult to handle than they usually are. So this chapter will concentrate on the methodological problems to which stress research is especially vulnerable. It must be noted that these are by no means the only methodological problems with which stress researchers need be concerned.

In this chapter I will present a conceptual framework that defines the context of stress research, discuss several important clusters of methodological issues, and present a general strategy for simultaneously and systematically dealing with several of those clusters of methodological issues.

A CONCEPTUAL FRAMEWORK FOR ANALYSIS OF STRESS RESEARCH

It is now trite to comment that *stress* is a much used and much misused term in the behavioral science literature. Many researchers (e.g., Appley & Trumbull, 1967; Cofer & Appley, 1964; Kahn, 1970; McGrath, 1970; Sells, 1970; Weitz, 1970) have commented upon the frequency and imprecision of use of the term. At the editor's request I include here a definition borrowed from an earlier chapter (McGrath, 1976), even though I prefer to define *stress research* and leave the rubric, stress, undefined: "there is a potential for stress when an environmental situation is perceived as presenting a demand which threatens to exceed the person's capabilities and resources for meeting it, under conditions where . . . (the person) . . . expects a substantial differential in the rewards and costs from meeting the demand versus not meeting it" (McGrath, 1976, p. 1352).

By and large this chapter will be limited to consideration of stress in the context of person-to-person behavior, which I will call social-psychological stress (see McGrath, 1970, p. 4). That term is intended to mean roughly what Cofer and Appley (1964, p. 441) mean by psychological as distinct from systemic stress, and what Lazarus (1966) means by psychological and sociological, as distinct from physiological, levels of stress. But, as Lazarus (1966) has argued, the distinction has to do not so much with the classes of measures to be considered as with the manner in which they will be interpreted. For example, physiological data (such as GSR) will be regarded as evidence of psychological and social-psychological states or processes (e.g., arousal) rather than as a basis for investigation of the physiological processes and mechanisms that underlie those indexes. Similarly, purely physical variables (e.g., cold, noise) will be dealt with as antecedent conditions contributing to social-psychological events. In short, all factors involved in the stress event cycle will be interpreted from a social-psychological perspective.

Some Propositions about Stress

Although empirical research on social-psychological factors in stress has been relatively inconclusive to date, one can induce several general themes or propositions from that research literature that are worth noting. Six such themes, all of which have received some empirical support, are presented here.[1] These six themes are not unequivocally supported in the literature; and they certainly do not constitute the basis for a fully articulated theory. But they may serve as a useful set of working hypotheses; and some of them raise important methodological problems for the area.

Theme 1: Cognitive Appraisal

Subjectively experienced stress depends on the person's perception and interpretation of the "objective" or external stress situation.

Theme 2: Experience

An individual's familiarity with the situation, past exposure to the stressor conditions, and/or prior practice or training in responses to deal with the situation can influence his or her level of subjectively experienced stress.

Theme 3: Reinforcement

An individual's past successes and failures in a given type of situation can operate to reduce or enhance, respectively, the level of subjectively experienced stress for that individual in that type of situation. (This is an extension of Theme 2.)

Theme 4: The Inverted U

At low levels of subjectively experienced stress (arousal), task performance is poor; increases in stress up to some level (a level that is optimal for a particular individual regarding performance of a particular task) enhance task performance; further increases in stress beyond that optimal level lead to performance decrements. (For contrary evidence for at least some classes of stress settings, see McGrath, 1976).

---

[1] For further discussion of these themes and references to research evidence about them, see McGrath, 1970. The list is paraphrased from McGrath, 1976.

Theme 5: Task Differences

The relationships among subjectively experienced stress, task performance, and ensuing consequences depend on type of task and how that task relates to the stressor conditions being investigated. (See Hackman, 1970, and McGrath, 1976, for elaboration of task-based stress effects.)

Theme 6: Interpersonal Effects

Presence and activities of other persons in the situation may influence the subjective experience of stress and may also influence responses to stress and the consequences of these responses. These influences may operate in several partially conflicting ways. Presence of other people may increase arousal level. Other people may be sources of potential affiliative, self-esteem, and other interpersonal rewards (see Kahn & French, 1970). Other people may also be sources of potential irritation and antagonism, especially when exposure is for long periods of time and/or under conditions in which the focal person does not fully control when and with whom those interactions will take place. The focal person's task performance may be directly and/or indirectly helped or hindered by other people who are interdependent with focal person with respect to task performance. Some of these effects may operate to increase arousal, some to reduce it. Some may modify task performance and its consequences independent of arousal levels. How strongly each of these functions operates in a given situation depends on the task structure and interpersonal composition of that situation.

Descriptive Model of a Stress Cycle

A stress situation begins with some set of circumstances in the sociophysical environment. It becomes a stress situation for a given individual (the focal person) if he or she perceives it as leading to some undesirable state of affairs if left unmodified (or to some desirable state of affairs if modified). This holds whether or not that perception is veridical. The focal person then "chooses" some response alterative(s) (including escape or inaction) and executes that response with the intention of changing his or her relation to the situation (in a favorable direction). That response does in fact have *some* consequences, both for the focal person and for the situation, though not necessarily the intended ones.

This description views a stress situation as a *four-stage, closed-loop cycle*. These four stages are connected by *four linking processes*, which provide the substance for the study of stress. Figure 1 presents a visual representation of this four-stage model. The link between stage A (the objective situation) and stage B (the perceived situation) is what Lazarus (1966) has called "cognitive appraisal," what Hackman (1970) has called redefinition, and what will here be called simply the *appraisal process*. Appraisal can result in the experience of stress or threat, as a subjective state.

The second process link, between stage B and stage C, is a *decision-making process*. It involves relating the situation (as perceived) to the available alternatives and "choosing" a response or set of responses intended to modify the situation. Lazarus (1966) has used the term "secondary appraisal" to refer to this

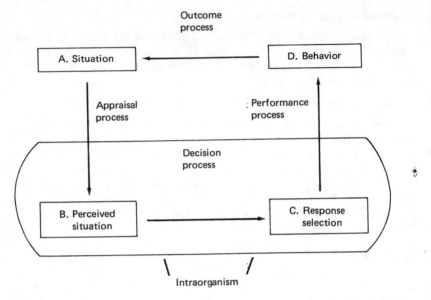

Outcome
process

A. Situation   ←────────────   D. Behavior

Appraisal   Performance
process   process

Decision
process

B. Perceived   ────────→   C. Response
situation   selection

Intraorganism

Figure 1   A representation of the stress event cycle.

process. The operation and effectiveness of this process will depend on (1) the outcome of the prior appraisal process and (2) the focal person's past experiences, current state (e.g., fatigue), response repertoire, and available resources.

The third link, between stage C (response selection) and stage D (behavior) is the response process or *performance process*. Effectiveness of that performance depends on ability, task difficulty, and the performance standards against which it is compared.

The fourth link, between stage D (behavior) and stage A (the objective situation) is the *outcome process*, representing the effects of the behavior of the focal person on the situation. This link is often ignored. The extent to which the focal person's behavior results in desired or undesired changes in the situation (link 4) depends not only on the focal person's level of performance but also on several other factors not under his or her control, notably: (1) the performance level and timing of behavior of others in the situation, both those in facilitative interdependence with the focal person (teammates) and those in competition with the focal person (opponents); (2) the nature, strength, and certainty of the behavior-situation linkage.

The outcome link has often been ignored, and to do so poses both substantive and methodological problems. Laboratory studies often arrange conditions so that the behavior-to-situation (or outcome) link is assured to be perfect ($r = 1.00$) in order to study the performance link or the decision link. In this way the "cycle" of behaving system becomes, in the laboratory experiment, the stimulus-response sequence of a trial. Field studies, on the other hand, often ignore the distinction between performance and outcome, tending to state hypotheses about performance (link 3, the relation of response choice to behavior), but to test them by observing the combined (and confounded) double link of performance and outcome (relation of response choice to situation effect). If outcomes are influenced by other factors (e.g., actions of teammates and opponents and chance), then such a strategy gives very low-grade information about both the performance link and the outcome link.

In the present framework there might well be different functional relations for stress at each of the links. One would expect a positive linear relation for the first link (from objective situation to perceived situation): the greater the real demand of the situation, the greater the perceived demand, other things being equal. But this relation must be viewed as quite imperfect, to the extent that individual factors (e.g., experience) affect the appraisal process. Moreover, the individual has to care about meeting the demand (i.e., the consequences) before there will be stress.

The second link (from perceived situation to response selection) might well relate to stress either positively or negatively, depending on other conditions. Zajonc's (1965) work on social facilitation suggests that increased arousal functions so as to make the response hierarchy even more hierarchical, thereby making well-learned responses even more dominant over less well-learned ones. If the best learned responses are the "right" ones, such stabilizing of the response hierarchy would enhance the effectiveness of the response choice. But if the best learned responses are not correct (from the point of view of the investigator), results will likely be scored as poor performance (of the "right" response). Perhaps one of the reasons why experience seems to modify stress (or the effects of stress) is that prior practice in appropriate responses makes them more likely to be selected under arousal conditions.

It is the third link (from response selection to behavior) to which the inverted U function would seem to apply if it applies at all. The rationale here is that a moderate amount of arousal would enhance the quality of performance because of its activating effect (cf. Scott, 1966) but that further increases in arousal would degrade performance, presumably because of the interference of fear or anxiety or disorganization. But the better learned the chosen response (stage C) the better it will be executed (stage D). Hence, considering what was said about link two, this might lead to better performance when the best learned responses are correct and poorer performance when they are not correct, rather than to a U-shaped function. This very crucial third link is the focus of continuing controversy (see McGrath, 1976).

For the fourth or outcome link we can posit no general expected relation. The shape of the outcome relation depends in large part on factors in the situation: whether outcome success is entirely dependent on the focal person's performance level or also on that of others, whether the effect of the focal person's behavior is influenced by chance, and the like. Each of these may represent a different functional relation.

The themes listed earlier therefore can serve as guiding hypotheses only if we first spell out where each theme fits within the four-stage framework, that is, which process link(s) it affects. Stress research has not always done so. For example, studies supporting the "experience" theme have not always been clear about whether past experience is expected to affect the appraisal process (i.e., lead to less subjectively experienced stress), the response selection process (i.e., increase the probability of selecting the correct response), or the performance process (i.e., increase the quality of performance, perhaps by increasing ability), or two or all three of these processes.

The same lack of precision regarding locus of effect could be noted with regard to much of the evidence supporting the other five themes, especially the inverted U hypothesis. Clarification of these matters is one major conceptual problem facing this area, and it is in some respects tied to some of the methodological problems to be considered later in this chapter.

AN ANALYSIS OF THE STRESS LITERATURE FROM A METHODOLOGICAL VIEWPOINT

A great range and diversity of methodological approaches have been used in the study of stress. This section presents classifications and brief discussions of (1) types of research settings used in the study of stress and, from these, some underlying types of stressor conditions; and (2) types of measures of stress response or stress effects and some of the limitations of each of those types of measures.[2] This much-condensed tour of the methodological terrain of the stress research field provides the foundation for a more systematic discussion of certain fundamental methodological problems, which will be the topic of later sections of the chapter.

Types of Research Settings and Types of Stressor Conditions

Studies in the stress research literature can easily be classified on the basis of whether the research was done in real-life settings or in experimentally contrived settings. The crucial distinction here is not what data collection methodology was used (that is, whether it was a laboratory experiment or a correlational or field study), but rather how the study situation fit into the ongoing life of the focal person(s). In effect it is the answer to the question: Is the focal person in the situation mainly (or merely) in order to be in an experiment or is the situation an integral part of his or her ongoing life?

Studies of stress, done either in real-life settings or in experimentally contrived ones, can be further subdivided into a number of classes based on the nature of the situation or condition(s) giving rise to the stress.

Seven such classes for *studies done in real-life settings* are:

Type 1: Studies of stress in combat situations or in hazardous military training (e.g., survival training, parachute training, simulated hazards in normal training situations).

Type 2: Studies of stress in isolated work and living sites (e.g., the arctic, isolated military bases, submarines, Sealab).

Type 3: Studies of stress in involuntary internment and custody (e.g., prisons, concentration camps, refugee camps).

Type 4: Studies of stress resulting from community disasters (e.g., floods, tornadoes).

---

[2] Much of the material in this section is drawn from prior research, which involved a systematic review of over 200 books and articles dealing with stress research. Some of that prior work is reported in McGrath (1970, ch. 5). For further detail and for documentation of studies fitting various categories of these classifications, see that source.

Type 5: Studies of stress resulting from person disasters, so-called life stresses (e.g., crippling accidents or illnesses, surgery, loss of loved ones, divorce).

Type 6: Studies of stress in occupational settings and in formal evaluation settings (e.g., tests, hiring interviews).

Type 7: Studies of stress arising from the individual's general sociocultural context (e.g., poverty, slum or ghetto residence, cultural deprivation).

The following list gives three such classes, each with major subclasses, for *studies done within experimentally contrived situations*:

Type 1: Studies of stress based on manipulation of physical stimuli or conditions
   a. Reactions to painful stimuli (actual, threatened, or vicarious) (e.g., shock, lacerations, injections).
   b. Effects of conditions or agents that alter sensorimotor processes (e.g., drugs, sleep deprivation, visual or auditory stimulation or distraction).
   c. Effects of restricted physical environments (e.g., sensory deprivation, perceptual impoverishment, physically constraining environments).

Type 2: Studies of stress based on manipulation of psychological and social-psychological conditions
   a. Evaluation threat.
   b. Task failure.
   c. Social reinforcement anomalies (e.g., limitations of social interactions, presence/absence of pleasant/permissive atmosphere, interpersonal disagreement, conformity pressures).
   d. Role- and status-based stress (e.g., role conflict, role ambiguity, status incongruence).
   e. Vicarious stress based on anxiety-arousing stimuli whose content implies socioemotional rather than physical threat (e.g., discussion of emotionally arousing materials).

Type 3: Studies of stress based on manipulation of task-inherent conditions
   a. Decision-making and risk-taking tasks, where presumed stress lies in the decision itself.
   d. Task parameters (e.g., complexity, ambiguity, conflicting or non-discriminable cues, time pressure) in which the presumed stress lies in the difficulty of the task.
   c. Dull and repetitive tasks.

While this classification of stress studies, in real-life and in experimentally contrived settings, is really just a loose taxonomy, it suggests certain underlying types of stress-inducing conditions. First, a number of the categories seem to involve stress based on actual or anticipated physical injury, pain, or death—a *physical threat* to the intact organism. Second, many of the categories seem to involve stress based on actual or anticipated injury or pain to the psychological self (e.g., negative self-evaluation because of task failure)—*ego threat*, as distinct from physical threat. A third form of stress seems to involve the actual or anticipated disruption of social relationship—*interpersonal threat*.

While these three types of stress all involve the actual (or anticipated) impingement of a threatening object, condition, or event, studies in some of the categories involve a type of stress that has to do with constriction, deprivation, or lack of certain kinds of stimuli, conditions, or events. This lack can have to do with deprivation of physical needs (e.g., sleep deprivation, constricted movement); deprivation of psychological needs (e.g., lack of varied stimulation); or deprivation of interpersonal needs (e.g., restricted interaction, social isolation). Thus there are three types of *deprivation* stress (physical, psychological, and interpersonal). This classification of types of stressor conditions is shown in Table 1.

These types of stress are not totally independent classes of events to be sure. Some situations of grave physical threat may also contain ego and interpersonal threat. Studies of stress in combat, for example, suggest that loss of self-esteem and threat of loss of interpersonal esteem are major sources of stress in what is basically a physical threat situation. Some stress situations may represent deprivations (underloads) in some respects and overloads in other respects. For example, some studies of isolated sites indicate that stress arises both from the physical and psychological deprivations and from the interpersonal over-stimulation of continual, enforced, extensive contacts with the same small set of others. Indeed studies done in real-life settings frequently involve relatively high levels of several of these forms of stress. Studies done in experimentally contrived settings, of course, usually attempt to involve only one form of stress in the interest of precision and interpretability (and, incidentally, usually involve only relatively moderate levels of stress for both practical and ethical reasons).

These distinctions between different forms of stress can serve as focal concepts (classes of stressor conditions) when we examine methodological problems later in the chapter. Their *comparability* as conditions inducing stress is one key question. To what extent are there similar effects from stress as represented by an electric shock or threat of an injection compared to stress as represented by auditory distraction, failure on a performance task, or threat of failing an examination? To the extent that research findings show convergence of effects over these different forms of stress (or, for that matter, over some other set of types of stress), to that extent are we justified in considering them as in some sense "the same thing" and in seeking general theoretical formulations about social-psychological stress. To the extent that research findings do not show convergence over these (or other) different forms of stressor conditions,

Table 1 A classification of types of stressor conditions with examples of each

Nature of the stressing agent	Role of the stressing agent in the situation		
	Actively impinging	Anticipated	Constraint/Deprivation
Physical	Shock	Anticipated shock	Physical isolation, confinement
Psychological	Task failure	Evaluation threat	Isolation from sensory inputs
Interpersonal	Feedback about disagreement	Fear of inter-personal rejection	Social deprivation

then we must take seriously the idea that we have included several empirically and theoretically distinct phenomena under our broad rubric *stress*.

A Catalog of Some Indexes of Stress Response

Thus far we have been dealing with the input side, or antecedent conditions involved in stress research situations. Equally important is the matter of different measures of stress response or stress effects and of the convergence of empirical findings (or lack of such convergence) across different types of measures.

Indexes used to measure stress response, or the direct effects of stress, can be categorized in terms of two facets as indicated in Table 2. The first facet has to do with the functional level, or system level, that the measure is presumed to reflect. The second facet deals with the operational procedures used to collect the data.

There are four readily discernible system levels used in measures of stress. One is the *physiological* level having to do with body functions and conditions. The second is the *psychological* level, having to do with cognitive, emotional, and motivational functions and conditions. The third is the *task behavior* level, having to do with overt responses of the organism in relation to instrumental aspects of the setting. The fourth is the *interpersonal behavior* level, having to do with overt responses of the individual to the social aspects of the environment. In principle, one can postulate a group, organization, or larger *social system* level of measures of stress response. But in fact very few stress studies use measures at such macrosystem levels. Studies of macrosystems most often use measures that are averages or comparable aggregations of individual measures (for an exception, see Haas & Drabek, 1970).

For the second facet of this classification of stress response indexes, dealing with the operations or methods used in obtaining the measure, the categories and terminology follow Webb, Campbell, Schwartz, and Sechrest (1966). Major classes are: subjective reports (questionnaires, ratings, and so forth); observations (with or without instruments); trace measures (indexes of accretions or erosions); and analysis of archival records (documents, production records, and so forth). These four classes of measures have been used with different frequencies for stress response indexes at the different functional levels, but in principle all are applicable for measures at all levels.

Table 2 gives examples of the types of indexes of stress that fit within each of the four levels for each of the four operational forms. This section presents a discussion of the particular strengths and weaknesses of measures of each type and some of the methodological problems they raise for the stress research enterprise. (For more detail and documentation of these categories of stress indexes, see McGrath, 1970.)

Indexes of Physiological Properties

Subjective reports. Somatic symptom checklists are often used in studies of sensory restriction and social isolation, but otherwise subjective report measures are seldom used for physiological indexes of stress. The other three operational forms—observation, trace measures, and archival records—are all used with considerable frequency.

Observation measures. Direct visual observation of external signs of stress are

Table 2   A classification of indexes of stress response

System level of measure	Operational form of measure			
	Subjective reports	Observations	Trace measures	Archival records
Physiological	Somatic symptom checklists.	Direct observations of physical tension. Instrumental measures of physiological processes (e.g., GSR, EEG).	Biochemical analyses of body products (e.g., blood, urine).	Medical records of physical disorders.
Psychological	Personality tests (e.g., MMPI, Taylor MAS). Checklist/direct report of stress (e.g., SSS)	Direct observations of psychological disturbance (e.g., stammer, hostility). Task-performance measures of psychological decrement.	Content analyses of projective tests (e.g., TAT).	Medical-psychiatric records of psychological disturbance.
Task performance	Questionnaires/interviews re task performance evaluation, level of aspiration, etc.	Observation of performance effectiveness on setting relevant tasks.	Analysis of group decision, task products.	Production records, supervisor evaluation, academic achievement records.
Interpersonal behavior	Questionnaire/interview re role perceptions, interpersonal relations.	Observation of interpersonal behavior (e.g., Bales IPA).	Analysis of group structure, role changes.	Records of interpersonal discord, group structure, etc.

Note. This table is adapted from Table 5–1 in McGrath, 1970.

occasionally used. Most observational measures at the physiological level, however, use relatively sophisticated biomedical instruments. The most common are measures of electrical conductivity of the skin, galvanic skin response (GSR). GSR actually subsumes a family of measures that vary in location on the body, parameters of conductivity used (e.g., resistance, conductivity, change in resistance), whether time-specific or general level potentials are used, and the temporal relation of the measure to experimental events. (Indexes that measure amount of sweat or number of active sweat glands, PSI or related measures, are conceptually related to GSR but are trace measures in terms of the present classification.) Other measures, in order of decreasing frequency of use in stress research, include: measures dealing with the cardiovascular system (pulse rate, heart rate, blood pressure, etc.); measures of respiration (rate and/or volume); measures of electrical activity of the brain; and measures of body temperature.

Virtually all of these measures have serious problems of reliability. Most reflect a wide range of differences among individuals, unrelated to specific stressor conditions, and an equally wide range of differences within the individual, related to diurnal cycles or other temporal or environmental conditions orthogonal to specific stressors. These problems require elaborate design controls and counterbalancing, as well as careful calibration of the instruments themselves. Moreover, some of these measures (GSR, pulse rate, perhaps others) are probably vulnerable to testing or reactivity effects (see Webb et al., 1966); that is, the measurement procedures themselves alter the levels of the properties that they measure. There is a considerable lack of convergence, or correlation, among these measures (see Mandler, Mandler, Kremen, & Sholiton, 1961; Holtzman & Bitterman, 1956). This is not surprising, since each of these reflect complex and specific physiological processes sensitive to many ongoing body functions and environmental conditions. But since all these have been used as indexes of the effects of stress, such lack of convergence poses substantial conceptual and methodological problems for stress research. The lack of convergence of multiple measures that are presumed to measure the same thing (namely, effects of stress) is a problem that will recur in several different aspects throughout the rest of this chapter.

Trace measures. The most commonly used trace measures at the physiological level are biochemical analyses of body products, usually blood cells and plasma, and urine (e.g., accretion levels of eosinophils, corticosteroids, adrenaline products, ATP, sugar, cholesterol, CO_2, free fatty acids). These trace measures are less likely to be vulnerable to reactivity effects than are observations or subjective reports. But they are accretions (or erosions) over time; many require sizable portions of time for substantial accretions to occur. Hence they are more useful in studies involving more macrotemporal intervals (e.g., effects of prolonged exposure to combat conditions). In contrast, observational measures of ongoing physiological processes (e.g., GSR, pulse rate) are more useful in studies of short time intervals (e.g., cue-to-onset anticipation intervals). These trace measures also do not correlate highly with one another, as they would be expected to do if each were a valid index of generalized stress. Nor do they correlate very highly with observational measures of physiological processes, but that is not surprising in view of the temporal differences noted.

Archival records. This class of measures has included medical reports of occurrence and severity of a number of symptoms and diseases thought to be at least partially caused, or aggravated, by stress (e.g., ulcers and related alimentary disorders, arthritis). These measures reflect long-run consequences rather than more immediate effects of stress. They can enter stress research in either of two roles: as prestudy measures used as independent or control variables, and as dependent variables measuring long-run consequences of major stress situations. In the latter capacity such measures are usually compared for populations undergoing different circumstances (e.g., persons in occupational roles with high versus low conflict, as in Kahn, Wolfe, Quinn, Snoek, & Rosenthal, 1964). Such archival records are fairly invulnerable to reactivity effects but are quite vulnerable to content, population, and observer biases and restrictions (see Webb et al., 1966). And archival records, even more than trace measures, are limited to studies involving macrotemporal contexts. They are also subject to some of the problems of effects of extraneous variables discussed for observational measures, since there are presumably many causal influences for disorders such as ulcers or arthritis, and some of them are probably unrelated to environmentally based stressor conditions. But archival records of this kind are in a sense ultimate criteria, involving indexes of permanent, irreversible tissue damage. As such, their importance and validity cannot be contested.

Indexes from archival records are also not highly correlated with one another, but this is to be expected if we consider ulcers and allergies as alternative and substitutable reactions to stress. The idea that multiple measures of stress ought to represent alternative (equipotential) response patterns, rather than convergent measures of the same thing, is also applicable to indexes using the other operational forms (subjective reports, observations, trace measures). The possibility of there being alternative, differential response patterns to the same stressor poses even more complex and difficult methodological problems than the already demanding need for multiple convergent measures of stress. This issue will be the subject of discussion later in this chapter.

Indexes of Psychological Properties

Subjective reports. This class of measures includes two distinctive types. The first, *trait* measures, are presumed to be relatively stable and enduring properties of the individual (e.g., anxiety, stress-proneness) and are usually measured by means of subscales from standardized personality tests (e.g., MMPI, Edwards, Bell, Taylor MAS). Such trait measures represent indexes of properties of the individual rather than of the individual-situation interaction, and as such their use in stress research has mostly been in the role of independent or control variables. The second type of subjective report measures at the psychological level, *state* measures, reflect the subjective stress accruing from the interaction of the individual and the situation and include: self-report of symptoms (e.g., hallucinations, delusions, etc.) and direct ratings of situation anxiety or related properties (e.g., fear, guilt).

Both types of subjective reports are especially vulnerable to reactivity effects. The respondent is aware that he or she is being tested, and responses are likely to be affected by the social-psychological demands of that situation. But since our four-stage conceptualization of the stress cycle hinges on the concept of subjectively experienced stress, it seems crucial that our measures include some direct reports of the individual's threat experience in the situation of concern— preferably *along with* measures using other operational forms and system levels (e.g., physiological level of observations of arousal).

Observation measures. While there have been a few uses of direct observation of signs of psychological stress (e.g., blushing, fidgeting), most measures in this category are indexes of psychological process inferred from performance of especially inserted tasks. Some comment is needed to clarify why such measures are placed here rather than under the task behavior level. Many stress studies make subjects perform certain tasks (e.g., digit-symbol substitution, perceptual recognition) at crucial points in time as a device for obtaining a measure of the deterioration of some psychological process. These involve measures of overt behavior on a task. Nevertheless, they are interpreted here as indexes at the psychological level. Such tasks are not relevant to the stressor conditions, nor are they indigenous to the setting. They are merely "instruments" inserted into the situation as a means for measurement of some psychological process. As such they are analogous to giving the subject a questionnaire. On the other hand, when a study involves performance of a task indigenous to the setting (e.g., completing an assigned mission) and/or that directly pertains to a stressor condition (e.g., learning a discrimination to turn off a shock), measures of these task performances are, of course, classified as at the task behavior level.

A very wide range of measures of psychological function, inferred from such imposed tasks, have been used in stress research. They include measures of shifts in visual, auditory, and tactual thresholds; latency and errors in recall of stress-relevant stimulus material; decrements in cognitive functioning (e.g., learning, short- and long-term memory, problem solving, reasoning); and decrements in performance of psychomotor tasks (e.g., pursuit rotor).

Measures based on direct observation of symptoms of psychological stress are vulnerable to observer biases, often involving considerable inference. Indexes inferred from performance of inserted tasks minimize vulnerability to such observer effects. But they are vulnerable to reactivity effects because the very nature of this procedure imposes a kind of artificiality even on studies done in real-life settings. Consider the combat pilot, just back from a dangerous mission, who is asked to perform a pursuit rotor task or an anagrams problem! We can scarcely assume that he will take the matter very seriously.

These measures also pose some very difficult conceptual problems. What are the psychological functions that, when degraded, are evidence of stress or of its effects? Should we expect them *all* to show decrements for *any* stressor condition? Or are these decrements more or less mutually exclusive alternative reactions to stress (the problem of alternative response patterns again)? Furthermore, it is likely that there are vast interindividual and intraindividual differences in these psychological processes, quite apart from the effects of stress on them. This raises for these measures the same problems noted above in regard to differential stability-lability of physiological indexes.

Trace measures. There are apparently no true trace measures of stress at the psychological level, but there are what might be called quasitrace measures in the form of projective tests. For example, the subject may be asked to write a story to a TAT picture. The investigator later scores that story in terms of aggression, discomfort-relief, anxiety, or the like. This is not a true trace measure because the subject knows he or she is performing in an experiment. But it does share some of the features of trace measures since the attributes on which responses are to be scored are generally unknown to the respondent, and those attributes are somewhat a by-product of the performance being deliberately produced. For example, the subject may be instructed to write a creative story, although the investigator will later score that story with respect to aggression or anxiety. In any case, there has been very limited use of such measures in stress studies.

Archival records. There has been only limited use of medical-psychiatric records of symptoms of psychological disturbance or of psychological functioning (e.g., ability or achievement tests). When used they are usually in the role of independent variables in relation to some other class of stress measure (e.g., differential performance of neurotics vs. normals on easy vs. difficult tasks).

Indexes of Task Behavior

Subjective reports. The measures in this class include self-report indexes of level of aspiration, own task ability, and the like. They represent the more or less direct assessment of perceptions of demands, and perceptions of demand-capability imbalances, that are crucial in the four-stage conceptual model of the stress problem. As with other subjective report measures, these are vulnerable to reactivity effects.

Observation measures. Measures of this class include indexes of speed, quality, accuracy (or error), or success in performance of setting-relevant tasks (e.g., radio repair, or escape, in appropriate hazardous military training situations). These are usually obtained by direct observation, though sometimes cameras, tape recorders, or other specialized sensing devices are used. These measures are relatively nonreactive, provided the measurement operations are carried out so that they are relatively unobtrusive in the setting. But they are vulnerable to content biases and restrictions (see Webb et al., 1966).

Trace measures. Task behavior indexes seldom are trace measures. Analysis of group decisions or other task products can be considered quasitrace measures that have the same strengths and weaknesses as quasitrace measures at the psychological level.

Archival records. This class of measures includes production records, supervisor ratings gathered for administrative rather than research purposes, and academic achievement records. These measures pose problems of content and population restrictions (see Webb et al., 1966). They are especially vulnerable to contamination from extraneous variables, since many things besides situational stress play a part in industrial production or academic achievement. Like other archival records they require long-duration studies. They leave a large gap between impact of stressor and ultimate consequences and thus tell us nothing about the experience of stress or about the processes involved in coping with stress.

Indexes of Interpersonal Behavior

Subjective reports. The measures in this class include self-report indexes of subject perceptions of the interpersonal milieu (e.g., perceived role conflict, ambiguity, or overload; perceptions of power and attraction in the group). These, along with subjective reports of task behavior, are crucial to examination of results of the appraisal process in the stress cycle; but, like other subjective report measures, they are highly vulnerable to reactivity effects.

Observation measures. Measures in this class include indexes of type and amount of communication, territoriality behavior, influence behavior, and expressions of positive and negative affect. These are usually obtained by direct observation, with the observer utilizing some standard set of observation categories. These, of course, pose problems of observer bias and reliability, which are more or less stringent depending on the level of inference required by the category system. They also pose the same kinds of conceptual and methodological problems as raised for observation measures at the psychological level: Just what are the parameters of interpersonal relationships that are affected by stressor conditions? How do those effects vary over individuals? and How are those effects mediated by the individual's perceptions, expectations, and capabilities?

Trace measures. As with indexes at the psychological and task behavior level, trace measures are seldom used as indexes of stress at the interpersonal behavioral level. Some studies using later analyses of "products" that are evidences of group structure or of interpersonal communication might qualify as trace or quasitrace measures. (For a good example of use of such measures, see Clore, Bray, Itkin, & Murphy, 1978).

Archival records. For stress research this is virtually an empty class. It would be exemplified by the use of records or documents to develop indexes of interpersonal discord, or communication rate, or the like. Records of participation in extracurricular activities in an educational setting or in extra work activities in a job setting, might be some exemplars of the class. Such indexes would have the same potential advantages and suffer the same vulnerabilities as indexes derived from archival records at the other functional levels.

Concluding Comments

This section has offered a brief tour of some of the main methodological aspects of the stress research area. It provides a fairly representative picture at one level, although it of course does not reflect many complex and subtle aspects of stress research. But even this brief picture should make it clear that the voluminous work done under the stress rubric, considered collectively, poses some serious substantive and methodological problems for researchers in that area. The next section presents a brief discussion of four clusters of methodological problems that are relatively pervasive within stress research.

SETTINGS, VALUES, TIME, AND MEASUREMENT: FOUR CLUSTERS OF METHODOLOGICAL PROBLEMS IN STRESS RESEARCH

Keeping in mind the conceptual and substantive picture of stress research presented in the first section, and the methodological catalog of stress research presented in the second section, we can now address directly several major clusters of methodological problems more or less endemic to stress research. The first of these has to do with the selection of appropriate settings for conducting stress research. In part this is the familiar "lab versus field" question, but in the case of stress research it is somewhat more complex than that. A second cluster of methodological problems is related to the value-laden nature of stress—the term, the concept, and the body of theory associated with the research—and how that value-toning affects the way stress research is done and interpreted. A third cluster of methodological problems stems from the crucial role that various temporal factors play in the occurrence of and reaction to stress and in the conduct and interpretation of stress research. A fourth cluster has to do with a complex array of problems of design and measurement. These revolve around the convergent validity of stress measures, the comparability of stressor conditions, and individual difference factors within stress research studies. Each of these four clusters of methodological problems will be discussed in relatively brief form here. Then the last section presents a strategy for systematic attack on the fourth of these clusters.

Problems Related to Choosing Appropriate Research Settings

In any empirical research, selection of a laboratory or a field research setting involves a trade-off of realism versus precision and control. That trade-off is present, of course, in the case of stress research; but in the stress area the issue is further complicated by several somewhat special circumstances.

First of all, the existence and degree of the phenomenon being studied, stress or arousal, depends on the individual's interpretation of the situation. (Note that in our discussion of some propositions about stress the substantive themes 1, 2, and 3, and the first process link in the stress event cycle all involve the individual's interpretation of the situation.) Therefore experimental realism is even more important than is usually the case. If the subject sees the situation as unreal or just a game, in many cases it would not be appropriate to talk about the existence of a stress condition at all. For example, a number of studies in the stress literature deal with laboratory tasks in which the stressfulness hinges on on the subject being motivated to try to do the task well. If subjects see the task as trivial, the idea that they are "aroused" or "activated" or "stressed" by increasing the difficulty of the task, or by giving failure feedback, or by increasing or decreasing the number of points that can be won is simply not to be taken seriously.

It is also the case, of course, that the laboratory scientist cannot impose very high degrees of intensity of conditions on subjects—both because it would be unethical to do so and because the scientist usually does not have strong stressor conditions under his or her control.

But stress is not always at maximum strength in natural settings either. For one thing, the strength of any stressor conditions is not under control of the researcher. Hence it is hard to know in advance that it will or will not be at some particular level on a given occasion. But even more importantly, natural systems and the populations in them tend to be mutually selective, so to speak. The level of ambient stress in real and ongoing systems tends (virtually by definition) to stay within bounds that are tolerable for the sets of people who continue in that setting. Those levels may or may not be high enough to provide a high-stress condition for comparison against a control condition. It is by no means the case that natural settings always have higher intensity stress conditions than laboratory situations. Often the participants have already successfully attenuated the effects of stress: they have coped it out of the situation, so to speak.

Nor is the experimenter without ethical problems when he or she works in the field setting. If it is a field experiment, of course, the investigator has the same ethical problems that would exist for a lab experiment, though probably in stronger form because the field experiment is probably dealing with a stronger manipulation. If the study is a so-called natural experiment, in which one group is going to get a stress condition from some source other than the experimenter, the investigator may have some obligation to help attenuate negative effects of such stressful conditions (if indeed they are inevitably "bad"). If there is to be a control condition or no-stress comparison group, then it must be possible to avoid the stressor condition; and therefore the researcher must decide whether or not it is ethical to stand by and permit "it" to happen to the experimental group (if "it" is bad).

Presumably a researcher working in the field is trying to maximze realism of the situation for the participants. But the realism of the situation can be dissipated a great deal by the use of highly reactive or obtrusive operations within what would otherwise be both a realistic and a stressful situation. Examples of obtrusive operations that spoiled an otherwise realistic situation were mentioned earlier: use of a pursuit rotor task immediately after return from a dangerous bombing mission; and use of a stress questionnaire for individuals who had been led to believe that they were about to crash in an airplane.

So while the natural setting offers the *possibility* of a more natural level of motivation and a stronger manipulation of stress, it does not always provide such high levels of stress. Furthermore, its potential realism may be attenuated by reactive elements of the research process; and realism is always purchased dearly, in terms of a sacrifice of precision and control, compared to what could have been obtained in the laboratory. All strategies—field and lab—bring with them certain inevitable costs and potential benefits. Whichever choice the researcher makes, one must make sure to reap the potential benefits of the chosen strategy, because one surely will reap the costs associated with that strategic choice.

Problems Arising from the Value-laden
Nature of the Stress Concept

The stress research area is one in which the value positions of the researchers seem to have a profound effect. First of all, the very term *stress* is perjorative, at least in its connotations in English. By the very choice of the word *stress*, researchers have in effect asserted that the phenomenon they are studying is bad. (There are several quasisynonyms though, such as *activation, arousal, challenge,* that have neutral or good connotations.) Since stress is bad, then the object of the enterprise must be to learn ways to get rid of it. Hence we have concepts like stress resistant (a good thing to be), stress prone (a bad thing to be), adaptation and coping (good things because they "get rid of" stress).

If instead the researchers in this area were studying *challenge* or *activation* or some other "good" term, we might think that the object of the enterprise was to keep it and/or get more of it. Being stress prone now becomes being motivated; adaptation becomes habituation; coping becomes decay of motivation or some such concept. In such a case it is not unlikely that the theories and research paradigms of the area also would be modified.

One of the strongest theoretical propositions in the stress area (strong in terms of its widespread belief and staunch defense, though not necessarily in terms of its empirical support) is the hypothesized inverted U relation between stress level and task performance. Its theoretical base seems to be that task performance is low at low levels of stress because of low activation/drive/motivation; and that performance is low at very high levels of stress mainly because "it stands to reason" that if you increase stress enough performance will deteriorate. But the latter only "stands to reason" because our choice of terms has led us to conclude in advance that "it"—stress—is a bad thing. If the term were *motivation,* or *challenge,* or *activation,* I doubt if it would stand to reason that increasing it *must* eventually lead to deterioration. It is my opinion that the evidence supporting the U-shaped curve is highly equivocal; and that the inverted U relation has become true by assumption largely because of the perjorative nature of the concept labels used in the stress area.

There is another somewhat subtler form in which the researcher's values alter the concepts and procedures invoked: the researcher's choices of criteria. If we assume that stress is bad and coping with it is good, then we should note that sometimes what is effective coping for a person is stress-producing for a larger system of which that person is a part, and vice-versa. For example, when a person is faced with a difficult and stress-producing task and performs it well (presumably at a cost), the larger unit has effectively coped; if instead the person simply avoided the task—yielding a stress-producing situation for the larger unit because the task remains unaccomplished—the person may well have coped more effectively from a personal point of view. Besides this difference in terms of system level of the criterion focus, there also can be a difference regarding whether the criterion will take a short-term or long-term focus. In the above example, for instance, by avoiding the difficult or noxious task the person may have a successful short-run solution (from his or her point of view though not from the larger unit's point of view) but might well have a very unsuccessful long-run solution even from that person's point of view (for example, if failure to do the task got that person fired or caused the power plant to explode). In all these cases the researcher imposes some value judgments to decide whose stress is to be reduced at whose expense—whose axe is to be ground, whose ox is to be gored.

Problems Arising from the Crucial Role of Temporal Factors

Temporal factors play an important role in the stress event cycle in several ways, and those temporal factors have been largely ignored in stress research. First of all, as noted earlier, the stress cycle is itself a dynamic and time-based process. Within that stress cycle are a number of factors operating at what might be called a microtemporal level. Among these are: anticipation intervals (from cue to onset of stress), duration of (stressing) stimulus, expected duration of that stimulus, duration of situation (or of person's presence in it), expected duration of person's presence in situation, time intervals involved in the interruption of whatever activity was ongoing before the introduction of a stress stimulus, and the like.

In addition there are a number of facets of the stress event cycle that reflect more or less macrotemporal aspects. Among these are such matters as the person's past experience with the stimulus, the situation, and the response; the person's level of maturation; and time intervals involved in the operation of coping mechanisms. It is useful to view some activities as anticipatory coping (such as what happens during intervals when an S is anticipating onset of a stressor but has not yet received it) and others as reactive coping (such as what the person does after receiving the stressor). Furthermore, some coping activities are immediate—like lifting your finger from a hot stove—and others take substantial time to bring about—like developing an ulcer. Moreover, it seems useful in some contexts to talk about certain kinds of events or structures as representing preventive coping. For example, there is some indication in studies of isolated pairs that early development of clear territorial patterns was a device that helped some pairs prevent later interpersonal conflict (Altman & Lett, 1970). We can consider various aspects of coping as laid out on a temporal continuum, from preventive coping long before the event, to anticipatory coping just before the event, to reactive coping just after the event, to delayed reactive coping long after the event. There are other major explanatory concepts within the stress area, in addition to coping, that have important temporal aspects; for example, learning, adaptation, adjustment, and fatigue.

There are also some important temporal aspects involved in the measurement of stress, as was noted earlier. Some measures reflect small and immediate (microtemporal) segments of time (e.g., individual GSR spikes); others reflect stress response over longer time intervals (e.g., task performance scores). In some cases important time lags exist between the event producing the stress and the availability of the measure of stress. Blood or urine deposits would be a case in point; so would the development of an ulcer. In other cases the measure has an important time-decay function (e.g., GSR readings), which may or may not be reflecting a similar time-decay function for the stressor condition being assessed.

All these temporal considerations deserve attention, but temporal factors have received very little attention in the stress area (and, to be sure, throughout many areas of social psychology). Not only is there a need for more long-term and longitudinal studies of stress and its effects, but there is also a pressing need for conceptual work to clarify these and other temporal aspects and relate them to one another. The last section of this paper touches upon these problems slightly, although it largely deals with some of the design and measurement problems that are described next.

Problems of Design and Measurement

There are, of course, a host of problems of design and measurement in the stress area, just as there are in other areas of study. Certain of these problems seem to take on an especially virulent form in the case of stress research. These problems derive from the substantive and methodological state of the field as presented in the beginning of this chapter.

One recurring theme has been the *importance of establishing convergent and discriminant validity of stress measures* (see Campbell & Fiske, 1959). This can be restated as a question: Do different measures of stress, by different operational forms, at different system levels, all measure the same thing (as indicated by their convergence)? Such convergence is an essential condition if we are to be able to separate that part of the variation in our data associated with the particular method of measurement from the part that reflects variation in the phenomenon we are trying to measure (namely stress).

But a particular theoretical viewpoint within the stress field holds that certain measures of stress are substitutes for one another, not parallel indicators of stress. From this viewpoint we would expect a person under stress either to develop ulcers or to exhibit excessive anger and aggressiveness but probably not to do both. From this viewpoint then we would not expect measures of such alternative stress responses to converge in the sense of showing high positive correlations. They might well show high negative correlations—if one occurs the other does not. But if there are more than two alternatives, as would usually be the case, they would likely show no correlation at all (that is, they would appear to show low convergent validity in the usual sense). This question of *convergence of measures* versus *differentiation of types of measures* therefore has both methodological and theoretical import.

There is a parallel problem with regard to stressor conditions. A wide variety of conditions, stimuli, and circumstances have been used as "stressors" (see Tables 1, 2 and 3). Are they all comparable? There are really two levels of question here. The first is the question of convergent validity of stressors of different types: Do different stressors correlate highly in terms of the resulting stress they produce? The second question is: Given an acceptable degree of convergent validity, can we calibrate these stressor conditions with respect to one another? (To put the matter in partly facetious terms: How many "ergs" of task failure equal one unit of arctic cold or one volt of electric shock?)

But again it is not necessarily theoretically compelling to expect that all stressor conditions will show convergence. Such would be the proper expectation if we hold a stress-is-general viewpoint (such as most interpretations of Selye's early formulations). But other views (e.g., Lacey, Lazarus) would hold that there are probably different "kinds" of stress and that we should not expect stressor conditions from these different kinds to act in the same way, that is, to show convergence. (Presumably, though, we still should expect two or more stressors of the same kind to converge with one another, even though they do not converge with stressors of a different kind.) Here again we have the question: Do these stressor conditions converge—in which case they may be regarded as *alternative indicators of the same thing*—or do they diverge, in which case they must be regarded as *indicators of different things*?

Besides the question of convergence versus differentiation of types for stressor conditions (and for stress responses, as indicated above), we have a parallel question with regard to the individuals or population units involved in the study. One way to pose this question is to ask: Are individuals all alike in regard to these matters, or do individuals differ in, say, their stress proneness? That is, do individuals differ in the degree to which a given intensity of a given kind of stressor will have a given effect? This could occur because individuals differ in sensitivity to different stressor conditions. Or it could occur because, given the same amount of stress, individuals differ in reactivity, or stress response amplitude. (The latter is similar to the question of stability—lability of physiological reactivity raised earlier.) So again we have an opposition of viewpoints: To what extent is there convergence among individuals in their stress reactions? Or do different types of individuals show more, or less, reactivity to stress? (Again we would presumably expect individuals of the same type to show convergence with one another, even if not with individuals of other types.)

In addition to these three questions about convergence or lack of it for stress measures, stressor conditions, and individuals, respectively ("main effects," so to speak), we need to consider the possibility of two-way interactions: Are there stressor-by-person-type interactions? That is, are different types of persons differentially sensitive to different types of stressor conditions? Are there stress-response-by-person-type interactions? That is, do different types of persons react to the same stressor with different response patterns? Are these stressor-condition-by-stress-response interactions? That is, are certain stress measures affected by one type of stressor condition, while other stress measures are not responsive to the first but are responsive to some other type of stressor condition? All three of these interaction effects have been postulated in recent stress literature under such labels as "fractional differentiation," "differential response patterns," and "stress proneness." We also need to consider the possibility of a three-way interaction of stressor-conditions-by-person-types-by-stress-responses. That is, does one type of person react to a given type of stressor condition with a particular stress response pattern, while another type of person reacts to the same or different stress condition with another response pattern, and so on? This entire cluster of questions derives from the juxtaposition of the basic methodological requirement for convergent validity with the conceptual arguments for multiple types of stressor conditions, of stress responses, and of population units. They pose a very formidable set of methodological hurdles for stress research. It is toward the solution of these problems that the next section of this paper is aimed.

THE P-B-S MATRIX: A GENERAL STRATEGY FOR DEALING WITH SOME FUNDAMENTAL METHODOLOGICAL PROBLEMS IN STRESS RESEARCH

The preceding sections should make it apparent that the methodological problems besetting research on stress are many, varied, complex, and relatively intractable. Furthermore, as is probably always the case, a good many of those fundamental methodological problems are very closely intertwined with fundamental conceptual problems. The problems furthermore tend to come in clusters; and the application of methodological techniques for dealing with one problem of a cluster still leaves—and often aggravates—the other problems of that cluster. There exists, for example, a long-established paradigm for dealing with the problem of method variance of stress measures by seeking to establish the convergent and discriminant validity of a series of measures of two or more "traits" (Campbell & Fiske, 1959). But the application of the Campbell and Fiske multitrait-multimethod (MT-MM) paradigm to determine the convergent and discriminant validity of stress response measures would have to be done while assuming: (1) that we already know the validity of particular stressor conditions that we would use in that determination, and (2) that we already have a resolution for the questions raised about individual differences. Furthermore, if one takes the position (for good conceptual reasons; see earlier discussion) that different people may use different forms of stress response as *alternative* coping strategies, then nonconvergence of these measures would be assessed as theoretically positive rather than as methodologically negative evidence. Such a view is in direct conflict with the logic of the MT-MM paradigm, and the issue between them cannot be resolved at that level by evidental means.

To some extent we can resolve these issues by applying the MT-MM logic to an array of stressor conditions, on the one hand, and to an array of person types on the other hand—in each case, assuming that we already have knowledge of the validity of the stress measures we would use in those applications. The problem here, of course, is that we really need to do these several things simultaneously and interdependently.

To that end this section will present a very general methodological strategy for simultaneously dealing with the issues of convergent and discriminant validity of: stress responses (behavior variables); stressor conditions (setting variables); and individual differences (population variables). I call the approach the *population-behavior-setting strategy* (or P-B-S matrix). It is a generalization and extension of the logic of the Campbell and Fiske (1959) MT-MM matrix paradigm. More generally, it is a systematic application of *multiple operationalism,* which has been advocated by Campbell and Fiske (1959), Webb et al. (1966), by Runkel and McGrath (1972), and others.[3] In an even broader sense it is a general strategy for systematic analysis of patterns of social-psychological behavior in concrete settings over time. While the P-B-S strategy is broadly applicable to a number of areas of social-psychological behavior, it seems especially useful in the stress research area because it represents a direct means for dealing with a number of the most crucial methodological issues in that area. In particular it represents a means for calibrating stressor conditions and stress response measures; for studying temporal and individual differences factors; and for assessing the meaningfulness and boundary conditions for concepts such as differential sensitivity to stress and differential stress response patterns.

Some Basic Methodological Questions

Every observation (i.e., every data point) involves somebody doing something at some time and place. Thus we can view the whole problem of the study of stress and its effects (or indeed the measurement of any construct and its network of relations) as involving the joint consideration of variables from each of three domains:

1. A *population* domain: Measurement always involves one or more population units (individuals, dyads, groups, organizations, etc.).
2. A *setting* domain: Measurement always involves one or more situations or occasions (i.e., one or more time/place/condition combination).
3. A *behavior* domain: Measurement always involves one or more behaviors, properties, or events enacted by that (those) population unit(s) in that (those) situation(s).

We must always contend with a multiplicity of variables from each of those three domains, and we must do so by means of one or another of a relatively restricted set of alternatives (measurement, manipulation, control, randomization).

---

[3] The P-B-S strategy is in many ways similar to Tucker's (1963) three-mode factor analysis and may in fact be just one special case of the class subsumed by three-mode factor analysis.

In stress research, dealing with variables from each of these three domains poses special problems. In the population domain we must be concerned about a cluster of problems that have to do with individual differences—in sensitivity to various stressor conditions and in degree and patterning of stress responses. In the situation domain we must be concerned with at least two major clusters of problems—one having to do with variables involving specific stressors and stressor conditions and the other having to do with a myriad of temporal aspects of the problem. In the behavior domain we must deal with a cluster of problems that center around the concepts of convergent and discriminant validity and method variance and that present special difficulties in measuring and interpreting stress responses.

For purposes of analysis we can consider each of these three domains separately, as if the other two did not vary or varied in ways that did not make any difference. When we do so, three basic methodological questions arise:

1. From the behavioral domain: How do I establish measures of responses to stress that are reliable and valid; that is, that have adequate discriminant and convergent validity in terms of Campbell and Fiske's (1959) MT-MM paradigm? (Is there one kind of stress response or several?)

2. From the situation domain: How do I establish that a stress response is a function of stress in some general sense and not of a particular stressor condition? That is, how do I establish the convergence of different stressor conditions in the Campbell and Fiske sense? (Is there one type of stressor condition or several?)

3. From the population domain: How do I establish that different population units (i.e., different persons, different groups, or whatever) are alike (that is, show convergence) in the effects of the stressor(s) on them and in their responses to the stress? (Is there one type of person, regarding stress, or are there several stress types?)

If we consider each pair of these domains together (while acting as if the third did not vary or did not matter), we can specify another three basic methodological questions, of a somewhat higher order of complexity, that are also crucial in stress research:

4. From the behavior and population domains considered jointly: Do different kinds (i.e., types) of population units differ in how they react to a stressor? That is, are there different patterns of response to a given stressor that are characteristic of different sets of people? (Are some people more stress prone than others?)

5. From the situation and population domains considered jointly: Do different kinds of population units (i.e., different types of people) react differently to different types of stressor conditions? That is, are there different patterns of sensitivity to different types of stress conditions that are characteristic of different types of people? (Are different types of people sensitive to different types of stress?)

6. From the behavior and situation domains considered jointly: Do different kinds of stressor conditions produce effects involving different kinds of stress responses? That is, are there some kinds of stressors that affect certain stress

responses, and other kinds of stressors that do not affect these but do affect other kinds of response measures? (Is there fractional differentiation of responses?)

If we now consider all three domains at the same time, we can specify a seventh, and much more complex, methodological question:

7. From the behavior, situation, and population domains considered jointly: Are there interactions among population-types, stressor-types, and stress-response-types? That is, are certain types of people especially sensitive to certain types of stressor conditions and especially reactive to them along certain types of stress-response dimensions?

The P-B-S Strategy

The rationale for the P-B-S strategy begins with the premise that every specific datum, every observation, must be referenced with respect to three domains:

1. Population: What individual person, group, or organization is the source of the observed behavior?
2. Behavior: What specific behavior variable and measure does the observation represent?
3. Setting: From what situation, setting, condition, or occasion did the observation originate?

A further premise of the P-B-S strategy is that any systematic study should involve multiple measures from each of these three domains. Given such a multivariate set of observations, which are to be treated together as a set, we can construe variables from each of these domains in any one of the following three ways:

1. As a *constant*: that is, all observations in the set can be considered as alike on a given domain. (For example, All measures may be from the same individual or same group, or all may be from the same condition, or all may be about the same behavior.)
2. As a *correlation base*: that is, all observations in the set may be considered as potentially different from one another on a given domain. (For example, the observations may each be from a different subject, or they may each be from different trials or occasions, or they may be a series of items each measuring different behaviors.)
3. As a *trait-by-method matrix*: that is, for a given domain the set of observations may include a number of replicated cases (which will be treated as alike) within each of several differentiated subsets (which are presumed to be different). (For example, observations may be from a number of subjects of each of several subject types; or on a number of measures of each of several behavior traits; or on a number of "trials" in each of several settings or conditions.)

The multitrait-multimethod (MT-MM) paradigm as set forth by Campbell and Fiske (1959) is discussed in terms that use the population domain as a *correlation base*, the setting domain as a *constant*, and the behavior domain as the locus for a *trait-by-method (T X M) matrix*. That is, there is a battery of behavior measures that is considered to include two or more alternative methods of measurement of two or more traits. These are correlated with one another over a set of population units for a single occasion.

But the logic of the MT-MM paradigm is equally applicable if we arrange the three domains in other ways, as to which is the correlation base, which is a constant, and which is the locus of the T X M matrix. Specifically, there seem to be nine different arrangements that offer promise of fruitful analyses (see Table 3). Each of the nine cases opens up some new questions rarely asked in our empirical studies. Together they provide a systematic basis for dealing with the seven key methodological questions noted earlier in this section.

Case I is, of course, the standard MT-MM application that Campbell and Fiske (1959) present. It is a means of determining the convergent and discriminant validity of a set of behavior traits and measures for a population using a single setting or measurement occasion. We can call Case I a *response matrix analysis (over population units)*.

Case II is still concerned with the convergent and divergent patterning of a set of behavior traits and measures, but with respect to a time-ordered series of occasions using a single population unit. Case II is a *response matrix analysis (over occasions)*.

Cases III and IV are concerned with analysis of the pattern of convergence and divergence among a series of occasions, some of which are considered as replicated trials of the same situation or condition, and some of which are considered as different conditions. For Case III the patterning is sought for one behavior variable over a number of population units. Case III is a *situation*

Table 3 Some potential generalizations of the MT-MM paradigm

| | Which domain is used for | | |
Cases	Correlation base	T X M matrix	Constant
I: Response matrix (analyzed over population units)	Population	Behavior	Setting
II: Response matrix (analyzed over occasions)	Setting	Behavior	Population
III: Situation matrix (analyzed over population units)	Population	Setting	Behavior
IV: Situation matrix (analyzed over behavior measures)	Behavior	Setting	Population
V: Population matrix (analyzed over occasions)	Setting	Population	Behavior
VI: Population matrix (analyzed over behavior measures)	Behavior	Population	Setting
VII: Response-by-situation matrix (analyzed over population units)	Population	Behavior-x-Setting	None
VIII: Response-by-population-type matrix (analyzed over occasions)	Setting	Behavior-x-Population	None
IX: Situation-by-population-type matrix (analyzed over behavior measures)	Behavior	Population-x-Setting	None

matrix analysis (over population units). For Case IV the patterning is sought for one population unit over a battery of behavior measures. Case IV is a *situation matrix analysis (over behavior measures)*.

Cases V and VI are concerned with analysis of patterns of convergence and divergence among the members of a population; that is, a search for convergence within and divergence between subject-types. In Case V the patterning is examined for a single behavior variable over a series of occasions or settings. Case V is a *population matrix analysis (over occasions)*. In Case VI the patterning deals with a series of behavior variables within a single setting. Case VI is a *population matrix analysis (over behavior measures)*.

Cases VII, VIII, and IX are applications in which the T X M matrix is composed by "crossing" two of the facets, with the third serving as a correlation base. In Case VII a series of behavior traits is crossed with a series of situations, and that behavior-by-setting matrix is analyzed for patterns of convergence and divergence over a series of population units. Here there is no a priori decision as to whether the behavior variables or the settings are to be considered traits, with the other considered as alternative methods. Rather there is an empirical question: Which shows convergence, which divergence, the behavior traits or the situation types? The answer to the latter question bears on an issue that has been controversial in many areas of behavioral science: Can we best conceptualize our phenomena as involving trait continuity over situations or as involving stages or system states within which behavior shows interdependent patterns? Case VII is a *response-by-situation matrix analysis (over population units)*.

Case VIII builds the T X M matrix by crossing a set of behavior variables and a set of population-unit types. The subject-type-by-behavior-variable patterning (convergence and divergence) is examined over a series of occasions or settings. Here the outcome bears on the relative distinctiveness of the behavior traits versus the population-unit differences over time. Case VIII is a *response-by-population-type matrix analysis (over occasions)*.

Case IX involves crossing a set of population-units and a set of situations to form the T X M matrix and analysis of their patterning over a series of behavior variables. Here the key question involves the relative distinctiveness of subjects and settings with respect to a battery of behavior variables. Case IX is a *situation-by-population-type matrix analysis (over behavior measures)*.

These nine applications of the MT-MM logic together provide a means to attack many of the key methodological issues reviewed in the previous sections, as well as some more general issues. The relevance of this approach to the problem of method variance in measures of stress response should be apparent. For either Case I or Case II, if a series of conceptually distinctive traits is measured by means of a series of methodologically distinctive methods of measurement, then the within-trait convergence and the between-trait divergence obtained when these measures are correlated (over times or over population units) is an empirical definition of the functional unity of those traits.

The analyses of Case III and Case IV bear on the "methods variance" question of setting-specific versus general stressor effects. If there is convergence among replicated occasions within a setting and divergence across settings, then those settings represent distinctive or different stress conditions (for that set of behaviors or for that set of population units, whichever is used as the correlation base). Similarly, the analyses bearing on population units (Case V and Case VI) permit the systematic analysis of individual differences (divergences) and of individual similarities or population types (convergences), over behavior variables or over situations.

Several of the analyses (Cases II, V, and VIII) can deal directly with temporal aspects. These involve analyses of response, population types, or both, correlated over occasions. The occasions can have a meaningful temporal pattern. In addition, several more analyses (Cases III and IV) deal with temporal features in the sense of testing the convergence of trials or occasions within conditions.

Perhaps one of the most interesting aspects of the P-B-S matrix approach is its bearing on the perennial issue of nomothetic versus ideographic analyses. The nomothetic approach is characteristic of laboratory research. The ideographic approach is characteristic of field research. Case I, correlation of behavior traits by methods over a population, would normally be considered a nomothetic analysis even though it deals with data from only a single situation or occasion. Yet Case II, correlation of behavior traits and methods over occasions, would normally be considered as an ideographic case study because it deals with data from only a single population unit. A similar comparison would apply to Cases III and IV. But the logic of search for patterns of convergence and divergence is parallel for correlations over occasions and correlations over population units.

Another broad issue to which the P-B-S system relates is that of "stages" versus "trait continuity" in the analysis of human behavior. Bandura and Walters (1963) address this problem and argue for trait continuity over time as more prominent than trait convergence within stages. Case VII would permit a direct test of this question. On a related issue Barker (e.g., Barker & Gump, 1964) asserts that convergence among individuals within settings is more prominent than convergence across settings within population units. Case IX puts this to the test. These are broad issues, which have their counterparts in the stress area in such concepts as individual differences in response pattern or coping style, individual difference in stress tolerance, and individual difference in sensitivity to situational demands.

A Trial Application of the P-B-S Strategy and Some Implications for Stress Research

The key requirement for application of the P-B-S matrix as a research strategy is to obtain a comprehensive set of observations that can be referenced systematically to the population, behavior, and setting axes. More concretely this requires obtaining measures of a set of behavior traits carried out by each of a series of methods, for each of a series of replicated occasions or trials within each of a set of different situations or conditions, for each of a number of homogeneous population units of each of several population types. Having done so it is then possible to perform all nine analysis cases on the same set of data and thereby deal with a whole spectrum of research questions in an integrated fashion. In such an approach it is not necessary to begin with a fixed set of a priori hypotheses to be tested. Rather it is appropriate to ask the empirical question: Where is the convergence, where is the divergence, within this systematic set of data?

In an initial attempt to apply the P-B-S system, Stapert and McGrath (1969) conducted a study that had the following design. Each of a series of (18) four-person groups worked for 2 hours on performance of a series of (3 to 8) tasks during each of four sessions one week apart. The tasks that any given group performed, through all their sessions, were drawn from a pool of standardized tasks of a single task type, each with known difficulty level (see Hackman, 1968). Since there were three such task-type pools, there were three different sets of groups.

Three interpersonal behavior variables were chosen as the behavior constructs of interest. They were "activity," "influence," and "attraction." These three concepts have been shown to be prominent in a number of studies of group structure and group process (e.g., McGrath, 1963; Schutz, 1958).

An array of methods of measurement was developed such that each method could be applied to each trait. Following Webb et al. (1966), we used widely divergent types of methods; subjective reports, trace measures, observation measures, and archival records were all used for measuring each trait. Since the different methods have different and complementary sources of error, trait convergence of such independent methods would be more meaningful than if all measures had been of the same type (such as all questionnaires).

Because of the availability of a pool of comparable tasks and task product measures (see Hackman, Jones, & McGrath, 1967), it was possible to vary task loads from session to session in terms of time demands and in terms of difficulty levels. Hence we could vary the level of task-based stress in different sessions and be able to ask questions about the effects of those variations within the design.

The initial tryout of the P-B-S approach had some success. The body of data generated in that study is far too vast and complex to present in detail here. In general we found a disappointingly high level of method variance for, and lack of convergence among, the different measures of the three main behavior variables. We also found, as expected, a strong replication of Hackman's three task types and his findings regarding task difficulty (Hackman, 1968).

This study was done mainly as a pilot or demonstration study to determine whether the P-B-S strategy was possible to implement in a "real" study or only useful as a verbal description of one logically possible way to conceptualize certain research questions. That we executed the study and that we were able to draw useful conclusions about the methodological properties of our measures, our situations, and our populations is an indication that the P-B-S strategy does have some potential usefulness—although it has considerable cost, at least relative to the average laboratory study in the same area. Some of these costs come from the necessity to find an array of methods of different operational forms to measure each of the behavior variables (i.e., traits) to be studied. Very often concepts are virtually defined in terms of a single method. When that is the case, and is accepted as immutable, there is no way to separate the "trait variance" and the "method variance" components, thus no way to estimate the convergent or divergent validity of the trait (or the usefulness of the form of measurement). We found that, by setting ourselves the requirement to find a measure of each form for each of our traits, we forced ourselves to be more inventive in designing such measures and to attempt conceptual clarification of our trait concepts—with some worthwhile results. Another aspect of the high cost is the relatively large (and systematic) body of data the study generated. Aside from the costs of data collection, this huge body of data and the complex patterns of analysis called for by the P-B-S strategy pose an enormous burden for data analysis—and indeed some of the potentially fruitful analyses of the data of that study have not yet been carried out. But those same features—the use of multiple measures and the systematic form of resulting data—are also the source of some of the major benefits as well as some of the main costs of the P-B-S strategy.

The reader should recognize that I am *not* arguing that every study in the stress area ought to be done following the format of the P-B-S strategy. Nor am I arguing that fundamental methodological research in the stress area using the P-B-S strategy or something like it (such as Tucker's [1963] 3-mode factor analysis) ought to precede any further substantive-oriented stress research. The latter might be ideal but certainly would not be practical. Nor am I really arguing that anyone ever ought to use the P-B-S strategy, literally, in the study of stress or of other social-psychological phenomena. The central point of presenting the P-B-S strategy here—and in many ways, the central point of inventing it in the first place—is to provide a systematic conceptual framework for *thinking about* a whole battery of interconnected and crucial methodological problems. These problems—convergence and divergence of stressors, stress measures, and population types; individual differences, in general, in sensitivity to stressor conditions and in response patterns; and situational and temporal factors—are all interrelated. So it is worthwhile to cast them in a framework within which they are dealt with as interrelated.

Moreover, by contemplating all facets of the P-B-S matrix, one's attention gets drawn to some aspects that might otherwise be overlooked. For example, it is easy to concentrate on method variance and convergent and discriminant validity of stress measures, and even to see that the concepts apply to stressor conditions as well as to measures of stress response, without realizing that an analogous set of concepts applies to the population domain—individual differences and population-type convergences. It is also easy to overlook the importance of response patterning and of differential sensitivity to stressors if one approaches the matter in the more limited and more conventional terms of establishing the reliability and the validity of particular stress measures. Furthermore, without casting these issues within a systematic framework such as the P-B-S matrix, one would be very unlikely to attend to the quite important problem of nomothetic versus ideographic data, of traits versus types, or of stages versus trait continuity. In these latter cases, of course, one can argue that they are primarily substantive rather than methodological problems. To some degree the P-B-S strategy ties substance and method together—and that may turn out to be one of its most useful features.

REFERENCES

Altman, I., & Lett, E. E. The ecology of interpersonal relationships: A classification system and conceptual model. In J. E. McGrath (Ed.), *Social and psychological factors in stress*. New York: Holt, Rinehart & Winston, 1970.

Appley, M. H., & Trumbull, R. (Eds.) *Psychological stress*. New York: Appleton-Century-Crofts, 1967.

Bandura, A., & Walters, R. H. *Social learning and personality development*. New York: Holt, Rinehart & Winston, 1963.

Barker, R. G., & Gump, P. *Big school, small school*. Stanford: Stanford University Press, 1964.

Campbell, D. T., & Fiske, D. W. Convergent and discriminant validation by the multitrait-multimethod matrix. *Psychological Bulletin*, 1959, *56*, 81–105.

Clore, G. L., Bray, R. M., Itkin, S. M., & Murphy, P. Interracial attitudes and behavior at a summer camp. *Journal of Personality and Social Psychology,* 1978, *36,* 107–116.

Cofer, C. N., & Appley, M. H. *Motivation: Theory and research.* New York: Wiley, 1964.

Haas, J. E., & Drabek, T. E. Community disaster and system stress: A sociological perspective. In J. E. McGrath (Ed.), *Social and psychological factors in stress.* New York: Holt, Rinehart & Winston, 1970.

Hackman, J. R. Effects of task characteristics on group products. *Journal of Experimental Social Psychology,* 1968, *4,* 162–187.

Hackman, J. R. Tasks and task performance in research on stress. In J. E. McGrath (Ed.), *Social and psychological factors in stress.* New York: Holt, Rinehart & Winston, 1970.

Hackman, J. R., Jones, L. E., & McGrath, J. E. A set of dimensions for describing the general properties of group-generated written passages. *Psychological Bulletin,* 1967, *67,* 379–390.

Holtzman, W. H., & Bitterman, M. E. A factorial study of adjustment to stress. *Journal of Abnormal and Social Psychology,* 1956, *52,* 179–185.

Kahn, R. L. Some propositions toward a researchable conceptualization of stress. In J. E. McGrath (Ed.), *Social and psychological factors in stress.* New York: Holt, Rinehart & Winston, 1970.

Kahn, R. L., & French, J. R. P., Jr. Status and conflict: Two themes in the study of stress. In J. E. McGrath (Ed.), *Social and psychological factors in stress.* New York: Holt, Rinehart & Winston, 1970.

Kahn, R. L., Wolfe, D. M., Quinn, R. P., Snoek, J. E., & Rosenthal, R. A. *Organizational stress: Studies in role conflict and ambiguity.* New York: Wiley, 1964.

Lazarus, R. S. *Psychological stress and the coping process.* New York: McGraw-Hill, 1966.

Mandler, G., Mandler, J. M., Kremen, I., & Sholiton, R. D. The response to threat: Relations among verbal and physiological indices. *Psychological Monographs–General and Applied,* 1961, *75,* (9, Whole No. 513).

McGrath, J. E. A descriptive model for the study of interpersonal relations in small groups. *Journal of Psychological Studies,* 1963, *14*(3), 89–116.

McGrath, J. E. (Ed.) *Social and psychological factors in stress.* New York: Holt, Rinehart & Winston, 1970.

McGrath, J. E. Stress and behavior in organizations. In M. D. Dunnette (Ed.), *Handbook of industrial and organizational psychology.* Chicago: Rand McNally, 1976.

Runkel, P. J., & McGrath, J. E. *Research on human behavior. A systematic guide to method.* New York: Holt, Rinehart & Winston, 1972.

Schutz, W. C. *FIRO: A three-dimensional theory of interpersonal behavior.* New York: Holt, Rinehart & Winston, 1958.

Scott, W. E. Activation theory and task design. *Organizational behavior and Human Performance,* 1966, *1,* 3–30.

Sells, S. B. On the nature of stress. In J. E. McGrath (Ed.), *Social and psychological factors in stress.* New York: Holt, Rinehart & Winston, 1970.

Stapert, J. C., & McGrath, J. E. *Multiple methods in the longitudinal study of small groups under stress.* Technical Report AF 1161–67, AFOSR, 1969.

Tucker, L. R. Implications of factor analysis of three-way matrices for measurement of change. In C. W. Harris (Ed.), *Problems in measuring change.* Madison, Wis.: University of Wisconsin Press, 1963.

Webb, E. J., Campbell, D. T., Schwartz, R. D., & Sechrest, L. *Unobtrusive measures: A survey of non-reactive research in social science.* Skokie, Ill.: Rand McNally, 1966.

Weitz, J. Psychological research needs on the problems of human stress. In J. E. McGrath (Ed.), *Social and psychological factors in stress.* New York: Holt, Rinehart & Winston, 1970.

Zajonc, R. B. Social facilitation. *Science,* 1965, *149,* 269–274.

II

STRESS, COPING,
AND PERFORMANCE

3

Regulatory Activity during States of Stress

Peter Schulz and Wolfgang Schönpflug
Free University of Berlin

A GENERAL CONCEPTION OF STRESS AND AN EXPERIMENTAL PARADIGM

Uncertainty and Uncertainty Reduction

In this study stress is investigated as a complex state to which several phenomena contribute, not a phenomenon sui generis. This state typically originates in the context of goal-directed activities. A prerequisite for the occurrence of stress seems to be a perceived imbalance between subjective task demand and a person's subjective capacity; this has also been pointed out in earlier conceptions (Lazarus, 1966; McGrath, 1970, 1976).

Generally no stress is observed if the perceived capacity of an individual exceeds his or her perceived task demands. Critical, however, are states in which task demands equal or exceed the capacity of an individual involved. The demand/capacity ratio will have an impact on the individual's uncertainty of proceeding: The more demands are conceived of as outbalancing the capacities of an individual, the higher will be his or her lack of information about effective continuation of activity (see Figure 1). There are two ways of reducing the uncertainty of proceeding: by (1) removing the preponderance of demands over capacities by raising capacity. A person's capacity can be improved by practice (Vossel & Laux, 1978) or by increment of effort (Düker, 1963; Kahneman, 1973). Or the uncertainty can be reduced by (2) removing the preponderance of demands over capacities by reducing task demands. In many situations a person can reduce the individual task demands by lowering his or her aspiration level (Schönpflug, chapter 14 in this volume). In all situations the person can resign from the task (Averill, 1973), thereby reducing task requirements to zero.

There appears to be a complement to the uncertainty of proceeding: the uncertainty of nonproceeding. The more the uncertainty of proceeding increases, the more information will be available to the person involved that he or she better discontinue the ongoing activity and thereby terminate or avoid a period of stress. During phases in which an equilibrium of task demands and capacities

This study was supported by a grant to the second author from the Government of the Federal Republic of Germany (*Bundesminister des Inneren/Umweltbundesamt*).

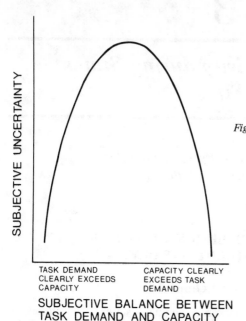

Figure 1 Relationship between the demand/capacity ratio and the subjective uncertainty of proceeding with a task. The more a person's subjective capacity is outbalanced by the task demands, the higher is his or her uncertainty of proceeding. On the other hand, a high imbalance in favor of demand will reduce one's uncertainty of nonproceeding. No stress is assumed to occur when a person knows how to proceed or when to resign: Critical for the occurrence of stress is, according to this assumption, a demand/capacity ratio in which the demand slightly outbalances capacity.

is approximated, a severe conflict between tendencies of proceeding and of nonproceeding can be expected.

As far as techniques of raising and applying one's own capacity are effective in reducing or avoiding the uncertainty of proceeding, they can be evaluated as adequate means of coping with stress. However, there are also other kinds of activities. In general during states of stress both physiological arousal (Selye, 1956) and overt behavior (Weiss, 1971a, 1971b) are increased. Primary activities, being effective in solving the problems at hand, are accompanied by additional controlling activities and ineffective problem-solving behavior. All kinds of coping attempts not effective in reducing or avoiding uncertainty of proceeding are evaluated here as inadequate coping.

That inadequate coping behavior is the main condition for the occurrence of stress is the central contention of this study. If attempted coping with a problem situation is not followed by success, the person involved is confronted with the experience of a sustained or even deteriorated ratio between task demand and capacity at a moment when he or she expects a change in favor of capacity. Subjective uncertainty is not reduced but rather increases during such a phase; furthermore, a continuation or even increment of uncertainty, despite coping attempts, gives rise to further inadequate reactions including affective responses. A state of stress due to inadequate coping attempts may last until the person involved finally succeeds in effective coping. Ineffective coping, while enhancing the uncertainty of proceeding, may also reduce the uncertainty of non-proceeding. When the uncertainty of nonproceeding reaches a liminal value, it can be assumed that the person involved will give up.

Techniques of adjusting task demands to capacities or even of escape from the task situation have not been considered as possible means of coping with stress in the preceding analysis. Although they are not classified among coping activities, their contributions to the reduction of uncertainty of proceeding should also be recognized. There will probably be cases in which downward shifts of subjective demands (or even complete resignation) can be evaluated as appropriate reactions; in other cases subjective reductions of demand will rather increase uncertainty and will therefore have to be evaluated as inappropriate.

Conditions of Uncertainty in Administrative Work and a Laboratory Analogue

Cases of balance and imbalance of capacity and task demand, as well as the resulting certainty and uncertainty about continuation of work, appeared to be common phenomena in field situations. It was decided to study these phenomena and the typical conditions under which they occur in an industrial setting before starting more detailed experimental studies in the laboratory. For this reason, 27 interviews were performed at a metalwork department of the Siemens Company in Berlin.[1] Selected for individual $1\frac{1}{2}$- to 2-hour interviews were members of the technical and administrative staff who were engaged in management tasks at the medium and lower level; their working place was located in or near the production halls.

Among the typical and common features of the clerical work required were the following characteristics:

1. The employees had to take notice of recent information regarding the work and decision problems at hand (e.g., specified orders, personal data); they had to keep this information in mind until completing their task.
2. The incoming information had to be evaluated on the basis of reference knowledge, for example, legal regulations, general directives, technical rules, tables, and the like. The reference knowledge is in part stored in the memory of the persons involved. It is totally stored in "external memories," such as books, files, and registers. If something is not available from the "internal" memory, it has to be searched for and retrieved from external sources.
3. On the basis of recent information and of reference knowledge the employees had to decide among a set of alternatives. At the medium and lower management level the alternatives, in general, are given within the incoming information or within the reference knowledge. The decisions therefore require mental operations combining recently incoming information both with each other and with reference knowledge.

Within this procedure three sources of mistakes can be found: (1) missing of incoming information, (2) lack of reference knowledge, (3) lack or insufficient use of mental operations.

Missing information and lacking reference knowledge can be compensated for by extended or replicated search and inquiry (e.g., asking a colleague by phone, looking up a number in a table repeatedly). By a compensatory search for information the time for reaching the decision is prolonged. There is also the

[1] The generous support of the Schaltwerk department of the Siemens Company (director: Dr. Diederichs) is gratefully acknowledged.

danger of retrieving irrelevant information, which is time-consuming and complicates the mental operations.

It was attempted to model an experimental situation after the observed industrial situation. Experimental tasks were constructed simulating the features of clerical work. Each task consisted of a problem, four alternative decisions (one being considered optimal), and five additional pieces of information (three being relevant, two irrelevant for reaching the optimal decision). An example of the tasks is given in Figure 2.

The problem, together with the four alternatives, was offered to the subjects. They were asked to make a decision on the optimal solution. Problem and alternatives were exposed to the subjects on a slide and the solution was signalled by the subjects to the experimenter by pressing one of four keys. The information presented on the problem slide was not sufficient to find the correct solution with a higher probability than chance. By pressing separate keys the subjects could order five slides containing additional information. Still another key was used to bring the problem slide back. Within the task interval the subjects were free to expose the problem and the additional information as long as they wanted; the only restriction was that only one slide could be exposed at a time.

During a perfect trial the subject memorized the content of the problem slide and consecutively pressed the keys to obtain the additional information. He memorized the relevant information and performed all operations to reach the optimal solution. If a subject, however, forgot or missed a piece of information

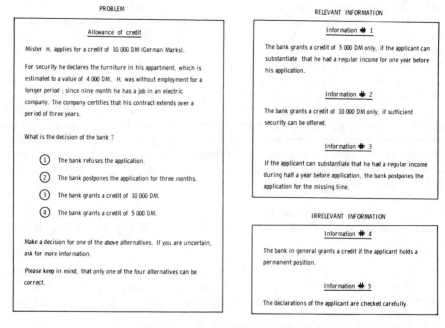

Figure 2 Example of an experimental task simulating features of clerical work. The subject is presented a slide with a problem and four alternatives for solution and is asked to find the optimal alternative. (In this example, alternative 2 is evaluated as optimal.)

on one slide, he either had to make a decision on the basis of insufficient information, or he had to compensate by ordering the slides with the missing information again. Since it was a waste of time and effort to order irrelevant information and even to repeat irrelevant information, the subjects could learn to avoid irrelevant information. A high rate of the slides containing irrelevant information were associated with keys number 4 and 5, whereas keys number 1 to 3 served for exposure of relevant additional information.

According to the theory introduced above, the exposition of a problem without sufficient information for a well-founded solution should create a state of uncertainty in the subject. By successively obtaining the information needed for a decision, the uncertainty should disappear and no stress should arise. If, however, information already obtained could not be retrieved or if the search for relevant information resulted in the supply of irrelevant bits, the amount of uncertainty should increase and thereby the degree of stress. These hypotheses were already anecdotically confirmed in the field study, and the experimental investigations were designed to corroborate them in a more systematic way.

Evidently the experience of uncertainty and stress develops over a longer period of time. The solution of the problem prepared for experimentation in general took just a few minutes. For this reason a larger series of problems was constructed. The problems were presented consecutively, and after giving his solution (or after termination of the time provided for each task), the subject received feedback from the experimenter; a green light indicated optimal solution, a red light a missing or incorrect solution. The subject was supposed to make inferences about task difficulty and his own competence from the light signals. It was expected that RIGHT-signals would shift his subjective demand/ capacity ratio toward dominance of the capacity estimate, whereas WRONG-signals would change the ratio in favor of the task demand.

Multiple Task Demands and the Role of Fatigue

In industrial settings as well as other life situations, the work problem is not the only source of stress. There are also working conditions that contribute to the degree of stress, for example, noise, time pressure, responsibility, and social conflicts. The work problem constitutes the primary task. Additional factors— being more or less contingent on the primary task—increase the number of demands and therefore the difficulty level of the total situation. (A more detailed analysis of multiple task demands in achievement situations is given in Schönpflug, chapter 14 in this volume.)

In the experimental research reported in this chapter two additional sources of stress were considered: noise and evaluative feedback. Different intensity levels of traffic noise were introduced and contrasted with a quiet situation. In the condition with evaluative feedback, subjects were exposed to a digital timer and received an extra payment for each correct decision within a standard time limit of 2 minutes. This condition was contrasted to a condition with nonevaluative feedback. Nonevaluative feedback consisted of right and wrong signals only; subjects had no time limit and received a fixed payment for the total experimental session independent of their performance.

Another factor of theoretical and practical importance seemed to be fatigue. Fatigue is a hypothetical process that diminishes an individual's psychophysical capacities in the course of prolonged activity. As the probability of inefficient behavior increases with the amount of fatigue, fatigue also had to be considered as one of the sources of stress. To account for this factor all experimental sessions were extended for 1 to 2 hours. For better comparison the experimental problems in the first and in the second half of each session were matched with respect to their difficulty.

General Classes of Regulatory Activity
and Individual Selection of Regulatory Acts

A problem or task situation can be conceived of as an actual state being discordant to a required state. In order to resolve discrepancies between actual and required states, regulatory acts can be performed. As also has been analyzed by Averill (1973), regulatory acts in stress situations can be grouped into three different classes:

1. External control,
2. Internal control,
3. Control of confrontation.

If there is a source of stress external to a system, the system can operate in such a way that the external source ceases to function as a stressing agent. This type of operation will be called *external control*. Thus if high work load is the stressing agent, external control will consist of applying effective methods of accomplishing the work assigned. If loud noise is the stressing agent, switching off the noise is an instance of external control. *Internal control,* on the other hand, is a regulatory activity directed toward agents within the system. Thus improvement of the manufacturing technique by mental training may be an example of internal control; diverting attention from an annoying noise is another example. External control leads to changes in structures being external to the operating system while the structure of the system itself remains unaffected; whereas internal control changes the structure of the operating system, leaving external structures unaffected.

During *control of confrontation* neither internal nor external structures are affected. Rather the system operates in such a way that a decision on time, locus, and circumstances of problem solution can be made. A typical case of the control of confrontation is the delay of action.

Regulatory acts belonging to different classes can very well go along with each other; also the timing of regulatory acts has to be considered. Some acts are concomitant or subsequent to the actual onset of stress. Other acts are preventive, exerting control before an actual onset of stress.

As already has been pointed out, effective coping with a problem situation is contingent on the choice of adequate regulatory activities. Whether there are adequate regulatory activities at the disposal of an individual and which activities are most adequate will both depend on the actual state of the individual and the specific situation. The individual involved will have to decide. But what can he use as the basis of his decision? He obviously has to refer to the nature of his uncertainty about effective continuation. He has to attribute causal factors to the observed imbalance between demand and capacity. And he will also have to form subjective estimates of the effectiveness of regulatory acts. Thus he may ask: "To what degree is my uncertainty due to work load, to my work strategy, to my state of fatigue, or to noise?" According to the answer he will tend to make his decision in favor of resigning the task, changing his work technique, getting rest, or switching off the noise. His final decision for a regulatory act will also consider positive and negative costs as well as positive and negative risks; in effect he may, for instance, rather wear earplugs than leave a noisy factory hall.

This study will have as one focus the role of causal attributions. In the same way that adequate attributions of the causes of uncertainty serve as necessary prerequisites for the choice of effective regulatory acts, inadequate attributions serve as a basis for the selection of ineffective procedures. As ineffective procedures tend to increase rather than decrease stress (an argument proposed in the beginning of this chapter), inadequate attributions of the causes of stress effects seem to play a prominent role among the conditions of occurrence and maintenance of states of stress.

The more an individual can use information from the actual task situation and from feedback of his or her own activity, the more he or she is likely to come to a correct evaluation of causal factors. However, since the person also introduces information from past experience, an attributional bias may result in deviations from a correct evaluation of causal factors. So the present study tries to investigate individual differences in coping with stress as due to a subjective attributional bias.

In general the following determinants in the choice of regulatory acts (or coping procedures) will be considered:

1. Causal factors for uncertainty in a problem situation as conceived of objectively (i.e., by the experimenter) and subjectively (i.e., by the subjects).

2. Availability of control activities for reducing uncertainty as conceived of objectively (i.e., by the experimenter) and subjectively (i.e., by the subjects).

3. The attributional bias on the side of the subjects (as a measure of individual differences).

REGULATORY ACTIVITY DURING NOISE STIMULATION

Specific Features of the Experimental Design and the Experimental Sample

Within the experimental paradigm described above several investigations were performed. A first study tested mainly two experimental factors: task difficulty and noise level. Each subject had to solve a series of 24 problems (as illustrated in Figure 2). The time limit for each problem was 120 seconds. There were three levels of task difficulty; the first half of the series included the same number of easy, medium, and difficult problems as did the second half of the series. Individual subjects had to work on the problems under one of the following conditions: a quiet experimental room; the same experimental room with traffic noise fluctuating between 30 and 40 dB(A); traffic noise between 50 and 60 dB(A); traffic noise between 70 and 80 dB(A).

Sixteen subjects were assigned to each of the four conditions, giving a total of

64 subjects. The subjects—unemployed technicians and office workers registered at a local labor agency—were selected on the basis of their extraversion-introversion score. Within each experimental group the subjects were divided into two subgroups of 8 each; the subjects in one of the subgroups had scores above the median of the total sample, the other half had scores below. A selection on the basis of extraversion-introversion was made because this measure seemed to be related to reactivity and causal attribution of success and failure (see Schönpflug & Heckhausen, 1976). In addition an intelligence test (Amthauer, 1953) was administered. All groups were matched with respect to intellectual abilities as measured in the test.

Noise and External Regulation of Noise as Sources of Stress

Often noise per se seems to interfere with ongoing primary activity. In such cases a detailed analysis reveals that interference occurs with internal (i.e., cognitive and emotional) reactions to noise rather than with noise as a physical event. In some situations reactions to noise also include motor or verbal components affecting the origin or propagation of noise; this has been called external regulation as we noted. Acts of external regulation can also interfere with ongoing primary activity (cf. McGrath, 1976).

In the present study it could be expected that the subjects would suffer from noise per se, especially during periods of information processing. For this reason subjects serving under noise conditions were asked at the end of the experimental session whether the noise was responsible for their failure. As can be seen from Figure 3, up to 80% of the subjects assented to the question. This effect highly depends on noise intensity ($p < .01$). Extraverts score higher than introverts under all noise conditions.

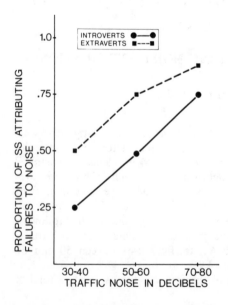

Figure 3 Proportion of subjects attributing failures to noise.

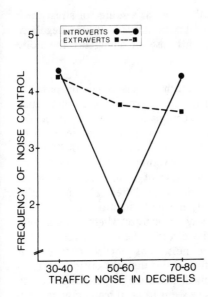

Figure 4 Frequency of operations on the noise control button (average for one problem).

However, the subjects were not only passively exposed to the noise; they were given the opportunity to control the duration of exposure. On the panel containing the response keys there also was a button for noise control. Pressing the button turned off the noise for 40 seconds. Subjects could press the button preventively (i.e., before starting out with a problem); they could also do it concomitantly (i.e., during the solution procedure). In general the time of 40 seconds did not suffice for the solution of a problem; thus for complete elimination of the noise, the subjects had to operate the noise control button repeatedly while working on a problem.

The frequency of operations on the noise control button (given in Figure 4) varies with noise intensity but not in a monotonous fashion. There is no straightforward relation to extraversion. Obviously the results in Figure 4 are not in full concordance with the subjective estimates of degree of interference (Figure 3). The main deviation is located in the 30–40 dB(A) noise condition, where the frequency of control operations is far above the value that could be predicted from the interference estimates.

Since the evaluation of adequacy of coping behavior is a central issue within the theory proposed in this chapter, a more detailed analysis is needed of the consequences of active noise control. In postexperimental interviews, three features were substantiated:

1. The decision for active control distracts attention from the primary task; and the control activity itself, although of short duration, interrupts ongoing primary activity.

2. Concomitant control is often triggered from peak events in the traffic noise (e.g., loud trucks, signals of ambulance cars). In such cases subjects experience a loss of control with respect to the timing of control activities. We even observed the phenomenon that subjects built up expectations for the next peak event to occur. This expectation was accompanied by tension and distraction from the primary task.

3. Execution of control activity eliminates the noise as a source of stress for a defined period. However, as this quiet period was limited, it was regularly followed by the return of traffic noise. In this case switching off the noise prevented adaptation to noise.

Already in this stage of data presentation it can be suspected that internal reactions to loud traffic noise may be beyond the active control of an individual. They may add up to such an amount that distractions and disturbances on the side of control activity are outbalanced. This contention does not seem to be valid in the case of weak traffic noise. Actually, noise at a range of 30-40 dB(A) is just above the threshold, and the subjects were exposed to an irregular series of acoustical events rather than a continuous flow of information. However, specific to the 30-40 dB(A) condition, subjects exhibited a rather active orientation toward the faint but discrete signals and built up strong expectations for the next peak event to occur. It is not easy to analyze whether distraction from weak traffic noise is outbalanced by the disturbances of control activity. But it can be stated that the weak traffic noise was not all obtrusive in intensity, and it did not yield any relevant information; thus the critical question has to be asked: Why did subjects pay so much attention to it rather than to divert attention or to habituate? In general there seem to be three components in the reaction to noise:

1. A less active component of internal responding, being most prominent with high intensity noise,
2. A high active orienting component, being most conspicuous with low intensity noise,
3. External noise control activity.

In the situation to be analyzed, solving mental problems was the primary task from the objective (i.e., the experimenter's) point of view; there were no specific demands related to the presentation of noise. From the objective point of view any active, orienting behavior toward noise could not be evaluated as adequate; and even if the occurrence of active orienting behavior could not be evaluated as adequate, it should be omitted rather than prevented by control of the object of orientation. Due to their disturbing and distracting features, external control activities are only adequate coping procedures in a few instances. They only become adequate means of responding if they compensate or even outbalance other internal stress effects; they can particularly be evaluated as adequate means for meeting the difficulties arising from less active components of internal responding. Following this line of argument, adequacy of external control seems to be more debatable under conditions of low than of high noise intensity.

Information Processing under Conditions of Internal and External Responding to Noise

Already in the first section some evidence of the applied field could be presented in favor of the contention that in the state of stress uncertainty is increased. This evidence should be corroborated in this section with reference to our experimental data. As the experimental task requires the collection of information and mental operations for reaching an optimal decision, uncertainty should lead to (1) loss of relevant information, (2) intrusion of irrelevant information, or (3) impairment of mental operations.

From the balance model of capacity and demand outlined in the first section, it could be predicted that subjects under uncertainty will either favor a risk-taking or a compensating strategy. In the course of the compensating strategy, subjects would try to reduce uncertainty by taking more time and making up for information loss by active information search; compensating procedures would allow them to maintain a high level of aspiration. A risk-taking strategy meant that subjects would try to operate on the basis of suboptimal information. Disregarding chance solutions the subjects should be prepared to accept a reduction of correct solutions.

In order to assess the degree of uncertainty, compensatory activity, risk taking, and effectiveness, four types of data are presented: frequency of calls for additional presentations of the problem and for additional information (Figure 5); time spent on additional information (Figure 6); probability of erros (Figure 7); and an index of efficiency (Figure 8). The data deserve a full presentation and analysis, but due to the complex design the results are rather heterogeneous. The problems classified as medium and high with respect to difficulty turned out to have a rather high error probability. The error probability ranged between .3 and .5 during the first half of the session and reached values beyond chance probability in some experimental conditions during the second half of the experiment. Many subjects reacted to their failures by concentrating on the initial presentation of the problem, which considerably reduced the time for additional calls. In general, effects of noise and personality are leveled off under conditions of higher difficulty, and the scores on compensatory activity are ambiguous. There is no such leveling in the scores for problems classified as easy, and the time spent on the initial presentation of the problem was short and

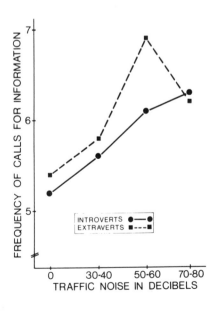

Figure 5 Number of calls for information following the initial presentation of the problem (average for one problem). (Data from conditions with lower task difficulty.)

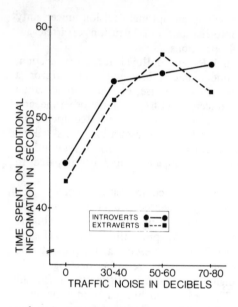

Figure 6 Time spent on additional information (average for one problem).
(Data from conditions with lower
task difficulty.)

rather invariant between experimental groups. Furthermore, differences between
the first and second half of the experimental session were small. Therefore
Figures 5–8 only present data for the problems initially classified as easy, and the
scores for the first and second half of the experimental session are combined.

Provided that calls for additional information (Figure 5) can be interpreted as
means of reducing uncertainty, traffic noise unrelated to a primary activity can
be stated as a factor inducing uncertainty. There is clear evidence that the
frequency of calls increases with noise intensity ($p = .01$) and so does the time
spent on information search (Figure 6) ($p < .05$). There is a remarkable

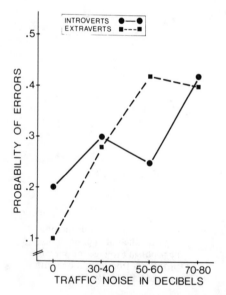

Figure 7 Probability of errors. (Data from
conditions with lower task difficulty.)

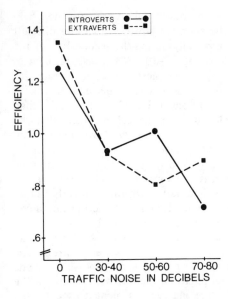

Figure 8 Index of efficiency based on the ratio of correct responses and number of calls for additional information. (Data from conditions with lower task difficulty.)

difference between introverts and extraverts: Whereas introverts continually extend their compensatory activity with increasing noise level, extraverts diminish their compensating activity with higher levels. It would be hard to believe that extraverts would suffer less from loud than from medium noise. Such a statement could not be substantiated by reference to their own judgments of disturbance by noise (Figure 3). Therefore, we conclude that with high external demand, extraverts shift toward risk-taking behavior. Their behavior can be interpreted as resignation toward matching their capacities to heavily increased external demands. Whereas introverts throughout and extraverts under low noise level try to regulate their demand-capacity ratio by increasing their capacity, extraverts under high noise conditions regulate by reducing the demand component, leaving capacity constant.

Obviously neither external control of noise nor compensatory activity completely succeeds in avoiding an increment of errors with increasing noise (Figure 7). There is an almost 100% increment of errors between the conditions without and with 30-40 dB(A) noise, and in general there is a monotonous relation between noise level and error probability ($p < .01$). Since adequacy of behavior is a central issue in this study, we also attempted to calculate an index of efficiency. This index relates the frequency of calls for information to the number of optimal decisions. Error probabilities and compensatory activities forming ascending functions of noise intensity combine to a descending function of efficiency (Figure 8). The relation of efficiency and noise intensity is significant at the .01 level. A remarkable feature of the function is the sharp drop between the conditions without and with 30-40 dB(A) traffic noise. Again it can be argued from the evaluative point of view that frequent external control of noise may have been more detrimental to performance than a tolerance of noise would have been; this supports the evaluation of external control of low noise as inadequate coping. Frequent control of loud noise, on the other hand, may have been beneficial for performance, as it reduces the need for further compensatory activity and prevents still larger deficits in efficiency.

The observations from the phases in which easier tasks were presented help clarify some of the processes that underlie states of stress. With more difficult tasks the effects become more dramatic, especially during the second half of the experimental session. Under these conditions and 70–80 dB(A) noise, differences between personality groups become more pronounced. The error rate for extraverts under these conditions rises to .67, which is slightly better than chance probability. Introverts under the same conditions managed to do worse than chance probability (.81). It can be concluded from the achievements that the subjects were operating outside the range of their capacity. Nevertheless they maintained their activity. Both introverts and extraverts ordered about six slides for additional information, but there was a marked difference between the time consumed for reaching the decision. Whereas the extraverts had decision times averaging at 85 seconds or 71% of the total time permitted, the introverts had an average of 103 seconds or 86% of the total time. Therefore the efficiency index of extraverts dropped to a value of .42, the introverts' index to .16.

We assume that subjects who are exposed to difficult tasks, high traffic noise, and who are in the last phase of their session are in a state of stress. The extravert group—compared to the introvert group—seems to show some tendencies to escape this state by earlier termination; the introvert group, on the other hand, seems to tolerate the existing state and even augment it by extended activity. Arguing again from the evaluative point of view, the critical observer would not resist the contention that compensatory behavior under these conditions of demand and capacity was not appropriate, and even an extreme risk-taking strategy (eventually going along with a strong control of external noise) would have been more advisable.

Causal Attribution, Choice of Regulatory Action, and Physiological Activity

The above interpretation of stress as a state in which inappropriate coping activity occurs remains inconclusive unless it can be shown that the decision time is indeed used for operations on the problem and that an extension of the time for reaching the decision is not due to (voluntary or unvoluntary) rest periods that actually reduce stress. Heart rate and skin resistance were continually monitored as measures of overall activity. The data are rather consistent as far as the impact of noise and introversion-extraversion is concerned. Interestingly enough, heart rate and skin resistance tend to decrease with both task difficulty and length of session. For a better comparison with the performance data, only the scores measured during presentations of tasks initially classified as easy are presented in Figures 9 and 10; scores from the second and the first half of the sessions are averaged.

The interaction between personality and noise for heart rate, and the overall difference between introverts and extraverts for skin resistance are of borderline significance ($p < .1$). If the data can be taken as indices of overall activity, effort, and emotional involvement, it appears that introverts rather than extraverts are getting involved in the conditions with traffic noise. Whereas introverts show only slight symptoms of reducing their involvement with increasing noise intensity, extraverts show a higher drop of involvement with high intensity. Thus there are signs of increasing arousal and motivation in the physiological data.

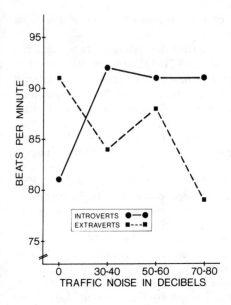

Figure 9 Heart rate in beats per minute, averaged over work periods.

Comparing the data for the conditions with noise, however, there is also evidence for a disengagement or demotivating process being more pronounced for extraverts.

The demotivating hypothesis receives further support from the subjects' judgment of degree of external control. The proportion of persons attributing their failures to noise rises dramatically with noise intensity ($p < .01$) and is higher for extraverts than for introverts ($p = .05$). These data are consistent with

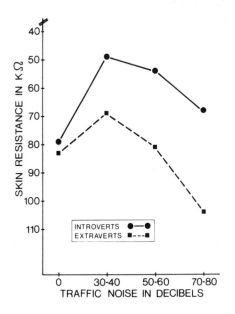

Figure 10 Skin resistance in kilo-ohms, averaged over work periods.

the judgments on interfering properties of noise presented earlier in this paper (Figure 2).

The demotivating effect of external control has already been analyzed elsewhere (e.g., Seligman, 1975; Weiss, 1971a, 1971b). In the model favored in this study, the concept of external or internal control reflects the internal representation of the demand/capacity ratio. The introverts—exhibiting symptoms of internal, labile control in the sense of Weiner (1974)—can be assumed to have a bias toward the capacity term, whereas the extraverts—displaying an external, labile attitude—are characterized by a bias toward the demand term (see Figure 1). All individuals shift the demand/capacity ratio toward the demand term if noise intensity increases.

Evidently external noise raises the uncertainty of proceeding and therefore induces stress as long as the capacity component dominates. If, however, the demand component sufficiently dominates, the external noise reduces the uncertainty of nonproceeding and finally leads to the termination of confrontation. Possibly, in the present study, introverts of the 50-60 dB(A) group have been most successful in their attempt to compensate for change of demand by change of capacity; by their activity they may have gained or at least prevented loss of efficiency and internal organization due to noise. Introverts with 30-40 dB(A) noise may have suffered more than gained from their extensive control activity, but due to the mild external noise their organization was not too severely affected. In summary, introverts with 70-80 dB(A) noise and/or high-task difficulty may even serve as examples of active but less organized systems. In contrast, extraverts show more characteristics of inactive but organized systems.

REGULATORY ACTIVITY AS A FUNCTION OF TIME-EVALUATIVE FEEDBACK

A Follow-up Study: Main Hypotheses and Experimental Design

One of the central issues to be elaborated in the analysis of the first experiment is the problem of timing. There seems to be a dramatic counterbalance in stress situations: On the one hand, in states of stress uncertainty of proceeding is increased, giving rise to time-consuming compensatory actions. On the other hand, increasing uncertainty of proceeding goes along with decreasing uncertainty of nonproceeding. The conflict between the tendency of gaining time for effective coping and time-saving escapism is apparently responsible for the high sensitivity to time pressure of stressed persons. In order to collect more detailed observations on this problem, it was decided to replicate the first study introducing a time-pressure technique.

As already mentioned above, time-evaluative feedback was contrasted with nonevaluative feedback. Subjects received a series of problems and indicated their solution by pressing a response key. After responding or failing to respond as scheduled, the subjects received a RIGHT/WRONG-signal. Under conditions of time-evaluative feedback, the subjects were permitted a time interval of 120 seconds for finding the optimal solution. In addition they were promised (and actually received) a premium of 1 German Pfennig (approximately $\frac{1}{2}$ U.S. cent) for each second saved on each 120 second-interval, if they still found the correct solution. On two digital displays they could monitor the time left during each interval and the total premium gained during the preceding part of the session. In the nonevaluative condition there was neither a time limit nor a premium. It was assumed that subjects receiving time-evaluative feedback would exhibit a stronger risk-taking behavior cutting short the time for compensatory actions. Assuming that the premium would serve as an incentive, it could be argued that time saving would constitute a demand additional to the primary task. The endeavor of meeting this additional demand would contribute to overcharging their capacities and both disorganize their performance and augment their state of stress.

In the second experiment 72 subjects were selected, mainly from the pool of unemployed technicians and office workers registered at the local labor agency. All were offered a sum of 20 German Marks for participation. One half of the sample (36 subjects) was also offered the extra payment as described above. Each group of 36 subjects was further divided into three subgroups of 12 subjects each. One of the subgroups was working in a quiet room (noise level approximately 35 dB[A]), the other two were exposed to traffic noise oscillating between 50–60 dB(A) and 70–80 dB(A), respectively. As in the first experiment they were given the opportunity to switch off the noise by pressing a button.

Again the subjects were classified and selected on the basis of a trait-anxiety test (German version of the A-Trait scale of the State-Trait Anxiety Inventory; Spielberger, Gorsuch & Lushene, 1970) and an intelligence test (Amthauer, 1953). Subjects were assigned to experimental conditions in such a way that six members of each subgroup had anxiety scores above the total median of the sample and six members had scores below the median. Anxiety was chosen as an independent factor within the experimental design because this score appeared to be related to the individual conception of demand characteristics and causal attribution (cf. Epstein, 1976). We hoped that control of this variable would help to explain a portion of the variance between individuals. The intelligence scores were used to match the subgroups in regard to intellectual capacity.

The subjects worked on the same type of problems as in the first experiment (see Figure 2). However, because the problems used in the first experiment turned out to be rather difficult, chance was taken for a revision. In the second experiment a modified series of problems was presented consisting of eight items classified as less difficult, eight items of medium, and eight items of higher difficulty.

Results

Effects of noise

As in the first experiment subjects spent some time on noise control and were still affected by interference. The effects were rather similar to those observed in the first experiment. Some significant interactions of noise intensity and both anxiety and time-evaluative feedback were observed. They will not be included, however, in the following report in order to present the effects of feedback and anxiety, which were not treated in earlier sections of this paper.

Information Processing under Conditions
of Time-Evaluative Feedback

The first effect of time-evaluative feedback was a 30% reduction in time spent for initial orientation to the task (Figure 11). The effect is highly significant. Highly anxious subjects tend to take more time for initial orientation ($p = .08$); and time spent on the first presentation of the problem also rises with problem difficulty ($p < .01$). The time taken for memorizing the problem was rather short for the group with evaluative feedback and resulted in an increased number of calls for repeated presentation of the problem ($p < .01$). As can also be seen from Figure 12, highly anxious subjects under time evaluation conditions exhibit a high rate of additional calls for the problem slide, whereas highly anxious subjects working without a time limit have the lowest number of additional calls ($p < .05$).

The additional calls for presentation of the problem slide can be interpreted as attempts to compensate for missing information due to time pressure during the first presentation. On the other hand, repeated presentations of the problem were not sufficient for reducing uncertainty of proceeding. A good indicator of this kind of uncertainty probably was the number of calls for irrelevant information. As will be recalled from an earlier section, subjects could learn to order three relevant pieces of information, thus avoiding presentations of irrelevant ones (see Figure 2). Ordering irrelevant information would either indicate a slow discrimination learning or a high uncertainty urging for more information; if relevant information is not used, the search passes over to irrelevant information. Indeed it can be shown that frequency of calls for irrelevant information tends to increase with time-evaluative feedback.

Although being more restricted in time, subjects with evaluative feedback in total ordered 10% more information, and after the presentation of the problem they used 10% more time until reaching a decision (Figure 13). The overall effect

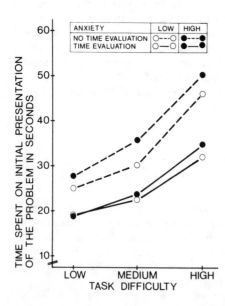

Figure 11 Time spent on the initial presentation of the problem (average for one problem).

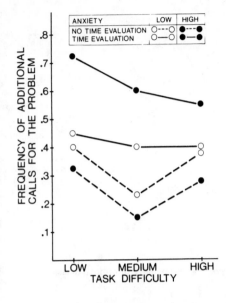

Figure 12   Frequency of additional calls for the problem (average for one problem).

of feedback conditions fails to be statistically significant. Nevertheless there remains the fact that those subjects who try to speed up and save time for each piece of information did not succeed and suffered an achievement loss (Figure 14). The probability of a correct solution is highly dependent on feedback conditions ($p < .05$), but also on task difficulty ($p < .01$) and interaction of anxiety and feedback ($p = .06$).

Obviously the effects of increasing task difficulty and time evaluation are not compensated for, although compensatory activity is not lacking. Attention should be drawn to the finding that the number of calls for the problem (Figure 12) is

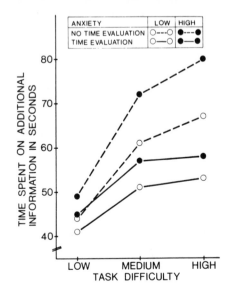

Figure 13   Time spent on additional information (average for one problem).

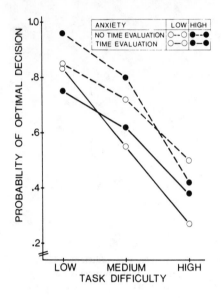

Figure 14   Probability of optimal decision.

not straightforwardly correlated with time expenditure (Figure 13). In groups with high task difficulty and time evaluation there is a tendency for a high number of calls going along with a comparatively short decision time. The tendency to cut short the average time spent on each item of information while still increasing the number of items called for can be interpreted as a symptom of impaired mental operations performed on the items and as another indicator of high uncertainty of proceeding. Interestingly enough, the total time consumed under conditions of time evaluation on the average remains far below the limit of 120 seconds for each problem. Thus there is evidence in favor of the conclusion that under high stress conditions subjects followed an avoidance strategy characterized by two properties: (1) compensation that was restricted to an external information search (cf. Lanzetta & Driscoll, 1966) and did not include full storage and utilization of the information available; and (2) preference for risk taking (actually, the nonanxious group with high difficulty and time evaluation approached the chance probability of .25).

Additionally, two kinds of efficiency scores have been calculated. The first score, which relates the amount of correct decisions to the amount of information ordered, clearly reveals a decline in efficiency with both increasing difficulty and time evaluation. The other score indicated the relation of correct decisions to decision time; according to this score, overall efficiency was reduced by difficulty but not by time evaluation. From the evaluative point of view the compensatory activity as exhibited under time evaluative feedback conditions cannot be accepted as appropriate. In addition the results cast some doubt on the appropriateness of the time-saving attitude of the subjects working under premium conditions. By their endeavor to save time and to raise their premium payment they actually faced a higher amount of stress and did not succeed in saving time; nevertheless they were breaking off their work period, took higher risks for their decision, and finally earned less money than they would probably have received if working without time pressure.

Casual Attribution, Choice of Regulatory Action, and Physiological Activity

As can be concluded from the results of a postexperimental questionnaire, the subjects rank both time pressure and task difficulty very high among the causes for their failures. Whereas it has to be accepted that choice of task difficulty was beyond their control, time pressure was self-imposed and a function of their unrealistic aspiration level. They would have maximized their monetary gain under premium conditions if they had set a lower goal and permitted themselves to consume more time. Since they failed to use this kind of regulation, they had to turn to compensatory techniques and risk-taking, which fell short of being effective.

There also seems to be a substantial difference between attributions of high- and low-anxious subjects. Whereas low-anxious subjects tend to attribute their failures to external factors, highly anxious subjects relate failures to lack of own ability. Disbelief in their own capabilities (cf. Sarason, 1975) seems to lead to demotivating effects during confrontation with a task. On the other hand—as can also be concluded from earlier studies (see Epstein, 1976)—the result of their activity is highly relevant for their self-esteem, and they may get rather involved with the appreciation of their achievement after confrontation with the task is over. This interpretation is in line with the heart-rate measures taken during and after confrontation with the task (Figure 15): Highly anxious subjects show a reduced heart rate during the work period ($p < .05$); if the work period is followed by evaluation, then their heart rate rises dramatically by an average of 10 beats per minute.

The differential heart-rate response of highly anxious subjects to the

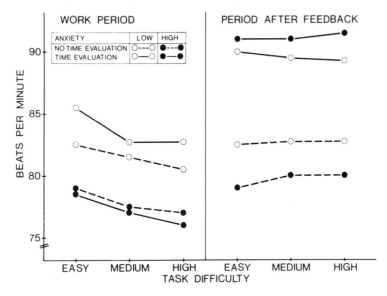

Figure 15 Heart rate in beats per minute, averaged over work periods and for a 30-second interval following (evaluative or nonevaluative) feedback.

confrontation with a problem and to confrontation with the outcome evaluation makes clear that neither high nor low heart rate is a stable characteristic of highly anxious individuals. Their heart rate is subjected to vigorous regulation. However, on the basis of their lowered arousal in task situations we cannot conclude that they spent less time in problem orientation. Actually, they spent more time on problem orientation than low-anxious subjects (Figure 11). Apparently, highly anxious individuals have lower premium expectations and therefore feel more free to engage in orienting activity, especially with difficult tasks (Figure 12). Their attitude operates against break-offs and risky decisions (Figure 13). In the absence of time evaluation, achievement of highly anxious subjects is slightly superior with easy problems but inferior with difficult ones; with time evaluation the differences between personality groups become inconclusive (Figure 14).

These data correspond to earlier findings (e.g., Gaudry & Spielberger, 1971; King, Heinrich, Stephenson, & Spielberger, 1976; Sarason, 1975) showing superiority of anxious over nonanxious individuals with easy but not with difficult tasks. According to the heart-rate scores presented in this section, this effect cannot be accounted for by a higher arousal level of highly anxious subjects being beneficial for simple tasks and detrimental for complex ones. Probably another consideration deserves some further testing: Highly anxious persons—due to their low confidence in their ability—employ more modes of control and orientation, while refraining from an early goal attainment; their behavior is extensive rather than intensive. The high degree of control that anxious persons gain can well be exerted in situations offering demands; it diminishes their uncertainty and enables them to meet high standards related to easy problems. In high-demand situations they cannot reach the same degree of control; they suffer from high uncertainty, are less efficient, and show inclinations to give up. Low-anxious individuals—relying more on their ability—seem to operate in a more selective, goal-oriented manner. Their control and orienting behavior is less extensive but more intensive. Their selective orientation and control may make them inferior to highly anxious individuals in low-demand situations but also helps them tackle high-demand situations. Possibly anxiety scores permit a classification along three dimensions: (1) rigidity of organization (high-anxious persons being more rigid); (2) range of adjustment (low-anxious individuals being more responsive to the whole range of information and demands); and (3) time allocation (low-anxious individuals being engaged in a higher number of diverse activities than persons with high anxiety).

REFERENCES

Amthauer, R. *Intelligenz-Struktur-Test.* Göttingen: Hogrefe, 1953.

Averill, J. R. Personal control over aversive stimuli and its relationship to stress. *Psychological Bulletin,* 1973, *80,* 286–303.

Düker, H. Über reaktive Anspannungssteigerung. *Zeitschrift für experimentelle und angewandte Psychologie,* 1963, *10,* 46–72.

Epstein, S. Anxiety, arousal, and the self-concept. In I. G. Sarason & C. D. Spielberger (Eds.), *Stress and anxiety* (Vol. 3). Washington, D.C.: Hemisphere, 1976.

Gaudry, E., & Spielberger, C. D. *Anxiety and educational achievement.* Sydney: Wiley, 1971.

Kahneman, D. *Attention and effort.* Englewood Cliffs, NJ: Prentice-Hall, 1973.

King, F. J., Heinrich, D. L., Stephenson, R. S., & Spielberger, C. D. An investigation of the causal influence of trait and state anxiety on academic achievement. *Journal of Educational Psychology,* 1976, *68,* 330–334.

Lanzetta, J. T., & Driscoll, J. M. Preference for information about an uncertain but unavoidable outcome. *Journal of Personality and Social Psychology,* 1966, *3,* 96–102.

Lazarus, R. S. *Psychological stress and the coping process.* New York: McGraw-Hill, 1966.

McGrath, J. E. A conceptual formulation for research on stress. In J. E. McGrath (Ed.), *Social and psychological factors in stress.* New York: Holt, Rinehart and Winston, 1970.

McGrath, J. E. Stress and behavior in organizations. In M. D. Dunette (Ed.), *Handbook of industrial and organizational psychology.* Chicago: Rand McNally, 1976.

Sarason, I. G. Anxiety and self-preoccupation. In I. G. Sarason & C. D. Spielberger (Eds.), *Stress and anxiety* (Vol. 2). Washington, D.C.: Hemisphere, 1975.

Schönpflug, W., & Heckhausen, H. *Lärm und Motivation.* (Forschungsbericht des Landes Nordrhein-Westfalen Nr. 2580). Opladen: Westdeutscher Verlag, 1976.

Seligman, M. E. P. *Helplessness. On depression, development, and death.* San Francisco: Freeman, 1975.

Selye, H. *The stress of life.* New York: McGraw-Hill, 1956.

Spielberger, C. D., Gorsuch, R. L., & Lushene, R. E. *Manual for the State-Trait Anxiety Inventory.* Palo Alto, CA: Consulting Psychologists Press, 1970.

Vossel, G., & Laux, L. The impact of stress experience on heart rate and task performance in the presence of a novel stressor. *Biological Psychology,* 1978, *6,* 193–201.

Weiner, B. *Achievement motivation and attribution theory.* Morristown, NJ: General Learning Press, 1974.

Weiss, J. M. Effects of coping behavior in different warning signal conditions on stress pathology in rats. *Journal of Comparative and Physiological Psychology,* 1971, *77,* 1–13. (a)

Weiss, J. M. Effects of coping behavior with and without a feedback signal on stress pathology in rats. *Journal of Comparative and Physiological Psychology,* 1971, *77,* 22–30. (b)

4

Psychophysiological Aspects of Performance and Adjustment to Stress

Ulf Lundberg
University of Stockholm

In human stress research particular interest has been paid to two problems: (1) the relation between stress and performance efficiency and (2) the relation between stress and mental and physical health. In the present chapter some results relevant to these problems will be presented and discussed from a psychophysiological point of view.

Both detrimental and beneficial effects of stress on performance have been reported. In the present article the role played by cognitive factors in these relationships will be emphasized. Adrenal medullary activity is a very important indicator of stress, and therefore I will review experiments illustrating the effects of emotional intensity and mental effort on adrenaline excretion. The possible harmful effects of frequently elevated or long-lasting high psychophysiological arousal will be discussed in relation to activation of the adrenal medullary and adrenal cortical systems.

STRESS AND PERFORMANCE

Stress and Arousal

The assumption that arousal (or activation) is a unidimensional continuum rests mainly on Selye's General Adaptation Syndrome (see e.g., Selye, 1974) and the fact that the reticular activating system of the midbrain has a general effect on the arousal level of the individual. Different types of stressful situations, physical and psychosocial stimulation, as well as demanding tasks are all assumed to contribute to an increase of the arousal level.

In experiments with several stressors the assumption of additive effects on

The research reported in this chapter has been supported by grants to Professor Marianne Frankenhaeuser from the Swedish Medical Research Council (Project No. 997), the Swedish Work Environment Fund, and the Swedish Council for Research in the Humanities and Social Sciences. The author is indebted to Professor Marianne Frankenhaeuser, Dr. G. Robert J. Hockey, and Dr. Richard H. Rahe for valuable comments and suggestions made on this paper.

arousal has not been confirmed (e.g., Lind, 1976). However, the conception of arousal as a unidimensional continuum has been supported by experiments involving combined effects on performance of stimulating and depressant factors. Corcoran (1962) showed that performance after sleep deprivation increased upon exposure to noise. Colquhoun and Edwards (1975) found beneficial effects of noise on performance during alcohol intoxication. The impairment of performance caused by alcohol was also found to be counteracted by electric shocks (Frankenhaeuser, Dunne, Bjurström, & Lundberg, 1974) and by a monetary reward (Myrsten, Lamble, Frankenhaeuser, & Lundberg, 1979). Wilkinson (1963) similarly reported interacting effects of noise, knowledge of results, and sleep deprivation, which in general support the idea of arousal as a single continuum.

Lacey (1967) has criticized the view of arousal as a unidimensional continuum and argued for a distinction between autonomic, electrocortical, and behavioral arousal. Although different indexes of physiological arousal tend to covary, Lacey (1967) reports experiments indicating independence between autonomic, electrocortical, and behavioral measures of arousal. Even correlations between various indicators of autonomic nervous arousal can be relatively low.

Performance and Arousal

It can be assumed that aversive stimulation (such as noise, heat, or vibration) impairs performance, but the experimental results are not consistent on this point (cf. Poulton, 1976). Performance seems to be relatively resistant to aversive stimulation, but negative as well as positive effects on performance have been reported. However, if one basically assumes that the intensity of unpleasantness or discomfort is inversely related to performance (as illustrated in the left-hand diagram of Figure 1) and, in addition, that discomfort can be induced by either too little or too much stimulation (Frankenhaeuser, 1980; Levi, 1972) (as illustrated in the middle diagram), the resulting relationship between performance and level of stimulation will be the inverted U curve presented in the right-hand diagram.

The inverted U curve is the best known model relating stress-induced arousal (or activation) to performance (Hebb, 1955). When arousal or activation is low, performance tends to be poor, and as arousal level increases, so does performance to an optimal level, after which a further increase in arousal results in deteriorated performance. The optimal level of arousal depends on the difficulty

Figure 1 (*left*) A hypothetical relation between performance and discomfort, and (*middle*) the relation between level of stimulation and discomfort. (*right*) The relation between performance and level of stimulation resulting from the other two diagrams.

of the task, being lower for difficult than for easy tasks. The latter relationship is consistent with the Yerkes-Dodson Law (Yerkes & Dodson, 1908).

One way that arousal level could affect performance was suggested by Easterbrook (1959), who hypothesized that selectivity in cue utilization is low during low arousal, thus impairing performance, while selectivity of relevant cues increases with arousal. At a very high arousal level selectivity is too great and restricts the range of cues so much that performance begins to deteriorate again. Several experiments by Hockey (1973) and Hockey and Hamilton (1970) support the idea of increased selectivity as a function of arousal. Their interpretation was that "with high arousal, subjects take in less information but pay more attention to it" (Hockey & Hamilton, 1970, p. 867). Easterbrook's (1959) hypothesis is consistent with the Yerkes-Dodson Law (1908), as narrowing of attention is beneficial to most simple tasks but impairs performance on complex ones.

Walker's (1958) action decrement theory relates arousal level to memory. He hypothesized that during the period of memory consolidation there is a temporary inhibition of retrieval. High arousal makes this process more active and results in better long-term memory but poorer short-term memory, while low arousal has the opposite effect. Experiments with noise-induced arousal (e.g., Berlyne, Borsa, Craw, Gelman, & Mandell, 1965) support this hypothesis. Similar results have been reported by M. Eysenck (1976), although his hypothesis suggests that it is the effects of arousal on storage rather than on retrieval that are of importance.

The inverted U model is very flexible and has been supported by many experiments (see e.g., Atkinson, 1974). Hockey (in press) has pointed out that "this advantage is also the major drawback to the theory: since almost any result can be explained it cannot easily be disproved." For example, when only two levels of arousal are used the inverted U curve will explain any effects on performance, while with three levels of arousal only two out of the six possible relations (excluding "equals") between performance (P) and arousal (A) are inconsistent with the model.[1] Therefore a critical test of this model must involve a systematic variation along the assumed arousal continuum, keeping other factors constant.

The inverted U curve describes the relationship between intensity of arousal (or activation, stress, etc.) and performance, but it does not account for possible temporal effects of stress on performance. A model suggested by Broverman, Klaiber, Vogel, and Kobayashi (1974) relates short-term and long-term stress to adrenal and cholinergic functions and to performance on different types of tasks. The theory states that short-term stress facilitates performance of serially repetitive and overlearned tasks but impairs performance of perceptual restructuring tasks. The effects of long-term stress are the opposite (i.e., facilitation of perceptual restructuring tasks and impairment of serially repetitive and overlearned tasks). The part of the model that describes the relationship between short-term stress and performance on serially repetitive and overlearned tasks is considered by them to be consistent with the inverted U curve model, while the part that relates long-term stress to performance on perceptual restructuring tasks is considered to be inconsistent with this relationship. However, it is difficult to

---

[1] If $A_1 < A_2 < A_3$, then $P_1 < P_2 < P_3$, $P_1 < P_3 < P_2$, $P_3 < P_1 < P_2$ and $P_3 < P_2 < P_1$ are consistent with the model, and $P_2 < P_3 < P_1$ and $P_2 < P_1 < P_3$ are not.

decide whether their model is contradicting or supporting the activation theory, as concepts such as "long-term stress" and "short-term stress" do not necessarily indicate whether arousal level is high or low. For example, when food deprivation is the stressor, the severity of the condition may increase over time, but the organism's psychological and physiological arousal level may decrease. With regard to other stressful conditions—such as noise exposure, electric shocks, and blood sampling—habituation to the situation (see Frankenhaeuser, Sterky, & Järpe, 1962; McGrath, 1970) reduces the stress response and accordingly the arousal level. Thus if long-term stress is associated with a decrease in arousal level, performance on complex tasks may improve and performance on simple tasks deteriorate, as indicated by the Yerkes-Dodson Law.

Stress and Adrenal Medullary Activity

A number of physiological variables have been used as indicators of stress, for example, heart rate, blood pressure, EEG, skin conductance, and muscular tension. However, the most important indicators of stress seem to be adrenal medullary and adrenal cortical activation (Mason, 1968a, 1968b). In our laboratory particular interest has been paid to the adrenal medullary activity in relation to various stressful conditions (for reviews see Frankenhaeuser, 1971, 1980). It has been demonstrated that the activity of the adrenal medulla, as reflected in the urinary excretion of adrenaline, is of importance for successful adaptation to various psychosocial stress situations and for maintaining a high performance level. However, although baseline levels of adrenaline excretion in relation to body weight are about the same for males and females, the adrenaline output during stress is usually less pronounced for females (Frankenhaeuser, Dunne, & Lundberg, 1976; Frankenhaeuser, Rauste von Wright, Collins, von Wright, Sedvall, & Swahn, 1978). To what extent this difference is determined psychosocially and/or biologically is not yet known (cf. Collins & Frankenhaeuser, 1978).

Emotional Intensity and Catecholamine Excretion

Various forms of aversive stimulation have been found to increase the urinary excretion of adrenaline (e.g., electric shocks, unpleasant films, gravitational stress, noise, repeated venipuncture, and crowdedness). There is usually a close relationship between subjective stress and adrenaline excretion (as illustrated in Figure 2). The particular relationship between a subjective variable indicating stress or arousal and adrenaline output can take various forms, as illustrated in the diagrams, because of the influence of other situational factors, for example. On the average the magnitude of the adrenaline response may vary from about three times the night-rest level during mild stress to eight to ten times during intense stress (cf. Frankenhaeuser, 1980; Johansson, 1977). However, the individual levels of excretion may vary much more.

The urinary excretion of adrenaline seems to reflect the intensity of the emotional response rather than the quality. This was demonstrated in an experiment by Pátkai (1971), in which subjects were exposed to a pleasant situation involving a "Bingo" game with monetary rewards and an unpleasant situation of watching medicosurgical films. Both situations were associated with higher adrenaline excretion than a neutral control situation. Similarly, Levi

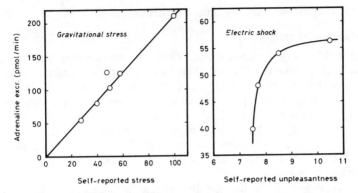

Figure 2 Mean values of adrenaline excretion plotted against self-reports of stress during a centrifuge ride (*left*) and against self-reports of unpleasantness during electrical stimulation (*right*). (The left-hand diagram is redrawn with permission on the basis of Frankenhaeuser, Sterky, and Järpe, *Perceptual and Motor Skills*, 1972, *15*, 63–72, and the right-hand diagram with permission on the basis of Frankenhaeuser, Fröberg, and Mellis, *Neuroendocrinology*, 1965, *1*, 105–112.)

(1972) has reported increased adrenaline output in both pleasant and unpleasant emotional situations and during sexual arousal induced by films.

In experiments in which adrenaline has been infused, the subjects have felt *as if* they were afraid, tense, restless, or the like. Schachter and Singer (1962) showed that it is the cognitive interpretation of the situation that determines the emotional quality accompanying the physiological arousal induced by adrenaline infusion.

Performance and Catecholamine Excretion

It is well known that physical work affects catecholamine excretion. However, mental work also has pronounced effects on adrenaline excretion. Frankenhaeuser, Nordheden, Myrsten, and Post (1971) showed that both a monotonous vigilance task and a complex choice reaction-time task induced an increase of adrenaline excretion. Increased output of adrenaline has also been reported during matriculation examination (Frankenhaeuser et al., 1978) and during the defense of a doctoral dissertation (Johansson, 1977). In the two latter cases the excretion was very high, indicating that mental effort is a very potent adrenaline stimulator, probably more so than physical effort.

It is obvious that in many situations in which mental effort is high there is a concomitant emotional reaction, for example, during an important examination. This makes it difficult to separate the effects on adrenaline output of emotional reaction on the one hand and mental effort on the other. However, in the same achievement situation it has been found that subjects with high adrenaline excretion perform better than subjects with low excretion (Frankenhaeuser et al., 1971; O'Hanlon & Beatty, 1976). It is very likely that better performance in these situations was the result of more mental effort invested and that this effort was reflected by the adrenaline output of the subjects.

Stress, Cognitive Factors, and Performance

Appraisal of Stress

In Lazarus' theory of stress (1966, 1976) the major determinant of the stress response is the appraisal of threat. This view has become generally accepted and is described by McGrath (1970) as an "emotional experience, and, to some extent, physiological, and performance measures are in part a function of the perceptions, expectations, or cognitive appraisal which the individual makes of the (stressing) situation" (p. 76). Cox (1978) similarly presents a transactional model of stress and emphasizes the imbalance between perceived demand and perceived capability, rather than actual demand and actual capability, as the determinants of stress.

Lazarus (1966, 1976) has divided coping mechanisms in stress into two classes: (1) direct actions in order to eliminate the factors causing stress, and (2) defense mechanisms such as denial, intellectualization, etc. However, in some cases one may distinguish a third class of coping strategies: the effort invested by the individual in counteracting the detrimental effects of stressful stimulation on behavior. These actions are directed, not toward the factors causing stress or on the perception of stress, but toward behavior during stress, for example, performance. This coping strategy probably leads to mental and/or physiological "costs." For example, where subjects have managed to maintain a high performance level during noise exposure, various negative "aftereffects" have been reported (Glass & Singer, 1972).

Coping with Noise Stress

Psychophysiological aspects of adjustment to noise exposure and the role played by cognitive set were illustrated in two of our own experiments. In the first (Frankenhaeuser & Lundberg, 1977) each of three groups of subjects performed mental arithmetic for 75 minutes while exposed in Session I to different noise intensities (56, 72.5, and 85 dB[A]) and in Session II to one and the same noise intensity (72.5 dB[A]). As shown in Figure 3, performance deteriorated with increasing noise level in Session I. In Session II, which was carried out on the next day and exposed all subjects to the same medium noise level, the subjects tended to maintain their relative performance level (i.e., the higher the noise level in Session I, the poorer the performance in Session II). In Session I the increase in adrenaline excretion from baseline was about the same in all three groups. However, self-reports indicated that more discomfort was experienced when noise was high. The results suggest that the subjects tended to slow down performance during more intense noise, thus making the "total mental load" about the same in all three groups.

In the second noise experiment (Lundberg & Frankenhaeuser, 1978) the same arithmetic task was performed during 60 minutes, and all subjects were exposed to one and the same low noise level (56 dB[A]) in Session I and to different noise levels in Session II. Figure 4 shows that subjects exposed to high noise (median level = 86 dB[A]) in Session II performed as well as subjects exposed to low noise (median level = 76 dB[A]). However, the data in Figure 4 also indicate that performance during high noise was associated with more effort and higher physiological arousal than performance during low noise.

These results indicate that an individual may cope with disturbing noise either

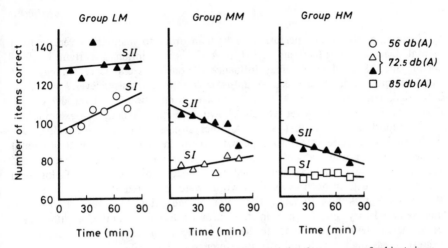

Figure 3   Successive mean scores in arithmetic performance for three groups of subjects in
each of two sessions (S I and S II). Group LM was exposed to low noise in S I and
medium noise in S II. Group MM to medium noise in both sessions, and Group HM
to high noise in S I and medium noise in S II. Low noise = 56 db(A); medium
noise = 72.5 db(A); high noise = 85 db(A). Straight lines have been fitted to the
data by the method of least squares. (Reprinted by permission of the publisher
from Frankenhaeuser and Lundberg, *Motivation and Emotion,* 1977, *1,* 139–150.)

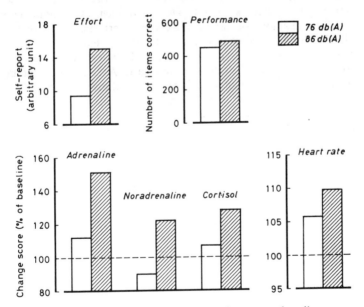

Figure 4   Mean values representing effort, performance, adrenaline,
noradrenaline, and cortisol excretion and heart rate of
subjects exposed to low (76 db[A]) and to high noise
(86 db[A]), respectively. Physiological scores have been
expressed in relation to baseline level.

by decreasing his or her performance level in order to maintain a certain total mental load or by increasing effort in order to maintain a certain level of performance. Several factors may influence the subject's choice of strategy. For example, pretraining on a task may induce a certain "normative level," which the individual tries to maintain when aversive stimulation is changed. This is illustrated by the carry-over effects shown in Figure 3 and, for example, by results reported by Gulian (1974). Another situation in which individuals are likely to invest more effort to cope with disturbing noise is when they cannot influence the stimulus rate of the task. In an experiment by Frankenhaeuser and Johansson (1976), subjects performed two versions of the Stroop Color-Word Interference Test. In both cases color words were presented at a certain rate, and the subject's task was to name the color of the print. One version, however, included auditory interference in the form of a voice naming a third color. Performance level was found to be the same in both cases, but adrenaline excretion was higher with auditory interference.

Other factors likely to influence the individual's choice of strategy are assumptions about the purpose of the experiment and about the general effects of aversive stimulation on performance. Beneficial effects of noise on performance efficiency may in some cases be explained by overcompensation, that is, the subject invests more effort than necessary to overcome the (assumed) effects of disturbing noise. This was probably the case in one of our earlier noise experiments (Frankenhaeuser & Lundberg, 1974), in which subjects performed significantly better during noise exposure than during a quiet condition in the first of two sessions. The performance level from the first session was then carried over to the second session regardless of changes in noise level. (The influence of anticipation of stress effects on performance during noise is discussed further by Schönpflug in chapter 14 of this volume.)

Thus Figure 3 suggests that subjects balance the effects of noise against their effort in order to optimize their total mental load. Assuming that the individual prefers an optimal level of mental load, one can tentatively suggest that with an easy task requiring only low effort, relatively high external stimulation (e.g., noise) may help to induce an optimal mental load, whereas with a difficult task and hence a high effort, external stimulation should be low if the total mental load is to be at an optimal level.

STRESS AND HEALTH

Nonspecific and Specific Effects

The possible harmful effects of psychological stress have been considered in a great many investigations (see e.g., Lazarus, 1974). According to a nonspecificity view, adaptation to stressful conditions may in a long-term perspective accentuate the wear and tear of the organism and may increase illness susceptibility in general. This view has been expressed by Levi (1972) and is based on Selye's General Adaptation Syndrome (Selye, 1974). The specificity view of stress and illness susceptibility has been emphasized by Lazarus (1966, 1976) and Mason (1974). They have argued that different physiological and endocrine systems are activated in different situations and that specific illnesses are connected to specific response patterns. Also, differences in appraisal of the same stimulus situation may induce different response patterns (cf. Sachar, 1970).

The nonspecificity view has been supported mainly by investigations of the relationship between life changes and onset of illness, while support for the specificity view has been obtained from studies of the role played by a specific behavior pattern (Type A) in the pathogenesis of coronary artery disease and of the selective effects of stress on the adrenal medullary and adrenal cortical systems.

Life Change

The basic assumption behind life change studies (for a review see Rahe, 1975) has been that adjustment to a new situation, regardless of the desirability of the change, involves some effort in terms of time and energy and that this "cost" appears as an elevated risk of illness onset. Psychophysical scaling techniques (e.g., the method of magnitude estimation) have been used to measure the readjustment necessary for various life changes. The importance of the individual's appraisal of life changes is indicated by Figure 5, in which the psychological "amount of life change" has been compared, retrospectively, between a group of myocardial infarction patients and a matched group of healthy control subjects (Lundberg, Theorell, & Lind, 1975). The difference between the patient group and the control group increases with the weight accorded to the individual's own perception of his life changes. The data also indicates that the amount of upset caused by a life change is more relevant for myocardial infarction than the amount of readjustment required.

There are many methodological problems involved in studies on life change, stress, and illness (see Rabkin & Struening, 1976). For example, it has been argued (Mechanic, 1976; Rabkin & Struening, 1976) that it is not necessarily the incidence of illness as such but rather the treatment-seeking behavior that increases with the amount of life change. Nevertheless there does seem to be evidence enough for a connection between life change and illness onset. There are, for instance, the accumulation of various life changes before the onset of coronary heart disease (e.g., Rahe, Romo, Bennett, & Siltanen, 1974) and the increase in mortality rate following the experience of even a single important life change such as death of one's spouse (Parkes, Benjamin, & Fitzgerald, 1969).

A physiological mechanism that might conceivably be involved in a relationship between life changes and susceptibility to illness in general is the immune response. Animal experiments (e.g., Monjan & Collector, 1977) support the assumption of reduced immune response during short-term stress; the effects of long-term stress are less clear. Monjan and Collector assume that adrenal cortical activity mediates the immunosuppression. However, circulating catecholamines could also be involved in such a mechanism, and Gruchow (1976) has found some evidence for a relationship between elevated catecholamine levels (as indicated by the metabolite vanilylmandelic acid [VMA]) and various kinds of chronic disease conditions. Support for general harmful effects of elevated catecholamines on several bodily functions has been obtained in other studies (e.g., Simpson, Olewine, Jenkins, Ramsey, Zyzanski, Thomas, & Hames, 1974). A relationship between life changes and adrenaline excretion was demonstrated by Theorell, Lind, Fröberg, Karlsson, and Levi (1972).

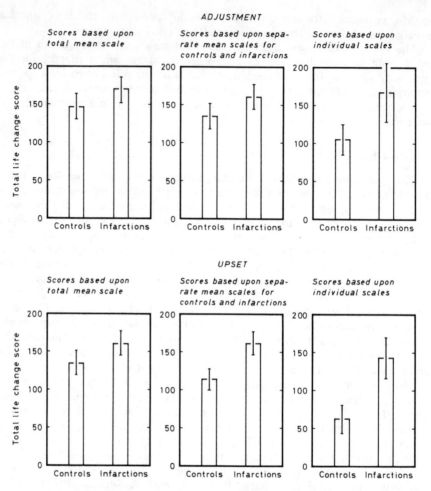

Figure 5 Mean values of total life change scores for control subjects and infarction patients regarding "adjustment" and "upset." The scores have been based alternatively upon a total mean scale, separate mean scales for controls and infarctions, and individual scales. (Reprinted by permission of the publisher from Lundberg, Theorell, and Lind, *Journal of Psychosomatic Research*, 1975, *19*, 27–32.)

The Coronary-prone Behavior Pattern

In studying the etiology of coronary heart disease, great interest has been paid to a particular response pattern, the coronary-prone or Type A behavior pattern (Friedman, 1969; Glass, 1977). The Type A individual is characterized by an extreme sense of time urgency, an excessive competitive drive, impatience, and job involvement. According to a follow-up of 3000 men (Rosenman, Brand, Sholtz, & Friedman, 1976), the incidence of coronary heart disease is about twice as high among Type A individuals as among persons without signs of this behavior pattern, that is, Type B individuals.

It has been assumed that high levels of circulating catecholamines play an important role in the pathogenesis of coronary heart disease (Raab, 1970), and there are data supporting the view that Type A individuals excrete more catecholamines than Type B individuals (Friedman, 1969; Friedman, Byers, Diamant, & Rosenman, 1975). The differences found between Type A and Type B individuals in terms of catecholamine excretion have generally been found for noradrenaline in plasma (e.g., Friedman et al., 1975). In a recent series of experiments, in which the urinary excretion of adrenaline and noradrenaline was investigated in Type A and Type B subjects (males and females) during different experimental conditions (Frankenhaeuser, Lundberg, & Forsman, in press; Lundberg & Forsman, 1979), it was found that there were no pronounced differences between Type A and Type B persons. In another experiment (Frankenhaeuser, Lundberg, & Forsman, 1980) physiological and subjective arousal was found to be consistently higher in Type A individuals during inactivity, as shown in the upper diagrams of Figure 6, but as shown in the lower diagrams, there was no systematic difference between Type A and Type B subjects during activity (i.e., performing mental arithmetic during noise exposure).

Selectivity in Endocrine Response

The review presented here of the relation between psychological stress and adrenal medullary activity shows that adrenaline and noradrenaline excretion in urine increase in a relatively nonspecific way in response to emotional intensity and mental effort. According to a theory proposed by Henry (1976), an aggressive and dominant response pattern is associated with activation of the sympathetic adrenal medullary system, while a passive and subordinate response

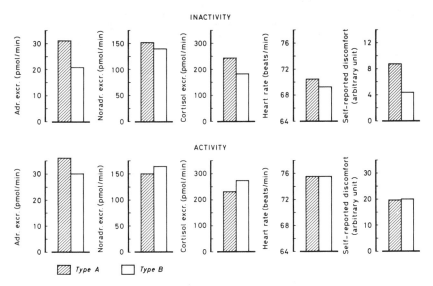

Figure 6   Mean values for adrenaline, noradrenaline, and cortisol excretion (pmol/min) and for heart rate (beats/min) and self-reported discomfort for Type A and Type B subjects exposed to conditions of inactivity and activity.

pattern is associated with activation of the pituitary adrenal cortical system. It is further assumed that the adrenomedullary response is related to coronary heart disease and the adrenocortical response to depression, and that both these response patterns are involved in the development of essential hypertension.

As indicated, the Type A pattern is characterized by a relatively dominant behavior and the Type B pattern by a more subordinate behavior. In a study by Friedman, Rosenman, and St. George (1969) it was shown that Type A individuals, who tend to excrete more catecholamines from the adrenal medulla, excreted less of the adrenal cortical hormone cortisol than Type B individuals when the subjects were challenged with large doses of adrenocorticotropin hormone (ACTH). A relationship between Type A behavior and cortisol excretion is also indicated by the data shown in Figure 6. During inactivity Type A subjects excreted more cortisol than Type B, while during activity the relation was reversed. These results have been analyzed and interpreted in terms of actual control over noise stimulation in relation to general attitudes toward control (cf. Lundberg & Frankenhaeuser, 1978), indicating an inverse relationship between cortisol excretion and control.

A recent series of experiments on adrenal medullary and adrenal cortical activation during different achievement situations provides further support for the idea that different physiological systems are activated (or suppressed) during psychologically different conditions and that control is one important aspect of these conditions. Figure 7 illustrates mean changes from baseline level in mood

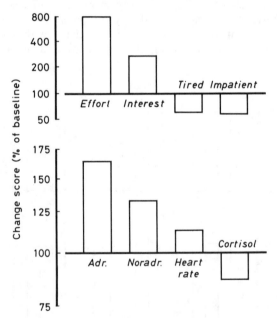

Figure 7 Mean changes (log scale) from baseline level in mood variables (upper diagram) and physiological variables (lower diagram) in an achievement situation characterized by high controllability (Frankenhaeuser, Lundberg, & Forsman, in press).

variables, adrenaline, noradrenaline, and cortisol excretion, and heart rate in an achievement situation characterized by high controllability (Frankenhaeuser, Lundberg, & Forsman, in press). It shows that increased effort and interest are related to adrenal medullary activation (e.g., adrenaline excretion) and adrenal cortical suppression (cortisol excretion).

CONCLUDING REMARKS

There is no simple relationship between stress (arousal) and performance as indicated by the results showing (1) a nonlinear relationship between stress and performance (the inverted U curve), (2) qualitatively different effects of stress on performance (e.g., narrowing of attention), and (3) different effects of stress on different performance tasks (e.g., on simple versus complex tasks). An additional factor complicating this relationship is that performance in itself may affect the organism in a way similar to that of a stressor, for example, by increasing the adrenaline output.

In the present paper it was tentatively suggested that an individual strives toward an optimal mental load and therefore may try to balance the influence from external (e.g., disturbing noise) and internal sources (e.g., mental effort). It was suggested that the individual can adopt one of two principal strategies while coping with aversive stimulation in an achievement situation: (1) keep effort constant and let performance deteriorate or (2) increase effort in order to keep the level of performance constant. Psychophysiological data indicate that the second strategy is associated with a greater mental and physiological load. There is also data showing that an individual tends to maintain the level of performance that he or she has already established.

With regard to the harmful effects of stress, there is evidence supporting both the nonspecificity and the specificity view. The research reported on the relation between life change and illness susceptibility appears to support the non-specificity view, and yet some illnesses (e.g., coronary heart disease) seem more closely related than other illnesses to psychological stress (as perceived by the individual) and to particular coping or behavior patterns. There is also evidence, for example, of a relationship between high levels of circulating catecholamines and different diseases such as myocardial infarction, hypertension, diabetes, and the like (cf. Gruchow, 1976).

According to Henry (1976) the active response of the dominant mode (high sympathetic adrenal medullary activity) should be less physiologically harmful than the subordinate response pattern (high pituitary adrenal cortical activity). As adrenal medullary activity seems to be closely related to mental effort and adrenal cortical activity to loss of control, a work situation in which control is possible and meaningful would be less harmful than one in which control is not possible. These ideas have been outlined in an ongoing research project that integrates social psychological and psychophysiological concepts and methods into a study of human adaptation to underload and overload in working life (Frankenhaeuser & Gardell, 1976).

The possibility that activation, mental effort, and concomitant catecholamine excretion have beneficial effects on health cannot be excluded (cf. Gal & Lazarus, 1975; Gruchow, 1976). A tentative hypothesis is that elevated adrenal medullary activity, induced by passive exposure to aversive stimulation, is more harmful to the organism than the same elevation induced by effort to perform well on a mental or physical task (cf. Stewart, 1975).

It may be noted that when particular factors within the coronary-prone behavior pattern (Type A) were investigated separately in relation to incidence of coronary heart disease, it was found that, although there was a significant relation between Type A behavior on the whole and coronary heart disease, one factor named Job Involvement tended to be related to coronary heart disease in the opposite direction (Jenkins, Zyzanski, & Rosenman, 1971; Kenigsberg, Zyzanski, Jenkins, Wardwell, & Licciardello, 1974). Individuals high in Job Involvement had less incidence of coronary heart disease than others. It is very likely that those individuals tend to invest more mental effort than others, but it seems as though their effort (involvement) does not necessarily increase the risk for coronary heart disease.

The potential harmful effects of a combination of (perceived) lack of control and lack of involvement (engagement) is illustrated further by the learned helplessness model (Seligman, 1975).

REFERENCES

Atkinson, J. W. Strength of motivation and efficiency of performance. In J. W. Atkinson & J. O. Raynor (Eds.), *Motivation and achievement*. Washington, D.C.: Hemisphere, 1974.

Berlyne, D. E., Borsa, D. M., Craw, M. A., Gelman, R. S., & Mandell, E. E. Effects of stimulus complexity and induced arousal on paired-associate learning. *Journal of Verbal Learning and Verbal Behavior*, 1965, *4*, 291–299.

Broverman, D. M., Klaiber, E. L., Vogel, W., & Kobayashi, Y. Short-term versus long-term effects of adrenal hormones on behavior. *Psychological Bulletin*, 1974, *81*, 672–694.

Collins, A., & Frankenhaeuser, M. Stress response in male and female engineering students. *Journal of Human Stress*, 1978, *4*(2), 43–48.

Colquhoun, W. P., & Edwards, R. S. Interaction of noise with alcohol on a task of sustained attention. *Ergonomics*, 1975, *18*, 81–87.

Corcoran, D. W. J. Noise and loss of sleep. *Quarterly Journal of Experimental Psychology*, 1962, *14*, 178–182.

Cox, T. *Stress*. London: Macmillan, 1978.

Easterbrook, J. A. The effect of emotion on cue utilization and the organization of behavior. *Psychological Review*, 1959, *66*, 183–201.

Eysenck, M. W. Arousal, learning, and memory. *Psychological Bulletin*, 1976, *83*, 389–404.

Frankenhaeuser, M. Behavior and circulating catecholamines. *Brain Research*, 1971, *31*, 241–262.

Frankenhaeuser, M. Psychoneuroendocrine approaches to the study of stressful person-environment transactions. In H. Selye (Ed.), *Selye's guide to stress research*. New York: Van Nostrand Reinhold, 1980.

Frankenhaeuser, M., Dunne, E., Bjurström, H., & Lundberg, U. Counteracting depressant effects of alcohol by psychological stress. *Psychopharmacologia*, 1974, *38*, 271–278.

Frankenhaeuser, M., Dunne, E., & Lundberg, U. Sex differences in sympathetic-adrenal medullary reactions induced by different stressors. *Psychopharmacologia*, 1976, *47*, 1–5.

Frankenhaeuser, M., Fröberg, J., & Mellis, I. Subjective and physiological reactions induced by electric shocks of varying intensity. *Neuroendocrinology*, 1965, *1*, 105–112.

Frankenhaeuser, M., & Gardell, B. Underload and overload in working life: Outline of a multidisciplinary approach. *Journal of Human Stress*, 1976, *2*(3), 35–46.

Frankenhaeuser, M., & Johansson, G. Task demand as reflected in catecholamine excretion and heart rate. *Journal of Human Stress*, 1976, *2*(1), 15–23.

Frankenhaeuser, M., & Lundberg, U. Immediate and delayed effects of noise on performance and arousal. *Biological Psychology*, 1974, *2*, 127–133.

Frankenhaeuser, M., & Lundberg, U. The influence of cognitive set on performance and arousal under different noise loads. *Motivation and Emotion*, 1977, *1*, 139–150.

Frankenhaeuser, M., Lundberg, U., & Forsman, L. Dissociation between adrenal-medullary and adrenal-cortical responses to an achievement situation characterized by high controllability: Comparison between Type A and Type B males and females. *Journal of Psychosomatic Research*, in press.

Frankenhaeuser, M., Lundberg, U., & Forsman, L. Note on arousing Type-A persons by depriving them of work. *Journal of Psychosomatic Research*, 1980, *24*, 45–47.

Frankenhaeuser, M., Nordheden, B., Myrsten, A.-L., & Post, B. Psychophysiological reactions to understimulation and overstimulation. *Acta Psychologica*, 1971, *35*, 298–308.

Frankenhaeuser, M., Rauste von Wright, M., Collins, A., von Wright, J., Sedvall, G., & Swahn, C. G. Sex differences in psychoendocrine reactions to examination stress. *Psychosomatic Medicine*, 1978, *40*, 334–343.

Frankenhaeuser, M., Sterky, K., & Järpe, G. Psychophysiological relations in habituation to gravitational stress. *Perceptual and Motor Skills*, 1962, *15*, 63–72.

Friedman, M. *Pathogenesis of coronary artery disease*. London: McGraw-Hill, 1969.

Friedman, M., Byers, S., Diamant, J., & Rosenman, R. H. Plasma catecholamine response of coronary-prone subjects (Type A) to a specific challenge. *Metabolism*, 1975, *23*, 205–210.

Friedman, M., Rosenman, R. H., & St. George, S. Adrenal response to excess corticotropin in coronary-prone men. *Proceedings from the Society of Experimental Biological Medicine*, 1969, *131*, 1305–1307.

Gal, R., & Lazarus, R. S. The role of activity in anticipating and confronting stressful situations. *Journal of Human Stress*, 1975, *1*(4), 4–20.

Glass, D. C. *Behavior patterns, stress, and coronary disease*. Hillsdale, NJ: Lawrence Erlbaum, 1977.

Glass, D. C., & Singer, J. E. *Urban stress: Experiments on noise and social stressors*. New York: Academic Press, 1972.

Gruchow, H. W. Catecholamine activity and reported morbidity. *Journal of Chronic Diseases*, 1976, *29* 773–783.

Gulian, E. Noise as a stressing agent. *Studia Psychologica*, 1974, *16*, 160–167.

Hebb, D. Drives and the C.N.S. (Conceptual Nervous System). *Psychological Review*, 1955, *62*, 243–254.

Henry, J. P. Understanding the early pathophysiology of essential hypertension. *Geriatrics*, 1976, *31*, 59–72.

Hockey, G. R. J. Changes in information-selection patterns in multisource monitoring as a function of induced arousal shifts. *Journal of Experimental Psychology*, 1973, *101*, 35–42.

Hockey, G. R. J. Effects of noise on human efficiency. In D. N. May (Ed.), *Handbook of noise evaluation*. New York: Van Nostrand Reinhold, in press.

Hockey, G. R. J., & Hamilton, P. Arousal and information selection in short-term memory. *Nature*, 1970, *226*, 866–867.

Jenkins, C. D., Zyzanski, S. J., & Rosenman, R. H. Progress toward validation of a computer-scores test for the Type-A coronary-prone behavior pattern. *Psychosomatic Medicine*, 1971, *33*, 193–202.

Johansson, G. *Case report on female catecholamine excretion in response to examination stress*. Reports from the Department of Psychology, University of Stockholm, 1977, No. 515.

Kenigsberg, D., Zyzanski, S. J., Jenkins, C. D., Wardwell, W. I., & Licciardello, A. T. The coronary-prone behavior pattern in hospitalized patients with and without coronary heart disease. *Psychosomatic Medicine*, 1974, *36*, 344–351.

Lacey, J. I. Somatic response patterning and stress. Some revisions of activation theory. In M. H. Appley & R. Trumbull (Eds.), *Psychological stress*. New York: Appleton-Century-Crofts, 1967.

Lazarus, R. S. *Psychological stress and the coping process*. New York: McGraw-Hill, 1966.

Lazarus, R. S. Psychological stress and coping in adaptation and illness. *International Journal of Psychiatry in Medicine*, 1974, *5*, 321–333.

Lazarus, R. S. *Patterns of adjustment* (3rd ed.). New York: McGraw-Hill, 1976.

Levi, L. Stress and distress in response to psychosocial stimuli. *Acta Medica Scandinavica*, 1972, *191*, Suppl. 528.

Lind, P. M. The behavioural effects of single and combined stressors: A test of arousal theory. *British Journal of Psychology*, 1976, *67*, 413–417.

Lundberg, U., & Forsman, L. Adrenal-medullary and adrenal-cortical responses to under-stimulation and overstimulation: Comparison between Type-A and Type-B persons. *Biological Psychology*, 1979, *9*, 79–89.

Lundberg, U., & Frankenhaeuser, M. Psychophysiological reactions to noise as modified by personal control over stimulus intensity. *Biological Psychology*, 1978, *6*, 51–59.

Lundberg, U., Theorell, T., & Lind, E. Life changes and myocardial infarction: Individual differences in life change scaling. *Journal of Psychosomatic Research*, 1975, *19*, 27–32.

Mason, J. W. A review of psychoendocrine research on the pituitary-adrenal cortical system. *Psychosomatic Medicine*, 1968, *30*, 576–597. (a)

Mason, J. W. A review of psychoendocrine research on the sympathetic-adrenal medullary system. *Psychosomatic Medicine*, 1968, *30*, 631–653. (b)

Mason, J. W. Specificity in the organization of neuroendocrine response profiles. In P. Seeman & G. M. Brown (Eds.), *Frontiers in neurology and neuroscience research. First International Symposium of the Neuroscience Institute*. Toronto: University of Toronto, 1974.

McGrath, J. E. Settings, measures and themes: An integrative review of some research on social-psychological factors in stress. In J. E. McGrath (Ed.), *Social and psychological factors in stress*. New York: Holt, Rinehart and Winston, 1970.

Mechanic, D. Stress, illness, and illness behavior. *Journal of Human Stress*, 1976, *2*(2), 2–6.

Monjan, A. A., & Collector, M. I. Stress-induced modulation of the immune response. *Science*, 1977, *196*, 307–308.

Myrsten, A.-L., Lamble, R., Frankenhaeuser, M., & Lundberg, U. Interactions of alcohol with reward in an achievement situation. *Psychopharmacology*, 1979, *62*, 211–215.

O'Hanlon, J. F., & Beatty, J. Catecholamine correlates of radar monitoring performance. *Biological Psychology*, 1976, *4*, 293–304.

Parkes, C. M., Benjamin, B., & Fitzgerald, R. G. Broken heart: A statistical study of increased mortality among widowers. *British Medical Journal*, 1969, *1*, 740–743.

Pátkai, P. Catecholamine excretion in pleasant and unpleasant situations. *Acta Psychologica*, 1971, *35*, 352–363.

Poulton, E. C. Arousing environmental stresses can improve performance, whatever people say. *Aviation, Space, and Environmental Medicine*, 1976, *47*, 1193–1204.

Raab, W. *Preventive myocardiology: Fundamentals and targets*. Springfield, IL: American Lecture Series, 1970.

Rabkin, J. G., & Struening, E. L. Life events, stress, and illness. *Science*, 1976, *194*, 1013–1020.

Rahe, R. H. Epidemiological studies of life change and illness. *International Journal of Psychiatry in Medicine*, 1975, *6*, 133–146.

Rahe, R. H., Romo, M., Bennett, L., & Siltanen, P. Recent life changes, myocardial infarction and abrupt coronary death. *Archives of Internal Medicine*, 1974, *133*, 221–228.

Rosenman, R. H., Brand, R. J., Sholtz, R. I., & Friedman, M. Multivariate prediction of coronary heart disease during 8.5 year follow-up in the Western Collaborative Group Study. *American Journal of Cardiology*, 1976, *37*, 903–910.

Sachar, E. J. Psychological factors related to activation and inhibition of the adrenal cortical stress response in man: A review. In D. de Wied & J. A. W. M. Weijnen (Eds.), *Progress in brain research* (Vol. 32). Amsterdam: Elsevier, 1970.

Schachter, S., & Singer, J. E. Cognitive, social, and physiological determinants of emotional state. *Psychological Reveiw*, 1962, *69*, 379–399.

Seligman, M. *Helplessness: On depression, development, and death*. San Francisco: Freeman, 1975.

Selye, H. *Stress without distress*. Philadelphia and New York: Lippincott, 1974.

Simpson, M. T., Olewine, D. E., Jenkins, C. D., Ramsey, F. H., Zyzanski, S. J., Thomas, G., & Hames, C. G. Exercise-induced catecholamines and platelet aggregation in the coronary-prone behavior pattern. *Psychosomatic Medicine*, 1974, *36*, 467–487.

Stewart, G. T. Stress in everyday life: A. Stress in society. *Royal Society of Health Journal*, 1975, *95*, 65–69.

Theorell, T., Lind, E., Fröberg, J., Karlsson, C.-G., & Levi, L. A longitudinal study of 21 subjects with coronary heart disease: Life changes, catecholamine excretion, and related biomedical reactions. *Psychosomatic Medicine,* 1972, *34*, 505–516.

Walker, E. L. Action decrement and its relation to learning. *Psychological Review,* 1958, *65*, 129–142.

Wilkinson, R. T. Interaction of noise with knowledge of results and sleep deprivation. *Journal of Experimental Psychology,* 1963, *66*, 332–337.

Yerkes, R., & Dodson, J. D. The relation of strength of stimulus to rapidity of habit-formation. *Journal of Comparative and Neurological Psychology,* 1908, *18*, 459–482.

5

Learned Helplessness, Anxiety, and Achievement Motivation

Neglected Parallels in Cognitive, Affective, and Coping Responses

Carol S. Dweck
University of Illinois

Camille B. Wortman
University of Michigan

In this chapter we will explore the cognitions that are associated with behavior in achievement settings and the coping strategies that are employed in such settings to minimize distress and maximize performance. There is a great deal of evidence to suggest that in challenging achievement settings some individuals are able to sustain high levels of motivation and vigor for a considerable period of time. They are not easily discouraged by difficulties or minor setbacks and generally regard failures as temporary and surmountable. They are able to concentrate fully on the task, enjoy working on difficult tasks, and normally show improvements in their performance over time. Other individuals find performance settings generally aversive and have difficulty sustaining motivation or interest on difficult achievement tasks. They often find it difficult to concentrate on the task at hand, as their thoughts frequently wander to task-irrelevant issues. These individuals are quickly discouraged by the slightest setback, viewing it as clear evidence of their inadequacy. Thus they often give up quickly or show striking performance decrements after initial failures have occurred.

We attempt to illustrate how these diverse reactions are mediated by the pattern of cognitions elicited in performance settings. We believe a careful analysis of the cognitive processes that occur during performance is essential if we are to understand the motivational determinants of achievement and if we are to devise effective ways of alleviating maladaptive behaviors in performance settings.

At least three major research areas have addressed the issue of performance in achievement settings: the achievement motivation area, the test anxiety field, and, more recently, the area of learned helplessness. For the most part, these fields have developed independently of one another. We feel that this is

Work on this paper was supported by National Science Foundation grant BNS 79-14252 and National Institute of Mental Health grant MH 31667 to the first author, and by National Science Foundation grant BNS 79-21450 to the second author. The authors thank Karen Mulhaney and David Reuman for critical comments on the manuscript.

unfortunate, since investigators in these areas have been concerned with problems and issues that are quite similar. We will first provide a brief overview of the theoretical and empirical work in each field that is most relevant to the question of performance in achievement settings. We will then summarize the strengths and weaknesses that have characterized research in each of these areas. Next we will draw from each of these research traditions to present a thorough account of the cognitive processes elicited in performance settings. We will conclude by identifying what we believe are the central questions raised by a joint consideration of these different research traditions and by suggesting some potentially fruitful avenues for subsequent research.

ACHIEVEMENT MOTIVATION

Research on achievement motivation has a long history (McClelland, Atkinson, Clark, & Lowell, 1953) and represents one of the first systematic attempts to conceptualize and predict behavior in achievement situations (Atkinson, 1957, 1964, 1966, 1974; Atkinson & Birch, 1974, Atkinson & Feather, 1966; Atkinson & Raynor, 1974). In this approach, domain-specific motives were postulated, and the relative strength of each motive at a given time in a given situation was viewed as determining what activity would be initiated. The theory of achievement motivation focusses on two motives: the motive to achieve success and the motive to avoid failure. These motives are generally viewed as relatively stable individual differences. In combination with the subjective probability of success, and the incentive value of the task, the strength of these motives determines the achievement tasks that are selected and the level of effort that will be shown on such tasks.

The theory has stimulated a considerable amount of research (see Atkinson & Raynor, 1974). For example, high need for achievement has usually been found to predict greater persistence and higher performance on tasks and examinations. Much of the research on the achievement motive has centered around the level of aspiration area, since the theory predicts differential risk preference among individuals differing in achievement motivation. Consistent with the original theory, early laboratory studies found that people with a high need for achievement generally show a preference for intermediate risks and moderately difficult tasks. They also tend to show more "typical" shifts of aspiration level (i.e., small increases after success and small decreases after failure), while individuals with a low need for achievement generally make more atypical shifts (see Atkinson & Raynor, 1974, for a review of this work). Recent research has suggested that as performance continues over time, individuals high in achievement motivation come to prefer increasingly difficult tasks (Kuhl & Blankenship, 1979).

Since the initial formulation of the theory, several refinements and modifications have been suggested, both by Atkinson and his associates. For example, Raynor (1974) has suggested that the tendency to undertake an achievement task is affected not only by the subjective probabilities of success on that task but also by the importance of success on the task to one's future goals. In support of this hypothesis individuals differing in achievement motivation show the greatest differences in anxiety and concern about achievement in a course when this course is seen as important to a student's long-term goals (Raynor,

Atkinson, & Brown, 1974). Moreover, students with a high resultant motive to achieve were found to perform better in an introductory psychology class if the course was relevant to their long-term goals, while students with a low resultant need for achievement performed better in courses that were unrelated to their long-term goals (Raynor, 1970). Raynor (1974) has discussed a number of intriguing implications of this modification for the area of motivation and career striving.

A second refinement in the theory that is relevant to the questions raised in this chapter was proposed by Atkinson and Birch (1970, 1974). These investigators have conceptualized behavior as a continuous stream of activity rather than as a series of discrete episodes. They maintained that a person's behavior at any given time is a function of action tendencies, which represents positive motivation to engage in particular behaviors, and negaction tendencies, which represent tendencies not to engage in those behaviors. According to Atkinson and Birch, behavior is determined by the resultant action tendency or the difference between the action and negaction tendency. The resultant action tendency for one activity competes with resultant action tendencies for other incompatible activities, and the strongest of them is expressed in behavior. Unlike prior versions of the model, this version is concerned with moment-to-moment changes in the strengths of these motives and thus with changes in an individual's activities over time.

A basic tenet of the theory is that an action tendency, once aroused, will tend to persist over time. For this reason, the strength of the motivation to achieve is a function of any previously aroused but unsatisfied motivation plus the additional strength of the tendency aroused by the immediate situation. For a positively motivated subject engaged in repeated trials on an achievement task, success on any one trial reduces achievement motivation, while failure does not. Therefore, positively motivated subjects should experience more motivation on a trial following a failure than on a trial following a success. In contrast, avoidance-motivated subjects should experience greater motivation after success trials than on failure trials. In support of this reasoning Weiner (1965, 1966) has found that for positively motivated subjects the speed of performance is greater following failure trials than following success trials.

This model suggests an experimental paradigm that differs from the traditional one in allowing for free expression of preference between a given set of alternatives over an extended period of time. It also suggests a change in emphasis from simple choice and effort measures to measures of latency and time spent. Some interesting implications can be derived from the theory and are presently being subjected to empirical test. For example, since they experience little resistance or negaction, positively motivated people should initiate achievement-oriented activities sooner, become more completely involved more quickly, and spend more time on such tasks than individuals who are more anxious or motivated to avoid failure. The motive to avoid failure increases the latency of initiating achievement tasks and increases the probability of choosing other, nonachievement tasks. Thus individuals motivated to avoid failure are more vulnerable to interrruptions that lead them completely out of the achievement situation. Once they begin the task, however, their negaction is gradually overcome. This means that performance decrements and, presumably, difficulties in concentration are most likely to occur at the initial stages of performance.

Although these modifications of the original model have important implications for the general problem of reactions to failure, this approach has devoted little attention to the cognitive processes of the subjects. In our judgment some of the most significant and exciting work in the area of achievement motivation has focused on the cognitions and causal judgments that may underlie various types of behavior in achievement settings (see, e.g., Heckhausen, 1968, 1975, 1977, chapter 12 in this volume; Weiner, Frieze, Kukla, Reed, Rest, & Rosenbaum, 1971; Weiner, 1974). In a reanalysis of the basis of achievement behavior, for example, Weiner et al. (1971) proposed that achievement motive differences may be related to differences in subjects' causal attributions. These investigators delineated a taxonomic scheme for the assignment of causality in achievement-related settings. They postulated that success or failure can generally be attributed to four causal elements: ability, effort, task difficulty, or luck. They defined ability and effort as internal attributions of causality or properties of the person, and task difficulty and luck as external attributions or properties of the environment or situation. They have further argued that ability and task difficulty are fixed in that they remain relatively unchanged over time, while effort and luck are variable and may change from moment to moment. Weiner et al. (1971) suggested that attributions to internal factors are associated with greater intensity of emotional response than attributions to external factors, and that attributions to stable factors are associated with greater changes in one's expectations for subsequent performance than attributions to variable factors.

Weiner and his associates have maintained that individual differences in achievement motivation are mediated by differences in causal attributions for success and failure, and that these causal inferences affect subsequent achievement behavior. These investigators have convincingly argued that individuals who are high in achievement motivation have more interest in achievement-related tasks because they attribute success at such tasks to their own ability and effort. This attribution presumably results in heightened pride in accomplishment. Such individuals should also show persistence in the face of failure since they generally ascribe failure to lack of effort, which they believe to be modifiable. They should respond to achievement tasks with greater vigor since they believe that their outcomes are determined by their efforts. Finally, they should select tasks of intermediate difficulty because such tasks yield the most self-evaluative feedback (see also Trope, 1975, 1979; Trope & Brickman, 1975). In contrast, individuals with low resultant achievement motivation should be less willing to engage in achievement-related activities. Since they tend to attribute their successes to external factors and failure to a lack of ability, successes are not particularly rewarding and failures are threatening. Because of their tendency to attribute their failures to lack of ability, which is presumably unchangeable, they should tend not to persist in the face of failure. They should perform most achievement tasks with relatively little intensity or vigor since they believe that their performance is less likely to be affected by their efforts. Finally, they should tend to select tasks that are either very easy or very difficult since such tasks provide a minimum of self-evaluative feedback. Although there have been inconsistencies from study to study, the available research evidence has provided much support for the utility of this approach. (See Heckhausen, 1975; Weiner, 1974; Weiner et al., 1971, for reviews.) Indeed, Weiner's attributional analysis has been invaluable in reawakening widespread interest in the study of achievement and its underpinning.

TEST ANXIETY

One of the earliest theoretical contributions in the field of test anxiety was made by Mandler and Sarason (1952) and was drawn heavily from Hullian drive theory. These investigators postulated that the chief differentiating characteristic of high-test-anxious persons is that when they are placed in an evaluative setting, a class of task-irrelevant or interfering responses is evoked. Mandler and Sarason (1952) designed an instrument to assess these interfering responses, the Test Anxiety Questionnaire (TAQ), and argued that these responses would be heightened as the testing situations become more evaluative or stressful.

Since that time, a considerable amount of theory-based research has been conducted (see I. G. Sarason, 1960, 1972a, 1972b, 1975a, 1975b; Spence & Spence, 1966; Spielberger, 1975; Wine, 1971, in press, chapter 10 in this volume, for reviews). A number of conclusions can be drawn from the available literature. First, high-test-anxious subjects tends to perform more poorly on cognitive tasks than do low-test-anxious individuals. Second, high-test-anxious subjects tend to report a greater incidence of task-relevant thoughts during performance, many of which are self-deprecating in nature. Third, differences in performance among high- and low-test-anxious individuals are enhanced if the task in question is difficult or complex. Finally, differences in performance are also enhanced if the test is taken under conditions that increase subjects' evaluation apprehension. Manipulations such as providing the subjects with ego-involving instructions, instructing them to complete the task under time pressure, or informing them that their performance will be observed by others generally result in performance decrements for high-anxious subjects and improved performance for low-anxious subjects.

As research findings have accumulated in this area, a number of investigators have begun to criticize the utility of viewing anxiety as a unitary state (see, e.g., Liebert & Morris, 1967; Sarason, 1966; Sarbin, 1968). An important theoretical distinction was drawn by Liebert and Morris (1967), who posited that there are two distinguishable components of test anxiety, one cognitive and the other emotional. The cognitive component, which they have labeled as "worry," was identified as cognitive concern about one's performance (e.g., thinking about the consequences of failure, expressing doubts about one's ability). The "emotionality" component referred to autonomic or physiological reactions that occur in the test situation. This distinction has been supported by a number of research studies. Worry scores show a consistent negative relationship to performance expectancies, as well as to actual performance on cognitive tasks. In contrast no consistent relationship has been found between emotionality scores and subjects' performance expectancies or actual performance (see Doctor & Altman, 1969; Liebert & Morris, 1967; Morris & Fulmer, 1976; Morris & Liebert, 1969, 1970; Morris & Perez, 1972; Spiegler, Morris, & Liebert, 1968).

Gradually researchers have begun to recognize the importance of the more cognitive components of test anxiety. A major impetus for this shift in focus has been the work of Wine (1971, in press, note 1; see also chapter 10 in this volume), who has proposed an attentional interpretation of the adverse effects test anxiety has on performance. Wine (1971) has suggested that highly test-anxious subjects perform poorly during task performance because they tend to divide their attention between self-relevant and task-relevant matters. In contrast, low-test-anxious subjects focus more of their attention on the task at hand. Drawing from a wide variety of research on test anxiety, including that of Liebert and Morris (1967), Wine was able to marshall an impressive amount of support for this hypothesis. Since the publication of her original paper (Wine, 1971), data have continued to accumulate in support of her view (see Wine, in press, and Wine's chapter in this volume for more recent reviews).

In each of her papers Wine has devoted considerable attention to the implications of her approach for the alleviation and treatment of test anxiety. In support of her reasoning she has presented evidence that therapies that direct attention away from self-preoccupied worry, help subjects to focus on the task at hand, and provide specific problem-solving strategies are the most helpful in improving the performance of test-anxious subjects. As Wine (in press) has noted, much of the treatment literature has been based on the erroneous assumption that emotional arousal is the major characteristic of test anxiety and has therefore been geared toward the reduction of arousal. Treatment practices focusing solely on emotionality reduction may produce self-reported reductions in anxiety, but they are unlikely to result in improved performance in the testing situation. Therapy modes that have included a component focusing specifically on subjects' cognitions are more likely to result in sustained improvements in performance (see Spielberger, Anton, & Bedell, 1976; Wine, in press; Note 1, for reviews).

Although the emphasis on cognitions in the anxiety literature has represented an important advance, two caveats must be raised regarding the nature and measurement of the anxiety construct. First, many researchers in the area speak as though anxiety predicts or explains self-preoccupation or rumination in achievement situations. However, it is only the cognitive or worry component of anxiety scales that has shown a consistent relationship to performance in test anxiety studies, and this component asks specifically about self-preoccupation (e.g., with consequences of failure, adequacy of abilities). Thus, it is more accurate to say that anxiety *is* self-preoccupation or rumination.

Second, and perhaps more important, there is evidence that the predictive power of test anxiety scales may come from a "poor self-evaluation" factor and not from the test anxiety (worry) factor at all. Working from the Test Anxiety Scale for Children (TASC) (Sarason, Lighthall, Davidson, Waite, & Ruebush, 1960), Nicholls (1976) unconfounded these two factors by constructing separate scales that assessed each independently. He found that those variables typically observed to be related to the original scale were more highly correlated with his self-evaluation scale than with his test anxiety scale. In fact, for girls, variables directly relevant to the construct validity of the TASC were largely unrelated to the unconfounded test anxiety scale. Thus, the question of what the anxiety construct represents or how it is operationalized is a serious one that should be addressed directly.

Since the publication of Wine's (1971) important article, investigators in this area have shown increasing interest in the nature of cognitions that underlie decrements in performance situations (see, e.g., Heckhausen, chapter 12 in this volume; Meichenbaum & Butler, in press; I. G. Sarason, in press). We focus quite heavily on this work in subsequent sections of this chapter, where we attempt to delineate the cognitions associated with adaptive and maladaptive behavior in performance settings.

THE LEARNED HELPLESSNESS APPROACH

The learned helplessness phenomenon, first studied systematically in research on fear conditioning in animals (e.g., Overmier & Seligman, 1967; Seligman, Maier, & Geer, 1968), has captured the interest of psychologists in many disciplines and has been applied to a wide variety of problem areas, including reactive depression (e.g., Klein & Seligman, 1976; W. R. Miller & Seligman, 1973, 1975, 1976; W. R. Miller, Seligman, & Kurlander, 1975; Seligman, 1974, 1975; Seligman, Klein, & Miller, 1976); stress and disease (e.g., Glass, 1977; Krantz, Glass, & Snyder, 1974; Krantz & Schulz, 1979); aging (e.g., Langer & Rodin, 1976; Rodin & Langer, 1977; Schulz, 1976); crowding and urban stress (e.g., Baum, Aiello, & Calesnick, 1978; Glass & Singer, 1972; Rodin, 1976); and educational and achievement issues (e.g., Dweck, 1975).

Because reviews exploring the relevance of the learned helplessness work for achievement behavior are generally not available, we will explore helplessness in some detail. We will review the history of the concept from the early work on animals to the more recent focus on the attributions and cognitions that may underlie helpless behavior. In so doing we will focus on problems that have emerged in the attempt to apply the animal research to human behavior and thus have prompted revision of the original model.

Previous Research Efforts

In the initial helplessness experiments with dogs and rats (e.g., Overmier & Seligman, 1967; Seligman, Maier, & Geer, 1968), it was found that exposure to uncontrollable aversive stimulation subsequently interferes with the acquisition of escape-avoidance learning. If naive dogs are placed in a two-compartment shuttlebox, they quickly learn to jump from one compartment to the other and thus avoid electric shocks. But this is not the case for dogs who have previously received uncontrollable electric shocks. These dogs are very slow to learn to avoid or escape the shock. Indeed, they appear to give up and passively accept as much shock as the experimenter chooses to administer.

On the basis of these data it was proposed that exposure to uncontrollable aversive outcomes results in "learned helplessness." The organism is said to have learned that its responses and outcomes are independent and to generalize this belief to situations in which control is, in fact, possible. Once outcomes are regarded as beyond one's control, active goal-oriented responding presumably drops out. According to Seligman, learned helplessness is characterized by a reduced incentive for responding, interference with the learning of new response-relief contingencies, passivity, and depression (Seligman, 1975; Seligman, Maier, & Solomon, 1971).

The learned helplessness model has generated an enormous body of research on infrahuman species as well as on humans too extensive to review here. In general the animal studies have provided fairly convincing evidence for the model (see Maier, Seligman, & Solomon, 1969; Maier & Seligman, 1976; Seligman, Maier, & Solomon, 1971, for reviews), although alternative explanations for these results have been proposed and inconsistencies in the findings have been noted (see e.g., Anisman & Waller, 1973; Levis, 1976; Weiss, Glazer, & Pohorecky,

1977). However, when the helplessness paradigm has been applied to research with human subjects, the evidence has been less clear-cut (see I. W. Miller & Norman, 1979; Roth, in press; and Wortman & Brehm, 1975, for reviews). In the typical experiment with humans, subjects are exposed to the experimental manipulation in the pretreatment or helpfulness training phase of the study. Performance decrements are assessed in a testing phase that follows helplessness training. In most cases the performance of subjects who have undergone helplessness training is compared with that of control subjects who do not receive the helplessness manipulation.

Some researchers have followed the animal model quite closely, employing uncontrollable aversive stimulation such as noise or shock in the training phase of the experiment (e.g., Cole & Coyne, 1977; Fosco & Geer, 1971; Gatchel, Paulus, & Maples, 1975; Gatchel & Proctor, 1976; Geer, Davison & Gatchel, 1970; Hiroto, 1974; Hiroto & Seligman, 1975; Klein & Seligman, 1976; Sherrod & Downs, 1974; Thornton & Jacobs, 1971, 1972). Since the animal work had demonstrated that it is not the aversiveness of the outcome but its uncontrollability that produces helplessness, other investigators have exposed subjects to various kinds of noncontingent outcomes, including insoluble problems (see, e.g., Dweck & Reppucci, 1973; Glass & Singer, 1972) and noncontingent feedback on problem-solving tasks (e.g., Benson & Kennelly, 1976; Cohen, Rothbart & Phillips, 1976; Douglas & Anisman, 1975; Griffith, 1977; Hanusa & Schulz, 1977; Hiroto & Seligman, 1975; Klein, Fencil-Morse, & Seligman, 1976; Roth & Bootzin, 1974; Roth & Kubal, 1975; Tennen & Eller, 1977). In general the studies that have employed an escape-avoidance learning situation highly similar to the animal paradigm have found performance decrements in helplessness testing. The results of studies exposing subjects to problem-solving tasks or failure without aversive stimulation are probably more relevant for understanding behavior in achievement settings however. In these studies the research findings have been more variable and have provided uneven support for the original model. For example, major questions have arisen regarding the size of helplessness effects, the generality of these effects, and the implications for the model of the *facilitating* effects sometimes obtained following helplessness pretreatment (see Miller & Norman, 1979; Roth, in press, and Wortman & Brehm, 1975, for a more detailed discussion of these issues).

Problems with the Original Helplessness Paradigm

One problem in interpreting the helplessness literature is the striking inconsistencies that have emerged among the results of the various studies. Many of the aforementioned studies have found performance decrements during helplessness testing. However, a sizable minority have reported no differences among conditions or have shown facilitation effects, with subjects exposed to helplessness training performing better than control subjects in the test situation (e.g., Hanusa & Schulz, 1977; W. R. Miller & Seligman, 1976; Roth & Bootzin, 1974; Roth & Kubal, 1975; Shaban & Welling, cited in Glass & Singer, 1972; Tennen & Eller, 1977; Thornton & Jacobs, 1972; Wortman, Panciera, Shusterman, & Hibscher, 1976). These latter effects are not easily derived from or explained by the original theory.

A second problem in interpreting these studies is that although subjects in the helplessness condition typically report feelings of helplessness and depression, they are equally likely to report other affective states, such as hostility (e.g., Gatchel, Paulus, & Maples, 1975; Krantz, Glass, & Snyder, 1974; W. R. Miller & Seligman, 1975; Roth & Bootzin, 1974; Roth & Kubal, 1975). Thus there seems to be a need to specify when exposure to uncontrollable outcomes is likely to produce depression and when it is likely to produce other kinds of negative affect.

A final issue regarding the significance of the helplessness phenomenon is that there is less evidence than one would wish that leaned helplessness generalizes to situations different from those in which it was produced. The vast majority of these experiments has tested for helplessness effects in a setting highly similar to the helplessness training situation, and thus provides little evidence for the generalizability of deficits. In most studies, helplessness effects have been assessed by asking subjects to continue with the same task (e.g., Fosco & Geer, 1971; Glass & Singer, 1972, pp. 78-86 and 109-120), a task that is very similar (e.g., Thornton & Jacobs, 1971), or a task administered in the same room by the same experimenter or both (e.g., Hiroto & Seligman, 1975). Yet, the most important feature of the helplessness phenomenon is that organisms supposedly learn that responses do not influence outcomes in one setting and then overgeneralize this belief to subsequent situations where control is, in fact, possible. Failure to respond in the same setting in which the phenomenon has been induced, and where one has already learned that behaviors do not influence outcomes, may in some cases be an adaptive way to behave. (For a more detailed discussion of the generalization issue, see Cole & Coyne, 1977; I. W. Miller & Norman, 1979; Roth & Bootzin, 1974; or Wortman & Brehm, 1975.)

To summarize thus far, the learned helplessness approach had its roots in laboratory research with animals and was based on the notion that certain experiences with uncontrollable outcomes lead to a generalized belief that outcomes are independent of responses. This belief was viewed as to leading, in turn, to a decrease in active, adaptive instrumental responding. Research within this paradigm, as well as attempts to extend the analysis to a variety of field settings, have both provided evidence for the utility of the approach and pointed up the need to revise and elaborate the model.

Toward a More Phenomenological Approach

As investigators struggled to reconcile the contradictory pattern of results that had emerged, it became clear that the objective noncontingency may be less important than how this noncontingency is experienced by the subject. Investigators began to search for new variables that would help to clarify how subjects interpret and hence respond to the uncontrollable outcome in question. Toward this end such factors as the subjects' initial expectations of control, the importance of the outcome, and subjects' attributions of causality for the outcome have received increasing attention from theorists and researchers.

The importance of these factors was discussed by Wortman and Brehm

(1975), who attempted to incorporate expectations of control, outcome importance, and amount of exposure to the outcome into a reformulation of the original model. They maintained that the stronger the expectation of control over the outcome, the longer it would take people to become convinced that they could not control the outcome, and the more anger, control motivation, and persistence they would show before giving up. Once they realized that the outcome was uncontrollable, repeated exposure to lack of control should result in lowered motivation, passivity, and depression. Wortman and Brehm predicted that the more important the outcome, the greater the magnitude of the initial facilitation effects as well as the subsequent decrements and depression. A strength of the model is that, unlike Seligman's formulations, it provides an explanatory mechanism for facilitation effects as well as performance decrements, and for hostility and anger as well as depression. Experiments that have manipulated or measured the relevant variables have generally found support for the model (see, e.g., Baum, Aiello, & Calesnick, 1978; Roth & Kubal, 1975).

The Focus on Attributions

As helplessness researchers began to focus more carefully on the subjects' interpretation of the uncontrollable stimulus rather than the stimulus itself, they naturally became interested in the attributions of causality that subjects may make for the uncontrollable outcomes they encounter (Wortman & Brehm, 1975). Investigators began to consider the possibility that an individual's reaction to an aversive event depends on his or her beliefs about the causes of that event. Attributional phenomena were also generating a great deal of interest among social psychologists working in other problem areas (see Jones, Kanouse, Kelley, Nisbett, Valins, & Weiner, 1972; and Harvey, Ickes, & Kidd, 1976, 1977; Weiner, 1972, 1974).

The relationships between attributions of causality for outcomes and subsequent performance decrements has been investigated extensively by Dweck and her associates. Their research has focused on a diverse set of problem areas, including the development of helpless response patterns, the nature of the cognitions underlying helpless behavior, and the alleviation of helplessness effects. Since this work has particular relevance for achievement settings, it will be discussed in some detail.

In the initial research linking attributions, helplessness, and response to failure, Dweck and Reppucci (1973) sought to explain why some children actively pursue and find alternative solutions when they encounter failure, wheras others become incapable of solving the very problems they solved easily shortly before. In this study, children were given a series of problems by two experimenters. One administered soluble problems, the other insoluble ones randomly interspersed. When the "failure experimenter" began to administer soluble problems, a surprising number of children failed to solve them, even though they were highly motivated, had solved similar problems from the "success experimenter," and continued to show gains on the problems given by the success experimenter.

When the characteristic attributions of the nonpersistent and persistent children were analyzed, a clear pattern emerged. Children who persisted in the face of failure (mastery-oriented children) placed far greater emphasis on motivational factors as determinants of outcomes. When failure is attributed to motivation, this implies that one can surmount the failure through one's efforts. In contrast, children who showed deterioration placed relatively more blame for their failures on less controllable factors (such as lack of ability). In other words they keyed on factors that imply that failure is unlikely to be reversed through effort. It is interesting that this helpless pattern of attributions was more typical of girls.

Numerous studies have substantiated this finding—when attributions for failure are assessed, whether in the actual performance situation or by means of an independent assessment, they rather reliably predict response to failure (e.g., Diener & Dweck, 1978; Dweck, 1975; Dweck & Bush, 1976; Weiner, 1972, 1974). It is important to note that the divergent reactions to failure occur in spite of equivalent performance prior to failure. It is the cognitions about the causes and controllability of failure, not the failure experience itself, that affects the likelihood of subsequent deterioration in performance.

A critical step in establishing the role of attributions in mediating responses to failure was to determine whether altering attributions would alter the impact of failure on performance. Toward this end Dweck (1975) studied a number of children identified as "helpless." All these children displayed the attributions characteristic of helplessness, and all showed severe disruption of performance when even mild failure occurred. Following an assessment of their response to failure, the children were exposed to one of two relatively long-term treatment procedures in a different situation (see Dweck, 1975, for details of procedures). Children in the first treatment, "attribution retraining," were taught to attribute the programmed failures they received to a lack of effort. Children in the second treatment, "success only," were provided with exclusively success experiences during the treatment phase. At the end of training, all children were again assessed in the original situation. The results indicated that among the children in the attribution retraining group, responses to failure had changed dramatically. For most of them failure now promoted an *improvement* in performance. In addition they showed a significantly greater tendency to emphasize effort over ability as a determinant of failure. In contrast the "success only" treatment group showed no such changes. In short, helpless children who were taught to attribute their failures in the manner of mastery-oriented children began to cope with failure in the mastery-oriented fashion as well.

Because the attributional analysis specified more precisely the cognitions assumed to underlie helplessness, it allowed researchers to focus on new questions with direct relevance to achievement settings. How does one's history of evaluative feedback teach attributions for failure? Is helplessness agent-specific and why? Do attributions mediate the generalization to failure effects across situations? These questions have been examined by Dweck and her associates in research on the development and generality of sex differences in helplessness.

In achievement situations with adult evaluators, girls consistently show greater helplessness than boys—they are more likely to see failure as indicating a lack of ability and to show disrupted performance. Moreover they are less likely to view success as reflecting high ability (Dweck & Reppucci, 1973; Nicholls, 1975). Boys, on the other hand, tend to attribute their failures to a lack of effort or to external factors rather than to lack of ability. Successes, however, are likely to be perceived by boys as indicants of competence. This occurs even though girls equal or surpass boys on virtually every index of academic achievement and even though teachers judge girls more favorably on most intellectual and social variables (see Dweck & Goetz, 1978; Dweck, Goetz, & Strauss, 1980). Why do girls blame their abilities for failure when the evidence seems to indicate high ability?

In an observational and an experimental study, Dweck, Davidson, Nelson, and Enna (1978) have shown how teachers' more favorable treatment of girls results in greater helplessness. First it should be pointed out that the typical sex difference in helplessness appears to occur only with adult evaluators. When the evaluators are peers (particularly male peers), the boys are the ones who are helpless in the face of failure feedback (Dweck & Bush, 1976). This finding implies that children's differing histories with different classes of evaluators lead them to attach different meanings to their evaluations. Whether feedback is taken as indicating that the failure is surmountable depends upon who is delivering the feedback.

To determine how negative feedback from adults comes to be seen as indicative of ability by girls, but positive feedback comes to be seen as indicative of ability by boys, Dweck et al. (Study 1) analyzed the contingencies of evaluative feedback in the classroom. Very briefly, the more frequent and diffuse use of negative feedback for boys (e.g., for conduct and nonintellectual aspects of work), combined with teachers' motivational attributions for boys' failures, makes failure more indicative of nonintellectual factors. However, negative feedback for girls was very specifically addressed to intellectual inadequacies on their academic work. Although they did not receive more of this type of feedback than boys, criticism was used almost exclusively for this purpose for girls. Moreover, girls' motivation was not called into question. Failure feedback is therefore more likely to be seen as an objective assessment of their ability. Essentially the opposite pattern occurred with positive feedback, making it more easily viewed as an assessment of competence by boys.

When these different "boy" and "girl" contingencies of negative feedback were programmed in an experimental situation (Dweck et al., Study 2), they *produced* the "girls" (helpless) or "boy" (mastery-oriented) attributions for failure regardless of the actual sex of the subject. Thus feedback patterns leading to helplessness can be identified and simulated. What are the long-term implications of the attributions communicated via this feedback? Recent research suggests that girls' attributions for failure not only lead them to react more poorly than boys to failure in a given situation. They also lead them to generalize their failures across situations (to ones involving new evaluators and new tasks) and over time (from one school year to the next) (Dweck, Goetz, & Strauss, 1980). Indeed this may be why girls lose their earlier edge over boys in achievement and fall increasingly behind them over the school years.

In short, Dweck's work suggests that attributions of causality should be given careful consideration by those interested in achievement behavior. Drawing from the work by Dweck, Wortman and Brehm (1975) had suggested that attributions of causality may not only affect the magnitude of helplessness effects but may also determine how far such effects generalize. Further evidence that attributions may be important was provided in a helplessness experiment conducted by Wortman, Panciera, Shusterman, and Hibscher (1976). Subjects who were unable to solve problems and thus stop aversive noise showed distress and negative affect only when they were led to attribute their poor performance to lack of ability. Subjects who were led to attribute their failure to factors in the situation showed no greater distress than subjects who were successful in solving the problems.

The Reformulated Helplessness Model

In response to the issues raised by the contradictory findings of helplessness experiments and to mounting evidence regarding the importance of attributions, Seligman and his associates have recently presented a reformulation of the original model that is based heavily on an attributional approach (Abramson, Seligman, & Teasdale, 1978). The reformulated model specified that when the individual learns that certain outcomes and responses are independent, he or she then makes an attribution about the cause. This attribution determines the person's subsequent expectation for lack of control. This expectation, in turn, determines both the kind of deficit that occurs and its generality and chronicity. Extending the work of Weiner et al. (1971), these investigators argued that people's attributions for their inability to control their outcomes can be classified along three orthogonal dimensions: internal-external (causes that stem from the person versus those that stem from the situation or environment); stable-unstable (long-lived and recurrent versus short-lived and intermittent); and global-specific (occurring across various situations versus unique to the situation in which helplessness was induced). According to the authors, attributions to internal factors are likely to be characterized by greater loss of self-esteem than attributions to external factors. Attributions to stable factors are expected to produce deficits of greater chronicity than attributions to unstable factors. Finally, deficits attributed to global factors are predicted to generalize further than those attributed to specific factors. Other revisions of the original model, also relying heavily on subjects' attributions about and interpretation of the outcome, have been proposed by I. W. Miller and Norman (1979) and by Roth (in press).

Wortman and Dintzer (1978) have recently raised a number of questions about Abramson, Seligman, and Teasdale's (1978) reformulated model. First, they have questioned some of the assumptions on which the reformulated model is based. Specifically, Wortman and Dintzer have summarized research suggesting that people may not always make attributions when they are confronted with failure, as will be discussed further below. How then would the model predict reactions to failures for which no attributions are made? Second, they have pointed out that even if the occurrence of attributions is assumed and a relationship between attributions and behavior is assumed, the model provides no basis for determining when a particular attribution (and hence particular behavioral responses) will occur. Unless it is possible to specify the conditions under which a given attribution will be made, the model loses much predictive power. Third, Wortman and Dintzer have noted that the model provides no explanatory mechanism to account for the so-called facilitation effect that has emerged repeatedly in experiments on helplessness. Improved performance following helplessness training has occurred in a relatively large number of experiments. In fact, facilitated performance has often been found in the very conditions predicted by the reformulated model to produce the strongest deficits: those in which subjects are led to attribute their poor performance to lack of ability (see

Roth, in press, for a review). Wortman and Dintzer concluded by praising Abramson et al. for their attention to attributions and expectations that may mediate helplessness effects. They suggested, however, that this focus should be broadened to include other cognitive processes that may underlie performance decrements and should be accompanied by a more careful elaboration of the relationship among cognitions, affective responses, and behavior.

Broadening the Approach: The Focus on Cognitions Underlying the Performance Decrements

Recent work by Diener and Dweck (1980, in press) is consonant with the argument that helpless and mastery-oriented children differ not just in their attributions but in the entire pattern of cognitions and problem-solving strategies that accompany their response to failure. Indeed Diener and Dweck (1978) found evidence to suggest that mastery-oriented children may often not even make attributions for their failures at an achievement task. Moreover, they may continue their achievement strivings regardless of the attribution they do make.

The Diener and Dweck studies were designed to answer a number of specific questions about the differences between helpless and mastery-oriented children. Do helpless children try sophisticated strategies but abandon them sooner, or revert to more immature strategies once failure occurs? Are they less capable of using feedback effectively? Is the deterioration they show in performance gradual or sudden? How does their strategy use change over time? Perhaps most importantly, what attributions and cognitions accompany these presumed differences between helpless and mastery-oriented children in strategy and in performance following failure?

In order to address these questions Diener and Dweck (1978) conducted two studies in which helpless and mastery-oriented children were trained to criterion on a series of eight fairly difficult discrimination-learning problems. This was followed by four failure problems on which changes in their problem-solving strategy could be monitored. In the first study, attributions for the failure were assessed at the end of these problems. The second study was identical except that prior to the seventh training trial, children were asked to begin to verbalize about whatever they were thinking about as they performed the task. They were assured that thoughts of any sort would be welcome. Strong and intriguing differences were found between the two studies, i.e., when attributions were elicited, as opposed to when children verbalized freely.

In both studies the typical group differences were obtained both in strategy change and in the attributions generated *when the children were asked*. Mastery-oriented children tended to stay at the same level or even to use *more* sophisticated strategies when failure was encountered. In contrast none of the helpless children showed any increase in sophistication as they attempted to deal with failure. Most of them manifested a progressive decrease in the use of legitimate strategies and an increase in completely ineffectual responses. Concerning their attributions, about 50% of the helpless children responded that they had failed because they were "not smart enough"; none of the mastery-oriented children provided this attribution. Mastery-oriented children divided their attributions between lack of effort, the experimenter, and increasing difficulty of the problems. These differences in attribution emerged despite the fact that all subjects had learned the initial problems equally well and all had an equal degree of success before the failure feedback.

Data from the second study, in which subjects verbalized their thoughts during the problem-solving task, provided a new picture of the differences among cognitions for helpless and mastery-oriented children. First, it should be noted that on the success trials there were no differences between the helpless and mastery-oriented in their verbalizations; yet once failure began to occur, marked changes took place. Both groups made many more achievement-related statements, but they differed considerably in their emphasis. The helpless children soon began to make attributions for their failures to a lack or a loss of ability, to express negative affect toward the task and to engage in more and more task-irrelevant statements. Some made what might be considered classic helplessness statements, such as "Nothing I do matters" or "I give up." In sharp contrast few of the mastery-oriented children make any attributions for failure. Rather their verbalizations consisted of self-instructions and self-monitoring specifically aimed at achieving success. They maintained very high expectations of success and expressed positive affect toward the task and the challenge it presented. Some even expressed delight that now they would really be able to test their powers. It appeared that they did not consider themselves to be failing but simply to be undergoing some temporary difficulties. They thus emphasized remedies and did not dwell on causes. The few attributions that were offered by mastery-oriented children did not fall into any particular category. Indeed, on the task at hand, isolating a causal factor (e.g., insufficient effort, bad luck, lower ability than realized, increased task difficulty) was largely irrelevant to finding a solution. Regardless of the cause the best tack was to sustain one's concentration and use the most sophisticated strategies possible.

Helpless and mastery-oriented children, then, differ not only in the attributions they make when asked to explain their failures. They show major differences in their performance strategies and in the classes of cognitions they entertain under failure.

What about success? As in the studies already discussed, helpless and mastery-oriented children showed equally proficient performance before failure occurred. Yet as soon as failure began, the helpless children behaved as though their successes had never existed. Mastery-oriented children used their prior success as evidence that future success was highly likely, e.g., "I did it before, I can do it again." A critical question is: What has happened to the successes for the helpless children? Do they process the successes differently to begin with or do they reevaluate them when failure occurs?

In research designed to explore this question Diener and Dweck (in press) again trained children on a difficult discrimination learning task. As before, all children solved eight problems successfully and then failed to solve four problems. Children were asked to evaluate their performance on the success problems either immediately after success or after failure. As in previous research, prefailure performance was equivalent; yet following success (1) helpless children had significantly lower expectancies of future success (6.04 versus 8.75 on a 10-point scale). In fact, when asked if they were to be given 15 more problems of the same type, how many they would expect to get right, helpless children said they would expect to get only half of them correct (7.64 versus

13.43 predicted by the mastery-oriented); (2) when asked how many problems they had gotten correct (i.e., eight), helpless children significantly underestimated (5.46 compared to 7.57 for the mastery-oriented); (3) when asked to choose an attribution for their successes, helpless children credited their abilities significantly less than did the mastery-oriented. In all, success was less indicative of competence for the helpless and less predictive of future success.

The picture became even more negative after failure. Helpless children revised their attributions for success in ways that made their prior successes even less reflective of ability. The mastery-oriented held fast to their view of success as reflecting competence. When asked about their current situation the helpless displayed a more negative view of their performance and more pessimistic thoughts about their future performance than they had before; the mastery-oriented were amazingly undaunted by the failures. Finally, when asked to report how many problems they had gotten wrong (i.e., 4), a highly significant difference emerged between the two groups. Helpless children overestimated by half (6.14), whereas the mastery-oriented were far more accurate (3.71). It would appear, then, that what little success the helpless children had acknowledged themselves to have attained, paled further in view of the failure. Moreover, their outlook was not aided by their tendency to exaggerate the magnitude of their failures.

In summary, the helpless children not only view their failures as indicative of incompetence and unsurmountable but also view their successes as irrelevant to their competence and unreplicable. The mastery-oriented take success as a sign of intelligence, believe that it will continue, and see no reason to revise this point of view in the face of obstacles.

RELATIVE STRENGTHS AND WEAKNESSES OF THE ACHIEVEMENT MOTIVATION, TEST ANXIETY, AND HELPLESSNESS APPROACHES

Although researchers in each of these areas have been interested in behavior in achievement settings, they have focused on different facets of this issue and have necessarily employed different paradigms to answer the questions of import to them. We believe that a careful comparison of these various approaches raises some intriguing theoretical and conceptual issues and suggests some new avenues for subsequent research. A brief discussion of the relative merits of the achievement motivation, test anxiety, and helplessness approaches is presented in turn.

A strength of many studies in the achievement area is that investigators have examined achievement behavior in actual performance settings outside the laboratory. For example, both Atkinson and Raynor (1974) and Heckhausen (in this volume) have attempted to test their theoretical notions by studying students' behavior, performance, and cognitions during important course examinations. Even more impressive in this regard is the research reviewed by Atkinson and Raynor (1974) that considers how the achievement motive affects a person over a lifetime. These investigators and their associates have attempted to apply the theory to such important problems as occupational choice and career striving. Although there are exceptions, most of the anxiety and helplessness studies have been more narrow in focus and have not examined behavior outside the laboratory.

Another feature that distinguishes the achievement motivation studies from those on test anxiety and attribution is that they have often assessed subjects' preferences for different kinds of achievement tasks. This focus on subjects' preferences and in changes in these preferences over time is particularly evident in the recent theoretical modification of Atkinson and Birch (1970). In order to test this model it is necessary to allow subjects free expression of preference over time. Most studies in the helplessness and anxiety areas have examined subjects' behavior in a highly prescribed setting and have not assessed changes over an extended period of time.

In our judgment this new paradigm raises some interesting questions about how the performance decrements associated with helplessness will be manifested in a less structured setting. What incentives will be required to induce a helpless child to work on a task? How do helpless children respond to interruptions or requests from their peers to engage in alternative activities? Under what conditions will they seek help from an authority figure or from their peers? When they have a task that must be completed by a specific point in time, how will they respond? Will they procrastinate, leaving the task for the very last minute and hence ensuring an aversive experience for themselves? We feel that these questions are important and can best be addressed in a less structured paradigm like that suggested by Atkinson and Birch (1970).

A general weakness of the research on achievement motivation is that until the last decade (e.g., Heckhausen, 1975, 1977, in this volume; Weiner, 1974; Weiner et al., 1971) investigators have relied heavily on overt behavior and have paid little attention to the cognitions underlying that behavior. For example, a large number of investigators have documented shifts in aspiration level or in subjects' tendencies to choose easier or more difficult tasks. Clearly there are many possible explanations for these patterns of behavior, and knowledge of the behavior tells us little about the underlying processes. For example, suppose subjects are found to select increasingly difficult tasks over time, as Atkinson and Birch (1970) would predict. Such a shift may be due to a stabilization of negaction tendency, as Atkinson and Birch (1970) have argued. Alternatively, selection of increasingly difficult tasks may reflect a general cognitive strategy to seek more information about one's abilities (Trope, 1975, 1979). Finally, it may stem from increasingly demanding standard-setting, which may occur because current successes do not have the same value for the individuals as they did initially (see Kuhl & Blankenship, 1979 and Revelle & Michaels, 1976, for other explanations of this finding).

A major strength of the research on test anxiety is the strong empirical focus on the cognitions associated with performance decrements that has characterized this research tradition from the beginning. Unlike the achievement and helplessness areas, many experiments on test anxiety have included dependent measures to assess subjects' cognitions. Most of these measures have been retrospective in that they have been administered following task performance and/or feedback. However, they have provided suggestive evidence that highly test-anxious subjects are more concerned about how well they are performing and entertain more self-devaluative cognitions during the task than their low-anxious counterparts (see e.g., Ganzar, 1968; Heckhausen, in this volume; Mandler & Sarason, 1952; Neale & Katahn, 1968).

As we noted earlier, this empirical focus on subjects' cognitive-attentional processes has been encouraged by important theoretical contributions by Liebert and Morris (1967) and by Wine (1971), emphasizing the strong cognitive component of performance decrements. The importance of subjects' focus of attention and information processing is also becoming increasingly apparent in the treatment area (see Wine, in press, for a review). Recent studies have demonstrated that treatments that involve the redirection of attention (see Dusek, Kermis, & Mergler, 1975; Dusek, Mergler, & Kermis, 1976; Edmunsen & Nelson, 1976; Mueller, 1978; Crossley, Note 2) or the use of memory supports (Sieber, 1969; Sieber, Kameya, & Paulson, 1970) are often highly effective in mitigating the adverse effects of test anxiety.

Another asset of the test anxiety literature is that because of the predictions originally derived from the theory (see S. B. Sarason, Mandler, & Craighill, 1952), researchers in this field have systematically examined the effect of a wide variety of situational variables on performance, including ego-involving instructions (S. B. Sarason et al., 1952), time pressure (Mandler & Watson, 1966), and the presence of an audience (e.g., Ganzer, 1968). These findings have played an important part in subsequent theorizing, research, and treatment applications (e.g., Meichenbaum & Butler, in press; Wine, 1971; Mahoney, Note 3) in that they have suggested that the performance of highly motivated or anxious subjects will suffer when attention is focused on the performer and when evaluative pressure is enhanced.

A weakness of the test anxiety literature is that with a few exceptions (see e.g., Marlett & Watson, 1968), there has been no careful analysis of the nature of the performance decrements that have repeatedly occurred in these studies. Moreover, little attention has been paid to the possibility that test anxiety may affect a wide range of behaviors other than simple task performance.

A major shortcoming of many of the learned helplessness studies is the extreme narrowness of the approach (see Wortman & Brehm, 1975; Wortman & Dintzer, 1978). As we have noted, the vast majority of these studies have used a procedure highly similar to the paradigm originally developed for animals. Deviations from this paradigm have often been associated with complex and contradictory results. Among researchers who have used a procedure that parallels the animal studies, the experimental findings that have emerged have been small in magnitude and have not been found to generalize to other settings.

Except for some of the studies reviewed above, little attention has been paid to the nature of the underlying cognitions associated with helplessness effects. When decrements in performance have occurred, it has not been possible to determine whether they stemmed from cognitive or motivational deficits. When a student makes errors on a proofreading task, for example, is this because he or she is unable to find the errors or unwilling to do so? (See Wortman & Brehm, 1975.) This lack of attention to the cognitive concomitants of helplessness may well stem from the animal origins of the theory and the original research (see Levis, 1976).

In response to these issues, the recent research discussed above has attempted to analyze the nature of the performance decrements, as well as to examine the underlying cognitions associated with helplessness (e.g., Diener & Dweck, 1978). Systematic research has also been conducted on the antecedents of helplessness (e.g., Dweck, Davidson, Nelson, & Enna, 1978). These investigators have studied the development of sex difference in helplessness by specifying how one's history of evaluative feedback can result in differences in interpreting and responding to such feedback. As Wine (in press) has noted, researchers in the anxiety area have almost completely ignored the question of how differences in test anxiety develop or why there are characteristic sex differences in response to failure and evaluative settings.

COMMON UNDERLYING COGNITIONS

On the basis of our review it is clear that despite their differences there are strong consistencies in the achievement motivation, test anxiety, and helplessness research in the cognitions associated with different reactions to performance outcomes. In this section of the chapter we will specify what we conclude to be the major differences in cognitive processes and coping strategies between those who show adaptive behavior in performance settings and those who react maladaptively.

Self-focus Versus Task Focus

Research is available from a wide variety of sources to suggest that the ability to concentrate and focus on the task at hand is associated with adaptive behavior in performance settings. In contrast the tendency to focus attention on oneself has generally been associated with performance decrements. The attentional basis for performance decrements was originally described by Wine (1971), who argued that the inferior performance of high-test-anxious subjects was a result of their tendency to divide their attention between the task and themselves. Her view was underscored by I. G. Sarason (1975a), who suggested that it is self-preoccupation or self-focusing rather than "anxiety" that is the more basic process underlying performance decrements. The importance of self-focused attention has also been apparent in the theory and research of Wicklund and his associates on objective self-awareness (see, e.g., Duval & Wicklund, 1972; Wicklund, 1975). These investigators have shown that self-focused attention is associated with a tendency to become self-critical. Subjects whose attention is focused on themselves by such manipulations as placing them in front of a mirror or telling them that they are being filmed, show higher discrepancies between real and ideal self-ratings than subjects whose attention is not self-focused. Moreover, it is possible to mute this self-critical reaction by distracting subjects and hence focusing attention away from themselves during the experimental session.

Many researchers have found evidence that focus of attention distinguishes between adaptive and maladaptive behavior in achievement settings. If subjects are asked at the conclusion of a task to indicate what they were thinking about during performance, Mandler and Watson (1966), Marlett and Watson (1968), Neale and Katahn (1968), and I. G. Sarason and Stoops (1978 all found that high-test-anxious subjects report a greater incidence of nontask-related thoughts than low-test-anxious subjects. Similarly, in a retrospective study investigating cognitions entertained by subjects during a course examination, Heckhausen (in this volume) has found that interference is associated with a tendency to focus attention on the self, and that cognitions reflecting self-concern are experienced as debilitating. Mahoney and his associates (Mahoney & Avener, 1977; Mahoney, Note 4) have reviewed a great deal of evidence to suggest that focus of attention differentiates between highly successful and less successful athletes. Superior performers are able to control their attention, remain task-oriented, and block out distractions. Athletes who focus attention on themselves and how they are doing and view themselves from the perspective of an external observer tend to perform less well. Experimental results summarized by Kimble and Perlmuter (1970) have suggested that self-focused attention may be particularly debilitating during the performance of automatic acts. These investigators have argued that since attention forces the individual to break the behavior into components, the smooth functioning of these acts is impaired when attention is focused on them.

Some of the most exciting work on self-focused attention has been conducted by Brockner and his associates (Brockner, 1979; Brockner & Hulton, 1978). In attempting to account for the relationship between self-focused attention and performance, Brockner and Hulton (1978) have noted that performance decrements may occur for two reasons: (1) because individuals are unable to devote adequate attention to the task or (2) because they focus on their own negative characteristics, thus engendering considerable feelings of anxiety. Their research on high- and low-self-esteem individuals has documented the impact of attentional focus on performance and has provided support for this latter explanation of the deficit (Brockner, 1979; Brockner & Hulton, 1978).

Self-doubt, Low Self-esteem, and Negative Interpretation of Self-information

A number of studies reviewed by I. G. Sarason (1960) have suggested that high-test-anxious subjects are less content with themselves than subjects lower in test anxiety. One might question whether people with high test anxiety are simply more negative in general, but research suggests that this is not the case. Sarason and Koenig (1965) have found that test anxiety is related to people's tendency to describe themselves negatively in an oral interview situation but not to their tendency to make negative references about others. Ganzer (1968) has also found evidence that high-test-anxious subjects tend to make self-devaluative statements (e.g., "my mind's a blank," "I feel really stupid"), particularly if they are being observed during performance.

More evidence regarding the role of self-critical cognitions has been obtained by Meichenbaum, Henshaw, and Himel (chapter 6 in this volume) in a study on the cognitive processes of high- and low-creative individuals. Not only do low-creative individuals make more negative self-statements while they are attempting to solve a problem, but they evidence more debilitation in performance following such statements. Meichenbaum found that after making such a statement, low-creative individuals were more likely than high creative ones to become silent or produce another negative statement and less likely to produce a strategy or facilitative statement. This suggests that low-creative individuals are less able to cope with self-imposed negative evaluation than high-creative individuals. Similar results were obtained by Heckhausen (in this volume), who found that for failure-motivated subjects, cognitions of self-concern or self-doubt were experienced as debilitating. Among success-motivated subjects there was no relationship between the frequency of such cognitions and subjective feelings of interference. These results are reminiscent of the findings of Diener & Dweck (1978), in which helpless children were both more likely to make self-disparaging attributions and more likely to show performance decrements concurrent with such attributions.

Additional evidence that feelings of self-doubt and low self-esteem are important has been presented by Meunier and Rule (1967), who found that on no-feedback trials, high-test-anxious subjects reported extremely low confidence in their ability. Similarly, Diener and Dweck (1980, in press) found that helpless subjects underestimated the number of problems they had gotten correct on a problem-solving task and overestimated the number they had gotten wrong by one-half. Mastery-oriented subjects were more accurate in their estimates of their prior performance.

The tendency to misinterpret or distort the feedback one receives has drawn relatively little attention from investigators in areas of achievement motivation or test anxiety. However, some interesting research in the area of social anxiety is relevant. Smith and Sarason (1975) found that high-socially-anxious people perceived the same feedback from another person as more negative than low-socially-anxious people. Similarly, O'Banion and Arkowitz (Note 4) found that high-socially-anxious people remember negative feedback more accurately and positive feedback less accurately than do low-socially-anxious individuals.

Self-blame

One of the first studies to examine subjects' attributions of causality was conducted by Doris and Sarason (1955), who found that high-test-anxious subjects blamed themselves for programmed failure more than low-test-anxious subjects. Since that time, causal attributions have generated little interest among test anxiety researchers. As we noted earlier, however, some theorists have taken an attributional approach to the area of achievement motivation, arguing that causal attributions underlie differences in achievement behavior (see Weiner, 1974; Weiner et al., 1971). The research evidence has suggested that individuals with a high need for achievement tend to attribute their successes to high ability and effort and their failures to lack of effort. In contrast, low need for achievement people ascribe their successes to luck or other variable factors and attribute their failure to low ability (see Heckhausen, 1977, or Weiner, 1974, for reviews). Dweck and her associates have extended this work by demonstrating that (1) mastery-oriented subjects attribute success to their abilities and failures to changeable factors, while helpless subjects do just the reverse (e.g., Dweck & Reppucci, 1973); (2) when helpless children are taught to attribute failure to changeable factors, improvements occur in subsequent performance (Dweck, 1975); and (3) mastery-oriented subjects may not even make attributions of causality during performance unless circumstances make it necessary to do so. Helpless children do tend to identify lack of ability as a cause of failure. This attribution does not appear to be the result of a careful causal analysis, however, but rather an "automatic" response to failure among helpless children (Diener & Dweck, 1978).

Thus certain individuals are not only more negative about themselves and about their performance, but they also put the two together in a causal fashion and view their poor performance as resulting from their lower competence.

Worry and Concern about Evaluation

In a number of studies in the test anxiety literature, subjects have been questioned retrospectively about their thoughts while performing the task. These studies suggest that worry and concern about evaluation are important determinants of behavior in the performance setting. High-test-anxious subjects have said that they thought more about how well or badly they were doing (Mandler & Watson, 1966), wondered how well others were performing (Mandler & Watson, 1966; Neale & Katahn, 1968), felt it was more important to do well (Mandler & Watson, 1966), glanced at the experimenter more often (Nottleman & ·Hill, 1977), and wondered what the experimenter would think of them (I. G. Sarason & Stoops, 1978). There is also evidence to indicate that success and failure have a greater impact on the subsequent performance of high-test-anxious subjects (Weiner, 1966; Weiner & Schneider, 1971) and that these subjects conform more to others' opinions in making perceptual judgments. These latter findings suggest that high-test-anxious subjects are more attentive to evaluative cues.

Negative Attitude toward the Task

Neale and Katahn (1968) found that high-test-anxious subjects retrospectively reported more unpleasant affect during a performance task than low-test-anxious subjects. Similarly, Meichenbaum et al. (in this volume) have found that low-creative individuals manifest more negative ideation while they are trying to come up with a creative solution to a problem than high-creative individuals. Diener and Dweck (1978) have reported that during failure helpless children are more likely to verbalize negative attitudes toward a problem-solving task while working on the task than mastery-oriented children. Finally, Nottleman and Hill (1977) found that high-test-anxious children glanced away from an anagram task more frequently than middle- or low-test-anxious children, suggesting a desire to avoid the task.

Expectations and Aspirations

Within the achievement literature a number of studies have supported the assertion that individuals with a low resultant need for achievement make more "atypical" shifts in their expectations or aspirations following performance. For example, such subjects tend not to raise their expectations following success (see Weiner, 1974, for a review). As noted earlier, Weiner (1974) has argued convincingly that these shifts in level of aspiration stem from subjects' attributions of causality. If success is attributed to variable factors such as luck, no changes in level of aspiration are expected to occur.

Trapp and Kausler (1958) have reported similar results with high-test-anxious subjects. In this study these subjects tended to lower their goals or aspirations over time even though their objective performance was not different from low-test-anxious subjects. Parallel findings have emerged from Dweck's work on helplessness. Diener and Dweck (1978) found that helpless children have significantly lower expectations for future success at a problem-solving task on which they have been successful. They expected to get only half as many problems right in the future as mastery-oriented children did, despite the fact that their prefailure performance was equivalent.

The Self-perpetuating Nature of These Cognitions

Perhaps the most intriguing feature of the cognitions that underlie maladaptive reactions in performance settings is their self-perpetuating nature. This has been noted by individuals working in all the research traditions we have discussed. To begin to understand this, one must examine (a) the nature of the self-statements that accompany maladaptive responding, (b) the way in which the processing of success and failure information perpetuates maladaptive cognitions, and (c) the ways in which the individual's behavior eliminates sources of counterevidence.

First, with the notable exception of Beck (1976), there is a tendency among many psychologists to assume that cognitions or "self-statements" are similar in character to overt statements. However, the purpose of overt statements is to communicate. Private statements do not have to serve this goal and as such are likely to be more poorly formulated, less explicit, and less accessible to conscious scrutiny (see Langer, 1979), making it difficult to formulate counterarguments or to seek counterevidence. Moreover, unlike public statements, one is not called upon to defend the reasoning behind private statements.

Second, maladaptive responders appear to process both positive and negative outcomes in a way that tends to confirm self-denigrating cognitions. Not only are failures taken as evidence of incompetence, but the threshold for perceiving failure appears lower. Not only are successes likely to be discounted as reflections of ability, but the threshold for perceiving themselves as successful is higher among these individuals (Diener & Dweck, in press). Thus even if evidence of competence were abundant, its impact might be minimized (see Dweck, 1975).

Finally, the maladaptive responder may avoid the very situations that would yield evidence of competence. For example, Marlett and Watson (1968) have pointed out that failure leads high-test-anxious individuals to avoid the situation, which therefore increases the probability of more failure. In the achievement motivation area, Heckhausen (1968) has noted that individuals with a high fear of failure choose goals in a way that contributes to their problems. Because they select very easy or very difficult tasks, they tend to attribute any successes to the task or to luck. Such successes, of course, are not particularly rewarding, and are unlikely to affect the subject's assessment of his or her competence. Heckhausen (1968) has also noted that since high-fear-of-failure subjects generally regard effort and persistence as ineffective, they often reduce their exertion and thus ensure a mediocre performance.

Problems associated with the avoidance of a task or situation have been eloquently discussed by Bandura (1977) in a review of his research on coping with phobias. Bandura has pointed out that avoidance of stressful situations impedes the development of coping skills, and that the resultant lack of competence can provide a realistic basis for one's anxieties and fears. Those who cease coping efforts prematurely will retain their self-debilitating expectancies and fears, since they never allow themselves to attain any evidence to the contrary.

Conclusions Regarding the Cognitions Associated with Adaptive and Maladaptive Behaviors in Performance Settings

Taken as a whole the evidence we have reviewed here suggests that reactions to success or failure in a performance setting depend on the meaning of the outcome for the person. For the maladaptive responder—characterized by high fear of failure, high test anxiety, and helplessness—failure has self-evaluative meaning. For the adaptive responder—who is achievement oriented with low test anxiety—failure has task-relevant information value. Since failure signifies a lack of ability to the maladaptive responder, it implies that further effort would not be worthwhile (even risky). For the adaptive responders, however, the attribution is short-circuited. Failure appears to be a direct signal to them to vary their strategy. Identifying a causal factor appears largely irrelevant in their search for a solution. If one has the view that outcomes are modifiable, even poor ability can be compensated for by additional effort. In essence the adaptive responder does not ask whether he or she is capable of surmounting the failure or whether the failure is surmountable but rather how it is to be surmounted (see Langer & Dweck, 1973).

If one believes that failure is an indication of ability but that success is not, then one's competence is on the line in every new achievement situation. Under these circumstances it is not surprising to find maladaptive responders concerned with issues of competence. When negative outcomes occur and are seen as signs of inadequacy and as predictors of continuing failure, it is not surprising to find a scarcity of solution-oriented strategies. Indeed one would expect maladaptive responders to feel that they are "at risk" in achievement situations and therefore try to avoid these situations, even at the cost of precluding success. Such avoidance might take the form of simply giving up, of directing attention away from the task and its solution (and hence away from oneself and one's ability), or of devaluing the task.

In contrast the competence of adaptive responders is not at risk in achievement settings; only successes are relevant to their conceptions of their ability. When one defines competence in terms of successes, one can only gain as a result of achievement strivings, both in terms of one's view of his or her ability and in terms of other, more concrete rewards that success might bring. One should therefore seek tasks that will maximize such gains. Since evaluation of self is not an issue, the adaptive responder can turn his or her attention to the task at hand. Failure, of course, may prompt greater engagement with the task because it signifies that new strategies must be devised to reach the solution.

Because mastery-oriented individuals view negative outcomes as signals to vary their strategy, mistakes are steps on the way to a solution and do not constitute a failure as long as there are remaining strategies to try. Their criterion for perceiving failure will therefore be higher than the helpless, for whom negative outcomes define the endpoint of their productive efforts. Adaptive responders may engage in some degree of worry or self-focus, but this will not trigger a chain of maladaptive ruminations about failure and incompetence. Because the adaptive responders see positive outcomes as a sign of ability and predictive of continuing positive outcomes, they will define themselves as having attained success sooner than the maladaptive responders, who do not ascribe the positive outcomes to stable factors.

ISSUES FOR SUBSEQUENT RESEARCH

Taken together, the research areas of achievement motivation, test anxiety, and attribution provide a fairly consistent picture of the cognitive processes associated with adaptive and maladaptive responses in performance settings. However, a joint consideration of these areas raises a number of intriguing conceptual issues that have not yet been resolved. In this section we will discuss some of these issues and examine their implications for subsequent research.

One issue raised by the preceding analysis concerns the relationships among the various classes of cognition that have been identified as important. How are an individual's attributions, expectations, self-evaluation, evaluation of the task, and tendencies to focus on various elements of the situation causally related to one another? Some of these classes of cognitions have been incorporated into an attribution model of achievement motivation (cf. Weiner et al., 1971; Weiner, 1974). The underlying assumption of this model is that individuals' attributions play a causal role in determining their expectations, self-evaluation, and emotional response. While we have reviewed some evidence to indicate that attributions influence behavior, no studies have yet focused on the relationship among classes of cognitions. Research that examines these cognitions over time in actual performance settings should be helpful in resolving this issue.

A related question concerns the relationship between the entire class of cognitions we have delineated and a person's emotional reaction to the performance setting. Do adaptive and maladaptive responders interpret initial signs of physiological arousal differently? Although we know of no research on this question, our guess is that those who interpret arousal as indicative of excitement and involvement will fare better than those who interpret it as a sign that they are in trouble. How does this initial interpretation affect subsequent emotional responsivity? What is the relationship between self-awareness of arousal and one's actual physiological state? Since there are indications in the literature that these indexes may be independent (see Morris & Liebert, 1970), it would be interesting to know how each of them are affected by the cognitions we have discussed. How do each of these indexes change over time as the individual encounters success or failure? How are these changes interpreted, and how do they affect subsequent motivation and performance?

In considering how emotional responses are interpreted by adaptive and maladaptive responders to failure, a third important question comes to mind: How do individuals make judgments about whether an event, an internal response or a feature of the environment or situation, represents a challenge or a threat (see Lazarus & Launier, 1979) or, put more broadly, what kinds of information from the environment do the adaptive and maladaptive responders notice? Do adaptive responders, for example, notice external factors that may be threatening and then minimize them or block them out, or do they fail to even notice them? More specific knowledge about how adaptive and maladaptive responders process, encode, and retrieve information available in the performance setting would clearly be useful.

Thus far we have raised a number of general issues about the cognitions, coping strategies, and emotional reactions that emerge during performance and the interrelationships among them. Two more specific questions are also worthy of consideration: First, what is the precise underlying mechanism for the performance deficits that have been found in achievement, test anxiety, and helplessness studies? Second, how do the processes we have been describing affect an individual's tendency to initiate and sustain interest in achievement-related activities outside the laboratory?

Researchers in each of these fields have conducted numerous studies demonstrating that performance deficits generally occur among high-fear-of-failure, high-test-anxious, or helpless persons. Since the underlying processes postulated by each of these research traditions are somewhat different, however, it may be useful to discriminate among them. To what extent does the deficit occur because one's responses become disorganized and one's thinking becomes confused? To what extent does it stem from one's learning that responses and reinforcements are independent, and consequently developing an expectancy of failure? Finally, to what extent are deficits due to the decision to avoid self-diagnostic information or the desire to avoid risking public embarrassment? Of course, these possibilities are by no means mutually exclusive. One may, for example, become confused, view failure as inevitable, and wish to avoid the risk of a public failure. Or one may abandon hopes for success, experience disorganized responding, and avoid further self-diagnostic information. Nonetheless, it appears critical to determine the circumstances under which each of these might operate either alone or in concert.

Interesting research designed to discriminate among some of these alternatives has recently been conducted by Snyder and his associates (Frankl & Snyder, 1978; Snyder, Smoller, Strenta, & Frankl, Note 5). Snyder has argued that deficits in helplessness experiments may occur not because one learns that there is no relationship between behaviors and responses but because individuals try half-heartedly on the test task. By expending little effort they presumably can protect their self-esteem in case failure should occur. In support of his reasoning, Snyder has found that such manipulations as describing the test task as highly difficult or playing distracting music during the test task can improve performance and reduce the deficit. Similar results have been obtained in the achievement area by Weiner (1966), who found that high-fear-of-failure subjects persist longer at difficult tasks than at easy tasks. Most versions of the learned helplessness model would predict that deficits will become even greater as the task becomes more difficult. Snyder would argue that if there are any characteristics of the performance situation that can serve as an excuse for failure (i.e., tasks known to be difficult, the presence of distractions), there is no way that the individual's performance can make him or her look bad. Presumably this vitiates the need to avoid risking one's competence by withdrawing from the task or putting forth low effort and frees the person to become involved in the task and try harder.

Snyder's research suggests that self-protective motivation deserves more attention as a cause of performance deficits than it has received from helplessness researchers. Studies that experimentally manipulate the importance of the task in question should enhance our knowledge about the self-protective process. Moreover, by experimentally manipulating others' awareness of the performance outcome, it should be possible to determine whether such behavior stems primarily from the desire to avoid self-diagnostic information or the desire to avoid public embarrassment.

The factors that affect an individual's inclination to select achievement tasks and sustain motivation on them is another issue we feel is in need of further attention. As we indicated earlier, researchers have focused primarily on performance in a highly structured setting, although achievement theorists have become quite interested in choice of achievement tasks and time voluntarily spent on each (cf. Atkinson & Birch, 1974). A number of more specific questions might be raised about achievement behavior in naturalistic settings. What cognitions are associated with the decision to continue working on a problem in the absence of external pressure or rewards (Niemark, 1976)? How is one's motivation to continue affected by such factors as the difficulty of the task and initial performance feedback? How do adaptive and maladaptive responders decide to reward themselves for good performance? What standards do they use to evaluate their own performance, and how do these standards change over time? (See Dweck, Goetz, & Strauss, 1980.) In an unstructured work situation, how do adaptive and maladaptive responders react to surveillance, supervision, or criticism by others?

In conclusion we believe that the cognitions and coping mechanisms that influence reactions to performance can best be understood by a joint consideration of past work in the achievement motivation, test anxiety, and helplessness areas. We feel that individuals working in each of these fields can profit substantially from a thorough awareness of the issues explored and the paradigms utilized in other areas. Moreover, we believe that a joint consideration of these areas is extremely valuable in identifying gaps in our current knowledge of behaviors in performance settings and in suggesting priorities for future research.

REFERENCES

Abramson, L. Y., Seligman, M. E. P., & Teasdale, J. D. Learned helplessness in humans: Critique and reformulation. *Journal of Abnormal Psychology,* 1978, *87,* 49–74.

Anisman, H., & Waller, T. G. Effects of inescapable shock on subsequent avoidance performance: Role of response repertoire changes. *Behavioral Biology,* 1973, *9,* 331–335.

Atkinson, J. W. Motivational determinants of risk-taking behavior. *Psychological Review,* 1957, *64,* 359–372.

Atkinson, J. W. *An Introduction to motivation.* Princeton, NJ: Von Nostrand, 1964.

Atkinson, J. W. An approach to the study of subjective aspects of achievement motivation. In J. Nuttin (Ed.), *Motives and consciousness in man.* Proceedings of the 18th International Congress in Psychology, Symposium 13, Moscow, 1966.

Atkinson, J. W. Strength of motivation and efficiency of performance. In J. W. Atkinson & J. O. Raynor (Eds.), *Motivation and achievement.* Washington, DC: Hemisphere, 1974.

Atkinson, J. W., & Birch, D. *The dynamics of action.* New York: Wiley, 1970.

Atkinson, J. W., & Birch, D. The dynamics of achievement-oriented activity. In J. W. Atkinson & J. O. Raynor (Eds.), *Motivation and achievement.* Washington, DC: Hemisphere, 1974.

Atkinson, J. W., & Feather, N. T. (Eds.). *A theory of achievement motivation.* New York: Wiley, 1966.

Atkinson, J. W., & Raynor, J. O. (Eds.). *Motivation and achievement.* Washington, DC: Hemisphere, 1974.

Bandura, A. Self-efficacy: Toward a unifying theory of behavioral change. *Psychological Review,* 1977, *84,* 191–215.

Baum, A., Aiello, J. R., & Calesnick, L. E. Crowding and personal control: Social density and the development of learned helplessness. *Journal of Personality and Social Psychology,* 1978, *36,* 1000–1011.

Beck, A. T. *Cognitive therapy and the emotional disorders.* New York: International University Press, 1976.

Benson, J. S., & Kennelly, K. J. Learned helplessness: The result of uncontrollable reinforcements or uncontrollable aversive stimuli? *Journal of Personality and Social Psychology*, 1976, *34*, 138-145.

Brockner, J. Self-esteem, self-consciousness, and task performance: Replications, extensions and possible explanations. *Journal of Personality and Social Psychology*, 1979, *37*, 447-461.

Brockner, J., & Hulton, A. J. B. How to reverse the vicious cycle of low self-esteem: The importance of attentional focus. *Journal of Experimental Social Psychology*, 1978, *14*, 564-578.

Cohen, S., Rothbart, M., & Phillips, S. Locus of control and the generality of learned helplessness in humans. *Journal of Personality and Social Psychology*, 1976, *34*, 1049-1057.

Cole, C. S., & Coyne, J. C. Situational specificity of laboratory-induced learned helplessness. *Journal of Abnormal Psychology*, 1977, *86*, 615-624.

Diener, C. I., & Dweck, C. S. An analysis of learned helplessness: Continuous changes in performance, strategy, and achievement cognitions following failure. *Journal of Personality and Social Psychology*, 1978, *36*, 451-462.

Diener, C. I., & Dweck, C. S. An analysis of learned helplessness: II. The processing of success. *Journal of Personality and Social Psychology*, in press.

Doctor, R. M., & Altman, F. Worry and emotionality as components of test anxiety: Replication and further data. *Psychological Reports*, 1969, *24*, 563-568.

Doris, J., & Sarason, S. B. Test anxiety and blame assignment in a failure situation. *Journal of Abnormal and Social Psychology*, 1955, *50*, 335-338.

Douglas, D., & Anisman, H. Helplessness or expectation incongruency: Effects of aversive stimulation on subsequent performance. *Journal of Experimental Psychology: Human Perception and Performance*, 1975, *1*, 411-417.

Dusek, J. B., Kermis, M. D., & Mergler, N. L. Information processing in low- and high-test anxious children as a function of grade level and verbal labelling. *Development Psychology*, 1975, *11*, 651-652.

Dusek, J. B., Mergler, N. L., & Kermis, M. D. Attention encoding and information processing in low- and high-test anxious children. *Child Development*, 1976, *47*, 201-207.

Duval, S., & Wicklund, R. A. *A theory of objective self-awareness*. New York: Academic Press, 1972.

Dweck, C. S. The role of expectations and attributions in the alleviation of learned helplessness. *Journal of Personality and Social Psychology*, 1975, *31*, 674-685.

Dweck, C. S., & Bush, E. S. Sex differences in learned helplessness: I. Differential debilitation with peer and adult evaluators. *Developmental Psychology*, 1976, *12*, 147-156.

Dweck, C. S., Davidson, W., Nelson, S., & Enna, B. Sex differences in learned helplessness: II. The contingencies of evaluative feedback in the classroom, and III. An experimental analysis. *Developmental Psychology*, 1978, *14*, 268-276.

Dweck, C. S., & Goetz, M. Attributions and learned helplessness. In J. Harvey, W. Ickes, & R. F. Kidd (Eds.), *New directions in attribution research*, Vol. II. Hillsdale, NJ: Erlbaum, 1978.

Dweck, C. S., Goetz, T. E., & Strauss, N. Sex differences in learned helplessness: IV. An experimental and naturalistic study of failure generalization and its mediators. *Journal of Personality & Social Psychology*, 1980, *38*, 441-452.

Dweck, C. S., & Reppucci, N. D. Learned helplessness and reinforcement responsibility in children. *Journal of Personality and Social Psychology*, 1973, *25*, 109-116.

Edmunsen, E. D., & Nelson, D. L. Anxiety, imagery and sensory interference. *Bulletin of the Psychonomic Society*, 1976, *8*, 319-322.

Fosco, E., & Geer, J. H. Effects of gaining control over aversive stimuli after different amounts of no control. *Psychological Reports*, 1971, *29*, 1153-1154.

Frankl, A., & Snyder, M. L. Poor performance following unsolvable problems: Learned helplessness or egotism? *Journal of Personality and Social Psychology*, 1978, *36*, 1415-1423.

Ganzer, V. J. Effects of audience presence and test anxiety on learning and retention in a serial learning situation. *Journal of Personality and Social Psychology*, 1968, *8*, 194-199.

Gatchel, R. J., Paulus, P. B., & Maples, C. W. Learned helplessness and self-reported affect. *Journal of Abnormal Psychology*, 1975, *84*, 732-734.

Gatchel, R. I., & Proctor, J. D. Physiological correlates of learned helplessness in man. *Journal of Abnormal Psychology*, 1976, *85*, 27–34.

Geer, J., Davison, G. C., & Gatchel, R. I. Reduction of stress in humans through nonveridical perceived control of aversive stimulation. *Journal of Personality and Social Psychology*, 1970, *16*, 731–738.

Glass, D. C. *Behavior patterns, stress, and coronary disease.* Hillsdale, NJ: Erlbaum, 1977.

Glass, D. C., & Singer, J. E. *Urban stress: Experiments on noise and social stressors.* New York: Academic Press, 1972.

Griffith, M. Effects of noncontingent success and failure on mood and performance. *Journal of Personality*, 1977, *45*, 442–457.

Hanusa, B. H., & Schulz, R. Attributional mediators of learned helplessness. *Journal of Personality and Social Psychology*, 1977, *35*, 602–611.

Harvey, J. H., Ickes, W., & Kidd, R. F. (Eds.). *New directions in attribution research* (Vol. 1). Hillsdale, NJ: Erlbaum, 1976.

Harvey, J. H., Ickes, W. J., & Kidd, R. F. (Eds.). *New directions in attribution research* (Vol. 2). Hillsdale, NJ: Erlbaum, 1977.

Heckhausen, H. Achievement motive research: Current problems and some contributions towards a general theory of motivation. In W. J. Arnold (Ed.), *Nebraska Symposium on Motivation.* Lincoln: University of Nebraska Press, 1968.

Heckhausen, H. Fear of failure as a self-reinforcing motive system. In I. G. Sarason & C. D. Spielberger (Eds.), *Stress and anxiety* (Vol. 2). Washington, DC: Hemisphere, 1975.

Heckhausen, H. Achievement motivation and its constructs: A cognitive model. *Motivation and Emotion*, 1977, *1*, 283–329.

Hiroto, D. S. Locus of control and learned helplessness. *Journal of Experimental Psychology*, 1974, *102*, 187–193.

Hiroto, D. S., & Seligman, M. E. P. Generality of learned helplessness in man. *Journal of Personality and Social Psychology*, 1975, *31*, 311–327.

Jones, E. E., Kanouse, D., Kelley, H. H., Nisbett, R. E., Valins, S., & Weiner, B. (Eds.). *Attribution: Perceiving the causes of behavior.* Morristown, NJ: General Learning Press, 1972.

Kimble, G. A., & Perlmuter, L. C. The problem of volition. *Psychological Review*, 1970, *77*, 361–384.

Klein, D. C., Fencil-Morse, E., & Seligman, M. E. P. Learned helplessness, depression, and the attribution of failure. *Journal of Personality and Social Psychology*, 1976, *33*, 508–516.

Klein, D. C., & Seligman, M. E. P. Reversal of performance deficits and perceptual deficits in learned helplessness and depression. *Journal of Abnormal Psychology*, 1976, *85*, 11–26.

Krantz, D. S., Glass, D. C., & Snyder, M. L. Helplessness, stress level, and the coronary-prone behavior pattern. *Journal of Experimental Social Psychology*, 1974, *10*, 284–300.

Krantz, D. S., & Schulz, R. Life crisis, control, and health outcomes: A model applied to cardiac rehabilitation and relocation of the elderly. In A. Baum & J. E. Singer (Eds.), *Advances in environmental psychology* (Vol. 2). Hillsdale, NJ: Erlbaum, 1979.

Kuhl, J., & Blankenship, V. Behavioral change in a constant environment: Shift to more difficult tasks with constant probability of success. *Journal of Personality and Social Psychology*, 1979, *37*, 551–563.

Langer, E. Playing the middle against both ends: The usefulness of adult cognitive activity as a model for cognitive activities in childhood and old age. In S. R. Yussen (Ed.), *The development of reflection.* New York: Academic Press, 1980.

Langer, E., & Dweck, C. S. *Personal politics.* New Jersey: Prentice Hall, 1973.

Langer, E. J., & Rodin, J. The effects of choice and enhanced personal responsibility for the aged: A field experiment in an institutional setting. *Journal of Personality and Social Psychology*, 1976, *34*, 191–198.

Lazarus, R. S., & Launier, R. Stress-related transactions between person and environment. In L. A. Pervin & M. Lewis (Eds.), *Perspectives in interactional psychology.* New York: Plenum, 1979.

Levis, D. J. Learned helplessness: A reply and an alternative S-R interpretation. *Journal of Experimental Psychology: General*, 1976, *105*, 47–65.

Liebert, R. M., & Morris, L. W. Cognitive and emotional components of test anxiety: A distinction and some initial data. *Psychological Reports*, 1967, *20*, 975–978.

Mahoney, M. J., & Avener, M. Psychology of the elite athlete: An exploratory study. *Cognitive Therapy and Research,* 1977, *1,* 135–141.

Maier, S. F., & Seligman, M. E. P. Learned helplessness: Theory and evidence. *Journal of Experimental Psychology: General,* 1976, *105,* 3–46.

Maier, S. F., Seligman, M. E. P., & Solomon, R. L. Pavlovian fear conditioning and learned helplessness. In B. A. Campbell & R. M. Church (Eds.), *Punishment.* New York: Appleton-Century-Crofts, 1969.

Mandler, G., & Sarason, S. B. A study of anxiety and learning. *Journal of Abnormal and Social Psychology,* 1952, *47,* 166–173.

Mandler, G., & Watson, D. L. Anxiety and the interruption of behavior. In C. D. Spielberger (Ed.), *Anxiety and behavior.* New York: Academic Press, 1966.

Marlett, N. J., & Watson, D. L. Test anxiety and immediate or delayed feedback in a test-like avoidance task. *Journal of Personality and Social Psychology,* 1968, *8,* 200–203.

McClelland, D. C., Atkinson, J. W., Clark, R. A., & Lowell, E. L. *The achievement motive.* New York: Appleton-Century-Crofts, 1953.

Meichenbaum, D., & Butler, L. Toward a conceptual model for the treatment of test anxiety. In I. G. Sarason (Ed.), *Test anxiety: Theory, research, and application.* Hillsdale, NJ: Erlbaum, in press.

Meunier, C., & Rule, B. G. Anxiety, confidence and conformity. *Journal of Personality,* 1967, *35,* 498–504.

Miller, I. W., III, & Norman, W. H. Learned helplessness in humans: A review and attribution-theory model. *Psychological Bulletin,* 1979, *86,* 93–118.

Miller, W. R., & Seligman, M. E. P. Depression and the perception of reinforcement. *Journal of Abnormal Psychology,* 1973, *82,* 62–73.

Miller, W. R., & Seligman, M. E. P. Depression and learned helplessness in man. *Journal of Abnormal Psychology,* 1975, *84,* 228–238.

Miller, W. R., & Seligman, M. E. P. Learned helplessness, depression, and the perception of reinforcement. *Behavior Research and Therapy,* 1976, *14,* 7–17.

Miller, W. R., Seligman, M. E. P., & Kurlander, H. M. Learned helplessness, depression, and anxiety. *Journal of Nervous and Mental Disease,* 1975, *161,* 347–357.

Morris, L. W., & Fulmer, R. S. Test anxiety (Worry and emotionality) changes during academic testing as a function of feedback and test importance. *Journal of Educational Psychology,* 1976, *68,* 817–824.

Morris, L. W., & Liebert, R. M. Effects of anxiety on timed and untimed intelligence tests. *Journal of Consulting and Clinical Psychology,* 1969, *33,* 240–244.

Morris, L. W., & Liebert, R. M. Relationships of cognitive and emotional components of test anxiety to physiological arousal and academic performance. *Journal of Consulting and Clinical Psychology,* 1970, *35,* 332–337.

Morris, L. W., & Perez, T. L. Effects of test interruption on emotional arousal and performance. *Psychological Reports,* 1972, *31,* 559–564.

Mueller, J. H. The effects of individual differences in test anxiety and type of orienting task on levels of organization in free recall. *Journal of Research in Personality,* 1978, *12,* 100–116.

Neale, J. M., & Katahn, M. Anxiety, choice, and stimulus uncertainty. *Journal of Personality,* 1968, *36,* 235–245.

Nichols, J. G. Causal attributions and other achievement related cognitions: Effects of task outcomes, attainment value and sex. *Journal of Personal and Social Psychology,* 1975, *31,* 379–389.

Nichols, J. G. When a scale measures more than its name denotes: The case of the test anxiety scale for children. *Journal of Consulting and Clinical Psychology,* 1976, *44,* 976–985.

Niemark, M. *Personality orientation.* Englewood Cliffs, NJ: Educational Technology Publications, 1976.

Nottleman, E. D., & Hill, K. T. Test anxiety and off-task behavior in evaluative situations. *Child Development,* 1977, *48,* 225–231.

Overmier, J. B., & Seligman, M. E. P. Effects of inescapable shock upon subsequent escape and avoidance learning. *Journal of Comparative and Physiological Psychology,* 1967, *63,* 23–33.

Raynor, J. O. Relationships between achievement-related motives, future orientation, and academic performance. *Journal of Personality and Social Psychology,* 1970, *15,* 28–33.

Raynor, J. O. Future orientation in the study of achievement motivation. In J. W. Atkinson & J. O. Raynor (Eds.), *Motivation and achievement.* Washington, DC: Hemisphere, 1974.

Raynor, J. O., Atkinson, J. W., & Brown, M. Subjective aspects of achievement motivation immediately before an examination. In J. W. Atkinson & J. O. Raynor (Eds.), *Motivation and achievement.* Washington, DC: Hemisphere, 1974, 155-171.

Revelle, W., & Michaels, E. J. The theory of achievement motivation revisited: The implications of inertial tendencies. *Psychological Review,* 1976, *83,* 394-404.

Rodin, J. Crowding, perceived choice, and response to controllable and uncontrollable outcomes. *Journal of Experimental Social Psychology,* 1976, *12,* 564-579.

Rodin, J., & Langer, E. Long-term effects of a control-relevant intervention with institutionalized aged. *Journal of Personality and Social Psychology,* 1977, *35,* 897-902.

Roth, S. Learned helplessness in humans: A review and a revised model. *Journal of Personality,* in press.

Roth, S., & Bootzin, R. R. Effects of experimentally induced expectancies of external control: An investigation of learned helplessness. *Journal of Personality and Social Psychology,* 1974, *29,* 253-264.

Roth, S., & Kubal, L. The effects of noncontingent reinforcement on tasks of differing importance: Facilitation and learned helplessness. *Journal of Personality and Social Psychology,* 1975, *32,* 680-691.

Sarason, I. G. Empirical findings and theoretical problems in the use of anxiety scales. *Psychological Bulletin,* 1960, *57,* 403-415.

Sarason, I. G. Experimental approaches to test anxiety: Attention and the uses of information. In C. D. Spielberger (Ed.), *Anxiety and behavior: Current trends in theory and research* (Vol. 2). New York: Academic Press, 1972. (a)

Sarason, I. G. Anxiety and self-preoccupation. In I. G. Sarason & C. D. Spielberger (Eds.), *Stress and anxiety* (Vol. 2). Washington, DC: Hemisphere, 1975. (a)

Sarason, I. G. Test anxiety and the self-disclosing coping model. *Journal of Consulting and Clinical Psychology,* 1975, *43,* 148-153. (b)

Sarason, I. G. *Test anxiety: Theory, research, and application.* Hillsdale, NJ: Erlbaum, in press.

Sarason, I. G., & Koenig, K. P. The relationship of test anxiety and hostility to description of self and parents. *Journal of Personality and Social Psychology,* 1965, *2,* 617-621.

Sarason, I. G., & Stoops, R. Test anxiety and the passage of time. *Journal of Consulting and Clinical Psychology,* 1978, *46,* 102-109.

Sarason, S. B. The measurement of anxiety in children. Some questions and problems. In C. D. Spielberger (Ed.), *Anxiety and behavior.* New York: Academic Press, 1966.

Sarason, S. B., Davidson, K. S., Lighthall, F. F., Waite, R. R., & Ruebush, B. K. *Anxiety in elementary school children.* New York: Wiley, 1960.

Sarason, S. B., Mandler, G., & Craighill, P. G. The effect of differential instructions on anxiety and learning. *Journal of Abnormal and Social Psychology,* 1952, *47,* 561-565.

Sarbin, T. R. Ontology recapitulates philology: The mythic nature of anxiety. *American Psychologist,* 1968, *23,* 411-418.

Schulz, R. Effects of control and predictability on the physical and psychological well-being of the institutionalized aged. *Journal of Personality and Social Psychology,* 1976, *33,* 563-574.

Seligman, M. E. P. Depression and learned helplessness. In R. J. Friedman & M. M. Katz (Eds.), *The psychology of depression: Contemporary theory and research.* Washington, DC: Hemisphere, 1974.

Seligman, M. E. P. *Helplessness. On depression, development, and death.* San Francisco: Freeman, 1975.

Seligman, M. E. P., Klein, D. C., & Miller, W. R. Depression. In H. Leitenberg (Ed.), *Handbook of behavior modification and behavior therapy.* Englewood Cliffs, NJ: Prentice-Hall, 1976.

Seligman, M. E. P., Maier, S. F., & Geer, J. The alleviation of learned helplessness in the dog. *Journal of Abnormal Psychology,* 1968, *73,* 256-262.

Seligman, M. E. P., Maier, S. F., & Solomon, R. L. Unpredictable and uncontrollable aversive events. In F. R. Brush (Ed.), *Aversive conditioning and learning.* New York: Academic Press, 1971.

Sherrod, D. R., & Downs, R. Environmental determinants of altruism: The effects of stimulus overload and perceived control on helping. *Journal of Experimental Social Psychology,* 1974, *10,* 468-479.

Sieber, J. E. A paradigm for experimental modification of the effects of test anxiety on cognitive processes. *American Educational Research Journal,* 1969, *6,* 46–61.

Sieber, J. E., Kameya, L. J., & Paulson, F. L. Effect of memory support on the problem-solving ability of test-anxious children. *Journal of Educational Psychology,* 1970, *61,* 159–168.

Smith, R. E., & Sarason, I. G. Social anxiety and the evaluation of negative interpersonal feedback. *Journal of Consulting and Clinical Psychology,* 1975, *43,* 429.

Spence, J. T., & Spence, K. W. The motivational components of manifest anxiety: Drive and drive stimuli. In C. D. Spielberger (Ed.), *Anxiety and behavior.* New York: Academic Press, 1966.

Spiegler, M. D., Morris, L. W., & Liebert, R. M. Cognitive and emotional components of test anixety: Temporal factors. *Psychological Reports,* 1968, *22,* 451–456.

Spielberger, C. D. Anxiety: State-trait-process. In C. D. Spielberger & I. G. Sarason (Eds.), *Stress and anxiety* (Vol. 1). Washington, DC: Hemisphere, 1975.

Spielberger, C. D., Anton, W. D., & Bedell, J. The nature and treatment of test anxiety. In M. Zuckerman & C. D. Spielberger (Eds.), *Emotions and anxiety: New concepts, methods, and applications.* Hillsdale, NJ: Erlbaum, 1976.

Tennen, H., & Eller, S. J. Attributional components of learned helplessness and facilitation. *Journal of Personality and Social Psychology,* 1977, *35,* 265–271.

Thornton, J. W., & Jacobs, P. D. Learned helplessness in human subjects. *Journal of Experimental Psychology,* 1971, *87,* 367–372.

Thornton, J. W., & Jacobs, P. D. The facilitating effects of prior inescapable/unavoidable stress on intellectual performance. *Psychonomic Science,* 1972, *26,* 185–188.

Trapp, E. P., & Kausler, P. H. Test anxiety level and goal-setting behavior. *Journal of Consulting Psychology,* 1958, *22,* 31–34.

Trope, Y. Seeking information about one's own ability as a determinant of choice among tasks. *Journal of Personality and Social Psychology,* 1975, *32,* 1004–1013.

Trope, Y. Uncertainty-reducing properties of achievement tasks. *Journal of Personality and Social Psychology,* 1979, *37,* 1505–1518.

Weiner, B. The effects of unsatisfied achievement motivation on persistence and subsequent performance. *Journal of Personality,* 1965, *33,* 428–442.

Weiner, B. Role of success and failure in the learning of easy and complex tasks. *Journal of Personality and Social Psychology,* 1966, *3,* 339–344.

Weiner, B. *Theories of motivation: From mechanism to cognition.* Chicago: Markham, 1972.

Weiner, B. (Ed.). *Achievement motivation and attribution theory.* Morristown, NJ: General Learning Press, 1974.

Weiner, B., Frieze, I., Kukla, A., Reed, L., Rest, S., & Rosenbaum, R. M. *Perceiving the causes of success and failure.* Morristown, NJ: General Learning Press, 1971.

Weiner, B., & Schneider, K. Drive versus cognitive theory: A reply to Boor and Harmon. *Journal of Personality and Social Psychology,* 1971, *18,* 258–262.

Weiss, J. M., Glazer, H. I., & Pohorecky, L. A. Coping behavior and neurochemical changes: An alternative explanation for the original "learned helplessness" experiments. In G. Serban & A. Kling (Eds.), *Relevance of the animal model to the human.* New York: Plenum, 1977.

Wicklund, R. A. Objective self-awareness. In L. Berkowitz (Ed.), *Advances in experimental social psychology* (Vol. 9). New York: Academic Press, 1975.

Wine, J. D. Test anxiety and direction of attention. *Psychological Bulletin,* 1971, *76,* 92–104.

Wine, J. D. Cognitive-attentional theory of test anxiety. In I. G. Sarason (Ed.), *Test anxiety: Theory, research, and application.* Hillsdale, NJ: Erlbaum, in press.

Wortman, C. B., & Brehm, J. W. Responses to uncontrollable outcomes: An integration of reactance theory and the learned helplessness model. In L. Berkowitz (Ed.), *Advances in experimental social psychology* (Vol. 8). New York: Academic Press, 1975.

Wortman, C. B., & Dintzer, L. Is an attributional analysis of the learned helplessness phenomenon viable? A critique of the Abramson-Seligman-Teasdale reformulation. *Journal of Abnormal Psychology,* 1978, *87,* 75–90.

Wortman, C. B., Panciera, L., Shusterman, L., & Hibscher, J. Attributions of causality and reactions to uncontrollable outcomes. *Journal of Experimental Social Psychology,* 1976, *12,* 301–316.

REFERENCE NOTES

1. Wine, J. D. *Cognitive-attentional approaches to test anixety modification.* Paper presented at the annual conference of the American Psychological Association, Montreal, August 1973.
2. Crossley, T. *The examination and validation of attentionally based test anxiety reduction on college freshman.* Unpublished MA thesis, University of New Brunswick, 1977.
3. Mahoney, M. J. *Cognitive skills and athletic performance.* Penn State University. Paper presented at the eleventh annual meeting of the Association for the Advancement of Behavior Therapy, Atlanta, 1977.
4. O'Banion, K., & Arkowitz, H. *Social anxiety and selective memory for positive and negative information about the self.* Unpublished manuscript, University of Oregon, 1975.
5. Snyder, M. L., Smoller, B., Strenta, A., & Frankl, A. *A comparison of eogtism, negative and learned helplessness as explanations for poor performance after unsolvable problems.* Unpublished manuscript, University of Texas, Austin, 1979.

6

Coping with Stress
as a Problem-Solving Process

Donald Meichenbaum, David Henshaw, and Norman Himel
University of Waterloo

INTRODUCTION

Adults dealing with the stress of parenting, subjects enduring laboratory-induced pain, and college students performing creative problem-solving tasks represent the populations my students and I have been studying recently. Anger control, pain tolerance, and creative problem-solving—where lie the communalities? One central commuality has been our approach to these problems. This approach can be summarized under the heading "cognitive ethology," which describes a host of assessment techniques designed to assess the flow of the subject's ideation. A variety of techniques described below are designed to record the subject's feelings, thoughts, and images that precede, accompany, and follow task performance. In the present chapter we will discuss the research potential of such cognitive assessment devices and indicate the common thought patterns that seem to accompany failure versus success at each of the tasks we have been researching. The treatment implications of these findings will be examined as well. Since the focus of the present book is on achievement, let us begin by considering the thought processes of high-versus low-creative college students.

CREATIVE PROBLEM SOLVING

Imagine being asked to perform several "creativity" tasks, such as telling all the unusual uses of common objects (e.g., bricks) or how a stuffed monkey can be changed so it is most interesting and unusual for children to play with and finally being asked to generate captions for a *Punch* cartoon. As you do these tasks we would like you to think aloud, sharing with us any feelings, thoughts, and images you may have. Such a think aloud study was conducted in our laboratory by David Henshaw.

The think aloud procedure is a time-honored assessment device in psychology. It is, however, fraught with dangers, yet at the same time it has not been fully exploited as an assessment device. An immediate caveat must be offered about the think aloud procedure, namely, one should *not* equate language with thought, and quite likely the creative process is changed when the subject is asked to think aloud. But even with this reservation, what can we learn about the thought processes of subjects who are creative, who achieve on such problem-solving tasks versus those who falter? In other words, how does the stream of consciousness differ for individuals whose achievement performance varies? What would your think aloud protocol look like for the various problem-solving tasks?

Consider the following think aloud protocols.

> *Okay, list as many interesting and unusual uses as you can think of for bricks....*
> *Well, what do you think of for bricks? You think of concrete bricks laid in houses,*
> *but there's also bricks of ice-cream, there's also bricks of gold, so I'll keep that in*
> *mind. Do not limit yourself to any one size of bricks.... Okay, try to think of*
> *something far off, something unusual.*

This subject then continued for a 10-minute period to provide a variety of creative responses. In contrast consider a student who begins her think aloud process in a potentially creative manner, but note the changes that take place.

> *Okay, the first thing I think about when I hear bricks is the three little pigs when*
> *the wolf couldn't huff and puff and blow the third house down because it was made*
> *of bricks. They also remind me mostly of somebody's back yard.... Only if Mary*
> *Jane was here she could think of anything to do with bricks because she's an*
> *architect. ... she's got to know about all these materials and stuff and she would be*
> *able to do it.*

After a few rather common responses the student states: "I don't know I'm probably wasting time on the tape recorder. I can't think about stuff." This self-denigrated theme persists as the subject continues to doubt her performance: "I wish I could put myself in Mary Jane's place right now or something and, she'd be able to think of tons of things." The subject's last few minutes were spent in task-irrelevant ideation.

Another uncreative subject offers the following thoughts:

> *I don't know, I just can't seem to think of anything else, I can't seem to think of*
> *anything period, really. Um, bricks, bricks are such stupid things ... I don't like*
> *thinking about this, it frustrates me because I can't think of anything to do with*
> *them ... that's probably why I feel pressured ... I keep thinking about the time*
> *limit ... more than I'm thinking about what I can do with bricks.*

In contrast, consider how a high-creative individual deals with such frustrations:

> *I just can't think of any ... my mind's just blank, it's really bothering me. It's*
> *just kind of building up through all the tests. I can't think of anything.... Probably,*
> *two million different ideas and I've got my nerve to say to myself that I can't think*
> *of anything. Wow.*

The subject then goes on to produce several creative responses. One final example taken from the protocol of a high-creative individual while doing the toy-monkey task provides a further example of the nature of the data.

> *Okay, um, once again I'll re-read the question but for the sake of brevity I'll just*
> *read it in my mind instead of out loud, all I'm doing in my mind is re-reading the*

*question. . . . Okay, I'm done reading the question and now I'm thinking, first of all,
I'm thinking what age group would it be for.*

Many more examples of the subjects' think aloud protocols could be offered, but
the point to be made is that substantial differences were found between the
thought processes of high- and low-creative subjects. In order to illustrate how
the think aloud protocols were collected and analyzed, let us consider the study
in more detail.

Collecting and Analyzing the Protocols

The subjects were separated into a high- and a low-creative group ($N = 10$) on
the basis of their performance on a number of creativity tests. The tests included
a wide-ranging battery, namely, the revised scale of the Welsh Art Scale (Barron
& Welsh, 1952) that assessed the subjects' general type of stimulus preference;
the Consequences Test (Guilford, 1967) and the Barron Inkblot Test of Human
Movement (Barron, 1955). The subjects' performance on each of these tasks were
standardized and a composite creativity scale was used for selection purposes.
The high- and low-creativity groups did not differ in their grade-point average or
in general verbal facility.

All subjects were tested individually in the think aloud tasks. The think aloud
protocols were obtained by leaving the subject alone in the laboratory room with
a tape recorder for 10 minutes for each of the three tasks. The major instruction
to the subject was to report "everything that comes to mind while you are
working on the task. We are less interested in final products than in the way
people arrive at them." Prior to the recording of the formal protocol all subjects
received preliminary exposure to similar training tasks in order to further clarify
the demands of the think aloud procedure. (See Henshaw, 1978, for details of
the assessment and scoring procedures.) In general, subjects were quite capable of
performing the tasks while thinking aloud.

The subjects' taped protocols were transcribed verbatim by a typist. The
procedure for analyzing this mass of data included two initial steps: (1) the
development of a unitizing system by which each of the transcripts could be
divided into units for subsequent scoring, and (2) the development of a scoring
system for assigning a score to each unit in a transcript.

Two methods for unitizing private speech are discernible in the literature. The
first method uses an arbitrarily selected time period to define the boundaries of
any given unit. Goor and Sommerfeld (1975), for example, unitized protocols of
high- and low-creative subjects using a time period of 3 seconds. Employing this
method, each transcribed protocol was divided at every 3-second interval. A
major disadvantage of this method is its arbitrariness with respect to protocol
content. The use of an external time parameter is artificial to the extent that the
time interval selected fails to contain within its boundaries the subject's naturally
occurring ideational units. Since naturally occurring units vary greatly in
duration, no single time parameter can contain all of them. A second method of
unitizing think aloud protocols circumvents this problem by making unitizing
decisions contingent on parameters contained in the subject's own thought
processes. For example, separate units were denoted in Henshaw's (1978) study
by any one or combination of the following: sentence structure, naturalistic

phrasing, changes in content, pauses in subject's ideational flow. The following two protocol segments exemplify the application of the unitizing system (separate units are denoted by slash marks):

or you could use bricks as a candle holder/ (pause) stick a candle in the holes in the middle/ you could even use the big bricks as a lamp/ put a light bulb in each of the separate hollow parts in the center/ silence/ um let's see/ (pause) you could scrape things with bricks/ silence/ I'm trying to think of what else they could be used for/ (pause) to heat hot water, like boil water/ (pause) you heat up a brick/ (pause) and drop it in a pot of water/ (pause) and the water will boil/

I'm just trying to think of something different from what I've already seen toys do/ it should be able to make it somehow run up the wall or something/ or jump like monkeys do/ (pause) make its eyes cross/ that would look cute/ or its tongue stick out/ its ears wiggle/ silence/ I thought for a minute it didn't have ears/ (pause) but it does/ (pause) it has a bow on it/ (pause) let's see/ (pause) what's it made out of/ (pause) it doesn't really say/

It should be noted that reliable unitizing cannot be done on the basis of content alone. Paralinguistic cues such as pauses, shifts in rate, tone, inflection, and volume of speech are important discriminators used by raters in the unitizing procedure. Since these cues are not evident in content, unitizing of transcripts was done while raters simultaneously listened to the taped verbal protocols. Similar scoring procedures have been used by Martin and Murray (Note 1) and Meichenbaum and Goodman (1978) to score childrens' spontaneous private speech.

In order to score the unitized protocols in the creative problem-solving think aloud study, a scoring system was developed based on Goor's (1974) system. Six general categories of verbal behavior were employed. They are: (1) reviewing given information, (2) strategy units, (3) solution units, (4) facilitative mediation, (5) inhibitive mediation, and (6) silence. Since one objective of the present chapter is to illustrate how thought processes can be scored, a brief example of each of the categories will be offered.

1. *Reviewing given information.* This category is comprised of two types of given information: (a) information provided concretely by the experimental task itself, and (b) any restatement of strategy or solution units. The subject's attention is directed to the information directly and concretely provided by the problem. Under this category the subject may make a restatement of a previously stated solution. For example: "Do not limit yourself;" "List as many unusual uses as you can think of."

2. *Strategy units.* This category is comprised of two types of units: (a) statements of a strategy, hypothesis, or approach to the experimental task that is new for the subject, and (b) the subject elaborates or develops a stated strategy. For example: "What do most people do with bricks?" "How about doing something with the size of this monkey?" "I'm thinking in terms of heavy compression, heavy weight." "Well, if I was a small child, how would I like it?"

3. *Solution units.* This refers to the subject's statements that constitute a solution to the task. For example: "Use bricks to make bookshelves." "Giving a cartoon caption." The strategy unit and solution unit scores taken together constitute what is most often scored as "creativity" on paper-and-pencil tests.

4. *Facilitative mediation.* This refers to the subject's statements aimed at

controlling his or her attention and promoting continued effort at task solution, as well as statements that reflect or imply a positive attitude toward or positive evaluation of the subject's abilities, personality, task strategies and solutions, the task itself, or the experiment as a whole. Included are expressions of positive affect including surprise and delight. For example: "Let me see." "What else can I do with it?" "Just trying to think of possibilities." "Okay, so I'll go with that idea some more." "Hey, I'm pretty good at this." "Ya, that's a great idea."

5. *Inhibitive mediation.* This refers to statements that reflect or imply a negative attitude toward or negative evaluation of the subject's personality or ability, task strategy or solution, the task itself, or the experiment as a whole. Expressions of negative affect included frustration, anger, and boredom, as well as statements that reflected the subject's inability to maintain attention to the task demands such as task-irrelevant ideas and associations. For example: "I don't think I could ever be a caption writer." "I wish my friend Mary Jane were doing this instead of me." "That's pretty common." "I don't like thinking about this." "I'm dumb." "I was thinking about that math test I took yesterday. I blew it."

6. *Silence.* Each 5-second interval of silence was scored as a discrete unit. This time interval was chosen in order to distinguish it from a pause, namely, a period during which some information processing seemed likely to be occurring. Pilot work indicated that subjects were more likely to change the content in their train of thought when this nonverbalization period was more than 5 seconds than they were following periods of nonverbalization of less than 5 seconds duration.

This detailed scoring system proved quite reliable, yielding 96% agreement for attempts at unitizing and 94% agreement for scoring categories. These reliabilities compare favorably with those reported by Goor (1974), who used a similar scoring system.

Results

Now that we have described in some detail how the think aloud protocols were collected and scored, we can deal with the results by describing the frequency and temporal (or probabilistic) relationships between the various classes of thought categories for the high- versus low-creative individuals. The data are quite rich.

High-creative subjects differed significantly from low-creative subjects in the categories of producing more instances of reviewing given information and producing significantly more new strategies, strategy elaborations, new solutions, and solution elaborations. A similar difference was evident for the facilitative mediation category, while the converse held for negative, inhibitive mediation. The low-creative subjects evidenced more negative evaluation and affect and higher frequencies of irrelevant ideas and associations than the high-creative subjects.

The results thus far have indicated that high- and low-creative subjects differed significantly in the frequencies with which they emitted various categories of verbal behavior. These results, however, leave open the question of how high- and low-creative subjects might differ in their patterns of verbal behavior. One way of addressing this question is to compare high- and low-creative subjects on the frequencies of the various categories of response that follow each specific category. This provides an opportunity to examine the patterning of thoughts over time.

In summary the results indicated consistent differences between high- and low-creative subjects across the three tasks. Following every major category of verbal behavior, high-creative subjects were significantly more likely than low-creative subjects to emit a facilitative statement and less likely than low-creative subjects to become silent. High-creative subjects were *more* likely than low-creative subjects to be "creatively productive" following every major category except facilitative mediation and *less* likely than low-creative subjects to produce inhibitive mediation following categories of reviewing given information, solution units, and inhibitive mediation. Of particular interest is the finding that facilitative mediation functioned similarly in both groups, while inhibitive mediation functioned differentially in the two groups. The low-creative subjects evidenced more debilitation in performance following an inhibitive statement than did the high-creative subjects. In effect the production of a facilitative statement was followed by a similar pattern of responses in both high- and low-creative subjects. For high-creative subjects, averaging across the three tasks, 46% of their responses following a facilitative statement fell into the creative productivity category (i.e., strategy and solution units). The comparable figure for low-creative subjects was 38%, not a significant difference. In general, for both groups, facilitative mediation tended to lead to units believed to contribute to creative performance.

The results for the distribution of responses following inhibitive mediation provide an interesting contrast. While facilitative mediation led to similar consequences for both groups, inhibitive mediation led to different consequences for the two groups. Following an inhibitive statement, low-creative subjects were more likely than high-creative subjects to become silent or to produce another inhibitive statement and less likely than high-creative subjects to produce a strategy unit or a facilitative statement. Across the three tasks, 84% of the responses of low-creative subjects following an inhibitive statement fell into the category of inhibitive mediation and silence, 6% fell into the category of strategy and solution units, while another 6% were followed by facilitative statements. The comparable data for high-creative subjects is 36%, 22%, and 17%, respectively. The two groups also differed in their reactions to silence. High-creative subjects were more likely than low-creative subjects to review given information and produce strategy units, solution units, and facilitative mediation following silence, whereas low-creative subjects were more likely to remain silent. Stated in other terms, over one-third of high-creative subjects' verbalizations following inhibitive mediation were task-relevant and facilitative, while less than one-eighth of low-creative subjects' verbalizations fell into these categories. High-creative subjects appeared to cope more successfully than low-creative subjects with self-imposed negative evaluation and wandering attention by emitting facilitative statements and continuing their efforts at the task solution. In order to further analyze the nature of the differences between high- and low-creative individuals, the 10-minute intervals for the three tasks were divided into two segments of 5 minutes each. The analyses of the frequency and temporal relationship data indicates that the largest differences appeared during the last 5 minutes. Most interestingly, it is during the last 5 minutes that the high-creative subjects produce significantly greater frequencies of facilitative mediation and less inhibitive mediation, while the low-creative individuals show the converse. These results concerning the role of negative ideation take on added meaning when compared with Goor's (1974) findings. Goor found that during a think aloud problem-solving session high-creative university students tended to follow instances of "self-reference and self-criticism" with more task-relevant and creatively productive thoughts than did their less creative counterparts. Thus the incidence and role of negative self-statements in the problem-solving performance takes on particular meaning. Patrick in 1935 and 1937 found that uncreative artists, when faced with a new task, referred less readily than creative artists to their own experience and imposed stricter standards on their productions. When they failed to meet those standards, uncreative artists engaged in task-irrelevant, unproductive, and self-defeating thoughts.

Development of a Self-report Scale

Since negative inhibitive and facilitative ideation seems to play such a prominent role in distinguishing between high- and low-creative individuals, an attempt was made to develop a self-report scale that would permit subjects to report, following performance, the incidence of their thoughts. The format of the self-report scale was taken from the work of Schwartz and Gottman (1976). A brief description of their work will provide a useful background.

In trying to understand the nature of social anxiety, Schwartz and Gottman conducted a task analysis of the behavioral deficit of low assertiveness. They identified groups of low-assertive and high-assertive individuals and then conducted multiple assessments in order to discern the role cognitive factors might play in the behavioral deficit. They found that low-assertive individuals did not differ from their more outgoing counterparts with regard to knowledge of what was an appropriate response. Moreover, when both groups were placed in a hypothetical behavioral role-playing situation of having a friend ask how he could handle specific assertive situations, once again the two groups did not differ in their knowledge or in the behavioral expression of assertion. Then what is the nature of the deficit? If both groups know *what* to do and *can* do it under the circumstance of a "safe" role-playing situation, then what is the nature of the initial behavioral deficit? To answer this question Schwartz and Gottman performed one more assessment. This time the assessment was in the form of role-playing in a situation that approximated a real-life situation of having the subject imagine himself being confronted by an unreasonable request. It is in regard to this last assessment that the low-assertive, highly socially anxious subjects manifested a deficient repertoire. Why? Schwartz and Gottman did an ingenious thing. They asked the subjects; they asked them in the form of a questionnaire designed to assess the subject's thoughts and feelings (i.e., their internal dialogues) during the respective role-playing scenes. Subjects were asked to fill out a 34-item questionnaire (an Assertive Self-Statement Test) that included 17 positive self-statements that would make it easier to refuse an unreasonable request and 17 negative self-statements that would make it harder to refuse. The subjects were asked to indicate on a scale from 1 to 5 how frequently these self-statements characterized their thoughts during the preceding assertive situations, with 1 = hardly ever and 5 = very often.

The moderate- and high-assertive subjects had significantly more positive than negative self-statements, whereas low-assertive subjects did not differ in their positive and negative self-statements. For the high-assertive subjects there was a marked discrepancy between positive and negative self-statements and usually little doubt in their minds about the appropriateness of their action. In contrast, the low-assertive subject could be characterized by an "internal dialogue of conflict," in which positive and negative self-statements competed against one another, interfering with interpersonal behavior. That cognitive factors may play such a directive role in social anxiety was underscored by studies conducted by Glass (Note 2) and Schmurak (1974), who found that cognitive modeling therapy in the form of alteration of self-statements was most effective in reducing nonassertiveness.

This detour into the literature on nonassertiveness was offered because we have adopted the format of the Schwartz and Gottman postperformance self-report scale to develop an instrument to assess the subject's thinking process while performing creativity tests. Space does not permit an extensive description of the instrument (see Henshaw, 1978), but a brief account can be offered. The scale consists of 15 self-statements believed to be facilitative of creative performance and 15 self-statements believed to be inhibitive of creative performance. Over 70% of a sample of 205 undergraduate student raters concurred with both the relevance and directionality of these self-statements. For each item in the scale the subject indicates the frequency with which the self-statement occurred while working on a battery of creativity tasks. Illustrative negative-inhibitive items include: "I was thinking that I'm not a very creative person." "I was worried about what others would think of my ideas." "I was preoccupied with how much time I had left." Illustrative facilitative items include: "I was thinking that no matter how far-fetched my idea was, it was worth pursuing." "I was thinking that the more ideas I thought up, the better my ideas would be."

A number of validity and reliability studies have been conducted on the self-instructional creativity scale. For example, Henshaw (1978) found that while the subject's facilitative and inhibitive self-report scores were both significantly related to his or her performance on a variety of creativity measures, the subject's overall self-instructional style (i.e., the difference score between endorsements of positive and negative items) was most highly correlated with performance. Moreover, the test-retest reliability of the self-report scale was found to be quite acceptable, with the difference score showing the most reliability.

In a related study the relationship between the self-instructional self-report scale and Gough and Heilbrun's (1965) adjective checklist was examined. Whereas the subject's performance on the creativity measures showed few significant relationships to personological variables, the self-instructional self-report scale demonstrated the most significant relationships with personality characteristics that have demonstrated relevance to creativity.

A good deal of research has yet to be conducted on the self-instructional creativity scale, but for now it demonstrates another promising way to assess the subject's thought processes. Surely one can raise questions about the subject's ability and willingness to accurately report his or her thoughts, especially on a postperformance basis. Do such self-reports constitute postperformance rationalizations, inferential reconstructions, or accurate accounts of ideation? These are important questions to be explored and teased apart, if possible. But no matter what these self-reports represent, the question is whether they have predictive and explanatory value. The intriguing question concerning the creativity scale is whether such self-reports of ongoing cognition will prove to be a better predictor of external (real-life) criteria of creativity than are the subject's performance on the actual creativity tests. It is suggested that if we are to understand the nature of achievement we have to develop instruments that will begin to assess the subject's ideation as well as his or her performance. That such a cognitive approach can have an heuristic impact is evident in a study of Meichenbaum (1975), who helped subjects enhance their creative problem-solving ability by learning to alter their self-statements.

Two additional examples can be offered of the potential of such self-report scales for understanding of competent performance. Recently, Kendall, Williams, Pechacek, Graham, Shisslak, & Herzoff (Note 3) developed a self-instructional self-report scale (similar in format to Schwartz and Gottman's) to assess hospital patients' reactions to catheterization procedures. The patients' negative self-statement scores were found to be significantly and negatively correlated with both the physicians' ratings of patient adjustment and the technicians' ratings of patient adjustment. Positive self-statements were not significantly related to either rating of adjustment. No data is reported on the difference score. Once again the higher the incidence of negative self-statements the poorer the rating of adjustment. Moreover, Kendall et al. report that cognitive behavior modification (CBM) procedures were most effective in fostering adjustment. The CBM procedure involved aiding the patients in labeling the stress, identifying stress-related cues, discussing cognitive coping procedures, reinforcing individual coping styles, and modeling and rehearsing cognitive coping skills. Meichenbaum (1977) has discussed the value of such CBM procedures in some detail. Sarason (1978) has also developed a postperformance cognitive interference self-report scale that has been employed in the study of test-anxious subjects, while Bruch (Note 4) has used such a self-report scale by having subjects interrupt their task performance reporting on their ideation.

A second example in which the assessment of subject's cognitions elucidates achievement performance is offered by Mahoney and Avener (1977), who studied elite athletes. The study of athletes provides a unique opportunity to examine the relationship between the stream of ideation and performance. In Mahoney and Avener's study 13 male gymnasts were given a standard questionnaire and interview before, during, and after the final trials of the U.S. Olympic team. They found that self-verbalizations and the form of mental imagery differentiated the best gymnasts from those who failed to make the Olympic team. Even though one must be cautious in interpreting such a correlational study, a similar pattern of results as those reported above with the creative problem-solving task is beginning to emerge. The better gymnasts tended to be more self-confident, and they "tended to use their anxiety as a stimulant to better performance. The less successful gymnasts seemed to arouse themselves into near-panic states by self-verbalizations and images which belied self-doubts and impending tragedies" (Mahoney & Avener, 1977, p. 140). Mahoney and Avener report many other correlations, but perhaps we are beginning to see some communality, some pattern of the role of specific ideation in contributing to poor performance in diverse achievement situations. Surely the studies reported in this chapter are too preliminary to draw such conclusions, but hopefully these results will encourage us to look further.

Our work with two other problems should provide even further challenging material. These will be presented only briefly in order to provide space for a discussion of the implications of this research for treatment.

LABORATORY-INDUCED PAIN

Meichenbaum (1977) has discussed the substantive evidence for the role cognition plays in the experience of pain. In order to further understand this role we have been employing a videotape *reconstruction* procedure with volunteer adult subjects who undergo a cold-pressor test. Subjects are asked to tolerate the pain of holding their arm in a tub of cold circulating water (2°C). The maximum allowable time is 5 minutes but the subjects do not know this. To tap cognitions we videotape each subject while engaged in the cold-pressor task. The subject's task is to keep her arm in the water as long as possible, although it could be voluntarily removed at any time. At various points during the tolerance period a pain intensity rating was requested by the experimenter. Following the cold-pressor assessment the subject was asked to watch herself on the videotape, reporting aloud the feelings and thoughts she had experienced. A small segment of tape is played, then stopped by the subject as she reconstructs her thoughts and feelings. The subject's verbal protocols can be analyzed in a microscopic manner, as in the creative problem-solving tasks, or by means of overall clinical ratings involving the presence or absence of particular thoughts and feelings. In our laboratory Myles Genest has been conducting this research.

The preliminary analyses indicate that the subjects who could tolerate the pain for the full 5 minutes did *not* differ from those who dropped out in the use of potentially coping self-statements and images per se, but instead differed in what they said to themselves about the use of such procedures to cope with the pain stressor. For example, one subject began with an image of falling out of a boat in the arctic and feeling the cold. From the perspective of coping with pain, such an attentionally diverting image should lead to enhanced tolerance. In fact this subject withdrew her arm within 2 minutes. Thus it does not appear to be the mere presence of potential coping stratagems per se that determine tolerance. Something more is needed. The analysis of the videotapes suggests that the difference lies in the subject's expression of belief that she can use such stratagems to handle the stressor.

The results remind us of the recent writings of Bandura (1977), who indicated that the expectation of personal efficacy determines whether coping behavior will be initiated and how much effort will be expended and how long it will be sustained in the face of obstacles and aversive experiences. One can ask exactly what internal dialogue interferes with and prevents the expression of such expectancy. The subjects who tolerated the cold pressor least tended to "catastrophize" and to see themselves as being overwhelmed, as having little ability to do anything to tolerate the pain. In contrast, those who remained longest tended to see the stressor as a challenge, as a *problem* to be solved.

Turk (1976, 1977) has demonstrated that a cognitive behavior modification procedure of stress inoculation can be successfully employed to significantly enhance subjects' tolerance for experimentally induced pain, in this case the ischemic blood-pressure cuff. He found that the expanded skills training program led to an increase in percentage of time subjects engaged in active coping strategies as opposed to cognitions concerning negative aspects of the task (i.e., perserverance in spite of the desire to stop, and noncoping cognitions).

Importantly, the results of Genest's study suggest that some subjects may have coping strategems already within their repertoire, and the focus of treatment should be on what subjects say to themselves about implementing such strategems. All too readily therapists assume that clients lack specific behavioral and cognitive skills. The general thrust of the results summarized in this chapter questions this assumption or at least calls for a careful task analysis. Such an analysis must include the nature of what the subject *is* and *is not* saying to himself.

ANGER CONTROL

Perhaps the role of such cognitive processes is most clearly articulated in the work on anger control conducted by Novaco (1975). In a series of studies Novaco (1977a, 1977b) has demonstrated that a valuable way to teach subjects (including child-abuse parents) to control anger is for them to reappraise the nature of provocations. Each provocation must come to be viewed as a problem to be solved rather than a stimulus against which to react. A variety of different CBM techniques were employed in order to make the subject task oriented when presented with a provocation, thus defining the situation as a problem that calls for a solution rather than a threat that calls for attack. In this way the client was led to focus attention on the issues involved and avoid responding in ways that would escalate the provocation sequence.

In our own lab we are following up Novaco's work by focusing on a slightly different version of the same question. Instead of teaching parents who have problems with anger control various scoping procedures, we are studying "normal" parents and trying to understand why the incidence of child abuse or the loss of anger control is not higher. We have been interviewing parents of children from 1 month to 16 years to determine situations that are viewed by parents as provoking as well as those situations that are rewarding. The question is, how do parents behave in response to such provocations? A description of this data could constitute a chapter in itself. One prominent observation is that a useful and important coping device is to see the provocation as a *problem to be solved*. Once the parent adopts this cognitive set, a whole host of interpersonal and intrapersonal coping behaviors may be enacted.

PROBLEM–SOLVING TRAINING

It is the contention of the present chapter that a theme that undercuts the myriad of coping devices is a "problem-solving set." In order to further underscore the potential of such a problem-solving view of the coping process, we will present a brief account of the burgeoning literature on problem-solving training.

A series of investigations conducted by Spivack, Shure, and their collaborators provide evidence that deficiencies in problem-solving thinking are associated with behavioral maladjustment. Deficits in problem-solving cognition, as assessed by performance on a projective-like task, were found among diverse socially incompetent populations including poorly adjusted preschool children from disadvantaged environments (Shure, Spivack, & Jaeger, 1971); emotionally disturbed 10- to 12-year-old children (Shure & Spivack, 1972); impulsive teenagers institutionalized for remedial purposes (Spivack & Levine, 1963); adolescent psychiatric patients (Platt, Altman, & Altman, Note 5); youthful incarcerated heroin addicts (Platt, Scura, & Hannon, 1973); and adult psychiatric patients (Platt & Spivack, 1972a, 1972b, Note 6). These studies have certain methodological limitations, which necessarily restrict the generalizability of results and the kinds of conclusions that may be validly drawn. For example, the assessment of problem-solving thinking was based upon the scoring of subjects' verbal responses to hypothetical problematic situations primarily of an inter-personal nature. There were no procedures for directly assessing how subjects think, feel, and behave when actually confronted with real-life problematic circumstances. Moreover, the data derived from these studies are correlational and therefore are insufficient for inferring any definitive causal relationship between problem-solving ability and social competence.

More convincing evidence comes from recent investigations assessing the efficacy of an educational intervention program concerned with teaching cognitive problem-solving skills to preschool children (Shure, Spivack, & Gordon, 1972; Spivack & Shure, 1974). It was found that the intervention program significantly improved certain dimensions of problem-solving thinking in young children with behavioral difficulties (i.e., impulsive and overinhibited pre-schoolers), and this resulted in significant improvements in the social adjustment of these children. Follow-up studies conducted 6 months after training confirmed that positive therapeutic effects were maintained and generalized to situations different from the training setting. Furthermore, even children originally con-sidered to be well-adjusted seemed to benefit from the intervention program (i.e., they were less likely to develop behavioral difficulties at a later point in time as compared to initially well-adjusted subjects who were not exposed to training). Thus Spivack and Shure (1974) conclude that an educational program designed to improve cognitive skills pertaining to interpersonal problem-solving can (1) effectively enhance the social adjustment of moderately disturbed children and (2) increase the likelihood that "normal" children will continue to maintain a level of good social adjustment. The latter inference suggests the potential utility of such cognitively oriented didactic procedures for *preventing* the development of behavioral disturbance.

The measures used to assess interpersonal problem-solving are not redundant with measures of general intelligence, academic achievement, or creativity (Platt & Spivach, 1972a). There appear to be several specific though interrelated cognitive abilities that are required for effective interpersonal problem-solving, and these component skills include the following (Spivack & Shure, 1974):

1. Ability to recognize the presence of social problems.
2. Ability to think of general alternative solutions to social problems.
3. Ability to consider specific alternative means for solving problems (i.e., means-ends thinking) and to evaluate these means in terms of their probable effectiveness and social acceptability.
4. Ability to consider alternative consequences.
5. Ability to perceive cause-and-effect relations in interpersonal events.

Spivack and Shure (1974) point out that the relative importance of these component skills for good social adjustment may vary developmentally, though the capacity for alternative solution thinking seems to be necessary for efficient interpersonal problem solving across all ages. These investigators further note that different people, within any age group, may be socially maladjusted because of different kinds of deficits in their thought processes. Thus educative-remedial procedures should be tailor-made for each person in order to rectify the *specific cognitive deficiency* that underlies the person's impaired capability to solve interpersonal problems.

The notion that psychological stress and social maladjustment can arise from ineffective problem solving has also been discussed by other researchers (D'Zurilla & Goldfried, 1971; Goldfried & D'Zurilla, 1969; Goldfried & Goldfried, 1975; Howard & Scott, 1965; Lukton, 1974; Mahoney, 1974; Mechanic, 1968, 1970, 1974; Scott & Howard, 1970). Using principles of cognitive behavior modification, D'Zurilla and Goldfried (1971) outline therapeutic guidelines for helping clients improve their skills in solving social problems. First these investigators suggest that the therapist should encourage the development of an appropriate general orientation or problem-solving mental set within the client. This mental set involves an appreciation that problematic situations occur commonly in life and can usually be coped with adequately. Moreover, the client is instructed that it is important to be able to recognize a problem when it occurs and to refrain from reacting impulsively or pessimistically. Following the formation of this general orientation the client is taught how to proceed independently through a series of specific cognitive operations and overt behaviors that are essential for efficient problem solving. The cognitive operations include:

1. Formulating and defining the problem as precisely as possible.
2. Generating a list of alternative solutions including both general strategies and specific tactics.
3. Deciding which procedure should be used to solve the problem. This decision-making process requires the client to assess the likelihood of various consequences (personal, social, short-term, long-term) of each alternative and to evaluate the relative utility and desirability of these consequences. The client attempts to select that course of action most likely to solve the initial problem, maximize positive consequences, and minimize negative consequences.
4. Verifying the efficacy of the procedure that is selected. This step requires the client to implement the chosen course of action and to assess whether its consequences are in accordance with what had been anticipated. A discrepancy between actual and predicted outcome suggests that the selected procedure may not be the most appropriate. The client should then use this feedback information constructively and return to an earlier stage in the sequence of problem-solving operations.

In essence, interpersonal problem-solving training involves teaching the client general coping skills that he or she can apply independently to deal with diverse problematic situations encountered in daily living. The client is taught how to think and behave in an autonomous, flexible, and scientific manner. Indeed Mahoney (1974) metaphorically depicts problem-solving therapy as an educational process whereby the client learns how to function as his or her own "personal scientist."

Although some clients may learn how to solve interpersonal problems symbolically, they still might have difficulty in actually executing their strategies because of interfering emotional inhibitions (e.g., excessive anxiety) or performance deficits (e.g., lack of assertiveness). In these cases, problem-solving training may be supplemented with behavior modification procedures that assist the client to overcome the emotional inhibition or rectify the performance deficit.

It is evident that several factors are essential for developing competence in solving interpersonal problems. According to Mechanic (1968, 1970, 1974), effective instrumental problem solving can occur only if the following conditions are fulfilled:

1. The person must have certain relevant problem-solving skills (cognitive, motoric, social) in his or her behavioral repertoire to apply under appropriate circumstances.

2. The person must be sufficiently motivated to deal directly with the problematic situation.

3. The person must have the capacity to regulate his or her affective arousal within a noninterfering moderate range in order to facilitate the implementation of direct coping skills.

4. The person must have an adequate amount of practice and experience in applying skills to cope directly with particular problematic situations.

Meichenbacum (1977) and Meichenbaum and Novaco (1978) have described how cognitive behavior modification procedures can be employed to teach such problem-solving skills on a therapeutic as well as preventive basis to high-risk populations. Such problem-solving training procedures follow nicely from the research discussed earlier on the nature of the internal dialogue that contributes to inadequate performance. Such cognitive behavior modification procedures or problem-solving training techniques are designed to alter the client's internal dialogue and thus his or her performance.

REFERENCES

Bandura, A. Self-efficacy: Toward a unifying theory of behavioral change. *Psychological Review,* 1977, *84*, 191–215.

Barron, F. The disposition toward originality. *Journal of Abnormal and Social Psychology,* 1955, *51*, 478–485.

Barron, F., & Welsh, G. Artistic perception as a possible factor in personality style: Its measurement by a figure preference test. *Journal of Psychology,* 1952, *33*, 199–203.

D'Zurilla, T. J., & Goldfried, M. R. Problem-solving and behavior modification. *Journal of Abnormal Psychology,* 1971, *78*, 107–126.

Goldfried, M. R., & D'Zurilla, T. J. A behavioral-analytic model for assessment of competence. In C. D. Spielberger (Ed.), *Current topics in clinical and community psychology* (Vol. 1). New York: Academic Press, 1969.

Goldfried, M. R., & Goldfried, A. P. Cognitive change methods. In F. H. Kanfer & A. P. Goldstein (Eds.), *Helping people change.* New York: Pergamon, 1975.

Goor, A. *Problem-solving processes of creative and non-creative students.* Doctoral dissertation, University of North Carolina at Chapel Hill, 1974.

Goor, A., & Sommerfeld, R. A comparison of problem-solving processes of creative students and non-creative students. *Journal of Educational Psychology,* 1975, *67*, 495–505.

Gough, H. G., & Heilbrun, A. B. *The adjective check list manual.* Palo Alto, CA: Consulting Psychologists Press, 1965.

Guilford, J. P. Some theoretical views of creativity. In H. Helson & W. Bevan (Eds.), *Contemporary approaches to psychology.* New York: Von Nostrand, 1967.

Henshaw, D. *A cognitive analysis of creative problem-solving.* Unpublished dissertation, University of Waterloo, 1978.

Howard, A., & Scott, R. A proposed framework for the analysis of stress in the human organism. *Behavioral Science,* 1965, *10,* 141-160.

Luckton, R. Crisis theory: Review and critique. *Social Science Review,* 1974, *48,* 384-402.

Mahoney, M. J. *Cognition and behavior modification.* Cambridge, Ma.: Ballinger, 1974.

Mahoney, M. J., & Avener, M. Psychology of the elite athlete: An exploratory study. *Cognitive Therapy and Research,* 1977, *1,* 135-142.

Mechanic, D. The study of social stress and its relationship to disease. In D. Mechanic (Ed.), *Medical sociology.* New York: Free Press, 1968.

Mechanic, D. Some problems in developing a social psychology of adaptation to stress. In J. E. McGrath (Ed.), *Social and psychological factors in stress.* New York: Holt, Rinehart & Winston, 1970.

Mechanic, D. Social structure and personal adaptation: Some neglected dimensions. In G. Coelho, D. M. Hamburg, & J. E. Adams (Eds.), *Coping and adaptation.* New York: Basic Books, 1974.

Meichenbaum, D. Enhancing creativity by modifying what subjects say to themselves. *American Educational Research Journal,* 1975, *12,* 129-145.

Meichenbaum, D. *Cognitive-behavior modification: An Integrative approach.* New York: Plenum Press, 1977.

Meichenbaum, D., & Goodman, S. Critical questions and methodological problems in studying private speech. In G. Zivin (Ed.), *Development of self-regulation through speech.* New York: Wiley, 1978.

Meichenbaum, D., & Novaco, R. W. Stress inoculation: A preventative approach. In C. D. Spielberger & I. A. Sarason (Eds.), *Stress and anxiety* (Vol. 5). Washington, D.C.: Hemisphere, 1978.

Novaco, R. W. *Anger control: The development and evaluation of an experimental treatment.* Lexington, MA: Heath, 1975.

Novaco, R. W. Stress inoculation: A cognitive therapy for anger and its application to a case of depression. *Journal of Consulting and Clinical Psychology,* 1977, *45,* 600-608. (a)

Novaco, R. W. A stress inoculation approach to anger management in the training of law enforcement officers. *American Journal of Community Psychology,* 1977, *5,* 327-346. (b)

Patrick, C. Creative thought in poets. *Archives of Psychology,* 1935, *178,* 74-99.

Patrick, C. Creative thought in artists. *Archives of Psychology,* 1937, *4,* 35-73.

Platt, J. J., Scura, W., & Hannon, J. Problem-solving thinking of youthful incarcerated heroin addicts. *Journal of Community Psychology,* 1973, *1,* 278-281.

Platt, J. J., & Spivack, G. Problem-solving thinking of psychiatric patients. *Journal of Consulting and Clinical Psychology,* 1972, *39,* 148-151. (a)

Platt, J. J., & Spivack, G. Social competence and effective problem-solving thinking in psychiatric patients. *Journal of Clinical Psychology,* 1972, *28,* 3-5. (b)

Sarason, I. G. The Test Anxiety Scale: Concept and research. In C. D. Spielberger & I. G. Sarason (Eds.), *Stress and anxiety* (Vol. 5). New York: Hemisphere, 1978.

Schwartz, R. M., & Gottman, J. M. Toward a task analysis of assertive behavior. *Journal of Consulting and Clinical Psychology,* 1976, *44,* 910-920.

Scott, R., & Howard, A. Models of stress. In S. Levine & N. Scotch (Eds.), *Social stress.* Chicago: Aldine, 1970.

Shmurak, S. *Design and evaluation of three dating behavior training programs utilizing response acquisition and cognitive self-statement modification techniques.* Unpublished doctoral dissertation, Indiana University, 1974.

Shure, M. B., & Spivak, G. Means-ends thinking, adjustment, and social class among elementary school-aged children. *Journal of Consulting and Clinical Psychology,* 1972, *38,* 348-353.

Shure, M. B., Spivack, G., & Gordon, R. Problem-solving thinking: A preventive mental health program for preschool children. *Reading World,* 1972, *11,* 259-273.

Shure, M. B., Spivack, G., & Jaeger, M. A. Problem-solving thinking and adjustment among disadvantaged preschool children. *Child Development,* 1971, *42,* 1791-1803.

Spivack, G., & Levine, M. *Self-regulation in acting out and normal adolescents.* Washington, D.C.: Report M-4531, National Institute of Health, 1963.

Spivack, G., & Shure, M. B. *Social adjustment of young children: A cognitive approach to solving real-life problems.* San Francisco: Jossey-Bass, 1974.

Turk, D. C. *Cognitive control of pain: A skills training approach for the treatment of pain.* Unpublished masters thesis, University of Waterloo, 1976.

Turk, D. C. *An expanded skills training approach for the treatment of experimentally induced pain.* Unpublished doctoral dissertation, University of Waterloo, 1977.

REFERENCE NOTES

1. Martin, R., & Murray, J. *Manual for scoring private speech.* Unpublished manuscript, University of Rochester, 1975.
2. Glass, C. R. *Response acquisition and cognitive self-statement modification approaches to dating-behavior training.* Unpublished manuscript, Notre Dame University, 1974.
3. Kendall, P. C., Williams, L., Pechacek, T., Graham, L. E., Shisslak, C., & Herzoff, N. *Cognitive-behavioral and patient education in catheterization procedures.* Unpublished manuscript, University of Minnesota, 1978.
4. Bruch, M. *Type of cognitive modeling, observers' imitation of modeled strategies, and modification of test anxiety.* Unpublished manuscript, Bradley University, 1976.
5. Platt, J. J., Altman, N., & Altman, D. *Dimensions of interpersonal problem-solving thinking in adolescent psychiatric patients.* Paper presented at the Eastern Psychological Association Meeting, Washington, DC, May 1973.
6. Platt, J. J., & Spivack, G. *Means-end problem-solving procedure (MEPS): Manual and tentative norms.* Philadelphia, PA: Department of Mental Health Sciences, Hahnemann Medical College and Hospital, 1974.

III

ANXIETY AND COPING IN ACHIEVEMENT SITUATIONS

7

Anxiety and Complex Learning

Darlene L. Heinrich
Florida State University

Charles D. Spielberger
University of South Florida

In this chapter we will review and evaluate the research literature on anxiety and complex learning. The conceptual framework for this review is provided by Spence-Taylor Drive Theory (Spence, 1958; Spence & Spence, 1966; Taylor, 1956) and Spielberger's (1966a, 1972a, 1972b) Trait-State Anxiety Theory. In selecting the studies to be reviewed, complex learning was defined as consisting of the three highest categories of learning as conceptualized by Gagné and Briggs (1974). These are: concept learning, rule learning, and problem solving, that is, the learning of higher order rules.

The chapter is organized into three sections. In the first, Drive Theory and Trait-State Anxiety Theory are described, and the major variables investigated in research guided by these theories are identified. The definition and measurement of state and trait anxiety are also discussed in the first section. Research findings on anxiety and complex learning are described and evaluated in the second section. In the final section, the implications of these findings for Drive Theory and Trait-State Anxiety Theory are critically examined.

DRIVE THEORY AND TRAIT–STATE ANXIETY THEORY

Drive Theory (K. W. Spence, 1958; Taylor, 1951), an extension of Hullian Learning Theory, has served as the conceptual framework in a majority of the experimental investigations of anxiety and learning. More recently, Trait-State Anxiety Theory (Spielberger, 1966a, 1972a) has been used to supplement Drive Theory in the design and interpretation of research on anxiety and learning. This theory distinguishes between anxiety as a transitory emotional state (A-State) and as a relatively stable personality trait (A-Trait), and specifies the conditions under which different levels of A-State are aroused in persons who differ in A-Trait. In order to clarify the theoretical frame of reference for this review and evaluation of research on anxiety and complex learning, the major postulates of Drive Theory and Trait-State Anxiety Theory will be briefly described.

Work on the chapter was facilitated by a grant (MDA 903–77–C–0190) to the second author from the U. S. Department of Defense, Advanced Research Products Agency.

Drive Theory

Drive Theory proposes that the strength of a given response, R, in any learning situation, is a multiplicative function of habit strength, H, and total effective drive state, D. This relationship may be expressed as follows: $R = f(H \times D)$. H is defined as the strength of the tendency to make a particular response to a specific stimulus or stimulus pattern. In animal learning studies H is operationally defined in terms of the number of reinforced stimulus-response trials. In human learning H is empirically or intuitively defined in terms of the strength of a "correct" response relative to all other possible response tendencies.

The concept of *drive* refers to the various need states of an individual (i.e., hunger, thirst, sex) that combine to determine his or her total level of motivation at a particular time. Drive Theory assumes that noxious or aversive stimuli arouse a hypothetical emotional response (r_e) that contributes to drive level. Since this emotional response is similar to the clinical concept of anxiety, individual differences in drive level are traditionally inferred from self-report measures of anxiety such as the Taylor (1953) Manifest Anxiety Scale (MAS). The following predictions with regard to the effects of habit strength and anxiety (drive) level on learning can be derived from Drive Theory:

1. For simple or easy learning tasks, in which correct responses are dominant and competing error tendencies are minimal, the performance of high-anxious subjects will be superior to that of low-anxious subjects.
2. For difficult learning tasks, in which competing error tendencies are strong relative to correct responses, high drive will activate these error tendencies, and the performance of high-anxious subjects will be inferior to that of low-anxious subjects.
3. For tasks of intermediate difficulty the *stage of learning* must be taken into account. High anxiety will be detrimental to performance early in learning when the strength of correct responses is weak relative to competing error tendencies. Later in learning, high anxiety will begin to facilitate performance as correct responses are strengthened and error tendencies are extinguished.

The effects of anxiety on learning may also be influenced by the type of response required of the subject. While high anxiety will generally facilitate performance on simple tasks when *number of errors* is used as the performance measure, response latency appears to be a more sensitive measure of covert error tendencies than number of errors. For example, high anxiety was found to impair *speed of response* early in learning and to facilitate speed later in learning for a very easy task in which there were few errors (Gaudry & Spielberger, 1971).

Spielberger (1966b) has shown that learning is influenced by both the ability of the learner and the characteristics of a learning task. He contends that the intelligence of a subject determines, in part, the relative strengths of correct and competing response tendencies that are elicited by a learning task. Thus tasks of intermediate difficulty may be relatively easy for bright subjects for whom correct responses become dominant more rapidly, but quite difficult for subjects with limited ability for whom error tendencies are initially stronger and less easily extinguished.

The impact of anxiety on learning for subjects who differ in ability will depend upon the complexity of a learning task and the stage of learning investigated (Speilberger, 1971). When students of comparable ability learn difficult materials, Drive Theory would predict that the performance of low-anxious students would be superior to that of high-anxious students, especially in the early stages of learning. As learning progresses and the task becomes easier with repeated practice, high anxiety would eventually be expected to facilitate the performance of subjects with high intelligence. For persons of average or low ability, high anxiety would only facilitate performance if the subjects gained sufficient mastery of the task so that "correct" responses became dominant relative to error tendencies.

The following predictions concerning the effects of anxiety and intelligence on performance on learning tasks that vary in difficulty may be derived from Spielberger's (1966a, 1971) extension of Spence-Taylor Drive Theory:

1. For subjects with superior intelligence, high anxiety will facilitate performance on most learning tasks. While high anxiety may initially cause performance decrements on very difficult tasks, it will eventually facilitate the performance of bright subjects as they progress through the task and correct responses become dominant.

2. For subjects of average intelligence, high anxiety will facilitate performance on simple tasks and, later in learning, on tasks of moderate difficulty. On very difficult tasks, high anxiety will generally lead to performance decrements.

3. For low intelligence subjects, high anxiety may facilitate performance on simple tasks that have been mastered. However, performance decrements will generally be associated with high anxiety on difficult tasks, especially in the early stages of learning.

Trait-State Anxiety Theory

Trait-State Anxiety Theory begins with the conceptual distinction between anxiety as a transitory state and as a relatively stable personality trait. According to Spielberger, Gorsuch, and Lushene (1970):

> State anxiety (A-State) may be conceptualized as a transitory emotional state or condition of the human organism that varies in intensity and fluctuates over time. This condition is characterized by tension and apprehension, and activation of the autonomic nervous system. . . . Trait anxiety (A-Trait) refers to relatively stable individual differences in anxiety proneness, that is, to differences between people in the tendency to respond to situations perceived as threatening with elevations in A-State intensity. (1970, p. 3)

The terms *stress* and *threat* are used by Spielberger (1972a) to refer to different aspects of a temporal sequence of events that results in the evocation of an anxiety state. *Stress* refers to the objective stimulus properties of situations that naturally occur or that are manipulated by an experimenter. *Threat* refers to the subjective appraisal of a situation as physically or psychologically dangerous, and *state anxiety* is directly related to perceived threat. The intensity of an anxiety state will be higher in situations that are perceived as more threatening, regardless of the objective danger (stress). State anxiety will be low in nonstressful situations and in situations in which an existing danger is not perceived as threatening.

Spielberger et al. (1970) note that persons high in trait anxiety tend to perceive a greater number of situations as more dangerous or threatening than persons who are low in A-Trait and to respond to threatening situations with A-State elevations of greater intensity. The nature or type of stress associated with a situation is also important in determining the likelihood that high-A-Trait individuals will respond with higher elevations in state anxiety. Differences in performance on learning tasks for subjects differing in trait anxiety have been observed primarily when experimental conditions involve some form of psychological stress, such as direct or implied threats to self-esteem, ego-involving instructions, or failure feedback. In contrast, persons with high trait anxiety do not perceive physical dangers such as pain or the threat of pain as any more threatening than low-A-Trait persons.

A number of self-report scales have been constructed to measure individual differences in anxiety. The Taylor (1953) MAS was specifically developed to assess the strength of the hypothetical emotional response, r_e. While the MAS has proved useful as an index of the drive level evoked by psychological stress, it does not appear to be related to drive in physical stress situations (Spielberger, 1972a). Other A-Trait scales that have been widely used in research on anxiety and learning include the IPAT Anxiety Scale (Cattell & Scheier, 1963) and the State-Trait Anxiety Inventory (STAI) (Spielberger et al., 1970).

The assessment of anxiety states is a recent development in psychological research. Since state anxiety scales assess the intensity of A-State reactions at a particular moment in time, such measures are logically more closely related to drive level than trait anxiety measures. Scales constructed to measure state anxiety typically require the subject to respond according to how he or she feels at a specific moment. The Today Form of the Multiple Affect Adjective Check List (Zuckerman, 1960) and the STAI A-State Scale (Spielberger et al., 1970) are examples of scales designed to assess state anxiety.

Most published studies of anxiety and complex learning were carried out before the trait-state distinction was widely accepted; hence trait anxiety measures have often been inappropriately used as indicants of drive level. Nevertheless, the results of a number of studies in which drive was measured with A-Trait scales have supported a Drive Theory interpretation of anxiety and complex learning. The reasons for this will be considered when studies concerned with stress, anxiety, and task difficulty are examined in the following section.

RESEARCH ON ANXIETY AND COMPLEX LEARNING

In this review the effects of anxiety and task difficulty on complex learning will be examined first. Next we will consider studies in which the effects of various types of stress on anxiety and learning were investigated. Finally, studies concerned with stress, anxiety and task difficulty are reviewed.

Anxiety, Task Difficulty, and Complex Learning

Task difficulty is typically defined in terms of four general classes of variables: (1) task complexity, (2) stages of the learning process, (3) memory support or conceptual aids for the learner, and (4) individual differences in intelligence. Investigations of anxiety and complex learning related to each of these four aspects of task difficulty will be evaluated in the context of predictions from Drive Theory. Studies in which the results are consistent with theoretical expectations will be considered first, followed by investigations at variance with theoretical expectations and those with nonsignificant outcomes. Important methodological issues that are encountered in these studies will also be discussed.

Anxiety and Task Complexity

Drive Theory predicts that high anxiety will facilitate performance in learning easy materials. While strict operational control over difficulty level can be maintained in research with simple conditioning and learning tasks, it is generally not possible to accurately determine the strength of correct and incorrect (competing) response tendencies on complex learning tasks. Rather, the "difficulty" of a given task is generally established to be relatively easier or more difficult than another similar task. For tasks that clearly vary in difficulty, Drive Theory predicts that high anxiety will facilitate performance on easy tasks and lead to performance decrements on the difficult tasks.

Drive Theory predictions of the effects of anxiety on performance for easy and difficult tasks were partially supported in two studies reported by Maltzman, Fox, and Morrisett (1953). In one study Maltzman et al. (1953) used training procedures to establish a dominant set that was congruent with the correct solutions for a set of anagrams tasks, which turned out to be extremely easy, with a mean error rate of only about 10%. They found that high anxiety even facilitated the performance of subjects given training on unrelated anagrams as well as those who were given training on the related anagrams. Since habit strength was very high for both groups, high drive activated "correct" response tendencies and training apparently did little to improve performance.

In a second study Maltzman et al. (1953) used a Luchin's Water Jar problem to establish a mental set that would lead to an *indirect* solution rather than to the preferred *direct* solution. The results showed that the greater the anxiety level (as measured by the MAS), the less often the direct solution to the problem was used. These findings were in accord with expectations from Drive Theory that high-anxious subjects perform more poorly on tasks in which incorrect (indirect) responses are dominant.

Van Buskirk (1961) found similar results in an investigation of the effects of anxiety and fear of failure on complex figure analogies and logical deduction tasks. On the logical deduction task, high-fear subjects performed better than low-fear subjects on an easy subtest, but both groups performed comparably on the more difficult subtest. On the easier figure analogies subtest, high- and low-fear-of-failure subjects performed comparably, but high-fear subjects performed more poorly than the low-fear subjects on the more difficult figure analogies subtest. These results show an interactive effect of anxiety and task difficulty that is consistant with Drive Theory.

Poorer performance for high-anxiety subjects on difficult tasks has been a common finding in the research literature, whereas facilitative effects of anxiety on easy tasks are found less often. An investigation by Romanow (1958) is typical of studies in which Drive Theory predictions were supported for difficult tasks but not for easy tasks. In this study the effects of concept dominance on learning were investigated for subjects who differed in drive level as measured by the MAS. Two of the concepts to be learned were highly dominant, two were of moderate dominance, and two were of low dominance. On the difficult, low-dominance tasks, the high-anxious subjects performed significantly more poorly than the low-anxious subjects. For the easier tasks (moderate or high levels of concept dominance), high- and low-anxious subjects did not differ in their performance. Thus the results supported Drive Theory predictions for the difficult tasks but not for the easy tasks.

Lipman and Griffith (1960) suggested that Romanow's failure to find facilitative effects of anxiety on the high-dominance items might have resulted from selecting concepts that were moderately difficult rather than easy. If the concepts were moderately difficult, then anxiety would not be expected to facilitate learning. Therefore Lipman and Griffith used tasks with even higher concept dominance for their subjects, in order to provide a more sensitive test of the effects of anxiety on the learning of easy concepts. They found that high-anxious subjects performed more poorly than low-anxious subjects irrespective of the degree of concept dominance, but the relative advantage of the low-anxious subjects increased as the task became more difficult.

The results of Romanow and of Lipman and Griffith are in general agreement. Both studies confirmed Drive Theory predictions with regard to the debilitating effects of anxiety on performance on difficult tasks, and both failed to reveal any facilitative effects on an easier task. While these investigators employed tasks that were presumed to be easy for their subjects, it was nevertheless possible that correct responses were not actually dominant on these tasks. An adequate test of Drive Theory requires the selection of tasks that vary substantially in level of difficulty for the subject population.

Katahn and Branham (1968) investigated the effects of anxiety on the acquisition and generalization of information. They found that high anxiety interfered with generalization but had no effects on performance during acquisition. Assuming that generalization is a higher order, more difficult task than original learning, these findings were consistent with Drive Theory predictions for the "difficult" task but not for the "easy" task.

Wolfgang, Pishkin, and Lundy (1962) investigated the effects of anxiety, task complexity, and misinformation feedback on a concept identification task. On the basis of Drive Theory the authors predicted that high-anxious subjects would show greater impairment in performance than low-anxious subjects with increasing complexity and misinformation feedback. The results failed to support these predictions. There were no significant differences in performance due to anxiety, nor were there any differences in the performance of high- and low-anxious subjects as a function of increasing task complexity or greater misinformation feedback.

The Wolfgang et al. (1962) study contains several methodological weaknesses that are frequently encountered in research on anxiety and complex learning. First, drive level was assessed using a measure of anxiety proneness (trait anxiety) rather than a measure of state anxiety. Therefore, in the absence of stressful instructions, it was possible that the two groups did not differ in state anxiety, in which case no difference in performance would be expected. Second, since level of task difficulty was not carefully defined, one cannot be sure that correct responses were more dominant for the "easiest" problems nor that incorrect responses were dominant for the difficult problems. Indeed the data suggested that the so-called difficult items were quite easy for some of the subjects in this study. If correct responses on the difficult task were actually dominant for some subjects and incorrect responses were dominant for other subjects, group differences on performance would not necessarily be expected for subjects who differed in level of state anxiety because facilitating and debilitating effects would cancel out. The result would be greater variability but no group differences in performance.

Tecce (1965) reported findings that were consistent with the Yerkes-Dodson Law. According to this law, there is an optimal level of drive for any given task, and levels of drive above or below the optimal level result in less efficient performance. In Tecce's study high-, medium-, and low-anxious groups attempted to solve Duncker's candle problem: half of each group was assigned to the "boxes empty" condition, and half were assigned to the "boxes full" condition. All three anxiety groups performed equally well in the boxes empty condition, in which correct responses to the problem were dominant. In the boxes full condition, the high- and low-anxious groups showed significant impairment in performance as compared to the medium-anxiety group. Thus persons with very low or very high anxiety performed less well than subjects with a moderate (more optimal) level of anxiety. These results suggest that Drive Theory should be modified to take into account research findings consistent with the Yerkes-Dodson Law.

Anxiety and Performance at Different Stages of Learning

In complex learning tasks the early stages of learning are more difficult than the later stages because the strength of correct responses is low and error tendencies are relatively strong. As learning occurs, the strength of correct responses increases and error tendencies are extinguished. Therefore Drive Theory predicts that high anxiety (high drive) will impair performance in the early stages of learning a complex task and facilitate performance later in learning.

Wesley (1953) investigated the relationship between anxiety and performance on a task that required subjects to form concepts and then shift to new concepts. As the task progressed, high-anxious subjects required fewer trials to shift set and made fewer perseverative responses than low-anxious subjects. Since differences between the high- and low-anxiety groups increased with successive shifts, these results suggested that the task became "easier" as the subjects progressed through various stages of learning and that high anxiety became increasingly facilitative, as would be predicted by Drive Theory.

O'Neil, Spielberger, and Hansen (1969) investigated the learning of difficult and easy mathematical concepts at different stages of learning. In this study, a computer with teletype terminals was used to administer the learning materials and the state anxiety measures while the subjects actually performed on the learning task. On the difficult learning task, students with high A-State made more errors than low A-State students during the early stages of learning; later in learning, the high A-State students improved and made fewer errors than low A-State students. These findings were replicated by O'Neil, Hansen, and Spielberger (Note 1) in a follow-up study that used essentially the same procedures except that the learning materials were presented via a cathode ray tube (CRT) instead of a teletype. In the early stages of learning, high-A-State subjects made more errors than low-A-State subjects. The high-A-State subjects also made more errors early in learning than they did in the later stages of learning, whereas there was little change in the relatively low error rate of the low-A-State subjects as they progressed through the task.

Anxiety and Conceptual Aids to Learning

Educators and psychologists have become increasingly concerned with creating environments that reduce the adverse effects of anxiety on learning. In contrast to psychologists, who typically use counseling and behavior therapy to reduce anxiety, educators and instructional designers have attempted to modify the demands of the learning task. Providing students with memory support and conceptual aids for organizing information have proved effective in reducing the debilitating effects of anxiety and improving learning. Since most conceptual aids are designed to eliminate or reduce error tendencies that compete with correct responses, high anxiety would be expected to facilitate performance when such aids are provided.

Sieber, Kameya, and Paulson (1970) used a Chinese-checkerlike marble puzzle in examining the effects of test anxiety and memory support on problem solving. In one version of this task, memory support was provided by displaying previous attempts to solve the puzzle that had resulted in an impasse. In a second version all previous solutions were removed from view. Without memory support, high-anxious students made more memory errors than low-anxious students. With memory support there were fewer errors, and the difference between high- and low-anxious subjects was reduced. Similar findings were reported in a second study (Sieber et al., 1970), which required subjects to specify the rule by which concept cards were classified. After training, students were presented with one of two versions of the task: a cumulative presentation in which exemplars remained exposed after presentation (memory support condition) or successive presentations in which each exemplar was removed before the next was presented (no memory support). Differences due to anxiety were greater in the no memory support condition in which the high-anxiety subjects made nearly twice as many errors as subjects with low anxiety.

Leherissey, O'Neil, and Hansen (Note 2) noticed an interesting parallel between the findings of Sieber et al. (1970) and the results reported by O'Neil et al. (1969, Note 1) in two earlier studies of anxiety and computer-assisted learning. The high-A-State students in both of the O'Neil et al. studies made more errors on a difficult learning task than the low-A-State students, but the error rate for high-A-State students in the second study was approximately twice as great as in the first. The learning materials were presented in the first study by a typewriter printout, which provided each student with a permanent record of all his or her previous responses. In the second study the same learning materials were presented via a cathode ray tube, which was erased immediately after each response. Leherissey et al. reasoned that the greater memory load associated with the CRT presentation of the learning materials in the second study could have accounted for the higher mean error rate for the high-A-State students.

Leherissey et al. (Note 2) used the same difficult learning task employed in the O'Neil et al. studies to investigate the effects of anxiety and memory load on computer-assisted learning. In a no memory support condition the learning materials were presented on the CRT in the same manner as in O'Neil et al.'s second study. In the memory support condition, earlier incorrect responses were presented before the student attempted to answer questions that were previously missed. Memory support had different effects on high- and low-A-State students. High-A-State students with no memory support made almost twice as many errors per correct response as did those with memory support. In contrast, the performance of low-A-State students in the Leherissey et al. study was about the same with and without memory support. Even with memory support, however, high-A-State students made significantly more errors than low-A-State students, and, surprisingly, state anxiety was highest in the memory support condition. Thus while memory support improved the performance of high-A-State students, it also induced higher levels of state anxiety. Quite possibly the latter finding resulted from reminding the students of their previous mistakes. Thus less aversive memory aids might produce more beneficial effects on performance without negative side effects.

In summary, memory support and conceptual aids generally facilitate the learning process. This is especially true for highly anxious students as reflected in better performance on complex learning tasks. Sieber et al. (1970) interpret these findings as providing evidence that memory support: (1) permits more efficient information processing; (2) reassures the individual and thereby reduces his or her level of anxiety; and/or (3) reduces the interfering cognitive components of anxiety (e.g., intrusive unpleasant thoughts) without reducing the drive or arousal component. Leherissey et al. (Note 2) found that state anxiety was higher in their memory support condition. Thus while memory support improves the performance of high-A-State students, it may also induce higher levels of state anxiety. While these findings appear to rule out Sieber et al.'s second alternative, the other two explanations appear equally viable and merit further investigation.

Anxiety, Intelligence, and Complex Learning

Prior to reviewing research on anxiety, intelligence, and complex learning, the relationship between anxiety and intelligence will be examined. In most studies no relationship was found between measures of trait anxiety and intellectual ability (e.g., Lipman & Griffith, 1960; Merrill, Kalish, Towle, & Steve, 1972; Merrill & Towle, 1971) or academic achievement (e.g., Wiggins, 1957). Small to moderate negative correlations of test anxiety with intelligence have been reported in a number of studies (e.g., Flynn & Morgan, 1966; Klein, Fredericksen, & Evans, 1969), while no relationship was found in others (Doyal & Forsyth, 1972; Greenberger, O'Conner, & Sorenson, 1971). Such findings are typical in studies of college students in which there was a restricted range of ability. However, when a sample includes a wide range of intelligence and a sizable proportion of low-ability students, small but usually significant negative correlations are reported (e.g., Grice, 1955; Kerrick, 1955).

The effect of range of ability on correlations between measures of anxiety and intelligence was demonstrated by Spielberger (1958). He obtained MAS and ACE scores in six consecutive semesters for college students enrolled in introductory psychology courses. As mean ACE scores increased over time (reflecting higher university admissions standards), the size of the negative correlation between MAS and ACE scores decreased from −.34 to .04. Feldhusen and Klausmeier (1962) also found that correlations between the MAS and intelligence, as measured by the Wechsler Intelligence Scale for Children (WISC), varied as a function of ability. Correlations of −.28, −.35 and −.07, respectively, were reported for school children with low (56–81), average (90–110), and high (120–146) WISC scores.

Several investigators have examined the effects of anxiety and intelligence on learning. Denny (1966) divided a sample of college students into high- and low-anxious and high- and low-intelligence groups according to their scores on the MAS and the College Entrance Examination Board. These students were given stressful (ego-involving) instructions prior to a concept formation task designed to be relatively easy for bright college students and difficult for low-ability students.

Consistent with Spielberger's (1966b) extension of Drive Theory, Denny predicted and found a transverse interaction between intelligence and anxiety. The performance of high-anxious students with high intelligence was superior to that of low-anxious, highly intelligent students. Conversely, the performance of the high-anxious students with low intelligence was inferior to that of low-anxious students.

Meyers and Dunham (1972) also found that performance on a concept-learning task of subjects with high general reasoning ability was facilitated by high anxiety, and that high anxiety resulted in performance decrements for low-ability students. However, no relationship was found between anxiety and performance on this same concept-learning task for subjects who were high or low in other cognitive abilities.

Rappaport (1971) investigated the effects of trait anxiety and mathematical ability on a complex numbers task. While no relationship was found between A-Trait and number of errors, college students with high A-State and low math ability made more errors than did those low in A-State and math ability. For students high in math ability, no performance differences were found as a function of anxiety.

Stevenson and Odom (1965) compared the effects of anxiety on the performance of fourth- and sixth-grade children on a variety of problem-solving tasks. In general it would be expected that these tasks would be easier for sixth- than for fourth-grade children. Stevenson and Odom's results were clearly consistent with predictions from Drive Theory for a moderately difficult concept formation task: low-anxious fourth graders performed better on this task than high-anxious fourth graders, while high-anxious sixth graders out-performed their low-anxious counterparts. Low anxiety was associated with better performance on paired-associates and anagrams tasks for sixth graders; for fourth graders low anxiety was associated with better performance on the paired-associates task but not on the anagrams task, for which performance was uniformly low.

Mazzei and Goulet (1969) and Fischer and Awrey (1973) attempted to replicate Denny's findings, but were unsuccessful. Using the Test Anxiety Questionnaire (TAQ) to measure anxiety, Mazzei and Goulet (1969) found that high-anxious/low-IQ subjects did better than low-anxious/low-IQ subjects, which was contrary to expectation. Fischer and Awrey (1973) used both the MAS and the TAQ to measure anxiety and found performance differences only for their low-intelligence groups, for whom high anxiety facilitated performance relative to low anxiety. This finding was consistant with Mazzei and Goulet (1969) but not with Denny nor with Drive Theory.

In summary, the effects of anxiety and ability on complex learning are quite complicated and not fully explained by Drive Theory conceptions. The possible influence of uncontrolled variables such as experimenter effects was raised by several investigators (Gonzalez-Reigosa, 1972; Meyers & Dunham, 1972). Such effects would be especially important in studies in which the investigator was in direct one-to-one contact with the subjects, as was the case in the Mazzei-Goulet and Fischer-Awrey studies.

Anxiety and Academic Achievement

A substantial amount of the research on anxiety and learning has appropriately taken place in school settings. These studies focus on: (1) the effects of student anxiety on course grades and grade-point averages (GPAs); and (2) the correlation between anxiety and standardized tests of scholastic achievement. As might be anticipated by now, the findings are mixed, but some consistencies emerge as the entire literature is considered.

Low negative correlations between anxiety and achievement are frequently found for elementary- and secondary-school students (e.g., Bauermeister & Berlingeri, 1974; Cowen, Zax, Klein, Izzo, & Trost, 1965) and occasionally for college students (e.g., Hountras, Grady, & Vraa, 1970; Spielberger & Katzenmeyer, 1959). However, most investigators have reported no differences in the grades of high- and low-anxious college students (e.g., Khan, 1969; Matarazzo, Ulett, Guze, & Saslow, 1954; Robinson, 1966; S. B. Sarason & Mandler, 1952), and a few investigators have been reported facilitating effects of anxiety (e.g., Gulo, 1973; S. B. Sarason & Mandler, 1952). Sharma (1970) reported that Indian adolescents with moderate anxiety outperformed their high- and low-anxious peers on an annual exam, as would be predicted by the Yerkes-Dodson Law but not by Drive Theory.

Low-anxious students tend to perform better on standardized achievement tests than high-anxious students. This is consistently found in third grade through high school in studies that have employed different measures of trait anxiety. Negative relationships have been reported between various measures of anxiety and a variety of achievement tests such as: the Stanford Achievement Test (Mulroy, 1968; Sarason, Davidson, Lighthall, Waite, & Ruebush, 1960), the Iowa Test of Basic Skills (Stevenson & Odom, 1965), the ETS Achievement Test (Barton, Bartsch, & Cattell, 1974), and the Metropolitan Achievement Test (Lunneborg, 1964). Only rarely do high-anxious students achieve at a higher level than low-anxious students (e.g., Barton et al., 1974; Khan, 1969).

Stress, Anxiety, and Complex Learning

In this section we will consider investigations of the effects of stress and trait anxiety on state anxiety and complex learning. According to Trait-State Anxiety Theory (Spielberger, 1966a, 1972a), individuals high in A-Trait will experience greater elevations in A-State than low-A-Trait persons when the experimental conditions involve some form of psychological stress such as direct or implied threats to self-esteem, ego-involving instructions, or failure feedback. Once an anxiety state is aroused, predictions of the effects of differences in A-State on performance for easy and difficult tasks can be derived from Drive Theory (K. W. Spence, 1958; Taylor, 1956).

I. G. Sarason (1961) investigated the effects of stress and individual differences in trait anxiety on the solution of a difficult anagrams task. Half the subjects received ego-threat instructions, which related success on the anagrams task to intelligence; the other half received nonthreatening instructions. Trait anxiety was measured by the Taylor (1953) MAS and Sarason's (1957) Test Anxiety Scale (TAS). High test anxiety facilitated performance under neutral conditions but was associated with performance decrements under stress conditions. Similar results were found for the MAS, but the stress-by-anxiety interaction effect was not statistically significant. It is interesting to note that the TAS, a situation-specific A-Trait measure, was a better predictor of the effects of stress on performance in a test like learning situation than the MAS, a measure of general trait anxiety.

Sutter and Reid (1969) also obtained a stress-by-test-anxiety interaction for students assigned either to work with partners on a difficult Computer Aided Instruction (CAI) problem-solving task or to work alone on this same task. High-test-anxious students performed better working alone; low-test-anxious students performed better when they worked with a partner. These results suggested that the presence of a partner was more stressful than working alone. Apparently the partner evoked task-irrelevant anxiety responses in the high-anxious subjects whereas low-anxious subjects seemed to be motivated by the partner to work harder and to produce more task-relevant responses.

Tomasini (1973) reported similar findings for high- and low-anxiety college students who were given 25 relatively easy anagrams to solve in 15 minutes. In the no-stress condition each subject worked alone. In the stress condition the subject and another student, a confederate of the experimenter, were assigned to work independently on the task. After 7 minutes the confederate left the room, giving the impression that he had completed all 25 anagrams. When performing alone (no stress) the high-A-Trait subjects made fewer errors than the low-anxious subjects. However, when the confederate was present (stress) the high-A-Trait subjects made more errors than low-anxious subjects. Interestingly, stress had greater influence on the performance of the low-A-Trait subjects than on that of high-A-Trait subjects. While high-anxious subjects performed comparably in both conditions, low-anxious subjects performed better when the confederate was present than when they worked alone.

The stress manipulations in the studies described above involved the threat of evaluation or unfavorable comparison with others. These ego-threat stress-induction procedures, which can be broadly classified as *psychological stress*, resulted in significant stress-by-trait-anxiety interaction effects in all three studies that were reviewed (I. G. Sarason, 1961; Sutter & Reid, 1969; Tomasini, 1973). In general, high-A-Trait subjects performed better than low-A-Trait subjects under low stress conditions, whereas low-A-Trait subjects did better than high-A-Trait subjects under high stress conditions. These results provide evidence that psychological stress results in greater increases in state anxiety for high-A-Trait persons than for those who are low in trait anxiety.

Snyder and Katahn (1970) evaluated the effects of positive and negative feedback (stress) on a concept-learning task for low-, middle-, and high-test-anxious students. Test anxiety was assessed using the STAI A-State scale, with instructions for the students to respond according to how they usually feel when they are about to take a classroom examination. The negative feedback consisted of reporting, after each trial, the "average" score attained by other students, which was in fact one standard deviation *above* the actual mean. A positive feedback group was given an "average" score that was one standard deviation *below* the actual mean. As in most of the studies previously described, high anxiety was associated with poorer task performance in the negative-feedback (stress) condition, but the stress-by-trait-anxiety interaction was not statistically significant.[1]

Ray, Katahn, and Snyder (1971) investigated the effects of test anxiety on acquisition, retention, and generalization, using the same concept-learning task as Snyder and Katahn (1970). One group of subjects was tested immediately after each of five learning trials, while a second group was tested only once, at the

---

[1] In a follow-up study with similar methodology, Snyder and Katahn (1973) found no relationship between test anxiety and performance.

end of the five trials. All subjects were tested for retention and generalization after 48 hours. The performance of subjects tested during acquisition after each trial was superior to that of subjects tested after the completion of five trials. With repeated testing the performance of low-anxious subjects was superior to that of high-anxious subjects. When differences in acquisition were statistically controlled, the retention and generalization of low-anxious subjects was superior to that of high-anxious subjects.

Meyers and Martin (1974) investigated the impact of stress and trait anxiety on state anxiety and performance on a concept-learning task. For the high-stress group, A-State increased following ego-involving instructions and remained at a high level throughout the task. In contrast, low-stress subjects who received nonego-involving instructions showed esentially no change in A-State as they worked on the task. While performance was not directly related to either ego-involving instructions or trait anxiety during learning, the subjects who reported higher state anxiety made significantly more errors than low-A-State subjects. On a transfer task the subjects in the stress group who were high in A-State performed more poorly; there was no relationship between A-State and performance in the low stress condition.

Though not entirely consistent, the findings of Snyder and Katahn, Ray et al., and Meyers and Martin provide evidence that high anxiety is detrimental to acquisition, retention, and generalization (transfer) when relatively difficult concept-learning tasks are given in stressful testlike, evaluative situations. These findings are generally consistent with Drive Theory.

Stress, Anxiety, and Task Difficulty in Complex Learning

Complex-learning studies involving stress, state and trait anxiety, and task difficulty are examined in this section. Dunn (1968) investigated the effects of stress, task complexity, and individual differences in trait anxiety on concept learning. Subjects in the stress condition were shocked during the presentation of half the instances of the verbal concepts they were required to learn, and a chime sounded on a specified proportion of correct responses. In the nonstress condition the shocks were omitted. The performance of the low-anxious subjects in the nonstress condition was comparable at all levels of task complexity, whereas high-anxious subjects learned fewer difficult than easy concepts. In the stress condition both high- and low-anxious subjects learned fewer difficult than easy concepts.

Trait-State Anxiety Theory posits that pain stressors, such as electric shock, will *not* differentially affect high- and low-A-Trait individuals (Spielberger, 1972a, 1972b). However, if shock is interpreted as an indication of failure, then persons high in trait anxiety would be expected to show greater elevations in state anxiety than low-A-Trait persons. The findings in Dunn's study suggested that his subjects interpreted the shock as an indication of failure. For high- and low-anxious subjects, stress had a negative effect on learning difficult concepts but facilitated the learning of easy concepts. For concepts of intermediate difficulty, stress facilitated learning for the low-anxious subjects but contributed to the performance decrements of high-anxious subjects. The finding that stress produced performance decrements in high-A-Trait subjects at lower levels of task difficulty than for low-A-Trait subjects was consistent with Drive Theory.

Grant and Patel (1957) employed the Wisconsin Card-Sorting Test, a concept-learning task, to investigate stress effects on the learning of subjects who were required to make five conceptual shifts while sorting the stimulus cards. High- and low-anxious subjects were assigned to treatment conditions that received either no shock, 2 shocks, or 12 shocks. In the no-shock condition, the subjects were told they would be shocked but actually received no shock. The subjects in the 2-shock condition received 2 painful shocks on correct responses during the first stage of the task. Subjects in the 12-shock condition received 2 shocks while learning the concepts during each of the six stages of the task.

Number of perseverative errors was the most sensitive performance measure in the Grant and Patel study. High-anxiety subjects who received either no shock or 12 shocks made more perseverative errors in the later stages of learning than the corresponding low-anxiety groups. In contrast, high-anxiety subjects in the 2-shock condition were equal to or superior to low-anxiety subjects. These results suggested that the no-shock and 12-shock conditions were more stressful for the high-anxiety subjects than the 2-shock condition. Subjects in the 12-shock condition were repeatedly stressed by the delivery of frequent shocks, whereas the anticipation of shock was apparently sufficient to sustain the high level of state anxiety that contributed to the performance decrements of the no-shock group.[2]

Romanow (1958) investigated the effects of stress on concept formation tasks that varied in difficulty. The subjects were divided into low-, medium-, and high-stress groups, each given different ego-involving instructions. In the low-stress group, subjects were told that the task was an indicator of clerical aptitude; the instructions for the medium-stress group described the task as a good indicator of curiosity; the high-stress instructions informed the subjects that the task was highly correlated with intelligence. For easy and moderately difficult concepts, differences in the performance of the three stress groups were small. For the difficult concepts, the low-stress group gave fewer correct responses and made significantly more errors than either the moderate- or high-stress groups. Clearly, these outcomes did not support Drive Theory. A possible explanation is that the low-involvement condition resulted in carelessness in some subjects because of lack of motivation to perform. A minimal amount of stress may be required in order to stimulate students to perform optimally.

The importance of assessing the amount of state anxiety experienced while subjects worked on a rule-learning task was demonstrated by Etaugh and Graffam (1973). High- and low-A-Trait college students were exposed to failure feedback (e.g., "You're not doing very well, you can do better than that") or given no feedback while they worked on a paired-associates rule-learning task. In the no-feedback condition, trait anxiety did not affect learning for the easy pairs, but high-anxious students made more errors and required more trials to learn the difficult pairs than low-anxious students. In the stress condition all subjects tended to make fewer correct responses than in the no-stress condition, but the negative effects of stress on performance that were anticipated for the high-A-Trait subjects were not observed.

In postexperimental interviews, Etaugh and Graffam found that almost all of

---

[2] The interpretation is based on the descriptive information provided by Grant and Patel. It should be noted, however, that Grant and Patel appear to have mislabeled the performance curves that are reported in their paper.

their high-anxious subjects were disturbed by the failure feedback, but 60% of the low-anxious subjects also reported that failure feedback was disturbing. In order to determine whether the disturbance reported by low-A-Trait subjects was related to their performance, the following groups of low-anxious subjects were compared: stress-disturbed, stress-not disturbed, and no-stress. The three groups performed equally well on the easier task, but subjects who reported being disturbed by failure feedback (ie., low-A-Trait/high-A-State) made significantly more errors on the difficult task. Etaugh and Graffam's results suggested that high state anxiety adversely influenced the performance of those low-A-Trait students who were disturbed by failure feedback.

O'Neil (1972) investigated the effects of ego-threat instructions on the performance of high- and low-A-Trait college women who were presented a concept-learning task via computer-assisted instruction (CAI). Subjects in O'Neil's stress condition were told that performance on the CAI task was related to the ability to do well in college courses. They also received periodic feedback indicating that their work was not good and that other students were more accurate and faster. Subjects in the nonstress condition had brief rest periods that corresponded in time with the negative feedback.

Consistent with predictions from Trait-State Anxiety Theory, O'Neil (1972) found that the stress instructions induced greater initial increments in A-State in the high-A-Trait (HA) students than in low-A-Trait (LA) students. The HA students in the stress condition also showed a greater decline in A-State than LA students as learning progressed. In the nonstress condition, HA and LA students showed parallel increases in A-State from pretask levels and parallel changes in A-State while they worked on the learning task. O'Neil also found that students reported higher levels of A-State while working on the more difficult tasks than on the easier tasks. The students with higher A-State scores also made more errors at all stages of learning than low-A-State students, a finding that was generally in accord with Drive Theory predictions for a difficult learning task.

While the relation between stress, state and trait anxiety, task difficulty, and performance on complex learning tasks is quite complicated, some tentative conclusions can be drawn from the research literature. First, psychological stress generally results in performance decrements, but some stress may be required to motivate people to perform at an optimal level. Second, psychological stress evokes higher levels of state anxiety in persons who are high in trait anxiety than in low-A-Trait persons. Third, high levels of state anxiety have drive properties that typically result in performance decrements on difficult learning tasks. Finally, psychological stress tends to facilitate the performance of persons who are high in A-State on easy learning tasks, but this is often difficult to demonstrate because of ceiling effects.

The research literature provides strong evidence that the impact of stress and task difficulty on complex learning is mediated by state anxiety. But the level of A-State in most studies must be inferred from stress manipulations and trait anxiety scores, and this practice often leads to incorrect conclusions. A better alternative is to actually measure A-State during learning. It has been demonstrated that brief, reliable, self-report A-State measures can be administered to subjects as they work on a learning task without interfering with their performance (Spielberger, O'Neil, & Hansen, 1972).

IMPLICATIONS OF THE RESEARCH FOR DRIVE THEORY AND TRAIT–STATE ANXIETY THEORY

The role of psychological stress in the arousal of state anxiety (drive) is a critical factor in research on anxiety and complex learning. When experimental conditions involve mild to moderate psychological stress, persons high in trait anxiety tend to perceive such situations as more threatening and to experience greater elevations in state anxiety than low-A-Trait individuals. When high-A-Trait individuals are told, for example, that intelligence is being assessed, they generally perform more poorly than low-A-Trait persons given these same instructions (I. G. Sarason, 1961; Sutter & Reid, 1969; Tomasini, 1973). Such findings are consistent with Drive Theory and Trait-State Anxiety Theory.

A major conceptual weakness in most studies of anxiety and complex learning is the failure to distinguish between trait and state anxiety. Measures of triat anxiety have been widely used to select subjects who are presumed to differ in drive level. While trait anxiety scores provide an index of individual differences in the potential for manifesting elevations in state anxiety, there is no assurance that a particular stress situation will be perceived as personally threatening. However, as previously noted, the intensity and duration of A-State reactions can be assessed by monitoring physiological indicators of autonomic arousal such as blood pressure, or by obtaining self-report measures of state anxiety (Spielberger et al., 1972; O'Neil et al., 1969, Note 1).

In studies in which state anxiety was actually measured, it has been shown that difficult learning materials induce higher levels of A-State than easy materials (O'Neil, 1972), the high-A-Trait subjects respond with greater initial increments in A-State than low-A-Trait subjects in evaluative stress situations (O'Neil, 1972), and that persons high in A-State make more errors than low-A-State persons on most learning tasks (Meyers & Martin, 1974; O'Neil, 1972). Such findings are generally consistent with Trait-State Anxiety Theory and Drive Theory and attest to the importance of distinguishing between the concepts of trait and state anxiety.

Task difficulty is one of the principal variables that has been investigated in research on anxiety and complex learning. In the context of Drive Theory, task difficulty refers to the relative strength of the correct responses and competing error tendencies that are associated with a learning task. The difficulty of a task may vary as a function of the inherent complexity of a task, the stage of learning, the availability of memory support or conceptual aids to learning, and the intelligence of the subject.

Drive Theory predictions were supported with regard to the effects of anxiety on difficult and easy tasks by Van Buskirk (1961) and in two studies reported by Maltzman, Fox, and Morrisett (1953). In these studies, high-anxious subjects made fewer errors on an easy task for which correct response tendencies were strong. In contrast, on difficult tasks where incorrect responses were dominant, the high-anxious subjects made more errors and generally performed more poorly.

Performance decrements for high-anxious subjects have also been reported on difficult tasks in a number of studies in which no facilitative effects were found for easier tasks (Katahn & Branham, 1968; Lipman & Griffith, 1960; Romanow, 1958). There are two possible explanations for these results. First, most complex learning tasks are inherently difficult. Therefore unless a subject has had prior experience on a learning task or training on a related task, correct responses will be low in his or her response hierarchy, and competing error tendencies will be activated by high anxiety. Second, the influence of stress on performance is greater on difficult tasks than on easy learning tasks. For difficult tasks, high trait anxiety is consistently negatively related to performance under stress conditions (Dunn, 1968; Etaugh & Graffam, 1973; O'Neil, 1972), while the influence of stress and trait anxiety on state anxiety and performance on easy tasks appears to be minimal (Etaugh & Graffam, 1973; O'Neil, 1972).

The interactive effects of trait anxiety and stress on complex learning were clearly demonstrated in the study by Dunn (1968) in which three levels of task difficulty were investigated. On an easy task, both high- and low-anxious subjects tended to perform better under stress. On a moderately difficult task, low-anxious subjects performed better under stress whereas high-anxious individuals did better in a nonstress condition. On a difficult task, low-anxious subjects did better in a nonstress condition than in a stress condition, while the performance of high-anxious subjects was uniformly low under both conditions. Similar findings were reported by Ray, Katahn, and Snyder (1971) and Meyers and Martin (1974) for easy and difficult acquisition, retention, and generalization tasks. These results suggest that stress has an adverse influence on high-anxious subjects at lower levels of task difficulty than is the case for low-anxious subjects.

Research on anxiety and performance at different stages of learning also strongly supports Drive Theory. In studies by Wesley (1953) and O'Neil et al. (1969), high-anxious subjects made more errors than low-anxious subjects during the early stages of learning, and high-anxious subjects showed greater improvement and made fewer errors than low-anxious subjects later in learning. On a more difficult task, O'Neil et al. (Note 1) found that high-A-State subjects made more errors than low-A-State subjects early in learning, whereas there was no difference between these groups later in learning. Thus in all three studies high anxiety was consistently associated with performance decrements in the early stages of a complex learning task, when correct responses were relatively weak and high drive would be expected to activate error tendencies.

In recent research that has focused on facilitating learning by reducing the adverse effects of anxiety, Sieber et al. (1970) and Leherissey et al. (1970) have reported results that were consistent with Drive Theory. Students who were provided with memory support or conceptual aids for organizing information did better than students without this assistance. In both studies, high-anxiety students with no memory support made almost twice as many errors per correct response as did those with memory support. In contrast, the performance of low-anxiety students was about the same with and without memory support. Interestingly, Leherissey et al. found that subjects given memory support reported *higher* levels of anxiety than those in the no-memory support condition, indicating that the improved performance did not result from reduced anxiety as was expected. It has been suggested by Sieber et al. (1970) that memory support permits more efficient information processing and/or reduces the interfering cognitive components of anxiety. However, Leherissey et al.'s findings suggest that memory support may actually increase the affective or emotional component of anxiety by calling attention to the complexity of the learning task. Ideally, memory support techniques should be developed that facilitate learning without increasing state anxiety.

The results in four studies have supported predictions based on Spielberger's extension of Drive Theory, which specifies that task difficulty may vary as a function of individual differences in intelligence. Stevenson and Odom (1965) found that low-anxious fourth graders performed better than high-anxious fourth graders on a concept formation task that was relatively difficult for them. On the other hand, high-anxious sixth graders outperformed their low-anxious counterparts on this same task. Denny (1966) found that high-anxious/high-intelligence subjects performed better on a concept attainment task than low-anxious/high-intelligence subjects, whereas low-intelligence subjects with high anxiety did more poorly than low-intelligence/low-anxious subjects. Rappaport (Note 3) and Meyers and Dunham (1972) have also reported transverse interactions that were consistent with Spielberger's extension of Drive Theory. But in two studies that attempted to replicate Denny's results (Fischer & Awrey, 1973; Mazzei & Goulet, 1969), the findings were contradictory and unexplainable in terms of Drive Theory. It should be noted, however, that these studies have been criticized because of the small sample size and the possibility that experimenter effects may have influenced the results (Gonzalez-Reigosa, 1972; Meyers & Dunham, 1972).

Occasionally, when three levels of anxiety are represented in an experimental study, the performance of subjects with a moderate level of anxiety was found to be superior to that of high- and low-anxious subjects (e.g., Tecce, 1965). While these results are in accord with the Yerkes-Dodson Law, they can also be interpreted as supporting Drive Theory, which would predict that persons with moderate anxiety would be superior to low-anxious persons on tasks of intermediate difficulty. However, in order to explain the inferior performance of high-anxious subjects on these same tasks, it must be assumed that high states of anxiety generate task-irrelevant, internal physiological responses and worry reactions that interfere with performance.

When supplemented by Trait-State Anxiety Theory and extended to incorporate individual differences in intelligence, Drive Theory provides a useful framework for clarifying the research findings on stress, anxiety, and task difficulty. While nonsignificant results have been reported in a number of studies and there are many contradictory findings, it seems apparent that a great deal of progress has been made over the past decade in explaining the effects of stress and anxiety on complex learning.

REFERENCES

Barton, K., Bartsch, T., & Cattell, R. B. Longitudinal study of achievement related to anxiety and extraversion. *Psychological Reports*, 1974, *35*, 551–556.

Bauermeister, J. J., & Berlingeri, N. C. Rendimiento academico en funcion del nivel de ansiedad-rasgo, sexo y habilidad general. *Revista Interamericana de Psicologia*, 1974, *8*, 1–2.

Cattell, R. B., & Scheier, I. H. *Handbook for the IPAT Anxiety Scale Questionnaire*. Champaign, IL: IPAT, 1963.

Cowen, E. L., Zax, M., Klein, R., Izzo, L. D., & Trost, M. A. The relation of anxiety in school children to school record, achievement, and behavioral measures. *Child Development*, 1965, *36*, 685–695.

Denny, J. P. Effects of anxiety and intelligence on concept formation. *Journal of Experimental Psychology*, 1966, *72*, 596–602.

Doyal, G. T., & Forsyth, R. A. The effect of test anxiety, intelligence and sex on children's problem solving ability. *Journal of Experimental Education*, 1972, *41*, 23–26.

Dunn, R. F. Anxiety and verbal concept learning. *Journal of Experimental Psychology*, 1968, *76*, 286–290.

Etaugh, C. F., & Graffam, K. A. Role of anxiety level and stress in rule acquisition. *Journal of Personality and Social Psychology*, 1973, *27*, 180–183.

Feldhusen, J. F., & Klausmeier, H. J. Anxiety, intelligence, and achievement in children of low, average, and high intelligence. *Child Development*, 1962, *33*, 403–409.

Fischer, D. G., & Awrey, A. Manifest anxiety, test anxiety and intelligence in concept formation. *Journal of Social Psychology*, 1973, *89*, 153-154.

Flynn, J. T., & Morgan, J. H. A methodological study of the effectiveness of programmed instruction through analysis of learner characteristics. *Proceedings of the 74th Annual Convention of the American Psychological Association*, 1966, 259-260. (Summary)

Gagné, R. M., & Briggs, L. J. *Principles of instructional design*. New York: Holt, Rinehart & Winston, 1974.

Gaudry, E., & Spielberger, C. D. *Anxiety and educational achievement*. Sydney: Wiley, 1971.

Gonzalez-Reigosa, F. The anxiety arousing effect of taboo words in bilinguals. (Doctoral dissertation, Florida State University, 1972). *Dissertation Abstracts International*, 1973, *33*, 3303B. (University Microfilms No. 73-00210).

Grant, D. A., & Patel, A. S. Effect of electric shock stimulus upon the conceptual behavior of anxious and non-anxious subjects. *Journal of General Psychology*, 1957, *57*, 247-256.

Greenberger, E., O'Connor, J., & Sorensen, A. Personality, cognitive, and academic correlates of problem solving flexibility. *Developmental Psychology*, 1971, *4*, 416-424.

Grice, G. R. Discrimination reaction time as a function of anxiety and intelligence. *Journal of Abnormal and Social Psychology*, 1955, *50*, 71-74.

Gulo, E. V. An examination of the relationship between selected personality factors and academic achievement in an undergraduate instructional television course. *College Student Journal*, 1973, *7*, 89-93.

Hountras, P. T., Grady, W. E., & Vraa, C. W. Manifest anxiety and academic achievement of American and Canadian college freshmen. *The Journal of Psychology*, 1970, *76*, 3-8.

Katahn, M., & Branham, L. Effects of manifest anxiety on the acquisition and generalization of concepts from Hullian Theory. *American Journal of Psychology*, 1968, *81*, 575-580.

Kerrick, J. S. Some correlates of the Taylor Manifest Anxiety Scale. *Journal of Abnormal and Social Psychology*, 1955, *50*, 75-77.

Khan, S. B. Affective correlates of academic achievement. *Journal of Educational Psychology*, 1969, *60*, 216-221.

Klein, S. P., Frederiksen, N., & Evans, F. R. Anxiety and learning to formulate hypotheses. *Journal of Educational Psychology*, 1969, *60*, 465-475.

Leherissey, B. L., O'Neil, H. F., & Hansen, D. N. *Effects of memory support on state anxiety and performance in computer assisted learning*. Technical Memorandum No. 20. Tallahassee: CAI Center, Florida State University, 1970.

Lipman, R. S., & Griffith, B. C. Effects of anxiety level on concept formation: A test of drive theory. *American Journal of Mental Deficiency*, 1960, *65*, 342-348.

Lunneborg, P. W. Relations among social desirability, achievement, and anxiety measures in children. *Child Development*, 1964, *35*, 169-182.

Maltzman, I., Fox, J., & Morrisett, L., Jr. Some effects of manifest anxiety on mental set. *Journal of Experimental Psychology*, 1953, *46*, 50-54.

Matarazzo, J. D., Ulett, G. A., Guze, S. B., & Saslow, G. The relationship between anxiety level and several measures of intelligence. *Journal of Consulting Psychology*, 1954, *18*, 201-205.

Mazzei, J., & Goulet, L. R. Test anxiety and intelligence in concept formation. *Psychological Reports*, 1969, *24*, 842.

Merrill, P. F., Kalish, S. J., Towle, N. J., & Steve, M. H. The interactive effects of the availability of objectives and/or rules on computer-based learning. *Proceedings of the 80th Annual Convention of the American Psychological Association*, 1972, *7*, 497-498. (Summary)

Merrill, P. F., & Towle, N. J. Interaction of abilities and anxiety with availability of objectives and/or test items on computer-based task performance. *Proceedings of the 79th Annual Convention of the American Psychological Association*, 1971, *6*, 539-540. (Summary)

Meyers, J., & Dunham, J. L. Anxiety-aptitude interactions in concept learning. *Proceedings of the 80th Annual Convention of the American Psychological Association*, 1972, *7*, 485-486. (Summary)

Meyers, J., & Martin, R. Relationships of state and trait anxiety to concept-learning performance. *Journal of Educational Psychology*, 1974, *66*, 33-39.

Mulroy, I. The relationship between anxiety and scholastic success in junior school children. *Papers in Psychology*, 1968, *2*, 32-33.

O'Neil, H. F. Effects of stress on state anxiety and performance in computer-assisted learning. *Journal of Educational Psychology*, 1972, *63*, 473-481.

O'Neil, H. F., Hansen, D. N., & Spielberger, C. D. *Errors and latency of response as a function of anxiety and task difficulty.* Paper presented at the Annual Meeting of the American Educational Research Association, Los Angeles, February 1969.

O'Neil, H. F., Spielberger, C. D., & Hansen, D. N. Effects of state anxiety and task difficulty on computer-assisted learning. *Journal of Educational Psychology*, 1969, *60*, 343–350.

Rappaport, E. *The effects of trait anxiety and dogmatism on state anxiety during computer assisted learning.* Technical Memorandum No. 33. Tallahassee: CAI Center, Florida State University, 1971.

Ray, W. J., Katahn, M., & Snyder, C. R. Effects of test anxiety on acquisition, retention and generalization of a complex verbal task in classroom situations. *Journal of Personality and Social Psychology*, 1971, *20*, 147–154.

Robinson, B. W. A study of anxiety and academic achievement. *Journal of Consulting Psychology*, 1966, *30*, 165–167.

Romanow, C. V. Anxiety level and ego involvement as factors in concept formation. *Journal of Experimental Psychology*, 1958, *56*, 166–173.

Sarason, I. G. Test anxiety, general anxiety and intellectual performance. *Journal of Consulting Psychology*, 1957, *21*, 485–490.

Sarason, I. G. The effects of anxiety and threat on the solution of a difficult task. *Journal of Abnormal and Social Psychology*, 1961, *62*, 165–168.

Sarason, S. B., Davidson, R. S., Lighthall, F. F., Waite, R. R., & Ruebush, B. R. *Anxiety in elementary school children*, New York: Wiley, 1960.

Sarason, S. B., & Mandler, G. Some correlates of test anxiety. *Journal of Abnormal and Social Psychology*, 1952, *47*, 810–817.

Sharma, S. Manifest anxiety and school achievement of adolescents. *Journal of Consulting and Clinical Psychology*, 1970, *34*, 403–407.

Sieber, J. E., Kameya, L. I., & Paulson, F. L. Effect of memory support on the problem solving ability of test-anxious children. *Journal of Educational Psychology*, 1970, *61*, 159–168.

Snyder, C. R., & Katahn, M. The relationship of state anxiety, feedback, and ongoing self-reported affect to performance in complex verbal learning. *American Journal of Psychology*, 1970, *83*, 237–247.

Snyder, C. R., & Katahn, M. Comparison levels, test anxiety, ongoing affect and complex verbal learning. *American Journal of Psychology*, 1973, *86*, 555–565.

Spence, J. T., & Spence, K. W. The motivational components of manifest anxiety: Drive and drive stimuli. In C. D. Spielberger (Ed.), *Anxiety and behavior.* New York: Academic Press, 1966.

Spence, K. W. A theory of emotionally based drive (D) and its relation to performance in simple learning situations. *American Psychologist*, 1958, *13*, 131–141.

Spielberger, C. D. On the relationship between anxiety and intelligence. *Journal of Consulting Psychology*, 1958, *22*, 220–224.

Spielberger, C. D. Theory and research on anxiety. In C. D. Spielberger (Ed.), *Anxiety and behavior.* New York: Academic Press, 1966. (a)

Spielberger, C. D. The effects of anxiety on complex learning and academic achievement. In C. D. Spielberger (Ed.), *Anxiety and behavior.* New York: Academic Press, 1966. (b)

Spielberger, C. D. Trait-state anxiety and motor behavior. *Journal of Motor Behavior*, 1971, *3*, 265–279.

Spielberger, C. D. Anxiety as an emotional state. In C. D. Spielberger (Ed.), *Anxiety: Current trends in theory and research* (Vol. 1). New York: Academic Press, 1972. (a)

Spielberger, C. D. Conceptual and methodological issues in anxiety research. In C. D. Spielberger (Ed.), *Anxiety: Current trends in theory and research* (Vol. 2). New York: Academic Press, 1972. (b)

Spielberger, C. D., Gorsuch, R. L., & Lushene, R. E. *Manual for the State-Trait Anxiety Inventory.* Palo Alto, CA: Consulting Psychologists Press, 1970.

Spielberger, C. D., & Katzenmeyer, W. G. Manifest anxiety, intelligence, and college grades. *Journal of Consulting Psychology*, 1959, *23*, 278.

Spielberger, C. D., O'Neil, H. F., & Hansen, D. N. Anxiety, drive theory, and computer-assisted learning. In B. A. Maher (Ed.). *Progress in experimental personality research* (Vol. 6). New York: Academic Press, 1972.

Stevenson, H. W., & Odom, R. D. The relation of anxiety to children's performance on learning and problem-solving tasks. *Child Development*, 1965, *36*, 1003–1012.

Sutter, E. G., & Reid, J. B. Learner variables and interpersonal conditions in computer-assisted instruction. *Journal of Educational Psychology*, 1969, *60*, 153–157.

Taylor, J. A. The relationship of anxiety to the conditioned eyelid response. *Journal of Experimental Psychology*, 1951, *41*, 81-92.

Taylor, J. A. A personality scale of manifest anxiety. *Journal of Abnormal and Social Psychology*, 1953, *48*, 285-290.

Taylor, J. A. Drive theory and manifest anxiety. *Psychological Bulletin*, 1956, *53*, 303-320.

Tecce, J. J. Relationship of anxiety (drive) and response competition in problem solving. *Journal of Abnormal and Social Psychology*, 1965, *70*, 465-467.

Tomasini, J. Effect of peer-induced anxiety on a problem-solving task. *Psychological Reports*, 1973, *33*,·355-358.

Van Buskirk, C. Performance on complex reasoning tasks as a function of anxiety. *Journal of Abnormal and Social Psychology*, 1961, *62*, 201-209.

Wesley, E. Perseverative behavior in a concept formation task as a function of manifest anxiety and rigidity. *Journal of Abnormal and Social Psychology*, 1953, *48*, 129-134.

Wiggins, J. G. Multiple solution anagram solving as an index of anxiety. *Journal of Clinical Psychology*, 1957, *13*, 391-393.

Wolfgang, A., Pishkin, V., & Lundy, R. M. Anxiety and misinformation feedback in concept identification. *Perceptual and Motor Skills*, 1962, *14*, 135-143.

Zuckerman, M. The development of an affect adjective checklist for the measurement of anxiety. *Journal of Consulting Psychology*, 1960, *24*, 457-462.

REFERENCE NOTES

1. O'Neil, H. F., Hansen, D. N., & Spielberger, C. D. *Errors and latency of response as a function of anxiety and task difficulty.* Paper presented at the Annual Meeting of the American Educational Research Association, Los Angeles, February 1969.

2. Leherissey, B. L., O'Neil, H. F., & Hansen, D. N. *Effects of memory support on state anxiety and performance in computer-assisted learning.* Memorandum No. 20. Tallahassee, FL: CAI Center, Florida State University, 1970.

3. Rappaport, E. *The effects of trait anxiety and dogmatism on state anxiety during computer-assisted learning.* Technical Memorandum No. 33. Tallahassee, FL: CAI Center, Florida State University, 1971.

8

Repression-Sensitization
as a Central Construct
in Coping Research

Heinz W. Krohne and Josef Rogner
University of Osnabrück

Investigations and theorizing on the relationship between stress (situation), anxiety, and performance have changed by taking into consideration the influence of anxiety-coping mechanisms on behavior. Questions concerning the form of the direct relationship between anxiety and performance have been replaced by the following problems (among others): (1) What makes a situation a threat situation for a certain person? (2) In a certain situation, which mechanisms reduce the threat experience successfully, and which mechanisms are unsuccessful? (3) What role do attention and information use play in reducing threat? (4) What are the consequences of certain coping mechanisms on behavioral outcome (e.g., on a required performance)? This chapter will try to systematically analyze these problems.

ANXIETY AND PERFORMANCE: FROM A MECHANISTIC TO A COGNITIVE VIEWPOINT

In anxiety research the relationship between level of anxiety and quality of performance (e.g., in problem solving) forms a major part of empirical analysis and theory formation. This field of research is dominated by a focus on the processes that mediate either a debilitating or facilitating influence of anxiety on performance.

Since the first presentation of the Spence-Taylor theory of anxiety (K. W. Spence & Taylor, 1951), this area has been heavily influenced by concepts developed within the mechanistic concept of anxiety based on Hull's behavioristic learning theory (Hull, 1943, 1952). In this context the so-called drive theory of anxiety (J. T. Spence & Spence, 1966; K. W. Spence, 1958; Taylor, 1956) postulated a facilitating effect of increased anxiety for simple tasks (with low response competition) and a debilitating effect for difficult tasks (with high response competition). The rise of an unspecific activation level (drive) was supposed to be the process by which this effect is produced.

The response interference hypothesis, also conceived on the basis of Hull's theory (Mandler & Sarason, 1952), however assumes that under aversive

Preparation of this chapter was facilitated by a grant from the Deutsche Forschungs-gemeinschaft (Kr 490/3) to the first author.

conditions task-related as well as anxiety-related habits are activated. Anxiety-related habits can have a facilitating effect, for example if reactions of being incited or of being relaxed are evoked. Anxiety-related habits, however, can also result in debilitating achievement, for example if reactions of worry, despair, or emotional arousal are produced. Such "task-irrelevant," anxiety-related habits affect the accomplishment of a task by interfering with task-related habits. Under achievement conditions individuals are supposed to show a relatively consistent, person-specific reaction tendency, which can vary between the manifestation of facilitating and debilitating reactions.

The response interference hypothesis postulates two processes affecting achievement: (1) a process of activation increase and (2) a process of worrying (see Liebert & Morris, 1967). Recent cognitive approaches to the relationship between anxiety and achievement have accentuated this cognitive process, particularly its debilitating component (Morris & Fulmer, 1976; Sarason, 1975; Spielberger, Gonzales, Taylor, Algaze, & Anton, 1978; Wine, 1971). For example, Wine argues that certain individuals react with "evaluative anxiety" in achievement situations (Wine, 1971; see also Wine's contribution, chapter 10, in this volume). (Incidentally, this anxiety is not confined to task-related situations but can also be evoked in other, e.g., interpersonal, settings. However, a person is not necessarily dispositionally anxious across different evaluative situations.) Individuals with high dispositional evaluation anxiety respond to cues that indicate an evaluation by directing their attention away from task-related information and toward self-centered cognitions, which result in raised emotional reactivity on their part. A deterioration of achievement is supposed to be produced by this deficient attention to task-relevant information.

Sarason (1975) postulates an interfering effect of self-preoccupation reactions in at least three stages of processing task-relevant information: (1) attending to relevant information; (2) processing information already taken in (for example, processing between different storage systems); and (3) selecting an overt response.

The common basis of these cognitive approaches is that they conceive comparatively consistent individual differences in susceptibility to stressors (in this case, evaluative threat). In terms of Spielberger's (1966) Trait-State Theory of Anxiety these differences refer to the concept of trait anxiety (A-Trait). A problem, however, is conceptualizing the relationship of these trait differences to differences in state anxiety (A-State), especially if one takes into account the concept of coping.

Krohne (1978), taking the lead from authors dealing primarily with the process of coping with anxiety (e.g., Epstein, 1972; Lazarus, 1966), pointed out that the arousal and persistence of elevated state anxiety in a stress situation is only to be expected with persons who either are not experienced in dealing with a certain stressor (e.g., novice parachutists, Fenz & Epstein, 1967) or who have not succeeded in establishing a coping system for certain classes of stressors. In several experiments Epstein could demonstrate that individuals—as a consequence of frequent confrontation with a stressor—established a coping system that is either flexible and situation-adequate ("modulated" coping) or comparatively rigid ("defensive" coping).

Since we have to assume that achievement situations represent a type of stressor familiar to almost every member of our society, we can conclude that the occurrence of (state) anxiety in test situations is generally a symptom of a person's inability to establish a coping system for this stressor. When dealing with the relationships between anxiety and achievement we will have to observe, not only the effects of emotional and cognitive anxiety reactions on achievement, but also the impact that certain coping strategies (e.g., defensive coping) exert on problem-solving behavior. The analysis of this problem represents a prime concern of this chapter. However, since there exist hardly any elaborated theoretical approaches or empirical results on this problem, we will primarily have to confine ourselves to speculations. In doing so we will also use conclusions from related studies.

THE CONCEPT OF COPING

Definition

In the mechanistic model little attention has been paid to how coping systems have been established. At best, conceptions of avoidance or escape learning (Miller, 1951; Mowrer, 1950) and of "preparatory" responses (Perkins, 1968) can be considered as steps in this direction. Only in later cognitive theories is the concept of coping with anxiety given more attention (Epstein, 1967, 1972; Eriksen, 1966; Lazarus, 1966).

In a first approximation, coping can be considered as "the sum total of all the strategies employed by an individual to deal with a significant threat to his psychological stability" (Chodoff, Friedman, & Hamburg, 1964, p. 744). These strategies include the preferred use of overt responses (such as avoidance, escape, or attack) as well as covert (intrapsychic) processes (e.g., redefinition or denial) (Lazarus, 1966; Lazarus, Averill, & Opton, 1974.) A person's coping behavior can refer to the handling of an *external* fact appraised as threatening, as well as dealing with *internal* emotional and cognitive processes evoked by threat appraisal (Chodoff et al., 1964; Haggard, 1943; Lazarus, 1974; Mechanic, 1962).

Without doubt the conceptualization of coping strategies represents an important extension of anxiety research stimulated by cognitive approaches. However the following topics (among others) remain to be addressed:

1. Can actual coping behavior (coping state) be described by typical strategy patterns?
2. How can these patterns be related to dispositional (trait) antecedents?
3. How do characteristics of the actual situation (eventually in interaction with specific coping dispositions) contribute to eliciting coping behavior?
4. How can we conceptualize the relationship of both coping trait and coping state to characteristics of performance behavior? What kind of predictions about performance in threat situations can be derived from this conceptualization (different from predictions from the mechanistic model of anxiety)?

In the following sections we will deal with these topics. Since the first three questions have been discussed in various previous reports (Krohne, 1975, 1976, 1978), we will especially concentrate on question 4. We will present a model for the interaction of coping and performance in which coping is related to the possibility of controlling information and/or behavior in threat situations. In this context coping is regarded as a special aspect of problem-solving behavior.

Patterns of Coping Behavior

Covariations between specific responses for coping with (or controlling) threat were first registered in experiments carried out to examine psychoanalytic statements about the effects of so-called anxiety defense mechanisms (A. Freud, 1946; S. Freud, 1926/1940–1942). Since emphasis was upon studying the fundamental defense mechanism of repression (e.g., Zeller, 1950; for an overview see Holmes, 1974), those reactions were primarily analyzed according to how threat or anxiety was controlled by a more or less marked distortion of reality.

However, even in this context it became evident that the assumption of a single defensive (or coping) process (namely repression) was not sufficient to account for the observed behavioral variance. So Bruner and Postman (1947), in their well-known studies, found that certain subjects did not respond to threatening stimuli with repression (operationalized by the perceptual threshold at tachistoscopic presentations) but, contrary to expectation, with increased vigilance. A multitude of systematic studies, especially by Eriksen and his co-workers (Eriksen, 1951a, 1951b, 1952a, 1952b; Lazarus, Eriksen, & Fonda, 1951), confirmed the existence of a vigilant ("sensitive") pattern of defensive coping reactions that is in many behavioral aspects opposed to the "repressive" pattern. (For more recent results see Averill, O'Brien, & DeWitt, 1977.)

The repressive coping pattern is characterized by the following reactions (among others) to threatening, as compared to neutral, stimuli: decreased amount of anxiety- and conflict-related word associations with the presentation of threatening verbal or visual stimulus material; increased recognition time with tachistoscopic presentation of such material; improved memorization of success-related and deteriorated memory of failure-related material; impaired learning of potentially threatening words.

The first studies on coping primarily observed two contrasting strategies—repression and vigilance. This result may primarily be due to the fact that such material as aggressive, sexual, often homosexual stimuli was used. Either such stimuli were only appraised as threatening (and hence evoked coping behavior) by subjects with more severe conflicts related to these topics, or the experimental design hardly allowed any other modes of responding. Since this procedure was also transferred to respective research in the achievement area, here, too, repressive and sensitive (vigilant) coping strategies were studied first (see, e.g., Eriksen, 1954a; Fulkerson, 1960; Truax, 1957). The various other possibilities of coping with achievement-related threat (e.g., increased attention to the task, seeking support, lowering level of aspiration, passivity, anger) were primarily studied within test anxiety research (for overviews see, e.g., Sarason, 1975; Wine, 1971) and achievement motivation or attribution theory (see Heckhausen, 1975; Weiner, 1972) and have only recently been perceived to be important in coping research (see Houston, 1977, and chapters 5, 9, 11, 12, and 13 in this volume).

Dispositional Antecedents of the Use of Coping Strategies

From a methodological point of view the two patterns of defensive coping behavior ("coping state") described above represent *descriptive constructs*. A descriptive construct describes a particular, rather consistently observed constellation of empirical data but does not explain what the antecedents of these data are. This means that the empirical relationships presented earlier are described as repressive (or sensitive) coping but are not explained by the construct of repression (or sensitization). A theory of the occurrence and interconnection of empirical facts is provided by the *explicative construct* (see Krohne, 1975).

A first step toward the development of an explicative construct could be the conceptualization of a personality dimension of which the empirical indicators are systematically related to the observed coping-state variables. The personality dimension "repression-sensitization" (R-S) represents such a construct.

Starting with studies that relate the described patterns of defensive coping behavior to clinical descriptions and tests of the respective subjects (Alper, 1948; Eriksen, 1954a, 1954b; Eriksen & Browne, 1956; Eriksen & Davids, 1955; Lazarus et al., 1951), R-S was developed as a unidimensional, bipolar personality construct (Altrocchi, 1961; Byrne, 1961, 1964; Gordon, 1957; Ullmann, 1958). At each pole of this continuum are located individuals who generally react with defensive coping in danger situations. A defensive coping tendency is defined by the properties *rigidity, frequent manifestation,* and *easy release* (see Krohne, 1978). Persons at the sensitive pole ("sensitizers") are generally characterized by appraising many situations as threatening and by accentuating information that indicates the (supposed or factual) imminent threat. Persons at the repressive pole ("repressers") are generally characterized by appraising relatively few stimuli as threatening and by avoiding information associated with threat.

Various procedures have been used as empirical indicators of the R-S dimension the validity of which, however, proved to be unsatisfactory (see Bell & Byrne, 1978; Byrne, 1964). Especially the *discriminant validity* seems to be insufficient, as in general these procedures are highly correlated with anxiety questionnaires. For example, the R-S Scale (Byrne, 1961), the most widely used test for assessing repression-sensitization, correlates with the Manifest Anxiety Scale (MAS) with $r = 0.75$ on the average (see, e.g., Golin, Herron, Lakota, & Reineck, 1967; Krohne, 1975).

From a strict methodological point of view the conceptualization of a R-S dimension does not represent an explicative construct. The concept would become explicative if it dealt with the following questions: (1) Can a general psychological theory be formulated from which one can stringently derive why a certain person responds with behavior R_A within the behavioral class A (e.g., recall of success) and with behavior R_B within the behavioral class B (e.g., identification of tachistoscopically presented threatening stimuli)? (2) If such a behavior-controlling mechanism can be described, what are the conditions of its development?

Both questions were more extensively discussed in different reports (Krohne, 1978, 1980). Therefore we will present only some central ideas on this topic here. These ideas will be discussed in connection with the third problem mentioned earlier (the interaction of situation and person characteristics in the release of coping behavior).

Disposition-Situation Interaction in Eliciting Coping Behavior

The low validity of instruments for measuring the R-S dimension is only to a small degree caused by unsatisfactory test construction. Rather the main reason seems to be insufficient elaboration of the central assumption of the construct concerning the conditions under which a behavior tendency (e.g., vigilance) manifests itself in actual behavior.

The R-S construct shares this difficulty with many other dispositionally (trait) oriented approaches. Mischel (1968) called attention to the fact that most tests constructed within the traditional trait approach to personality are only weakly correlated with those behavior characteristics that, according to the assumptions of the underlying "theory," should be manifestations of the respective disposition. Taking the lead from Mischel's arguments we therefore believe that the relevant theoretical units concerning coping do not consist of dispositions in a classical trait-theoretical sense but of cognitive activities (cognitions) of the individual that, related to specific situations, function as mediators between changes in the environment and behavioral manifestations.

Such a coping theory is *interactionally* oriented. Interactional approaches assume that situation characteristics and acquired, and therefore dispositional, cognitions of a person determine initial appraisal of situations and selection of responses. The executed (overt or intrapsychic) reaction on its part changes the situation either by active modification (by overt reactions) or by redefinition (by intrapsychic reactions). Subsequently, it depends on the "resistance" of the situation to the selected response mode (for example, not every threat can be reduced by redefinition) whether the situational change moves in a direction corresponding with the content of a person's cognition. The resulting situation reappraisal can or cannot confirm the cognitions brought by the person. In the latter case lasting alterations of both cognitions and actual behavior will result (see Krohne, 1977, and the concept of "transaction" by Lazarus and Launier, 1980).

In these approaches the central cognitions are the *expectancies* an individual has established about certain consequences of both environmental events and the person's own reactions. In addition, situation appraisal and response selection are governed—often in interaction with the elicited expectancies—by the following cognitive characteristics: *competencies* of an individual to construe different behavioral modes under respective conditions; the way a person generally *categorizes* situational characteristics; *values* that certain expected consequences have for the person; *self-regulatory* systems and plans (see Mischel, 1973).

In his coping theory Lazarus (1966, Note 1) attempts to systematically interrelate these (and additional) parameters. Whether a stimulus is appraised as threatening ("primary appraisal") depends (apart from characteristics of the situation) on the outcomes of the following cognitive activities: the way in which a person preferredly categorizes stimuli and the expectancies about the consequences of a stimulus categorized in a certain way.

In our approach we consider the *discriminative ability* of a person to be the basis for the establishment and elicitation of expectancies. Persons at the two poles of the R-S continuum are presumably characterized by a low ability to discriminate between dangerous and nondangerous cues. While repressers indiscriminantly appraise relatively many situations as nondangerous, sensitizers, on the other hand, experience many situations as threatening.

Expectancies, however, are not confined to stimulus-outcome sequences but can also refer to the consequences of a person's own actions. In the latter case threat appraisal depends on whether the person disposes of responses in his or her repertoire that allow for control of the situation. Lazarus calls this determinant of threat appraisal "relationship of stimulus noxity to counterharm resources of the individual."

If a stimulus is appraised as threatening, the consequent cognitive activities are directed toward the search for possibilities to eliminate threat (Lazarus: "secondary appraisal"). As long as this search proves unsuccessful these activities are accompanied by state anxiety with its cognitive and emotional component. In this case coping reactions are also directed toward the reduction of state anxiety. Parameters being crucial in this process are the *values* certain outcomes have for the person concerned (in the sense of cost and profits of the states attained) and self-regulatory systems and plans of the individual (e.g., self-set standards).

In case overt coping behavior (e.g., escape) cannot be carried out (eventually because the costs of its outcome are higher than the anticipated profit) Lazarus postulates that so-called intrapsychic activities are elicited. Examples of such activities are denial, redefinition, or intellectualization.

REPRESSION-SENSITIZATION AND PERFORMANCE

In the preceding section we argued that the elicitation of reactions that can be attributed to a certain class of intrapsychic coping mechanisms depends on (1) the presence of specific situation characteristics (as they are appraised by the person concerned) and (2) dispositional conditions of the person. Extreme manifestations on the R-S dimension (either at the repressive or at the sensitive pole) can be considered as indicators of an individual's tendency to react relatively independently of the situation either with sensitive or repressive coping once he or she has appraised the situation as threatening.

We will now raise the question of which mediating processes can account for the influence of repressive or sensitive reaction tendencies on performance. Can mediating processes be conceptualized for effects that are to be seen as analogous to the anxiety components of "worrying" or "emotionality"? In the following we will first present some empirically found relations between R-S indicators and performance measures. Then we will speculate about processes possibly mediating these relationships. Finally we will analyze how far these speculations are supported by empirical findings.

Empirical Results

Clark and Neuringer (1971) reported significantly higher verbal abilities (Cooperative School and College Ability Test) with repressers as compared to nondefensive or sensitive individuals when the effects of general aptitude and age were controlled. However, Byrne (1961), Lomont (1965), and Krohne (1974) could not find significant relationships between R-S values and any verbal abilities. Similar negative results were obtained in a study by Krohne (1974) on the relationships between repression-sensitization and different indicators of "cognitive complexity," and by Kirschenbaum and Karoly (1977) comparing R-S and quantitative performance under various self-monitoring conditions.

Although Bergquist, Lewinsohn, Sue, and Flippo (1968) found indications of a better short-term memory with sensitizers, this result could not be supported in other studies (Bergquist, 1972; Bergquist, Lewinsohn, & Benson, 1971). It seems noteworthy that in these studies no interaction between the R-S dimension and the emotional content of the stimulus material could be observed.

Differences between repressers and sensitizers were attained in the area of information processing. When solving a problem (e.g., judging other persons) sensitizers search more information than repressers but also are more disturbable when integrating this information into concepts. They then drop to a lower level of processing than repressers (Krohne & Schroder, 1972). When identifying ambiguous stimuli, repressers, as compared to sensitizers, report a higher degree of subjective certainty concerning the correctness of their own identification (Krohne, 1974). Moreover, repressers tend to manifest a higher degree of leveling and generalizing of information, show a strong tendency to reduce ambiguity, and are also less open to new information (Altrocchi, 1961; Dublin, 1968; Nalven, 1967; Weissman & Ritter, 1970). Accordingly, repressers show a lower cognitive flexibility with concept information tasks (Bergquist, Lloyd, & Johansson, 1973) and pay less attention to peripheral stimuli in anagram solutions (Mendelsohn & Griswold, 1967). Finally, Markowitz (1969) attained a significant interaction effect of repression-sensitization and stress condition on the rate of incidental learning. Under ego threat, as compared to a neutral situation, sensitizers showed an increase in learning while repressers manifested a decrease. With the exception of Nalven (1967), who used a sentence-completion method, all studies cited assessed repression-sensitization by the R-S scale (Byrne, 1961; Byrne, Barry, & Nelson, 1963).

Repression-Sensitization and Attentional Redirection

As already mentioned above (see page 171) one essential difference between repressive and sensitive coping behavior in threat situations was supposed to be in the directing of attention and, correspondingly, the searching for information. According to our conception of coping (Krohne, 1978) this *redirection* of attention after threat appraisal is viewed as the mediating process between the R-S behavioral tendency and interindividual differences in performance. In extreme cases attention can—at least temporally—be withdrawn from a danger stimulus (repression) or it can be directed more intensely toward those aspects of a situation (sensitization).

However, this redirection hypothesis alone does not yet account for the observed performance differences between repressers and sensitizers. We therefore introduce as an additional explicative concept *costs of attentional redirection*. These can be short- or long-term costs. One *long-term* cost of a person's tendency in threat situations to redirect attention in a specific way (focusing = sensitization, or withdrawal = repression) would be the inhibition of constructing a flexible, situation-adequate coping system. Such a deficient construction can manifest itself in the system of physiological arousal, in cognitive processes, or in open (motoric) reactions. By *short-term* costs we understand an influence exerted on cognitive processes carried out simultaneously with repressive or sensitive attention redirection. In achievement-related situations such an influence could be exerted, for example, on task-solving behavior.

The use of special coping modes in a threat situation presumably depends, not only on automatized behavioral tendencies (as conceptualized in the repression-sensitization disposition, for example), but also on the anticipated costs of a certain coping behavior (see Glass & Singer, 1972; Lazarus, 1966, chapter 6). This anticipation in its turn depends on different factors: the information available or the behavior alternatives open to a person in a certain threat situation. It also has to be taken into consideration that coping behavior in a threat situation is no one-shot event. In order to better understand how coping behavior is steered by anticipations and which kind of consequences are elicited by a special coping mode, we will now turn to an analysis of the following problems: How can situations appraised as threatening be classified? Which sequence of elements in a threat situation, especially an evaluative situation, can be identified?

THE THREAT SITUATION

Classification of Situations with Threat Character

Principally, two ways of classifying threat situations exist: a posteriori and a priori classifications. In the a posteriori approach, for example, by dimension-analytic procedures (Ekehammar, Magnusson, & Ricklander, 1974; Endler, Hunt, & Rosenstein, 1962; Endler & Okada, 1975; see also chapter 15 by Magnusson & Stattin in this volume), the generalizability of the results is limited by the population dependency of the measurement and by a rather arbitrary selection of the variables used in an investigation. Therefore, we prefer the a priori approach, in which classifications are established on the basis of theoretical considerations concerning the elicitation of threat appraisal.

We consider a central theory-related classification variable of threat situations to be the degree of potential *controllability* of the situation by the person exposed to it (Averill, 1973; Glass & Singer, 1972). Theoretical constructs supporting our view are, for example: desire for certainty (Brim & Hoff, 1957), mastery motive (de Charms, 1968; Kelly, 1955: White, 1959), perceived freedom (Brehm, 1966; Steiner, 1970), or predictability and controllability (Seligman, 1975).

Analogous to the useful distinction between "perception response' and "executive response" proposed for the analysis of information-processing behavior (see, e.g., Streufert & Driver, 1967), we conceive two dimensions of control: *information control* and *behavior control* (see Averill, 1973; Furedy & Doob, 1972). Informational control refers to the variable access to information (e.g., a warning signal) about an aversive event prior to its onset (*predictability*, Glass & Singer, 1972; Seligman, 1975). Behavioral control refers to the variable availability of reactions influencing a noxious stimulus once it has been signalled or encountered (*controllability*).

Both forms of control can be split into several dimensions (see Averill, 1973; Monat, 1976; Monat, Averill, & Lazarus, 1972). Information about the aversive event can reduce *temporal uncertainty* (knowing *when* the stressor will be applied) or *event uncertainty* (knowing *which kind of stressor* will be encountered). Behavioral control can refer to a person's influence upon the administration of the noxious stimulus (e.g., administration by the person himself or by another person; *regulated administration*) or to a person's ability to modify the stimulus by some direct action (e.g., avoidance, escape, attack; *stimulus modification*).

A problem seems to be the conceptualization of the relationship between informational control (predictability) and behavioral control (controllability). The most simple approach would be a conception of the two dimensions as varying independently of each other. However, at least in stress experiments, a separation of the effects of both modes of control seems to be almost impossible (see Averill, 1973; Mineka & Kihlstrom, 1978; Seligman, 1975). Generally, controllable events involve a certain amount of predictability. The subject not only assumes that he or she will encounter a certain stressor (e.g., an electric shock, a problem-solving task) but also knows that in the case of the onset of an aversive event he or she can react in a certain way. Many everyday stress situations, however, illustrate that the assumption of an independent variation of both dimensions is meaningful (see Glass & Singer, 1972, p. 63). There are predictable aversive events that either allow for behavioral control (an epidemic disease like the Asian flu) or do not permit control (a hurricane). There are also unpredictable aversive events that can be controlled (a flat tire) or that do not allow for control (being put in jail after a car accident in an isolated place in a remote foreign country).

For the aim of our analysis we therefore conceive the two dimensions of control as varying independently of each other. When realizing, in each case, two steps of control (possible vs. impossible control) we obtain four modes of control in threat situations:

1. *Informational control and behavioral control possible.* The danger stimulus can be predicted and reacted to accordingly. Such a stimulus may be appraised as threatening, but since its mode and the time of its impact are known and possibilities of responding are available (e.g., avoidance or escape), an anxiety reaction will not result. (Example: an exam for which the student is informed about time, the required knowledge, and the way of solving the tasks.)

2. *Informational control possible, behavioral control impossible.* In this case, information about the danger stimulus (mode, intensity, and/or impact conditions) is provided but the person cannot influence this stimulus at the moment. As overt behavior is not possible, manifestations of intrapsychic reactions (redefinition, repression, intellectualization) are to be expected. (Example: a surgical operation for which the patient is psychologically prepared.) State anxiety should increase when the intrapsychic reactions prove to be ineffective in eliminating threat.

3. *Informational control impossible, behavioral control possible.* Within the context of a general (vague) appraisal of threat there are no concrete cues to the danger stimulus. However, a reaction can be executed after its occurrence. That means that in such situations escape but not avoidance reactions are possible. Therefore fear instead of anxiety or intrapsychic reactions should be observed. (Example: the paradigm used in some experiments on stress to apply an unpredictable stressor—e.g., shock—after the onset of which an instrumental response—e g., escape—is possible; see Weiss, 1971.)

4. *Informational control and behavioral control impossible.* The aversive event can neither be predicted nor influenced after its occurrence. This situation should result in the syndrome Seligman (1975) called "learned helplessness." An example would be a child who is inconsistently punished by severe parents, and who therefore cannot predict and avoid these punishments. This example demonstrates the necessity to distinguish within the class of informational

control between general, temporal, and event uncertainty. The child may know that he or she will be punished rather frequently (no general uncertainty), but he or she may not know the time (temporal uncertainty) or the form of the next punishment (event uncertainty).

Sequence of Elements in Performance Situations

Having classified situations with threat character, we will now investigate where informational control and where behavioral control can preferably be realized in the course of a performance situation. From this analysis we will learn (1) which types of loss of control are responsible for the threat appraisal of these situations, and (2) which costs originate from repressive or sensitive coping.

A performance situation can be characterized by the following sequence of elements:

1. Announcement of a performance evaluation
2. Execution of preparatory reactions
3. Realization of the proper performance behavior
4. Feedback of results to the performing person

This analysis separates the stage of preparation from the stage of performance. To a large extent this distinction seems to parallel our differentiation of informational control and behavioral control presented above.

The stage of preparation is characterized by the fact that performance reactions (e.g., answering a sequence of test questions) have to be postponed. Thus the feedback concerning the adequacy of these reactions is also delayed. Doubtlessly, apart from the anticipation of being evaluated, this delay contributes to the stress character of a performance situation. By blocking a direct response to obtain feedback, the stage of preparation can be identified as a case of insufficient (or at least limited) behavioral control. On the other hand, information about different aspects of the performance situation, although to a variable extent, can be obtained. Thus the preparation stage in a performance situation (frequently) realizes the mode "informational control possible, behavioral control impossible." In this context a distinction has to be made between information necessary for task solution (e.g., consulting a textbook = *task-relevant information*) and information referring to the performance situation in general (e.g., questions like "How well will I do?" "What happens if I fail;" "Will I get difficult questions?" = *task-irrelevant information*). In the following we will especially consider interindividual differences in the search for task-irrelevant information, as it is this search that essentially produces interference with performance.

EFFECTS OF VARIABLE INFORMATIONAL CONTROL

Preference for Information versus Noninformation about an Aversive Event

The state of being informed about an unavoidable aversive event is generally to be preferred to the state of being uninformed (see, among others, Averill, 1973;

D'Amato, 1974). The concepts of "preparatory response" (Perkins, 1968) and "safety signal" (Seligman, 1975) present possible explanations for this phenomenon. However, it has to be taken into account that in many experiments on this topic the aversive event was nearly always the application (or at least threat) of a pain stimulus, rarely of an evaluative stimulus. Ratings of the degree of aversiveness, preference for a certain experimental condition (receiving information such as a signal vs. being uninformed about the aversive stimulus), and physiological or subjective-verbal reactions represented the dependent variables in those experiments.

Threat and/or the application of a pain stimulus (pain-threat) undoubtedly both represent a situation very different from the threat and/or the application of an evaluation (ego-threat). Not only do persons differ dispositionally in their responsiveness to pain- versus ego-threat (Kendall, 1978), but also the temporal and functional relationship between stimulus announcement, waiting period, and stimulus application are very different. If we nevertheless base some of our assumptions also on experiments with pain-threat, we do so because we consider the relationship between different preferences for informational states (approach vs. withdrawal from the threat-relevant information) and resulting performance as a general one, comparatively independent of the source of threat. Although according to our knowledge this topic has not yet been investigated, we assume that preferences for modes of information in evaluative situations follow similar rules as in pain-threat situations.

In reviewing experiments on information preference it is notable that always a relatively large number of subjects behave contrary to the above-mentioned hypothesis of a preference for the state of being informed. Those subjects prefer the state of not being informed about a forthcoming aversive event (see Table 1). In the investigations cited the stressor-related information had no instrumental value for an avoidance or escape response. (Similarly, task-irrelevant information has no instrumental value in performance situations.) However, we can assume that for both types of situations this information facilitates the establishment of preparatory responses, the reduction of uncertainty (see Berlyne, 1960), or the

Table 1   Investigations Showing Number of Subjects with Preference for Informational Control versus Subjects with Preference for Information Rejection in Threat Situations

Investigation	Preference for control	Information rejection	No decision
Badia, Suter & Lewis (1967)	27	13	
	22	13	
Ball & Vogler (1961)	28	11	
Breznitz (1967)	47	13	
Cook & Barnes (1964)	17	3	
	16	4	
D'Amato & Gumenik (1960)	16	2	2
Furedy & Dobb (1972)	13	5	14
	9	10	13
	3	3	10
	19	14	15
	10	10	12
Jones, Bentler, & Petry (1966)	24	8	
Lanzetta & Driscoll (1966)	19	5	
Monat, Averill, & Lazarus (1972)	35	5	

shortening of an "anxiety inducing waiting period" (see Averill, 1973; Sarason & Stoops, 1978).

When comparing the consequences of the state of present information to the state of limited access to information, present information was found to be accompanied by lower physiological arousal and cognitive disturbance *during* the application interval of the stressor (Monat, Averill, & Lazarus, 1972), by a faster habituation to the stressor (Maltzman & Wolff, 1970), by a higher stress tolerance (Staub & Kellett, 1972), and a lower *subsequent* disturbance of frustration tolerance and performance (Glass, Singer, & Friedman, 1969). Thus there exists some empirical evidence for the hypothesis that the state of informational control has positive consequences for subsequent processes (e.g., task solutions). Why do approximately one-third of the subjects (at least in pain-threat experiments) do without this information?

The following explanation can be derived from the results of postexperimental inquiry: *The intake of information about an aversive event is accompanied by high emotional arousal experienced as unpleasant.* In the cited experiments this arousal increase could be avoided by turning attention away from these stimuli (preference for the state of not being informed). In doing so, subjects have to compare *costs* (especially short-term costs) and *gain* of information control. Especially with low intensity of the signalled stressor, the immediate costs of arousal increase after information intake can exceed the profit of informational control. So Furedy (1975) reports that preference for information was clearly a function of the intensity of the stressor (see also Averill & Rosenn, 1972). With high intensity of shock or noise the phenomenon of signal preference could be secured, with medium intensity no clear preference was observed, while with low intensity there was a preference for not being informed. "The interpretation assumes that Ss believe both that signal-elicited preparation reduces aversiveness (i.e., a form of preparatory response theory), and that this preparation takes some effort" (Furedy, 1975, p. 72). When extending these investigations to situations of ego-threat, one would have to examine whether there are corresponding preferences as a function of the importance (= intensity of the stressor) of the announced performance evaluation (see Morris & Fulmer, 1976, for the relationship between importance of performance, feedback, and anxiety).

In the studies mentioned above the preference reactions of many subjects varied with the intensity of the aversive event. Following Epstein (1972) we can speak here of a "modulated" stress coping system. Such a system is characteristic of persons in the medium part of the repression-sensitization continuum (nondefensive individuals). But there are also subjects who—situation invariant—show a preference either for information control or for noninformation. Such reactions seem to be characteristic of persons with a sensitive or a repressive anxiety-defense system. Several authors, however, found no relationship between these control preferences and indicators of repression-sensitization (Averill & Rosenn, 1972; Ball & Vogler, 1971; Monat, 1976; Monat et al., 1972, using the Rorschach Index according to Levine & Spivack, 1964; the Sentence Completion Test of Goldstein, 1959; and Welsh's R-Scale, 1956). These negative results can, on the one hand, be due to the already mentioned insufficient validity of the R-S indicators used; on the other hand, however, it can be caused by the fact that phenotypically equal reactions can result from different mediation processes. This cannot definitely be determined in a posteriori analyses of information preference. We can expect, however, that one condition are differences (state or trait) on the R-S dimension. This expectancy is based on the observations (1) that sensitizers generally turn to threat-related information while repressers reject this information and (2) that repressers generally tend to underestimate and sensitizers to overestimate threat (for empirical results see Byrne, 1964; Bell & Byrne, 1978; Krohne, 1974, 1978). But as information preference covaries with the appraised stressor intensity, we deduce that repressers more than sensitizers should renounce threat-related information. Thus we will next deal with the question of the effects of repressive or sensitive use of information upon performance.

When analyzing this problem the following facts have to be distinguished: (1) the influence of repressive or sensitive coping during the anticipation period both on the attention to task-irrelevant information and on the use of task-relevant information, and (2) the effect of repressive or sensitive coping in the task-solution period.

The Influence of Repression-Sensitization in the Anticipation Period

Attention to Task-Irrelevant Information

Focusing attention on threat-related but not necessarily task-relevant aspects of the situation (vigilance or sensitization) could facilitate the establishment of a person-internal stress regulation, for example by redefining the situation ("threat redefinition," Holmes & Houston, 1974). Moreover, an arousal increase during anticipation—as a consequence of attention focusing—could already to inhibited when confronted with the stressor so that a relatively low reactivity ensues (see Janis, 1958). So, for instance, Niemelä (1974) found two different patterns of reaction in the periods of anticipation and confrontation with a pain stressor. While one subject group showed high physiological arousal (GSR) during anticipation and relatively low autonomic responsiveness during confrontation (the vigilant pattern), another group manifested exactly the opposite pattern; that is, low responsiveness during the anticipation period and high arousal during confrontation (the avoidant pattern). Postexperimental assessment of the cognitions during anticipation supported the interpretation of these two patterns as vigilance and avoidance. Similar results were obtained by Monat et al. (1972).

If task-solution behavior is included in the analysis, the following relationships are expected: Learning of complex and novel material should be disturbed by sensitive coping during the anticipation period (with its high arousal). This disadvantage cannot be compensated for by relatively low arousal during the confrontation period (test situation) because the necessary knowledge could not be adequately acquired. On the other hand, such tasks should be learned relatively well by repressers. Here the reproduction during the test situation should be impaired because of the high arousal level. Compared to persons with a modulated stress-coping system, both groups should score lower in new, complex tasks with test character; sensitizers because they do not learn the material adequately, repressers because they cannot reproduce it undisturbedly (at least in very threatening situations). With simple routine tasks no negative effect should be expected. However, according to our knowledge, no systematic investigations of these supposed relationships have been carried out so far.

Unfortunately, the theory-conforming results reported above could not be replicated by other authors. So Averill and Rosenn (1972) found that persons who preferred an avoidance strategy during shock anticipation (by concentrating on music instead of a warning signal) manifested higher physiological arousal (GSR, heart rate) than vigilant persons (who listened to the warning signal). Concerning self-reported tension and occurrence of nonshock-related thoughts (attention deployment), no differences between vigilant and avoidant individuals were observed. There was also no relationship between these characteristics and trait measures of defensiveness. Similar results are reported by Hare (1966).

Obviously the Averill and Rosenn results contradict our earlier theorizing concerning the relationship between attention focusing and physiological arousal during the anticipation of danger stimuli. However, these authors observed a relationship between *perceptual concentration* and lower physiological arousal during the anticipation period. This relation is supported by results of Lacey, Kagan, Lacey, and Moss (1963). These authors postulate that the autonomic responses (especially heart rate) will be relatively low, particularly with the perceptual focusing on a signal (information orientation), whereas attention diversion (information rejection) will be accompanied by a rise of autonomic responsiveness. Just this relationship was observed by Averill and Rosenn. If, however, there is no clear danger signal and the person is only preoccupied with the threat-related information ("worrying," as observed in anticipating perform-ance evaluation), an arousal increase should occur, as many anxiety experiments have demonstrated (see, e.g., Averill, 1973).

Houston and Holmes (1974) report a result largely corresponding to that of Averill and Rosenn. During the anticipation period their subjects (Ss) were exposed to either an *information-avoidant* (reading aloud a story) or a threat-centered condition. (Thus the Ss could not determine their coping style on their own.) The investigators found higher physiological arousal in the informa-tion-avoidance condition. Postexperimental analyses concerning the cognitive activities of the Ss during the anticipation period yielded that those Ss whose attention remained focused on the threat took the opportunity to redefine the characteristics of the anticipated stressor (in the sense of threat reduction). This should result in a decrease in physiological arousal. The authors assume that this redefinition connected with the focusing of attention is only successful with *ambiguous* threat. However, it must be pointed out that the results can also be explained by the physiological assumptions of Lacey et al., that is, without referring to relatively complex cognitive processes.

The result of Houston and Holmes could not be replicated in a subsequent similar experiment by Bloom, Houston, Holmes, and Burish (1977). The authors used three different coping conditions: *Attentional diversion* (reading a story and thinking about it), *redefinition* (writing down reasons why the application of shock in this experiment does not matter), and *control* (no manipulation of coping strategies). The attentional diversion condition resulted in a significantly lower level of physiological arousal than the other two conditions, which did not differ in this respect. However, the experimental design differed in essential points from that of Houston and Holmes: (1) A sample shock was applied prior to anticipation. (2) Redefinition was induced by a corresponding cognitive activity and not merely made possible by attentional focusing. (3) Attentional diversion was achieved via *silent* reading and *evaluating* a story. No check was applied whether subjects in this condition also tried to redefine the situation. In interpreting their result the authors assume that when threat is nonambiguous (quality and intensity of the shock were known beforehand), redefinition is less effective than attentional diversion.

Thus the question arises: How comparable are the experiments on the function of attentional focusing in the anticipation period? In some investigations a sample stressor was presented, in others this was not done. In some studies an aversive event was only announced, not applied. In several experiments the Ss were selected according to their preferred coping strategy (however, usually by assessment during the experiment, not via preexperimental assessment), in other studies the Ss were assigned to respective experimental treatments. For the latter case it has to be checked, of course, whether a respective coping strategy (e.g., redefinition) had at all been implemented in the subject. This was not carried out in every case. The activities that should make possible the use of a certain coping strategy (e.g., the strategy of attentional diversion through the activity of reading a story) are not always comparable. Frequently, there are no conclusive theoretical deductions how certain activities are associated with the preferred use of a coping strategy. Furthermore, it is often not analyzed how far this activity itself (e.g., reading aloud) has a stress-inducing or at least activating effect.

The Use of Task-Relevant Information

The use of task-relevant information has thus far been discussed primarily as a function of different levels of anxiety arousal (see Easterbrook, 1959; Wine, 1971). This relationship shall not be discussed here in detail (see also Wine's chapter in this volume). Instead we will analyze the following problems: How much does repressive or sensitive attentional focusing influence the use of relevant information? Do dispositional (repression-sensitization) and situational characteristics (e.g., task complexity, length of the anticipation period) have interactive effects on performance in task solutions?

A plausible assumption is that under certain conditions the repressive and sensitive coping strategies are inferior to modulated coping in the use of task-relevant information. As mentioned above, sensitive coping means increased attention to those aspects of a performance situation that represent a possible threat to self-esteem. In complex problem-solution processes, in which the person must be fully engaged in the reception and processing of task-relevant information, this implies a loss of information.

Repressive coping means that the aspects of a performance situation threatening to the self-esteem are being understated. Here the effect on the quality of performance should primarily be mediated by motivational processes. The low involvement of the represser in the performance situation could result in a decreased effort and hence an impaired preparation for the task-solution period. This would be especially the case with tasks evaluated as simple, that is, with tasks presenting few incentives. More complex, intrinsically motivating tasks should be solved comparatively well by repressers.

As mentioned above, sensitizers should score comparatively low on complex tasks. However, the requirements of the simple, routine tasks should match the information-processing structure of sensitizers rather well. The structure of these tasks frequently complies with the predominant characteristic of the sensitizer: the compulsive preoccupation with information related to threat (Cornsweet, 1964; Fulkerson, 1960; Mendelsohn & Griswold, 1967). Sensitive coping, with its permanently renewed dealing with threat-related information, is very time-consuming. If, however, a task is structured in such a way that this compulsive dealing increases the performance standard (e.g., in tasks in which utmost perfection is required), this task should be particularly well achieved by sensitizers. This should especially be the case if there is sufficient time for this activity. Time pressure, however, should unfavorably influence the sensitive system.

An investigation by Vagt and Kühn (1976) illustrates these considerations. (It ought to be noted that the authors used high-anxious Ss instead of sensitizers; however, the operational separation of these two groups has been insufficient so far, see Krohne, 1978.) Vagt and Kühn found that Ss with high test anxiety did not differ from those with low test anxiety in school test grades. If, however, the amount of preparation for classes in general was taken into account, high-anxious Ss reported significantly longer preparation. In our opinion this result illustrates nicely how an extended use of time may compensate for the interfering effects of paying too much attention to threat-related aspects of a performance situation.

Schaffner, Krohne, and Seveker (Note 2) investigated the relationships between dispositional variables (R-S trait, trait anxiety, and test anxiety), state variables (R-S state, state anxiety, and degree of cognitive interference), and length of preparation for as well as performance on a school test (essay writing) with 41 students of the ninth grade.[1] (Trait and state measures were applied immediatedly after the school test.) Causal relationships between these variables were anlayzed by means of path analysis (see Figure 1).

It is obvious that repression-sensitization is the basic disposition by which other characteristics are influenced. The manifestation of test anxiety, state anxiety, cognitive interference, and actual coping behavior (R-S state) depends on this variable. It is noteworthy that the performance level also depends on R-S trait but is mediated by test anxiety and R-S state, with repressers showing higher performances than sensitizers. Surprisingly, performance is not significantly influenced by cognitive interference or state anxiety. For preparation

[1] Test anxiety was measured by a German version of the Test Anxiety Inventory (Spielberger et al., 1978). The other dimensions were assessed by newly constructed tests of the authors' not yet published. (A high test grade means a low performance.)

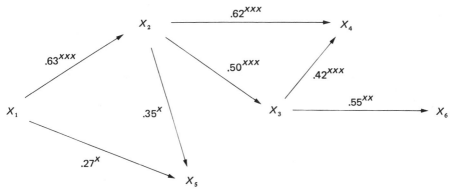

Figure 1 Path diagram for the data of Schaffner, Krohne, and Seveker (Note 2). (X_1 = R-S trait, X_2 = test anxiety, X_3 = R-S state, X_4 = cognitive interference, X_5 = state anxiety, and X_6 = performance on a school test. $^x p < .10$, $^{xx} p < .05$, $^{xxx} p < .01$).

time, only correlations with the other variables were calculated. Preparation time is significantly associated with repression-sensitization ($r = .46$) and test anxiety ($r = .40$), with sensitizers and high-anxiety Ss preparing longer for a school test. No significant correlation was found between preparation time and school performance.

Essay writing represents a task for which a student cannot prepare very well. Accordingly, a lower scoring of sensitizers was to be expected. A different type of task is represented by grammar tests, which generally require the student to apply the grammatical rules learned during the preceding lessons. Here a superiority of sensitizers compared to repressers should be expected. First results of the study by Schaffner et al. demonstrate the validity of this assumption: Preparation time for a grammar test is significantly longer than for an essay test ($p < .05$). Interestingly, performance on a grammar test seems to be directly dependent on R-S trait. This could mean that when a person can prepare well for a task, the elicitation of actual coping mechanisms does not influence his or her performance level.

The Influence of Repression-Sensitization in the Task-Solution Period

Krohne and Hudson (1979) systematically varied the type of task (routine tasks such as proofreading or finding mistakes in calculations versus creative tasks such as person descriptions or finding uses for things) and the length of time available for task solution. One hypothesis was that sensitizers under the condition of "routine task with extended length of time" should do better than the groups of nondefensive Ss or repressers. This hypothesis could not be confirmed. The authors argue that this negative result is primarily due to the use of a pure trait measure of repression-sensitization (R-S Scale of Byrne, 1961). In future investigations, first a trait measure of repression-sensitization more *specific* to the threat should be used, based on the well-established distinction between ego-threat and pain-threat (Endler, 1975; Kendall, 1978), and second, in addition to a trait test, a measure of actual coping behavior (coping state) should be applied. (See, for example, the study of Cohen and Lazarus, 1973, who found significant differences between sensitizers, nondefensives, and repressers only for a state measure of coping—coping with the threat of undergoing surgery—and not for a trait test of coping dispositions or anxiety.)

Houston and Hodges (1970) studied the effect of failure-threat and pain-threat on "Digits Backward" performance of "accentuators" (sensitizers), nondefensives, and "deniers" (repressers). The three groups were defined on the basis of discrepancies between self-report and physiological measures of stress. While no performance differences related to type of stress were observed, accentuators scored significantly lower than the other two groups, for which no differences were obtained.

A corresponding result was observed by Houston (1971) who only applied failure-threat. The author differentiated the Ss on the basis of a trait measure *and* a state measure of repression. As in the study by Krohne and Hudson (1979), the trait measure proved to be a weak predictor of differential performance under stress, whereas the state measure yielded significantly better performance by repressers as compared to nondefensive persons.

In the experiments described, the anticipation (or preparation) period consisted only of the announcing of threat and a subsequent (short) waiting for the task to be presented (confrontation). Since no task-relevant information was presented during the preparatory period the performance differences observed cannot be accounted for by a differential use of this information. The fact that sensitizers scored lower than repressers (or repressers better than nondefensive persons) contradicts our expectations mentioned earlier. According to these expectations, attention to threat-relevant aspects of the situation (sensitization) should foster the establishment of a person-internal stress-regulation system. During threat confrontation this regulation should result in a lower rise of arousal and thus (compared to repressers) better performance.

The following circumstances could have produced the results presented: (1) The preparation phase was too short to establish an effective regulation (e.g., redefinition). That means that sensitizers would still have reacted during confrontation in the way (with increased arousal and preoccupation with threat-related information) that they generally react during preparation. Repression, on the other hand, seems to control threat efficiently by a relatively simple mechanism (attentional diversion) if this threat is not too strong. (2) Establishment and operation of the sensitive stress-regulation system obviously requires that the individual is able to actively master the environment by seeking information and by manipulating things. If sensitizers are forced to be dependent and passive, as in many stress experiments, they cannot actively master their environment and fully establish their coping system. (For similar considerations of the role of the sensitizer's active mastery in a postoperative context, see Cohen and Lazarus, 1973.) (3) One can doubt whether the operational definition of repression and sensitization in the last two studies mentioned (Houston & Hodges, 1970; Houston, 1971) is especially advantageous. In order to define repression and sensitization, Houston and Hodges derived for each subject a change score in self-reported arousal (AACL) between rest and confrontation periods. The corresponding change score was calculated for physiological arousal (heart rate). The final repression-sensitization score is then the difference between these two change scores. Thus a subject with a *high* difference between test and rest period in AACL and a *low* difference in heart rate was defined as a sensitizer ("accentuator") and vice versa. Apart from the fact that the reliability of this difference measure is presumably rather low, assumptions of the nature of cognitive and physiological arousal patterns are already included in this analysis the validity of which has not yet been proven. Therefore it would be desirable to develop a state measure of repression-sensitization that is related in a more direct way to the presently secured theoretical basis of this concept.

CONCLUDING REMARKS

The results of investigations on the interactive effects of characteristics of the threat situation and the disposition repression-sensitization on level of performance are not completely uniform. In concluding we therefore want to elaborate some viewpoints that we think are crucial for a better understanding of this interactive process.

The joint classification of situations with threat character along the dimensions of informational control (predictability; variable access to information about a forthcoming aversive event) and behavioral control (controllability; variable availability of reactions for reducing threat after being informed about a forthcoming aversive event or after onset of this event) has been proven meaningful. On principle, an independent variation of both dimensions seems to be possible.

A division of the threat situation into a preparation period and a confrontation period is also useful. This division, first applied to pain-threat situations, can also be transferred to achievement situations (evaluative threat).

Elicitation of threat appraisal and coping reactions in achievement situations obviously depends to a high degree on the structure of the preparation period. In achievement situations this period frequently is one in which behavioral control is limited or impossible and informational control is variable.

Depending on how much information (task-relevant and task-irrelevant) is accessible, an internal stress-regulation system can be constructed during preparation. This system can neutralize stress reactions in the confrontation stage. However, intake of threat-related information (as well as its rejection) during preparation can have advantages as well as disadvantages for task-solution (confrontation).

Increased attention to threat-relevant information (sensitive coping) during preparation can facilitate the construction of stress regulation. This regulation in turn can be helpful in dealing with the danger during confrontation. A disadvantage of the increased attention to threat information is that the person has to put up with a heightened arousal level during preparation. This arousal can eventually impair the use of task-relevant information. On the other hand, the advantage of rejecting threat information (repressive coping) lies in comparatively low arousal and hence rather undisturbed preparation for the task. A disadvantage represents the possibility of being overwhelmed by a stressor for which no regulatory system has been elaborated. Besides, the repressive coping system during preparation has disadvantageous motivational consequences. A too low arousal level during preparation implies little motivation to prepare appropriately for the performance situation (e.g., to search for task-relevant information).

The systems of repressive or sensitive informational use, respectively, not only imply different cost-profit balances, they also require different situations for their optimal functioning. From the investigations described the following situation parameters seem to be crucial:

1. The length of time available for constructing the stress-regulation system during the preparation period.
2. The degree of activity (e.g., exploratory activity) allowed for a person during preparation.
3. The structure of the task to be solved during performance.
4. The strength of the stressor (in achievement situations, the importance of the evaluation implied in the achievement).

1. The elaboration of a stress-regulation system that is based on the attention and use of threat-relevant information during preparation (sensitive coping) obviously requires a certain amount of time. If this time is too short, only simple regulatory mechanisms, if any, are successful (e.g., denial; repressive coping). For a too short preparation period a sensitive orientation is not only inefficient, it presumably has even negative consequences for further performances, because an

interruption of the reactions of constructing the regulatory system poses an additional stress on the individual.

What is the optimal length of preparation time for constructing an adaptive regulatory system? A general answer would be that the optimal time varies with the range of possible adaptive reactions. If only one reaction (e.g., denial, avoidance, or escape) is adaptive, the optimal time length is comparatively short. If the situation demands a more complex pattern of preparatory reactions (e.g., search for additional information plus subsequent redefinition of the stressor), more time is needed for elaborating this behavior.

Investigations of pain stressors allow for the conclusion that eventually a curvilinear relationship exists between length of preparation and optimal adaptation to a stressor. As mentioned above, a short preparation period rarely permits the elaboration of adaptive responses. On the other hand, an extended preparation period does not seem to be optimal either. One reason for this could be the lack of feedback about the efficacy of the stress regulation elaborated. It is also possible that the extended preparation time serves as a further danger cue, suggesting that anything one had to await so long for cannot be minor. However, it seems questionable whether these relationships are also true of evaluative threat. Here one can suppose that a built-up regulation system can be maintained by self-generated feedback.

2. The sensitive coping system is more "active" than the repressive one. That means that the sensitive system demands an active access to information as well as the possibility to influence the environment according to the information received. If one of these possibilities is blocked, the sensitive system is little efficient in dealing with the stressor.

3. Two characteristics of the task structure especially interact with the repression-sensitization dimension in determining performance level: (a) The degree to which compulsive and cautious preparation behavior is advantageous for solving the presented tasks. For certain tasks (e.g., proofreading) a high performance level can be achieved by the utmost cautiousness in handling the task (e.g., frequent comparisons between task stimuli and solution responses). Since in these cases the task structure fits the preferred task-solution style of sensitizers, those individuals should score higher than nondefensives or repressers. (b) The degree to which incidental cues contribute to task-solution. It is characteristic of many tasks that incidentally presented information adds to the level of performance. For example, in an oral exam an examiner might help a student who is in trouble by giving him or her hidden clues for the solution. As mentioned above, sensitizers use those incidental cues better than repressers. Hence, in performance situations providing this additional information, sensitizers should score higher than their repressive counterparts.

4. As described earlier, building up a stress-regulation system by focusing on threat-related information during the preparation period implies costs and gains with respect to the resulting performance level. Whether the cost-gain balance is profitable or not depends especially on the strength of the stressor (i.e., complexity of the task and importance of the evaluation implied in it). If the stressor is strong, focusing on threat-related information during preparation and, as a consequence, suffering from increased arousal (sensitive orientation) can be advantageous. If, however, the stressor is only minor (e.g., the task to be solved is comparatively easy), then building up a stress-regulatory system would be unnecessary. In this case the represser's comparatively simple approach would be more advantageous.

In this chapter we intended to demonstrate that an individual's threat-coping mechanisms present important mediators between the stress situation and the performance level achieved. However, there is no general answer as to which coping mechanism is most beneficial for high achievement. Obviously, there are complex causal relationships and interactions between different aspects of the evaluative threat situation and coping mechanisms employed in this situation in determining the final performance.

REFERENCES

Alper, T. G. Memory for completed and incompleted tasks as a function of personality: Correlation between experimental and personality data. *Journal of Personality*, 1948, *17*, 104-137.

Altrocchi, J. Interpersonal perceptions of repressors and sensitizers and component analysis of assumed dissimilarity scores. *Journal of Abnormal and Social Psychology*, 1961, *62*, 528-534.

Averill, J. R. Personal control over aversive stimuli and its relationship to stress. *Psychological Bulletin*, 1973, *80*, 286-303.

Averill, J.R., O'Brien, L., & DeWitt, G. W. The influence of response effectiveness on the preference for warning and on psychophysiological stress reactions. *Journal of Personality*, 1977, *45*, 395-418.

Averill, J. R., & Rosenn, M. Vigilant and nonvigilant coping strategies and psychophysiological stress reactions during the anticipation of electric shock. *Journal of Personality and Social Psychology*, 1972, *23*, 128-141.

Badia, P., Suter, S., & Lewis, P. Preference for warned shock: Information and/or preparation. *Psychological Reports*, 1967, *20*, 271-274.

Ball, T. S., & Vogler, R. E. Uncertain pain and the pain of uncertainty. *Perceptual and Motor Skills*, 1971, *33*, 1195-1203.

Bell, P. A., & Byrne, D. Repression-sensitization. In H. London & J. E. Exner (Eds.), *Dimensions of personality*. New York: Wiley, 1978.

Bergquist, W. H. Short-term memory for word lists of varying contextual constraint as a function of repression-sensitization. *Psychological Reports*, 1972, *30*, 536.

Bergquist, W. H., Lewinsohn, P. M., & Benson, B. Further study of short-term memory for various types of stimuli as a function of repression-sensitization. *Psychological Reports*, 1971, *29*, 1163-1169.

Bergquist, W. H., Lewinsohn, P. M., Sue, D. W., & Flippo, F. R. Short- and long-term memory for various types of stimuli as a function of repression-sensitization. *Journal of Experimental Research in Personality*, 1968, *3*, 28-38.

Bergquist, W. H., Lloyd, J. T., & Johansson, S. L. Individual differences among repressors and sensitizers in conceptual skills. *Social Behavior and Personality*, 1973, *1*, 144-152.

Berlyne, D. E. *Conflict, arousal and curiosity*. New York: McGraw-Hill, 1960.

Bloom, L. J., Houston, B. K., Holmes, D. S., & Burish, T. G. The effectiveness of attentional diversion and situation redefinition for reducing stress due to nonambiguous threat. *Journal of Research in Personality*, 1977, *11*, 83-94.

Brehm, J. W. *A theory of psychological reactance*. New York: Academic Press, 1966.

Breznitz, S. Incubation of threat: Duration of anticipation and false alarm as determinants of the fear reaction to an unavoidable frightening event. *Journal of Experimental Research in Personality*, 1967, *2*, 173-179.

Brim, O. G., & Hoff, D. B. Individual and situational differences in desire for certainty. *Journal of Abnormal and Social Psychology*, 1957, *54*, 225-229.

Bruner, J. S., & Postman, L. Tension and tension release as organizing factors in perception. *Journal of Personality*, 1947, *15*, 300-308.

Byrne, D. The Repression-Sensitization Scale: Rationale, reliability and validity. *Journal of Personality*, 1961, *29*, 334-349.

Byrne, D. Repression-sensitization as a dimension of personality. In B. A. Maher (Ed.), *Progress in experimental personality research* (Vol. 1). New York: Academic Press, 1964.

Byrne, D., Barry, J., & Nelson, D. Relation of the revised Repression-Sensitization Scale to measures of self-description. *Psychological Reports*, 1963, *13*, 323-334.

Chodoff, P., Friedman, S. B., & Hamburg, D. A. Stress, defenses and coping behavior: Observations in parents of children with malignant disease. *American Journal of Psychiatry*, 1964, *120*, 743-749.

Clark, L. F., & Neuringer, C. Repressor-sensitizer personality styles and associated levels of verbal ability, social intelligence, sex knowledge, and quantitative ability. *Journal of Consulting and Clinical Psychology*, 1971, *36*, 183-188.

Cohen, F., & Lazarus, R. S. Active coping processes, coping dispositions, and recovery from surgery. *Psychosomatic Medicine*, 1973, *35*, 375-389.

Cook, J. O., & Barnes, L. W. Choice of delay of inevitable shock. *Journal of Abnormal and Social Psychology*, 1964, *68*, 669-672.

Cornsweet, D. *Use of cues in the visual periphery under conditions of arousal.* Unpublished doctoral dissertation, University of California, Berkeley, 1964.

D'Amato, M. R. Derived motives. *Annual Review of Psychology*, 1974, *25*, 83-106.

D'Amato, M. R., & Gumenik, W. E. Some effects of immediate versus randomly delayed shock on an instrumental response and cognitive processes. *Journal of Abnormal and Social Psychology*, 1960, *60*, 64-67.

deCharms, R. *Personal causation: The internal affective determinants of behavior.* New York: Academic Press, 1968.

Dublin, J. E. Perception of and reaction to ambiguity by repressors and sensitizers: A construct-validity study. *Journal of Consulting and Clinical Psychology*, 1968, *32*, 198-205.

Easterbrook, J. A. The effect of emotion on cue utilization and the organization of behavior. *Psychological Review*, 1959, *66*, 183-201.

Ekehammar, B., Magnusson, D., & Ricklander, L. An interactionist approach to the study of anxiety. *Scandinavian Journal of Psychology*, 1974, *15*, 4-14.

Endler, N. S. A person-situation interaction model for anxiety. In C. D. Spielberger & I. G. Sarason (Eds.), *Stress and anxiety* (Vol. 1). Washington, DC: Hemisphere, 1975.

Endler, N. S., Hunt, J. McV., & Rosenstein, A. J. An S-R inventory of anxiousness. *Psychological Monographs*, 1962, *76* (17, Whole No. 536).

Endler, N. S., & Okada, M. A. A multidimensional measure of trait anxiety: The S-R Inventory of General Trait Anxiousness. *Journal of Consulting and Clinical Psychology*, 1975, *43*, 319-329.

Epstein, S. Toward a unified theory of anxiety. In B. A. Maher (Ed.), *Progress in experimental personality research* (Vol. 4). New York: Academic Press, 1967.

Epstein, S. The nature of anxiety with emphasis upon its relationship to expectancy. In C. D. Spielberger (Ed.), *Anxiety: Current trends in theory and research* (Vol. 2). New York: Academic Press, 1972.

Eriksen, C. W. Perceptual defense as a function of unacceptable needs. *Journal of Abnormal and Social Psychology*, 1951, *46*, 557-564. (a)

Eriksen, C. W. Some implications for TAT interpretation arising from need and perception experiments. *Journal of Personality*, 1951, *19*, 282-288. (b)

Eriksen, C. W. Defense against ego-threat in memory and perception. *Journal of Abnormal and Social Psychology*, 1952, *47*, 230-235. (a)

Eriksen, C. W. Individual differences in defensive forgetting. *Journal of Experimental Psychology*, 1952, *44*, 442-447. (b)

Eriksen, C. W. Psychological defenses and "ego strength" in the recall of completed and incompleted tasks. *Journal of Abnormal and Social Psychology*, 1954, *49*, 45-50. (a)

Eriksen, C. W. Some personality correlates of stimulus generalization under stress. *Journal of Abnormal and Social Psychology*, 1954, *49*, 561-565. (b)

Eriksen, C. W. Cognitive responses to internally cued anxiety. In C. D. Spielberger (Ed.), *Anxiety and behavior.* New York: Academic Press, 1966.

Eriksen, C. W., & Browne, C. T. An experimental and theoretical analysis of perceptual defense. *Journal of Abnormal and Social Psychology*, 1956, *52*, 224-230.

Eriksen, C. W., & Davids, A. The meaning and clinical validity of the Taylor Anxiety Scale and the hysteria-psychasthenia scales from the MMPI. *Journal of Abnormal and Social Psychology*, 1955, *50*, 135-137.

Fenz, W. D., & Epstein, S. Gradients of physiological arousal in parachutists as a function of an approaching jump. *Psychosomatic Medicine*, 1967, *29*, 33-51.

Freud, A. *The ego and the mechanisms of defense.* New York: International Universities Press, 1946.

Freud, S. Hemmung, Symptom und Angst. In S. Freud, *Gesammelte Werke* (Vol. 14). London: Imago, 1940–1942. (First published in 1926.)

Fulkerson, S. C. Individual differences in reaction to failure-induced stress. *Journal of Abnormal and Social Psychology,* 1960, *60,* 136–139.

Furedy, J. J. An integrative progress report on informational control in humans: Some laboratory findings and methodological claims. *Australian Journal of Psychology,* 1975, *27,* 61–83.

Furedy, J. J., & Doob, A. N. Signaling unmodifiable shocks: Limits on human informational cognitive control. *Journal of Personality and Social Psychology,* 1972, *21,* 111–115.

Glass, D. C., & Singer, J. E. *Urban stress: Experiments on noise and social stressors.* New York: Academic Press, 1972.

Glass, D. C., Singer, J. E., & Friedman, L. N. Psychic cost of adaptation to an environmental stressor. *Journal of Personality and Social Psychology,* 1969, *12,* 200–210.

Goldstein, M. J. The relationship between coping and avoiding behavior and response to fear-arousing propaganda. *Journal of Abnormal and Social Psychology,* 1959, *58,* 247–252.

Golin, S., Herron, E. W., Lakota, R., & Reineck, L. Factor analytic study of the manifest anxiety, extraversion, and repression-sensitization scales. *Journal of Consulting Psychology,* 1967, *31,* 564–569.

Gordon, J. E. Interpersonal predictions of repressers and sensitizers. *Journal of Personality,* 1957, *25,* 686–698.

Haggard, E. A. Experimental studies in affective processes: I. Some effects of cognitive structuring and active participation on certain autonomic reactions during and following experimentally induced stress. *Journal of Experimental Psychology,* 1943, *33,* 257–284.

Hare, R. D. Denial of threat and emotional response to impending painful stimulation. *Journal of Consulting Psychology,* 1966, *30,* 359–361.

Heckhausen, H. Fear of failure as a self-reinforcing motive system. In I. G. Sarason & C. D. Spielberger (Eds.), *Stress and anxiety* (Vol. 2). Washington, DC: Hemisphere, 1975.

Holmes, D. S. Investigations of repression: Differential recall of material experimentally or naturally associated with ego threat. *Psychological Bulletin,* 1974, *81,* 632–653.

Holmes, D. S., & Houston, B. K. Effectiveness of situation redefinition and affective isolation in coping with stress. *Journal of Personality and Social Psychology,* 1974, *29,* 212–218.

Houston, B. K. Trait and situational denial and performance under stress. *Journal of Personality and Social Psychology,* 1971, *18,* 289–293.

Houston, B. K. Dispositional anxiety and the effectiveness of cognitive coping strategies in stressful laboratory and classroom situations. In C. D. Spielberger & I. G. Sarason (Eds.), *Stress and anxiety* (Vol. 4). Washington, DC: Hemisphere, 1977.

Houston, B. K., & Hodges, W. F. Situational denial and performance under stress. *Journal of Personality and Social Psychology,* 1970, *16,* 726–730.

Houston, B. K., & Holmes, D. S. Effect of avoidant thinking and reappraisal for coping with threat involving temporal uncertainty. *Journal of Personality and Social Psychology,* 1974, *30,* 382–388.

Hull, C. L. *Principles of behavior.* New York: Appleton-Century-Crofts, 1943.

Hull, C. L. *A behavior system.* New Haven, CT: Yale University Press, 1952.

Janis, I. L. *Psychological stress.* New York: Wiley, 1958.

Jones, A., Bentler, P. M., & Petry, G. The reduction of uncertainty concerning future pain. *Journal of Abnormal Psychology,* 1966, *71,* 87–94.

Kalveram, K. T. Über Faktorenanalyse: Kritik eines theoretischen Konzepts und seine mathematische Neuformulierung. *Arehiv für Psychologie,* 1970, *122,* 92–118.

Kelley, G. A. *The psychology of personal constructs.* New York: Norton, 1955. 2 vols.

Kendall, P. C. Anxiety: States, traits—situations? *Journal of Consulting and Clinical Psychology,* 1978, *46,* 280–287.

Kirschenbaum, D. S., & Karoly, P. When self-regulation fails: Tests of some preliminary hypotheses. *Journal of Consulting and Clinical Psychology,* 1977, *45,* 1116–1125.

Krohne, H. W. Untersuchungen mit einer deutschen Form der Repression-Sensitization Skala. *Zeitschrift für Klinische Psychologie,* 1974, *3,* 238–260.

Krohne, H. W. *Angst und Angstverarbeitung.* Stuttgart: Kohlhammer, 1975.

Krohne, H. W. *Theorien zur Angst.* Stuttgart: Kohlhammer, 1976.
Krohne, H. W. Persönlichkeitstheorie. In T. Herrmann, P. R. Hofstätter, H. P. Huber, & F. E. Weinert (Eds.), *Handbuch psychologischer Grundbegriffe.* Munich: Kösel, 1977.
Krohne, H. W. Individual differences in coping with stress and anxiety. In C. D. Speilberger & I. G. Sarason (Eds.), *Stress and anxiety* (Vol. 5). Washington, DC: Hemisphere, 1978.
Krohne, H. W. Parental child-rearing behavior and the development of anxiety and coping strategies in children. In I. G. Sarason & C. D. Spielberger (Eds.), *Stress and anxiety* (Vol. 7). Washington, DC: Hemisphere, 1980.
Krohne, H. W., & Hudson, J. R. *Art der Angstverarbeitung und Leistungen bei verschiedenen Typen von Problemlöseaufgaben.* Psychologische Forschungsberichte aus dem Fachbereich 3 der Universität Osnabrück. No. 11. Osnabrück, 1979.
Krohne, H. W., & Schroder, H. M. Anxiety defense and complex information processing. *Archiv für Psychologie,* 1972, *124,* 50–61.
Lacey, J. I., Kagan, J., Lacey, B. C., & Moss, H. A. The visceral level: Situational determinants and behavioral correlates of autonomic response patterns. In P. H. Knapp (Ed.), *Expressions of emotions in man.* New York: International Universities Press, 1963.
Lanzetta, J. T., & Driscoll, J. M. Preference for information about an uncertain but unavoidable outcome. *Journal of Personality and Social Psychology,* 1966, *3,* 96–102.
Lazarus, R. S. *Psychological stress and the coping process.* New York: McGraw-Hill, 1966.
Lazarus, R. S. Cognitive and coping processes in emotion. In B. Weiner (Ed.), *Cognitive views of human motivation.* New York: Academic Press, 1974.
Lazarus, R. S., & Averill, J. R. Emotion and cognition: With special reference to anxiety. In C. D. Spielberger (Ed.), *Anxiety: Current trends in theory and research* (Vol. 2). New York: Academic Press, 1972.
Lazarus, R. S., Averill, J. R., & Opton, E. M. The psychology of coping: Issues of research and assessment. In G. V. Coelho, D. M. Hamburg, & J. E. Adams (Eds.), *Coping and adaptation.* New York: Basic Books, 1974.
Lazarus, R. S., Eriksen, C. W., & Fonda, C. P. Personality dynamics and auditory perceptual recognition. *Journal of Personality,* 1951, *19,* 471–482.
Lazarus, R. S., & Launier, R. Stress-related transactions between person and environment. In L. A. Pervin & M. Lewis (Eds.), *Perspectives in interactional psychology.* New York: Plenum, 1980.
Levine, M., & Spivack, G. *The Rorschach Index of Repressive Style.* Springfield, IL: Thomas, 1964.
Liebert, R. M., & Morris, L. W. Cognitive and emotional components of test anxiety: A distinction and some initial data. *Psychological Reports.* 1967, *20,* 975–978.
Lomont, J. F. The repression-sensitization dimension in relation to anxiety responses. *Journal of Consulting Psychology,* 1965, *29,* 84–86.
Maltzman, I., & Wolff, C. Preference for immediate versus delayed noxious stimulation and the concomitant GSR. *Journal of Experimental Psychology,* 1970, *83,* 76–79.
Mandler, G., & Sarason, S. B. A study of anxiety and learning. *Journal of Abnormal and Social Psychology,* 1952, *47,* 166–173.
Markowitz, A. Influence of the repression-sensitization dimension, affect value, and ego threat on incidental learning. *Journal of Personality and Social Psychology,* 1969, *11,* 374–380.
Mechanic, D. *Students under stress.* New York: The Free Press of Glencoe, 1962.
Meichenbaum, D. *Cognitive-behavior modification: An integrative approach.* New York: Plenum Press, 1977.
Mendelsohn, G. A., & Griswold, B. B. Anxiety and repression as predictors of the use of incidental cues in problem solving. *Journal of Personality and Social Psychology,* 1967, *6,* 353–359.
Miller, N. E. Learnable drives and rewards. In S. S. Stevens (Ed.), *Handbook of experimental psychology.* New York: Wiley, 1951.
Mineka, S., & Kihlstrom, J. F. Unpredictable and uncontrollable events: A new perspective on experimental neurosis. *Journal of Abnormal Psychology,* 1978, *87,* 256–271.
Mischel, W. *Personality and assessment.* New York: Wiley, 1968.
Mischel, W. Toward a cognitive social learning reconceptualization of personality. *Psychological Review,* 1973, *80,* 252–283.
Monat, A. Temporal uncertainty, anticipation time, and cognitive coping under threat. *Journal of Human Stress,* 1976, *2*(2), 32–43.

Monat, A., Averill, J. R., & Lazarus, R. S. Anticipatory stress and coping reactions under various conditions of uncertainty. *Journal of Personality and Social Psychology*, 1972, *24*, 237–253.

Morris, L. W., & Fulmer, R. S. Test anxiety (worry and emotionality) changes during academic testing as a function of feedback and test importance. *Journal of Educational Psychology*, 1976, *68*, 817–824.

Morris, L. W., & Liebert, R. M. Relationship of cognitive emotional components of test anxiety to physiological arousal and academic performance. *Journal of Consulting and Clinical Psychology*, 1970, *35*, 332–333.

Mowrer, O. H. *Learning theory and personality dynamics*. New York: Ronald, 1950.

Mowrer, O. H. *Learning theory and behavior*. New York: Wiley, 1960.

Nalven, F. B. Some perceptual decision making correlates of repressive and intellectualizing defenses. *Journal of Clinical Psychology*, 1967, *23*, 446–448.

Niemelä, P. Coping patterns in shock anticipation and in everyday stress. *Scandinavian Journal of Psychology*, 1974, *15*, 268–272.

Perkins, C. C. An analysis of the concept of reinforcement. *Psychological Review*, 1968, *75*, 155–172.

Rothbart, M., & Mellinger, M. Attention and responsivity to remote dangers: A laboratory simulation for assessing reactions to threatening events. *Journal of Personality and Social Psychology*, 1972, *24*, 132–142.

Sarason, I. G. Anxiety and self-preoccupation. In I. G. Sarason & C. D. Spielberger (Eds.), *Stress and anxiety* (Vol. 2). Washington, DC: Hemisphere, 1975.

Sarason, I. G., & Stoops, R. Test anxiety and the passage of time. *Journal of Consulting and Clinical Psychology*, 1978, *46*, 102–109.

Seligman, M. E. P. *Helplessness: On depression, development, and death*. San Francisco: Freeman, 1975.

Spence, J. T., & Spence, K. W. The motivational components of manifest anxiety: Drive and drive stimuli. In C. D. Spielberger (Ed.), *Anxiety and behavior*. New York: Academic Press, 1966.

Spence, K. W. A theory of emotionally based drive (D) and its relation to performance in simple learning situations. *American Psychologist*, 1958, *13*, 131–141.

Spence, K. W., & Taylor, J. A. Anxiety and strength of UCS as determiners of amount of eyelid conditioning. *Journal of Experimental Psychology*, 1951, *42*, 183–188.

Spielberger, C. D. Theory and research on anxiety. In C. D. Spielberger (Ed.), *Anxiety and behavior*. New York: Academic Press, 1966.

Spielberger, C. D., Gonzales, H. P., Taylor, C. J., Algaze, B., & Anton, W. D. Examination stress and test anxiety. In C. D. Spielberger & I. G. Sarason (Eds.), *Stress and anxiety* (Vol. 5). Washington, DC: Hemisphere, 1978.

Staub, E., & Kellett, D. S. Increasing pain tolerance by information about aversive stimuli. *Journal of Personality and Social Psychology*, 1972, *21*, 198–203.

Steiner, I. D. Perceived freedom. In L. Berkowitz (Ed.), *Advances in experimental social psychology* (Vol. 5). New York: Academic Press, 1970.

Streufert, S., & Driver, M. J. Impression formation as a measure of the complexity of the conceptual structure. *Educational and Psychological Measurement*, 1967, *27*, 1025–1039.

Taylor, J. A. Drive theory and manifest anxiety. *Psychological Bulletin*, 1956, *53*, 303–320.

Truax, C. B. The repression response to implied failure as a function of the hysteria-psychasthenia index. *Journal of Abnormal and Social Psychology*, 1957, *55*, 188–193.

Ullmann, L. P. Clinical correlates of facilitation and inhibition of response to emotional stimuli. *Journal of Projective Techniques and Personality Assessment*, 1958, *22*, 341–347.

Vagt, G., & Kühn, B. Zum Zusammenhang zwischen Ängstlichkeit und Schulleistung: Die Berücksichtigung des Ausmasses der häuslichen Vorbereitung auf schulische Prüfungssituationen. *Zeitschrift für experimentelle und angewandte Psychologie*, 1976, *23*, 163–173.

Weiner, B. *Theories of motivation: From mechanism to cognition*. Chicago: Markham, 1972.

Weiss, J. M. Effects of coping behavior in different warning signal conditions on stress pathology in rats. *Journal of Comparative and Physiological Psychology*, 1971, *77*, 1–13.

Weissman, H. N., & Ritter, K. Openness to experience, ego strength and self-description as a function of repression and sensitization. *Psychological Reports*, 1970, *26*, 859–864.

Welsh, G. S. Factor dimensions A and R. In G. S. Welsh & W. G. Dahlstrom (Eds.), *Basic readings on the MMPI in psychology and medicine*. Minneapolis: University of Minnesota Press, 1956.

White, R. W. Motivation reconsidered: The concept of competence. *Psychological Review*, 1959, *66*, 297-333.

Wine, J. Test anxiety and direction of attention. *Psychological Bulletin*, 1971, *76*, 92-104.

Zeller, A. An experimental analogue of repression: II. The effect of individual failure and success on memory measured by relearning. *Journal of Experimental Psychology*, 1950, *40*, 411-422.

REFERENCE NOTES

1. Lazarus, R. S. *The stress and coping paradigm*. Paper presented at the conference on "The Critical Evaluation of Behavioral Paradigms for Psychiatric Science," Glenedan Beach, Oregon, November 1978.
2. Schaffner, P., Krohne, H. W., & Seveker, W. *Zusammenhänge zwischen Angst, Angstverarbeitung, kognitiver Interferenz and Leistung*, in preparation.

9

Trait Anxiety and Cognitive Coping Behavior

B. Kent Houston
University of Kansas

In recent years there has been considerable interest in trait anxiety (Spielberger, 1975) and in cognitive coping behaviors (Krohne, 1978; Lazarus, Averill, & Opton, 1974), though little attention has been given to the relation between trait anxiety and cognitive coping behaviors. The question to be examined here is whether high-trait-anxious and low-trait-anxious individuals differ with respect to the cognitive coping behavior they exhibit in stressful situations. The answer to this question may have not only theoretical significance but implications for treatment as well.

For the purposes of this paper, the following terms are defined as indicated. *Stress* is any one or a combination of negative emotional states (e.g., apprehension, anger, depression, etc.). Such states are regarded as being negative in that people typically prefer to avoid or reduce experiencing them. *Coping* refers to avoiding or reducing stress. A *cognitive coping maneuver* or *strategy* is an organized cognitive coping response or set of cognitive coping responses. The term *cognitive coping behavior* is used to indicate that in the course of the paper, reference is made not only to cognitive coping strategies but also to stress-induced cognitive responses whose coping function is unclear (e.g., worry or preoccupation) and to the absence of cognitive coping strategies in situations in which such strategies are appropriate.

On the basis of clinical evaluations and/or intercorrelations of MMPI scales, Deese, Lazarus, and Keenan (1953) and Eriksen and Davids (1955) suggest that high-trait-anxious individuals are characterized by the use of intellectualization and rationalization for cognitively coping with stress, whereas low-trait-anxious individuals are characterized by the use of repression and other cognitive avoidance maneuvers. Another viewpoint is that high-trait-anxious individuals fail to employ or lack cognitive maneuvers for coping with stress (Silverman & Blitz, 1956). Yet another position is that high-trait (test)-anxious individuals, whether or not they lack cognitive meneuvers for coping with stress, habitually respond cognitively to stressful situations by being self-preoccupied (Sarason, 1975; Wine, chapter 10 in this book).

Two studies were conducted in an attempt to shed light on these diverse views. In one study the relationship between trait anxiety and cognitive behaviors for coping with stress was investigated (Houston, 1977). In a second study, the authors investigated whether experimentally reducing trait anxiety would predictably change individuals' cognitive coping behaviors (Hutchings, Denney, Basgall, & Houston, Note 1).[1]

STUDY I

In the first study the relationship between trait anxiety and cognitive coping behaviors was investigated in two stress situations: a laboratory situation in which stress was generated by telling subjects that avoidance of shock was contingent upon good performance on a memory task, and a classroom situation in which stress was generated by students' taking the final examination in one of their college courses. Even though the two situations differed in setting (laboratory vs. classroom), they were similar in that negative consequences for poor performance were anticipated in both (failure and physical shock in the laboratory setting, and failure and other ramifications of poor performance in the classroom setting). The reason for investigating two stress situations was to evaluate the consistency of findings across different stress situations.

In both situations the cognitive coping behaviors with which a subject coped, or failed to cope, with the stressful aspects of the situation were inferred from a post-experimental questionnaire by two judges. (See Table 1 for the list of cognitive coping behaviors that were considered.) Then a judgment was made for each subject concerning which one of the cognitive coping behaviors appeared to predominate. Trait anxiety scores were also obtained from the subjects, and biserial correlations were computed between subjects' trait anxiety scores and presence or absence of the various cognitive coping behaviors. A cognitive coping behavior was regarded as

[1] The first study was supported by Biomedical Sciences Support Grant RR07037 to B. K. Houston. The second study was supported by University of Kansas General Research allocations #3129-x038 to Douglas R. Denney and #3293-x038 to B. K. Houston. Thanks are due to David S. Holmes and Claire Selzer for the helpful comments on the manuscript.

TABLE 1   Categories of Cognitive Behavior for Coping or Not Coping with Stress

Category	Description of cognitive behavior
Intellectualization	Taking analytic or intellectual orientation toward stressful aspects of the situation or whole situation in general
Isolation	Taking detached or indifferent attitude toward stressful aspects of the situation or whole situation in general
Denial	Not regarding the situation as stressful
Rationalization	Providing plausible reasons why potentially stressful aspects of the situation should not be regarded as upsetting
Reversal of affect	Reacting with positive affect toward potentially stressful aspects of the situation or whole situation in general
Supplementary projection	Projecting negative emotions, not acknowledged by self, onto others
Complementary projection	Projecting malevolence onto the experimenter
Active mastery	Trying hard to do well on the task
Resignation	Patiently enduring or submitting to the experience
Avoidant thinking	Thinking about things not relevant to the stressful and/or task-relevant aspects of the situation
Search for strategy	Alternating between or intermittently using coping strategies
Lack of strategy	Not attempting to employ a cognitive strategy nor obsessing about the situation
Preoccupation	Ruminating about various aspects of the stressful experience

"present" if it was the predominant behavior, and it was regarded as "absent" if it was not the predominant behavior.

In the laboratory setting the trait anxiety scores obtained were from the State-Trait Anxiety Inventory (Spielberger, Gorsuch, & Lushene, 1970), and in the classroom setting they were the debilitating anxiety scores from the Achievement Anxiety Test (Alpert & Haber, 1960). The Achievement Anxiety Test was employed for the classroom situation rather than the trait form of the State-Trait Anxiety Inventory because measures of test anxiety have been found to be more appropriate to test situations than are measures of general anxiety (Alpert & Haber, 1960; Sarason. 1957).

Results

Results from the laboratory situation indicated that the manipulation of stress was successful. Subjects in the threat of shock condition (121 males) reported significantly more anxiety and manifested significantly higher pulse rates than subjects in a nonthreat, control condition (20 males).

Biserial correlations computed between subjects' trait anxiety scores and the presence or absence of each cognitive coping behavior revealed that higher trait anxiety scores were associated with:

1. Lack of strategy ($r_b = +.16, p < .05$)
2. Preoccupation ($r_b = +.15, p < .10$)
3. Not using intellectualization ($r_b = -.18, p < .05$).

Although it sounds undesirable for trait anxiety to be associated with the cognitive coping behaviors described above, it is important to know whether preoccupation, lack of strategy, and not using intellectualization is indeed maladaptive. An analysis for the threat condition of the relationship between cognitive coping behaviors and scores for self-report of anxiety and pulse rate revealed that both lack of strategy and preoccupation (referred to as "worry" in Houston, 1977) were generally associated with greater stress response than the other cognitive coping behaviors and therefore may be regarded as being maladaptive. In addition, use of intellectualization was found to be related to less-stress response, so, by inference, not using intellectualization could be maladaptive depending on what other cognitive coping strategies were used instead. Since high-trait-anxious subjects were likely to be preoccupied and lack cognitive coping maneuvers, not using intellectualization was maladaptive for them.

Results from the classroom situation revealed that the subjects (33 males and 51 females) reported significantly more anxiety at the time of the examination than during a nonstressful time of the semester several weeks earlier, suggesting that indeed the final examination was stressful.

Biserial correlations computed between subjects' debilitating anxiety scores and the presence or absence of each cognitive coping behavior revealed that higher debilitating anxiety was associated with preoccupation, ($r_b = +.27, p < .01$). Furthermore, an analysis of the relationship between cognitive coping behaviors and scores for the examination and self-report of anxiety revealed that preoccupation was generally associated with greater stress response than the other cognitive coping behaviors. Thus preoccupation may be regarded as maladaptive.

Discussion

Both measures of trait anxiety (the trait form of the State-Trait Anxiety Inventory and the debilitating anxiety scale) were related to cognitive coping behaviors. The higher individuals scored on these measures, the more they tended to respond with maladaptive cognitive coping behavior (viz., being preoccupied). In addition, in the laboratory situation the higher the individuals' trait anxiety scores, the more they tended to lack organized ways of coping with stress as indicated by lower frequency of use of intellectualization and greater overall lack of strategy.

The consistency of findings concerning trait anxiety and preoccupation increases confidence about the generalizability of this relationship to other stressful situations. The failure in the classroom situation to find a significant relation between trait anxiety and either lack of strategy or intellectualization is disconcerting, though it may have been due to one or more technical reasons: (1) fewer subjects were used in the classroom than the laboratory situation, thus making it more difficult to demonstrate significant relationships; (2) a group rather than an individual procedure was used in the classroom situation to obtain information relevant to coping behavior during the stressful experience, which may have reduced the fidelity of the information obtained; and the like.

Taken together the results from the two situations suggest that highly trait-anxious individuals tend to lack organized ways of coping with stress and instead ruminate about themselves and the situation in which they find themselves. These general findings are congruent with both the perspective that high-anxious individuals tend to be preoccupied in stressful situations (cf. Sarason, 1975; Wine, chapter 10 in this book) and the perspective that such individuals lack cognitive maneuvers for coping with stress (cf. Silverman & Blitz, 1956). Further, these findings, particularly from the laboratory situation, are contrary to the expectation concerning highly trait-anxious individuals derived from Deese, Lazarus, and Keenan (1953) and Eriksen and Davids (1955). Specifically, it was found that the higher the subject's trait anxiety score, the less likely he was to employ intellectualization; and in neither study was a relation found between trait anxiety scores and measures of either rationalization or cognitive avoidance maneuvers.

STUDY II

The results of the first study must be regarded as encouraging though tentative because the observed relation between trait anxiety and cognitive coping may be spurious; that is, triat anxiety and cognitive coping may in fact not be directly related, rather both may be related to a common, third variable. One way to corroborate that trait anxiety and cognitive coping behavior are indeed related is to experimentally change people's trait anxiety and then determine whether there is a predictable change in their cognitive coping behaviors. The approach of the second study, then, was to investigate the effect on high trait anxiety and cognitive coping behaviors of interventions that might be expected to reduce trait anxiety and that do not focus on cognitive coping behaviors. The two interventions chosen for study were applied relaxation and Anxiety Management Training.

In applied relaxation (Goldfried, 1971), individuals are taught to use relaxation as an active response for coping with anxiety-provoking situations. Individuals receive intensive training in relaxation, and additional instructions and discussions are devoted to the application of relaxation as a coping skill outside the context of treatment. Since several investigations have shown applied relaxation to be effective in reducing specific trait anxieties, namely test anxiety (Chang-Liang & Denney, 1976; Russell, Wise, & Stratoudakis, 1976) and speech anxiety (Goldfried & Trier, 1974; Russell & Wise, 1976; Zeisset, 1968), it seems reasonable to expect that it would reduce general trait anxiety, although no published study reports on its effectiveness for this purpose.

Anxiety Management Training (AMT; Suinn & Richardson, 1971) bears many similarities to applied relaxation. Individuals are taught to use relaxation as an active response for coping with anxiety-provoking situations. Similar to applied relaxation, individuals are trained in relaxation and are given assistance and encouragement for applying relaxation as a coping skill in actual anxiety-provoking settings. However, AMT also includes rehearsal of the use of relaxation skills for coping with anxiety within the treatment setting. Clients are asked to visualize anxiety-provoking scenes, experience the anxiety associated with the scene, and then apply their relaxation coping skills to reduce their anxiety. Again similar to applied relaxation, since several investigations have shown AMT to be effective in reducing specific trait anxieties, namely test anxiety (Suinn & Richardson, 1971) and speech anxiety (Nicoletti, 1972), it seems reasonable to expect that it would reduce general trait anxiety, although again no published study reports on its effectiveness for this purpose. (Two dissertations, however, Nicoletti, 1972, and Edie, 1972, indicate that AMT may be useful for reducing chronic anxiety.)

To the extent that rehearsal of coping skills would be expected to be beneficial, AMT could be expected to be more effective in reducing trait anxiety than applied relaxation. One of the purposes of this study then was to investigate this possibility. Thus the study had two major purposes. One was to investigate whether applied relaxation and AMT were more effective than placebo and relaxation-only conditions in reducing high trait anxiety and changing highly trait-anxious individuals' cognitive coping behaviors. The second purpose was to compare the relative effectiveness of applied relaxation and AMT in accomplishing these changes. Considering the results of the first study reported here, it was expected that an intervention that was effective in reducing high trait anxiety should also reduce highly trait-anxious subjects' tendencies to be preoccupied and/or to lack coping strategies in stressful situations. It should be noted that neither applied relaxation nor AMT deal with *cognitive* coping behaviors. Rather they focus on relaxation, ostensibly a somatic response, as coping behavior.

Method

The Taylor Manifest Anxiety Scale (TMAS; Taylor, 1953) and the Neuroticism Scale of the Eysenck Personality Inventory (Eysenck, 1968) were administered to approximately 800 students enrolled in general psychology at the University of Kansas. Sixty-three high-trait-anxious subjects who scored in the upper 15% of the distribution of scores on each scale were selected to participate in the study. (The reason for employing the Neuroticism Scale in addition to a measure of trait anxiety, namely, the TMAS, was to provide for the selection of neurotically inclined high-trait-anxious subjects.) These subjects were randomly assigned to AMT ($n = 14$), applied relaxation ($n = 10$), relaxation-only ($n = 10$), placebo ($n = 14$), and untreated control ($n = 15$) conditions. The subjects in each of the four treatment conditions were further assigned to one of two treatment groups, composed of 5 to 8 subjects. Each treatment group was led by one of two experimenters, a male or a female graduate student in clinical psychology, and received a total of six 1-hour treatment sessions.

Subjects in the AMT and the applied relaxation groups received the procedures described earlier, with AMT consisting of training in relaxation, instructions regarding its application, and structured rehearsal; and applied relaxation consisting of training in relaxation and instructions regarding its application but no structured rehearsal. Subjects in the relaxation-only groups were trained in relaxation using the same audiotapes employed in the AMT and applied relaxation groups. Unlike AMT and applied relaxation subjects, who had been given a rationale concerning their treatment that emphasized the need for actively employing relaxation as a coping response, relaxation-only subjects were given a passive rationale indicating that relaxation would automatically supplant anxiety as the subject continued in relaxation training. Subjects in the placebo condition were shown videotaped programs dealing with topics such as depression, hostility, and sexuality, and were told that subliminal frames containing a variety of anxiety-provoking stimuli had been implanted in the tapes. Although these frames were not perceptible at a conscious level, they purportedly would serve to "unconsciously extinguish" the subject's anxiety. (In actuality no such subliminal frames had been included.) Measures concerning expectancy for change were administered after the first and second treatment sessions for subjects in these four treatment conditions. Subjects in the untreated control condition provided information on the same outcome measures (described below) as subjects in the other conditions, but they received no intervening treatment.

All subjects completed the trait form of the State-Trait Anxiety Inventory at a session conducted one week before the start of treatment and a session one week after termination of treatment. (Additional measures were obtained at these times that, however, are not germane to the purposes here and will be reported separately.)

Two weeks after termination of treatment, all subjects were individually scheduled for a laboratory session, the purpose of which was to see how subjects in the different conditions coped with and physiologically and affectively responded to a stressful situation. The laboratory session was described to the subjects as merely an opportunity to measure their physiological responses.

The laboratory session, somewhat similar to the laboratory stress situation in the first study, was divided into four periods: base, assessment of limit for digits backward, first performance, and second performance. During the base level period, initial levels of four physiological measures were obtained: pulse rate, finger pulse volume, skin resistance, and blood pressure. In addition a base level measure of anxiety was obtained by having subjects fill out the Today form of the Affect Adjective Check List (AACL, Zuckerman, 1960) by checking those words that described how they felt at that moment.

After completing the AACL, the Digits Backward Test from the Wechsler Adult Intelligence Scale (WAIS) was given with standard instructions (Wechsler, 1955, p. 41). Each subject was given digit series of increasing length until reaching his or her own limit, defined as the level at which he or she failed two successive series of a specified number of digits. Then the subject was given two practice sets of digits, each set containing one less digit than his or her limit. (For example, if a person's limit had been seven digits, he or she would be given sets containing six digits to repeat.) While determining a subject's limit for repeating digits backward, the manual for the WAIS was prominently displayed to impress upon the subjects the importance of the task.

During the first performance period the subject was given six more sets of digits to repeat that were each one digit less than his or her limit. The number of sets the subject correctly repeated out of the six constituted his or her digits backward score for the first performance period. Following this, stress-inducing instructions were given all subjects except seven subjects in the placebo and six subjects in the untreated control conditions who were assigned to a nonstress condition. The purpose of the nonstress condition was to allow an opportunity to check on the effectiveness of the stress manipulation.

Each subject receiving the stress-inducing instructions was told that although he was not doing too badly, he could do better and that other students seemed to have done better than he had done. These instructions had been successfully employed by Hodges (1968) in an experiment to induce stress in high-trait-anxious individuals. In the nonstress condition the subject was merely told that the experimenter would give him or her more digits like the ones that he or she had just been doing.

During the second performance period all subjects were given six more sets of digits of the same length as in the first performance period. The number of sets the subject correctly repeated out of the six constituted his or her digits backward score for the second performance period. At the conclusion of this period, subjects who had received the stress instructions were given a questionnaire, like the ones used in the first study, asking them to describe their thoughts and feelings about various aspects of the experiment during this last (i.e., second performance) period, which was after they had received the stress-inducing instructions. Subjects' responses to this questionnaire were used to infer the cognitive behaviors by which subjects coped, or failed to cope, with the stressful aspects of the second performance period.

Measures of the four physiological responses (pulse rate, finger pulse volume, skin resistance, and blood pressure) were taken during the period of assessment of limit for digits backward and the two performance periods as well as just after the stress-inducing instructions were delivered between the two performance periods. In addition, AACL measures were obtained (retrospectively) for the assessment of limit for digits backward period, right after delivery of the stress instructions between the two performance periods, and (retrospectively) for the second performance period.

Results and Discussion

Expectancy Measures

Analyses of the three questions contained in the first expectancy measure (given after the first treatment session) and the one question in the second expectancy measure (given after the second treatment session) revealed that there were no significant differences between conditions for three out of four of the questions. However, for one question from the first expectancy measure, subjects in the placebo condition indicated that they expected significantly less improvement than subjects in the other treatment conditions. Thus we were somewhat less successful than anticipated in devising a placebo treatment condition that would consistently generate positive expectancies comparable to those generated by the other treatment conditions. It should be noted, however, that subjects' expectations concerning their treatment in the relaxation-only condition were comparable to those of subjects in the applied relaxation and AMT conditions.

Trait Anxiety

Since base-free measures of change are desirable (Tucker, Damarin, & Messick, 1966), "residualized" posttest scores (cf. Cronbach & Furby, 1970) were derived for the trait anxiety data. A residualized posttest trait anxiety score consisted of the difference between the obtained posttest trait anxiety score and that predicted on the basis of linear regression from the respective pretest score. Preliminary analyses (two therapist-groups by four treatment conditions: AMT, applied relaxation, relaxation-only, and placebo) performed on the residualized posttest trait anxiety scores revealed no significant main effects or interactions involving therapist-group, hence therapist-group was eliminated as a factor in subsequent analyses of the data. The residualized posttest trait anxiety scores were then subjected to a one-way analysis of variance comparing all five experimental conditions (condition means presented in Table 2). This analysis revealed a significant conditions effect, $F(4,58) = 4.37, p < .004$.

Further analyses[2] revealed that subjects in the AMT condition obtained significantly ($p < .05$) lower posttest trait anxiety scores than subjects in the relaxation-only, placebo, and untreated control conditions. Subjects in the applied relaxation condition obtained significantly ($p < .05$) lower posttest trait anxiety scores than subjects in the untreated control condition. There were no significant differences between the remaining three conditions nor between the AMT and applied relaxation conditions.

Laboratory Measures of Stress

All analyses of the AACL and physiological data were performed on residualized scores that were derived in the same fashion as described above. That the stress instructions were effective in inducing stress during the laboratory session was indicated by the following. Subjects in the nonstress condition reported significantly ($p < .05$) less anxiety than subjects in the placebo and relaxation-only condi-

---

[2] Pairwise t tests were used to evaluate differences between means whenever an analysis of variance revealed a significant F. The use of pairwise t tests in this manner has been supported by recent Monte Carlo studies (Bernhardson, 1975; Carmer & Swanson, 1973).

TABLE 2   Mean Residualized Posttest Trait Anxiety Scores for Five
Experimental Conditions

AMT	Applied relaxation	Relaxation only	Placebo	Untreated control
57.86	61.75	63.22	63.91	67.36

Note. Any two means not underlined by the same line differ at least at the .05 level of statistical significance.

tions. In addition, although subjects in the nonstress condition did not differ significantly in their performance from subjects in the other conditions during the first performance period (before the other subjects received the stress-inducing instructions), they performed significantly ($p < .05$) better during the second performance period than subjects in either the placebo or relaxation-only conditions (interaction between treatment conditions and performance periods one and two, F [5,57] = 2.69, $p = .03$). No significant differences, however, were found between nonstress and any of the other treatment conditions on the physiological measures. Although disconcerting the latter finding is not critical because Hodges (1968), who employed the same procedure as was used in the present study, found no significant difference in physiological arousal between his nonstress and false feedback, stress conditions.

To the extent that AMT and/or applied relaxation reduced trait anxiety and possibly changed cognitive coping behaviors, one would expect that subjects in one or both of these conditions would be less upset in the stressful laboratory situation than subjects in the control conditions. With regard to measures reflecting stress response, the analyses revealed the following condition differences. Subjects in the AMT and applied relaxation conditions reported less anxiety than subjects in either the placebo or relaxation-only conditions. These differences were statistically significant ($p < .05$) for the AMT but not for the applied relaxation condition. Subjects in the AMT and applied relaxation conditions performed better during the second performance period than subjects in either the relaxation-only or placebo conditions. These differences were statistically significant ($p < .05$) for the applied relaxation but not for the AMT condition. In general then it appears that subjects in the AMT and applied relaxation conditions were less upset in the stressful laboratory session than subjects in the control conditions. No significant differences, however, were found between any of the conditions for any of the psysiological measures. Since trait anxiety has not been found to be related to physiological measures in previous studies using similar procedures (Hodges, 1968; Houston, 1977), it may not be reasonable to expect an intervention to influence high-trait-anxious individuals' physiological responses to stress.

It should be noted that the untreated control condition did not differ significantly from the AMT, applied relaxation, or nonstress conditions in the comparisons reported above. In other words the subjects in this condition in the laboratory session were not very distressed. The reason for these anomalous results is not clear. Further, this anomaly is not congruent with the other results of the study. Posttest trait anxiety scores were higher in the untreated control condition than in any other condition, significantly higher than in the AMT and applied relaxation conditions (see Table 2). It is possible that after removing six subjects from the untreated control condition to form the nonstress condition for the laboratory session, the small sample size and/or idiosyncracies of the remaining subjects in the untreated control condition precluded attaining statistically significant results.

Coping Behaviors

Since the results of the first study suggested that preoccupation and lack of coping strategies characterized high-trait-anxious subjects in stressful situations, these two characteristic coping behaviors were considered together in evaluating the effect of the interventions on cognitive coping behavior. Thus two raters independently read the postexperimental questionnaires and judged for each subject which of the following two groups of cognitive coping behaviors predominated during the experimental period: (1) preoccupation with self and/or the situation, or lack of strategy for coping with stress; or (2) use of some kind of strategy or strategies for coping with stress. The judgments made by one rater agreed with those made by the other rater for 70% of the subjects, indicating a significant degree of interrater reliability ($p < .02$), and disagreements between the two raters as to which group of coping behaviors had predominated were subsequently resolved by conference. This procedure, then, associated one grouping of cognitive coping behavior (the one judged to have been predominant) with each subject.

Next, the proportion of subjects in a treatment condition for whom preoccupation or lack of strategy had predominated was compared with the proportion of such subjects in every other treatment condition. The results of these comparisons (using tests for independent proportions, McNemar, 1969, pp. 58–63) indicated that the proportion of subjects for whom preoccupation or lack of strategy had predominated was lower in AMT (converting the proportion to percent = 14%) than in applied relaxation (40%, $< .15$), relaxation-only (60%, $< .02$), placebo (57%, $< .05$), and the untreated control (33%, $< .29$). The results also indicated that preoccupation and lack of strategy occurred less frequently for subjects in the applied relaxation condition than in either the relaxation-only or placebo conditions, though none of these comparisons approached statistical significance.

CONCLUSIONS

AMT was found to be significantly more effective than placebo and relaxation-only conditions in reducing high trait anxiety (and state anxiety in the laboratory session) and changing highly trait-anxious individuals' maladaptive cognitive coping behaviors, namely, reducing their preoccupation and lack of coping maneuvers. The results for applied relaxation tended to parallel those for AMT, though considerably fewer statistically significant differences were observed. Although none of the differences between AMT and applied relaxation were statistically significant, the results for AMT were considerably more robust. On the basis of this, one can conclude that AMT is somewhat more effective than applied relaxation. Thus it appears from this study that the provision of structured rehearsal in the recognition and reduction of anxiety during treatment sessions in AMT is a valuable additional component over what is involved in applied relaxation.

Further, by experimentally reducing trait anxiety and witnessing a predicted change in cognitive coping behaviors, one is more confident that highly trait-anxious individuals are indeed characterized by either preoccupation or lack of coping strategies in stressful situations. As was mentioned in the first study, these findings are congruent with Sarason's (1975), Wine's (chapter 10 in this book), and Silverman and Blitz's (1956) views of highly trait-anxious individuals though are contrary to the speculations of Deese, Lazarus, and Keenan (1953) and Eriksen and Davids (1955). The results of the studies presented here suggest that psychological treatments, such as the procedures suggested by Meichenbaum (Meichenbaum, Turk, & Burstein, 1975), that would specifically focus on highly trait-anxious individuals' tendencies to be preoccupied and/or lack cognitive coping strategies under stress may be particularly beneficial. A treatment that added such a focus to the procedures contained in AMT would be expected, then, to be more effective than AMT alone for the treatment of high trait anxiety. This expectation remains to be tested.

REFERENCES

Alpert, R., & Haber, R. N. Anxiety in academic achievement situations. *Journal of Abnormal and Social Psychology*, 1960, *61*, 207-215.

Bernhardson, C. S. Type I error rates when multiple comparison procedures follow a significant *F* test of ANOVA. *Biometrics*, 1975, *31*, 229-232.

Carmer, S. G., & Swanson, M. R. An evaluation of ten pairwise multiple comparison procedures by Monte Carlo methods. *Journal of the American Statistical Association*, 1973, *68*, 66-74.

Chang-Liang, R., & Denney, D. R. Applied relaxation as training in self-control. *Journal of Counseling Psychology*, 1976, *23*, 183-189.

Cronbach, L. J., & Furby, L. How we should measure change—or should we? *Psychological Bulletin*, 1970, *74*, 68-80.

Deese, J., Lazarus, R. S., & Keenan, J. Anxiety, anxiety reduction, and stress in learning. *Journal of Experimental Psychology*, 1953, *46*, 55-60.

Edie, C. *Uses of anxiety management training in treating trait anxiety.* Unpublished doctoral dissertation, Colorado State University, 1972.

Eriksen, C. W., & Davids, A. The meaning and clinical validity of the Taylor anxiety scale and the hysteria-psychastenia scales from the MMPI. *Journal of Abnormal and Social Psychology*, 1955, *50*, 135-137.

Eysenck, H. J. *Eysenck Personality Inventory.* San Diego, CA: Educational and Industrial Testing Service, 1968.

Goldfried, M. R. Systematic desensitization as training in self-control. *Journal of Consulting and Clinical Psychology*, 1971, *37*, 228-234.

Goldfried, M. R., & Trier, C. S. Effectiveness of relaxation as an active coping skill. *Journal of Abnormal Psychology*, 1974, *83*, 348-355.

Hodges, W. F. Effects of ego threat and threat of pain on state anxiety. *Journal of Personality and Social Psychology*, 1968, *8*, 364-372.

Houston, B. K. Dispositional anxiety and the effectiveness of cognitive coping strategies in stressful laboratory and classroom situations. In C. D. Spielberger & I. G. Sarason (Eds.), *Stress and anxiety* (Vol. 4). Washington, DC: Hemisphere, 1977.

Krohne, H. W. Individual differences in coping with stress and anxiety. In C. D. Spielberger & I. G. Sarason (Eds.), *Stress and anxiety* (Vol. 5). Washington, DC: Hemisphere, 1978.

Lazarus, R. S., Averill, J. R., & Opton, E. M., Jr. The psychology of coping: Issues of research and assessment. In G. V. Coelho, D. A. Hamburg, & J. E. Adams (Eds.), *Coping and adaptation.* New York: Basic Books, 1974.

McNemar, Q. *Psychological statistics* (4th ed.). New York: Wiley, 1969.

Meichenbaum, D., Turk, D., & Burstein, S. The nature of coping with stress. In I. G. Sarason & C. D. Spielberger (Eds.), *Stress and anxiety* (Vol. 2). Washington, DC: Hemisphere, 1975.

Nicoletti, J. *Anxiety management training.* Unpublished doctoral dissertation, Colorado State University, 1972.

Russell, R. K., & Wise, F. Treatment of speech anxiety by cue-controlled relaxation and desensitization with professional and paraprofessional counselors. *Journal of Counseling Psychology*, 1976, *23*, 583-586.

Russell, R. K., Wise, F., & Stratoudakis, J. P. Treatment of test anxiety by cue-controlled relaxation and systematic desensitization. *Journal of Counseling Psychology*, 1976, *23*, 563-566.

Sarason, I. G. Test anxiety, general anxiety, and intellectual performance. *Journal of Consulting Psychology*, 1957, *21*, 485-490.

Sarason, I. G. Anxiety and Self-preoccupation. In I. G. Sarason & C. D. Spielberger (Eds.), *Stress and anxiety* (Vol. 2). Washington, DC: Hemisphere, 1975.

Silverman, R. E., & Blitz, B. Learning and two kinds of anxiety. *Journal of Abnormal and Social Psychology*, 1956, *52*, 301-303.

Spielberger, C. D. Anxiety: State-trait-process. In C. D. Spielberger & I. G. Sarason (Eds.), *Stress and anxiety* (Vol. 1). Washington, DC: Hemisphere, 1975.

Spielberger, C. D., Gorsuch, R. L., & Lushene, R. E. *Manual for the State-Trait Anxiety Inventory.* Palo Alto, CA: Consulting Psychologists Press, 1970.

Suinn, R., & Richardson, R. Anxiety management training: A non-specific behavior therapy program for anxiety control. *Behavior Therapy*, 1971, *4*, 498–511.

Taylor, J. A. A personality scale of manifest anxiety. *Journal of Abnormal and Social Psychology*, 1953, *48*, 285–290.

Tucker, L., Damarin, F., & Messick, S. A base-free measure of change. *Psychometrika*, 1966, *31*, 457–473.

Wechsler, D. *Manual for the Wechsler Adult Intelligence Scale.* New York: Psychological Corporation, 1955.

Zeisset, R. M. Desensitization and relaxation in the modificiation of psychiatric patients' interview behavior. *Journal of Abnormal Psychology*, 1968, *73*, 18–24.

Zuckerman, M. The development of an affect adjective checklist for the measurement of anxiety. *Journal of Consulting Psychology*, 1960, *24*, 457–462.

REFERENCE NOTE

1. Hutchings, D., Denney, D. R., Basgall, J., & Houston, B. K. *Anxiety management and applied relaxation in reducing chronic anxiety.* Unpublished manuscript, University of Kansas, 1978.

10

Evaluation Anxiety

A Cognitive-Attentional Construct

Jeri Dawn Wine
Ontario Institute for Studies in Education

The self-report anxiety scale literature has become voluminous since its inception in 1952 with the presentation of the Test Anxiety Questionnaire (TAQ; Mandler & Sarason, 1952) and related validational research (S. B. Sarason, Mandler, & Craighill, 1952), followed shortly by the publication of the Taylor Manifest Anxiety Scale (MAS; 1953). A major reason these scales inspired so much research was that their publication was accompanied by carefully articulated minitheories. In the case of the MAS the theoretical model was derived from Hullian Drive Theory. The MAS was intended as a measure of drive level and constructed in order to test predictions regarding relationships between drive level and task variables in their effects on task performance or learning. Drive level as measured by the MAS was expected to combine multiplicatively with response strength. In simple tasks, in which the correct response is dominant, persons high in MAS are expected to perform at a higher level than persons low in MAS. In more complex tasks, drive level was hypothesized to strengthen the incorrect interfering responses dominant in the response hierarchy, thus high-MAS individuals are expected to perform worse than low.

The minitheory underlying the development of the TAQ has been labeled the "interfering response hypothesis" (I. Sarason, 1960) and was also derived from Hullian Learning Theory. Mandler and Sarason (1952) assumed that two kinds of drives are evoked in testing situations: (1) a learned task drive directed toward task completion and (2) a learned anxiety drive that can elicit responses related to task completion *or* responses that interfere with task completion. It is the latter interfering response class, consisting of habitual responses readily elicited in testing situations, that the TAQ was intended to measure. It was expected that situational conditions, varying on an evaluative stress dimension, would interact with test anxiety in affecting task performance.

Both the TAQ and the MAS have been supplanted by more carefully constructed and adequately standardized instruments, for example, I. G. Sarason's Test Anxiety Scale (TAS; 1972a) and Spielberger, Gorsuch, and Lushene's State-Trait Anxiety Inventory (STAI; 1970). Test anxiety theory and manifest anxiety theory have undergone revision and elaboration, while the two streams of research have cross-fertilized each other. The task variables of prime importance to MAS drive theorists were investigated by test anxiety theorists, who interpreted them as stress variables (I. G. Sarason, 1960). MAS researchers learned that differences in learning rates between high anxious and low anxious persons appeared only when instructions or other situational conditions emphasized that subjects were being evaluated; threat of physical danger did not elicit differences in the performance of high anxious and low anxious individuals (Hodges & Spielberger, 1966; Spence & Spence, 1966; and Spielberger, 1975). Though the scales inspired an enormous amount of shotgun research, a good deal of theory-based research has also been published. Some major empirical generalizations can be drawn from the early research that apply to both the general anxiety and test anxiety literature. High-anxious subjects, on both kinds of scales, tend to perform more poorly on cognitive tasks than do low-anxious. The difference in their performance levels is exacerbated if the task is a difficult or complex one and if it is completed under evaluatively stressful situational conditions (for representative reviews of this literature see I. G. Sarason, 1960, 1972a; Spence & Spence, 1966; Spielberger, 1975; and Wine, 1971).

In the present chapter a cognitive-attentional interpretation of the effects of self-reported anxiety level is presented. It is proposed that the component common to self-reported anxiety on measures of general and test anxiety may be labeled "evaluation anxiety." Persons high in evaluation anxiety react to cues that indicate they are being evaluated with an habitual, overlearned set of self-oriented cognitions. The precise nature of these cognitions vary from one individual to another but tend to be constant within an individual. The cognitions serve as a trigger for heightened emotional reactivity. Persons low in evaluation anxiety react to performance evaluation with an external, situational, task focus, generating cognitions about the task or situation conducive to task completion or heightened understanding of the situation. This "direction of attention" hypothesis was first described in a review of the test anxiety research literature (Wine, 1971). A number of other specific evaluation anxieties have been explored in the literature, including speech anxiety (e.g., Meichenbaum, Gilmore, & Fedoravicius, 1971), audience anxiety (e.g., Paivio & Lambert, 1959; Paivio, 1965), social anxiety (e.g., Watson & Friend, 1969), and dating anxiety (e.g., McGovern, Arkowitz, & Gilmore, 1975). The differences between these anxieties are the specific situational circumstances that elicit the anxiety. The "performance anxiety" reported by Masters and Johnson (1970) as being characteristic of persons who are sexually dysfunctional is a specific evaluation anxiety. Performance anxiety refers to the tendency to observe and evaluate one's own actions when engaging in sexual activity. Though controlled research on its effects have not been reported, Masters and Johnson state that performance anxiety is very debilitating to sexual functioning.

Persons high in one form of evaluation anxiety are not necessarily prone to anxiety in all other kinds of evaluative situations. The individual's social learning history determines the cues that elicit evaluation anxiety and shapes the precise nature of the cognitions identifying it. For example, in the case of a highly specific test anxiety, a single very traumatic experience with a specific teacher and a specific stressful examination in a particular subject area may predispose an individual to react with self-devaluing cognitions and resulting high emotionality in other situations very similar to the original one on all dimensions. In the extreme case of very generalized evaluation anxiety, a child may be tuned through parental child-rearing practices to interpret a wide range of environmental cues as evaluatively stressing. Evaluation anxiety cuts across the trait-state anxiety distinction. Individuals who score high on self-report measures of trait anxiety, whether general or situationally specific, are prone to becoming worried and tense, to report high levels of state anxiety given the appropriate situational circumstances.

TEST ANXIETY:
A SPECIFIC CASE OF EVALUATION ANXIETY

The most heavily researched of the specific evaluation anxieties is test anxiety. Test anxiety research has lent itself readily to cognitive analyses, since the dependent measures most widely used have been cognitive performance on a variety of tasks. The early test anxiety research investigated the debilitating effects of test anxiety on cognitive task performance as a function of situational conditions varying on an evaluative stress dimension. These included instructional variations, performance feedback, and audience presence. Highly test-anxious persons perform more poorly on cognitive tasks than less anxious individuals, especially if the tasks are difficult and are given in evaluatively stressful circumstances. The direction-of-attention hypothesis regarding the effects of test anxiety has been supported by research indicating that: (1) Test-anxious persons are generally more self-preoccupied than less anxious persons: and self-focused, task-irrelevant cognitions are specifically elicited in test-anxious persons in cognitive-evaluative situations. (2) Test anxiety reduces the range of task cues used in cognitive task performance, probably as a function of the division of attention between task-relevant and self-relevant variables. (3) Test anxiety is composed of cognitive and physiological components. It is the cognitive component, consisting of self-preoccupied worry, that interferes most directly with cognitive performance, is the more stable of the two components, and serves as a trigger for heightened physiological reactivity. (4) The test-anxious individual's cognitive task performance is improved by experimental and treatment manipulations designed to enhance attention to task-relevant cues and reduce self-preoccupied worry. The following sections summarize and update the evidence bearing upon a cognitive-attentional interpretation of test anxiety.

Test Anxiety and Self-focusing

I. G. Sarason has reported two literature reviews (1960, 1975) supporting the proposition that high levels of self-reported test anxiety are associated with negative self-descriptions on other paper-and-pencil personality measures. A recent large-scale investigation of this sort by Many and Many (1975) found a significant negative relationship between self-reported self-esteem and test anxiety. In another recent study (Nicholls, 1976) in which factors of the Test Anxiety Scale for Children (S. B. Sarason, Davidson, Lighthall, Waite, & Ruebush, 1960) were examined, it was concluded that negative self-evaluation was the major component of the scale.

Evidence for the general self-devaluing tendencies of highly test-anxious persons comes from studies completed by I. G. Sarason and his colleagues (Sarason & Ganzer, 1962, 1963; Sarason & Koenig, 1965). Using a verbal conditioning paradigm in unstructured interview situations, they found that highly test-anxious persons made many more negative self-references than low, that they increased negative self-reference as a function of reinforcement, but they did not increase positive self-references when reinforced for them.

Of greater concern to the direction-of-attention hypothesis are studies reporting assessment of the cognitions of persons differing in test anxiety level while performing tasks under evaluative stress. These studies are rarer but their results instructive. Several studies have examined levels of aspiration, confidence levels, or attribution of responsibility for task performance. Doris and Sarason (1955) arbitrarily failed persons at extremes in TAQ scores on a number of tasks, and then asked them to assign responsibility of their failures. The high TAQ subjects were significantly more likely to assign responsibility to themselves than were the low-anxious subjects. Trapp and Kausler (1958) compared the levels of aspiration of high- and low-test-anxious persons in digit symbol performance. Though actual performance levels did not differ, the high-test-anxious subjects progressively reduced their levels of aspiration over trials until the levels were significantly lower than those of the low-anxious individuals. Meunier and Rule (1967) examined the confidence levels of high- and low-test-anxious subjects in their judgments of the length of lines as a function of positive, negative, or no feedback. On no-feedback trials, highly test-anxious persons reported low confidence levels equivalent to their confidence levels on negative feedback trials. The reverse was true for the low-test-anxious individuals, who reported high confidence levels on no-feedback trials, equivalent to their confidence levels on positive feedback trials.

Several studies provide even more direct support for the contention that high test anxiety is associated with preoccupation with self-devaluing cognitions during task performance. Mandler and Watson (1966), Neale and Katahn (1968) and Marlett and Watson (1968) administered several tasks to high- and low-test-anxious individuals. In each investigation post-task questionnaires asked subjects to indicate the incidence of self-devaluing cognitions during task performance. In all three studies, to the question "How often during the testing did you find yourself thinking how well, or how badly you were doing?", the high-test-anxious subjects reported a significantly higher incidence of such thoughts than did the low-test-anxious persons.

I. G. Sarason and Stoops (1978) constructed a cognitive interference questionnaire consisting of items assessing the incidence of interfering thoughts during task performance. Representative items are: "I thought about how poorly I was doing" and "I wondered what the experimenter would think of me." The questionnaire was completed following performance on an anagram task administered with several different sets of instructions varying on an evaluative stress dimension. The high-test-anxious subjects reported much higher cognitive interference scores than the low. There was also a significant interaction between test anxiety and the instructional conditions, largely as a function of the very high incidence of interfering thoughts reported by high-test-anxious subjects in the most evaluatively stressful achievement-oriented condition.

The most direct evidence for the high incidence of interfering self-relevant thoughts during the test-anxious person's task performance was reported by Ganzer (1968). He recorded the task-irrelevant comments of high- and low-test-anxious individuals during a serial verbal-learning task. The high-test-anxious subjects made many more irrelevant comments than did the low, and the comments were mostly of an apologetic self-deprecatory nature.

It is clear that, not only is test anxiety associated with a general tendency to be self-deprecatory, but that negative, self-devaluing cognitions are elicited in test-anxious individuals during evaluatively stressful cognitive task performance.

Test Anxiety and Task Cue Utilization

Easterbrook's (1959) now-classic review of the literature bearing on the relationship between arousal level and range of cue utilization presented an empirical generalization quite consistent with the direction-of-attention hypothesis. The studies reviewed by Easterbrook indicated that emotional arousal is consistently associated with a narrowing of the range of task cues used during task performance. The emotional arousal dimension referred to is very broad; anxiety level was included as a representative of the dimension. The effects of experimentally manipulated arousal level on performance of two types of tasks were reported in the reviewed studies. In one type, subjects responded to a continuous central or focal task while simultaneously responding to occasional peripheral stimuli. In the second type of task, intentional versus incidental learning was compared. Emotional arousal reduced peripheral task performance and incidental learning, while maintaining or improving central and intentional learning.

Several researchers have also examined relationships between self-reported anxiety level and range of cue utilization. Wachtel's research (1968) reported relationships between subjects' self-reported test anxiety level and the first type of task examined by Easterbrook (i.e., performance on a continuous focal tracking task) and reaction times to occasional peripheral lights. The tasks were administered under three instructional conditions, two of which appropriately engaged test anxiety by manipulating evaluative stress. In these two conditions, test anxiety was negatively correlated with speed scores on the peripheral task; in one of the conditions test anxiety was positively correlated with accuracy of performance on the central task. These results are generally in support of the cue utilization hypothesis.

Zaffy and Bruning (1966) devised an ingenious task variation for examining the cue utilization hypothesis. Though the anxiety scale used in their study was the MAS, and thus not directly relevant here, the general type of task has been used in two test-anxiety studies and deserves mention. Their variation involves presenting subjects with a task under three different conditions. In the relevant-cue condition, additional task cues are provided that are relevant or helpful for performing the task; in the irrelevant-cue condition the additional task cues provided are irrelevant or directly interfere with successful task performance, while in the no-cue condition no additional task cues are provided. Evidence in support of the cue utilization hypothesis would indicate that highly anxious subjects use the added task cues less than low-anxious subjects, or, stated in the reverse, the performance of low-anxious subjects should show greater improvement as a function of the presence of relevant cues, and greater deterioration as a function of added irrelevant cues. Zaffy and Bruning's results were in support of the cue utilization hypothesis. The two test-anxiety studies in which this type of task was used were reported by West, Lee, and Anderson (1969) and Geen (1976). The results of both studies were in support of the cue utilization hypothesis, indicating that the performance of high-test-anxious subjects was less likely than that of low-test-anxious subjects to reflect utilization of the added relevant and irrelevant task cues.

The present paper suggests an explanation for the difference in the range of task cues used by high- and low-test-anxious individuals. Under evaluative testing conditions the attention of high-test-anxious persons is divided between task cues and internally focused self-deprecatory thinking and perception of autonomic reactivity, while the attention of the low-test-anxious person is focused more fully on task cues.

Cognitive and Physiological Components
of Test Anxiety

The overriding importance of cognitive factors in self-reported test anxiety level, in contrast to emotional reactivity, was recognized in a thoughtful review by S. B. Sarason in 1966. He noted that children who score high on test anxiety scales rarely experience the absorbing, unambiguous painful distress of a total anxiety reaction. In his view such painful emotional reactivity plays an indispensable role in the origins of test anxiety, but:

> the cognitive consequences of anxiety in children affect personality development to a greater degree than does the anxiety to which they were a response. It is these cognitive consequences—involving attitude formation, social perceptions, fantasy, judgemental processes and the like—which take on a kind of pattern or organization that will itself affect the nature of subsequent experience at the same time that it will be changed by it. (S. B. Sarason, 1966, p. 78)

Sarason's insights regarding the relative importance of cognitive and physiological factors in test anxiety foreshadowed an important development in test anxiety theory advanced by Liebert and Morris (1967). These authors suggest that test anxiety is composed of two major components: *worry*, which they describe as cognitive concern over performance, and *emotionality*, which is the autonomic arousal aspect of anxiety. They constructed a self-report situational measure of these two components of test anxiety, which requires subjects to report on worry and emotionality in specific testing situations, as well as a more general measure (Morris & Liebert, 1969).

The results of a series of studies using the worry-emotionality distinction are instructive regarding the relative roles of cognitive and emotional factors in test anxiety (Doctor & Altman, 1969; Liebert & Morris, 1967; Morris & Fulmer, 1976; Morris & Liebert, 1969, 1970; Morris & Perez, 1972; and Spiegler, Morris & Liebert, 1968). With regard to specific testing situations, worry scores are fairly constant across time, but emotionality scores reach a peak immediately before the testing situation and fall off rapidly immediately after. Worry scores are reduced by performance feedback, a cognitive informational variable, while emotionality scores are not. Worry scores are negatively related to performance expectancies and to actual performance, while emotionality scores bear no consistent relationship to expectancies or test performance.

The combined results of this series of studies suggest that emotionality has a transient, fleeting quality and is confined to the testing situation. Worry, the cognitive component, is a stable disposition that interferes directly with cognitive performance, triggers the autonomic reactivity, and plays a major role in the maintenance of test anxiety.

The relationship between the worry-emotionality analyses of test anxiety and the direction-of-attention hypothesis is obvious. Worry refers to attentionally demanding cognitive activity going on during task performance. Autonomic reactivity is less likely to be demanding of attention except at extremely high levels "where physiological reactivity may be distractive and annoying" (Doctor & Altman, 1969, p. 364).

Cognitive-Attentional Experimental Manipulations

The bulk of the early laboratory research in test anxiety was concerned with experimental manipulations designed to evoke test anxiety and demonstrate its debilitating effects on task performance. Recent cognitively based theoretical reviews of the literature (I. G. Sarason, 1972a, 1975, 1978; Sieber, 1969), including the earlier direction-of-attention review by this author (Wine, 1971), have provided an impetus for the examination of means for improving the test-anxious individual's task performance.

Sieber and her colleagues (Paulson, Note 1; Sieber, 1969; Sieber, Kameya, & Paulson, 1970) completed several studies on the effects of memory supports on the task performance of highly test-anxious children. In multistage tasks, memory supports consist of visual displays of earlier stages of the task. Sieber (1969) noted that test anxiety is associated with faulty short-term memory. She hypothesized that providing test-anxious children with visual aids to their memory would improve their performance and reduce the discrepancy between the performance of high- and low-test-anxious subjects on tasks relying on short-term memory. These hypotheses were confirmed in several studies with differing kinds of task materials and different kinds of memory supports. The faulty short-term memory of test-anxious subjects, most likely, is a result of the cognitive interference of negative self-preoccupation. Memory supports are means of sustaining attention to task variables and minimizing the effects of self-directed thinking.

I. G. Sarason and his colleagues have completed a number of investigations of pretask manipulations intended to facilitate high-test-anxious subjects' performance on a variety of cognitive tasks. These manipulations include instructional variations and exposure to models with differing characteristics. A series of studies (I. G. Sarason, 1958, 1972b, 1978) explored reassuring, task-orienting, and informational properties of instructions. The instructions labeled "reassuring" may be described as attention-directing, since they suggested that the subject concentrate on the task rather than worrying about how he or she was doing. These instructions facilitated the verbal learning performance of test-anxious subjects.

The second study in this series (I. G. Sarason, 1972b) compared several sets of pretask instructions on the verbal learning performance of high- and low-test-anxious subjects. The performance of high-test-anxious subjects was facilitated most by instructions labeled "motivating task-orientation," surpassing their performance even in a "reassurance" condition. The motivating task-orientation instructions informed subjects that the experimenter was interested in the shape of learning curves rather than the individual subject's performance but that the subject would find the task interesting and worthwhile. In another study (1978) Sarason compared several instructional manipulations interpolated between two anagram tasks, after subjects had been arbitrarily failed in the first task. Test-anxious subjects performed best on the second anagram task, following instructions that combined worry-reducing reassurance with hints on specific problem-solving strategies. The combined results of these studies indicate clearly that instructions that direct attention away from self-preoccupied worry, are task-oriented, and give information about appropriate problem-solving strategies are helpful to the test-anxious individual's cognitive functioning.

The results of a series of studies (I. G. Sarason, 1972b, 1973, 1975; I. G. Sarason, Pederson & Nyman, 1968) examining the impact of exposure to models confirm and extend these conclusions. The results of these studies suggest, in general, that exposure to models who are task-oriented and provide attention-directing cognitive structuring clues is beneficial to the performance of test-anxious persons. Of additional benefit is evidence in the behavior of the model that he or she is successfully coping with the worry and tension associated with test anxiety.

Cognitive-Attentional Treatment Research

The test-anxiety treatment literature is comprehensively reviewed by Spielberger, Anton, and Bedell (1976). Thus the studies reviewed in this section are only those specifically derived from an attentional approach. It is interesting to briefly note, regarding the general test-anxiety treatment literature, that several reviewers (Allen, 1972; Spielberger et al., 1976; and Wine, Note 2) have reached essentially the same conclusion regarding the effects of treatment (such as systematic desensitization) specifically designed to reduce emotional arousal. These treatment approaches have consistently positive effects on self-report anxiety level but typically have little or no impact on cognitive performance. In order to consistently elicit cognitive performance change, procedures specifically focused on cognitive modification are required.

The earlier direction-of-attention review (Wine, 1971), stated that an attentional approach is explicitly concerned with cognitive activity going on during task performance, while autonomic reactivity is irrelevant unless the individual attends to the arousal. It was suggested that attentional training should enhance the test-anxious subject's cognitive task performance as well as reduce self-reported worry and tension. Procedures intended to reduce autonomic arousal, though likely to be reflected in self-reported anxiety level, were not expected to enhance cognitive performance. These propositions were investigated in a small exploratory treatment study and received tentative support.

Several researchers have replicated the results of the exploratory study in larger scale studies. Crossley (Note 3) completed a carefully controlled experimental analogue of the exploratory treatment study. The effects of attentional training, relaxation training, and a placebo treatment condition were examined on the performance of both high- and low-test-anxious subjects. The task was the Thurstone two-second Hidden Digits test, which is very sensitive to attentional interference. Neither the self-report anxiety level nor the cognitive performance of low-test-anxious subjects was affected by any of the conditions. The self-reported anxiety level of high-test-anxious subjects was reduced by both attentional training and relaxation training, but only the attentional training had positive effects on performance of the Thurstone Hidden Digits test.

Little and Jackson (1974) and Holroyd (1976) completed treatment studies that essentially replicate these results and extend the findings to academic tests and to academic performance. However, Little and Jackson found that a condition combining attentional training with relaxation training was more beneficial than attentional training alone. Holroyd (1976) used a more general cognitive therapy approach that included attentional training, comparing it to systematic desensitization and a combination of cognitive therapy, systematic desensitization, and pseudotherapy. The cognitive therapy was more effective than any of the other conditions in reducing anxiety and improving grade-point average.

The combined results of these studies are strongly in support of the proposition that treatment procedures designed to enhance attention to task-relevant cues and reduce self-preoccupied worry have positive effects on the cognitive task performance and self-reported anxiety levels of highly test-anxious subjects.

OTHER EVALUATION ANXIETIES

The test anxiety literature bearing upon the direction-of-attention hypothesis was reviewed in some detail in the preceding section, partially because the relevant research is so extensive but also because of the peculiar nature of test anxiety as a theoretical construct. Theoretical models have hypothesized that test anxiety interacts with cognitive variables, such as intelligence, to determine cognitive performance. Thus the literature has readily lent itself to cognitive-attentional analysis. Research on other specific evaluation anxieties is much less extensive, has typically not involved assessment of cognitive variables, nor has it typically been generated from unified theoretical positions.

In order to establish some communality among test anxiety and other evaluation anxieties it is important to demonstrate that self-reported anxiety regarding specific evaluating situations interferes with performance in those situations. Criteria for adequate performance are less clear than is the case for correlates of test anxiety. For example, indexes for the measurement of social competence are less likely to be generally agreed upon than is the measurement of cognitive task performance. In spite of the criterion problem, social-anxiety researchers have established some relationships between self-reported social anxiety and overt social behaviors. Arkowitz, Lichtenstein, McGovern, and Hines (1975) reported that scores on the Social Avoidance and Distress scale, the Fear of Negative Evaluation scale (Watson & Friend, 1969), and the S-R Inventory of Anxiousness in interpersonal situations (Endler, Hunt, & Rosenstein, 1962) differentiated between high- and low-frequency daters and correlated with peer ratings of social skills and with observational behavioral measures. Other social-anxiety researchers have reported similar results regarding relationships between social-anxiety self-report measures and social skill (for review see Hersen & Bellack, 1977). Similarly, audience anxiety scores have been demonstrated to correlate negatively with observers' ratings of willingness to speak before evaluating audiences, as well as with length of oral stories as a function of approval and disapproval (Paivio, 1965). Speech anxiety self-report has been shown to correlate with behavioral observations of adequacy of speech behaviors (Meichenbaum et al., 1971). However, the relationship between self-reported anxiety level and measures of adequacy of performance has not been as consistent in the investigations of other evaluation anxieties as in test anxiety (e.g., Borkovec, Fleischmann, & Caputo, 1973).

Self-report social-evaluation anxiety measures interact with situational conditions varying on an evaluative dimension and relate to other cognitive variables. Smith and Sarason (1975) found that socially anxious individuals perceived the same feedback from another individual as being more negative than did low-socially-anxious individuals. Smith (1972) found that socially anxious subjects, in comparison to those low in social anxiety, were extremely sensitive to evaluative cues from others. In one experiment they showed greater attraction than lows toward agreeing strangers than disagreeing strangers; in another experiment they showed more significant learning effects as a function of agreeing and disagreeing statements made by another person. O'Banion and Arkowitz (Note 4) found that high-socially-anxious individuals remembered negative feedback more accurately and positive feedback less accurately than low-socially-anxious individuals. Clark and Arkowitz (1975) found that high- and low-socially-anxious persons differed in their ratings of their own conversational skills, with high-socially-anxious subjects reporting overly negative self-evaluations, while the self-ratings of low-socially-anxious individuals were more positive and more consistent with external judges' ratings. Smye (1977) and Wine and Smye (Note 5) report that the verbal behaviors in simulated social interactions of high-socially-anxious adolescents, in comparison to lows, reflected concern over evaluation and cautious, positive self-presentation.

The evidence indicates, in the case of social-evaluation anxiety, that individuals who report themselves to be highly anxious make different inferences regarding cues presented to them by others than do low-socially-anxious individuals; that is, they are more likely to interpret the behaviors of others as negatively evaluating. They also are self-devaluing of themselves and their own social behaviors. Argyle (1969) reports that high-socially-anxious persons are more likely to see themselves as "observed" rather than "observers" in social situations, reminiscent of the extreme self-consciousness referred to by other social-anxiety researchers (e.g., Zimbardo, 1977). The highly socially anxious individual appears to have a stable set of self-devaluing cognitions readily elicited in social-evaluative situations and appears to be more likely to be a self-observer and evaluator than an accurate observer of the behavior of others. It is logical to presume that persons high in other forms of evaluation anxiety, such as speech and audience anxiety, have negative self-devaluing cognitions that are elicited under the appropriate situational conditions.

Cognitive modification treatment procedures have been used with evaluation anxieties other than test anxiety with positive results. Meichenbaum et al. (1971), Casas (1975), and Di Loreto (1971) found cognitive restructuring procedures to be highly effective with speech-anxious individuals, especially with those individuals who were generally anxious about the evaluations of others. Similarly, Kanter and Goldfried (Note 6) found rational restructuring to be highly effective in treating interpersonal anxiety, as did Glass, Gottman, and Shmurak (1976), in the treatment of dating anxiety.

An attentional analysis of evaluation anxiety may provide direction to a search for procedures for modifying the anxious individuals' anxiety level and performance. The analysis suggests that the evaluation-anxious individual is excessively self-preoccupied with negative self-devaluing cognitions and makes inaccurate inferences regarding the behavior of others. Training in inhibition of negative self-relevant thinking, combined with training in observational skills of others' behaviors and in generating accurate inferences regarding those behaviors should be helpful to persons high in any form of evaluation anxiety.

REFERENCES

Allen, G. J. The behavioral treatment of test anxiety: Recent research and future trends. *Behavior Therapy*, 1972, *3*, 253–262.

Argyle, M. *Social interaction.* Chicago: Aldine, 1969.

Arkowitz, H., Lichtenstein, E., McGovern, K. B., & Hines, P. The behavioral assessment of social competence in males. *Behavior Therapy*, 1975, *6*, 3–13.

Borkovec, T. D., Fleischmann, D. J., & Caputo, J. A. The measurement of anxiety in an analogue social situation. *Journal of Consulting and Clinical Psychology*, 1973, *41*, 157–161.

Casas, J. *A comparison of two mediational self-control techniques for the treatment of speech anxiety.* Unpublished doctoral dissertation, Stanford University, 1975.

Clark, J. V., & Arkowitz, H. Social anxiety and self-evaluation of interpersonal performance. *Psychological Reports,* 1975, *36,* 211–221.

Di Loreto, A. O. *Comparative psychotherapy: An experimental analysis.* Chicago: Aldine-Atherton, 1971.

Doctor, R. M. & Altman, F. Worry and emotionality as components of test anxiety: Replication and further data. *Psychological Reports,* 1969, *24,* 563–568.

Doris, J., & Sarason, S. B. Test anxiety and blame assignment in a failure situation. *Journal of Abnormal and Social Psychology,* 1955, *50,* 335–338.

Easterbrook, J. A. The effect of emotion on cue utilization and the organization of behavior. *Psychological Review,* 1959, *66,* 183–201.

Endler, N. S., Hunt, J. McV., & Rosenstein, A. J. An S-R inventory of anxiousness. *Psychological Monograph,* 1962, *76* (17, Whole No. 536).

Ganzer, V. J. The effects of audience presence and test anxiety on learning and retention in a serial learning situation. *Journal of Personality and Social Psychology,* 1968, *8,* 194–199.

Geen, R. G. Test anxiety, observation and range of cue utilization. *British Journal of Social and Clinical Psychology,* 1976, *15,* 253–259.

Glass, C. R., Gottman, J. M., & Shmurak, S. H. Response acquisition and cognitive self-statement modification approaches to dating skills training. *Journal of Counseling Psychology,* 1976, *23,* 520–526.

Hersen, M., & Bellack, A. S. Assessment of social skills. In A. R. Ciminero, K. S. Calhoun, & H. E. Adams (Eds.), *Handbook of behavioral assessment.* New York: Wiley, 1977.

Hodges, W. F., & Spielberger, C. D. The effects of threat of shock on heart rate for subjects who differ in manifest anxiety and fear of shock. *Psychophysiology,* 1966, *2,* 287–294.

Holroyd, K. A. Cognition and desensitization in the group treatment of test anxiety. *Journal of Consulting and Clinical Psychology,* 1976, *44,* 991–1001.

Liebert, R. M., & Morris, L. W. Cognitive and emotional components of test anxiety: A distinction and some initial data. *Psychological Reports,* 1967, *20,* 975–978.

Little, S., & Jackson, B. The treatment of test anxiety through attentional and relaxation training. *Psychotherapy: Theory, research and practice,* 1974, *11,* 175–178.

Mandler, G., & Sarason, S. B. A study of anxiety and learning. *Journal of Abnormal and Social Psychology,* 1952, *47,* 166–173.

Mandler, G., & Watson, D. L. Anxiety and the interruption of behavior. In C. D. Spielberger (Ed.), *Anxiety and behavior.* New York: Academic Press, 1966.

Many, M. A., & Many, W. A. The relationship between self-esteem and anxiety in grades four through eight. *Educational and Psychological Measurement,* 1975, *35,* 1017–1021.

Marlett, N. J., & Watson, D. Test anxiety and immediate or delayed feedback in a test-like avoidance task. *Journal of Personality and Social Psychology,* 1968, *8,* 200–203.

Masters, W. H., & Johnson, V. E. *Human sexual inadequacy.* New York: Little, Brown, 1970.

McGovern, K. B., Arkowitz, H., & Gilmore, S. K. Evaluation of social skill training programs for college dating inhibitions. *Journal of Counseling Psychology,* 1975, *22,* 505–512.

Meichenbaum, D. H., Gilmore, B. J., & Fedoravicius, A. Group insight vs. group desensitization in treating speech anxiety. *Journal of Consulting and Clinical Psychology,* 1971, *36,* 410–421.

Meunier, C., & Rule, B. G. Anxiety, confidence, and uniformity. *Journal of Personality,* 1967, *35,* 498–504.

Morris, L. W., & Fulmer, R. S. Test anxiety (worry and emotionality) changes during academic testing as a function of feedback and test importance. *Journal of Educational Psychology,* 1976, *68,* 817–824.

Morris, L. W., & Liebert, R. M. Effects of anxiety on timed and untimed intelligence tests: Another look. *Journal of Consulting and Clinical Psychology,* 1969, *33,* 240–244.

Morris, L. W., & Liebert, R. M. Relationship of cognitive and emotional components of test anxiety to physiological arousal and academic performance. *Journal of Consulting and Clinical Psychology,* 1970, *35,* 332–337.

Morris, L. W., & Perez, T. L. Effects of test-interruption on emotional arousal and performance. *Psychological Reports,* 1972, *31,* 559–564.

Neale, I. M., & Katahu, M. Anxiety, choice, and stimulus uncertainty. *Journal of Personality*, 1968, *36*, 235–245.

Nicholls, J. G. When a scale measures more than its names denotes: The case of the Test Anxiety Scale for Children. *Journal of Consulting and Clinical Psychology*, 1976, *44*, 976–985.

Paivio, A. Personality and audience influence. In B. A. Maher (Ed.), *Progress in experimental personality research* (Vol. 2). New York: Academic Press, 1965.

Paivio, A., & Lambert, W. E. Measures and correlates of audience anxiety ("stage fright"). *Journal of Personality*, 1959, *27*, 1–17.

Sarason, I. G. The effects of anxiety, reassurance, and meaningfulness of material to be learned on verbal learning. *Journal of Experimental Psychology*, 1958, *56*, 472–477.

Sarason, I. G. Empirical findings and theoretical problems in the use of anxiety scales. *Psychological Bulletin*, 1960, *57*, 403–415.

Sarason, I. G. Experimental approaches to test anxiety: Attention and the uses of information. In C. D. Spielberger (Ed.), *Anxiety: Current trends in theory and research* (Vol. 2). New York: Academic Press, 1972. (a)

Sarason, I. G. Test anxiety and the model who fails. *Journal of Personality and Social Psychology*, 1972, *22*, 410–413. (b)

Sarason, I. G. Test anxiety and cognitive modeling. *Journal of Personality and Social Psychology*, 1973, *28*, 58–61.

Sarason, I. G. Test anxiety and the self-disclosing coping model. *Journal of Consulting and Clinical Psychology*, 1975, *43*, 148–153.

Sarason, I. G. The Test Anxiety Scale: Concept and research. In C. D. Spielberger & I. G. Sarason (Eds.), *Stress and anxiety* (Vol. 5). Washington, DC: Hemisphere, 1978.

Sarason, I. G., & Ganzer, V. J. Anxiety, reinforcement, and experimental instructions in a free verbilization situation. *Journal of Abnormal and Social Psychology*, 1962, *65*, 300–307.

Sarason, I. B., & Ganzer, V. J. Effects of test anxiety and reinforcement history on verbal behavior. *Journal of Abnormal and Social Psychology*, 1963, *67*, 513–519.

Sarason, I. G., & Koenig, K. P. The relationship of test anxiety and hostility to description of self and parents. *Journal of Personality and Social Psychology*, 1965, *2*, 617–621.

Sarason, I. G., Pederson, A. M. & Nyman, B. A. Test anxiety and the observation of models. *Journal of Personality*, 1968, *36*, 493–511.

Sarason, I. G., & Stoops, R. Test anxiety and the passage of time. *Journal of Consulting and Clinical Psychology*, 1978, *46*, 102–109.

Sarason, S. B. The measurement of anxiety in children: Some questions and problems. In C. D. Spielberger (Ed.), *Anxiety and behavior*. New York: Academic Press, 1966.

Sarason, S. B., Davidson, K. S., Lighthall, F. F., Waite, R. R., & Ruebush, B. K. *Anxiety in elementary school children*. New York: Wiley, 1960.

Sarason, S. B., Mandler, G., & Craighill, P. G. The effect of differential instructions on anxiety and learning. *Journal of Abnormal and Social Psychology*, 1952, *47*, 561–565.

Sieber, J. E. A paradigm for experimental modification of the effects of test anxiety on cognitive processes. *American Educational Research Journal*, 1969, *6*, 46–61.

Sieber, J. E., Kameya, L. J., & Paulson, F. L. Effect of memory support on the problem-solving ability of test-anxious children. *Journal of Educational Psychology*, 1970, *61*, 159–168.

Smith, R. E. Social anxiety as a moderator variable in the attitude similarity-attraction relationship. *Journal of Experimental Research in Personality*, 1972, *6*, 22–28.

Smith, R. E., & Sarason, I. G. Social anxiety and the evaluation of negative interpersonal feedback. *Journal of Consulting and Clinical Psychology*, 1975, *43*, 429.

Smye, M. D. *Verbal, cognitive and behavioral correlates of social anxiety in adolescents.* Unpublished doctoral dissertation, Ontario Institute for Studies in Education, 1977.

Spence, J. T., & Spence, K. W. The motivational components of manifest anxiety: Drive and drive stimuli. In C. D. Spielberger (Ed.), *Anxiety and behavior.* New York: Academic Press, 1966.

Spiegler, M. D., Morris, L. W., & Liebert, R. M. Cognitive and emotional components of test anxiety: Temporal factors. *Psychological Reports*, 1968, *22*, 451–456.

Spielberger, C. D. *Anxiety: Current trends in theory and research* (Vols. 1 & 2). New York: Academic Press, 1972.

Spielberger, C. D. Anxiety: State-trait-process. In C. D. Speilberger & I. G. Sarason (Eds.), *Stress and anxiety* Vol. 1). Washington, DC: Hemisphere, 1975.

Spielberger, C. D., Anton, W. D., & Bedell, J. The nature and treatment of test anxiety. In M. Zuckerman & C. D. Spielberger (Eds.), *Emotions and anxiety: New concepts, methods and applications.* Hillsdale, NJ: Lawrence, 1976.

Spielberger, C. D., Gorsuch, R. L., & Lushene, R. E. *Manual for the State-Trait Anxiety Inventory.* Palo Alto, CA: Consulting Psychologists Press, 1970.

Taylor, J. A. A personality scale of manifest anxiety. *Journal of Abnormal and Social Psychology*, 1953, *48*, 285–290.

Trapp, E. P., & Kausler, P. H. Test anxiety level and goal-setting behavior. *Journal of Consulting Psychology*, 1958, *22*, 31–34.

Wachtel, P. L. Anxiety, attention and coping with threat. *Journal of Abnormal Psychology*, 1968, *73*, 137–143.

Watson, D., & Friend, R. Measurement of social-evaluative anxiety. *Journal of Consulting and Clinical Psychology*, 1969, *33*, 448–457.

West, C. K., Lee, J. F., & Anderson, T. H. The influence of test anxiety in the selection of relevant from irrelevant information. *The Journal of Educational Research*, 1969, *63*, 51–52.

Wine, J. D. Test anxiety and direction of attention. *Psychological Bulletin*, 1971, *76*, 92–104.

Zaffy, D. J., & Bruning, J. E. Drive and the range of cue utilization. *Journal of Experimental Psychology*, 1966, *71*, 382–384.

Zimbardo, P. G. *Shyness: What it is, what to do about it.* Reading, MA: Addison-Wesley, 1977.

REFERENCE NOTES

1. Paulson, F. L. *Memory support as a way of reducing the undesirable effects of anxiety on children's learning.* Paper presented at the meeting of the Western Psychological Association, Vancouver, BC, June 1969.

2. Wine, J. D. *Cognitive-attentional approaches to test anxiety modification.* Paper presented at the annual conference of the American Psychological Association, Montreal, August 1973.

3. Crossley, T. *The examination and validation of attentionally based test anxiety reduction on college freshman.* Unpublished MA thesis, University of New Brunswick, 1977.

4. O'Banion, K., & Arkowitz, H. *Social anxiety and selective memory for positive and negative information about the self.* Unpublished manuscript, University of Oregon, 1975.

5. Wine, J. D., & Smye, M. D. *Social anxiety and social behavior in adolescents.* Unpublished manuscript, Ontario Institute for Studies in Education, 1978.

6. Kanter, N. J., & Goldfried, M. R. *Relative effectiveness of rational restructuring and self-control desensitization in the reduction of interpersonal anxiety.* Unpublished manuscript, State University of New York at Stony Brook, 1976.

IV

ACHIEVEMENT MOTIVATION, CAUSAL ATTRIBUTION, AND ANXIETY

11

An Attribution Theory of Motivation and Emotion

Bernard Weiner
University of California, Los Angeles

The attribution approach to motivation and experience has proven exceedingly rich. In this article I will examine the particular attributional path I have followed and document its richness by outlining a few of the empirical and theoretical relations in the achievement area that appear to be conclusive. The extensiveness of the theoretical network suggests that a general theory of motivation is under development. I also will speculate about the potential role of anxiety in this formulation.

Some of the thoughts expressed in this article have been voiced in previous reviews (Weiner, 1972, 1974, 1976). With each opportunity to take stock of where we are, some ideas become more firmly fixed, others are discarded and new presumptions take their place, some earlier evidence grows in stature, and other prior data require reinterpretation. There certainly is some advantage to the dictum of publish *and* perish, which allows one to convey one's ideas in a single, self-contained, and final package. Like most others, however, I communicate my thoughts as they evolve, and prior questionable truths give way to new, equally uncertain laws, while other notions remain unchanged.

THE SEARCH FOR CAUSES

A central assumption of attribution theory, which sets it apart from pleasure-pain theories of motivation, is that the search for understanding is the (or *a*) basic "spring of action." This does not imply that humans are not pleasure seekers or that they never bias information in the pursuit of hedonic goals. Rather, information seeking and veridical processing are believed to be normative, may be manifested in spite of a conflicting pleasure principle, and, at the least, comprehension stands with hedonism among the primary sources of motivation (see W. Meyer, Folkes, & Weiner, 1976).

In an academic setting the search for understanding often leads to the attributional question: "Why did I succeed (or fail)?" or more specifically "Why did I flunk math?" or "Why did Mary get a better mark on this exam than I?" But classrooms are environments for the satisfaction of motivations other than achievement. Thus attributional questions might also pertain to, for example,

This article was written while the author was supported by a grant from the Spencer Foundation. Substantial portions of the manuscript previously appeared in the *Journal of Educational Psychology*, 1979, 71.

interpersonal acceptance or rejection, such as "Why doesn't Johnny like me?" However, for the time being attention will be centered on achievement concerns.

Among the unknowns of this attributional analysis is a clear statement of when people ask "why" questions. It has been demonstrated that this search is more likely given failure (rejection) than success (acceptance) (Folkes, 1978). Furthermore it is plausible to speculate that unexpected events are more likely to lead to "why" questions than expected events (Lau & Russell, 1980) and that subjective importance also will influence the pursuit of knowledge. Finally, it has been demonstrated that during task performance failure-oriented or "helpless" students especially tend to supply attributions (Diener & Dweck, 1978). Diener and Dweck also intimate that a subset of students, called "mastery-oriented," do not engage in attribution making. However, I suspect that attributional inferences often are quite retrospective, summarize a number of experiences, take place below a level of immediate awareness, and are intimately tied with self-esteem and self-concept. Thus I believe that attributions are supplied by the mastery-oriented as well, although not necessarily during or immediately following all task performances.

Our initial statement regarding the perceived causes of success and failure (Weiner, Frieze, Kukla, Reed, Rest, & Rosenbaum, 1971) was guided by Heider (1958) as well as our own intuitions. We postulated that in achievement-related contexts the causes perceived as most responsible for success and failure are ability, effort, task difficulty, and luck. That is, in attempting to explain the prior success or failure at an achievement-related event, the individual assesses his or her level of ability, the amount of effort that was expended, the difficulty of the task, and the magnitude and direction of experienced luck. We assumed that rather general values are assigned to these factors and that the task outcome is differentially ascribed to the causal sources. In a similar manner, future expectations of success and failure would then be based upon one's perceived level of ability in relation to the perceived difficulty of the task (labeled by Heider as "can"), as well as an estimation of the intended effort and anticipated luck.

In listing the four causes reported above we did not intend to convey that they were the *only* perceived determinants of success or failure, or even that they were the most salient ones in all achievement situations. In later work (e.g., Weiner, 1974; Weiner, Russell, & Lerman, 1978), we explicitly indicated that factors such as mood, fatigue, illness, and bias could serve as necessary and/or sufficient reasons for achievement performance. Research restricting causality to the four causes given above at times might give rise to false conclusions. For example, assume that one is testing the hedonic bias notion that success primarily is self-ascribed. By not including help from others, for example, among the alternative causes, the hedonic bias hypothesis might be supported, because the given external causes (task difficulty and luck) do not adequately capture the phenomenology of the subject.

In the last few years intuition has given way to empirical studies attempting to identify the perceived causes of success and failure. At least four investigations of academic attributions (Elig & Frieze, 1975; Frieze, 1976; Bar-Tal & Darom, Note 1; Cooper & Burger, Note 2) have been conducted (there undoubtedly are many more unknown to me), and there have been a number of studies that examine attributions outside the classroom context (e.g., work experiences and athletics). The methodologies of the classroom inquiries have minor variations, with students or teachers stating the causes of success or failure at real or imagined events and judging themselves or others. The responses are then categorized and tabulated.

Cooper and Burger (Note 2) provide a concise summary of the data from three of the studies (see Table 1). It is evident that ability, effort (both typical and immediate), and task difficulty are among the main perceived causes of achievement performance. Thus the prior intuitions of Heider (1958) and my colleagues and me were not incorrect. In addition Table 1 shows that others (teachers, students, and family), motivation (attention and interest), and what Cooper and Burger label "acquired characteristics" (habits and attitudes) and "physiological processes" (mood, maturity, and health) comprise the central determinants of success and failure. Luck is not included with the dominant causes but could be prominent on specific occasions, particularly in career or athletic accomplishments (see Mann, 1974).

In sum there are a myriad of perceived causes of achievement events. In a cross-cultural study it was even reported that patience (Greece and Japan) and tact and unity (India) are perceived as causes of success and failure (Triandis, 1972). But there is a rather small list from which the main causes repeatedly are selected. Furthermore, within the list, ability and effort appear to be the most salient and general of the causes. That is, outcomes frequently depend upon what we can do and how hard we try to do it. A clear conceptual analysis of only ability and effort would greatly add to our knowledge, given an attributional perspective.

Before moving on to this conceptual formulation, it should be recognized that Table 1 presents only a description of the perceived reasons for success and failure in achievement settings. Although attribution theory often is referred to as a naive conception, using the language of the person on the street, it also has been appreciated that science has to go beyond mere phenomenology. That is,

Table 1 A Summary of Previous Coding Systems

Frieze (1976)	Bar-Tal & Darom (1977)	Cooper & Burger (1978)
Ability	Ability	Academic ability
Stable effort	Effort during test	Physical and emotional ability
Immediate effort	Preparation at home	Previous experience
Task	Interest in the subject matter	Habits
Other person	Difficulty of the test	Attitudes
Mood	Difficulty of material	Self-perceptions
Luck	Conditions in the home	Maturity
Other		Typical effort
		Effort in preparation
		Attention
		Directions
		Instruction
		Task
		Mood
		Family
		Other students
		Miscellaneous

Note. Adapted from Cooper and Burger, 1978.

order must be imposed using scientific terminology that may not be part of the logic of the layperson. This is implicit in, for example, the work of Kelley (1967, 1971). Heider also clearly acknowledged the distinction between a naive psychology and a scientific psychology. He stated: "There is no prior reason why the causal description [scientific language] should be the same as the phenomenal description [naive language], though, of course, the former should adequately account for the latter" (Heider, 1958, p. 22).

I turn now from the layperson's perception of causality to the scientific language that is imposed on these causes. In this article I completely neglect the process by which causal beliefs are reached, although this is the most common problem in the attributional field and is what is meant by the *attribution process* (see Kelley, 1967, 1971; Weiner, 1974). This void is left so that full space can be devoted to the psychological consequences of perceived causality, the topic most central to my concerns.

DIMENSIONS OF CAUSALITY

Inasmuch as the list of conceivable causes of success and failure is infinite, it is essential to create a classification scheme or a taxonomy of causes. In so doing, similarities and differences are delineated and the underlying properties of the causes are identified. This is an indispensable requirement for the construction of an attributional theory of motivation.

The prior theoretical analyses of Rotter (1966) and Heider (1958) were available to serve as our initial guides in this endeavor. Rotter and his colleagues proposed a one-dimensional classification of causality. Causes either were within (internal) or outside (external to) the person. In a similar manner Heider (1958) as well as de Charms (1968), Deci (1975), and many others have articulated an internal-external classification of causality. Rotter labeled this dimension *locus of control*, whereas in the present context locus is conceived as a backward-looking belief and therefore is referred to as *locus of causality*. Indeed I contend that the concepts of *locus* and *control* must be separated.

The causes listed in Table 1 can be readily catalogued as internal or external to the individual. From the perspective of the student, the personal causes include ability, effort, mood, maturity, and health, while teacher, task, and family are among the external sources of causality. But the relative placement of a cause on this dimension is not invariant over time or between people. For example, health might be perceived as an internal ("I am a sickly person") or as an external ("The flu bug got me") cause of failure. Inasmuch as attribution theory deals with phenomenal causality, such personal interpretations must be taken into account. That is, the taxonomic placement of a cause depends upon its subjective meaning. Nonetheless, in spite of possible individual variation, there is general agreement when distinguishing causes as internal or external.

A second dimension of causality, which we have come to perceive as increasingly important, is labeled *stability* (Weiner et al., 1971). The stability dimension defines causes on a stable (invariant) versus unstable (variant) continuum. Again Heider (1958) served as our guide, for he contrasted dispositional and relatively fixed characteristics such as ability with fluctuating factors such as effort and luck. Examining Table 1, ability, typical effort, and family would be considered relatively fixed, while immediate effort, attention, and mood are more unstable. Effort and attention may be augmented or decreased from one episode to the next, while mood is conceived of as a temporary state. However, as indicated previously, the perceived properties of a cause can vary. For example, mood might be thought of as a temporary state or as a permanent trait. In addition, experimenters can alter the perceived properties of a cause. For example, although difficulty level of a task generally is considered a stable characteristic (Weiner et al., 1971), Valle and Frieze (1976) portrayed task difficulty as unstable by anchoring this concept to assigned sales territory, which could be shifted for any salesperson. At times task difficulty is classified as stable, while the experimental manipulation strongly suggests that subjects would perceive this factor as unstable (see Riemer, 1975).

Still a third dimension of causality identified by Heider and later incorporated into the achievement domain by Rosenbaum (1972) was labeled *intentionality*. Causes such as effort or the bias of a teacher or supervisor were categorized as intentional, whereas ability, the difficulty of the task, mood, and so on were specified by Rosenbaum to be unintentional.

In prior writings this distinction was accepted (e.g., Weiner, 1974, 1976). But following a suggestion of Litman-Adizes (Note 3), it is now apparent that Rosenbaum (1972) mislabeled this dimension. Rosenbaum argued that the dimension of intentionality is needed to differentiate, for example, mood from effort. Both of these are internal and unstable causes, yet intuitively they are quite distinct. Rosenbaum invoked the intent dimension to describe this difference, with mood classified as unintentional and effort classified as intentional. However, it seems that the dimension Rosenbaum had identified was that of control. Failure attributed to a lack of effort does not signify that there was an intent to fail. Intent connotes a desire or want. Rather, effort differs from mood in that only effort is perceived as subject to volitional control. Hence I propose that a third dimension of causality categorizes causes as *controllable* versus *uncontrollable*.

Causes theoretically can be classified within one of eight cells (2 levels of locus X 2 levels of stability X 2 levels of control). Among the internal causes, ability is stable and uncontrollable; typical effort is stable and controllable; mood, fatigue, and illness are unstable and uncontrollable; and temporary exertion is unstable and controllable. Among the external causes, task difficulty is stable and uncontrollable; teacher bias may be perceived as stable and controllable; luck is unstable and uncontrollable; and unusual help from others is unstable and controllable (see Table 2).

Some problems with this classification scheme remain unsolved, particularly among the external causes. For example, can an external cause be perceived as

Table 2 Causes of Success and Failure Classified According to Locus, Stability, and Controllability

	Internal		External	
	Stable	Unstable	Stable	Unstable
Uncontrollable	Ability	Mood	Task Difficulty	Luck
Controllable	Typical effort	Immediate effort	Teacher bias	Unusual help from others

controllable? The answer to this question depends on how far back one goes in a causal inference chain as well as whether controllability assumes only the perspective of the actor, which is not the case in Table 2 (e.g., teacher bias may be controllable from the vantage point of the teacher but not given the perspective of the pupil). These questions, as well as the proposed independence of the dimensions, are difficult issues for future thought and research.

Although the main dimensions of causality in achievement-related contexts may have been identified, other dimensions are likely to emerge with further analysis and will raise additional problems about the independence of the dimensions. Intention may be one of these dimensions and logically could be separable from control (although causes are certain to correlate highly on these two dimensions). A causal statement regarding a neglected homework assignment illustrating the separation of intent from control is "I wanted to study but could not control myself from going out." A conceptually similar example disassociating intent from control concerns a criminal who does not want to commit a crime but cannot control his compulsion. Criminal justice also accepts the possibility of control without intent, as in negligence.

Still another possible dimension of causality, identified by Abramson, Seligman, and Teasdale (1978), has been labeled *globality*. The global versus specific ends of this dimension capture the concept of stimulus generalization (while stability expresses temporal generalization). For example, one's ability may be perceived as task-specific ("I failed because I am poor at math") or as a general trait influencing performance in a wide variety of settings ("I failed because I am dumb").

The dimensions of causality introduced above were derived from a logical examination of perceived causes. More recently, a number of investigators have employed techniques such as factor analysis or multidimensional scaling to discover the dimensions of causality (e.g., J. Meyer, 1980; Passer, 1977; Michela, Peplau, & Weeks, Note 4). In the inceptive study by Passer, male and female subjects rated the similarity of the causes of either success or failure. Eighteen causes were presented in all possible pairs to the subjects. The similarity judgments provided the input for a multidimensional scaling procedure. This method is akin to a cluster analysis and depicts the underlying judgment dimensions.

Passer found two clear dimensions of causality: (1) a locus dimension, anchored at the internal end with causes such as bad mood and no self-confidence and at the external extreme with causes such as bad teacher and hard exam; and (2) an intentional-unintentional dimension (which I will call controllable-uncontrollable), anchored at the controllable end with causes such as never studies hard and lazy, and at the controllable extreme with causes such as nervous and bad mood. The findings reported by Passer (1977) were similar for males and females in both the success and failure scaling solutions.

The proposed third dimension of causality, stability, was not displayed. Nevertheless Passer's results are encouraging in that two of the three dimensions that had been presumed did emerge and other unanticipated dimensions that had not been part of the logical analysis did not appear.

The data reported by Michela et al. (Note 4) were equally promising. Although they were concerned with the causes of loneliness, two familiar dimensions emerged in their study—stability and locus. There was some indication that control also appeared in the data, although it did not come through as an independent dimension and was more evident among the internal causes. This suggests that perhaps control cannot be paired with externality.

The investigation by J. Meyer (1980) provides the best evidence for the dimensions portrayed in Table 2. Meyer gave subjects information relevant to the judgment of the causes of success and failure, such as past history and social norms (Kelley, 1967). The subjects then rated nine possible causes of the outcomes, including ability, effort, task difficulty, luck, mood, and teacher. A factor analysis of these ratings yielded the three dimensions suggested in Table 2.

It therefore appears that what dimensions emerge in part depends on the empirical procedure that is used. Given a multidimensional scaling method in which subjects rate the similarity of the causes, the dimensions generated by the logical analysis may not be identical to those emerging with the empirical procedure. For example, as shown in the Passer (1977) data, a naive person may not spontaneously recognize that mood, luck, and effort are similar because they are unstable, and thus a stability dimension of causality will not be evident. On the other hand, factor-analytic procedures are not subject to this limitation as J. Meyer (1980) has demonstrated. This procedure has yielded results fully supporting the logical analysis. For the scientist these dimensions are second-order concepts (Schütz, 1967, p. 59); they are concepts used by attribution theorists to organize the causal concepts of the layperson.

CONSEQUENCES OF CAUSAL PROPERTIES

I turn now from the dimensions of causality to the consequences or the implications of these dimensions for thought and action. I contend that each of the three dimensions of causality has a primary psychological function or linkage, as well as a number of secondary effects. The primary relation of the *stability* dimension is to the magnitude of expectancy change following success of failure. The *locus* dimension of causality has implications for self-esteem, one of the emotional consequences of achievement performance; affect also is a secondary association for causal stability. The dimensional linkages with expectancy and affect (value) integrate attribution theory with expectancy-value formulations of motivation as outlined by Atkinson (1964), Lewin (1935), and others (see Weiner, 1972, 1974), although this unification is not examined in this article. Finally, perceived *control* by others relates to helping, evaluation, and linking. The theory thus addresses both self- and other-perception and intra- as well as interpersonal behavior. The locus and control dimensions have a number of secondary effects that also will be very briefly considered.

Stability

The primary conceptual linkage of the stability dimension with expectancy of success was first explored by Weiner et al. (1971) and has not greatly changed since that time (see Weiner, 1972, 1974, 1976). I now more fully perceive the implications of this association, other secondary linkages with causal stability have been uncovered, and the empirical data have grown in clarity. But the following discussion is consistent with prior statements and is partially redundant with these earlier writings.

Research in the attributional domain has proven definitively that causal ascriptions for past performance are an important determinant of goal expectancies. For example, failure that is ascribed to low ability or to the difficulty of a task decreases the expectation of future success more than failure that is ascribed to bad luck, mood, or a lack of immediate effort. In a similar manner, success ascribed to good luck or extra exertion results in lesser increments in the subjective expectancy of future success at that task than does success ascribed to high ability or to the ease of the task. More generally, expectancy shifts after success and failure are dependent upon the perceived stability of the cause of the prior outcome; ascription of an outcome to stable factors produces greater typical shifts in expectancy (increments in expectancy after success and decrements after failure) than do ascriptions to unstable causes. Stated somewhat differently, if one attains success (or failure) and if the conditions or causes of that outcome are perceived as remaining unchanged, then success (or failure) will be anticipated with a greater degree of certainty. But if the conditions or causes are subject to change, then there is some doubt that the prior outcome will be repeated.

Empirical Evidence

A large number of research investigations support the above theoretical contentions (e.g., Fontaine, 1974; McMahan, 1973; J. Meyer, 1980; Ostrove, & Goldstein, 1976; Meyer, Note 5; Pancer & Eiser, Note 6). In the Weiner et al. (1976) investigation it was demonstrated that expectancy changes are related to the dimension of stability and are not associated with the locus of causality. This is an important finding, not only because two attributional dimensions are discriminated, but also because a vast competing literature relates expectancy changes to the dimension of locus (see Weiner et al., 1976, for a review).

Weiner et al. (1976) gave subjects either 0, 1, 2, 3, 4, or 5 consecutive success experiences at a block-design task, with different subjects in the six experimental conditions. Following the success trial(s), expectancy of success and causal ascriptions were assessed. Expectancy of future success was determined by having subjects indicate "how many of the next ten similar designs you believe that you will successfully complete" (Weiner et al., 1976, p. 61). To assess perceptions of causality, subjects were required to mark four rating scales that were identical with respect to either the stability or locus dimensional anchors but differing along the alternate dimension. Specifically, one attribution question was "Did you succeed on this task because you are always good at these kinds of tasks, or because you tried especially hard on this particular task?" "Always good" and "tried hard," the anchors on this scale, are identical on the locus of causality dimension (internal), but they differ in perceived stability, with ability a stable attribute and effort an unstable cause. In a similar manner, judgments were made between "lucky" and "tried hard" (unstable causes differing in locus), "these tasks are always easy" and "lucky" (external causes differing in stability), and "always good" and "always easy" (stable causes differing in locus). Thus the judgments permitted a direct test of the locus versus stability interpretation of expectancy change.

Expectancy estimates were examined separately for each of the causal judgments. The data revealed that within both the internal and the external causes, expectancy increments were positively associated with the stability of the ascription; that is, there were higher expectancies given ability and task ease ascriptions than given effort or luck attributions. Contrasting locus of causality differences within either the stable or the unstable ascriptions disclosed that the disparate causal locus groups did not differ in their expectancies of success.

Locus of Control Controversy

One of my disappointments has been that investigators associated with social learning theory and locus of control have failed to recognize or admit the stability-expectancy linkage and the existence of other dimensions of perceived causality. Some researchers (e.g., Lefcourt, von Baeyer, Ware, & Cox, Note 7) are incorporating the stability dimension into perceived causality scales. But this is in contrast with the position of other investigators. For example, Phares (1978) states, "At the present time there does not appear to be a convincing body of data supporting the utility of adding the stability dimension. . . . Even should the addition of stability find support in laboratory studies of expectancy changes, it is not clear that . . . [broader] demonstrations of utility will be forthcoming" (p. 270).

In opposition to this statement the literature associating stability with expectancy change is unequivocal, and the findings generalize outside the laboratory as well as beyond the achievement domain (see Weiner, 1979). It may indeed be that the concept of locus of control has great utility; my modest hope is that individuals in this area will acknowledge some of the prior shortcomings in the conceptual analysis of expectancy shifts at skill and chance tasks and in their limited approach to causality (for a fuller discussion of these issues, see Weiner et al., 1976).

Formal Analysis and Self-Concept Maintenance

McMahan (1973) and Valle and Frieze (1976) have developed formal models of expectancy shifts based on the concept of causal stability. Valle and Frieze postulate that predictions to expectancies (P) are as a function of the initial expectancy (E) plus the degree to which outcomes (O) are attributed to stable causes (S):

$$P = f\{E + O[f(S)]\}$$

In addition, Valle and Frieze (1976) also note that the perceived causes of success and failure are related to the initial expectancy of success. It has been clearly documented that unexpected outcomes lead to unstable attributions, particularly luck (Feather, 1969; Feather & Simon, 1971; Frieze & Weiner, 1971). Hence, Valle and Frieze (1976) conclude: "There is some value for the difference between the initial expectations and the actual outcome that will maximally change a person's predictions for the future. If the difference is greater than this point, the outcome will be attributed to unstable factors to such a great extent that it will have less influence on the person's future predictions (p. 581)."

These ideas have important implications for the maintenance of one's self-concept and for attributional change programs (see Weiner, 1974, 1976). For example, assume than an individual with a high self-concept of ability believes that he or she has a high probability of success at a task. It is probable that failure then would be ascribed to unstable causes such as luck or mood, which may not reduce the subsequent expectancy of success and sustains a high-ability self-concept. On the other hand, success would be ascribed to ability, which increases the subsequent expectancy (certainty) of success and confirms one's high self-regard. The converse analysis holds given a low self-concept of ability and a low expectancy of success: Success would be ascribed to unstable factors, and failure to low ability. These attributions result in the preservation of the initial self-concept (see Ames, 1978; Fitch, 1970; Gilmore & Minton, 1974; Ickes & Layden, 1978). In addition, the above analysis suggests that in change programs involving expectancies of self-concept the perceived causes of performance must be altered, and a modification in self-perception would have to involve a gradual process (Valle & Frieze, 1976).

In one research investigation guided by the above reasoning, Ames, Ames, and Garrison (1977) had children of high or low social status in the classroom attribute causality for positive and negative interpersonal outcomes. For example, the children were given situations such as, "Suppose you meet a new student at school and you become friends quickly"; or "Imagine you ask someone to play with you after school, but they say they cannot play." The children then attributed causality for each situation either to an internal, external, or mutual cause. The data indicated that given negative interpersonal outcomes, high-social-status children made greater use of external causal ascriptions, and given positive interpersonal outcomes they made more internal attributions than the low-social-status pupils.

Resistance to Extinction and Achievement Change

The stability concept is generalizable to the body of psychological literature concerning experimental extinction (see Rest, 1976). Experimental extinction often is defined as the cessation of a previously instrumental response following the permanent withholding of the reward. It is reasonable to presume that when a response is perceived as no longer instrumental to goal attainment, the organism will cease making that response. Hence any attribution that maximizes the expectation that the response will not be followed by the goal should facilitate extinction. On the other hand, attributions that minimize goal expectancy decrements after nonreward should retard extinction.

As discussed above, the stability or instability of the perceived causal factors influences the expectancy that the outcome of an action might change in the future. Therefore I suggest that resistance to extinction is a function of attributions to the causal dimension of stability during the period of nonrein-forcement. Ascriptions of nonreinforcement to bad luck, lack of immediate effort, or other unstable causes are hypothesized to minimize expectancy decrements and result in slower extinction than attributions of nonattainment of a goal to perceived stable factors, such as teacher bias, high task difficulty, or lack of ability. Rest (1976) has presented strong evidence confirming these hypotheses. Inasmuch as random reinforcement schedules elicit unstable causal attributions (Weiner et al., 1971), they also should (and do) increase resistance to extinction. In a similar manner, chance rather than skill instructions also increase resistance to extinction (Phares, 1957), presumably because failure is ascribed to unstable causes only given the chance instructions.

A related notion is that information generating lack of effort ascriptions for failure also should result in response maintenance (see Rest, 1976). There are data in the infrahuman experimental literature that may be interpreted as supporting this hypothesis. Lawrence and Festinger (1962), marshalling evidence to support their cognitive dissonance explanation of extinction, report that resistance to extinction is positively related to the effortfulness of a response. Our analysis suggests that when great exertion is required to attain a reward, the salience of effort as the cause of goal attainment is augmented. Thus the expectancy of reward following nonattainment of the goal should be compara-tively unchanged and extinction prolonged. With repeated nonreward, however, the ascription shifts from effort to ability and/or task difficulty, thus decreasing expectancy and producing extinction.

These ideas have more than just a passing relevance to educational practices. Many of the burgeoning achievement-change programs make direct or indirect use of attributional principles. These programs often attempt to induce students to attribute their failures to a lack of effort, which is both unstable and under volitional control (see Andrews & Debus, 1978; Chapin & Dyck, 1976; Dweck, 1975). This goal is expressly established for failure-oriented children, who apparently ascribe their failures to a lack of ability, which is a stable and uncontrollable cause (see Diener & Dweck, 1978). Presumably, inasmuch as effort can be increased volitionally, ascriptions of nonattainment of a goal to lack of effort will result in the sustaining of hope and increased persistence toward the goal. On the other hand, since ability is stable and not subject to volitional control, ascription of nonattainment of a goal to low ability results in giving up and the cessation of goal-oriented behavior.

In sum it is suggested that the relations between diverse independent variables (reward schedules, effortfulness of the response, and certain attributional biases) and the dependent variables of resistance to extinction or persistence in goal-related behavior are mediated by perceptions of causality:

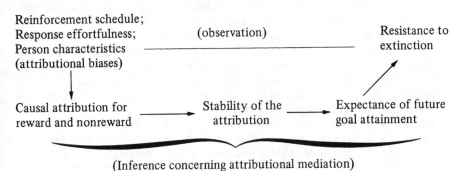

(Inference concerning attributional mediation)

Locus

In contrast to the rather stable beliefs about causal stability, our thoughts concerning locus of causality have fluctuated greatly. A temporary resolution is proposed here that is a synthesis of our previous antithetical positions and better accounts for the complexity of human affective responses.

Initially Weiner et al. (1971) postualted that locus of causality is related to the affective consequences of success and failure. Emotional reactions were believed to be maximized given internal attributions for success and failure and minimized given external attributions. Thus, for example, pride and shame, the alleged dominant affects in achievement situations (Atkinson, 1964; McClelland, Atkinson, Clark, & Lowell, 1953), would be most experienced given personal responsibility for success and failure, as opposed to instances in which external factors such as luck or others were perceived as the causal agents. This postulated relation seemed intuitively reasonable, was consistent with Atkinson's (1964) formulations concerning the incentive value of success and failure, and found support in a variety of research investigations. Because a detailed account of this position was recently presented (Weiner, 1977), I will not discuss it in further detail here.

Subsequently it became evident that it is incorrect to presume an invariant positive relation between internality and the magnitude of emotional reactions in achievement settings. For example, failure ascribed to others, such as the bias of a teacher or hindrance from students or family, will presumably generate great anger and hostility. In this event, externality is positively related to emotional intensity. Thus the position expressed in Weiner et al. (1971) cannot be correct (see Weiner, 1977; Weiner et al., 1978).

We therefore initiated a series of studies to determine the relation between attribution and affect (Weiner et al., 1978; Weiner, Russell, & Lerman, 1979). In our first investigation, subjects were given a scenario that depicted a success or failure experience at an exam, along with a causal attribution for that outcome (e.g., Joan failed because she did not have the ability). The subjects then reported the affects they surmised would be experienced in this situation. About 100 affects for success and 150 for failure were provided, with responses made on rating scales indicating the intensity with which the affects would be experienced.

There were two general findings of interest. First, there was a set of outcome-dependent, attribution-independent affects that represented broad positive or negative reactions to success and failure regardless of the "why" of the outcome. Given success, feelings of pleasure, happiness, satisfaction, goodness, and so on were reported as equally experienced in the disparate attribution conditions. In a similar manner, given failure, there were a number of outcome-linked emotions, such as feeling uncheerful, displeased, and upset. The outcome-dependent affects for both success and failure were reported as the ones that would be most intensely experienced.

But for both success and failure there were many emotions discriminably related to specific attributions. Given success, the unique attribution-affect linkages were the following: ability—competence and confidence; typical effort—relaxation; immediate effort—activation; others—gratitude; personality—conceit; and luck—surprise. That is, if one perceived that success was caused by ability, then competence and confidence were reported as intensely experienced; if one succeeded because of help from others, then the dominant reported affect was gratitude; and so on. In a similar manner, for failure, the attribution-affect linkages were the following: ability—incompetence; effort—guilt and shame; personality—resignation; others—aggression; and luck—surprise (see Weiner et al., 1978; 1979).

It is of interest to point out that at times causal attributions yield opposite reactions for success and failure, as would be expected given diametric outcomes (respectively, competence vs. incompetence given ability attributions; gratitude vs. agression given attributions to others). But at times the same emotion accompanies both positive and negative outcomes (surprise given a luck attribution); and given still other ascriptions, such as typical or immediate effort, the emotions that accompany success (respectively, relaxation and activation) are unrelated to the failure-tied affects (guilt and shame).

These data suggest we should reject the supposition that locus of causality mediates affective reactions in achievement contexts. Rather, emotions appeared to be either outcome or attributionally generated, without any intervening dimensional placement.

Additional evidence, however, has resulted in a synthesis of our prior antithetical stances. In a recent study (Weiner, Russell, & Lerman, 1979) subjects recreated a "critical incident" in their lives in which they succeeded (or failed) at an academic exam because of ability, typical effort, immediate effort, help (or hindrance) from others, personality, or luck. They then listed three affects they experienced in this situation. Table 3 includes only the emotions that were reported for *success* by more than 10% of the respondents for any particular attribution. The table shows the percentage of subjects in all the attribution conditions reporting these relatively shared experiences.

The data in Table 3 are consistent with our previous findings. The most dominant affect, happiness, is expressed regardless of the reason for the success. In addition to this outcome-linked emotion, there are significant attribution-affect linkages. These associations are as follows: ability—competence and pride; other people—gratefulness and thankfulness; stable effort—contentment; personality—pride; and luck—surprise, relief, and guilt (the linkages are based on comparisons within an emotion but across attributions).

The failure data also revealed systematic patterns. There were significant outcome-linked emotions including disappointment, as well as attribution-affect associations consistent with prior research: ability—incompetence and resignation; effort—guilt; other people—anger; and luck—surprise.

Additional analyses of these data also demonstrated that causal dimensions play an essential role in affective life. Given internal attributions for success (ability, effort, personality), the affects pride, competence, confidence, and satisfaction were reported more frequently than they were given external attributions (others, luck). Internal ascriptions for failure generated the emotions of guilt and resignation. In sum, particular affects clustered with the internal causes. Reanalysis of Weiner et al. (1978) revealed virtually identical results.

It therefore appears that in achievement situations there are (at least) three sources of affect. First there are emotions tied directly to the outcome. One feels "good" given success and "bad" given failure, regardless of the reason for the outcome. These probably are the initial and strongest reactions. Second, accompanying these general feelings are more distinct emotions, such as gratitude or hostility if success or failure, respectively, is due to others, surprise when the outcome is due to luck, and so on. Third, the affects that are associated with self-esteem, such as competence, pride, and shame, are mediated by self-ascriptions. Many emotional reactions are shared given success due to ability or

Table 3 Percentage of Respondents Stating a Particular Emotion for Success, as a Function of the Attribution for Success

Emotion	Causal attribution					
	Ability	Unstable effort	Stable Effort	Personality	Others	Luck
Competent	30	12	20	19	5	2
Confident	20	19	18	19	14	4
Content	4	4	12	0	7	2
Excited	3	9	8	11	16	6
Grateful	9	1	4	8	43	14
Guilty	1	3	0	3	2	18
Happy	44	43	43	38	46	48
Proud	39	28	39	43	21	8
Relieved	4	28	16	11	13	26
Satisfied	19	24	16	14	9	0
Surprised	7	16	4	14	4	52
Thankful	0	1	0	0	18	4

Note. From Weiner, Russell, and Lerman, 1979.

effort, the two dominant internal attributions. It therefore may be that the central self-esteem emotions that facilitate or impede subsequent achievement performance are dimensionally linked, referred by the actor to him- or herself. Some affects thus seem to be mediated by the locus dimension but in a manner much more complex than was originally posited. It is likely that these dimension-linked affects have the greatest longevity and most significance for the individual.

Stability and Affect

In addition to the locus-affect linkage, there also is a relation between causal stability and emotions. Weiner et al. (1978) found that the affects of depression, apathy, and resignation were reported primarily given internal and stable attributions for failure (lack of ability, lack of typical effort, personality deficit). This suggests that only attributions conveying that events will not change in the future beget feelings of helplessness, giving up, and depression. Perhaps the control dimension also plays a role in generating these particular emotions. Hence the dimensions of causality relate to different sets of emotions.

In another research investigation supporting a stability—emotion union, Arkin and Maruyama (1979) assessed students' attributions for their success or failure in a college class. In addition, anxiety associated with school performance was measured. It was found that among successful students the stability of their attributions was negatively correlated with anxiety. That is, when success was ascribed to stable causes, students reported relatively little anxiety. On the other hand, among the unsuccessful students, attributional stability and anxiety correlated positively; most fear was reported when failure was perceived as likely to recur in the future.

Cognition-Emotion Sequence in Achievement Contexts

On the basis of the above discussion, I suggest that in achievement-related contexts (and, in particular, school settings), the actor progresses through something like the following cognition-emotion scenarios:

> 1. "I just received a D in the exam. That is a very low grade." (This generates feelings of being frustrated and upset.) "I received this grade because I did not try hard enough" (followed by feelings of shame and guilt). "There really is something lacking in me, and it is permanent" (followed by low self-esteem or lack of worth and hopelessness).
> 2. "I just received an A on the exam. That is a very high grade" (generating happiness and satisfaction). "I received this grade because I worked very hard during the entire school year" (producing contentment and relaxation). "I really do have some positive qualities, and will continue to have them in the future" (followed by high self-esteem and feelings of self-worth, as well as optimism for the future).

Secondary Linkages

Because of the vast literature in the locus of control area, it might be anticipated that causal locus is directly linked with many psychological reactions in addition to esteem-related affects. This indeed is likely to be the case. For example, it has been reported that locus of control relates positively to behaviors such as information seeking and to experiences such as feeling like an "origin" (de Charms, 1968). In most of this research, however, the concepts of *locus* and *control* are united. It is not reasonable to expect individuals who attribute failure to a lack of ability, which is internal but uncontrollable, to seek out information or feel like origins. Rather it seems that the experiential state of an origin and correlated behaviors are exhibited because of the perceived personal control of the situation or the belief that causality is both internal *and* controllable. Thus the discussion of the secondary linkages with locus is postponed until the presentation of the control dimension of causality.

Control

Attribution theory as formulated by Heider (1958), Jones and Davis (1965), and Kelley (1967) primarily concerns person perception, or inferences about the intentions and dispositions of others. But thus far in this article I have only been concerned with self-perception. I believe that one of the main contributions of our work has been the adaptation of some principles of social perception for the construction of a theory of motivation that has the individual as the unit of analysis.

In the discussion of the implications of causal dimensions, self- and other-perception were not distinguished. Considering changes in the expectancy of success, the same cause-effect logic pertaining to causal stability should hold when considering oneself or others. The discussion of affect also is equally applicable to both the self and others, although, of course, the emotional experiences are limited to the self and inferred about others. But if success or failure is perceived as being due to certain causes, then particular affective experiences should follow.

The following examination of the dimension of control centers upon inferences about others and how beliefs about another's responsibility for success and failure influence an actor's reactions toward that person. The reactions examined are helping, evaluation, and sentiments.

Helping

Ickes and Kidd (1976), guided by Weiner et al. (1971) and Rosenbaum (1972), proposed an attributional analysis of helping behavior. A number of investigators prior to Ickes and Kidd (1976) had established that the tendency to help is influenced by the perceived cause of the need for aid (e.g., Berkowitz, 1969; Ickes, Kidd, & Berkowitz, 1976; Piliavin, Rodin, & Piliavin, 1969; Schopler & Matthews, 1965). The majority of these experiments concluded that help is more likely when the perceived cause of the need is an environmental barrier, as opposed to being internal to the person desirous of aid. For example, Berkowitz (1969) reported that individuals are more inclined to help an experimental subject when the experimenter caused a delay in the subject's response, in contrast with a condition in which the subject is perceived as personally responsible for falling behind in the experiment.

In their review, Ickes and Kidd (1976) argued that this locus of control explanation of helping confounds the causal dimensions of locus and intentionality (which I again will call controllability). They suggest that in the study conducted by Berkowitz (1969), the causal ascription to the experimenter is both external and uncontrollable (from the perspective of the actor), whereas an attribution to the subject's own mismanagement is internal to the actor and is perceived by the potential helper as under volitional control. Hence two dimensions of causality are confounded, and it it impossible to determine which of the two causal dimensions is responsible for the differential help-giving. Ickes and Kidd, in contrast with Berkowitz, suggest that it is the controllable aspect of the perceived cause, and not the locus, that mediated the disparate help-giving. The reader should note how similar this analysis is to the one pertaining to expectancy shifts in skill and chance tasks. Both controversies point out that the locus of control literature has been plagued by an inadequate analysis of perceived causality. Furthermore, what is required is research that separates the various causal dimensions.

Other data support the Ickes and Kidd (1976) interpretation of helping behavior. For example, Piliavin et al. (1969) found that there is a bias toward aiding an ill person in distress as opposed to helping a drunk. According to the above argument this is because drunkenness is perceived as subject to volitional control whereas illness is not. When a failure is perceived as controllable, then help is withheld; the persons presumably should help themselves. For this reason it is much easier to raise charity funds for battered children or blindness than for alcoholism centers (see Weiner, 1980).

Guided by the prior research of Barnes, Ickes, and Kidd (1979), Weiner (1980) then applied these ideas to one instance of altruism in the classroom—lending class notes to an unknown classmate. In this investigation two themes were created for a student's failure to take class notes. One theme involved a professor, and the second concerned an employer. In the professor theme the students always (stable) or sometimes (unstable) did not take notes because of something about himself (internal) or something about the professor (external). Either he was unable to take good notes (uncontrollable) or he did not try (controllable), while the professor either was unable to give a clear lecture or did not try. Thus, for example, an internal, stable, and uncontrollable cause was that the student never was able to take good notes (low ability), while an external, unstable, and uncontrollable cause was that the professor at times could not give a clear lecture. Each story within the eight possible causal combinations (2 levels of stability X 2 levels of locus X 2 levels of control) elaborated the basic scenario. The second theme involved a work situation in which the student did not have the notes because he (or the boss) always (sometimes) was responsible for his coming late to school, which could (could not) have been avoided.

Following each causal statement the subjects rated the likelihood of lending their notes to the student. Judgments were made on a 10-point scale anchored at the extremes with "definitiely would lend my notes" and "definitely would not lend my notes."

The mean helping judgments for four conditions (2 levels of locus X 2 levels of control) are shown in Table 4. Stability did not affect the judgments and thus is ignored in the analysis. Table 4 reveals that helping is reported to be relatively equal and reasonably high in all conditions except when the cause is internal and controllable, in which case aid is unlikely to be given. That is, if the student did not try to take notes (professor theme) or could have avoided being absent (employer theme), then help is withheld. The findings concerning the influence of intent information on moral judgments and criminal justice support this line of reasoning (see Caroll & Payne, 1976, 1977).

Table 4 Mean Likelihood of Helping as a Function
of Perceived Locus of Causality
and Controllability

	Controllable	Uncontrollable
Internal	3.13[a]	6.74
External	7.35	6.98

Note. From Weiner (1980).
[a]High numbers indicate greater likelihood of note-lending.

Evaluation

Some of the early experimental work conducted by me and my colleagues was undertaken to promote the distinction between various causes of success and failure. In particular we attempted to provide evidence that ability and effort should be distinguished, although both are internal in locus of causality.

In one reference experiment that was employed, subjects were asked to pretend that they were teachers and were to provide evaluative feedback to their pupils (e.g., Eswara, 1972; Kaplan & Swant, 1973; Rest, Nierenberg, Weiner, & Heckhausen, 1973; Weiner & Kukla, 1970, Weiner & Peter, 1973). The pupils were characterized in terms of effort, ability, and performance on an exam. The data from these investigations conclusively demonstrated that effort is of greater importance than ability in determining reward and punishment. High effort was rewarded more than high ability given success, and lack of effort was punished more than lack of ability given failure. To explain these findings, I stated:

> There appear to be two reasons for the discrepancy between ability and effort as determinants of reward and punishment. First, effort attributions elicit strong moral feelings—trying to attain a socially valued goal is something that one "ought" to do. Second, rewarding and punishing effort is instrumental to changing behavior, inasmuch as effort is believed to be subject to volitional control. On the other hand, ability is perceived as nonvolitional and relatively stable and thus should be insensitive to external control attempts. (Weiner, 1977, p. 508)

Thus both the moral and control aspects of evaluation were considered. But it was not realized that evaluation is conceptually similar to behaviors and feelings such as help-giving, altruism, liking, and blame. That is, there is a pervasive influence of perceived controllability or personal responsibility on interpersonal judgments in achievement-related contexts, including how students are graded.

Sentiments

Investigations linking liking to perceptions of controllability primarily have been conducted in the area of loneliness (see Peplau, Russell, & Heim, 1979). Michela, Peplau, & Weeks (Note 4) found that persons lonely for reasons thought to be controllable (e.g., does not try to make friends) are liked less than individuals lonely for uncontrollable reasons (e.g., no opportunity to meet people). In addition, when a lonely person puts forth effort to make friends, that person is liked and elicits sympathy (Wimer & Peplau, Note 8). In contrast, if it is believed that the lonely individual is responsible for his or her plight, then sympathy is not forthcoming, and respondents indicate they would avoid such persons. I assume that this pattern of results will also be evident in achievement-related contexts. Surely a teacher will not particularly like a student who does not try, and failure perceived as due to lack of effort does not elicit sympathy.

Self-Perception of Control

While perceived control in others relates to interpersonal judgments, self-perceptions of control have quite a different array of consequences. These intrapersonal effects appear to be vast, ranging from experiential states, such as feeling as an origin (de Charms, 1968) and perceiving freedom of choice (Steiner, 1970), to specific behaviors, such as information search (see Rotter, 1966) and normal functioning rather than learning, cognitive, and motivational deficits that are postulated to accompany the loss of control (Seligman, 1975). This is a complex subject matter in need of systematic examination and synthesis that goes well beyond the scope of our present knowledge.

Summary

A variety of sources of information (not discussed here) are used to reach causal inferences in achievement-related contexts. The perceived causes of success and failure primarily are ability and effort but also include a small number of salient factors such as home environment and teacher and a countless host of idiosyncratic factors. These causes can be comprised within three primary dimensions of causality: stability, locus, and control. There also are an undetermined number of subordinate causal dimensions, including perhaps intentionality and globality. The three main dimensions, respectively, are linked to expectancy changes, esteem-related affects, and interpersonal judgments (decisions about helping, evaluation, and sentiments). In addition, there are secondary linkages between the causal dimensions and psychological effects: stability relates to depression-type affects, and control is associated with particular feeling states and behaviors. The dimension-consequence linkages influence motivated behaviors such as persistence and choice. This theory is depicted in Table 5.

ANXIETY

Little attention has been given to the place of anxiety within the attributional conception that has been advocated. However, it is possible to speculate upon the various roles that anxiety may play in this framework.

Anxiety as a Causal Antecedent

Anxiety (an independent variable) is likely to be included among the antecedents that influence causal decision making. Anxiety can interfere with information search and processing and bias the information that is selected and retained.

Anxiety and Perceived Causality

The above analysis suggests that anxiety may impede veridical causal inference making, perhaps resulting in ego-defensive or even self-deprecating causal biases. For example, one might falsely conclude that failure was due to "bad luck" or

Table 5 Partial Representation of an Attributional Theory of Motivation

Antecedent conditions →	Perceived causes →	Causal dimensions →	Primary effects →	Other consequences
	Ability	Stability	Expectancy change	Performance intensity
	Effort (typical and immediate)	Locus	Esteem-related affects	Persistence
	Others (students, family, teacher)	Control	Interpersonal judgements; intrapersonal feeling states	Choice
	Motivation (attention, interest)	Intentionality		Others
	Etc.	Globality		

241

"interference from others" rather than being caused by a lack of ability. These external causal inferences respectively produce feelings of surprise and anger rather than the feeling of incompetence. (One is reminded of the well-known Freudian position regarding the vicissitudes of the instincts, for in the event that an attribution to low ability is altered to one of interference from others, there should be a corresponding change from "aggression turned inward" to "aggression turned outward.")

Anxiety, Expectancy, and Affect

The shifting of causal inferences, in turn, produces alterations in expectancy and affect. Some of these consequences have already been intimated. For example, if anxiety is related to low self-esteem, then given high anxiety, a low level of expectancy is likely to be maintained in achievement-related contexts. This could be mediated, for example, by ascription of failure to low ability and ascription of success to good luck.

Anxiety is also a consequence (dependent variable) of causal ascriptions. My colleagues and I (Weiner, Russell, & Lerman, 1978, 1979) have found that affective experiences are in part dependent upon how one evaluates achievement outcomes. As just indicated, failure ascribed to bad luck or interference from others primarily elicits the respective affects of surprise and aggression rather than fear. But causal ascriptions of failure to the internal factors of ability, effort, and mood do produce anxiety-related affects (e.g., panicky, shaken, troubled). Furthermore, depressive-type affects (e.g., resigned, helpless, apathetic) are reported only when causal ascriptions are made to internal and stable factors (ability, intrinsic motivation, personality). The general message of this analysis is merely that anxiety and related mood states such as depression are strongly influenced by causal cognitions, which comprise one cognitive component of the evaluation of the physical and social world.

REFERENCES

Abramson, L. Y., Seligman, M. E. P., & Teasdale, J. D. Learned helplessness in humans: Critique and reformulation. *Journal of Abnormal Psychology*. 1978, *87*, 49–74.

Ames, C. Children's achievement attributions and self-reinforcement: Effects of self-concept and competitive reward structure. *Journal of Educational Psychology*, 1978, *70*, 345–355.

Ames, R., Ames, C., & Garrison, W. Children's causal ascriptions for positive and negative interpersonal outcomes. *Psychological Reports*, 1977, *41*, 595–602.

Andrews, G. R., & Debus, R. L. Persistence and causal perception of failure: Modifying cognitive attributions. *Journal of Educational Psychology*, 1978, *70*, 154–166.

Arkin, R. M., & Maruyama, G. M. Attribution, affect, and college exam performance. *Journal of Educational Psychology*, 1979, *71*, 85.

Atkinson, J. W. *An introduction to motivation*. Princeton, NJ: Van Nostrand, 1964.

Barnes, R. D., Ickes, W. J., & Kidd, R. F. Effects of perceived intentionality and stability of another's dependency on helping behavior: A field experiment. *Personality and Social Psychology Bulletin*, 1979, *5*, 367–372.

Berkowitz, L. Resistance to improper dependency relationships. *Journal of Experimental Social Psychology*, 1969, *5*, 283–294.

Carroll, J. S., & Payne, J. W. The psychology of the parole decision process: A joint application of attribution theory and information processing psychology. In J. S. Carroll & J. W. Payne (Eds.), *Cognition and social behavior*. Hillsdale, NJ: Erlbaum, 1976.

Carroll, J. S., & Payne, J. W. Judgements about crime and the criminal: A model and a method for investigating parole decision. In B. D. Sales (Ed.), *Prospectives in law and psychology, Vol. 1: The criminal justice system*. New York: Plenum, 1977.

Chapin, M., & Dyck, D. G. Persistence in children's reading behavior as a function of N length and attribution retraining. *Journal of Abnormal Psychology*, 1976, *85*, 511–515.

de Charms, R. *Peronal causation*. New York: Academic Press, 1968.

Deci, E. L. *Intrinsic motivation*. New York: Plenum, 1975.

Diener, C. I., & Dweck, C. A. An analysis of learned helplessness: Continuous changes in performance, strategy, and achievement cognitions following failure. *Journal of Personality and Social Psychology*, 1978, *36*, 451–462.

Dweck, C. S. The role of expectations and attributions in the alleviation of learned helplessness. *Journal of Personality and Social Psychology*, 1975, *31*, 674–685.

Elig, T. W., & Frieze, I. H. A multidimensional scheme for coding and interpreting perceived causality for success and failure events: The Coding Scheme of Perceived Causality (CSPC). *JSAS Catalog of Selected Documents in Psychology*, 1975, *5*, 313. (Ms. No. 1069)

Eswara, H. S. Administration of reward and punishment in relation to ability, effort, and performance. *Journal of Social Psychology*, 1972, *87*, 139–140.

Feather, N. T. Attribution of responsibility and valence of success and failure in relation to initial confidence and task performance. *Journal of Personality and Social Psychology*, 1969, *13*, 129–144.

Feather, N. T., & Simon, J. G. Causal attributions for success and failure in relation to expectations of success based upon selective or manipulative control. *Journal of Personality*, 1971, *39*, 527–541.

Fitch, G. Effects of self-esteem, perceived performance, and choice on causal attributions. *Journal of Personality and Social Psychology*, 1970, *16*, 311–315.

Folkes, V. S. *Causal communication in the early stages of affiliative relationships*. Unpublished doctoral dissertation, University of California, Los Angeles, CA, 1978.

Fontaine, G. Social comparison and some determinants of expected personal control and expected performance in a novel task situation. *Journal of Personality and Social Psychology*, 1974, *29*, 487–496.

Frieze, I. H. Causal attributions and information seeking to explain success and failure. *Journal of Research in Personality*, 1976, *10*, 293–305.

Frieze, I. H., & Weiner, B. Cue utilization and attributional judgments for success and failure. *Journal of Personality*, 1971, *39*, 591–605.

Gilmore, T. M., & Minton, H. L. Internal versus external attributions of task performance as a function of locus of control, initial confidence and success-failure outcome. *Journal of Personality*, 1974, *42*, 159–174.

Heider, F. *The psychology of interpersonal relations*. New York: Wiley, 1958.

Ickes, W. J., & Kidd, R. F. An attributional analysis of helping behavior. In J. H. Harvey, W. J. Ickes, & R. F. Kidd (Eds.), *New directions in attribution research* (Vol. 1). Hillsdale, NJ: Erlbaum, 1976.

Ickes, W. J., Kidd, R. F., & Berkowitz, L. Attributional determinants of monetary help-giving. *Journal of Personality*, 1976, *44*, 163–178.

Ickes, W. J., & Layden, M. A. Attributional styles. In J. H. Harvey, W. J. Ickes, & R. F. Kidd (Eds.), *New directions in attribution research* (Vol. 2). Hillsdale, NJ: Erlbaum, 1978.

Jones, E. E., & Davis, K. E. From acts to dispositions: The attribution process in person perception. In L. Berkowitz (Ed.), *Advances in experimental social psychology* (Vol. 2). New York: Academic Press, 1965.

Kaplan, R. M., & Swant, S. G. Reward characteristics of appraisal of achievement behavior. *Representative Research in Social Psychology*, 1973, *4*(2), 11–17.

Kelley, H. H. *Attribution in social interaction*. Morristown, NJ: General Learning Press, 1971.

Lau, R. R., & Russell, D. Attributions in the sports pages: A field test of some current hypotheses in attribution research. *Journal of Personality and Social Psychology*, 1980, *39*, 29–38.

Lawrence, D. H., & Festinger, L. *Deterrents and reinforcement*. Stanford, CA: Stanford University Press, 1962.

Lewin, K. *A dynamic theory of personality*. New York: McGraw-Hill, 1935.

Mann, L. On being a sore loser: How fans react to their tesm's failure. *Australian Journal of Psychology*, *1974, 26*, 37–47.

McClelland, D. C., Atkinson, J. W., Clark, R. A., & Lowell, E. L. *The achievement motive*. New York: Appleton-Century-Crofts, 1953.

McMahan, I. D. Relationships between causal attributions and expectancy of success. *Journal of Personality and Social Psychology*, 1973, *28*, 108–114.

Meyer, J. P. Dimensions of causal attribution for success and failure: A multivariate investigation. *Journal of Personality and Social Psychology*, 1980, *38*, 689–703.

Meyer, W. U., Folkes, V. S., & Weiner, B. The perceived information value and affective consequences of choice behavior and intermediate difficulty task selection. *Journal of Research in Personality*, 1976, *10*, 410–423.

Ostrove, N. Expectations for success on effort-determined tasks as a function of incentive and performance feedback. *Journal of Personality and Social Psychology*, 1978, *36*, 909–916.

Passer, M. W. *Perceiving the causes of success and failure revisited: A multidimensional scaling approach.* Unpublished doctoral dissertation, University of California, Los Angeles, 1977.

Peplau, L. A., Russell, D., & Heim, M. An attributional analysis of loneliness. In I. Frieze, D. Bar-Tal, & J. Carroll (Eds.), *Attribution theory: Applications to social problems.* San Francisco: Jossey Bass (1979).

Phares, E. J. Expectancy changes in skill and chance situations. *Journal of Abnormal and Social Psychology*, 1957, *54*, 339–342.

Phares, E. J. Locus of control. In H. London & J. E. Exner, Jr. (Eds.), *Dimensions of personality.* New York: Wiley, 1978.

Piliavin, I. M., Rodin, J., & Piliavin, J. A. Good Samaritanism: An underground phenomenon? *Journal of Personality and Social Psychology*, 1969, *13*, 289–299.

Rest, S. Schedules of reinforcement: An attributional analysis. In J. H. Harvey, W. J. Ickes, & R. F. Kidd (eds.), *New directions in attribution research* (Vol. 1). Hillsdale, NJ: Erlbaum, 1976.

Rest, S., Nierenberg, R., Weiner, B., & Heckhausen, H. Further evidence concerning the effects of perceptions of effort and ability on achievement evaluation. *Journal of Personality and Social Psychology*, 1973, *28*, 187–191.

Riemer, B. S. Influence of causal beliefs on affect and expectancy. *Journal of Personality and Social Psychology*, 1975, *31*, 1163–1167.

Rosenbaum, R. M. *A dimensional analysis of the perceived causes of success and failure.* Unpublished doctoral dissertation, University of California, Los Angeles, 1972.

Rotter, J. B. Generalized expectancies for internal versus external control of reinforcement. *Psychological Monographs*, 1966, *80*(1, Whole No. 609).

Schopler, J., & Matthews, M. W. The influence of the perceived causal locus of partner's dependence on the use of interpersonal power. *Journal of Personality and Social Psychology*, 1965, *2*, 609–612.

Schütz, A. *Collected papers. I. The problem of social reality.* The Hague, Martinus Nijhoff, 1967.

Seligman, M. E. P. *Helplessness: On depression, development, and death.* San Francisco: Freeman, 1975.

Steiner, I. D. Perceived freedom. In L. Berkowitz (Ed.), *Advances in experimental social psychology* (Vol. 5). New York: Academic Press, 1970.

Triandis, H. *The analysis of subjective culture.* New York: Wiley-Interscience, 1972.

Valle, V. A. *Attributions of stability as a mediator in the changing of expectations.* Unpublished doctoral dissertation, University of Pittsburgh, 1974.

Valle, V. A., & Frieze, I. H. Stability of causal attributions as a mediator in changing expectations for success. *Journal of Personality and Social Psychology*, 1976, *33*, 579–587.

Weiner, B. *Theories of motivation: From mechanism to cognition.* Chicago: Rand McNally, 1972.

Weiner, B. (Ed.). *Achievement motivation and attribution theory.* Morristown, NJ: General Learning Press, 1974.

Weiner, B. An attributional approach for educational psychology. In L. Shulman (Ed.), *Review of research in education* (Vol. 4). Itasca, IL: Peacock, 1976.

Weiner, B. Attribution and affect: Comments on Sohn's critique. *Journal of Educational Psychology*, 1977, *69*, 506–511.

Weiner, B. A theory of motivation for some classroom experiences. *Journal of Educational Psychology*, 1979, *71*, 3–25.

Weiner, B. A cognitive (attribution)-emotion-action model of motivated behavior: An analysis of judgments of help-giving. *Journal of Personality and Social Psychology*, 1980, *39*, 186–200.
Weiner, B., Frieze, I. H., Kukla, A., Reed, L., Rest, S., & Rosenbaum, R. M. *Perceiving the causes of success and failure.* Morristown, NJ: General Learning Press, 1971.
Weiner, B., & Kukla, A. An attributional analysis of achievement motivation. *Journal of Personality and Social Psychology*, 1970, *15*, 1–20.
Weiner, B., Nierenberg, R., & Goldstein, M. Social learning (locus of control) versus attributional (causal stability) interpretations of expectancy of success. *Journal of Personality*, 1976, *44*, 52–68.
Weiner, B., & Peter, N. A cognitive-developmental analysis of achievement and moral judgments. *Developmental Psychology*, 1973, *9*, 290–309.
Weiner, B., Russell, D., & Lerman, D. Affective consequences of causal ascriptions. In J. H. Harvey, W. J. Ickes, & R. F. Kidd (eds.), *New directions in attribution research* (Vol. 2). Hillsdale, NJ: Erlbaum, 1978.
Weiner, B., Russell, D., & Lerman, D. The cognition-emotion process in achievement-related contexts. *Journal of Personality and Social Psychology*, 1979, *37*, 1211–1220.
Wong, P. T. P. & Weiner, B. When people ask why questions and the heuristics of attributional search. *Journal of Personality and Social Psychology*, in press.

REFERENCE NOTES

1. Bar-Tal, D., & Darom, E. *Causal Perceptions of pupils' success or failure by teachers and pupils: A comparison.* Unpublished manuscript, University of Tel-Aviv, Israel, 1977.
2. Cooper, H. M., & Burger, J. M. *Internality, stability, and personal efficacy: A categorization of free response academic attributions.* Unpublished manuscript, University of Missouri, Columbia, 1978.
3. Litman-Adizes, T. *An attributional model of depression: Laboratory and clinical investigations.* Unpublished manuscript, University of California, Los Angeles, 1977.
4. Michela, J., Peplau, L. A., & Weeks, D. *Perceived dimensions and consequences of attributions for loneliness.* Unpublished manuscript, University of California, Los Angeles, 1978.
5. Meyer, W. U. *Selbstantworlichkeit und Leistungsmotivation.* Unpublished doctoral dissertation, Ruhr-Universität, Bochum, West Germany, 1970.
6. Pancer, S. M. & Eiser, J. R. *Expectations, aspirations, and evaluations as influenced by another's attributions for success and failure.* Paper presented at the 83rd Annual Meeting of the American Psychological Association, Chicago, September 1975.
7. Lefcourt, H. M., von Baeyer, C. L., Ware, E. E., & Cox, D. J. *The multidimensional-multiattributional causality scale: The development of a goal-specific locus of control scale.* Unpublished manuscript, University of Waterloo, Ontario, Canada, 1978.
8. Wimer, S. W., & Peplau, L. S. *Determinants of reactions to lonely others.* Paper presented at the 58th Annual Meeting of the Western Psychological Association, San Francisco, April 1978.

12

Task-Irrelevant Cognitions during an Exam

Incidence and Effects

Heinz Heckhausen
University of Bochum

Instead of hyperactivity, the inadequate use of time spent on a task is currently regarded as the performance-interfering effect of anxiety in self-esteem threatening stress situations. It is assumed that anxious persons pay too much attention to task-irrelevant cognitions that deal with self-concern, so that they are distracted from actual problem solving (see review by Sarason, 1975; Wine, 1971). In agreement with this attention hypothesis several authors have found that in a postexperimental questionnaire highly anxious as compared to low-anxious persons report a higher frequency of thoughts about succeeding or failing (Mandler & Watson, 1966; Marlett & Watson, 1968).

Other authors found that postexperimental reports can be divided into a cognitive and an affective component of anxiety (two-component hypothesis). The cognitive component includes self-concern cognitions (worry), while the affective component includes the awareness of emotionality symptoms. Both components have different effects: First, emotionality is high only during the test period, whereas self-concern already exists before the exam and persists after the exam (Spiegler, Morris, & Liebert, 1968). Second, expectation of failure before an exam covaries with self-concern cognitions during the exam but not with emotionality (Liebert & Morris, 1967; Morris & Liebert, 1970; Spiegler et al., 1968). Third, self-concern cognitions—but not emotionality—during the test correlate with poor performance, especially if the test-taking time is limited (Doctor & Altman, 1969; Morris & Liebert, 1969, 1970).

The following study attempts to assess the frequency and effects of various types of task-irrelevant cognitions during an oral exam. For this purpose a questionnaire was administered immediately after the oral examination. Eleven types of cognitions were designated "task-irrelevant." These cognitions do not directly contribute to the intended solution of the problem. In this case, problem solution consisted of answering exam questions. In general the level of interference of task-irrelevant cognitions is expected to increase with their frequency and to be accompanied by poor exam results. But such a general relationship probably varies in two respects: first, in regard to different types of task-irrelevant cognitions, and second, because of differences in the motivation of the candidates.

The present study is designed to elaborate the predicted overall relationship between the frequency of task-irrelevant cognitions and the extent of their interference. It also searches for moderating main effects of "cognition type" and of individual motivation as well as for possible interaction effects. For this reason, possible contents of cognitions were divided beforehand into different categories. The categorization was done on a strictly theory-oriented basis, that is, according to an extended process-model of motivation (Heckhausen, 1973, 1977). In order to determine the effects of individual motivation differences, two additional sets of motivation variables were assessed with the same postexamination questionnaire.

The first set of variables includes determinants of the motivation process *before* and *after* the exam. Therefore it will be called "motivation process." These variables are: aspiration level (before the exam), the grade received, the causal attribtuion of this grade, and self-evaluation (after the exam). It was expected that a "negative motivation syndrome" consisting of these four variables (i.e., an unrealistic aspiration level, poorer grades, more external causal attribution, and more negative self-evaluations) goes along with an increasing incidence and a more adverse effect of task-irrelevant cognitions. According to the two-component hypothesis this negative motivation syndrome should be related more closely to self-doubt cognitions than to neutral task-irrelevant cognitions or to cognitions indicating awareness of an emotional state.

The second set of variables refers to the motivation *during* the exam. These variables indicate whether a success- or a failure-oriented motivation state predominated (S- vs. F-state). In addition, motivation state is also differentiated into its factor-analyzed affective and cognitive components. An F-state is expected to correlate with frequency and interference level of task-irrelevant cognitions (especially those of the self-doubt type). The variables of "motivation process" and "motivation state" should covary. A negative motivation syndrome should be associated with F-state, and a positive motivation syndrome with S-state.

According to the two-component hypothesis of test anxiety, only the cognitive and not the affective components of the motivation state should correlate with poor exam grades. Finally, among the task-irrelevant cognitions, specific contents should relate to specific emotions. Possible relationships between different kinds of causal attribution cognitions and emotions will be investigated.

METHOD

Subjects were 70 psychology students who were examined by the author in developmental psychology during one exam period. They had been asked some weeks before if they were willing to participate in this study. Strict anonymity was assured. Of the 70 subjects 65 (36 females, 29 males) filled out the questionnaire completely or almost completely. Since they did not always answer all the items, the number of subjects is somewhat smaller in most cases.

Immediately after the oral exam and after being informed about the grade attained the examinee was directed into a separate room where he or she was to complete a three-piece questionnaire. The first part referred to the motivation process before and after the exam, the second to the motivation state during the exam, and the third to the frequency and the effects of the various cognitions during the exam.

Cognitions during the Exam

In accordance with the mentioned process model of motivation (Heckhausen, 1973, 1977) ten types of cognitions were distinguished. The third part of the questionnaire consisted of 40 different thoughts phrased in the form of running heads. These thoughts referred to the exam situation. Every thought was to be rated on a 4-point scale ("never" vs. "often"), according to its frequency, and then on a 5-point scale ("very distracting" vs. "very helpful") according to the influence it had on exam performance. Two of the ten cognition types (or content categories) referred to the task, whereas the other eight were task-irrevelant, that is, they did not contribute to answering the exam questions. One of these eight categories concerned "irrelevancies," the remaining seven were designed as categories of self-concern. Within each of these seven categories there was an equal number of negative and positive items that were in one way or another related to poor or good exam performance. The negative items all dealt with cognitions of self-doubt. A ninth category included "performance intentions" for the improvement of the achievement process. The last category, "self-forgetfulness," referred to the incidence rate of task-related information processing and thereby to the absence of cognitions of self-concern and their interfering influence. In detail, these categories were:

1. Causal attribution of the possible performance results: content vs. discontent with one's exam preparations; satisfied vs. unsatisfied with one's ability (9 items).
2. Incentive values of the possible consequences of performance results: expecting to be positively or negatively evaluated by oneself or by others after the exam (8 items).
3. The standards set by the examinee: accomplishing, nonaccomplishing, or overaccomplishing aspiration level; comparison of own exam results with those of others and with one's earlier results (5 items).
4. The course of performance: ascending-descending trend of performance (3 items).
5. Action-outcome expectancies: confidence in, doubts about being successful (2 items).
6. General emotional state: tension vs. relaxation; positive vs. negative emotional states (6 items).
7. Performance intentions: to concentrate more (2 items).
8. Situation-outcome expectancies: to get it over with somehow; looking forward to the end of the exam. These two items are similar to those of the action-outcome expectancies and, if not mentioned otherwise, are combined with them.
9. Irrelevancies: unimportant externals of the situation (2 items).
10. Self-forgetfulness. One item: "I was concentrating on the problem so much that I totally forgot myself."

Motivation State

Analogous to the procedure of Spielberger (1966), who assesses anciety as a temporary state (state anxiety) in a circumscribed situation, the second part of the questionnaire determined a success-oriented (12 items) and a failure-oriented motivation state (15 items; S- and F-state). Both sets of items were designed according to the TAT procedure of determining the motive tendencies "hope of success" (HS) and "fear of failure" (FF) (see Heckhausen, 1963) and also according to the construct validation of these two variables (see especially Schmalt, 1976). Both sets of items were first tested with an independent sample of examinees for response distribution and item-test correlations, and in some cases rephrased. Every item referred to the preceding exam. As expected, there was little homogeneity in both item sets (average inter-item correlation for S-state: $r = .20$; for F-state: $r = .25$). The scores for both motivation states are not independent of each other, as are the TAT scores for HS and FF. A negative correlation rather suggests a bipolarity of the S- and F-states. The difference between the sums of S-item and F-item scores was taken as an individual's index of his or her motivation state. Since female subjects showed a higher average HS score than male students, S- and F-state groups were formed according to separate medians or terciles for males and females. This was done in order to ensure that there would be the same number of males and females in the groups to be compared.

All 27 items were factor analyzed. Since answers were probably influenced by the grade just received and by the sex of the examinee, both variables were considered as heterogeneity factors whose variance component was extracted according to a method of Overall (1962; Cooley & Lohnes, 1971). The exam grade accounted for 8.4% and the sex for 6.7% of the variance in the correlation matrix. The residual correlation matrix was analyzed into its main components, and the obtained factorial structure was varimax-rotated. Five bipolar factors and one unipolar factor were obtained. Each factor could easily be interpreted in agreement with the construct dimensions of HS and FF. Nineteen of the 27 items loaded at least .50 on one of the six factors. Only 2 of the remaining 8 items showed a factor-loading of below .40 (but above .30). In the following the single factors are listed and marked with items of high positive or negative factor-loadings. The sequence was chosen so that the factors 1–3 can be classified as being more "cognitive" and the factors 4–6 as being more "affective."

1. *Experiencing competence vs. incompetence* (10.5%, total amount of variance accounted for). "I was often not satisfied with my performance" (factor-loading: +.76). "I was often uncertain whether I had answered sufficiently" (+.61). "I was altogether content with my answers to the exam questions" (−.69).

2. *Failure expectancy vs. anticipation of success* (8.3%). "I thought: if only the exam were over" (+.57). "I was sure I would make it" (−.72).

3. *Negative vs. positive self-evaluation* (9.4%). "In between I thought: Am I prepared enough for this exam?" (+.47). "I already saw myself satisfied after passing the exam" (−.73).

4. *Nervousness vs. calmness* (9.3%). "I was worried because of the lack of feedback from the examiner" (+.69). "I felt my performance ability constrained on account of my nervousness" (+.61). "I felt fully up to the situation" (−.44).

5. *Feeling overtaxed vs. enjoying mastering difficulties* (9.9%). "I hoped to get easy questions" (+.76). "At first some questions appeared to be just too difficult for me" (+.74). "I enjoyed answering questions that were somewhat more difficult" (−.55).

6. *Cool and objective response control* (6.7%), unipolar. "When difficult questions were posed I thought about the problem first, in order to explain it correctly (+.76). "I was very cool during the exam" (+.44). "I was worried that I would do something wrong" (+0.40). In the following, the absence of this factor will be called *lack of response control.*

Motivation Process

The first part of the questionnaire assessed the essential determinants of the motivation process before and after the exam (22 items). The most important variables in detail were:

1. Aspiration level before the exam; satisfactory or unsatisfactory grade-level goal discrepancy; the grade achieved minus the unsatisfactory grade.
2. Causal attribution of the received grade after the exam: ability for this subject area, amount and intensity of study and exam preparation, unfavorable physical condition, examiner, chance (bad vs. good luck) (5 five-point scales).
3. Self-evaluation after the exam: contentment with the exam performance, relief, annoyance (3 five-point scales).

RESULTS

Motivation Process and Motivation State

Before we present the main results concerning incidence and effect of different types of task-irrelevant cognitions, let us turn to the results indicating the construct validity of the variables of motivation process and motivation state. Theory requires relations both within as well as between the two sets of variables.

As far as the relations among the variables of the motivation process are concerned, the variable "self-evaluation" plays a central role, because it is dependent on aspiration level, achievement level, and causal attribution. These are three determinants among the other variables (see Heckhausen, 1973, 1975). By means of a multiple-regression analysis it could be demonstrated that these theoretically essential variables account for 51% of the self-evaluation variance: 29% are due to the difference between aspiration level and the grade achieved (goal discrepancy), and additional 22% are due to different factors of the causal attribution (and among those "unfavorable physical condition" accounted on its own for 16%). Furthermore, goal discrepancy as an indicator of an unrealistic (namely a too low) aspiration level correlates with the compound variable "feeling overtaxed," that is, with the difference between the estimated minimum degree of actual ability and the minimum degree of ability estimated to be necessary to pass the exam.

Taking a look at the motivation state, one can say that the factor-analytically derived components all seem theoretically meaningful and are easily interpreted (see above). As we will see, the variables of the motivation state (as well as those of the motivation process) account considerably for the variance of frequency and interference of task-irrelevant cognitions.

As expected the two sets of variables converge with regard to their meaning as constructs. This is demonstrated by covariations between single variables of the motivation process and state. Table 1 differentiates the correlations among the two sets of variables. Instead of the comprehensive S- and F-states, the six factors of the motivation state are used. The three motivation factors "experiencing incompetence," "failure expectancy," and "feeling overtaxed" covary most closely with aspiration level and causal attribution of achieved exam results. The more marked these factors are the lower is the grade level with which one would be satisfied and the poorer are the attained grades.

The more the F-state is based on a "negative self-evaluation" the less is "ability" used as a factor for causal attribution. This might be an indication that one's own ability concept is a problematical issue of one's self-image. In attributing causes, biases are most likely to occur in connection with the causes "intensity of exam preparations" (effort) and "luck" (good or bad luck). Generally, the belief that the amount of effort during the exam preparations does not influence the grade increases together with the distinctiveness of five of the six factors of the F-state. In addition, the factor "unfavorable physical condition" is included as an explanation of (obviously disappointing) exam performance. As expected, this causal factor correlates rather closely (.50) with the motivation factor "nervousness." By and large, the preference for external causal attributions (for diminishing the perceived self-responsibility) increases with F-state. Such an externalizing tendency correlates especially with "negative self-evaluation" and with "experiencing incompetence."

Finally, let us look at self-evaluation. With low aspiration level and grade attained, contentment and relief after the exam are higher the stronger the motivation factor "experiencing incompetence" is. The relationship is not paradoxical but rather plausible if one considers that nobody failed, not even the examinees with intense "feelings of incompetence."

Similar covariations are obtained if, in terms of motivation state, one merely differentiates between the summarized S- and F-states. Some of these results indicate effects of sex differences. In the causal attribution of the attained exam grades the F-group, in comparison to the S-group, emphasizes much less intensive exam preparation ($F[1.61] = 13.92$; $p < .001$), much more unfavorable physical condition ($F = 4.92$; $p < .05$), and more luck ($F[1.41] = 7.46$; $p < .01$). Both groups attribute the same amount of influence to the examiner. In most cases the differences are somewhat greater for the male candidates, so that significant interaction effects exist between motivation state and sex. The difference between internal (ability, exam preparation) and external causal factors (examiner, luck) shows a strong main effect of the motivation state ($F[1.52 = 13.08$; $p < .001$). The F-group refers more often to external causal factors (mainly good or bad luck), and the S-group explains the outcome more often in terms of internal factors (especially intensity of exam preparation). Since the references to causal factors by the females of both motivation groups are more evenly distributed than those of the male subjects, we also find a strong interaction effect of motivation state and sex ($F[1.52] = 8.11$; $p < .01$). In contrast to male subjects female examinees of both motivation groups do not differ in the attribution of success or failure to good or bad luck. Males of the F-group attribute far more to luck than those of the S-group ($p < .001$).

As far as self-evaluation is concerned, the S-group reports more contentment with their exam performance than the F-group ($F[1.61] = 4.93$; $p < .05$). The

Table 1 Correlations (p < .10) of Variables of the Motivation Process with the Various Failure-oriented Factors of the Motivation State

| | | Variables of the motivation state | | | | | |
| | | Cognitive components | | | Affective components | | |
Variables of the motivation process	N	1 Experiencing incompetence	2 Negative self-evaluation	3 Failure expectancy	4 Nervousness	5 Feeling over-taxed	6 Lack of reaction control
Aspiration level							
1. Grade level with which satisfied	49	-.25		-.56ss		-.52ss	
2. Grade level with which dissatisfied	51	-.27		-.48ss		-.54ss	
3. Attained grade level	65	-.41ss	-.37ss	-.33ss			
4. Goal discrepancy (3 minus 2)	51				-.23	-.31s	
Causal attribution							
5. Ability	65		-.27s				
6. Degree of exam preparation	65	-.31s	-.45ss	-.27s	-.36ss	-.25s	
7. Unfavorable physical condition	44	.26		.27	.50ss		
8. Examiner	62				.25		
9. Luck	57	.26s	.25	.30s		.31s	
10. Externalizing tendency ((8 + 9) − (5 + 6))	56	.39ss	.47ss		.37ss	.28ss	
Self-evaluation							
11. Contentment	65	.32s					
12. Relief	65	.30s					.22

Note. s:p < .05; ss:p < .01.

two groups do not differ significantly in terms of feelings of relief and/or anger. With regard to anger there is a sex related main effect: Male subjects report having been more annoyed than females $(F[1.61] = 5.08; p < .05)$. That is, the males of the F-group are more angry than those of the S-group $(p < .05)$.

Frequency and Interference of the Various Types of Cognitions

The results confirm, as expected, a remarkably high frequency and great variety of task-irrelevant cognitions. However, the results also show that the adverse influence depends very much upon the content of the cognitions. This influence is subject to considerable individual differences, even with equal frequency.

Let us first look at the *differences between the types of cognitions*. The estimated interference of most of them grows with increasing frequency, in the following order: Irrelevancies $(r_s = .70)$, causal attribution $(r_s = .50)$, incentive values of the consequences $(r_s = .36)$, affective state $(r_s = .34)$, course of performance $(r_s = .28)$, and action-outcome expectancies, the latter being only significant at the 10% level. As expected, performance intentions were not thought to have an adverse effect. Among self-concern cognitions there were only two categories, "norm-setting" and "situation-outcome expectancies," that were not considered to be interfering in spite of high frequencies. All the cognition types, taken together, show a higher level of experienced interference with increasing frequency $(r_s = .52)$.

Frequency and level of interference should correlate more closely if only self-doubt cognitions are considered, because these are more straining and impairing in their effects as compared to neutral or self-assurance contents. This is confirmed by correlations between the interfering influence of the various cognitions and the frequency of their self-doubt contents. The correlations increase for "causal attributions" from .50 to .57 (internal, negative) and to .61 (external), for "incentive values" from .34 to .64, for "course of performance" from .21 to .65, and for "norm-setting" from .06 to .50.

The small increase of several correlation coefficients demonstrates that, with growing frequency, positive contents of causal-attribution cognitions are hardly less interfering than negative ones. This applies in almost the same degree to the positive contents of incentive values and affective state. On the other hand, it hardly applies to the positive contents of course of performance and action-outcome expectancies, and it does not at all apply to norm-setting. If we also add to self-doubt the frequency of those cognitions that cannot be divided into positive and negative contents (i.e., irrelevancies, performance intentions, and situation-outcome expectancies), the correlation with the summarized interference effect increases from .52 to .78. That means, it is essentially the negative self-doubt contents that lead to the covariation of cognition frequency and adverse effect. But the relationship between frequency and interference is still not as close as the attention hypothesis suggests. Assuming that the questionnaire data reflect what actually happened, there must be considerable individual differences as to the extent that the frequency of task-irrelevant cognitions is interfering, even if the contents of these cognitions are self-centered. Let us now turn to the sources of these individual differences.

Frequency of Cognitions
and Motivation Process Variables

If we examine the overall frequency of each task-irrelevant cognition (i.e., without distinguishing whether contents refer to positive or negative self-concern), then frequency increases the more the single process variables add to a negative motivation syndrome (i.e., unrealistic aspiration level, high goal discrepancy, poor grades, external causal attribution, and negative self-evaluation). The correlations, however, are almost all insignificant.[1] Conversely, the frequency of self-forgetfulness (i.e., the absence of task-irrelevant cognitions) correlates significantly with variables of the positive motivation syndrome: with good grades ($r = .20$; $p < .10$), with attribution of the grade to one's ability ($r = .29$; $p < .05$), with internal factors ($.30$; $p < .02$), with lack of externalizing tendencies ($-.27$; $p < .05$), and with contentment about the achieved grade ($.22$; $p < .10$).

In line with our hypothesis, all motivation variables covary with cognition frequency as soon as the items of each cognition type are divided into "positive," "negative," and "open" contents; that is, success-oriented, failure-oriented (self-doubt), and neither success- nor failure-oriented. This categorization refers to all cognition contents with the exception of "performance intentions," the items of which are already failure-oriented; and with the exception of "irrelevancies" because these items are neither success- nor failure-oriented. Within the category "causal attribution," only the internal factors are divided into positive and negative contents. All the external factors (task difficulty, examiner, chance, momentary disposition) are combined into one single category.

The frequencies of failure-oriented (self-doubt) and success-oriented contents (self-confidence) of the various cognitions are conversely related to the variables of the motivation process. In detail: The lower the *aspiration level,* the more causal attribution draws on external factors ($-.34$), and the less positive incentives of the consequences ($.47$) and success expectancies play an important role ($.50$). That means, the lower the aspiration level, the more often one doubts a satisfactory course of performance. The greater the goal discrepancy, the more frequently consequences having negative incentive values come to mind ($.31$).

The relatively poorer the attained grade is, the more the following effects are observed: external factors (such as lack of ability and insufficient exam preparation) are considered as causal factors during the exam ($.40$); anticipated incentive values of the consequences are negative ($.23$) and not positive ($-.22$); the examinee is aware of not having achieved the set standard ($.26$); he or she doubts a satisfactory course of performance ($.38$) and gives up to failure expectancies ($.42$); the examinee becomes aware of a negative affective state ($.29$) and less so of a positive affective state ($.23$).

The more the exam result is attributed to *ability,* the more the following data are registered: causal attribution cognitions refer less frequently to internal factors ($.23$); the examinee experiences more often the feeling before the exam that he or she would reach the standard set ($.35$); an unfavorable course of performance is noticed less frequently ($-.21$) and a positive affective state more so ($.29$).

----

[1] Since several variables were not distributed normally, the data of each variable were dichotomized and point-biserial correlations were computed.

The more the exam outcome is attributed to the intensity of the *exam preparation* (effort), the more the following effects are noted: The incentive values of the anticipated consequences are positive (.30) and not negative (−.36); failure expectancies do not occur (−.33); an unsatisfactory course of performance is noticed less frequently (−.27) and a positive affective state more so (.24).

The more one attributes the exam outcome to *unfavorable physical condition*, the more the following effects are stated: the examinee is concerned with internal causal attributions during the exam (.43); failure expectancies occur more often (.46); a negative emotional state is noticed (.26), whereas a positive emotional state is absent (−.38).

The more the *examiner* is held to be responsible for the grade attained, the more often the examinee engages in external causal attributions during the exam (.23) and experiences positive feelings (.27).

The more often the grade is ascribed to *good or bad luck*, the more the following effects are noticed: the examinee is concerned with external causal attributions during the exam (.31); failure expectancies occur (.27); the examinee thinks less frequently that he or she would attain the norm set (−.27).

The more the exam result is afterwards attributed to *internal factors* and the less to *external factors*, the more the following manifestations are observed: internal (−.26) as well as external factors (−.29) are considered; negative consequences (−.25), failure expectancies (−.35), and the feeling of having had an unsatisfactory course of performance (−.23) occur less frequently; on the other hand, anticipations of positive consequences (.30) and of positive feelings (.34) are more frequent; the examinee is certain to achieve the aspiration level set (.40).

With increasing experience of *satisfaction* with the attained grade, doubts about one's ability and exam preparation (−.28) and failure expectancies (−.35) decrease, but certainty to attain the aspiration level (.32), as well as awareness of a favorable course of performance (.22) and of positive feelings (.45) increases.

Similar relations exist for the *feeling of relief* after the exam. The more one feels relieved, the more frequently one anticipates positive consequences during the exam (.29), is certain to attain the goal set (.40), notices a favorable course of performance (.39) and positive feelings (.38), and experiences fewer failure expectancies (−.23).

The greater one's *annoyance* is after the exam, the more often one thinks of negative consequences during the exam (.30), doubts the goal attainment (.23), compares the goal setting with one's own earlier performances and with achievements of others (.28), notices an unsatisfactory course of performance (.26), anticipates failure (.37), and experiences negative feelings (.41).

The results can be summarized as follows: It is not simply the frequency of task-irrelevant cognitions but mainly the occurrence of self-doubt contents during the exam that correlates with a straining motivation process before and after the exam. A low aspiration level before the exam correlates especially with the following self-doubts: degree to which internal (perceived as insufficient) and external factors are considered, negative incentive values and failures are anticipated, and an unfavorable course of performance is noticed. Furthermore, a low aspiration level correlates with discontent, lack of relief, annoyance, and a bias for attributing the attained grade more often to external (unfavorable physical condition or chance) than to internal factors (ability or exam preparation).

If some of the motivation variables (aspiration level, goal discrepancy, and the various causal attribution factors) are taken as predictors of the frequency of self-doubt cognitions, multiple-regression analyses account, on the average, for 22% of the total variance of the self-doubt frequency within the single cognition types; e.g., for cognitions about negative incentive values ($R^2 = .33$), external causal factors ($R^2 = .26$), the setting of standards ($R^2 = .13$), and affective states ($R^2 = .18$). As expected, we do find that the motivation process variables covary more closely with self-concern cognitions (such as behavior-outcome expectancies, course of performance, and causal attributions) than with cognitions about one's emotionality (nervousness, test anxiety).

Adverse Effects of Cognitions and Motivation Process Variables

The estimated adverse effect of cognitions, divided up into positive and negative content, shows far more relations to the variables of the motivation process than does the total frequency of cognitions. Table 2 shows how their interfering effect correlates with the variables of the motivation process. Included are only correlations of the cognition categories "causal analysis," "course of performance," "action-outcome expectancies," and "affective state"; and only those pairs of correlation coefficients for positive and negative contents are considered of which at least one coefficient reached a significance level of 10% or less. (In the category "norm-setting" there are no significant correlations with negative contents; in the category "incentive of the consequences" there was only one correlation with the examination grade.)

Table 2 presents some remarkable relations. Comparing the columns for each type of cognition, causal attribution stands out because here negative and positive contents hardly differ in their interfering influence. As for the positive motivation syndrome (high aspiration level, good grade, internal attribution, positive self-evaluation), neither the negative nor the positive contents of causal attribution are perceived as debilitating. For the negative motivation syndrome the opposite is true. (The factor "luck," however, is an exception, also in relation to the other types of cognitions as will be discussed later.)

In contrast, the remaining cognition types show an asymmetry in the degree of interference of negative and positive contents. Remarkably, the negative contents of cognitions about the course of performance, action-outcome expectancies, and affective states are regarded as less interfering or even more facilitative the higher the aspiration level and the attained grade level rise. Occasional negative cognitions about performance feedback, a momentary failure expectation, and uneasiness seem to have a welcome and useful guiding and motivating function for people with high aspiration levels and high ability (good grades). This function is less often observed with positive performance feedback, success expectancies, and positive affective states. Conversely, persons with low aspiration levels and poorer grades—obviously those with a self-concept of low ability—describe the negative contents of failure feedback, failure expectancies, and negative affective states (all supporting their own self-doubts) as disturbing and debilitating. (These correlations increase even more if one sorts out those subjects who do not report these kinds of cognitions.)

The effects of negative and positive contents tend to converge if they are associated with certain preferred explanations of the exam outcome. The effects

Table 2 Correlations (r_{pb}; $p < .10$) of Variables of the Motivation Process with the Estimated Amount of Adverse Effects of Negative and Positive Contents of Four Cognition Types

| Variables of the motivation process | N | Adverse effects of different contents | | | | | | | |
| | | Causal attribution | | Course of performance | | Action-outcome expectancy | | General affective state | |
		Negative	Positive	Negative	Positive	Negative	Positive	Negative	Positive
Aspiration Level									
1. Grade level with which satisfied	47			−.40ss	.05	−.45ss	.01		
2. Grade level with which dissatisfied	47	−.39ss		−.37ss	−.09	−.48ss	−.01	−.33s	.14
3. Attained grade level	61		−.25s	−.37ss	.04	−.23	−.23	−.25s	−.20
4. Goal discrepancy (3 minus 2)	47				−.23			−.07	.24
Causal attribution									
5. Ability	61	−.23	−.16	.01		−.26s	−.30s	.00	−.26s
6. Degree of exam preparation	61			−.31s	−.17			−.16	−.28s
7. Unfavorable physical condition	41			.38s	.01	.13	.28	.39ss	.30s
8. Examiner	59		.43ss			.04	.23		
9. Luck	53	.06		.20	.21	.16	.35s	−.02	.27s
10. Externalizing tendency ((8 + 9) − (5 + 6))	53	.33ss	.32ss				−.28		
Self-evaluation									
11. Contentment	61	−.38ss	−.27s	−.12	−.24	−.09		.14	.37ss
12. Relief	61	−.30s	−.31s	.07	−.37ss	.13	−.51ss	−.19	−.45ss

of both negative and positive contents become more adverse the more an externalizing attribution tendency prevails. This relation also holds for subjects who attribute their grades especially to an unfavorable physical condition. The attribution of the exam grade to luck deserves special mention. The more the exam outcome is ascribed to good or bad luck the more it is the positive contents of causal attribution, action-outcome expectancies, and affective states that are experienced as impairing performance. The following interpretation seems plausible: Persons who tend to attribute their success to luck (this matches the failure-oriented achievement motive, see Heckhausen, 1975) experience cognitions that assure success as contrary to their expectation. This dissonance presumably creates some disturbance or even threat during the performance because cognitions assuring success suggest a higher responsibility for the outcome.

Finally, as far as the two self-evaluation variables are concerned, it is the positive contents that are related to performance facilitation. The more satisfied and relieved one is after the exam the more success-oriented cognitions about the course of performance, success expectancies, and positive affective states are regarded as helpful during the exam.

Using again as predictors several of the motivation variables (aspiration level, goal discrepancy, and the various causal attribution factors for the attained grade) one can account, on the average, for 29% of the total variance of the debilitating effect of self-doubt contents. That is 7% more than for the *frequency* of self-doubt contents. The highest amount of interference variance can be accounted for by cognitions about affective states ($R^2 = .44$), external causal factors ($R^2 = .34$), and course of performance ($R^2 = .32$), and the lowest for cognitions dealing with norm-setting ($R^2 = .19$).

Interference as an Effect of Cognition Frequency and of Motivation Process Variables

Since the frequency of cognitions—especially of self-doubt cognitions—covaries with variables of the motivation process and also with the *degree of interference*, we must examine whether interference still correlates with motivational variables after cognition frequency is partialled out. For this purpose the interference scores of the negative contents of the various cognitions were examined by analysis of variance for effects from frequency (high vs. low) and from four motivation variables. The following motivation variables were selected: aspiration level (the grade with which one is satisfied), grade attained, the tendency to externalize causal attribution, and contentment with grade (each factor divided into high vs. low).

First, frequency of self-doubt has a significant main effect on the degree of interference for each type of cognition. However, among the four motivation variables only aspiration level has a main effect in five out of the six cognition types. Grade and contentment each produce one main effect in one category. Let us begin with aspiration level: With a higher level of aspiration there is a decline in the adverse effects of negative incentive values ($p < .10$), of failing to reach the set norm ($p < .10$), and of failure-expectancy ($p < .10$). Each effect is independent of the particular cognition frequency. The same applies for negative internal causes ($p < .05$) and for negative affective states ($p < .05$), although it is only true for that subgroup with a high frequency in the corresponding cognition group.

As for the two other motivation variables, the adverse effect of negative incentive values declines with an increasing grade ($p < .05$), and the adverse effects of causal attribution and of questioning one's ability and preparedness decrease with greater contentment ($p < .10$). A significant interaction between frequency and motivation variables exists only for two cognition types and for the motivation variable "aspiration level." The higher the aspiration level the less does interference increase with a growing frequency of negative causal-attribution cognitions and of failure expectancy.

To summarize, the motivation variables are not the only factors that, independent of cognition frequency, influence the degree of interference of self-doubt cognitions. The motivation variable "aspiration level" is an exception. A high aspiration level weakens the interference of self-coubt cognitions in five of the six cognition categories, namely incentive values, norm-setting, failure-expectancy, causal attribution, and affective state.

Frequency and Interference of Cognitions as a Function of S- and F- States

In order to account for individual differences let us direct our attention to the second set of variables (motivation state during the exam). As expected, S- and F-state groups differ in frequency and influence of all cognition types, even if these are not categorized according to positive, negative, and open contents. Self-forgetfulness occurs much more often in the S-state than in the F-state ($\bar{x} = 3.23$ vs. 2.00; $t = 5.03$; $p < .001$). All other cognition types occur significantly more often in the F-state except for norm-setting. The results become even more clear-cut if both groups are confined to the upper and lower third of the S-F-difference scores. Figure 1 shows that all types of cognitions, except for norm-setting, occur more often in the F-state, especially causal attribution of the possible action-outcomes and performance intentions. Figure 1 also includes the estimated amount of interference for each cognition type in both groups. Frequency and interference only covary in the F-state ($r_s = .56$; $p < .02$; for the S-state: $r_s = .11$, ns). In the S-state all cognition types occur less often and none of them is perceived as disturbing. A covariation between frequency and interference does not exist for any type of cognition. This is different in the F-group; all the self-concern cognitions (categories 1–6), the performance intentions (category 7), and the irrelevant cognitions (category 8) are experienced as debilitating. Frequency and interference correlate more closely for irrelevant cognitions ($r_s = .81$; $p < .01$), for incentive value of possible con-sequences ($r_s = .54$; $p < .02$), and for causal attribution ($r_s = .41$; $p < .10$).

If both groups are divided according to sex the following differences result within the F-group: Female candidates report a lower frequency of self-concern cognitions than males. Females of the F-group match females of the S-group far more than their male counterparts of the same motivation state, at least for the categories "incentive values," "norm-setting," "course of performance," and "action-outcome expectancies." The frequency curve in Figure 1 represents average scores that are considerably higher for the male subgroup in the above-mentioned categories. As far as the interference is concerned, no similar sex

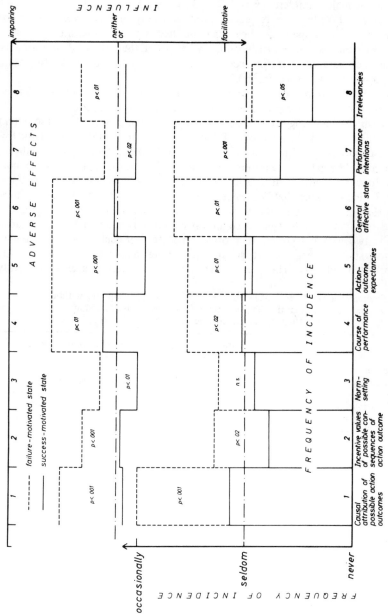

Figure 1 Frequency and interference effects of different types of cognition contents for two groups of subjects with prevailing failure-motivated or a prevailing success-motivated state during an oral exam.

261

differences are obtained. In accordance with the lower frequency of self-concern cognitions the female candidates of the F-group attain significantly better exam grades than the male candidates ($\bar{x} = 2.5$ vs. 3.2).

Interestingly, F-state subjects became aware not only of their own nervousness (affective state) as impairing; they also ascribed similar impairment to such cognitive activities as causal attribution, awareness of the course of performance (including the evaluation of the exam answers), and expectation of the exam result (action-outcome expectancies).

As already mentioned, the amount of interference results not only from higher frequency of corresponding cognition types but also covaries with the degree to which these cognitions are more negative than positive (i.e., the extent to which they are failure-oriented). Table 3 presents more information on this fact for the various cognition categories. Each of these categories is divided into failure-oriented (negative) self-doubt contents, success-oriented (positive) contents, and open contents (neither success- nor failure-oriented items).

Table 3 demonstrates that for each cognition category the F-group has more negative than positive contents, while the reverse is true for the S-group. The incidence of positive and negative cognition contents is equal if they are added up for the two extreme groups of motivation state. For each cognition category failure-motivated subjects report significantly more negative contents than do success-oriented subjects. They also scale the negative contents as significantly

Table 3 Frequency and Influence of Positive, Negative, and Open Contents within the Self-concern Cognition Types in the F-Group ($N = 21$–22) and in the S-Group ($N = 19$–21), and the Significance of the Mean Score Differences

Self-concern cognition types	Frequency			Negative or positive influence		
	F–group	S–group	P	F–group	S–group	P
1. Causal attribution						
Internal Negative	1.95	0.92	< .001	−1.11	+0.05	< .001
Positive	1.25	1.85	< .01	+0.41	+1.24	< .01
External	1.94	0.96	< .001	−1.11	−0.39	< .01
2. Incentive values						
Negative	1.25	0.53	< .01	−0.92	−0.11	< .01
Positive	1.02	1.38	ns	+0.32	+0.64	ns
Open	1.49	0.74	< .001	−0.65	−0.06	< .01
3. Norm-setting						
Negative	1.68	0.75	< .01	−1.30	−0.23	< .01
Positive	0.95	1.00	ns	+0.75	+0.68	ns
Open	1.20	0.97	ns	−0.23	+0.38	< .01
4. Course of performance						
Negative	1.93	1.03	< .001	−1.53	−0.75	< .01
Positive	0.77	1.10	ns	+0.41	+0.83	ns
5. Action-outcome expectancy						
Negative	2.05	0.50	< .001	−1.84	−0.30	< .001
Positive	1.09	1.90	< .01	+0.07	+1.05	< .05
6. General affective state						
Negative	2.12	0.96	<.001	−1.64	−0.71	< .001
Positive	0.81	1.50	< .01	+0.57	+1.29	< .01

more debilitating. Compared with the S-group. F-state subjects report significantly less positive contents in three of the six cognition categories: causal attribution (e.g., feeling good about one's own ability), action-outcome expectancies (e.g., feeling confident that the exam will be successful), and affective state (e.g., feeling relaxed and calm). Correspondingly, F-state subjects do not estimate the facilitative effect of the positive contents as high as do S-state subjects. Within the other cognition categories (incentive values, norm-setting, and course of performance) the F-group does not differ significantly in positive contents from the S-group. Accordingly, both groups do not differ in their estimation of the facilitative influence. In general it can again be stated that the interference of self-concern cognitions does not only depend on their absolute frequency but also on the predominance of negative contents (self-doubt cognitions).

What about those contents that cannot be classified as either positive or negative (open contents)? Causal attribution cognitions in the F-group deal twice as often with external factors than those in the S-group, and those factors are experienced as being far more impairing. (In agreement with the result, Piehl, 1976, found that anxious as compared with nonanxious examinees attribute the exam outcome more often to luck and the examiner.) The F-group also reports twice as many open contents about incentive values of possible consequences (e.g., getting more information on one's own ability or the importance of the exam for long-term study goals). Open norm-setting cognitions (e.g., comparison with one's own earlier exam performance and with the performance of others) are equally frequent in both groups, but they differ significantly in their effect. F-state subjects describe them as more interfering, S-state subjects as more facilitative. Evidently, the evaluation of the expected performance-outcome, based on individual and social reference norms, is more disturbing in an F- than in an S-state.

The question is still open as to what extent the different degrees of interference in the F- and S-group result not only from different frequencies of positive and negative contents in both groups but also from the motivation state as a main effect in itself. Therefore analyses of variance were performed with motivation state (S vs. F) and cognition frequency (low vs. high) as independent factors. Table 4 contains the results for the whole sample. The various self-concern cognitions are divided into positive, negative, and open types. Again *cognition frequency* produces the strongest effect; the more frequently negative or positive cognition contents prevail, the more is their influence described as impairing or facilitative, respectively. This applies especially to the cognition types "course of performance," "causal attribution," and "affective state." It applies less markedly to "action-outcome expectancies," "norm-setting," and "incentive values." The main effect of *motivation state* is less distinct but mostly reaches at least the 10% level of significance. Negative contents are always perceived as more interfering in the F-group than in the S-group. Positive contents are perceived as more facilitative. Only in one case ("course of performance") did the motivation state have no effect, because here a frequency effect is overwhelming.

Again it is striking how much the influence of open contents is dependent on the motivation state. Open incentive values (getting more information on one's competence, the subjective value of the exam, importance of the exam for

Table 4 Results of Analyses of Variance of the Estimated Influence of Negative, Positive, and Open Contents of Self-concern Cognition Types: Main Effects of Cognition Frequency (Fr) and of Motivation State (St; S-state vs. F-state) and their Interactions (Fr × St)

Self-concern cognition types	Frequency (Fr)		Motivation State (St)		Fr × St	
	F	P	F	P	F	P
1. Causal attribution						
Internal Negative	14.15	< .001	2.99	< .10	0.42	ns
Positive	15.31	< .001	6.30	< .01	0.41	ns
External	9.95	< .01	2.90	< .10	0.02	ns
2. Incentive values						
Negative	4.91	< .05	3.55	< .10	0.05	ns
Positive	10.22	< .01	2.71	< .25	1.44	< .25
Open	2.31	< .25	14.22	< .001	14.88	< .001
3. Norm-setting						
Negative	2.84	< .10	5.87	< .05	1.32	ns
Positive	14.79	< .001	0.18	ns	2.54	< .25
Open	0.26	ns	3.76	< .10	0.48	ns
4. Course of performance						
Negative	38.66	< .001	1.08	ns	0.05	ns
Positive	34.42	< .001	0.99	ns	1.65	< .25
5. Action-outcome expectancy						
Negative	4.02	< .05	3.02	< .10	1.32	ns
Positive	3.54	< .10	4.48	< .05	3.99	< .06
6. General affective state						
Negative	9.55	< .01	3.09	< .10	0.19	ns
Positive	43.39	< .001	5.19	< .05	4.01	< .05

Note. df between 1;61 and 1;58.

long-term study goals) are experienced by the S-group as being more promoting the more frequently they occur. The F-group, however, experiences them as being more interfering. This produces a strong interaction effect. The open norm-setting cognitions (comparison with one's earlier exams or with those of others) are perceived in the S-state as facilitative, independent of their frequency; in the F-state, however, they are experienced as more interfering the more frequent they are. There are two remaining interaction effects: Even when occurring less frequently, success expectancy and positive affective states are experienced by the S-group as much more promoting than by the F-group.

In summary, negative cognition contents are less disturbing and open ones more facilitative in a success-oriented than in a failure-oriented motivation state. Among the motivation variables it is only high aspiration level that has the same effect; it diminishes the interfering effect of self-doubt.

Frequency and Interference of Self-doubt Cognitions as a Function of Motivation State Factors

Instead of considering the summarized S- and F-states, we will now have a look at the various factors of the motivation state. We will examine whether these factors can account for individual differences in frequency and interference of (negative) self-doubt contents. Table 5 shows the correlations between the failure-oriented manifestation of the six motivation-state factors and the frequency of the various self-doubt cognitions. Additionally, the variance accounted for by all six factors is noted for each type of cognition.

The affective motivation factor "nervousness" shows the closest and most frequent relations. A high factor score in nervousness entails an increased frequency of all types of self-doubts. But the correlative data do not enable us to decide whether nervousness produces self-doubt cognitions or vice versa, or whether they are mutually responsible for their increase. The two cognitive motivation factors "experiencing incompetence" and "negative self-evaluation" also correlate with the higher frequencies of any type of self-doubt. If we take a look at the cognition types in the columns of Table 5, we find that especially action-outcome expectancies, internal and external causal attribution, and affective state occur more frequently when the failure-oriented motivation factors increase (whereas self-forgetfulness occurs less often). Taken together the six motivation factors account on the average for no less than 46% of the variance (R^2) of the self-doubt frequency within the various cognition types.

With interference, however, the amount of variance accounted for is much smaller, namely 29% on the average (see Table 6). Again the motivation factors "nervousness," "experiencing incompetence," and "negative self-evaluation" are not only associated with a higher frequency but also with a stronger interference of all self-doubt cognitions. As far as the various types of cognitions are concerned, those subjects whose motivation factors were failure-oriented report as impairing especially self-doubt contents concerning internal and external causal attribution, action-outcome expectancies, and affective states.

Cognitive versus Affective Factors of Motivation State and Exam Performance

As expected, the three cognitive factors of the motivation state correlate significantly with poor exam grades. Table 7 contains the correlations for the single factors, for the summarized cognitive and affective factors, and for the difference scores of S- and F-state items. Dividing the subjects into an S- and an F-state group, the first group has significantly better grades (mean: 2.21 vs. 2.80; $p < .01$), and its members feel more content and relieved $p < .01$). All these results confirm the two-component hypothesis of Morris and Liebert (1969, 1970): Self-doubts dealing with a self-concept of low ability are more closely correlated with poor exam grades than cognitions that refer to the awareness of one's nervous and helpless state.

Relations between Causal Attribution Cognitions and Emotions

We have seen that causal attribution cognitions play a particular role among the task-irrelevant cognitions. Task-performance is perceived to be strongly influenced by the frequency of this cognition type (Table 4). Frequency and effect of cognitions about internal positive, internal negative, and external causes vary with different motivation states (Table 3). Their frequency correlates very

Table 5 Correlations between the Frequency of Self-doubt Contents of Various Cognition Types and the Failure-oriented manifestation of the Six Motivation State Factors and the Explained Variance (R^2) of the Frequency of Self-doubts within each Cognition Type

Motivation state factors	Negative cognition contents of							
	Causal attribution		Incentive of consequences	Norm-setting	Course of performance	Action-outcome expectancy	Affective state	Mean r
	Internal	External						
Cognitive factors								
1. Experiencing incompetence	.54ss	.43ss	.47ss	.47ss	.55ss	.53ss	.55ss	.51
2. Negative self-evaluation	.64ss	.51ss	.32s	.49ss	.46ss	.64ss	.46ss	.50
3. Failure expectancy	.19	.34ss	.29s	.10	.29s	.38ss	.29s	.27
Affective factors								
4. Nervousness	.49ss	.65ss	.43ss	.55ss	.55ss	.74ss	.64ss	.58
5. Feeling overtaxed	.18	.37ss	.03	.06	.29s	.29s	.18	.20
6. Lack of reaction control	.32s	.21	.20	.31s	.23	.31s	.39ss	.28
Explained variance (R^2)	.48	.50	.31	.40	.40	.64	.48	.46

Note. $N = 62$–65.

Table 6 Correlations between the Adverse Effects of Self-doubt Contents of Various Cognition Types and the Failure-oriented Manifestation of the Six Motivation State Factors and the Explained Variance (R^2) of the Adverse Effects of Self-doubts within each Cognition Type

Motivation state factors	Negative cognition contents of							
	Causal attribution		Incentive of consequences	Norm-setting	Course of performance	Action-outcome expectancy	Affective state	Mean r
	Internal	External						
Cognitive factors								
1. Experiencing incompetence	.42ss	.35ss	.47ss	.34ss	.46ss	.51ss	.38ss	.42
2. Negative self-evaluation	.51ss	.21	.35ss	.29s	.22	.49ss	.40ss	.35
3. Failure expectancy	.26s	.17	.31s	.10	.15	.27s	.16	.20
Affective factors								
4. Nervousness	.39ss	.52ss	.36ss	.35ss	.36ss	.37ss	.55ss	.41
5. Feeling overtaxed	.35ss	.27s	.22	.23	.22	.31s	.27s	.27
6. Lack of reaction control	.38ss	.20	.18	.19	.06	.26s	.25s	.22
Explained variance (R^2)	.35	.32	.26	.18	.25	.34	.34	.29

Note. N = 62–65.

Table 7 Correlations of the Failure-oriented Manifestation of the Various Motivation State
Factors and of the F- and S-States (Failure- or Success-motivated State)
with Poor Exam Grade. ($N = 65$).

Cognitive factors			Affective factors		
1 Experiencing incompetency	2 Negative self- evaluation	3 Failure expectancy	4 Nervousness	5 Feeling overtaxed	6 Lack of reaction control
.41ss	.37ss	.33ss	.23ns	.16ns	.13ns
	.48ss			.25s	

Note. F-state: —.17ns; S-state: —.43s.

closely with the motivation-state factor "nervousness" (Table 5), and their
estimated debilitating effect (no matter whether the assumed causes are positive
or negative) correlates negatively with contentment and relief after the exam
(Table 2). These and other results suggest that causal attribution cognitions leave
emotions in their wake. Although our data do not give us any information on
sequences, they do allow us to examine relations. We can differentiate causal
attribution cognitions and emotions with more accuracy than we have been able
to do so far.

The causal-analysis cognitions were divided according to Weiner's classification
scheme of the internal versus external and stable versus variable dimensions (see
Weiner, 1974). The cognition questionnaire allows us to distinguish between the
following types of causes (see Table 8): ability (internal and stable, self-concept
of ability), exam preparation and concentration (internal and variable, persistence
and effort before and/or during the exam), physical condition (variable, questionable whether internal or external, i.e., to what extent one feels responsible), difficulty of the exam questions (external and stable), examiner (external, questionable
whether seen as stable or variable), chance (external and variable).

The reported emotions were divided into four different types (see Table 8)
according to a process model of motivation (Heckhausen, 1977):

1. Motivating incentive emotions. These refer to the consequences of the
expected action-outcome (i.e., to positive or negative self-evaluation or evaluation
by others).

2. Emotions referring to a candidate's expectations. These refer to the
expectations of a positive or negative action-outcome (i.e., feeling confident of
attaining a set goal or worrying about failing).

3. Emotions referring to a candidate's general condition. These do not refer
to future events but describe momentary, especially physical, conditions, such as
relaxation versus tension, anger, exam anxiety with all of its various physical
sensations.

4. Emotional shift. This refers to experienced shifts of the emotional state
(i.e., relief, pleasant surprise vs. disappointment).

For each type of causal attribution cognition and emotion, subjects were
divided at the median of the frequency scores into a high versus low group.

Table 8 Significant Covariation (Chi-Square) between Types of Causal Attribution Cognitions and Types of Emotions during the Exam

Types of causal attribution cognitions	Emotion Types			
	Motivating incentive emotions (positive or negative self-or other-evaluation after exam)	Expectancy emotions (confidence or worry)	State emotions (relaxation vs. tension; exam anxiety; anger)	Emotional shift (positive: relief; negative: disappointment)
Ability (self-concept of high-ability)	*Positive self-evaluation* (S)			*Relief* (S)
Exam preparation (fully sufficient)	*Positive other-evaluation*	*Confidence* (S) *Worry*	*Relaxation* (S) No exam-anxiety (S)	*No disappointment* (S)
Concentration during exam (disturbed and concerned about improvement)				
State (feeling dependent on)	F: Negative other-evaluation			F: Disappointment
Task difficulty (of exam question)		Worry (S)	*Tension* *Exam anxiety* *Exam anxiety* (S) S: Tension F: Anger	
Examiner (feeling dependent on)		*Worry* (S)		F: *Relief*
Chance (feeling dependent on)		*Worry* (F)	*Exam anxiety* (S) Anger	Disappointment

Note. S = success subgroup, being satisfied with the achieved exam grade; F = failure subgroup, being dissatisfied with exam grade. S or F in parenthesis: closer covariation in S or F subgroup, respectively. S or F put in front: covariation only in S or F subgroup significant. The closest relations are italicized.

Chi-square analyses examined the relationship between every cognition type of causal attribution and every type of emotion. The same was carried out separately for two halves of the total sample, those who were content with the exam outcome (success group) and those who were discontent (failure group). Table 8 contains the significant results. The underlined emotions show especially close relations to the listed cognitions. A relation that is closer for one of the two subgroups (success or failure group) is indicated with an S or F behind the emotion noted. A relation produced by only one subgroup is marked with an S or F in front of the emotion noted.

In Table 8 one main difference stands out. Whereas five of the seven causal-attribution cognitions are associated with emotions referring to expectations and to general conditions, the motivating incentive emotions of the anticipated (positive or negative) self-evaluation and evaluation by others are related to only one causal factor—the consideration of one's own ability, of one's competence. (For the success group self-evaluation is more important than evaluation by others. This seems to be one of the differences between success- and failure-motivated persons; see Heckhausen, 1977). Remarkably, it is the factor of one's ability (internal and stable) and not the factor of effort (internal and variable) that is associated with the anticipation of motivating incentive values of self-evaluation and evaluation by others (and is also connected with a positive emotional shift). Thus it is not the amount of effort but the self-concept of ability brought into question that has reinforcement value, that is, is motivating in its effect (see also Heckhausen, 1978; Meyer, 1973).

The two effort factors (exam preparation and concentration) refer to the expectancy emotions of confidence and worry. A fully satisfactory exam preparation seems to be particularly conducive to emotions, since it covaries with three kinds of emotions (especially in the success group): with a confident expectancy emotion, a relaxed state emotion, and a nonnegative emotional shift. If one more often feels dependent on one's physical condition, then state emotions of tension and exam anxiety come to the fore. This applies similarly to the external stable factor of difficulty of the exam question. Here the success- and the failure-group differ as follows: Those who are satisfied with the exam outcome report more tension, those who are dissatisfied report more anger. The two external (and not controllable) factors "examiner" and "luck" arouse more often the expectancy emotion of worry. At the same time, luck correlates in this case with exam anxiety (especially in the success group) and with anger.

Without going into detail we can state that characteristic relations exist between various types of causal attribution cognitions and types of emotions. Cognitions about one's ability play a crucial role, because they obviously provide the basis for the motivating incentive emotions of self-evaluation and evaluation by others, which are the reinforcing consequences of the attained exam result. All the other types of causal cognitions refer to a shorter span in future orientation since they are associated with expectancy emotions (hope or fear with regard to the exam outcome) and/or with state emotions (relaxed vs. tense). Among the cognition types, considerations of a sufficient amount of exam preparation seem to have the broadest effect: This type contributes to an increase in emotions referring to expectations, general conditions, and emotional shift. Finally, the awareness of the dependency on momentary physical condition stands out. This kind of cognition is mainly associated with the state emotions of tension and test anxiety.

DISCUSSION

The purpose of this study was to differentiate task-irrelevant cognitions during achievement stress situations more incisively than has been attempted so far and to do so according to theory-based content categories. Let us summarize the more important results.

The attention hypothesis, according to which self-concern cognitions impair the course of performance in stress situations, needs to be differentiated. Various types of cognitions, apart from the actual problem-solving processes, have to be distinguished. First, they all have different functions. There are cognitions dealing with the course of performance and with norm-setting. These cognitions result in performance intentions. Their function is to monitor and guide the course of performance. In this respect they are helpful. However, if those types of cognition become too dominant they may also impair the problem-solving process.

A facilitative function cannot be ascertained with the other types of cognition, especially causal attribution of the possible outcomes, incentive values of the possible consequences of action-outcomes, action-outcome expectancies (including the situation-outcome expectancies), and awareness of a general affective state. Except for awareness of the affective state, the listed cognition types transcend the momentary problem-solving process in prospective and retrospective terms; none of them contributes to the task-solving process; they can all result in massive self-doubt contents; can accentuate concerns about one's self-esteem; and can debilitate, interrupt, and impair behavior during the task. Considering the close covariation of frequency and interference, particularly adverse are cognitions about unimportant externals of the situation. Although irrelevancies are not related to self-esteem, they nevertheless distract from the task.

These various types of cognitions need not be disturbing in any case. In fact one can even experience them as facilitative. It depends on three factors whether and to what extent one regards these various cognition types as impairing: their frequency; the predominance of failure-oriented contents of self-doubt compared with success-oriented contents of self-confidence; and individual differences in motivation. First of all there is a general tendency for the interfering effect to increase when frequency increases. Such a covariation is very close only in some cases (e.g., for cognitions of causal attribution and incentive values of the consequences). The covariation is limited by individual differences in motivation. It exists only for examinees in a failure-oriented state of motivation, obviously because it exceeds a threshold value above which the course of performance is increasingly impaired. In a success-oriented motivation state, frequency of the various cognition types does not covary with the influence of these cognitions.

The relation between frequency and influence can further be differentiated if within the single cognition categories those cognitions that are success oriented (self-confidence) are distinguished from failure-oriented cognitions (self-doubt). The factors of the failure-oriented state of motivation can account for almost 50% of the variance in frequency and for 30% of the variance in interference of self-doubt cognitions. This applies especially to the frequency and degree of interference of three self-doubt cognition types: failure-expectancy, causal attribution (internal-negative and external), and awareness of negative affective states. The following three (out of six) factors of the failure-oriented motivation state account for most of the individual differences in frequency and interference: experiencing incompetence, negative self-evaluation, and nervousness.

In general an impairing influence increases with failure-oriented cognitions of self-doubt, and a favorable influence increases with success-oriented cognitions. However, both correlations are moderated by the state of motivation. Regardless of their frequency, self-doubt cognitions are comparatively more disturbing in a failure-oriented than in a success-oriented state of motivation. And open cognitions as well as success cognitions prove to be more helpful in a success-oriented than in a failure-oriented motivation state. Furthermore, it is necessary to differentiate between a positive and a negative syndrome of the variables of the motivation process before and after the exam. With a negative syndrome both negative and positive contents of causal attribution cognitions have adverse effects. Among the various motivation variables it is a high aspiration level that decreases or suspends the otherwise general debilitating effect of self-doubt contents.

Under special conditions, positive cognition contents can be experienced as disturbing, and negative cognition contents as helpful. In the first case the exam result is attributed to luck. The more an examinee attributes the result to luck, the more he or she feels disturbed by the incidence of success-related (and not failure-related) cognitions. The second case applies to an examinee with a high aspiration level and a good exam grade. The higher both of these are, the more are occasional failure feedback, failure expectancy, and negative affective states (and not their positive counterparts!) experienced as helpful.

Among the motivation variables two results deserve notice. First, the two-component hypothesis of test anxiety by Morris and Liebert was confirmed: The attained examination grades covary with the cognitive (self-doubt) but not with the more emotional components of the motivation state. On the other hand, we again find a close relation between biases in causal attribution and individual differences in motivation. The more the state of motivation during the exam was failure-oriented, the more is the examinee convinced that luck, but not the amount of preparation, did have an influence on the grade. If this relation is not just a result of ex post facto self-justification, we face again that fatal and self-perpetuating mechanism of failure-motivated persons: Effort and persistence are regarded as so ineffective that in view of a possible failure one is very much tempted to reduce one's exertion (Heckhausen, 1975; Meyer, 1973).

The results of this study provide suggestions for intervention programs in cases of exam anxiety. Such interventions can use self-instructions, for example, that are incompatible with self-doubt cognitions (see Meichenbaum, 1972). They should aim at reducing certain kinds of self-doubt cognitions, especially causal-attribution considerations (lack of ability and insufficient exam preparation), failure expectancy, the anticipation of the incentive values of possible consequences, and the awareness of a tense or nervous state. Especially the relations found between different kinds of causal-attribution cognitions and emotions give important clues for the construction of an intervention program. Since doubts about one's ability are associated with "motivating incentive" emotions of negative self-evaluation by others, these could be the main source of interference with a relaxed and self-forgetful problem-solving process. This is supported by the fact that the two corresponding factors of the motivation state, experiencing incompetence and negative self-evaluation, explain most of the individual differences in frequency and interference of self-doubt cognitions. It is therefore advisable to design an intervention program that aims primarily at reducing self-doubt about ability. In the second place, attention must be paid to the relations between the conviction of a sufficient exam preparation and confident-expectancy emotions, relaxed-state emotions, and a nonnegative emotional shift. These relations are not observed in the nonsuccessful group but clearly exist in the successful group. This underlines the above-mentioned fact that failure-motivated persons unfortunately regard persistence and effort as not having very much influence on the exam outcome.

To be sure, some reservations with respect to the collected self-report data are necessary. The data were all reported directly after the exam and the announcement of the grade. They are retrospective statements and refer to different points in time: prior to the exam (aspiration level), during the exam (cognitions), and after the exam (causal attribution and self-evaluation). As is always necessary with respondent data, we must ask how much the subjects were able and willing to report objectively and in detail, whether response tendencies were involved, and how adequate the questionnaire was for the subjects' experience. As far as the latter point is concerned, we tried to formulate the question in a situation-specific and naturalistic manner. But answering a questionnaire right after the announcement of the exam grade might be a problem. This later event could have influenced the subject's evaluation of earlier events (e.g., goal-setting before the exam and cognitions during the exam). The sequence of the questionnaire parts could also have caused systematic response effects. Other sequences, however, would probably create other problems. We tried to take some of these problems into consideration. Thus for the dimensional analysis of the motivation state we extracted the exam grade as a heterogeneity factor from the correlation matrix. Besides, the variables of the motivation process and of the motivation state show so many relations among and between each other predicted by motivation theory that one cannot deny a certain validity.

Another objection could be raised: Since the questions concerning the state of motivation and the cognition content refer to the same situation, they partly overlap in time and content. Presumably this already accounts for a certain part of the common variance of motivation state and frequency and interference of cognitions. But this cannot be solely an artifact of the method of questionnaire construction, as the variance of frequency and interference of the cognitions can be explained to a large extent by the variables of the motivation process before and after the exam.

Another question to be raised is whether the theory-based taxonomy of the cognition types that guided the construction of the questionnaire is thematically exhaustive or whether important cognition contents were omitted. The answer is that the cognition categories used cover at least the present range of motivation theory and they have proved to be important within the uncovered network of relations so far. An approach of separately assessing the various cognition types seems to be promising for future studies.

Finally it must be stated that the present study attempted to get hold of the flux of cognitions only in a static and elementary way by simply having subjects estimate retrospectively the frequency of incidence and intensity of influence on any task activity. This is a far cry from a process analysis, from sequencing events or from cause-effect relations within the flux of cognitions. Attempts in this direction would have to cope with many methodological difficulties. Nevertheless, this simple study might serve as a starting point, to demonstrate the impact or cognitions in the stream of behavior and also to help establish this empirically.

SUMMARY
REFERENCES

Cooley, W. W., & Lohnes, P. R. *Multivariate data analysis.* New York: Wiley, 1971.

Doctor, R. M., & Altman, F. Worry and emotionality as components of text anxiety: Replication and further data. *Psychological Reports,* 1969, *24,* 563–568.

Heckhausen, H. *Hoffnung und Furcht in der Leistungsmotivation.* Meisenheim: Hain, 1963.

Heckhausen, H. Intervening cognitions in motivation. In D. E. Berlyne & K. B. Madsen (Eds.), *Pleasure, reward, preference.* New York: Academic Press, 1973.

Heckhausen, H. Fear of failure as a self-reinforcing motive system. In I. G. Sarason & C. D. Spielberger (Eds.), *Stress and anxiety* (Vol. 2). Washington, DC: Hemisphere, 1975.

Heckhausen H. Achievement motivation and its constructs: A cognitive model. *Motivation and Emotion,* 1977, *1,* 283–329.

Heckhausen, H. Selbstbewertung nach erwartungswidrigem Leistungsverlauf: Einfluss von Motiv, Kausalattribution und Zielsetzung. *Zeitschrift für Entwicklungspsychologie und Pädagogische Psychologie,* 1978, *10,* 191–216.

Liebert, R. M., & Morris, L. W. Cognitive and emotional components of test anxiety: A distinction and some initial data. *Psychological Reports,* 1967, *20,* 975–978.

Mandler, G., & Watson, D. L. Anxiety and the interruption of behavior. In C. D. Spielberger (Ed.), *Anxiety and behavior.* New York: Academic Press, 1966.

Marlett, N. F., & Watson, D. Test anxiety and immediate or delayed feedback in a test-like avoidance task. *Journal of Personality and Social Psychology,* 1968, *8,* 200–203.

Meichenbaum, D. Cognitive modification of test anxious college students. *Journal of Consulting and Clinical Psychology,* 1972, *39,* 370–380.

Meyer, W. -U. *Leistungsmotiv und Ursachenerklärung von Erfolg und Misserfolg.* Stuttgart: Klett, 1973.

Morris, L. W., & Liebert, R. M. Effects of anxiety on timed and untimed intelligence tests. *Journal of Consulting and Clinical Psychology,* 1969, *33,* 240–244.

Morris, L. W., & Liebert, R. M. Relationship of cognitive and emotional components of test anxiety to physiological arousal and academic performance. *Journal of Consulting and Clinical Psychology,* 1970, *35,* 332–337.

Overall, J. E. Orthogonal factors and uncorrelated factor scores. *Psychological Reports,* 1962, *10,* 651–662.

Piehl, J. E. Bedingungen unterschiedlicher Ursachenerklärungen von Examensnoten. *Zeitschrift für Entwicklungspsychologie und Pädagogische Psychologie,* 1976, *8,* 51–57.

Sarason, I. G. Anxiety and self-preoccupation. In I. G. Sarason & C. D. Spielberger (Eds.), *Stress and anxiety* (Vol. 2). Washington, DC: Hemisphere, 1975.

Schmalt, H. -D. *Messung des Leistungsmotivs.* Göttingen: Hogrefe, 1976.

Spiegler, M. D., Morris, L. W., & Liebert, R. M. Cognitive and emotional components of test anxiety: Temporal factors. *Psychological Reports,* 1968, *22,* 451–456.

Spielberger, C. D. Theory and research on anxiety. In C. D. Spielberger (Ed.), *Anxiety and behavior.* New York: Academic Press, 1966.

Weiner, B. *Achievement motivation and attribution theory.* Morristown, NJ: General Learning Press, 1974.

Wine, J. Test anxiety and direction of attention. *Psychological Bulletin,* 1971, *76,* 92–104.

13

Fear Reactions and Achievement Behavior of Students Approaching an Examination

Peter Becker
University of Trier

This chapter deals with the theoretical and empirical analysis of two inter-dependent aspects of students' behavior prior to an examination: examination fear and achievement behavior. After a brief survey of some of the variables considered important for the description and explanation of examination fear and achievement behavior, an initial model will be presented for the prediction of students' levels of fear at different points in time before the examination. An empirical test of the model will then be conducted. The results of this test have interesting implications for our present understanding of the relationships between variables considered relevant to achievement behavior and those intimately associated with the phenomenon of fear. In the final section the findings and interpretations will be compared to those of Epstein and Fenz (1965), and some conclusions will be drawn with regard to the prevention and therapy of unusually high levels of examination fear.

A THEORETICAL ANALYSIS OF THE BEHAVIOR OF STUDENTS APPROACHING AN EXAMINATION

The model of behavior to be discussed here is based on concepts from cognitive theories of action and personality, in particular, those of Lewin (1951), Rotter (1954), Atkinson (1964), Heckhausen (1965), Mischel (1973), and Boesch (1975, 1976). Figure 1 schematically represents this author's view of the interaction between the individual and environmental determinants of behavior. It indicates that one must know the objective characteristics of the examination and the phase before an examination, the enduring traits of the examinees, and, most importantly, the "psychological situation" of each student.

The author is indebted to Prof. Johannes Engelkamp, University of Saarland, and to Diplom-Psychologe Donald Doenges, University of Trier, for their very valuable comments on an earlier draft of this article.

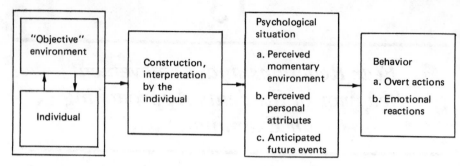

Figure 1 Schematic representation of the interaction of personality and environmental characteristics determining individual behavior.

By *objective environment* we mean the reliably observable characteristics of the examination including the following:

1. difficulty level (e.g., the failure rate)
2. form (oral or written)
3. student's prior experience in taking examinations
4. importance of passing the examination
5. opportunity to repeat in case of failing
6. preciseness of the information identifying the material to be tested
7. number of examinees

These characteristics influence the behavior of students with different personality traits in different ways. For example, some students prefer oral to written examinations. The objective characteristics of the situation are subjectively perceived. It is therefore necessary to take personality attributes into consideration. The author restricts himself to some enduring *traits* that might affect the behavior of students prior to an examination. These traits are:

1. *Achievement motivation.* The extensive literature on achievement motivation allows the following conclusions: Students high in achievement motivation would be expected to set higher goals than students low in achievement motivation; they should work harder and should probably earn higher grades. Students who tend to be successful should prefer goals of moderate difficulty, whereas students with a high motive to avoid failure should choose more extreme difficulty levels and should more often try to avoid examinations (see Birney, Burdick, & Teevan, 1969; Wilcke, 1976). As Entwisle (1972) and Schmalt (1976) have shown, there are many problems in measuring achievement motivation with sufficient reliability and validity. This is probably one of the main hindrances to an integration of the literature on achievement motivation. It is an open question, for example, as to whether the tendency to avoid failure is equivalent to examination fear or to test anxiety. Is it appropriate to measure the tendency to avoid failure using the Test Anxiety Questionnaire and to regard it as an inhibitory force, as Atkinson does?

2. *Emotional lability versus stability.* In Becker and Schneider's (1976) study, emotionally labile students experienced more fear, exhibited more intense stress reactions, and were more defensive than emotionally stable ones in the interval from 4 to 2 weeks prior to the examination.

3. *Intelligence.* The author is not aware of any investigation in which the influence of this variable upon the behavior of students approaching an examination was studied. It is reasonable to assume that the more intelligent students have experienced success more often, are more success-oriented, and have a higher achievement motivation than their less intelligent fellow students. From the arguments of Kukla (1972) and Meyer (1976) the conclusion can be drawn that more intelligent students should show more effort and persistence than less intelligent students when confronted with a difficult examination offering only two outcomes, namely success (= passing) or failure.

4. *Repression-sensitization.* For many students an examination represents a threatening situation triggering fear reactions and defense mechanisms (Becker & Schneider, 1976; Mechanic, 1962). Repressers and sensitizers very probably use different strategies in this situation (see Krohne & Rogner, chapter 8 of this volume).

5. *Locus of control.* People differ in the degree to which they believe they have control over reinforcement and feel personally responsible for what happens to them. Students with high internal control, compared to externals, would be expected to try more intently to gain control over their academic performance and grades, particularly under conditions that emphasize student control of contingencies. This hypothesis was confirmed by Allen, Giat, and Cherney (1974) (see also Bass, Ollendick, & Vuchinich, 1974). Subjects preferring an internal attribution of success or failure should show more intensive emotional reactions than externals (Weiner, 1974).

As far as the *psychological situation* of an examinee is concerned, the author considers at least the following determinants of a student's emotional reactions and achievement behavior to be important: the student's

1. estimation of his or her momentary level of competence, particularly in comparison to that of the other examinees
2. level of aspiration
3. estimation of the difficulty of the examination
4. probability estimate of success or failure
5. estimation of the grade he or she will attain
6. evaluation of the importance of reaching his or her goal

Another very essential determinant of behavior is the *temporal distance* to the examination. As the time of an examination approaches students usually begin to work harder to increase their level of competence. By comparing their knowledge with that of their fellow students or by participating in a trial examination, they are in a position to estimate more accurately their chance of passing the examination and of receiving a particular grade. Reaching a level of competence corresponding to one's aspiration should make one feel rather confident, whereas feeling unprepared could cause one to become panic-stricken or depressed.

Mechanic (1962) observed the behavior of students approaching an examination. With regard to the fear of examination he wrote:

As the examinations approached and as student anxiety increased, various changes occured in behavior. Joking increased, and, while students still sought social support and talked a great deal about examination, they began specifically to avoid certain people who aroused their anxiety. Stomachaches, asthma, and a general feeling of weariness became common complaints, and other psychosomatic symptoms appeared. The use of tranquilizers and sleeping pills became more frequent. (Mechanic, 1962, p. 142)

This passage gives the impression that the typical reaction of all students is to increasingly experience fear and stress before taking an important examination. This is what Miller's conflict model appears to suggest. On the other hand, the studies by Fisch (1970), Martin (1971), or Becker and Schneider (1976) could not replicate Mechanic's (1962) findings. Fisch (1970) and Martin (1971), who investigated students in the time interval before an examination, both found inverted U-shaped curves in retrospective self-ratings of avoidance or anxiety.

It was one of the aims of the present author's inquiry to develop a theoretical model that allows an understanding of the types of fear curves to be expected under different conditions. The study was also conceived as a contribution to the formulation of a somewhat more general theory of fear. In contrast to many other investigations, fear was the dependent variable in this study, and the author was searching for fear predictors. From the many variables determining the examination fear mentioned above, a selection had to be made for practical reasons. As will be seen, the author's interest was mainly focused upon some variables characterizing the psychological situation of the students. Before formulating a model of fear of examination the question was asked, What is examination fear? Is it equivalent to the fear of failing in the examination? Is it the uncertainty as to whether one will receive the grade envisaged? Is examination fear a unitary phenomenon or are there different kinds of fear?

A *first model* is based on the assumption that examination fear results from an estimated competence deficit leading to some insecurity about reaching the goal (grade) envisioned. Additional variables considered relevant, such as the personal importance of the examination, have been deliberately omitted for the sake of clarity and simplicity. It is assumed that all the students are taking the same (written) examination so that the influence of this important element of the objective environment is under control. The following predictions can be made with these restrictions:

$$F(T) = N(T) \cdot D(T) \qquad (1)$$

F(T) is the examination fear at date T. N(T) is the nearness of the examination at date T.

$$D(T) = C(G) - C(T) \qquad (2)$$

D(T) is defined as the *competence deficit* or the discrepancy between the competence one believes necessary for reaching the goal (grade) envisioned C(G) and the subjective estimate of competence one has at date T. In other words: One experiences more fear the higher one's level of aspiration, the lower one's subjective estimation of competence, and the nearer the examination.

In order to predict F(T), one additional assumption is necessary concerning the change in competence while approaching the examination: From the start of preparation to the date of examination there will be a linear increase in competence. Different students are expected to have competence gradients with different slopes, depending on the intensity of preparation, learning capacity, and so forth.

By increasing their level of competence as they approach the examination, the students should—according to equations 1 and 2—*reduce* one fear condition, namely D(T), the competence deficit. On the other hand, approaching the examination would *add to* another determinant of fear, namely the proximity of the examination. Thus there are two processes with opposite effects on the level of fear. This phenomenon can be expressed in a quadratic equation that results from mathematical transformations of equation 1 (see Becker, 1980). Using this quadratic equation the following predictions can be made: (1) There are inverted U-shaped and monotonously increasing fear curves during the last weeks before the examination. (2) Three important determinants of the fear curves are: the initial competence deficit D(0) (see Figure 2); the point of time at which one begins intensive preparation (see Figure 3); and the steepness of the competence gradient (see Figure 4). (3) At a great temporal distance from the examination all students are relatively free from fear. Shortly before the examination there are large differences between the fear levels of different students (see Figure 3). (4) Students asked to imagine that they had to take the examination the next day have high levels of fear at a great distance from the examination when their level of competence C(T) is still low. However, in approaching the examination this kind of hypothetical fear should diminish.

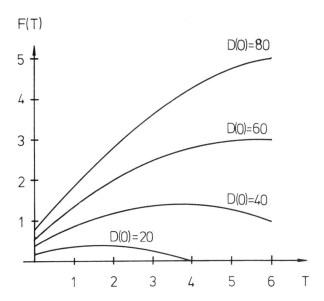

Figure 2 Prediction of the relationships between level of examination fear F(T) and imminence of examination T for individuals differing in the initial competence deficit D(0).

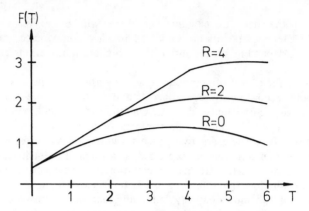

Figure 3 Prediction of the relationships between level of
examination fear F(T) and imminence of examination T for individuals who begin to prepare for the
exam at certain intervals before the date T_E. R = 0
(no delay, early beginning), R = 2 (delay of 2 weeks),
R = 4 (delay of 4 weeks).

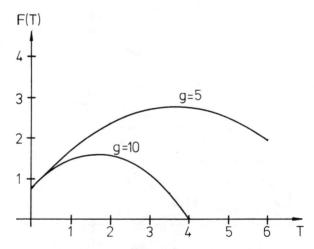

Figure 4 Prediction of the relationships between level of
examination fear F(T) and imminence of examination T for individuals differing in the gradient of
competence g. g = 10 (steep gradient of competence; learns quickly), g = 5 (flat gradient of
competence; learns slowly).

A STUDY OF STUDENTS
APPROACHING AN EXAMINATION

Plan of the Study

The aim of this longitudinal study was to survey the behavior of students at several points of time prior to an examination. The data gathered form the basis for investigating the relationships between several aspects of achievement behavior and for testing the model for predicting examination fear. The investigation was conducted in 1976 at the University of Saarland, Germany (see Becker, 1980). Subjects were 28 male students studying economics who intended to participate in their first academic examination at university level. This was a rather difficult written examination in industrial organization with a previous failure rate of 30-35%. Approximately 2 months before the examination the students had had an opportunity to participate in a sample exam in order to receive feedback about their level of competence. The 28 volunteer subjects were selected on the basis of extremely high or low scores in a test of emotional lability. All subjects received 25 German Marks (about 14 U.S. dollars) for their cooperation, and anonymity was maintained. The author constructed three inventories using items with response categories in the form of rating scales. Depending on the content of the inventories, the students had to answer the items at least once and up to five times (see Figure 5). For example, the students scaled their estimated competence and the amount of fear of examination at T1, T2, T3, T4, and T5.

From the many variables considered relevant for the description and explanation of achievement behavior and fear of examination a selection had to be made. The following list contains some of the most important variables and classes of variables used:

1. the momentary level of subjective estimate of competence
2. the momentary level of examination fear, as measured with a "fear thermometer" with a scale from 0 (free from fear) to 100 (panic fear)
3. the level of aspiration
4. the number of points one expects to gain
5. stress reactions (e.g., dysphoric reactions, psychosomatic symptoms, sleep disorders)
6. coping behavior (e.g., intensity of preparation)
7. defensive reactions (e.g., avoidance behavior, reduction of the level of aspiration, comforting cognitions)
8. attitudes and beliefs about the examination (e.g., critique of the examination, estimation of the failure rate)
9. self-evaluation (e.g., self-critique)
10. the number of points one has gained in the examination

An Empirical Test of the Model

It was found that the arithmetic means of the subjective competence $C(T)$ increased in an approximately linear fashion in the weeks before the examination (T1: 7,3: T2: 8,4; T3:9,2; T4: 9,5; T5: 10,9). A classification of the fear curves

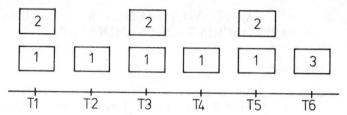

Figure 5 Course of the investigation. T1 = 4 weeks prior, T2 = 3 weeks
prior, T3 = 2 weeks prior, T4 = 1 week prior, T5 = 2 days
prior to the examination. T6 = day of examination. 1 = Inventory 1, containing 13 items, for example, the fear level
and the subjective estimate of competence. 2 = Inventory 2,
containing 67 items. 3 = Inventory 3 for stress reactions
immediately before and during the examination.

revealed that half the students ($N = 14$) had inverted U-shaped curves. Eight fear
curves had increasing gradients while the remaining profiles were U-shaped or
descending.

As expected, the standard deviations of the fear ratings increased from T1 to
T5 (T1: 11,04; T2: 13,81; T3: 15,93; T4: 18,42; T5: 22,01;). In line with a
deduction from the model, the fear of taking the examination the next day
decreased in an approximately linear fashion (T1: 56,1; T2: 47,5; T3: 46,8; T4:
41,1; T5: 34,6). So far the general assumptions and deductions of the model
were confirmed.

It had also been predicted that students differing in their initial competence
deficit D(0) should have different fear curves (see Figure 2). To test this
prediction the 28 students were divided into three groups, group G1 with a high
D(0), group G2 with a medium D(0), and group G3 with a low D(0). Each group
was further split into emotionally stable and emotionally labile students, because
Becker and Schneider (1976) had found that this trait correlated with the level
of examination fear. Figure 6 shows the fear curves of the six groups.

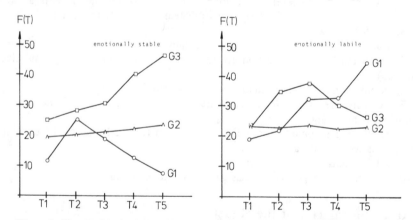

Figure 6 The empirical relationships between level of examination fear F(T) and
imminence of examination T in six groups of emotionally stable and
emotionally labile students. G1 = low, G2 = medium, G3 = high
initial competence deficit.

The three curves of the emotionally stable students corresponded rather well to the expectations. However, the curves of the emotionally labile students, particularly of the group with a small initial competence deficit, did not conform to the predictions. In order to find out the reasons for this, the emotionally labile group with a low D(0) was compared with the other five groups on a number of selected variables. The results of analyses of variance revealed that this group had a lower level of aspiration and a higher expectation of failure than most of the other groups. It was hypothesized that these students could be characterized as failure-oriented.

In order to test the influence of the variable *failure versus success orientation* the 28 students were divided into two groups with 14 students comprising the failure-oriented subjects (Ss) and 14 students making up the success-oriented Ss. The subjective probability of failing the examination was the selection criterion. Each group was further divided into those with high, medium, or low initial competence deficits. The predicted level of fear using equation 1 was compared to the observed fear level. In the three groups of success-oriented students there was a sufficiently close relationship between the arithmetic means of the predicted and the observed levels of fear $(r = .71; p < .01)$. In the three groups of failure-oriented students, however, the prediction model failed again $(r = .20; ns)$. As can be seen from Figure 7, two subgroups of success-oriented students have an inverted U-shaped fear curve, and the third group exhibits a similar trend. In contrast to the success-oriented students, the fear levels of the three failure-oriented subgroups tend to increase as the examination approaches. The arithmetic means of fear levels of the entire failure-oriented group increase in an approximately linear fashion, whereas those of all success-oriented Ss form an inverted U-shaped curve. This difference in trend represents a highly significant interaction effect in the analysis of variance $(p < .001)$. This effect will be interpreted in a later section.

The predicted and the obtained fear ratings were correlated in an attempt to

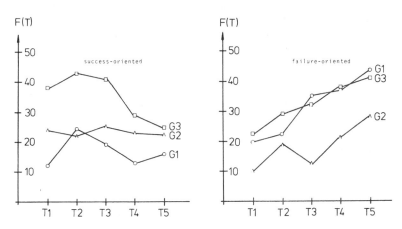

Figure 7 The empirical relationships between level of examination fear F(T) and imminence of examination T in six groups of success- and failure-oriented students. G1 = low, G2 = medium, G3 = high initial competence deficit.

test the capability of the model to predict the *individual* levels of fear at different points of time before the examination. For the entire group of 28 students, including both success- and failure-oriented examinees, the correlations were .37 ($p < .05$) at T1, .29 (*ns*) at T2, .18 (*ns*) at T3, .29 (*ns*) at T4, and .05 (*ns*) at T5. With the exception of T4, the correlations became increasingly smaller as the date of the examination approached. Thus shortly before the examination the prediction model failed completely.

An Extended Model of Examination Fear

The results emphasize that the phenomenon of examination fear cannot be reduced to the experience of a competence deficit. Obviously if this initial model is not to be rejected completely, it must be expanded to include further valid predictors. The variable "success versus failure orientation" was analyzed as a first step in this direction.

All 28 Ss had evaluated the probability of failing the examination (P_f) three times. Correlations of this variable with fear level were $-.32$ (*ns*) at T1, .18 (*ns*) at T3, and .44 ($p < .05$) at T5. Interestingly, the trend of the correlations of P_f is opposite to that of the correlations between the competence deficit and fear level. At T1 students with a high level of aspiration and a low P_f exhibited a relatively high examination fear. This kind of fear may be equivalent to insecurity about reaching one's (high) level of aspiration. At T5, however, the competence deficit $D(T5)$ was more or less irrelevant; here it was the expectation of failing the examination that seemed to produce fear. Thus it seemed probable that the predictability of the individual levels of fear could be improved by incorporating the variable $P_f(T)$ into the model. This was borne out by multiple correlations of .53 at T1 ($p < .05$), .21 at T3 (*ns*), and .46 at T5 ($p < .05$).

Another variable possibly influencing the level of fear of examination is the *personal importance* (PI) of success or failure (Atkinson, 1964; Halisch, 1976; Raynor, 1974). An individual who considered it highly important not to fail the examination should show a high degree of ego-involvement and emotionality, particularly when in doubt about reaching his goal. The item "failing the examination would be a great shock for me" was chosen as an indicator of the variable PI. It correlated with the level of fear .54 ($p < .01$) at T1, .29 (*ns*) at T3, and .28 (*ns*) at T5. When this particular index was used as a third predictor of individual levels of fear, still higher multiple correlations were found: $R = .68$ ($p < .01$) at T1, $R = .48$ (*ns*) at T3, and $R = .75$ ($p < .01$) at T5. Thus a further differentiation of the model again improved its capability of prediction.

One can draw the following conclusions from the initial and revised model for examination fear:

1. Other things being equal, fear will increase with (a) heightened personal importance of success or failure, (b) raised level of aspiration, (c) lowered momentary subjective estimate of competence, (d) increased estimated probability of failure, and (e) proximity to the examination.

2. Since these predictors are not independent of each other but form positive and negative intercorrelations that vary with the proximity of the examination, no simple formula can be devised allowing for an optimal prediction at each of the different points of time.

3. The type of fear curve evidenced before an examination is dependent on

the variable "success versus failure orientation." There were relatively many students ($N = 14$), especially among the success-oriented group, whose fear level reached a peak several days or weeks before the examination and then declined. Most of the failure-oriented students, however, were characterized by monotonously increasing levels of fear.

4. Two forms of examination fear must be differentiated. Several weeks prior to the examination the level of fear of all the students was lower than $F(T1) = 50$. At this time the student with a high level of aspiration is apparently uncertain about receiving the grade he or she considers satisfactory and becomes relatively fearful. This kind of fear can be called *uncertainty concerning success*; it characterizes most success-oriented students. It may be reduced by increasing one's level of competence, as the first model predicts (see Figure 7). A second kind of fear is more typical of failure-oriented Ss and may be called *fear of failure*. This fear showed a relatively monotonous increase as the examination approached. Further research may indicate the need to differentiate between types of fear of failure. In the present study, 7 students with scores indicating a high subjective probability of failing also had high levels of fear of failure ($F(T5) \geqslant 50$) shortly before the examination. Among these 7 students, two subgroups could be identified: those with a low subjective estimate of competence ($N = 4$) and those with a medium level of subjective estimate of competence. The latter were emotionally labile and considered it highly important not to fail the examination ($N = 3$). The high fear of these three emotionally labile Ss could be called irrational or neurotic.

Toward a More Comprehensive Analysis of Preexamination Behavior

It would be interesting to study the dynamics of preexamination behavior from a more comprehensive point of view and to examine possible relationships between variables in the extended model and other variables, such as amount of preparation, the individual's positive or negative feelings toward the examination, and the grade he or she finally received. As a first step, the Ss' self-ratings of their behavior and feelings were structured by a factor analysis of 71 items taken from two of the above-mentioned inventories (see Becker, 1980). Each student had responded to the items at T1, T3, and T5, and this information was used as though there were $3 \times 28 = 84$ individuals. Between three and eight factors were successively extracted and varimax-rotated. A 6-factor solution seemed psychologically most meaningful.

Factor 1, which accounted for 12.3% of the total variance, was interpreted as "failure versus success orientation." The items with the highest loadings were: dislike of written examinations (.80), belief that one's competence is lower than that of fellow students (.71), doubts about one's ability to pass the examination (.71), and indications of a high subjective probability of failing the examination (.64).

Factor 2 (12.1% of the total variance) consisted of "psychic and psychosomatic stress symptoms," for example, sleep disturbances, feelings of resignation, and gastrointestinal symptoms.

Factor 3, accounting for 10.6% of the total variance, was interpreted as "improper and inconsistent preparation." Some items with high loadings were:

studied only a few hours daily for the examination (.85), lack of perseverance (.77), and engaged in irrelevant activities (.49).

Factor 4, which accounted for 7.0% of the total variance, was interpreted as "high versus low achievement motivation." The marker items, among others, were: only a high grade would be considered as satisfactory (.74), failing the examination would be a great shock (.70), confidence that one will receive a high grade (.67), and succeeding in the examination was considered very important (.59).

Factor 5 (5.3% of the total variance) was interpreted as "criticism of the examination and the examiner." It consisted of items like: one agrees that the examinations should be modified (.68), the grade one earns is an unsatisfactory measure of one's competence (.63), good luck and one's personal condition on the examination day heavily influence the grade one will earn (.61), and examiners rarely strive for objectivity and fairness (.54).

Factor 6, accounting for 5.1% of the total variance, consisted of items pertaining to "examination fear."

In an extended empirical analysis the correlations between the scores in scales containing the marker variables of the six factors, single marker variables, and other selected variables were calculated (see Becker, 1980). The main results are schematically represented in Figure 8.

The similarities between factor 1 (failure versus success orientation), 4 (high versus low achievement motivation), and 6 (examination fear) and certain

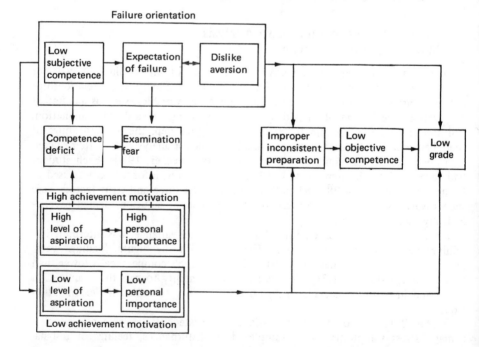

Figure 8 Schematic representation of some important variables characterizing the behavior of students before an examination and related to the level of examination fear and the grade received.

concepts in Heckhausen's theory of achievement motivation are noteworthy and invite further scrutiny. Heckhausen (1963, 1965) saw the necessity to differentiate between "hope of success," "fear of failure," "total level of achievement motivation," and "hope of success minus fear of failure." To measure these concepts he used a special form of the TAT and theoretically derived scoring keys. Heckhausen considered hope of success and fear of failure to be independent concepts and the total level of achievement motivation to be the sum of these two components.

The results of the preceding factor analysis as well as the relationships suggested in Figure 8 do in part corroborate Heckhausen's views. The factor analysis indicates that it is necessary to differentiate success versus failure orientation (a variable that corresponds to Heckhausen's hope of success) from examination fear (a variable that seems comparable to Heckhausen's concept of fear of failure). Similarly, it seems necessary to distinguish these two variables from the level of achievement motivation, a variable Heckhausen also uses. In this study, however, a high level of achievement motivation was not (in contrast to Heckhausen) the algebraic sum of hope of success and fear of failure but a new construct including both a high level of aspiration and high personal importance of the examination.

The author believes that the behavior of students before an examination can be understood rather well by focusing on the *subjective competence* of the examinees (see also Meyer, 1976).[1] Empirical evidence favoring this hypothesis is the fact that the two items with the highest loadings on the first *unrotated* factor were "Had many doubts about passing the examination" (.79) and "Belief that one's competence is lower than that of the fellow students" (.71). Feeling incompetent apparently increases the expectation of failure and heightens the aversion to the examination (see also Heckhausen, 1965). It also seems to influence the fear level, especially as the day of the examination approaches. Aversion to and dislike of examination is one factor probably responsible for an improper and inconsistent preparation: One experiences difficulties in commencing study, does not work with sufficient perseverance, and engages in irrelevant activities.[2] As a result of poor preparation, achievement potential is not fully utilized and one remains at a low level of objective competence. Under these circumstances, success is hardly to be expected. The correlations between the variable "Belief that one's competence is lower than that of the fellow students" and the number of points one actually received were $-.62$ ($p < .01$) at T1, $-.59$ ($p < .01$) at T3, and $-.71$ ($p < .01$) at T5. Subjective probability of failing the examination correlated significantly with the number of points achieved: $-.76$ ($p < .01$) at T1, $-.58$ ($p < .01$) at T3, and $-.66$ ($p < .01$) at T5. Thus two marker variables of the factor "success- versus failure-orientation" were reliable predictors of the grades received in the examination. Obviously the 28 students—most of whom had participated in a sample examination—had realistic ideas about their objective competence.

[1] As will be demonstrated the author regards subjective estimate of competence to be a key concept not only in relation to the theories of achievement motivation but also to the theories of anxiety.

[2] It has been postulated in the works of Kukla (1972) and Meyer (1976) and substantiated by the author's research that a positive relationship exists between low subjective competence and relatively low effort in confrontation with a difficult task.

Level of achievement motivation is another variable partially related to subjective estimate of competence. Students with low subjective estimates of competence tended to have low levels of achievement motivation. That is, their level of aspiration was low, and they considered the examination to be relatively unimportant.[3] Low achievement motivation was also a predictor of earning a low number of points. According to the author's theory of examination fear, a low level of achievement motivation is a defense against high fear. Maintaining low levels of achievement motivation would also tend to alleviate the disappointment of receiving a low grade.

As can be seen in Figure 8, there was no significant relationship between the level of examination fear as measured in the weeks prior to the examination and the grade actually received. None of the pertinent correlations were significantly different from zero. This can be better understood by closely examining the relationships between these two variables and the two other variables considered important in predicting the grade and the fear level, namely "success versus failure orientation" and "high versus low achievement motivation." Whereas a failure orientation was a common determinant of both fear and a *low* grade, leading to a positive correlation between the two, high achievement motivation correlated positively with fear but negatively with a low grade. In other words, students with low subjective and objective competence may remain relatively free from fear if they have low achievement motivation. On the other hand, students with high subjective and objective competence can become rather fearful if their level of achievement motivation is very high. It is interesting to note that Martin (1971), in a study on the anxiety of students anticipating an examination, also found no significant correlation between the preexamination level of anxiety (state as well as trait) and the final grades of the examinees.

DISCUSSION

The most interesting results of this study were the discovery of: (1) two types of examination fear, (2) inverted U-shaped curves characterizing fear levels of most of the success-oriented students prior to the examination, and (3) the monotonously increasing fear gradients of most of the failure-oriented students. These findings are strikingly similar to those of Epstein and Fenz (1965), which showed that experienced sport parachutists reach the peak of fear and stress reactions long before the jump, whereas novices exhibit either monotonously increasing curves or experience the greatest amount of fear shortly before the jump. In this respect success-oriented students may be comparable to experienced and failure-oriented students to inexperienced parachutists. Epstein (1967) explained the different fear curves by introducing the concept of "inhibition gradient," which is assumed to be steeper than the "gradient of fear." He observed that experienced parachutists control their level of fear by using well-developed coping and defense strategies (a modulated control system).

The present author's interpretation of the results of Epstein and Fenz is more in line with the arguments recently presented by Fenz (1975) and is based on a cognitive action model. According to this model the variable "subjective action

[3] This result confirms predictions made by Meyer (1976) in his theory of achievement motivation.

competence" is a key concept in any theory of anxiety (see also Boesch, 1976; White, 1959). This concept refers to the type of self-confidence and success orientation specific to a particular performance situation. An individual with a high subjective level of action competence believes that he or she can master this special situation. The opposite would be the feeling of helplessness (Mandler, 1972; Seligman, 1975). Both the present results and those of Fenz (1975) indicate that a high (subjective or objective) competence level is one factor favoring low fear levels, at least in the period closest to the critical event. It is interesting to note that Mechanic (1962) and Becker and Schneider (1976) also found that intensive preparation is one way to reduce one's examination fear.

With regard to the prevention and treatment of high examination fear, it is suggested that counselers, instructors, and students implement all measures conducive to increasing examinees' action competence and success orientation; e.g., students should acquire precise information about the contents of the examination, practice self-control techniques and efficient study habits, observe or simulate examinations, receive feedback about their competence, and, last but not least, prepare intensively.

A second fundamental variable contributing to the fear level in the extended model is an excessively high level of aspiration. Thus in some cases the main task of a counselor could be to help a student lower an unrealistic or unsound level of aspiration. In this regard the spontaneous reduction of the level of aspiration of many students as the examination approached ($p < .05$) should be mentioned. According to the extended model the third variable that should be taken into consideration is the personal importance of attaining a special goal (grade). On an organizational level it may be advisable to let the students choose between a single examination determining their final grade (= high personal importance condition) or a combination of several smaller tests of competence (= low personal importance condition).[4]

Although abnormally high levels of examination fear are detrimental to performance and should be reduced, one can ask if it is indeed possible or even beneficial to eliminate low or "normal" fear reactions. In contrast to Atkinson (1964), who considers fear of failure to be merely an inhibitory force leading automatically to avoidance behavior, the author believes that fear may have a useful adaptational function. As Freud described in his signal-function theory of anxiety, fear can be a warning signal making the individual aware that he or she must either avoid a situation that is too threatening, enhance his or her action competence, or reconsider and change his or her system of needs and values.

REFERENCES

Allen, G. J., Giat, L., & Cherney, R. J. Locus of control, test anxiety, and student performance in a personalized instruction course. *Journal of Educational Psychology,* 1974, *66,* 968–973.

Atkinson, J. W. *An introduction to motivation.* Princeton, NJ: Van Nostrand, 1964.

Bass, B. A., Ollendick, T. H., & Vuchinich, R. E. Study habits as a factor in the locus of control-academic achievement relationship. *Psychological Reports,* 1974, *34,* 906.

[4]The author realizes that such possibilities have already existed for some years in the U.S. and Canada, for example, but for West Germany they are relatively new.

Becker, P. *Studien zur Psychologie der Angst.* Weinheim: Beltz, 1980.

Becker, P., & Schneider, E. Persönlichkeitsspezifische Reaktionen auf eine Stresssituation: Studenten vor der Prüfung. *Zeitschrift für experimentelle und angewandte Psychologie,* 1976, *23,* 1–29.

Birney, R. C., Burdick, H., & Teevan, R. C. *Fear of failure.* Princeton, NJ: Van Nostrand, 1969.

Boesch, E. E. *Zwischen Angst und Triumph. Über das Ich und seine Bestätigung.* Bern: Huber, 1975.

Boesch, E. E. *Psychopathologie des Alltags. Zur Ökopsychologie des Handelns und seiner Störungen.* Bern: Huber, 1976.

Entwisle, D. R. To dispel fantasies about fantasy-based measures of achievement motivation. *Psychological Bulletin,* 1972, *77,* 377–391.

Epstein, S. Toward a unified theory of anxiety. In B. A. Maher (Ed.), *Progress in experimental personality research* (Vol. 4). New York: Academic Press, 1967.

Epstein, S., & Fenz, W. D. Steepness of approach and avoidance gradients in humans as a function of experience: Theory and experiment. *Journal of Experimental Psychology,* 1965, *70,* 1–12.

Fenz, W. Strategies for coping with stress. In I. G. Sarason & C. D. Spielberger (Eds.), *Stress and anxiety* (Vol. 2). Washington, DC: Hemisphere, 1975.

Fisch, R. *Konfliktmotivation und Examen.* Meisenheim am Glan: Anton Hain, 1970.

Halisch, F. Die Selbstregulation leistungsbezogenen Verhaltens: Das Leistungsmotiv als Selbstbekräftigungssystem. In H. D. Schmalt & W.-U. Meyer (Eds.), *Leistungsmotivation und Verhalten.* Stuttgart: Klett, 1976.

Heckhausen, H. *Hoffnung und Furcht in der Leistungsmotivation.* Meisenheim am Glan: Anton Hain, 1963.

Heckhausen, H. Leistungsmotivation. In H. Thomae (Ed.), *Handbuch der Psychologie* (Vol. 2). Göttingen: Hogrefe, 1965.

Kukla, A. Foundations of an attributional theory of performance. *Psychological Review,* 1972, *79,* 454–470.

Lewin, K. *Field theory in social science.* New York: Harper & Row, 1951.

Mandler, G. Helplessness: Theory and research in anxiety. In C. D. Spielberger (Ed.), *Anxiety: Current trends in theory and research* (Vol. 2). New York: Academic Press, 1972.

Martin, R. P. The development of anxiety in persons anticipating a highly stressful event. *Dissertation Abstracts International,* 1971, *31(A),* 5854.

Mechanic, D. *Students under stress.* New York: Free Press of Glencoe, 1962.

Meyer, W.-U. Leistungsorientiertes Verhalten als Funktion von wahrgenommener eigener Begabung und wahrgenommener Aufgabenschwierigkeit. In H. D. Schmalt & W.-U. Meyer (Eds.), *Leistungsmotivation und Verhalten.* Stuttgart: Klett, 1976.

Mischel, W. Toward a cognitive social learning reconceptualization of personality. *Psychological Review,* 1973, *80,* 252–283.

Raynor, J. O. Future orientation in the study of achievement motivation. In J. W. Atkinson & J. O. Raynor (Eds.), *Motivation and achievement.* New York: Wiley, 1974.

Rotter, J. B. *Social learning and clinical psychology.* Englewood Cliffs, NJ: Prentice-Hall, 1954.

Schmalt, H. D. *Die Messung des Leistungsmotivs.* Göttingen: Hogrefe, 1976.

Seligman, M. E. P. *Helplessness: On depression, development and death.* San Francisco: Freeman, 1975.

Weiner, B. An attributional interpretation of expectancy-value theory. In B. Weiner (Ed.), *Cognitive views of human motivation.* New York: Academic Press, 1974.

White, R. W. Motivation reconsidered: The concept of competence. *Psychological Review,* 1959, *66,* 297–333.

Wilcke, B. A. *Studienmotivation und Studienverhalten.* Göttingen: Hogrefe, 1976.

14

Aspiration Level and Causal Attribution under Noise Stimulation

Wolfgang Schönpflug
Free University of Berlin

VARIETIES OF STRESS WITHIN THE ACTIVITY CHAIN

The Concept of Activity Chain and a Definition of Stress

The theoretical analyses and empirical investigations reported in this chapter are based on an information-processing model. The essential features of the model are demonstrated in Figure 1. Two sources of information are included in the model: the subject's environment and the subject him- or herself. Reference to the subject as his or her own source of information has a twofold impact. On the one hand the model considers the role of interoceptive stimulation (which will not be followed up in this study); on the other hand it introduces the subjective memory as an information source (which will prove to be of major importance to this study).

Incoming information is assumed to be processed within three stages: a modeling stage, a task-building stage, and a stage of strategy formation. Modeling means the construction of invariant units and features, for example, reconstruction of objects, persons (including the subject), events and their attributes. The concept of modeling is supposed to serve as a unifying label for cognitive processes commonly referred to as perception, imagery, concept formation, even fantasy production. Internal models can be modified, contrasting versions may originate. All the generated alternatives may be evaluated and compared. The result is the selection of a required state of the subject and the environment. Further activity may be directed toward conservation of this state (if it is conceived of as existing) or toward its

This chapter is based mainly on a study documented in Schönpflug and Heckhausen (1976). The study was supported by a grant from the State Government of Nordrhein-Westfalen, Germany (*Ministerium für Wissenschaft und Forschung/Landesamt für Forschung*) to Dr. Heinz Heckhausen and the author (both at that time members of the Institute of Psychology, Ruhr-Universität Bochum). The contributions of Heinz Heckhausen to the research reported in the following chapter as well as his comments on an earlier version of this paper are gratefully acknowledged.

SOURCES OF   P R O C E S S I N G   EXECUTION
INFORMATION

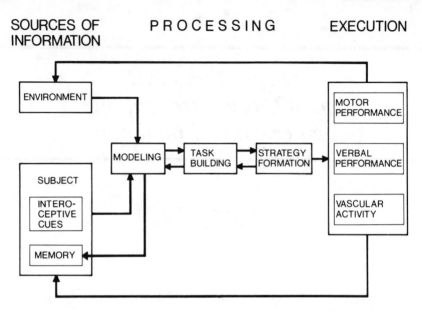

Figure 1 The activity chain. Modeling leads to an internal representation of the
subject's environment and state. During task building, requirements and
goals are selected, and strategies are elaborated for attaining the goals. At
the end of the chain, performance is executed that either conserves or
changes the subject and his or her environment.

production (if it is conceived of as missing). This stage is designated as task building
(alternative concepts: problem formation, goal setting). Generation and elaboration
of activity patterns suitable for solving the task and of conceptual preparatory
actions may constitute a third processing stage that will be designated here as
strategy formation. Task building and strategy formation may become the basis for
motor, vascular, and verbal performance, thus leading to an execution stage.

Modeling, task building, strategy formation, and execution seem to be crucial
components within what can be called the activity chain. Obviously the activity
within the chain is not just linear but also recursive. In particular, modeling and
task building seem not only to follow each other in consecutive stages; sometimes
the order may also be reversed, as emerging goals affect perception as well (cf.
Tajfel, 1969). Also, the existence of elaborated strategies may bias the process of
task building (e.g., Allport's, 1937, principle of functional autonomy). As a
consequence of executed actions the environment and the subject are actually
affected, and modeling increases the input of the subject's memory. In addition, a
full analysis will have to make provisions for the fact that the subject as a source of
information also encompasses the states of the behavior chain itself, and that in acts
of self-regulation modeling, task building and strategy formation may also be
directed toward selected states of behavior chain. The system described in Figure
1 therefore appears to be a highly complex and refined regulatory structure.

Stress is assumed to occur if activity within this system reaches or exceeds the
limits of its regulation range (cf. Teichner, 1968), and/or if disregulations can be
observed (cf. Schulz & Schönpflug, chapter 3 in this volume).

The Single Task and the Dual Task Case

As disregulation may take place during any phase of the activity chain, several types of stress are to be defined. One type of stress results from failures or complications during modeling. Stress of this kind can be due to information overload (e.g., Streufert & Streufert, 1968), to lack of information (e.g., Rausch, Hoeth, Reisse, & Meyer, 1965), or to ambiguous information (cf. Cobb, 1974; Kahn, 1973; Shavit, 1975). Modeling stress may go along with stress during task building, but task-building stress may still be separated out. Paradigms of task-building stress are the incapability of deciding between alternative models—one case of conflict (cf. Kahn, 1973; Levi & Benjamin, 1976)—and the unavailability of alternative models—one version of the case of helplessness (Seligman, 1975). Conflict between alternatives and unavailability of alternatives searched for may also be problems in strategy formation.

Some stress effects may be predominantly associated with the stage of execution. If there is too high a demand on muscular skill and on the capabilities for effort expenditure, if articulatory mechanisms are overcharged, if vascular responses have reached their reaction ceiling (cf. Borg, 1975; Teichner, 1968; Welford, 1976), then conditions of execution stress may exist. At least one type of stress extends over more than one component of the activity chain: the inability to attain preset goals despite availability of strategies and terminated performance—the case of frustration (Dembo, 1931).

Evidently all these stresses can originate from a single source, for example, a work problem or a threatening thought. They all are established within single task paradigms. Of course, there are also dual task cases (or multiple task cases, in general). Dual task situations (or multiple task situations, in general) include setups requiring incompatible responses or competition for limited capacities (e.g., Laabs & Stager, 1976; see also Welford, 1976), task problems going along with conflicting threatening thoughts (Hamilton, 1975), as well as mental, verbal, or motor tasks accompanied by unspecific external stressors such as heat or noise (e.g., Poulton & Edwards, 1974). The dual task case is characterized by the need for parallel processing and simultaneous execution as indicated in Figure 2.

One way of overcoming the difficulties of parallel processing and execution is obviously an increment in effort (Kahneman, 1973). In addition the possibilities of coordinating otherwise interfering processes are to be considered; in particular, internal time-sharing techniques deserve more attention. Coordination and organization of both parallel information processing and simultaneous executive activity seem to constitute a special kind of internal control process. Thus adding a second task to the first one not only duplicates the number of activity chains by requiring a coordinative control process but it also establishes the need for a third instance of information flow. Coordinating activity may solve capacity problems and create new ones at the same time. On the one hand it may succeed in optimizing utilization of available capacities, on the other hand it also requires some capacity, thereby reducing the total capacity left for the primary activity chains.

Since the empirical section of this paper will deal extensively with noise as an external stressor, attention should be drawn to the fact that this analysis is treating this stressor like a problem that has to be worked on. Indeed, external noise is conceived of as a source of information that can elicit an activity chain of its own.

SOURCES OF   PROCESSING   EXECUTION
INFORMATION

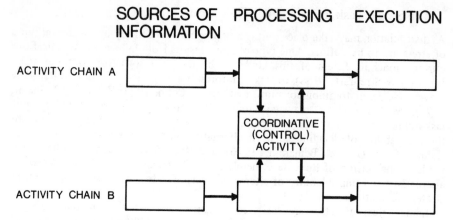

Figure 2 The dual task case. With two sources of information, two parallel activity chains
can be established. The parallel activity chains may compete for limited capacities.
Utilization of available capacities may be optimized by coordinative (control)
activity; this, however, introduces a new process that also chains a portion of the
available capacities.

It can be represented as an internal model, it can be evaluated, and response
strategies to noise can be elaborated and executed (e.g., retreat from the noisy
area, turning off the noise). The interfering effects of noise cannot be sufficiently
explained without reference to the cognitive, motor, and vascular processes brought
about by noise stimulation.

Shifts of Aspiration Level as a Function of Stress

It is a well-documented phenomenon that subjects lower their level of aspiration
when experiencing failure (Hoppe, 1931). A reduction of aspired goals is also a
possible response to increments in workload (Hacker, 1976). Obviously in such
cases shifts of aspiration have the function of preventing failure, disorganization of
behavior, and emotional imbalance. While the above-mentioned demonstrations
explicitly refer to single task cases, there is no reason to abstain from
generalizations in multiple task situations. The search for appropriate goals seems to
be a general principle in behavior regulation and stress prevention. Reykowski
(1972) reported some studies bearing on this issue. In these studies a series of tasks
had to be performed, for instance, identification and maze learning. After some
trials without stress, interruptions and pain stimuli were introduced. With this
treatment the time required for solving the tasks increased. The increment,
however, was higher for persons who had underestimated their performance during
the nonstress trials; those who had displayed no discrepancy between their
aspiration level and their achievement level during the nonstress trials were more
tolerant of stress.

In current theories of stress the role of aspiration shifts has not been sufficiently
recognized. Goal setting becomes a relevant process in all achievement situations.
Current theories dealing with stress in achievement situations restrict themselves to
mental and motor performance. Thus, these theorists prefer concepts like filtering,

interference, response incompatibility, pigeon-holing, and the like in order to explain deficits under stress (cf. Broadbent, 1971). This kind of theorizing centers on strategy formation and execution rather than on task building, and it is more inclined toward the actual impact of stress than toward anticipations of stress effects. In light of the activity chain model it would be precipitous to interpret every performance decrement under stress as due to disorganization or any other deterioration of mental operations and motor acts on which the performance is based; decrement of performance can very well go along with organized behavior if—in response to stress—the level of aspiration has been lowered. Shifts in level of aspiration can be assumed to occur in the phase in which stress is already experienced. Aspiration shifts can, however, also be expected to take place in anticipation of impending stress. In the latter case the aspiration shift not only precedes the onset of stress but there is also a stronger temporal dissociation between goal setting and the execution period.

Goal Setting and Attribution of Success and Failure under Stress

In the search for an optimal level of aspiration, subjects tend to take several factors into account. Causal attributions of success and failure include stable and variable factors in both the subject and his or her environment. Representative formulations of attribution theory (Kelley, 1972; Weiner, 1974) focus on the single task case but can easily be generalized to multiple task situations.

In general the outcome of an action can be described as contingent on the action itself or on the physical and social situation. The view that an outcome can depend directly on both internal control of a subject and control of agents external to him or her should be supplemented by the notion that a subject's characteristics and his or her actions can be influenced by the given situation. In the latter case the effect of external agents is mediated by the subject. This results in Heckhausen's (1977) schema of contingencies as depicted in Figure 3. The contingencies indicated in the

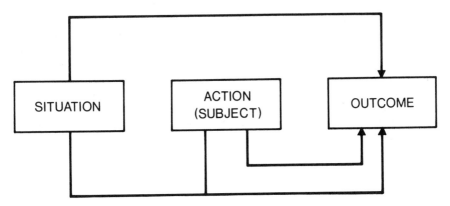

Figure 3 Contingency schema for determination of an outcome. An outcome may be contingent on the preceding action and/or on the given situation. The influence of the situation on the outcome may also be mediated by the subject and his or her action (after Heckhausen, 1977).

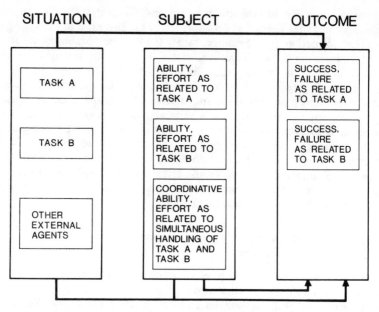

Figure 4 Causal attribution in the dual task situation. The situation offers two
tasks with their respective difficulties; also other external agents,
including global conceptions of good and bad luck, may be relevant.
Ability and effort on the subject's side have to be related to both
tasks separately, as well as to their simultaneous handling. Success
and failure are the most common indicators of outcome.

graph can form the basis for theoretical explanations as well as for subjective
expectations.

If the contingency schema is extended to represent two tasks with their
respective difficulties, the definition of personal control factors has to be adapted
to the duplication of requirements. Ability and effort are regarded as the most
prominent personal control factors. With more than one task, different ability and
effort components have to be distinguished. In addition the coordinating ability
and the effort in handling two tasks should be accounted for separately. For two
tasks the outcome on either task should also be registered separately. The extended
schema is illustrated in Figure 4. Success and failure are entered in the graph as
indicators of outcome. The situational factors given by task A and task B may be
complemented by an unspecified group of other external agents; in subjective
reports this group is often represented by global conceptions of "good luck" and
"bad luck."

AN EXPERIMENTAL STUDY:
HYPOTHESIS, DESIGN, METHOD

In an attempt to use the concepts and methods of achievement motivation and
causal attribution theories for a further advancement of stress theory (and in order
to extend the application of the theories of achievement motivation and causal
attribution to paradigms in the area of stress), a series of studies was performed at

the University of Bochum, Germany, which are fully documented in Schönpflug and Heckhausen (1976). The last of these studies will be reported in the following section.

Time Estimation as a Primary Task and Noise as an Additional Stressor

The time estimation task described in detail in the next paragraph was the task to be performed under all experimental conditions. In addition, subjects were exposed in different experimental sessions to white noise of varying intensity; in one control condition subjects made their estimates without being exposed to noise. There were several consecutive time estimates within each experimental session, and subjects received an immediate feedback on their hits and failures. Regarding the noise, the subjects could respond to it internally but there was no opportunity to control it externally (e.g., the subjects were not permitted to attenuate it). If the noise gave rise to interference, coping with it would be manifested most clearly in an increment in estimation efficiency. There was no doubt from the beginning that the estimation task could be accomplished and that it was terminated by an explicit response. Yielding a result that could be evaluated as success or failure, it had every chance of receiving a high ranking in the subjects' frame of reference for skilled performance. Coping with stressful noise can also be regarded as a task, as has already been contended in the theoretical analysis of the dual task situation. However, without being given the opportunity for an explicit response and without obtaining direct, immediate, and unambiguous feedback, subjects should be less inclined to focus on coping with the noise. In general the role of the primary task will presumably be assigned to time estimation, whereas coping with noise can be expected to become a secondary task.

The time estimation task was introduced as a test of practical intelligence. Subjects were repeatedly exposed to a white light signal; the duration of the light indicated the time interval to be judged. As the interval was supposed to be constant, the estimated duration could be stated by pressing a button at the bisection point of the interval. Immediately after pressing the button, a green or a red signal light appeared and continued until termination of the white light. Green lights were introduced as signals for correct estimates, red lights as signals for incorrect trials.

The critical interval in the main trials lasted for about 25 seconds. The subjects were told that their estimates were controlled electronically so that they would have practically no chance to hit the bisection point exactly (i.e., to less than .01 of a second) if there was no "safety margin" allowed. The safety margin was defined as the maximal deviation from the exact bisection point that would still be scored as correct. The subjects were permitted to choose one of the following three safety margins in different trials: 2 ($\pm$ 1) seconds, 3.5 ($\pm$ 1.75) seconds, and 7 ($\pm$ 3.5) seconds. The choice of safety margin should allow the subjects to select the difficulty level of the task, which seems to be an important variable for achievement motivation (cf. Atkinson, 1964; Weiner, 1974).

The temporal characteristics of the interval to be estimated and the signal lights are summarized in Figure 5. In all but the control sessions subjects wore earphones and were exposed binaurally to white noise of 60, 90, or 105 dB(A). Without presentation of noise there was a standard sound level lower than 45 dB(A) in the

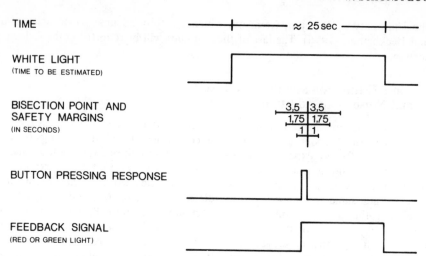

TIME ————————|———— ≈ 25 sec ————|——

WHITE LIGHT
(TIME TO BE ESTIMATED)

BISECTION POINT AND
SAFETY MARGINS
(IN SECONDS)

BUTTON PRESSING RESPONSE

FEEDBACK SIGNAL
(RED OR GREEN LIGHT)

Figure 5 The estimation task. The bisection point of a time interval (marked by a white light) had to be indicated by the pressing of a button. Three different safety margins were provided within which a response was to be scored as correct. Immediately after the response, subjects received a feedback signal indicating whether their response was scored as correct (green light) or incorrect (red light).

experimental room. The variation of sound level was explained to the subjects as an attempt to simulate "environmental conditions well-known from real-life situations."

Scoring Procedure and Feedback Conditions

The consecutive time estimates were performed in series. Eight estimates were combined to form one series. Thus the maximum number of correct estimates per series was eight. However, subjects were free to choose between three safety margins that also constituted different difficulty levels. A scoring system was developed to relate the number of hits and the task difficulty. Each correct estimate with a safety margin of 7 second (low difficulty) was scored 1 point; with a margin of 3.5 second (medium difficulty) 2 points were scored; and with a margin of 2 second (high difficulty) 3 points.

The pronounced effect of feedback rate (success and failure) on aspiration level and causal attribution (Karabenick, 1972; Meyer, 1973) had to be taken into account. Therefore feedback rate was introduced as an independent variable. In order to separate groups with high and low positive feedback, the feedback procedure described above could be varied without the subjects' awareness. Two different feedback conditions were defined. Under each condition subjects were run through six series of eight estimates. Thus a maximal score of 24 points per series could be achieved. As a guide for modification of feedback, prototypical scores for all sessions in all conditions were prepared. These prototypical scores started out with high values for the first series of the high-feedback condition and with low values for the first series of the low-feedback condition. With an increasing number of series the predetermined scores were only slightly rising in the low-feedback condition; they were steadily moving toward the maximal values in the high-feedback condition. From these prototypical performance curves, individual deviations were also predetermined in order to avoid subjective responses to feedback stereotypies in different sessions.

In individual trials actual feedback was adjusted by the experimenter to the corresponding prototypical curve. If the performance of a subject was not in accordance with the prototypical curve, manipulation of feedback was accomplished in the following way: By means of an additional electronic circuit the termination of the white light could be either advanced or postponed. Although the subjects were made to believe that the interval during which the white light was turned on was constant in all experimental trials, the interval actually varied within the limits of 20–30 second. This variation was not noticed by the subjects. If experimental conditions required the subjects to receive positive feedback, the green light went on after they had pressed the button (presumably marking the bisection point of a constant time interval), and the white light was left on for the same time that had elapsed between its onset and the time of pressing the button. In this way the time between the onset of the white light and the pressing of the button was duplicated to give the total duration of the white light, and the button pressing response was located precisely in the middle of the interval. If the subjects were to receive negative feedback, the red light appeared and the duration of the white light was prolonged for a period either shorter or longer than the prior interval between the onset of white light and the pressing of the button; the difference between the time before and after pressing the button exceeded the preselected safety margin. Under this condition it became fairly evident that the moment of pressing the button did not mark the bisection point between onset and offset of the white light.

Provision was made that extreme responses, like pressing the button with very short or very long delay after the onset of the white light, as well as missing responses were not evaluated as being correct. There were only a few extreme or missing responses under conditions of high positive feedback, and no subject had to be discarded due to considerable deviation from the corresponding prototypical curve. The final distribution of scores will be presented and analyzed in the results section.

Subjects, Personality Variables, and Experimental Design

Forty-eight students at the University of Bochum, Germany, were selected for participation in this study. They were not enrolled in psychology courses and received a small honorarium. Subjects with major hearing loss according to Bekésy's audiometric test were not included in the sample.

It was suggested that individual differences would account for a high proportion of variance in the data to be collected. In order to assess at least a part of the individual variation, a series of personality tests was administered, including a German version of the Maudsley Personality Inventory (Brengelmann & Brengelmann, 1960). The subjects could only be assigned to feedback conditions in such a way that just one of the tested personality variables was evenly distributed. The variable selected to be balanced within the experimental design was extraversion. Therefore extraversion will be the only personality variable that will be treated in this chapter.

It was decided to favor the dimension of extraversion-introversion among the tested personality variables because it seemed to be related to both goal setting and reactivity. Introverts are reported to prefer a higher level of aspiration than extraverts (Eysenck, 1953). Introverts also seem to react more strongly to external stimulation than extraverts (Uherik & Biro, 1973). It could be argued that both effects were due to internal control mechanisms also operating in the process of causal attribution (cf. Meyer, 1973).

The subjects were classified as introverts and extraverts depending on the median of the total sample. One half the introvert group and one half the extravert group were randomly assigned to the condition with high positive feedback and low positive feedback respectively. All subjects took part in four experimental sessions and were exposed to noise of 45, 60, 90, and 105 dB(A), each sound level being used in one session. From four different sound levels given in four consecutive sessions, 24 different sequences could be constructed. All 24 possible sequences were replicated for both high- and low-feedback conditions. The 24 sequences also appeared once in the group of 24 introverts as well as in the group of 24 extraverts. Thus the sequences were also equally distributed over the total personality groups. Within these limits the assignment of the subjects to sequences of sound levels varied by chance. This means that in the four independent groups of subjects defined by the combination of feedback conditions and personality groups the different sequences are not equally represented. The experimental design is summarized in Table 1.

Procedure and Measurements

During the presession, personality tests were administered and the subjects were introduced to the experimental situation. They were given some training trials on the time estimation task and shown the apparatus by which the time intervals and the signal lights were controlled. It was a setup constructed by means of Massey-Dickinson components. The subjects were encouraged to test the apparatus and check the precision of timing with their own watch. During the demonstration phase, of course, the device used for modification of feedback was inactive.

The subjects were informed about the choice of safety margins and the scoring procedure in general. They were also informed that they had to return for four more sessions and that they had to expect a training effect within each session but no carry-over effects between sessions.

After the introductory session the subjects actually returned four more times to the laboratory. Between sessions there was an interval of at least one week. The

Table 1 Experimental Design

Positive feedback	Extraversion	Sound level in dB(A)			
		45	60	90	105
Low	Low				
	High				
High	Low				
	High				

sessions lasted about one hour and the subjects took part individually. At the beginning of each session the general introduction was briefly repeated.

In each session the subjects had to perform 48 time estimates (organized in six series containing eight estimates each). Thus the subjects could score for one series 0–24 points. If there was an additional acoustical stimulation, the noise was turned on for approximately 15 second before each series and switched off shortly afterwards.

Prior to each series the subjects had to rate their expectations and aspirations on scales ranging from 0 to 24 points. They were asked to mark (a) the minimal and (b) the maximal score they expected to obtain, (c) the score they believed to obtain with highest probability, (d) the minimal score they actually wanted to obtain, and (e) the score that would fully satisfy them. Measures (a), (b), and (c) were supposed to indicate minimal, maximal, and medium level of expectation, measures (d) and (e) minimal and optimal level of aspiration.

After each series the subjects had to fill out another prepared form. The score they had actually received in the last series was entered on top of the sheet; in addition the experimenter repeated the score orally when addressing the subject after the termination of each series. The subjects were asked to rate (f) satisfaction with the last score, (g) annoyance of sound level during the last series, (h) disturbance by sound level, attribution of outcome to (i) ability and (j) effort, using 7-, 9-, or 11-point scales, respectively. They also estimated (k) the number of hits during the last series due to good luck or favorable uncontrolled factors in general and (l) the number of failures during the last series due to bad luck or unfavorable uncontrolled factors.

During the whole experiment heart rate and electrical skin resistance were registered as measures of involvement. Skin resistance was measured by means of Velcro electrodes attached to the second and fourth finger of the left hand. Pulse measures were continually taken from the thumb of the left hand.

After the termination of the last session there was a final interview that included a debriefing of the experimental procedure. A few subjects who had been under the failure condition stated they had incidentally suspected "that something may be wrong with the apparatus," but no subject ever believed in manipulations on the experimenter's side.

RESULTS

Statistical Treatment of Data

All data were submitted to an analysis of variance. Rate of positive feedback, sound level, and replication of series were defined as fixed variables, extraversion as a random variable. For this reason all effects except the effects of extraversion itself had to be tested against their interaction with extraversion (cf. Hays, 1963).

Scores Received, Expectations, and Aspirations

The scores varied significantly with feedback rate ($F = 715$; 1,1 df, $p < 0.05$) and with series within one session ($F = 20.4$; 5,5 df, $p < 0.01$). There was also a significant interaction between feedback rate and series ($F = 14.3$; 5,5 df,

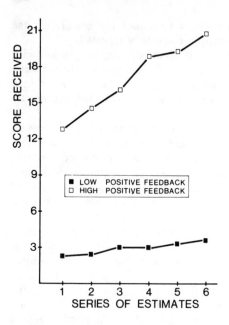

Figure 6 Scores received (number of hits weighted by safety margins) in six consecutive series of time estimates as a function of feedback.

$p < 0.01$). Increases of scores were accompanied by decreases in safety margin. Choice of safety margin varied consistently with feedback rate ($F = 3730$; 1,1 *df*, $p < 0.01$), series ($F = 14.1$; 5,5 *df*, $p < 0.01$), and their interaction ($F = 10.2$; 5,5 *df*, $p < 0.05$). The significant variations of scores and safety margins in seconds are presented in Figures 6 and 7.

Expected and aspired scores followed the actual scores; therefore a considerable portion of the variation in these data is due to feedback rate, replication of series,

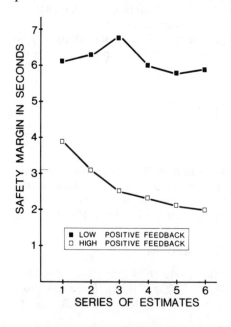

Figure 7 Safety margins in six consecutive series of time estimates as a function of feedback.

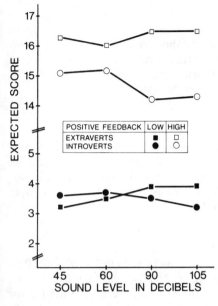

Figure 8 Score predicted with highest probability (medium expectation) as a function of sound level and extraversion.

and their interaction. The only other significant effect is the interaction between sound level and extraversion. The general trends are the same for minimal, medium, and maximal expectations on the one hand, and for minimal and optimal aspirations on the other. For the sake of parsimony Figures 8 and 9 present only the values for medium expectation (interaction of sound level and extraversion: $F = 3.9$; 3,1012 *df, p* < 0.01) and for optimal aspiration (interaction of sound level and extraversion: $F = 2.8$; 3,1012 *df, p* < 0.05).

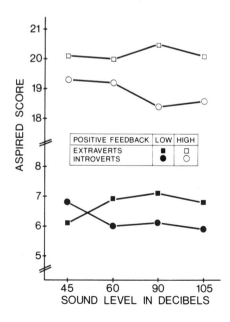

Figure 9 Score stated to be fully satisfying (optimal aspiration) as a function of sound level and extraversion.

Ratings of Satisfaction

The degree of satisfaction with the last score depended highly on the score actually received and therefore varied considerably with the rate of positive feedback with replicated series and the interaction between the two variables. In addition there was a significant increase of satisfaction ratings with sound level ($F = 18.9; 3,3$ df, $p < 0.05$). There was absolutely no effect of extraversion.

Evaluation of Sound Level

Judgments of annoyance and disturbance were highly correlated. Therefore analysis and presentation of data can be restricted to disturbance ratings. As can be seen from Figure 10, there is a strong influence of sound level ($F = 203.7; 1,3$ df, $p < 0.01$); the effect is modified by feedback and extraversion, giving rise to a triple interaction effect ($F = 4.1; 3,1012$ df, $p < 0.01$).

Attribution to Ability, Effort, and Chance

The interactions between feedback and sound level ($F = 30.0; 3,3$ df, $p < 0.01$), feedback and extraversion ($F = 4.4; 1,44$ df, $p < 0.05$), and sound level and extraversion ($F = 3.5; 3,1012$ df, $p < 0.05$) were significant sources of variation for the ratings of the contribution of ability to the attainment of scores. As shown in Figure 11, extraverts tend to rate contributions of their own ability higher than introverts if receiving high positive feedback. Their ratings, however, tend to be lower than those of introverts if they receive low positive feedback. With medium sound level the contribution of ability is judged to be highest, but this effect again is modified by feedback and personality.

Extraverts also seem to rate the role of effort higher than introverts if receiving high positive feedback, but lower if receiving low positive feedback. The effect,

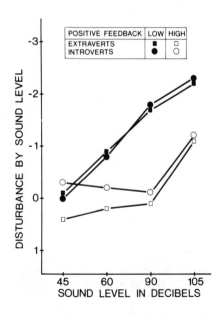

Figure 10 Rated disturbance by noise as a function of feedback, sound level, and extraversion.

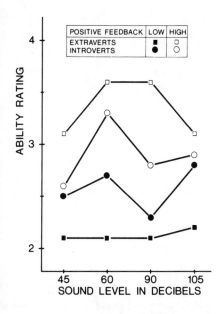

Figure 11 Ratings of ability as a function of feedback, sound level, and extraversion.

however, fails to be statistically significant, as do all other sources of variance.

Extraverts with high positive feedback attributed success more often to good luck than other subjects $(F = 4.5; 1,44$ *df,* $p < 0.05$) (see Figure 12); other effects were not significant. Extraverts also tended to attribute failures to bad luck rather than introverts; attributions to bad luck in low positive feedback situations in general tended to exceed those with high positive feedback (see Figure 13). These effects, however, failed to reach significance.

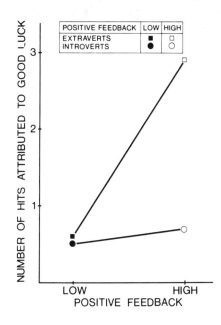

Figure 12 Number of hits per series attributed to good luck as a function of feedback and extraversion.

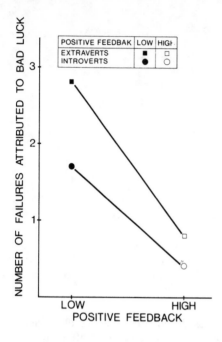

Figure 13 Number of failures per series attributed to bad luck as a function of feedback and extraversion.

Physiological Measures

Introverts exhibited higher increments of heart rate during experimental sessions if the rate of positive feedback was high; extraverts on the contrary showed higher increments of heart rate with low positive feedback ($F = 7.3$; 1,44 *df, p* < 0.01). In general, introverts seem to react to a variation in sound level more sensitive than extraverts ($F = 2.6$; 3,1012 *df, p* < 0.05). Similar observations could be made with galvanic skin resistance. The data as presented in Figures 14 and 15 are also consistent with the results from the preceding studies.

INTERPRETATION OF RESULTS
AND SOME ADDITIONAL EVIDENCE

Noise: A Conspicuous Stressor

Noise again turns out to be a substantial stressor. Negative evaluations, however, as indicated by the annoyance and disturbance ratings, are attenuated by high positive feedback (Figure 10). This gives good evidence of the task characteristics of noise.

The distinction introduced in the theoretical analysis of the problem remains valid in light of the data. Obviously there are noise-specific activities such as covert avoidance responses. Under conditions of a parallel dominating activity, as elicited by the time estimation task, these activities may be performed at a minimal level. This picture changes if sound stimulation approaches the pain threshold. Under this condition avoidance responses and other concomitant reactions are performed at a

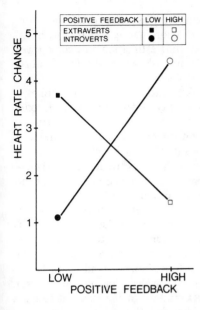

Figure 14 Heart rate change during experimental sessions as a function of feedback and extraversion.

higher rate. If performed at a higher rate, the dominance of parallel activities can be assumed to be reduced; and coping with the specific reactions to noise can even become a dominating process itself. Apparently, nonneutral ratings of annoyance under conditions of high positive feedback are indicators of noise-specific coping activities.

The same extent of noise-specific activities as observed under conditions of high feedback can be assumed to occur under conditions of low feedback. But as annoyance and disturbance ratings are more pronounced under low than under high

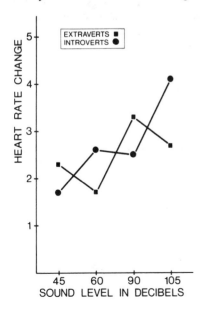

Figure 15 Heart rate change during experimental sessions as a function of sound level and extraversion.

feedback, there remains a portion that is accounted for by noise-specific activities. This portion can be interpreted as a correlate of coordinating activity. With high feedback, coordination of parallel processes (like time estimation and coping with noise) may be judged by the subjects as an irrelevant task, while with low feedback it may appear to be the crucial task.

The ratings of satisfaction also have to be taken into consideration. Ratings of satisfaction increased continuously with sound intensity under both feedback conditions. Since satisfaction ratings are explicitly related to the outcome, the portion of the satisfaction ratings that covaries with sound intensity can be interpreted as another correlate of coordinating activity. Interestingly enough, this correlate also changes for sound intensities below 105 dB(A) under high positive feedback when no change in annoyance and disturbance ratings is observed. Satisfaction ratings possibly reflect a special aspect of coordinating activity, for instance coordinating efficacy.

From the attribution theoretical point of view the extent of noise-specific and coordinating activities is closely associated with the difficulty created by introduction of noise. As the time estimation task remains at the same level of difficulty throughout the whole experiment, the total difficulty as induced by the experimenter increases with sound level. Thus the subjects could not fail to recognize the noise as an apparent source of aggravation, as a conspicuous stressor. Any achievement in a primary task also requires mastery of the external stressor. Therefore subjects seem to evaluate their scores higher in the presence of noise—as can be seen from the satisfaction ratings.

External Control and Uncertainty in Stress Situations

The finding that high positive feedback favors attribution to ability and good luck and reduces attributions to bad luck replicates earlier findings (e.g., Miller, 1976; Snyder, Stephan, & Rosenfield, 1976). The causal factor most clearly affected by noise intensity is ability. Noise effects on ability ratings, however, are only to be observed under conditions of high positive feedback. If subjects search for an explanation for continuous success (in spite of increasing difficulty due to medium noise intensities), they tend to attribute their success to improved utilization of capacities. This explanation, however, does not seem to hold for high noise intensities. At least under the condition of a 105 dB(A) noise the amount of difficulty as induced by noise-specific and coordinating activities seems to outbalance the subjects' capacities. Extraverts may explain their success in a highly difficult situation with good luck, although they do not attribute it more to good luck than in low-difficulty situations. Introverts, on the other hand, seem to refrain from attributions to good luck at all. As extreme noise itself cannot be made responsible for success, subjects should suffer from a lack of explanations for successes under high stress.

The amount of stress or task difficulty that can be balanced by skill seems to vary between individuals. According to the statements of introverts, improved utilization of capacities can merely compensate effects of 60 dB(A) noise, whereas, according to the statements of extraverts, 90 dB(A) noise is also compensated. This, however, is a postperformance judgment, just indicating that extraverts and introverts may have different attributional biases toward their own ability.

With extremely low positive feedback as given in some conditions of this study subjects explain their failures mainly by the influence of bad luck and lack of efficiency. These causal factors seem to leave no space for other explanatory concepts such as increment of difficulty induced by noise.

In general two characteristics stand out in situations that can be characterized as severely stressing: external control and uncertainty. External control is exerted by tasks that cannot be successfully solved, although the subject works on a solution. But using lack of efficiency and bad luck as causal factors of failure may at the same time be ambiguous and obscure. Even the experience of success may cause feelings of uncertainty if occurring under stressful conditions. If it occurs repeatedly, it cannot be attributed to an external temporary agent, such as incidental unexpected hits, and remains—if not attributed to competence—without sufficient explanation. In any case the lack of explanatory power may introduce an element of uncertainty into the situation, leading to conflict, emotional involvement, and feeling of discomfort (cf. Berlyne, 1960).

When lack of consistent explanations creates feelings of uncertainty, the search for causal attributions may become a technique of reducing uncertainty. It can be concluded from the verbal reports that extraverts make more extended use of this technique. They refer to good and bad luck more frequently and in addition show stronger tendencies to attribute success to their own abilities. From these observations it could also be concluded that extraverts are less tolerant of uncertainty than introverts.

Activation and Effort

Effort plays an important role in the generation of stress. A period of stress can easily be terminated if the stressing activities performed in this period are renounced. In contrast, a stressing situation is maintained if activities in this situation are sustained by individual effort. Heart rate as a physiological indicator of activation shows only weak reactions to increasing noise intensity; in particular, 105 dB(A) noise is distinctly responded to only by introverts (Figure 15). Thus the extraverts—relying on ability and good luck more than the introverts—may not have evaluated the task characteristics of the noise to the same extent as the introverts, and in consequence did not respond to it with the same increment of organismic activation.

Although all subjects tend to attribute experienced success more to effort than experienced failure to lack of effort, which has already been observed in former studies (e.g., Miller, 1976; Snyder et al., 1976), only introverts follow this trend as far as organismic activation is concerned (Figure 14). This result could be related to the introverts' stronger tendency for internal control (cf. Schulz & Schönpflug, chapter 3 in this volume). Internal control may coincide with higher physiological activation if control processes are reinforced by positive feedback. If, however, this reinforcement is lacking, control processes are diminished and activation in general is reduced.

In the experimental situation the extraverts' heart rate increased with low but not with high positive feedback. This reaction is more difficult to understand. The following interpretation may be offered: The extraverts are possibly guided by the attitude that their ability and their good luck are operating even without effort expenditure. This is evident for good luck being defined as an external agent per se.

Further interpretation is needed for ability. Ability is commonly regarded as an internal causal factor, and indeed it is a controlling agent located internally. This does not mean that ability should necessarily be regarded as an internally controlled agent (i.e., an agent activated by the subject). The subject may as well conceive of ability as a self-activating or an externally activated agent. Extraverts may have taken a rather relaxed attitude as long as they believed to profit from their self-activating or externally activated abilities. Under the experience of failure, however, extraverts may have suffered from the lack of supporting mechanisms. Under this condition they may strive to extend their own control of the situation, thereby raising their activation level.

This interpretation is in line with the ability and chance ratings but not with the effort ratings themselves. As measures of physiological activation and subjective indexes of effort do not validate each other, their divergence becomes another problem for further investigation.

The Crucial Question: Is There an Aspiration Shift in Stressful Situations?

Only the data of the introverts correspond to predictions from the theory: They lower their aspiration level with increasing total difficulty (Figure 9). This tendency is well in accordance with their expectations (Figure 8). Obviously, they react to the increased difficulty induced by increments of sound intensity. For introverts the external and negative influence of noise is neither compensated for by another external factor favorable to the outcome of performance (like good luck) nor by the factors of both ability and effort, which are conceived of by the introverts as internally controlled. For this reason the following generalization is proposed: Introverts who experience a stressful situation as externally controlled tend to lower their expectations of efficiency of their own control and reduce their level of aspiration.

The same tendencies are not to be observed with extraverts. This may be due to differences in the conception of internal control. One of the major reasons can be seen in their firmer belief in good luck. For extraverts, even perceived difficulties can be compensated for with good luck and therefore they show no downward shift of expectations and aspirations in a stressful situation as investigated in this study. Actually extraverts even exhibit tendencies of raising their expectations and aspirations with increasing difficulty and stress (Figures 8 and 9). This effect had not been predicted and is probably due to a special feature of the experimental treatment: The feedback given was rather invariant for each individual in consecutive sessions. As noise intensity varied, subjects had some reason to build up the conception of being resistant to stress. For extraverts this conception might have supported their belief in favorable self-activating or externally activated factors. Therefore the subjective experience of a constant outcome—despite a perceived variation in noisiness—may have produced a bias toward upward shifts or at least a bias against downward shifts in expectation and aspiration.

Some Recent Data on the Role of Feedback Conditions

The most important limitations of the series of studies performed at the Bochum laboratory derive from the exclusive use of manipulative feedback and lack of variation in feedback with experimental variation of stress conditions. Both conditions may lead to deviations from the subjects' expectancies and reduce both the subjects' objective control of the situation and their subjective perception of control. Evidence for these effects is reported in the literature (Feather & Simon, 1971; Wortman & Brehm, 1975); these effects also had to be dealt with in the preceding discussion. For this reason, Margarete Krenauer at the Institute of Psychology of the Free University of Berlin has recently performed another study, comparing the effects of manipulative feedback, realistic feedback, and no feedback on goal setting and causal attribution.

Krenauer used three series of pattern recognition tasks. Each subject had to undergo all series; between series the sound level in the experimental room was varied. During one series there was no extra stimulation (50 dB(A)), during the other two series traffic noise was introduced shifting the total sound level to 80 or 95 dB(A) respectively. Sound intensity in the three series was either ascending or descending for each subject. All subjects were familiarized with the task and the sound levels to be used; the sound level to come in the following series was regularly announced in advance.

Manipulated feedback had an effect on goal setting and attribution, but (as can be seen from Figure 16) without manipulated feedback the aspiration level was closely related to sound intensity (for all feedback conditions: $F = 60.1$; 2,422 df, $p < 0.01$). If the sound level was ascending during the experiment the aspired scores in general were lower than with descending intensities (for all feedback conditions: $F = 27.9$; 1,211 df, $p < 0.01$). These data give clear evidence that in highly predictable situations subjects adjust their aspiration to the amount of stress. They even seem to develop a long-term strategy for goal setting: If gradual increments of stress are impending, they tend to leave a higher margin of variation by choosing lower values.

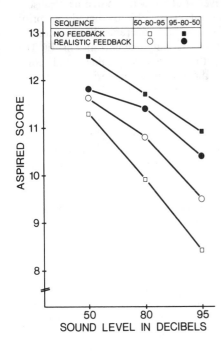

Figure 16 Scores stated to be fully satisfying (optimal aspiration) as a function of sound level, feedback, and sequence of sound levels (Krenauer's data).

Main Conclusion: Stress Reactions
Can Also Be Anticipatory

One of the most substantial contentions of the theory of achievement motivation has also to be taken into account in the theory of stress: namely, that individuals do not only react to the present situation but also to their anticipation of situations to come. Thus there is not only the actual experience of stress to be considered but the anticipation of stress as well. The anticipation of stress can be investigated as a phenomenon by itself. However, it may also help to explain the behavior in the actual stress situation. If execution conforms to goal setting, adjustment of aspiration level to anticipated stress will modify an individual's achievement-related behavior during the following stage of stress. And although this point has not yet been sufficiently investigated, there should be substantial differences between achievement-related behavior in stress situations with and without anticipatory adjustments of aspiration level.

Anticipation of stress effects also requires some knowledge about stress effects. Individuals may gain some knowledge about impending stress without prior experience. Stress theories, however, should also make provisions for individual acquisition of knowledge about stressors and stress effects by experience. (The theory of learned helplessness, Seligman, 1975, is a related approach.) In the theoretical model presented the assumption of an individual memory storing the contingencies between task situations (including stressors), difficulty levels, and own capacities has become indispensable. These contingencies seem to form the basis for anticipatory adjustments to forthcoming stress situations.

Stored contingencies may also become the basis for an individual's evaluation of his own achievement in or after a stressing situation. Self-evaluation in many cases is a function of the contrast between observed and expected outcome (Halisch, Butzkamm, & Posse, 1976). If anticipation of stress effects, based on prior experience or any other source of knowledge, results in decrements of aspiration level, then increments of self-evaluation of the actual outcome becomes likely. The positive correlation between satisfaction with the scores obtained and noise intensity as ascertained in this study supports the notion of long-term expectations of stress effects. It must be admitted that the positive correlation observed between satisfaction and noise intensity is only in line with the aspiration shift of introverts and their verbally expressed expectations. Extraverts seem to operate in a less straightforward way. As could already be shown in the analysis of causal attributions, extraverts take more causal factors into consideration than introverts. Extraverts possibly build up the same general expectancies as introverts, and they also use them for an evaluation of the outcome. However, in contrast to introverts they also rely on compensating factors (like luck), which may even lead to upward shifts of aspiration level and to short-term expectations in stress situations and thus to deviations of temporary aspirations and expectations from long-term expectations.

Shortcomings and Further Perspectives

Unfortunately the present study does not succeed in operationalizing all the processes and factors hypothesized in the underlying model. Although the model postulates three different and parallel processes of time estimation, noise-specific coping, and coordination, the present study did not allow the assessment of sufficiently differentiated objective and subjective measures related to those processes. According to the model the processes should be differentially described with their respective outcomes and their intrinsic goals. There should also be differential indexes of task requirements, capacities, exertion, and other factors contributing to the outcome.

As compared and contrasted to objective indexes, the following subjective estimates should be collected: perceived outcome of differential activities, aspiration level, perception of task requirements and task difficulties, attribution of outcomes to skills, and effort. Subjective judgments must not be expected to correspond fully to objective descriptions. In particular, the discrimination of task requirements may be weaker than in the model. It may depend on the situation and the subject's sophistication to what degree the difficulty of a primary task is discriminated from the difficulty induced by an additional acoustical stimulation. If there is a discrimination, the relative proportion of difficulties may be misjudged. The same holds true for causal attributions. The role of competence, effort, and other factors may not be discriminated for parallel activities and the process of their distinction, and, if so, their relative proportion may be misjudged. By a wrong evaluation the impact of noise may be overemphasized or underrated. The mechanisms leading to deviation of subjective judgments and attributions constitute a special field of investigation within the area of stress research (see also Weick, 1970).

REFERENCES

Allport, G. W. *Personality: A psychological interpretation.* New York: Holt, 1937.
Atkinson, J. W. *An introduction to motivation.* Princeton, NJ: Van Nostrand, 1964.
Berlyne, D. E. *Conflict, arousal, and curiosity.* New York: McGraw-Hill, 1960.
Borg, G. (Ed.). *Physical work and effort.* Oxford: Pergamon, 1975.
Brengelmann, J. C., & Brengelmann, L. Deutsche Validierung von Fragebogen der Extraversion, neurotischen Tendenz und Rigidität. *Zeitschrift für experimentelle und angewandte Psychologie,* 1960, 7, 291–332.
Broadbent, D. E. *Decision and stress.* London: Academic Press, 1971.
Cobb, S. A model for life events and their consequences. In B. S. Dohrenwend & B. P. Dohrenwend (Eds.), *Stressful life events: Their nature and effects.* New York: Wiley, 1974.
Dembo, T. Der Ärger als dynamisches Problem. *Psychologische Forschung,* 1931, 15, 1–144.
Eysenck, H. J. *The structure of human personality.* London: Methuen, 1953.
Feather, N. T., & Simon, J. G. Causal attributions for success and failure in relation to expectations of success based on selective or manipulative control. *Journal of Personality,* 1971, 39, 527–541.
Hacker, W. Psychische Regulation von Arbeitstätigkeiten: Innere Modelle, Strategien in Mensch-Maschine-Systemen, Belastungswirkungen. In W. Hacker (Ed.), *Psychische Regulation von Arbeitstätigkeiten.* Berlin: Deutscher Verlag der Wissenschaften, 1976.
Halisch, F., Butzkamm, J., & Posse, N. Selbstbekräftigung: I. Theorieansätze und experimentelle Erfordernisse. *Zeitschrift für Entwicklungspsychologie und Pädagogische Psychologie,* 1976, 8, 145–164.
Hamilton, V. Socialization anxiety and information processing: A capacity model of anxiety-induced performance deficits. In I. G. Sarason & C. D. Spielberger (Eds.), *Stress and anxiety,* (Vol. 2). Washington, DC: Hemisphere, 1975.
Hays, W. L. *Statistics for psychologists.* New York: Holt, Rinehart and Winston, 1963.
Heckhausen, H. Achievement motivation and its constructs: A cognitive model. *Motivation and Emotion,* 1977, 1, 283–329.
Hoppe, F. Erfolg und Misserfolg. *Psychologische Forschung,* 1931, 14, 1–62.
Kahn, R. L. Conflict, ambiguity, and overload: Three elements in job stress. *Occupational Mental Health,* 1973, 3, 2–9.

Kahneman, D. *Attention and effort.* Englewood-Cliffs, NJ: Prentice-Hall, 1973.

Karabenick, S. A. Valence of success and failure as a function of achievement motives and locus of control. *Journal of Personality and Social Psychology,* 1972, *21,* 101–110.

Kelley, H. H. *Causal schemata and the attribution process.* New York: General Learning Press, 1972.

Laabs, G. J., & Stager, P. Monitoring the information-processing demands of attention switching. *Canadian Journal of Psychology,* 1976, *30,* 47–54.

Levi, A. M., & Benjamin, A. Jews and Arabs rehearse Geneva: A model of conflict resolution. *Human Relations,* 1976, *19,* 1035–1044.

Meyer, W. U. *Leistungsmotiv und Ursachenerklärung von Erfolg und Misserfolg.* Stuttgart: Klett, 1973.

Miller, D. T. Ego involvement and attribution for success and failure. *Journal of Personality and Social Psychology,* 1976, *34,* 901–906.

Poulton, E. C., & Edwards, R. S. Interactions and range effects in experiments on pairs of stresses: Mild heat and low-frequency noise. *Journal of Experimental Psychology,* 1974, *102,* 621–628.

Rausch, E., Hoeth, F., Reisse, W., & Meyer, I. Kommunikationsstruktur und Gruppenleistung. *Psychologische Forschung,* 1965, *28,* 598–615.

Reykowski, J. Efficiency of self-regulation and tolerance for stress. *Studia Psychologica,* 1972, *14,* 294–300.

Schönpflug, W., & Heckhausen, H. *Lärm und Motivation.* Opladen: Westdeutscher Verlag, 1976.

Seligman, M. E. P. *Helplessness. On depression, development, and death.* San Francisco: Freeman, 1975.

Shavit, H. Personality adjustment as a function of interaction between locus of evaluation and tolerance for ambiguity. *Psychological Reports,* 1975, *37,* 1204–1206.

Snyder, M. L., Stephan, W. G., & Rosenfield, D. Egotism and attribution. *Journal of Personality and Social Psychology,* 1976, *33,* 435–441.

Streufert, S., & Streufert, S. C. Information load, time spent and risk taking in complex decision making. *Psychonomic Science,* 1968, *13,* 327–330.

Tajfel, H. Social and cultural factors in perception. In G. Lindzey & E. Aronson (Eds.), *The handbook of social psychology* (Vol. 3, 2nd ed.). Reading, MA: Addison-Wesley, 1969.

Teichner, W. H. Interaction of behavioral and physiological stress reactions. *Psychological Review,* 1968, *75,* 271–291.

Uherik, A., & Biro, V. Typological properties and intraindividual schema of bioelectric skin reactivity. *Studia Psychologica,* 1973, *15,* 24–36.

Weick, K. E. The "ess" in stress: Some conceptual and methodological problems. In J. E. McGrath (Ed.), *Social and psychological factors in stress.* New York: Holt, Rinehart and Winston, 1970.

Weiner, B. *Achievement motivation and attribution theory.* Morristown, NJ: General Learning Press, 1974.

Welford, A. T. *Skilled performance: Perceptual and motor skills.* Glenview, IL: Scott, Foresman, 1976.

Wortman, C. B., & Brehm, J. W. Responses to uncontrollable outcomes: An integration of reactance theory and the learned helplessness model. In L. Berkowitz (Ed.), *Advances in experimental social psychology* (Vol. 8). New York: Academic Press, 1975.

V

METHODS IN STRESS
AND ANXIETY
RESEARCH

15

Methods for Studying Stressful Situations

David Magnusson and Håkan Stattin
University of Stockholm

Though human beings have been acquainted with stress throughout evolution, the character and comprehension of the stressful components the environment imposes upon the individual have changed. We have witnessed how the transformation of the traditional agricultural community into the industrial, rationalistic, and urban society of today has brought with it new, highly stress-inducing factors—high social and geographical mobility, environmental pollution and destruction, crowding, and so forth. From society's point of view this development has already led to serious problems and will probably involve still more in the future. From the individual's point of view it is essential to consider whether the total load of stressful factors is too high to cope with and whether we have the capacity to develop appropriate, adapting reaction patterns. Whether we are interested in these problems from the viewpoint of society or of the individual, new paradigms and new methods must be developed for the urgently needed systematic investigation of the stressful environment.

Most researchers in the field of stress agree that stress experienced in a particular situation is a function of both situational characteristics and personal factors and that the behavior of the individual cannot be fully understood without considering both, yet systematic empirical analyses of situations are rare. We know a great deal about the individual's responses—overt and covert reactions and actions—to provocative events. But research on the structure and quality of stress situations and on situation dimensions affecting the behavior of the person is still neglected.

The task of determining psychologically relevant dimensions that could be used for description, categorization, and dimensionalization of stressful situations is a difficult one. But it is nonetheless important if we want to proceed in more fruitful research to a better understanding of the processes in which individual reactions and actions are formed in stressful situations. The present article aims at discussing different ways of approaching the problems of investigating the characteristics of stressful situations empirically, in order to arrive at systematic knowledge that can be used in theory, research, and application also in the field of stress.

THE ENVIRONMENT–THE SITUATION

The actual behavior of an individual in a certain stressful situation is dependent not only on person properties and the characteristic features of the particular moment-to-moment situation; for a full understanding of human behavior, aspects of the environment at different levels should be considered.

Jessor and Jessor (1973), Magnusson, Dunér, and Zetterblom (1975), and recently Bronfenbrenner (1977) have emphasized that the environment can be described on a continuum ranging from a macro- to a microlevel. The physical environment on the macrolevel consists of the typography of the landscape, parks, streets, homes, and so forth, and on the microlevel of the equipment of a room, objects, and the like. The social macrolevel is defined by the laws, norms, and values that are common to a whole society or a culture, while the social microlevel consists of the norms, attitudes, habits, and the like of the specific groups and persons involved in the situation.

At all levels the environment plays a very important role in determining an individual's behavior in a certain situation in two main ways. First, the environment at all these levels and in both its physical and its social properties influences the developmental learning process in which the individual's specific way of dealing with and reacting to environmental conditions of different kinds is formed. And second, it forms the frame of reference and offers the stimulus conditions (circumstances) for behavior in the specific situation. For a full understanding of an individual's behavior on a particular occasion in a specific situation we ought to know his or her life history, including the different types of environments at different levels he or she has encountered. In this article we will restrict ourselves to analyses of the environment that is present to the individual on a certain occasion in time, that is, what is referred to by Tolman as "the immediate situation" (Magnusson, 1980).

General Situation Factors and Within-Situation Factors

As a first crucial distinction when discussing situational effects on behavior, it has been proposed that situational influences can be thought of as *general situation factors* and *within-situation factors* (Magnusson, 1976; Magnusson & Endler, 1977). The situation affects behavior of an individual first as a general frame of reference. Being at church, attending a committee meeting, and playing on a sports ground form different frames of reference for behavior. Investigating situations at this level means a search for *general situation factors*. In an interactional model of behavior the interactions that are investigated and found between individuals and situations at this level may be denoted *across-situation interactions*.

In a certain situational setting there is a continuous flow of situational cues that influence and are affected by the person. Such factors, influencing behavior within the frame of reference of a certain general situation, can be denoted *within-situation factors* . (see e.g., conversation grammars studied by Duncan, 1972; Duncan & Fiske, 1977; social interaction studied by Rausch, Dittman, & Taylor, 1959; Raush, Farbman, & Llewellyn, 1960; interpersonal behavior studied by Peterson, 1977; generative rules in social behavior studied by Argyle,

1969, 1977). The continuous bidirectional interactions between the person and the cues in the situation may be called *within-situation interactions.*

It should be underlined that the traditional laboratory experiment is designed on the paradigm of controlling and examining within-situation factors. An experimental situation is set up and aspects of this situation are varied systematically. Within the frame of reference given by the total experimental situation, which can be thought of as the general situation, most of the within-situation factors are likewise held constant. One or two within-situation factors (stimuli) are altered objectively, and this variation is assessed on the subject side by means of data collection methods such as ratings, self-reports, or objective measures of physiological reactions. The stimulus variations are more quantitative than qualitative. In most cases the experimental process is also unidirectional more than bidirectional; that is, the subject reacts to the stressful stimuli that the researcher has built up in advance and is given no freedom to take action or to restructure the circumstances as defined by the experimenter.

The Objective and the Subjective Situation

In what terms are we to conceptualize the situation? An old distinction between the environment (1) as its actually is, without interpretation, and (2) as it is perceived and interpreted by individuals can be applied also to the conceptualization of situations.

In the following sections the analysis of situations in terms of their actual physical and social properties will be referred to as an *objective situation approach,* and the approach in which the analyses are made in terms of the situation's psychological significance to individuals will be referred to as *subjective situation approach.*

THE OBJECTIVE SITUATION APPROACH

Analyses of the situation as the objective "outer world" have a long history in the social sciences. For a long period this view was held by geographers, architects, culture anthropologists, and economists, among others. In these disciplines individual behavior is explained in terms of an environment that is objectively described and varied in objective terms. The environment is conceptualized in ecological structures, in spatial, geographical, architectural, or organizational dimensions, and is assessed independently of the interpretations made by the individuals involved.

In traditional laboratory research in psychology, under strong influence from psychophysics and classical behaviorism, quantifiable stimuli were set in relation to quantitative measures of individuals' reactions. Behavior was explained with reference to variation of objective stimuli, and the situation was defined as being "resolvable into a complex group of stimuli" (Watson, 1924). The view of the environment has changed considerably since then, but the conceptualizing of the situation has traditionally been preserved in physical or social terms (see e.g., Barker, 1965; Chein, 1954; Krause, 1970; Sells, 1963; Sherif & Sherif, 1956, 1974), in contrast to subjective or interpersonal terms. The notion that the situation is conceived and defined by inanimate physical features or some aspects of the observed physical setting is also a main thread in the growing field of environmental psychology (see Proshansky, Ittelson, & Rivlin, 1970).

Returning to the stress domain, the effect of objectively described or measured aspects of stressful situations on behavior has been discussed by Paykel, Myer, Dienelt, Klerman, Lindenthal, and Pepper (1969), McGrath (1970), Holmes and Rahe (1967b), Lazarus (1966), Levine and Scotch (1970), Mechanic (1975), Levi and Andersson (1975), Kagan and Levi (1974), among others. Examples of objective conditions that have been measured in relation to aspects of individual behavior are work and work conditions, schooling, socioeconomic standard, urbanization, migration, and social mobility (see Kagan & Levi, 1974, and Levi & Andersson, 1975, for extensive reviews).

An interesting approach that connects both objective and subjective situation descriptions can be found in empirical studies of *life stress*. In order to find a link between life stress and bodily disease, Holmes and Rahe (1967a, 1967b) developed the Social Readjustment Rating Scale, originally containing 43 common life events (change in residence, marriage, personal injury or illness, etc.) that had been found empirically to covary with psychophysiological stress symptoms. For each of the life event items in the inventory the subjects are asked to estimate, on a magnitude scale, the degree of adjustment that is necessary to cope with the event in question. By summing the readjustment ratings across the stressful life events it has been shown that individuals with a high total readjustment score (life change score) are more vulnerable to illness, bodily diseases like myocardial infarction, athletic injuries, and the like than individuals with low readjustment scores (Masuda, Wagner, & Holmes, 1975; Holmes & Rahe, 1967b; Lundberg & Theorell, 1976; Rahe, 1968; Rahe & Paasikivi, 1971; Theorell & Rahe, 1971, 1975).

The Social Readjustment Rating Scale emphasizes objective measures of life situations in that it assumes that a linear relation exists between the frequency of stressful events per se and the strength of stress symptoms. There is in addition an implicit assumption that the life events in question have a general impact on present somatic and psychic illness, only influencing the level of expression. The relation between the character of the stress symptoms and the character of the stressful situations still remains at issue. The subjective situation description enters the picture on the measurement side. The stressfulness of the events is measured on the person side by the subjectively experienced and reported amount of life change caused by each of the included stress events.

After Holmes and Rahe's introduction of the paper-and-pencil method of measuring life stress, other inventories with similar features and measurement directions have emerged: Recent Life Change by Rahe (1975) and the Life Event Inventory by Cochrane and Robertson (1973). These inventories yield summations of earlier stressful life events for the study of effects on present states.

Critics of the inventories have suggested that stress-relevant psychological characteristics other than amount of life change should be taken into consideration, such as anticipation of the situations and control over their outcome (Vinokur & Selzer, 1975) and the perception and interpretation by the subject (Lowenthal & Chiriboga, 1973; Rabkin & Struening, 1976; Sarason & Johnsson, 1976). These additional characteristics are part of the psychological situation, which is considered in the next section.

THE SUBJECTIVE SITUATION APPROACH

The psychological environment refers to the person's perception and construction of the physical and the social environment, and the subjective approach can be traced back to formulations by psychology theorists such as Koffka (1935), Lewin (1935), Murray (1938), and Rotter (1954). Recently the need to study situations in terms of their psychological significance has been advocated by Bowers (1973), Endler (1975), Jessor and Jessor (1973), Magnusson (1971, 1974, 1976, 1978), Mischel (1973), and Schneider (1973), among others.

Three Kinds of Subjective Situation Factors

In the subjective situation approach, situations as wholes and specific cues within situations can be described and categorized using three different kinds of person variables:

1. in terms of the cognitive-perceptual appraisal and construction of the situations—the *perceptual approach*
2. in terms of the person's spontaneous reactions: psychic (e.g., feelings and emotions) or somatic (hormonal excretion, pulse rate, skin conductance, etc.)—the *reaction approach*
3. in terms of manifest, molar behavior or actions—the *action approach*

The Perception Approach to Studies of Stressful Situations

It has been proposed that individual behavior and interindividual differences in spontaneous reactions and in molar behavior (actions) in a new situation can be predicted under three conditions: (1) if we know how situations of this kind are interpreted by the individual or groups of individuals, (2) if we know their dispositions to behave in the kind of situations being evaluated, and (3) if we have a theory providing a link between (1) and (2) (Magnusson, 1976). Lazarus (1966) underlined that the strength of the stress reaction and the kinds of adaptation mechanisms employed in the situation are determined by the way in which the individuals perceives, constructs, and evaluates the outer stress situation. Lowenthal and Chiriboga (1973) referred to social psychologists, sociologists, and anthropologists like Katz (1967), Maddox (1970), and Clark (Note 1), who emphasized that too little attention has been paid to individual variations in the perception of social and psychic structures.

What is stressed by these researchers and others, especially those advocating an interactional model of personality, is that the individual's perception and subjective construction of a situation (i.e., the situation in the eye of the beholder) is the important basis for his or her reactions and actions in the situation (see also Magnusson, 1976).

Such an assumption leads to a need for knowledge about how individuals perceive and interpret situations in order to describe, classify, and understand human behavior adequately. From this point of view, situation perception seems to be one of the most fruitful areas of research. However, though this need has been strongly underlined by many theorists and researchers, very few empirical studies have been made of situations in terms of perceptions and interpretations (see Magnusson, 1971; Sells, 1963; Brown & Fraser, Note 2). One obvious reason is the lack of appropriate methods for systematic use of the information stored in individuals' perceptions and interpretations of situations. Developing such methods is one of the more important and challenging tasks for psychological research directed at describing and understanding behavior.

Perceived Situation Outcome and Situation Control

When an individual confronts a stressful situation a crucial aspect of his or her perception and evaluation of the situation is the expectancies the person has of possible negative consequences and of possibilities of control by his or her own actions. An accumulating bulk of evidence points to the individual's perception of control of the stress situation as an important mediator between the stress-provocative environment and the adaptive behavior of the person. Results from recent studies of learned helplessness (Krantz, Glass, & Snyder, 1974; Seligman, 1975), locus of control (Houston, 1973; Lefcourt, 1966; Manuck, Hinrichsen, & Ross, 1975a, 1975b), and other work in the stress field (Averill, 1973; Glass, Singer, & Friedman, 1969; Klemp & Rodin, 1976; Monat, 1976; Neufeld, 1976; Schwartz, 1968) clearly indicate that perception of control over the environment is one of the strong variables in explaining the overt and covert behavior of the individual in a stressful situation.

Stress situations vary with regard to their appraised consequences. In a particular situation the consequences can be clear and easily interpretable for some individuals but more diffuse and difficult to trace for others. Thus the situational information input and the individual's accumulated knowledge and experience will determine which outcome the individual will expect. Given a certain expected outcome, persons will also differ in whether they expect to be able to influence the consequence.

Having knowledge of what will happen in a situation (the expected consequences) can be denoted *predictive control* of the situation. Expectancy of being able to influence the outcome behaviorally can be labeled *behavior control* of the situation. Both aspects of control are essential when it comes to interpreting the behavior that the individual expresses in the stress situation. Both predictive control and behavior control are useful perceptual compartments when trying to dimensionalize and categorize stressful situations on the basis of situational control.

Methodological Problems

The growing awareness of the role played by the psychological situation for stress symptoms makes it necessary to find methods that take into account the stress-provocative character of the situations in which behavior occurs. As in other empirical psychological research, we face two problems in trying to describe and categorize stressful situations in terms of situation perception: (1) We need appropriate methods by which we can collect the adequate information from the individuals about how they perceive and interpret the situations under study; that is, we need adequate methods for the collection of data, and (2) we need appropriate methods for the treatment of data.

Basically the problems connected with methods of data collection can be solved in the same way as in other research in which data for person variables are collected and treated. However, as long as we want to cover situation perception and interpretation of stressful situations directly, without using reactions as indicators, we are restricted to self-reports for data collection. In the next section attempts to use such methods for the collection of stressful situation perception data will be described and some main results presented.

Before we can analyze the role of the stress situation in determining individual behavior, we have to develop useful taxonomies of situations that help us to classify and reduce the number of stressful events that are within the researcher's larger pool of stress situations. This implies that the raw situation perception data have to be treated with adequate methods for finding the most appropriate categorization of the situations under study. Here the common set-up of multivariate statistical methods (factor analysis, cluster analysis, multidimensional scaling, and latent profile analysis) are examples of potentially helpful tools in categorizing and dimensionalizing stressful situations. When choosing among these methods of data treatment, the underlying psychological cognitive models should be considered (see e.g., Magnusson, 1971).

A Psychophysical Approach

A psychophysical approach to the study of situations in terms of situation perception was introduced by Magnusson (1971). The raw situation perception data that form the basis for the categorization of situations are obtained as similarity ratings. A set of verbally described situations is presented to the individual, two situations at a time, and the task is to rate the degree of perceived similarity between the two situations under consideration. Depending on the psychological model that is supposed to underly the individual's perception of situations, different multidimensional scaling methods can be used in order to classify situations in terms of basic situation dimensions or in terms of situation categories. The direct similarity estimate method for data collection was used by Magnusson (1971), Magnusson and Ekehammar (1973, 1975) and Ekehammar and Magnusson (1973) in studies of two situational domains, namely, situations common to university students and stressful situations. For common situations two bidirectional factors, a "positive-negative" and an "active-passive," and one unidirectional factor ("social") were obtained. In the study of stressful situations four factors were obtained; threat of punishment, threat of pain, inanimate threat, and ego threat.

The direct similarity estimate method was originally introduced in this field in order to analyze situations as wholes, leaving the interpretation of similarity open to the subject. Alternately we may also specify in advance in which terms (of perceived threat, perceived control, or expected outcome, for example) we want the subject to rate the degree of similarity.

Situation Perception Inventory

A more direct method for collecting data on situation perception is by applying the traditional inventory technique in situation perception inventories. Each situation is then rated by the subject on a number of relevant scales referring to different aspects of the situation perception process (e.g., perceived threat, perceived control, or expected outcome). The correlation matrix for scales can be factor analyzed and the situations described and classified in terms of profiles across different factors. Situations can also be categorized (1) by factor analysis of a matrix of coefficients for the correlation between situations, or (2) by latent profile analysis on the basis of situation profiles across scales.

Weyer and Hodapp (1975) started from concretely defined situation domains—job, household situations, and family life events—and constructed items within each domain measuring perceived stress as defined by Lazarus's psychological model of stress. After reliability and validity analyses, 9 of the original 14 situation scales were accepted as measuring perceived situational threat: professional and work disadvantages (*Berufs und Arbeitsbelastung*), leisure time and relaxation after work (*Freizeit und Entspannung von der Arbeit*), heavy demands from work (*Überforderung durch die Arbeit*), housewife burdens (*Hausfrauenspezifische Belastung*), unspecific work load (*Unspezifische Arbeitsbelastung*), heavy demands from housework (*Uberforderung durch Hausarbeit*), matrimonial burdens and conflicts (*Belastungen und Konflikte in der Ehe*), burdens and conflicts because of younger children (*Belastungen und Konflikte durch jüngere Kinder*), conflicts with older children (*Konflikte mit älteren Kindern*).

The situation perception inventory technique for data collection was also used by Moos (1972) in the construction of COPES (Community-Oriented Programs Environmental Scale) for measuring environmental press (or "beta press" in Murray's terminology).

Semantic Differential Approach

Individuals' interpretations of stressful situations can also be investigated by means of the semantic differential technique. This was used by Pervin and Rubin (1967) in their construction of TAPE (Transactional Analysis of Personality and Environment) for the investigation of college perception. They used the method for studying the way that students as individuals and as groups perceive the academic environment in general terms such as My College, Faculty, Students, and so forth. The technique seems to be fruitful also for the study of stressful situations in terms of subjective interpretation and meaningfulness. Categorization of the stressful situations can be made on the basis of profiles across scales on item or factor level.

The Reaction Approach to the Study of Stressful Situations

In the reaction approach, stressful situations are described and classified in terms of the spontaneous reactions they evoke in the individuals. We distinguish here between spontaneous reactions and actions without saying that there is a clear border between the two kinds of behavior. For the categorization of stressful situations it is of interest that dimensional analyses of variables for spontaneous reactions have revealed two main factors that have been found in a number of studies: a psychic reaction factor ("I become worried," "I become nervous," "I become anxious," etc.) and a somatic reaction factor ("My hands shake," "I get in a sweat," "My heart beats," also labeled "worry" and "emotionality" (see e.g., Ekehammar, Magnusson, & Ricklander, 1974; Endler & Magnusson, 1976; Endler, Magnusson, Ekehammar, & Okada, 1976; Fenz, 1967; Fenz & Epstein, 1965; Hagtvet, 1976; Liebert & Morris, 1967; Morris & Liebert, 1969, 1970).

For the study of stressful situations by means of situation reactions, all methods for collecting data on reactions to specific situations can be used: ratings, self-reports, and strictly objective methods such as devices for measuring hormonal excretion in the urine, skin conductance, or pulse rate. Until recently the most common approach to the study of situations by means of person reactions has been the reaction inventory approach.

The Reaction Inventory Approach

To be useful in the description and classification of stressful situations, an inventory of reactions needs to contain ratings of reactions for each of the situations under consideration. This implies that traditional reaction inventories in which the individual is asked to generalize his or her reactions across situations and time ("Do you usually . . . ?", "Do you often . . . ?") cannot be used. In these kinds of inventories the cross-situational variation of behavior is not taken into account. A formula that meets the requirement of yielding ratings for each of a set of situations was introduced by Endler, Hunt, and Rosenstein (1962). According to the technique employed in their S-R Inventory of Anxiousness, the subjects rate their reactions on a number of scales for each of a number of specified stressful situations, which are briefly described verbally. For classifications of the situations, the correlations between situations are calculated for averaged reaction scores across situations. Factor analysis can be applied to the resulting correlation matrix to extract the underlying situation dimensions.

Focusing on stress-inducing situations, Magnusson and Ricklander (1971) introduced the questionnaire Individual's Reactions to Situations (IRS-1), built on the same principles as Endler et al.'s inventory, with the purpose of determining dimensions in stress situations that adolescent pupils may encounter in their everyday life (see Ekehammar et al., 1974). Three main situation factors were isolated, interpreted as "threat of punishment" ("super ego threat"), "anticipation threat," and "inanimate threat." Interestingly, about the same factor pattern was revealed for pupils of the same age group in two other nations with quite different cultures (Magnusson & Stattin, 1977, 1978). A modified version of the inventory (IRS-2) yielded three interpretable situation factors: "threat of punishment" ("super ego threat"), "threat of pain," and "inanimate threat."

Hodges and Felling (1970) used a situation-bound inventory, the Stressful Situation Questionnaire, to investigate the impact of stressful college situations on undergraduates' anxiety reactions. Four situation factors were extracted, three associated with failure and ego threat and the fourth involving pain and physical danger.

In a large-scale research program on psychopathic behavior, Schalling (1977) developed a scale, Situational Unpleasantness Sensitivity scale (SUS), with which situations are grouped on the basis of ratings of aversiveness by different groups of subjects: students, conscripts, and criminals. Careful empirical analyses of ratings of aversiveness have yielded seven factors; Anticipation, Criticism, Aggression, Pain-medical, Pain, Thrill, and Boredom.

The Psychophysical Approach

A possible basis for the study of situations in terms of person reactions would be similarity ratings, in which similarity refers to reactions of different kinds. A study in which similarity ratings of different kinds of behavioral traits were used as stimuli, points to the usefulness of this kind of data (Magnusson & Ekman, 1970).

Comparisons between Classifications of Stressful Situations

From a psychological point of view it seems reasonable to assume that classifications of stressful situations in terms of situation perception data will be systematically related to classifications in terms of situation reaction data. In a couple of recent studies Magnusson and Ekehammar (1975) and Ekehammar, Schalling, and Magnusson (1975) compared the factor pattern of situation perception data with the factor pattern of situation reaction data for the same stress-provoking situations. Perception data were obtained with similarity ratings and reaction data with the situation-by-reaction inventory IRS-1. It was hypothesized that both methods of data collection would give the same main groupings of the situations in a factor analysis. The results pointed to considerable congruence in the factor pattern comparison.

In a third study (Magnusson & Ekehammar, 1978) it was hypothesized that an individual's reactions should be more similar across situations he or she perceived as similar than across situations perceived as dissimilar; that is, similar situations evoke similar reactions (cf. Frederiksen, 1972). Individual data were investigated and the overall outcome was in the predicted direction.

The Action Approach to the Study of Stressful Situations

Under this heading the description and classification of situations is discussed in terms of the actions taken by the individual in response to the situations. Rotter (1954) and Frederiksen (1972) suggested that situations can be described and categorized with reference to the behavior that individuals express in them. They proposed that situations can be grouped on the basis of the similarity of behavior they evoke in individuals. The role of activity has also been underlined by researchers within the field of stress research (see e.g., Averill, 1973; Coleman, 1973; Gal & Lazarus, 1975; Hamburg, 1974; Lazarus, 1966, 1974; Mason, 1971; Monat, Averill, & Lazarus, 1972; Sanchez-Craig, 1976). For some purposes it might be appropriate and useful to classify stressful situations on the basis of the kind and direction of the actions taken by the participants.

Using an action approach one can distinguish between *covert* and *overt* action tendencies. Two broad types of covert coping activities (intrapsychic coping mechanisms) have attracted particular attention in research on stress: "defense-vigilance" and "repression-sensitization" (Byrne, 1964; Monat, Averill, & Lazarus, 1972; Weinstein, Averill, Opton, & Lazarus, 1968; see also "situational denial," Houston, 1971).

The classical grouping of overt actions in anxiety and stress situations is trichotomized as (1) escape, (2) passivity, and (3) attack (see e.g., Horney, 1950). In an effort to study the relationship between threatening stimuli and action tendencies, Poetter and Gulas (1973) compared the tendency of individuals to go "toward," "away," and "against" hypothetical neutral and fear-arousing stimuli in the Fear Survey Schedule (Wolpe & Lang, 1964) with measures of general fear arousal for the same situations. The predominant response style was to move toward neutral stimuli but to move away or against threatening stimuli. Persons with a total high fear arousal were more likely to move away from all stimuli, irrespective of the cue properties, than persons with a low fear arousal level. Unfortunately the authors did not report the relation between the character of the threatening stimuli and the different action tendencies. However, the study indicates one possible way of categorizing situations on the basis of action tendencies.

CONCLUSIONS

It is an urgent task of our society to find ways to eliminate the consequences of stress emanating from modern technology and industrialization. In order to reach that goal we need ways to detect and measure factors in the environment that prevent human growth and development.

Our knowledge of the relationship between stress-provoking environments and human adaption ability is insufficient. In the introduction to this chapter we argued that systematic analyses of the environment on different levels, and especially of the situations in which actual behavior occurs, are highly needed and may serve as a bridge to wider practical utilization.

It is an interesting and somewhat puzzling fact that so little empirical research on stress situations has been presented, though the importance of situational factors in determining behavior has been pointed out by numerous theorists in the social sciences. One reason for this state of affairs may be that we have not been accustomed to thinking about "the situation" as a unit for research. Another obvious reason is the lack of methods that seem directly applicable.

In this chapter we have pointed to some methodological tools that have been used already and proved fruitful. In order to be effective, however, research on situations must be planned and performed along many lines, and it may be one of the challenging tasks in psychology of today to develop and apply adequate methods for that research.

REFERENCES

Argyle, M. *Social interaction.* Chicago: Aldine-Atherton, 1969.

Argyle, M. Predictive and generative rules models of P X S interaction. In D. Magnusson & N. S. Endler (Eds.), *Personality at the crossroads: Current issues in interactional psychology.* New York: Erlbaum, 1977.

Averill, J. R. Personal control over aversive stimuli and its relationship to stress. *Psychological Bulletin,* 1973, *80,* 286–303.

Barker, R. G. Explorations in ecological psychology. *American Psychologist,* 1965, *20,* 1–14.

Bowers, K. S. Situationism in psychology: An analysis and a critique. *Psychological Review,* 1973, *80,* 307–336.

Bramwell, S. T., Masuda, M., Wagner, N. D., & Holmes, T. H. Psychosocial factors in athletic injuries. *Journal of Human Stress,* 1975, *1*(2), 6–20.

Bronfenbrenner, U. Toward an experimental ecology of human development. *American Psychologist,* 1977, *32,* 513–531.

Byrne, D. Repression-sensitization as a dimension of personality. In B. A. Maher (Ed.), *Progress in experimental personality research* (Vol. 1). New York: Academic Press, 1964.

Chein, I. The environment as a determinant of behavior. *Journal of Social Psychology,* 1954, *39,* 115–127.

Cochrane, R., & Robertson, A. The life events inventory: A measure of the relative severity of psycho-social stressors. *Journal of Psychosomatic Research,* 1973, *17,* 135–139.

Coleman, J. C. Life stress and maladaptive behavior. *American Journal of Occupational Therapy,* 1973, *27,* 169–180.

Duncan, S. Some signals and rules for taking speaking turns in conversations. *Journal of Personality and Social Psychology,* 1972, *23,* 283–292.

Duncan, S., & Fiske, D. W. *Face-to-face interaction: Research, methods, and theory.* Hillsdale, NJ: Erlbaum, 1976.

Ekehammar, B., & Magnusson, D. A method to study stressful situations. *Journal of Personality and Social Psychology,* 1973, *27,* 176–179.

Ekehammar, B., Magnusson, D., & Ricklander, L. An interactionist approach to the study of anxiety. *Scandinavian Journal of Psychology,* 1974, *15,* 4–14.

Ekehammar, B., Schalling, D., & Magnusson, D. Dimensions of stressful situations: A comparison between response analytical and a stimulus analytical approach. *Multivariate Behavioral Research*, 1975, *10*, 155–164.

Endler, N. S. The case for person-situation interactions. *Canadian Psychological Review*, 1975, *16*, 12–21.

Endler, N. S., Hunt, J. McV., & Rosenstein, A. J. An S-R Inventory of Anxiousness. *Psychological Monographs*, 1962, *76* (17, Whole No. 536).

Endler, N. S., & Magnusson, D. Multidimensional aspects of state and trait anxiety: A cross-cultural study of Canadian and Swedish college students. In C. D. Spielberger & R. Diaz-Guerrero (Eds.), *Cross-cultural anxiety* (Vol. 1). Washington, DC: Hemisphere, 1976.

Endler, N. S., Magnusson, D., Ekehammar, B., & Okada, M. The multidimensionality of state and trait anxiety. *Scandinavian Journal of Psychology*, 1976, *17*, 81–96.

Fenz, W. D. Specificity in somatic responses to anxiety. *Perceptual and Motor Skills*, 1967, *24*, 1183–1190.

Fenz, W. D., & Epstein, S. Manifest anxiety: Unifactorial or multifactorial composition? *Perceptual and Motor Skills*, 1965, *20*, 773–780.

Frederiksen, N. Toward a taxonomy of situations. *American Psychologist*, 1972, *27*, 114–123.

Gal, R., & Lazarus, R. S. The role of activity in anticipating and confronting stressful situations. *Journal of Human Stress*, 1975, *1*(4), 4–20.

Glass, D. C., Singer, J. E., & Friedman, L. N. Psychic cost of adaptation to an environmental stressor. *Journal of Personality and Social Psychology*, 1969, *12*, 200–210.

Hagtvet, K. A. Worry and emotionality components of test anxiety in different sex and age groups of elementary school children. *Psychological Reports*, 1976, *39*, 1327–1334.

Hamburg, D. A. Coping behavior in life-threatening circumstances. *Psychotherapy and Psychosomatics*, 1974, *23*, 13–25.

Hodges, W. F., & Felling, J. P. Types of stressful situations and their relation to trait anxiety and sex. *Journal of Consulting and Clinical Psychology*, 1970, *34*, 333–337.

Holmes, T. H., & Rahe, R. H. *Booklet for Schedule of Recent Experience (SRE)*. Seattle: University of Washington Press, 1967. (a)

Holmes, T. H., & Rahe, R. H. The social and readjustment rating scale. *Journal of Psychosomatic Research*, 1967, *11*, 213–218. (b)

Horney, K. *Neurosis and human growth: The struggle toward self-realization*. New York: Norton, 1950.

Houston, B. K. Trait and situational denial and performance under stress. *Journal of Personality and Social Psychology*, 1971, *18*, 289–293.

Houston, B. K. Viability of coping strategies, denial, and response to stress. *Journal of Personality*, 1973, *41*, 50–58.

Jessor, R., & Jessor, S. L. The perceived environment in behavioral science: Some conceptual issues and some illustrative data. *American Behavioral Scientist*, 1973, *16*, 801–828.

Kagan, A. R., & Levi, L. Health and environment-psychosocial stimuli: A review. *Social Science and Medicine*, 1974, *8*, 225–241.

Katz, D. Group process and social integration. *Journal of Social Issues*, 1967, *23*, 3–22.

Klemp, G. O., & Rodin, J. Effects of uncertainty, delay, and focus of attention on reactions to an aversive situation. *Journal of Experimental Social Psychology*, 1976, *12*, 416–421.

Koffka, *Principles of gestalt psychology*. New York: Harcourt, Brace, 1935.

Krantz, D. S., Glass, D. C., & Snyder, M. L. Helplessness, stress level, and the coronary-prone behavior pattern. *Journal of Experimental Social Psychology*, 1974, *10*, 284–300.

Krause, M. S. Use of social situations for research purposes. *American Psychologist*, 1970, *25*, 748–753.

Lazarus, R. S. *Psychological stress and the coping process*. New York: McGraw-Hill, 1966.

Lazarus, R. S. Psychological stress and coping in adaptation and illness. *International Journal of Psychiatry in Medicine*, 1974, *5*, 321–333.

Lefcourt, H. M. Internal versus external control of reinforcement: A review. *Psychological Bulletin*, 1966, *65*, 206–220.

Levi, L., & Andersson, L. *Psychosocial stress: Population, environment and quality of life*. New York: Halsted, 1975.

Levine, S., & Scotch, N. A. *Social stress*. Chicago: Aldine, 1970.

Lewin, K. *A dynamic theory of personality*. New York: McGraw-Hill, 1935.

Liebert, R. M., & Morris, L. W. Cognitive and emotional components of test anxiety: A distinction and some critical data. *Psychological Reports*, 1967, *20*, 975-978.

Lowenthal, M. F., & Chiriboga, D. Social stress and adaption: Toward a life-course perspective. In C. Eisdorfer & M. P. Lawton (Eds.), *The psychology of adult development and aging*. Washington, DC: American Psychological Association, 1973.

Lundberg, U., & Theorell, T. Scaling of life changes: Differences between three diagnostic groups and between recently experienced and non-experienced events. *Journal of Human Stress*, 1976, *2*(2), 7-17.

Maddox, G. L. Themes and issues in sociological theories of human aging. *Human Development*, 1970, *13*, 17-27.

Magnusson, D. An analysis of situational dimensions. *Perceptual and Motor Skills*, 1971, *32*, 851-867.

Magnusson, D. The individual in the situation: Some studies on individuals' perception of situations. *Studia Psychologica*, 1974, *16*, 124-132.

Magnusson, D. The person and the situation in an interactional model of behavior. *Scandinavian Journal of Psychology*, 1976, *17*, 253-271.

Magnusson, D. On the psychological situation. Reports from the Department of Psychology, University of Stockholm, 1978, No. 544.

Magnusson, D. *Toward a psychology of situations*. Hillsdale, N.J.: Lawrence Erlbaum, 1980.

Magnusson, D., Dunér, A., & Zetterblom, G. *Adjustment: A longitudinal study*. Stockholm: Almqvist & Wiksell, 1975.

Magnusson, D., & Ekehammar, B. An analysis of situational dimensions: A replication. *Multivariate Behavioral Research*, 1973, *8*, 331-339.

Magnusson, D., & Ekehammar, B. Perceptions of and reactions to stressful situations. *Journal of Personality and Social Psychology*, 1975, *31*, 1147-1154.

Magnusson, D., & Ekehammar, B. Similar situations—similar behaviors? A study of the intraindividual congruence between situation perception and situation reactions. *Journal of Research in Personality*, 1978, *12*, 41-48.

Magnusson, D., & Ekman, G. A psychophysical approach to the study of personality traits. *Multivariate Behavioral Research*, 1970, *5*, 255-273.

Magnusson, D., & Endler, N. S. (Eds.) *Personality at the crossroads: Current issues in interactional psychology*. New York: Lawrence Erlbaum, 1977.

Magnusson, D., & Stattin, H. *Cross-national comparisons of anxiousness employing a situation by reaction inventory—IRS-1*. Reports from the Department of Psychology, University of Stockholm, 1977, No. 506.

Magnusson, D., & Stattin, H. *A cross-cultural comparison of anxiety responses in an interactional frame of reference. International Journal of Psychology*, 1978, *13*, 317-332.

Manuck, S. B., Hinrichsen, J. J., & Ross, E. O. Life stress, locus of control, and state and trait anxiety. *Psychological Reports*, 1975, *36*, 413-414. (a)

Manuck, S. B., Hinrichsen, J. J., & Ross, E. O. Life-stress, locus of control, and treatment-seeking. *Psychological Reports*, 1975, *37*, 589-590. (b)

Mason, J. W. A re-evaluation of the concept of "non-specificity" in stress theory. *Journal of Psychiatric Research*, 1971, *8*, 323-333.

McGrath, J. E. (Ed.) *Social and psychological factors in stress*. New York: Holt, Rinehart and Winston, 1970.

Mechanic, D. Some problems in the measurement of stress and social readjustment. *Journal of Human Stress*, 1975, *1*(3), 43-48.

Mischel, W. Toward a cognitive social learning reconceptualization of personality. *Psychological Review*, 1973, *80*, 252-283.

Monat, A. Temporal uncertainty, anticipation time, and cognitive coping under threat. *Journal of Human Stress*, 1976, *2*(2), 32-43.

Monat, A., Averill, J. R., & Lazarus, R. S. Anticipatory stress and coping reactions under various conditions of uncertainty. *Journal of Personality and Social Psychology*, 1972, *24*, 237-253.

Moos, R. Assessment of the Psychosocial Environments of Community-Oriented Psychiatric Treatment Programs. *Journal of Abnormal Psychology*, 1972, *79*, 9-18.

Morris, L. W., & Liebert, R. M. The effects of anxiety on timed and untimed intelligence tests: Another look. *Journal of Consulting and Clinical Psychology*, 1969, *33*, 240-244.

Morris, L. W., & Liebert, R. M. Relationship of cognitive and emotional components of test anxiety to physiological arousal and academic performance. *Journal of Consulting and Clinical Psychology*, 1970, *35*, 332–337.

Murray, H. A. *Explorations in personality*. New York: Oxford University Press, 1938.

Neufeld, R. W. Evidence of stress as a function of experimentally altered appraisal of stimulus aversiveness and coping adequacy. *Journal of Personality and Social Psychology*, 1976, *33*, 632–646.

Paykel, E. S., Myers, J. K., Dienelt, M. N., Klerman, G. L., Lindenthal, J. J., & Pepper, M. P. Life events and depression: A controlled study. *Archives of General Psychiatry*, 1969, *21*, 753–760.

Pervin, L. A., & Rubin, D. B. Student dissatisfaction with college and the college dropout: A transactional approach. *Journal of Social Psychology*, 1967, *72*, 285–295.

Peterson, D. R. A functional approach to the study of person-person interactions. In D. Magnusson & N. S. Endler (Eds.), *Personality at the crossroads: Current issues in interactional psychology*. New York: Erlbaum, 1977.

Poetter, R. A., & Gulas, I. The fear survey schedule: Response styles to fear-arousing stimuli. *Psychological Reports*, 1973, *32*, 731–737.

Proshansky, H. M., Ittelson, W. H., & Rivlin, L. G. (Eds.) *Environmental psychology: Man and his physical setting*. New York: Holt, Rinehart and Winston, 1970.

Rabkin, J. G., & Struening, E. L. Life events, stress, and illness. *Science*, 1976, *194*, 1013–1020.

Rahe, R. H. Life-change measurement as a predictor of illness. *Proceedings of the Royal Society of Medicine*, 1968, *61*, 44–46.

Rahe, R. H. Stress and strain in coronary heart disease. *Journal of the South Carolina Medical Association*, 1975, *72*, Suppl. 7–14.

Rahe, R. H., & Paasikivi, J. Psychosocial factors and myocardial infarction: II. An outpatient study in Sweden. *Journal of Psychosomatic Research*, 1971, *15*, 33–39.

Raush, H. L., Dittman, A. T., & Taylor, T. J. The interpersonal behavior of children in residential treatment. *Journal of Abnormal and Social Psychology*, 1959, *58*, 9–27.

Raush, H. L., Farbman, I., & Llewellyn, L. G. Person, setting and change in social interaction: II. A normal control study. *Human Relations*, 1960, *13*, 305–333.

Rotter, J. B. *Social learning and clinical psychology*. Englewood Cliffs, NJ: Prentice-Hall, 1954.

Sanchez-Craig, B. M. Cognitive and behavioral coping strategies in the reappraisal of stressful social situations. *Journal of Counseling Psychology*, 1976, *23*, 7–12.

Sarason, I. G., & Johnsson, J. H. *The life experiences survey: Preliminary findings*. Technical report No. SCS-LS-001. Department of Psychology, University of Washington, Seattle, 1976.

Schalling, D. The trait-situation interaction and the physiological correlates of behavior. In D. Magnusson and N. S. Endler (Eds.), *Personality at the crossroads: Current issues in interactional psychology*. New York: Erlbaum, 1977.

Schneider, D. J. Implicit personality theory: A review. *Psychological Bulletin*, 1973, *79*, 294–309.

Schwartz, S. H. Words, deeds, and the perception of consequences and responsibility in action situations. *Journal of Personality and Social Psychology*, 1968, *10*, 232–242.

Seligman, M. E. P. *Helplessness: On depression, development, and death*. San Francisco: Freeman, 1975.

Sells, S. B. Dimensions of stimulus which account for behavior variances. In S. B. Sells (Ed.), *Stimulus determinants of behavior*. New York: Ronald, 1963.

Sherif, M., & Sherif, C. W. *An outline of social psychology*. New York: Harper & Brothers, 1956.

Sherif, M., & Sherif, C. W. Crowding, perceived control, and behavioural after effects. *Journal of Applied Social Psychology*, 1974, *4*, 171–186.

Theorell, T., & Rahe, R. H. Psychosocial factors and myocardial infarction: An inpatient study in Sweden. *Journal of Psychosomatic Research*, 1971, *15*, 25–31.

Theorell, T., & Rahe, R. H. Life change events, ballistocardiography and coronary death. *Journal of Human Stress*, 1975, *1*(3), 18–24.

Vinokur, A., & Selzer, M. L. Desirable versus undesirable life events: Their relationship to stress and mental distress. *Journal of Personality and Social Psychology*, 1975, *32*, 329–337.

Watson, J. B. *Behaviorism.* New York: Norton, 1924.

Weinstein, J., Averill, J. R., Optom, E. M., & Lazarus, R. S. Defensive style and discrepancy between self-report and physiological indexes of stress. *Journal of Personality and Social Psychology,* 1968, *10,* 400–413.

Weyer, G., & Hodapp, V. Entwicklung von Fragebogeskalen zur Erfassung der subjektiven Belastung. *Archiv für Psychologie,* 1975, *127,* 161–188.

Wolpe, J., & Lang, P. J. A fear survey schedule for use in behavior therapy. *Behavioral Research and Therapy,* 1964, *2,* 27–30.

REFERENCE NOTES

1. Clark, M. M. *On the relationship between cultural anthropology and studies of adult development and aging.* Paper presented at the Conference on Anthropology and Mental Health, Center for Advanced Study in the Behavioral Sciences, Stanford, CA, October 1971.

2. Brown, P., & Fraser, C. *Speech as a marker of situation.* Paper presented at the Conference on Social Markers in Speech, Paris, October 1978.

3. Magnusson, D., & Ricklander, L. *Inventory of reactions to situations–IRS-1.* Unpublished manuscript, Department of Psychology, University of Stockholm, 1971.

16

Self-Report Measures in Research on Job-Related Stress

Geerd Weyer
University of Frankfurt

The workaday world is one source of stress with which most of us are familiar. Especially since working a job is so common, occupational stress and its long-range effects deserve special attention. Psychological disturbances and a number of somatic symptoms belong to the list of long-range effects. Coronary heart disease and circulatory problems such as high blood pressure are often mentioned, disturbances in other bodily systems, such as digestive or respiratory problems, have also been reported (e.g., Cooper & Marshall, 1976; French & Caplan, 1973; Zaleznik, De Vries, & Howard, 1977). Of all the different methods used to obtain data about pressures experienced by individuals in their natural job situations, questionnaires are probably the most common alternative. They are economical to use, can be scored objectively, and have a certain face validity since the subject is asked directly about how he or she feels toward various aspects of the job environment.

In the interpretation of questionnaire results it is not enough to consider the subject's statements as indications of inner feelings that cannot be further analyzed. Especially for the theoretical analysis it seems essential to specify—within a conceptual framework—the relevant variables that control the test scores and those variables that are related to the scores in some other specified way. Without a conceptual framework, which of course should be verified in the sense of construct validation, questionnaires can only be considered as structured interviews.

In the following some questionnaires on job stress are discussed. All of them are based on the generally accepted idea in recent psychological stress research that subjective feelings of pressure result from an interaction between person and environment (e.g., Appley & Trumbull, 1967; Cobb, 1974; Kahn, 1973; Lazarus, 1966; McGrath, 1970). Within this very general framework quite different assumptions and concepts will be discussed. The respective measuring instruments used to operationalize these theoretical assumptions are also quite varied.

Another point common to all tests discussed here is their area of application: They are suitable for use in epidemiological or field studies. In general, only those instruments that require the subject's response to certain situations described in the test items come into question. In other words the subject should

The author is indebted to Margund Brandt, Almut Krumpholz, Ingrid Lotz, Sabine Mackenrodt, and Hannelore Nitsch who helped with collecting the data, and to Susan Zorn who translated the manuscript.

indicate how he or she experiences a certain situation without actually experiencing it at the moment. Since experiencing the situation and reporting the experience do not occur at the same time, acute fluctuations in feelings cannot be measured by these techniques but, rather, the long-term effects of situational conditions on feelings.[1]

JOB–RELATED TENSION INDEX

The Job-related Tension Index is based on some items used by Gurin, Veroff, and Feld (1960) in a survey study. In the version by Kahn, Wolfe, Quinn, Snoek, & Rosenthal (1964) there are 14 or 15 items containing statements about possible job pressures and problems. The subject is to indicate the frequency of these pressures on a 5-point scale. The total score is the sum or average of the item ratings. Besides the item intercorrelations, no other item- or test-statistics are given by Kahn et al. (1964). (Coefficients of internal consistency between .77 and .86 were found for a 14-item German-language version of this questionnaire.)

Although construction was not based on an explicit theoretical model it becomes clear that the scale value is considered as a response variable dependent upon objective environmental conditions as well as personality traits. This is shown, for example, by the joint effect of the environmental variable "role conflict" and each of the following personality variables on the job tension scores: "neurotic anxiety," "extraversion-introversion," and "flexibility-rigidity." It should be noted that role conflict is a complex variable based on subjective information from the subject. The same is true regarding job tension and personality variables. The importance of job tension as an intervening variable is also referred to, since, besides showing its dependency on input variables, its possible influence on work performance, absenteeism, and staff turnover is also implied. Unfortunately, no data concerning this aspect are presented.

It is also interesting that another variable measured by questionnaires, namely "job satisfaction," is handled within the same framework of variable relationships and on the same level as job tension. This means that neither variable is seen as coupled with the other in a series of cause-and-effect relationships.

INDEX OF THE FREQUENCY
OF PERCEIVED JOB PRESSURE
AND DISCREPANCY INDEX OF JOB PRESSURE

Buck (1972) refers to Brehm's (1966) theory of psychological reactance in defining job pressure as "the resultant psychological state of the individual which exists when he perceives that (1) conflicting forces and incompatible demands are being made upon him in connection with his work; (2) at least one of these forces or demands is an induced one; (3) the forces are recurrent or stable over time" (Buck, 1972, p. 49).

Buck suggests two techniques to operationalize job pressure. The first, the index of the Frequency of Perceived Job Pressure (FPJP) is a factor score based on seven—as claimed by the author—synonymous items (frustration, pressure,

---

[1] Perhaps one could speak of "tonic" (prolonged) as opposed to "phasic" (short) state changes. This difference should not be confused with the difference between trait and state.

upset, jumpy-nervous, tense, stress, strain). The subject is to indicate how often each item is experienced on the job. The seven items were chosen according to their degree of homogeneity in a principal components analysis. The one-dimensionality of the scale was checked by the Guttman-Scalogram analysis.

As a complement to this global measure (a second index with a more direct relation to job pressure was used to gain a more differentiated measure. From a number of items the sum of the discrepancies between personal importance of a goal at work and the actual goal approach is built. For example, the discrepancy is measured between the subjective importance of "achieving good quality work or excellence of performance" and how this goal can be frustrated by various "sources of pressure," such as supervisor demands, company policy, and so forth. Between the two indexes of job pressure there is a moderate positive correlation ($r = .36$ for managers; $r = .40$ for workers).

To validate the FPJP (no values are given for the discrepancy measure), the relationships between personality variables (needs, internal factors, general traits and attributes after Murray, 1938) and environmental variables (e.g., job security, social aspects of the job, etc.) are given. Here also, all variables (environmental, personality, and job pressure) are gained through subjective information.

Personality and environmental variables are considered to be independent variables. Their combined influence on job pressure scores is demonstrated by a stepwise multiple regression analysis. With an optimal selection and combination of predictors from both groups of variables, a much greater portion of job pressure variances can be clarified than would be possible with a combination of predictors from only one of the groups.

Job satisfaction, mental health, and performance are investigated as possible consequences of job pressure. The first two variables were measured by questionnaire items. The correlations are in the expected direction; that is, poor states of mental health and dissatisfaction accompany job pressure. Buck not only considers dissatisfaction to be a result of pressure but also discusses the possibility that both conditions result simultaneously in response to common cues. No relationship was found between performance ratings and job pressure.

SYRACUSE INDEXES: ACTIVITIES INDEX AND ORGANIZATIONAL CLIMATE INDEX

Stern and his associates developed a series of measures, the Syracuse Indexes, based on Murray's need-press model (Stern, 1970). According to this model, behavior is determined by individual needs and environmental presses. Need and press variables are described in the same terms (need-press categories) within a common taxonomy. Environmental press is further divided into alpha and beta presses: objective stimulus configuration and subjectively perceived environment, respectively. Stern also distinguishes between private (idiosyncratic) and consensual (mutually shared) beta press.

Needs are measured by the Activities Index (AI). The most recent version contains 300 dichotomous items describing commonplace daily activities and feelings. The items are classified according to 30 need categories with 10 items in each need subscale.

Consensual beta press is measured by various environmental indexes. Besides several measures for college environments, there is also an Organizational Climate

Index (OCI) that can be used in administration settings and in industry. In accordance with the need-press model the general format of the OCI is the same as that of the AI: 30 scales with 10 items each. For both indexes, analyses of reliability (coefficients of consistency of medium degree and, in part, high retest coefficients) and validation data (only partially for the OCI) are available. As an illustration, one item from the need-press category "achievement" is presented from the AI and the OCI, respectively: need item (AI)—"Choosing difficult tasks in preference to easy ones." The corresponding press item (OCI) is "Standards set by the administrative staff are not particularly hard to achieve."

The intraindividual discrepancy between need and press can be considered as a direct measure of the quality of person-environment fit (e.g., French, Rodgers, & Cobb, 1974; Levi, 1975; Pervin, 1968) and thus as a measure of stress. The technical problem of building the discrepancy score is not solved at the scale level but, rather, much more elaborately by factor score comparisons.

Data concerning the effects of need-press discrepancies in the area of jobs are not available thus far. The relationships found between factor scores from a joint AI X OCI factor analysis and staff turnover and absenteeism are more or less indirect indications of validity.

WORK ENVIRONMENT SCALE

The Social Climate Scales by Moos and associates are designed to measure the perceived psychological characteristics of different environmental settings according to Murray's and Stern's beta press concept (Kiritz & Moos, 1974; Moos, 1974). The purpose is to obtain a very detailed (multidimensional) description of the setting, which is considered to be similar to the personality of an individual. The perceived social climate should indicate "a bridge between 'objective' environmental stimuli and physiological responses which are mediated by differences in perception, coping, and defense" (Kiritz & Moos, 1974, p. 111).

From the series of questionnaires developed for this purpose, the Work Environment Scale (WES) serves to characterize the social climate at work (Moos & Insel, 1974). This scale consists of ten subscales with nine items each. Dichotomous items were formulated "to identify characteristics of an environment which would exert a press toward peer cohesion or toward autonomy or toward work pressure" (p. 16). The inventory was divided into subscales according to content. Some of the scale labels are remindful of Stern's press factors. One of the subscales, Work Pressure, covers just about the same material as Kahn's Job Tension Index and Buck's Job Pressure Index. The scales themselves were constructed according to item-metric considerations. The scale reliabilities (coefficients of consistency) are quite high (.70 to .91), although in a German-language pilot version much lower values were obtained (.48 to .78). Even so, these reliabilities were usually sufficient for group comparisons (Weyer & Hodapp, 1978). Validation data for the WES are not given.

JOB–RELATED SUBJECTIVE THREAT AND DISSATISFACTION SCALES

The development of our scales was oriented toward Lazarus's psychological stress model. In this model the intervening variable "perceived threat" has a key position. It indicates a state that arises from cognitive appraisal of environmental events ("primary appraisal"), as a function of antecedent situational and dispositional variables.

If a situation is judged to be threatening, possibilities of reducing or eliminating the threat (coping) will be sought. Attempts can consist of intrapsychic maneuvers (for example, the activiation of perceptual defense mechanisms), as well as overt actions, for example, changing the situation or flight. In both cases, reactions can be observed on a subjective-verbal and a physiological level—in the latter case, of course, also on the level of open behavior. Besides changes in the setting as a consequence of these reactions, psychophysical changes in the individual should also be regarded in the long run.

Our questionnaire scales are supposed to measure the construct "subjective threat," as defined above, separately for several situational domains (Hodapp & Weyer, 1975; Weyer & Hodapp, 1975, 1980). Five scales that were especially constructed for job-oriented threats by methods of factor and item analysis are now available in German: the Job-related Subjective Pressure and Dissatisfaction Scales (*Subjektive Belastungs- und Unzufriedenheits-Skalen–Beruf* (SBUS-B), Hodapp, & Neuhäuser, 1980). They are as follows:

1. GJP General Job Pressure (*Arbeits- und Berufsbelastung*), 16 items, alpha = .86
2. GJD General Job Dissatisfaction, (*Arbeits- und Berufsunzufriedenheit*), 16 items, alpha = .86
3. RC Relationships to co-workers (*Belastendes Betriebsklima*), 12 items, alpha = .86
4. LRR Lack of Relaxation and Recreation (*Mangelnde Erholung von der Berufsarbeit*) 10 items, alpha = .78
5. CM Career Motivation (*Karrierestreben*) 5 items, alpha = .67.

Whereas the first two scales (GJP and GJD) contain rather global estimates of job pressure and job dissatisfaction, the third and fourth scales (RC and LRR) measure more specific aspects. The fifth scale (CM) does not exactly fit into the general concept of the other four scales. However, such a motivational variable can be useful as an additional differentiating aspect in certain questions.

The structural relationship between the scales is illustrated by a covariance selection model (see Figure 1). (For the method see Hodapp, chapter 18 in this volume.) According to this diagram there is no direct relationship between scale 1 (GJP) and scale 2 (GJD). The two general areas of "pressure" and "dissatisfaction" are clearly separated. A connection between the two is only present over certain sub-aspects of pressure and dissatisfaction (RC and LRR).

In the remaining part of this chapter a few points concerning the validity of the scales will be discussed. We will limit ourselves to a demonstration of some relationships between the two scales General Job Pressure (GJP) and General Job Dissatisfaction (GJD) and similar scales, and to a few other relevant variables.[2]

---

[2]When, in the following, independent, intervening, and dependent variables are mentioned, this refers to the theoretical assumed relations between the variables. Empirically based statements regarding cause and effect would in no way be justified due to the nature of the research designs and the methods of evaluation used.

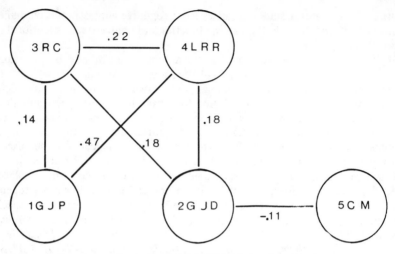

Figure 1 Covariance selection model (134/234/25) for the subjective pressure and dissatisfaction scales. The relationships between the scales are expressed by partial correlation coefficients. Sample on which construction of the scales was based, $N = 581$.

The correlation of the scales with the three other German-language questionnaires used for validation purposes are shown in Table 1. They need no further explanation.

However, meaningful interpretations of relationships to those variables that belong to the stress model on which the scales were based are more important than relationships to other techniques designed for the same purpose. Of interest, for example, is how the scale values relate to threatening conditions and personality variables thought to dispose toward the feeling of threat. Data from a sample of hospital personnel (doctors, nurses, and technicians, $n = 79$) serve to illustrate this point. Hours of overtime per week is used to indicate externally caused work pressure, and individual ability to tolerate pressure is measured by the N-score (Neuroticism) on the EPI (Eggert, 1974). The joint influence of both variables on the GJP scores is shown by contrasting the means in Table 2.

The sample is divided into the following four groups:

Table 1 Correlations of Scale 1 (General Job Pressure) and Scale 2 (General Job Dissatisfaction) with the Job Satisfaction Scale (SAZ, Fischer & Lück, 1972), the Job-Related Tension Index (JRTI, Kahn et al., 1964), and the Work Environment Scale 6: Work Pressure (WES 6, Moos & Insel, 1974).

	SAZ $n = 108$[a]	JRTI $n = 108$[a]	WES 6 $n = 101$[b]
1 GJP	−.36	.47	.72
2 GJD	−.70	.31	.46

[a]Employees from 3 different companies.
[b]Teachers.

Table 2 Means of General Job Pressure as a Function of Overtime per Week and Neuroticism (EPI–N)

EPI–N		Overtime per week (hours)	
		≥5	≤4
	Group	1	2
High	M	10.62	5.62
(≥11)	SD	3.47	3.99
	n	21	21
	Group	3	4
Low	M	8.85	4.94
(≤10)	SD	4.25	3.51
	n	21	16
Contrast		t	df	p
$L_1 : M_1 - M_4 = 5.68$		4.46	75	<.001
$L_2 : M_2 - M_3 = -3.23$		−2.73	75	<.01

Note. Sample: hospital staff ($N = 79$).

1. high N-scorers with much overtime
2. high N-scorers with little overtime
3. low N-scorers with much overtime
4. low N-scorers with little overtime.

A comparison of groups 1 and 4 shows a highly significant difference of the means (contrast L_1), which can be attributed to the convergent influence of both variables. In a comparison of groups 2 and 3 the divergent effects of both variables, which partially compensate each other, become apparent (contrast L_2). The difference between the means is, as expected, smaller than that of the first contrast but still meaningful. From the direction of the difference, situational influences seem to be stronger.[3]

The same analysis for the GJD scale likewise resulted in a significant, though weaker, convergent effect of neuroticism and overtime. Prestige, however, seems to have more influence on dissatisfaction (GJD) than work pressure. Under similar working conditions, workers lower in the hierarchy are more dissatisfied than those higher up. Among flight personnel of an airline, for example, copilots have higher GJD scores than captains; and stewards and stewardesses have higher GJD scores than pursers and purserettes.

Further relationships postulated by the model exist between pressure scores

[3] This sort of data analysis with orthogonal contrasts—as opposed to correlation methods and analyses of variance—assumes neither linear relationships between the variables nor special types of combined effects of the two independent variables. In particular, the interaction effect as implied by the interactional position in personality research (e.g., Ekehammar, 1974) is not treated as any more important than the main effects (Olweus, 1976). The convergent and divergent mean contrasts allow for the possibility of both an additive and a nonadditive combination of the independent variables.

and such variables that indicate a habitual tendency to deny pressure or perceive it only partially (coping disposition). Thus sensitizers (in the sense of Byrne, 1964, and Krohne, 1974, 1978) have somewhat higher GJP and GJD scores than repressers.

As long-range consequences of job stress, changes in well-being, physiological changes, and the development of somatic symptoms are expected. Correlations between our scales, complaint indexes, and blood-pressure scores, as well as group differences between hypertension patients and healthy subjects support this expectation. There is some indication that subjectively felt pressure is more important than dissatisfaction (Weyer & Hodapp, 1979; for the opposite view, see French & Caplan, 1973).

Further insights can be gained by considering not only single, isolated relationships between pressure scale values and response variables but also the joint effects of pressure and coping variables on different reaction levels. This is illustrated by data that show the joint influence of General Job Pressure (GJP) and the coping variable "Frankness" (FPI scale 9, Fahrenberg, Selg, & Hampel, 1973) on (1) the number of subjective complaints (FPI scale 1, "Nervousness") and (2) a physiological variable, diastolic blood pressure.

In Table 3 the average number of subjective complaints for four groups formed according to their respective GJP and FPI-9 scores are presented in the same manner as in Table 2. The largest mean difference (contrast L_1) occurs, as expected, between the high-pressure group with high "Frankness" scores, that is, weak defenses (group 1), and the low-pressure group with low "Frankness" scores, that is, strong defenses (group 4). The largest number of subjective

Table 3 Means of Subjective Complaints (FPI-Scale 1 "Nervousness") as a Function of General Job Pressure (GJP) and Frankness (FPI-Scale 9)

		General job pressure	
FPI–9		$\geqslant 6$	$\leqslant 5$
	Group	1	2
High	M	5.78	4.54
($\geqslant 5$)	SD	1.48	2.06
	n	33	26
	Group	3	4
Low	M	4.79	3.78
($\leqslant 4$)	SD	1.89	1.62
	n	19	27

Contrast	t	df	p
$L_1 : M_1 - M_4 = 2.00$	4.32	101	<.001
$L_2 : M_2 - M_3 = -0.25$	−0.48	101	ns

Note. Sample: University personnel who served as control for clinical comparison studies. (Total $N = 106$. One value is missing.)

Table 4 Means of Diastolic Blood Pressure as a
Function of General Job Pressure (GJP) and
Frankness (FPI-Scale 9)

FPI-9		General job pressure	
		$\geqslant 6$	$\leqslant 5$
	Group	1	2
High	M	80.58	75.75
($\geqslant 5$)	SD	10.00	8.85
	n	31	24
	Group	3	4
Low	M	87.40	80.28
($\leqslant 4$)	SD	12.96	11.23
	n	20	25

Contrast	t	df	p
$L_1 : M_1 - M_4 = 0.30$	.10	96	ns
$L_2 : M_2 - M_3 = -11.65$	-3.59	96	<.001

Note. Same sample as Table 3. (Total $N = 106$. Six
values are missing here.)

complaints is registered in group 1, the least in group 4. There is hardly any difference between the averages of groups 2 and 3 (contrast L_2). The diverging effects of both variables mutually compensate each other. The high-pressure group with strong defenses mentions hardly any more complaints than the low-pressure group with weak defenses.

The same analysis with diastolic blood pressure as the dependent variable presents a completely different picture (see Table 4). While there is no difference in blood pressure between groups 1 and 4 (contrast L_1), there is a very pronounced difference between groups 2 and 3 (contrast L_2). The high-pressure group with strong defenses has the highest diastolic pressure; the low-pressure group with weak defenses, the lowest diastolic pressure. This can be interpreted according to other results concerning the discrepancy between subjective verbal and physiological stress reactions (e.g., Krohne, 1978; Weinstein, Averill, Opton, & Lazarus, 1968). The tendency to deny the unpleasant or play it down results in lower scores on both the subjective pressure scales (GJP) and the subjective complaints scale (FPI-1). Such an effect, however, cannot be assumed for autonomic physiological functions such as blood pressure. In fact, just the opposite is to be expected; that is, the "true" relationship between subjective pressure and the physiological value is partially hidden by the one-sided depressing effect of defenses on subjective pressure scores.

CONCLUDING REMARKS

In the various questionnaires discussed, two different approaches to the measurement of job stress as a person-environment interaction can be distinguished.

1. Environmental conditions and individual variables are measured separately. The discrepancy between them indicates a state of stress as defined in the sense of a lack of fit between person and environment (Discrepancy Index of Job Pressure, Buck, 1972; Organizational Climate Index and Activities Index, Stern, 1970).

2. Only one measure is employed in which the state of stress as the result of the individual evaluation of the environment is asked for directly (Index of the Frequency of Job Pressure, Buck, 1972; Job-related Tension Index, Kahn et al., 1964; Job-related Subjective Pressure and Dissatisfaction Scales, Weyer et al., 1977).[4]

The advantage of the first approach lies in the possibility of learning something about the origins of stress states. However, the chances are quite slim, in our opinion, since both classes of variables are obtained separately but not independently of each other. Environmental and personality variables are both seen from the same person's subjective point of view. In the second approach, which is much simpler, questionnaires requiring the subject to give information about conditions causing stress states are dispensed with altogether. This problem is clarified by the validation of the questionnaire. The techniques discussed here handle this problem in a similar fashion. An attempt is made to show the relationship from scale values and important variables of influence, on the one hand, to dependent variables, on the other hand. Although causal relationships between the variables are usually assumed, they can in no way be proved by the research designs and methods of data evaluation employed. Improvements could be made by initiating longitudinal studies with a carefully planned choice of variables and with adequate methods of data analysis (also see Hodapp, chapter 18 in this volume and Weyer & Hodapp, 1979). The validity of data gained this way would allow statements that exceed the level of mere plausibility.

The usefulness of job stress questionnaires should also be demonstrated more clearly. Most convincing would be proof of their superiority to other techniques in predicting the consequences of job pressure on health.

REFERENCES

Appley, M. H., & Trumbull, R. On the concept of psychological stress. In M. H. Appley & R. Trumbull (Eds.), *Psychological stress: Issues in research*. New York: Appleton-Century-Crofts, 1967.

Brehm, J. W. *A theory of psychological reactance*. New York: Academic Press, 1966.

Buck, V. E. *Working under pressure*. London: Staples Press, 1972.

Byrne, D. Repression-sensitization as a dimension of personality. In B. A. Maher (Ed.), *Progress in experimental personality research* (Vol. 1). New York: Academic Press, 1964.

Cobb, S. A model for life events and their consequences. In B. S. Dohrenwend & B. P. Dohrenwend (Eds.), *Stressful life events: Their nature and effects*. New York: Wiley, 1974.

Cooper, C. L., & Marshall, J. Occupational sources of stress: A review of the literature relating to coronary heart disease and mental ill health. *Journal of Occupational Psychology*, 1976, *49*, 11–28.

Eggert, D. *Eysenck–Persönlichkeitsfragebogen EPI*. Göttingen: Hogrefe, 1974.

[4]The Work Environment Scale by Moos & Insel (1974) is an exception in that only environmental variables (similar to Stern's OCI) are to be measured without employing an additional measure to obtain personality variables.

Ekehammar, B. Interactionism in personality from a historical perspective. *Psychological Bulletin.* 1974, *81*, 1026-1048.

Fahrenberg, J., Selg, H., & Hampel, R. *Das Freiburger Persönlichkeitsinventar FPI.* Göttingen: Hogrefe 1973.

Fischer, L., & Lück, H. E. Entwicklung einer Skala zur Messung von Arbeitszufriedenheit (SAZ). *Psychologie und Praxis*, 1972, *16*, 64-76.

French, J. R. P. (Jr.), & Caplan, R. D. Organizational stress and individual strain. In A. J. Marrow (Ed.), *The failure of success.* New York: AMACOM, 1973.

French, J. R. P. (Jr.), Rodgers, W., & Cobb, S. Adjustment as person-environment fit. In G. V. Coelhoe, D. A. Hamburg, & J. E. Adams (Eds.), *Coping and adaptation.* New York: Basic Books, 1974.

Gurin, G., Veroff, J., & Feld, S. *Americans view their mental health.* New York: Basic Books, 1960.

Hodapp, V., & Weyer, G. Eine Fragebogenuntersuchung zur Erfassung der berufsbezogenen, psychischen Belastung bei älteren Männern. *Arbeitsmedizin Sozialmedizin Präventivmedizin*, 1975, 10, 219-222.

Hodapp, V., & Weyer, G. *Weiterentwicklung von Fragebogenskalen zur Erfassung der subjektiven Belastung und Unzufriedenheit von Hausfrauen (SBUS-H). Psychologische Beiträge*, 1980, *22*, 322-334.

Kahn, R. L. Conflict, ambiguity and overload: Three elements in job stress. *Occupational and Mental Health*, 1973, *3*, 2-9.

Kahn, L. R., Wolfe, D. H., Quinn, R. P., Snoek, J. D., & Rosenthal, R. A. *Organizational stress: Studies in role conflict and ambiguity.* New York: Wiley, 1964.

Kiritz, S., & Moos, R. H., Physiological effects of social environments. *Psychosomatic Medicine*, 1974, *36*, 96-114.

Krohne, H. W. Untersuchungen mit einer deutschen Form der Repression-Sensitization-Skala. *Zeitschrift für Klinische Psychologie*, 1974, *3*, 238-260.

Krohne, H. W. Individual differences in coping with stress and anxiety. In C. D. Spielberger & I. G. Sarason (Eds.), *Stress and anxiety* (Vol. 5). Washington, DC: Hemisphere, 1978.

Lazarus, R. S. *Psychological stress and the coping process.* New York: McGraw-Hill, 1966.

Levi, L. Parameters of emotion: An evolutionary and ecological approach. In L. Levi (Ed.), *Emotions: Their parameters and measurement.* New York: Raven Press, 1975.

McGrath, J. E. A conceptual formulation for research on stress. In J. E. McGrath (Ed.), *Social and psychological factors in stress.* New York: Holt, Rinehart and Winston, 1970.

Moos, R. H. *The social climate scales: An overview.* Palo Alto, CA: Consulting Psychologists Press, 1974.

Moos, R. H., & Insel, P. H. The work environment scale (WES). In R. H. Moos, P. M. Insel, & B. Humphrey, *Combined preliminary manual for family, work and group environment scales.* Palo Alto, CA: Consulting Psychologists Press, 1974, 16-25.

Murray, H. A. *Explorations in personality.* New York: Oxford University Press, 1938.

Olweus, D. Der "moderne" Interaktionismus von Person und Situation und seine varianzanalytische Sackgasse. *Zeitschrift für Entwicklungspsychologie und Pädagogische Psychologie*, 1976, *8*, 171-185.

Pervin, L. A. Performance and satisfaction as a function of individual-environment fit. *Psychological Bulletin*, 1968, *69*, 56-68.

Stern, G. G. *People in context.* New York: Wiley, 1970.

Weinstein, J., Averill, J. R., Opton, E. M., & Lazarus, R. S. Defensive style and discrepancy between self-report and physiological indexes of stress. *Journal of Personality and Social Psychology*, 1968, *10*, 406-413.

Weyer, G., & Hodapp, V. Entwicklung von Fragebogenskalen zur Erfassung der subjektiven Belastung. *Archiv für Psychologie*, 1975, *127*, 161-188.

Weyer, G., & Hodapp, V. Eine deutsche Version der "Work Environment Scale (WES)."– Erste Anwendungserfahrungen bei Lehrern und Vergleich mit den "Subjektiven Belastungs- und Unzufriedenheitsskalen im beruflichen Bereich (SBUS-B)." *Diagnostica*, 1978, *24*, 318-328.

Weyer, G., & Hodapp, V. Job stress and essential hypertension. In I. G. Sarason & C. D. Sarason & C. D. Spielberger (Eds.), *Stress and anxiety* (Vol. 6). Washington, DC: Hemisphere, 1979.

Weyer, G., Hodapp, V., & Neuhäuser, S. *Weiterentwicklung von Fragebogenskalen zur Erfassung der subjektiven Belastung und Unzufriedenheit im beruflichen Bereich (SBUS-B)*. *Psychologische Beiträge*, 1980, 22, 335-355.

Zaleznik, A., De Vries, M. F. R., & Howard, J. Stress reactions in organizations: Syndromes, causes and consequences. *Behavioral Science*, 1977, 22, 151-162.

17

Response Bias in the Measurement of Achievement and Stress

Applications of Signal Detection Theory

Manfred Velden
University of Mainz

The chief characteristic of signal detection theory (SDT) is that it allows us to isolate effects of response bias from measures of an individual's ability to detect signals or to discriminate between stimuli. We may say that for the psychophysics of detection and discrimination, the problem of response bias has been largely resolved by means of this theory (Green & Swets, 1966). Due to this particular capability SDT has in recent years been employed far beyond the field of psychophysics in order to arrive at achievement measures that are not confounded by the subject's response strategy or risk-taking behavior (Pastore & Scheirer, 1974; Swets, 1973). Before discussing applications of SDT in stress research, especially achievement under stress conditions, I will give a short presentation of the SDT rationale in its simplest form. This seems necessary in order to facilitate an understanding of the relevance of SDT applications in stress research and to enable the reader to critically appraise such applications.

THE SDT RATIONALE

Let us assume that two stimuli, S_1 and S_2, which differ with respect to some variable, for example intensity, are to be discriminated from each other. In this case the model assumes two distributions, $f_1(x)$ and $f_2(x)$, on an internal continuum, x (observation axis), statistically resulting from the repeated application of the stimuli (see Figure 1). If an x-value, resulting from the application of either S_1 or S_2, exceeds the value x_c (criterion point) on the observation axis, the subject (observer) decides that this value arose from S_2; if the x-value is less he or she concludes that it arose from S_1. From a number of such conditional decisions two parameters can be estimated. The first, d', represents the degree to which the two stimuli can be discriminated by the subject. It is defined as the distance between the means of the two distributions, $\mu_2 - \mu_1$. The value of d' depends on the objective difference between the stimuli and the sensory capacity of the observer. The second parameter, β, is defined as the ratio of the probability (probability density, to be exact) that a value of the magnitude of x_c arose from application of S_2 to the probability that it arose from S_1. It reflects the subject's general inclination to decide for S_1 or S_2. Its

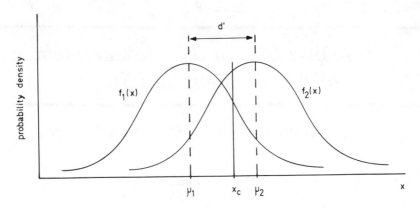

Figure 1 Psychophysical model of SDT discrimination task.

magnitude depends on nonsensory factors, that is, the subject's estimate of the a priori probabilities of occurrence of the stimuli and the consequences of his or her decisions (values and costs). According to the model it is independent from d' and thus represents response set isolated from discriminative ability.

APPLICATIONS

Reviewing the applications of SDT in stress research we may distinguish between (1) measurement of achievement under stress conditions and (2) measurement of stress, anxiety, aversiveness, and the like. In terms of experimental design, stress goes as the independent variable in the former studies and as the dependent variable in the latter.

An example of the former studies would be the measurement of recognition memory under the ego-involving instruction that intelligence is being measured. It would seem quite plausible in this situation if the subjects showed an increased tendency to report that the items had already been presented in order to attain a higher recognition score. It is therefore necessary to have a statistical model that allows a clear distinction between measurement of response tendency and actual recognition memory.

The latter studies deal with the problem of response set in rating responses, mostly self-ratings, that are used in the assessment of psychological states. If, for example, one is studying by means of self-ratings the effect of some form of treatment on the state anxiety of psychiatric patients, it may easily happen that, due to some biasing influence (for example social desirability), the patient's ratings deviate from what he or she actually feels. Therefore it would again be convenient to have a way to isolate response bias from the actual experience.

The problem of unbiased measurement of achievement is of particular relevance in the context of this book. A critical review of possible solutions of this problem therefore constitutes the largest part of the present contribution. As will be outlined in the last section the problem of unbiased measurement of negative sensations and emotions, in contrast to the measurement of achievement, remains unsolved.

Measurement of Achievement under Stress

For achievement tasks in which the subjects can make errors the problem of response bias is identical to the problem of how to incorporate the errors into the achievement score. Let us assume that in some task a great many items are presented to the subject that belong to class S_1, and that there are items of a second class, S_2, that are interspersed between the others. The subject's task is to mark those items belonging to class S_2. There are now four possible combined events: (1) the subject marks an item from class S_2 (a hit), (2) marks an item from class S_1 (a false alarm), (3) does not respond to an item from class S_2 (a miss), and (4) does not respond to an item of class S_1 (a correct rejection). Because it can be shown that the proportions of misses and correct rejections yield entirely redundant information if the proportions of hits and false alarms are given, let us only consider hits and false alarms.

A subject may do the task in quite different ways. He or she may, for example, be very careful not to make false alarms and therefore only mark an item when very sure that it actually belongs to class S_2. Keeping the amount of false alarms small by this strategy implies, however, that the amount of hits will be reduced too. On the other hand the subject may not find a false alarm too jeopardous and rather frequently mark an item even if he or she is not quite sure that it really belongs to class S_2. In this case the hit rate is greater than in the first case, but, of course, the false alarm rate is also greater. What index for the subject's achievement shall we take? Assuming that the subject's capability to do the task is the same in both cases and the difference is one of response strategy only, then this index should not be different under the two conditions. This means that the proportion of correctly marked items is obviously a biased index for achievement because it has a different value under the two conditions.

How about subtracting the false alarms from the hits? To analyze the adequacy of such a corrected index let us return to the simple psychophysical model presented above. Figure 2 (upper and lower half) again shows two functions that describe the distributions of values on some internal variable resulting from the repeated application of items of class S_1 and class S_2, respectively. The point x_{c_l} on the internal variable defines the subject's response strategy (criterion) when he or she is rather lax with respect to making false alarms; x_{c_s} is the criterion in case of a rather strict attitude toward this type of error. In both cases the area to the right of x_c under the $f_1(x)$ function represents the proportion of false alarms while the one under the $f_2(x)$ function represents the proportion of hits. So the area under $f_1(x)$ between the two criteria, x_{c_l} and x_{c_s}, respectively, represents the proportion of false alarms that the subject avoids under the strict criterion (upper half of Figure 2), while the area under $f_2(x)$ between the criteria represents the proportion of hits that he or she loses when reacting in the strict manner (lower half of Figure 2). Since the two areas differ in size, and the subject's capability for doing the task is identical under both conditions, the proportion of hits reduced by the amount of false alarms cannot be a fair index of achievement either. This type of treatment of errors is actually unfair to subjects using extreme criteria as compared to others. The reason for this is that when moving x_c away from the intersection of the two functions, either false alarms decrease more slowly than hits (i.e., when x_c is shifted to the right) or false alarms increase faster than hits (i.e., when x_c moves

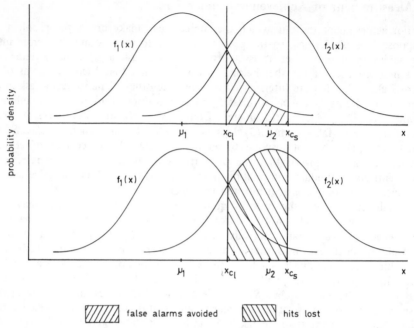

Figure 2   Change in hits and false alarms when shifting the criterion to an extreme position.

to the left). Stated in terms of errors (both false alarms and misses) and correct responses (both hits and correct rejections), the former increase disproportionately in relation to the latter if extreme criteria are employed. Thus if we observe an experimental effect on the proportion of correct responses or correct responses minus false responses, we cannot tell whether this is an effect on achievement, response strategy, or both. Achievement and response strategy are confounded in this index.

SDT makes a clear distinction between these two aspects of the subject's behavior by means of the two indexes d' and β that were defined above. Of course, the appropriateness of the psychophysical model has to be tested for each kind of achievement task when SDT is to be applied. Modifications of the model can be made and different indexes used.

Examples of applications of SDT in achievement measurement under stress conditions will now be given. They make the importance of independent indexes of achievement and set aspect of the subject's behavior quite clear.

Vigilance

In the vigilance tasks that are used in experimental psychology the subject is required to sustain his or her attention for about an hour or more. During this time the subject is supposed to detect signals (for example, short stops of a continuously moving clock hand) that occur irregularly and rather infrequently. The goal of many of these experiments has been to test whether and in what form attention declines over time, but the influence of stressing conditions in addition to the long duration (for example, the requirement to divide one's attention) has also been examined.

The first experiments (for example, N. H. Mackworth, 1948) and many others since have shown that there is a substantial drop in correctly detected signals in the first half hour of a vigilance task. This drop has been interpreted as a deterioration of performance and several theories were proposed to account for this assumed performance decrement (Frankman & Adams, 1962).

In the early 1960s it began to be questioned, however, whether performance is correctly represented by the number of signals detected. If the decrease in detected signals over time were accompanied by a decrease in false alarms, then a change in reaction strategy rather than performance decrement might have occurred. These considerations suggest application of SDT. Yet the classical vigilance paradigm, in which signals occur irregularly distributed over time, does not allow straightforward application of the theory. SDT discrimination and detection experiments imply a defined time interval in which either S_1 or S_2 occurs, or in which either a signal or no signal is present. Vigilance tasks in which the time intervals of possible signal occurrence (observation intervals) are not clearly marked for the observer or in which a response interval is not defined for each observation interval pose the problem of how to classify any given response—is it a hit or a false alarm? Egan, Greenberg, and Schulman (1961) were the first to apply SDT in vigilance research, and they actually used a task with undefined observation intervals. They arrived at estimates of hit and false-alarm proportions by cumulating rates of responding in two time intervals associated with each signal presentation, one immediately after signal occurrence, and the other one long after signal occurrence but before occurrence of the next signal. A response during the former interval was considered to be a hit, during the latter a false alarm. Comparison of the data with data from experiments with defined observation intervals showed this procedure to be legitimate.

Analysis of vigilance data by means of SDT has been made in many studies since (for an overview see Broadbent, 1971; J. F. Mackworth, 1970; Swets, 1977; Swets & Kristofferson, 1970). There is strong evidence now that there is no or only unsubstantial decrement in performance over time in most of the vigilance tasks used, but use of a progressively more strict decision criterion instead. This implies a drop in correctly detected signals as well as false alarms.

Let it be noted that vigilance tasks do not necessarily imply undefined observation intervals. A task may be easily conceived in which a background event is presented regularly and the subject is asked to tell whether some signal is given together with the background event. The background event is to be presented at a rate slow enough to permit defining a response interval for each such event. An experiment by Broadbent and Gregory (1965), in which the background event was a light that flashed regularly and the signal was an occasional brighter flash, is an example of this type of task.

Vigilance experiments in which stressors in addition to the long duration of the task were introduced are also good examples of the necessity to assess performance and risk-taking behavior independently. Wiener, Poock, and Steele (1964) carried out an experiment in which they examined the effect of adding a secondary mental arithmetic task to a vigilance task. The signals to be detected were larger movements of a voltmeter. For data analysis they used the simple index "percent signals detected." The only significant effect they observed was a decline in percentage of detections over time (48 minutes) for all groups, including two controls. A reanalysis of the data of this experiment in terms of SDT performed by M. M. Taylor (1965) revealed a completely different picture. In terms of d' there was no decline in performance over time whatsoever but a substantially inferior performance of the experimental group as compared to the controls. As can be inferred from the stable performance over time in combination with decreasing percentage of signals detected for all groups, an increasingly stricter criterion was used. In addition there was a substantially less cautious criterion used by the group that had to do mental arithmetic during the task. It seems that the subjects of this group tried to compensate for the detrimental effect of doing the arithmetic by giving more responses. In terms of signals correctly detected this strategy was quite effective, but not in terms of actual detection performance.

Broadbent and Gregory (1965) among other things examined the effect of high intensity noise (100 dB) on visual vigilance. SDT analysis showed that the effect of loud noise was, if anything, an improvement in d'. The fact that under some conditions it might give a loss in detections was because of their effect on the criterion.

The applications of SDT in vigilance research make it quite clear that response bias may present a critical problem in vigilance tasks with and without additional stressing conditions. No doubt SDT supplies the most powerful tool for coping with this problem.

For historical reasons vigilance tasks are often such that they do not allow straightforward application of SDT. The observation intervals are not defined and there are few sessions and low data rates. They often yield extreme proportions, especially for false alarms. Being based on very few signal presentations these proportions yield particularly unreliable indexes. Modifications of the current vigilance tasks in the direction of more standard SDT experiments should therefore be made as far as the behavior to be predicted from the task allows to do so. Selection of a specific type of task from the great amount of possible displays should, of course, not be based exclusively on methodological considerations as presented above. However, what we presently know about the effect of stressing conditions on criterion behavior in vigilance tasks makes some kind of control of this source of systematic error mandatory.

Verbal Learning and Memory

Verbal learning tasks are, as compared to vigilance tasks, still more unlike the standard psychophysical SDT experiments. Egan (1958) was the first to use SDT in this field too and thus demonstrated the great flexibility of the model with respect to its application to psychology.

Word recognition, a typical paradigm in verbal learning, allows quite straightforward application of the theory, even though it has at first glance little in common with the classical detection experiment in psychophysics. After a list of items has been presented to the subject he or she is confronted with a second list that includes both items from the first list and new items. The subject is requested to classify each item of the second list as either "old" (if it was in the first list) or "new." All we have to do in order to apply the psychophysical model of SDT (see Figure 1) is to consider the two *classes* of stimuli presented (old and new) as the two stimuli S_1 and S_2, with S_2 corresponding to the class of old items if the variable x is something like "familiarity." From the proportions of hits ("old"|old) and false alarms ("old"|new) the two SDT indexes may be computed, d' representing recognition memory and β representing the subject's cautiousness with respect to labeling a new item as "old."

Many applications of SDT in verbal learning and memory have now been made, both with the recognition (e.g., Clark & Greenberg, 1971) and the paired associates (e.g., Murdock, 1965) paradigm, for which some modification of the usual task is necessary. They supply good evidence that the model can be meaningfully applied in this field (for critical reviews of the matter see Banks, 1970; Lockhart & Murdock, 1970; Parks, 1966).

Studies in which verbal learning is used to examine the effect of stressful conditions on learning and memory have been rare, but they show quite clearly that such conditions are particularly apt to alter the subjects' response criterion. They therefore call for isolation of decision behavior from achievement.

In a recent study Miller and Lewis (1977) analyzed recognition memory (geometric designs) data of three groups of elderly people (depressive, demented, and normal persons) on the basis of SDT. In terms of d' there was no difference in recognition memory between the depressives and the normals but a highly significant difference between each of these groups and the demented group. On the other hand the demented persons and even more so the depressives used a much stricter decision criterion. To judge simply in terms of correct responses therefore means that the depressives may easily be misclassified as demented, a consequence of their extreme cautiousness with respect to false positive responses.

Clark and Greenberg (1971) examined the effect of stress and knowledge of results upon recognition memory (CVC trigrams). The stressed group was told that the number of correct identifications was related to intelligence and that most college students achieved a very high proportion of correct responses by the third trial. Data analysis in terms of SDT yielded some results that are of particular importance for the achievement under stress issue. It was found that recognition memory (d') decreased over trials under the stress condition, while it increased under the no-stress condition. Response criterion (β), on the other hand, decreased over trials under the stress condition and increased under the no-stress condition. This means that the stressed subjects showed an increasing tendency to report old items, probably because they felt intuitively that they might attain better scores by this strategy, while the unstressed subjects became more cautious over trials with respect to reporting false positives. The great difference in response criterion (1.05 and 2.15 for the stressed and the unstressed group, respectively) in the third trial indicates that when using achievement scores not based on SDT there would probably be a seemingly better achievement by the stressed group in this trial, while the actual recognition memory scores (d') are 1.09 and 1.47 for the stressed and the unstressed group, respectively. Lack of control of decision behavior in this experiment would have completely obscured the characteristic course of achievement over trials under the two conditions.

As a further result the authors found a particularly high amount of state anxiety (measured by Zuckerman's Affect Adjective Check List after the third trial) for the stressed group if knowledge of results was given. Because this group also showed a particularly low criterion value the authors assume that there is a close relationship between the response criterion and measures of state anxiety.

The Clark and Greenberg study is of specific importance in the context of this book because verbal learning tasks have frequently been used to test the hypotheses of Taylor and Spence (Spence & Spence, 1966; J. A. Taylor, 1956) and, on the basis of these hypotheses, to examine interrelationships between anxiety, stress, and achievement (for example Spielberger & Smith, 1966). An analysis of such studies with respect to possible confoundings of criterion and achievement behavior in the performance indexes that were used cannot be given here. However, effects of stressful conditions on decision behavior have consistently been found in studies that used SDT methodology (for example Broadbent & Gregory, 1965; Clark & Greenberg, 1971; Miller & Lewis, 1977; M. M. Taylor, 1965), and it is therefore very probable that such confoundings will occur unless the achievement and the decision aspect of the subjects' behavior can be separated from each other. For example, let the number of correct responses in a serial learning experiment be taken as an index of achievement. In this case we may presume that an instruction like "speed of learning increases with intelligence" will lead the subjects to accept a more lenient criterion, which means an increased risk to name false items but at the same time an increased number of items reported correctly.

It should be pointed out that in the Clark and Greenberg (1971) study it is the interaction between stress condition and trials with respect to the criterion that is particularly pertinent in connection with the Taylor-Spence theory. On the basis of this theory we can predict characteristic trends of performance over trials under different anxiety levels and/or stress conditions. If such specific trends over trials are to be expected with respect to response strategy also, then performance over trials may be biased or obscured if performance measures are used that are not criterion free. Clark and Greenberg's (1971) result of an increasingly lax criterion under the stress condition should be understood as a warning in this context.

Conclusions.

Applications that have been made thus far clearly show the usefulness of SDT for the assessment of stressor effects on achievement. This view has been taken by other authors before (Trumbo, 1973; Wilkinson, 1969). The general advantage that is implied in separate indexes for risk-taking behavior and achievement is also intuitively obvious. Therefore, if straightforward application of SDT is possible for a task (for example, recognition memory), it should be used. Difficulties may arise if the behavior to be predicted or the construct to be represented requires the use of a specific task that would have to be substantially altered in order to allow application of the SDT model. In this case the experimenter must consider carefully whether the control of response bias or the validity of the task is more important. It appears that in research on stress and achievement, especially where theoretical premises are to be tested, the range of usable tasks is rather broad and application of SDT would pose no problem. In many instances the classical SDT detection and discrimination experiments or slight modifications thereof can be used (for example, in vigilance research).

Measurement of Stress and Anxiety States

In recent years attempts have been made to use SDT in order to arrive at unbiased measures of stress variables such as anxiety, depression, or experienced aversiveness (Chapman & Feather, 1971; Clark, Kurlander, Bieber, & Glassman, 1977; Neufeld, 1975). Application of the SDT rationale in this context is based on the formal analogy between the ratings commonly used to measure these variables and the SDT rating experiment (Green & Swets, 1966). The psychophysical basis of the rating experiment is essentially the same as that presented above. For the sake of simplicity we may assume that the multiple response categories of the rating experiment are condensed such that there are only two categories left. In this case we have the binary decisions as in the model presented above.

It can be shown, however, that in the case of ratings of psychological objects (for example, images with respect to anxiety-provoking strength, dreadful pictures with respect to intensity of experienced aversiveness, or items describing an emotional state with respect to degree of agreement with the state of the rater), the psychophysical basis does not allow interpretation of the SDT indexes derived from such ratings in the strict sense of the model (Velden & Clark, 1979). The fact that the subject's task in these ratings is not to discriminate between the stimuli as such (the rater can discriminate perfectly between them) but only between their psychological impact as represented on some psychological continuum, enables him or her to make a stimulus-contingent bias, a possibility not given in the SDT detection and discrimination experiments. Let us take the example of a psychiatric patient whose depressive state has been treated in some way. In order to assess the state of the person's mood after the treatment, two sets of items are presented to him or her. One set consists of items describing a depressed state, while the other set contains items that describe a relaxed state. The patient is asked to rate each item with respect to whether it correctly describes his or her emotional state by saying "true" or "false." In terms of the SDT model (Figure 1) the set of depressed items may be considered to constitute S_1. the set of relaxed items S_2, and the internal continuum x is subjective trueness of an item with respect to the state of the patient. For x-values to the right of x_c the patient responds with "true" and to the left with "false." Positive d'-values will now reflect a relaxed state and negative ones a tense state. A neutral state is indicated by values around zero. If, for whatever reason, the patient has a tendency to appear emotionally rather stable after the treatment without actually feeling this way, he or she can set a stricter criterion for responding "true" if a depressed item is given than in the case of a relaxed item. By that the subject will appear to be in a better mood than he or she actually is. In an authentic SDT situation there is no such possibility of a stimulus-contingent choice of criterion because the subject has no knowledge about the stimuli beyond the sensory experience on x that they evoke. Because the main problem with ordinary ratings is the possibility of a stimulus specific bias these ratings continue to hold grave methodological problems.

REFERENCES

Banks, W. P. Signal detection theory and human memory. *Psychological Bulletin*, 1970, *74*, 81–99.

Broadbent, D. E. *Decision and stress*. London: Academic Press, 1971.

Broadbent, D. E., & Gregory, M. Effects of noise and of signal rate upon vigilance analyzed by means of decision theory. *Human Factors*, 1965, *7*, 155–162.

Chapman, C. R., & Feather, B. W. Sensitivity to phobic imagery: A sensory decision theory analysis. *Behavior Research and Therapy*, 1971, *9*, 161–168.

Clark, W. C., & Greenberg, D. B. Effect of stress, knowledge of results, and proactive inhibition on verbal recognition memory (d′) and response criterion (L_x). *Journal of Personality and Social Psychology*, 1971, *17*, 42–47.

Clark, W. C., Kurlander, R., Bieber, R., & Glassman, A. H. Signal detection theory treatment of response set in mood questionnaires. In C. D. Spielberger & I. G. Sarason (Eds.), *Stress and anxiety* (Vol. 4). Washington, DC: Hemisphere, 1977.

Egan, J. P. Recognition, memory, and the operating characteristic (Tech. Rep. AFCRC-TN-58-51). Bloomington: Indiana University, Hearing and Communication Laboratory, 1958.

Egan, J. P., Greenberg, G. Z., & Schulman, A. I. Operating characteristics, signal detectability, and the method of free response. *Journal of the Acoustical Society of America*, 1961, *33*, 993–1007.

Frankman, J. P., & Adams, J. A. Theories of vigilance. *Psychological Bulletin*, 1962, *59*, 257–272.

Green D. M., & Swets, J. A. *Signal detection theory and psychophysics*. New York: Wiley, 1966.

Lockhart, R. S., & Murdock, B. B. Memory and the theory of signal detection. *Psychological Bulletin*, 1970, *74*, 100–109.

Mackworth, J. F. *Vigilance and attention*. Harmondsworth, England: Penguin, 1970.

Mackworth, N. H. The breakdown of vigilance during prolonged visual search. *Quarterly Journal of Experimental Psychology*, 1948, *1*, 6–21.

Miller, E., & Lewis, P. Recognition memory in elderly patients with depression and dementia: A signal detection analysis. *Journal of Abnormal Psychology*, 1977, *86*, 84–86.

Murdock, B. Signal-detection theory and short-term memory. *Journal of Experimental Psychology*, 1965, *70*, 443–447.

Neufeld, R. W. J. Effect of cognitive appraisal on d′ and response bias to experimental stress. *Journal of Personality and Social Psychology*, 1975, *31*, 735–743.

Parks, T. E. Signal-detectability theory of recognition-memory performance. *Psychological Review*, 1966, *73*, 44–58.

Pastore, R. E., & Scheirer, C. J. Signal detection theory: Considerations for general application. *Psychological Bulletin*, 1974, *81*, 945–958.

Spence, J. T., & Spence, K. W. The motivational components of manifest anxiety: Drive and drive stimuli. In C. D. Spielberger (Ed.), *Anxiety and behavior*. New York: Academic Press, 1966.

Spielberger, C. D., & Smith, L. H. Anxiety (drive), stress, and serial position effects in serial verbal learning. *Journal of Experimental Psychology*, 1966, *72*, 589–595.

Swets, J. A. The relative operating characteristic in psychology. *Science*, 1973, *182*, 990–1000.

Swets, J. A. Signal detection theory applied to vigilance. In R. R. Mackie (Ed.), *Vigilance*. New York: Plenum Press, 1977.

Swets, J. A., & Kristofferson, A. B. Attention. *Annual Review of Psychology*. 1970, *21*, 339–366.

Taylor, J. A. Drive theory and manifest anxiety. *Psychological Bulletin*, 1956, *53*, 303–320.

Taylor, M. M. Detectability measures in vigilance: Comment on a paper by Wiener, Poock, and Steele. *Perceptual and Motor Skills*, 1965, *20*, 1217–1221.

Trumbo, D. A. Some laboratory tasks for the assessment of stressor effects. *Psychiatria, Neurologia, Neurochirurgia*, 1973, *76*, 199–207.

Velden, M., & Clark, W. C. Reduction of rating scale data by means of signal detection theory. *Perception and Psychophysics*, 1979, *25*, 517–518.

Wiener, E. L., Poock, G. K., & Steele, M. Effect of time sharing on monitoring performance: Simple arithmetic as a loading task. *Perceptual and Motor Skills*, 1964, *19*, 435–440.

Wilkinson, R. Some factors influencing the effect of environmental stressors upon performance. *Psychological Bulletin*, 1969, *72*, 260–272.

18

Causal Inference from Nonexperimental Research on Anxiety and Educational Achievement

Volker Hodapp
University of Mainz

Anxiety is a frequent accompanying phenomenon of regular achievement tests in the everyday life of students. Its relationship—mostly negative—to complex learning is often demonstrated (Gaudry & Spielberger, 1971; Heinrich & Spielberger, chapter 7 of this volume; for German studies, e.g., Schwarzer, 1975). Nevertheless the theoretical value of many studies, especially of correlative ones, remains controversial because the interrelationship between anxiety and achievement has not been clarified sufficiently, and the results may be looked at from the most varied theoretical points of view.

A special difficulty for correlative studies is the causal relationship between anxiety and achievement (e.g., Phillips, Martin, & Meyers, 1972; Ruebush, 1963). Gaudry and Spielberger (1971) observe on this point:

> The problem of causality is a difficult one in educational research, particularly where individual difference variables such as intelligence and anxiety are involved. Experimental studies which permit us to make causal statements are generally not feasible because true experiments require the random assignment of subjects to experimental conditions... The most reasonable approach is to conduct quasi-experiments which are designed to rule out rival hypotheses. (p. 80)

In this chapter I will present methods that make possible a more exact analysis of determining factors. They narrow down probable dependencies of variables even in cases of nonexperimental studies. The term *causal analysis* has become common for some of these methods (Heise, 1975) even though the concept of causality is encumbered with speculative philosophical convictions (cf. Bunge, 1959). It is common for the social sciences (e.g., Blalock, 1971) to speak of a causal relationship when the covariance of two events is characterized by an asymmetry of this relation. An asymmetrical variable relation exists when X produces Y, but not vice-versa. Furthermore, one cannot speak of a causal relationship when the common occurence of two events may be traced back to a third. Conceptions of causal models are also necessary in the realm of nonexperimental anxiety research. They lead to more precise hypotheses and more theory-oriented questioning.

I am indebted to Nanny Wermuth for her helpful comments and suggestions. I also wish to thank Professor C. D. Spielberger for his kind permission to reanalyze and describe his data.

COVARIANCE SELECTION

Method

The method of covariance selection makes possible a multivariate analysis of interdependence structures (Wermuth, 1976a). The conceptions of this model permit the attribution of correlative relationships between several normally distributed variables to the simplest possible pattern of (symmetrical) variable relationships, in which case those that are merely the results of other variables disappear. Starting from the theory of covariance selection by Dempster (1972), Wermuth (1976b) developed a model search procedure with the help of which a covariance selection model can be found that contains the greatest possible number of partial zero correlations and, on the whole, is still compatible with the data. Partial zero correlation means that a correlation may exist between two variables, however, this correlation can be totally explained by correlations of all other variables. Test statistics can be specified that show the compatibility of the model.

The starting point of covariance selection is the inverse of the correlation matrix whose elements are a multiple of partial correlation coefficients. Elements near zero point to conditional independence of variables (Wermuth, 1976b).

Looking at a simple example the two variable patterns in Figure 1 correspond to specified covariance selection models. Model 12/23 expresses that variables 1 and 3 are independent when variable 2 is taken into account. Conditionally independent variables or groups of variables are separated by (/). Variables not separated by this sign are therefore directly connected variables. This model would be acceptable, that is, it would be consistent with observations made, if the partial correlation $r_{13.2}$ would lie near zero. In model 123 it is, however, not possible to explain one of the three variable relationships by keeping constant one variable.

Models such as this with more than three variables can no longer be developed with the calculation of first-order partial correlations. The above manner of notation however, makes possible a simple presentation of complex structures of interdependence. In practice this method has been used only sporadically (Wermuth, 1978; Wermuth, Hodapp, & Weyer, 1976). Its application in the field of anxiety and stress research nevertheless seems to be very promising (Weyer & Hodapp, 1979).

An Example from Anxiety Research

Depending on the theoretical standpoint, the question of the relationship between anxiety and achievement has many different answers. The Trait-State Anxiety Theory, influenced by learning theory, postulates a direct, performance-

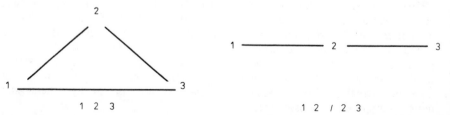

Figure 1 Covariance selection model notation for two simple variable patterns.

impairing effect of intensive increase in A-State, which augments the probability of incorrect responses in complex learning tasks (Spielberger, O'Neil, & Hansen, 1972). Morris and Liebert (1970), on the other hand, attempted to demonstrate that performance was not influenced by the emotional component of test anxiety but rather that an interfering effect on performance could be traced back to the worry component of test anxiety (i.e., cognitive concerns about the consequences of failure).

In their review Spielberger, Gonzales, Taylor, Algaze, & Anton (1978) emphasize that examination stress is characterized by heightened arousal and an accumulation of negative, self-centered reactions in persons especially afflicted with test anxiety. In order to test these hypotheses, Spielberger et al. (1978) developed a questionnaire that comprised an exhaustive study of test anxiety, separating emotionality and worry. Especially interesting in this case is the relationship between anxiety variables and academic achievement (Table 1). The high negative correlations between worry and achievement ($r = -.43$ and $r = -.30$) as well as the weak negative correlations of emotionality and achievement ($r = -.10$ resp. $r = -.01$) seem to corroborate Morris and Liebert's assertion, according to which only the worry component interferes with achievement.

A covariance selection according to the model search procedure of Wermuth (1976b) reached the following results: The simplest models proved to be model 134/234/245/246 ($p = .18$) for males and model 134/25/345/456 ($p = .06$) for females. These models are characterized by the fact that most relationships are independent without the whole model differing significantly from the data. Figure 2 is an illustration of the latter model. It shows groups of variables that are directly linked with each other. Correlations between such variables can therefore not be dissolved. Other correlations come into existence only through the fact that single variables within several subgroups are linked to other variables.

It is surprising that in both models achievement remains dependent on the two components of test anxiety, namely worry and emotionality (variable groups 134). Conditionally dependent are achievement and A-State, and also achievement and A-Trait. For example, in the case of males, A-Trait (5) and

Table 1 Correlations between Anxiety Measures, Study Skills, and Achievement as Stated by Spielberger

	1	2	3	4	5	6
	Ach	A-St	Em	Wo	A-Tr	St-Sk
1 Achievement	1.00	−.13	−.10	−.43	−.28	.29
2 A-State	−.14	1.00	.64	.47	.57	−.42
3 Emotionality (TAI)	−.01	.28	1.00	.65	.42	−.29
4 Worry (TAI)	−.30	.27	.56	1.00	.47	−.48
5 A-Trait	−.09	.54	.39	.39	1.00	−.38
6 Study Skills	.21	−.21	−.04	−.25	−.22	1.00

Note. Above the diagonal: male students ($n = 115$); below the diagonal: female students ($n = 185$).

Note. These correlations refer to data published by Spielberger et al. (1978) yet are based on an earlier scoring system of emotionality and worry with 5 items each. Calculations for the new system lead to very similar results and reach the same conclusions about anxiety-achievement relationships.

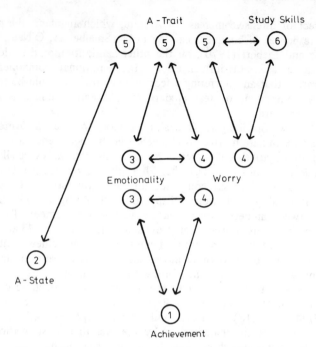

Figure 2 Covariance selection model for data of Spielberger,
female students.

achievement (1) are linked by variable 4 (worry) (see groups 245/134). In the
case of females, A-Trait and achievement are independent when worry as well as
emotionality are taken into account (see groups 134/345). The partial correlation
$r_{15.34}$ in this case is near zero. A further interesting result is the fact that study
skills are linked to the worry component rather than to emotionality.

The covariance selection makes no statement about the direction of influence.
However, statements are possible about spurious correlations and indirect
relationships between variables, decisive factors of a causal analysis (Suppes,
1975). According to this data a direct relationship between A-State and
achievement can be excluded. The same applies to the A-Trait/achievement
relationship when the more specifically situation-bound variables of test anxiety
are taken into account.

RECURSIVE SYSTEMS

Path Analysis

Method

Asymmetrical relationships are an essential determinant of causal models. In
experimental techniques the direction of variable linking is decided by the
manipulation of independent variables and the constancy of possible influencing
factors by randomizing. The analysis of functional relation in nonexperimental
research poses the problem of excluding influences in one direction. Within the

framework of recursive systems, this can be undertaken only with regard to theoretical a priori assumptions.

The technique of path analysis (Anderson & Evans, 1974; Dohrenwend, 1978; Duncan, 1975; Heise, 1975; Werts & Linn, 1970) opens the possibility of changing interdependencies into dependencies with the help of certain a priori assumptions and of judging the strength of linear, additive, asymmetrical relationships. Path analysis proceeds with a system of dependent relationships put into the form of a complete recursive system. Equations 1 and Figure 3 show such a recursive system. Each variable is taken to be in standardized form.

$$X_2 = a_{21} X_1 + U_2$$
$$X_3 = a_{31} X_1 + a_{32} X_2 + U_3$$

(1)

The path diagram in Figure 3 and equation system 1 make clear that a recursive system contains a sequence of regression equations such that variables in the system relate successively in the form of dependent variables to the preceding variables. Such a model could be illustrated by the variables A-Trait (X_1), A-State (X_2), and achievement (X_3) (cf. King, Heinrich, Stephenson, & Spielberger, 1976). In a complete recursive model all dependent variables in a system (the so-called endogenous variables) are respectively related to all preceding variables, so that equations 1 form a triangle, characteristic for a recursive system. The exogenous variable in our model (i.e., the variable that does not appear in any equation as a dependent variable) could be supplemented by other exogenous variables, which in a complete model should appear in all equations. U_2 and U_3 represent residual variables, which among themselves and with the regressors of the equation are considered independent. They substitute the variance parts not explained by the variables of the system. As they usually add little to the interpretation, they will be left out of the following diagrams.

Incomplete recursive systems are characterized by the fact that single coefficients of the equation system equal zero. It will therefore be necessary to allude to problems of estimation in path analysis, the problem of testing hypotheses, and to the relationships between covariance selection and recursive systems.

Statistical Problems of Path Analysis

All recursive systems, complete or incomplete, may be presented as an issue of multiple regression equations. Thereby the path coefficients are to be regarded

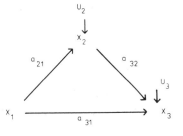

Figure 3 Path diagram of a recursive system.

simply as standardized multiple regression coefficients and to be calculated as least squares estimates (cf. Heise, 1975; or Kerlinger & Pedhazur, 1973). The results from a complete recursive model will, however, often be of only limited value, as each variable set with different variable orders may be formulated as a complete recursive system and made to fit the data perfectly. Therefore wrong model specifications concerning the order of variables cannot be detected by testing hypotheses. Thus, following the attribution theory (Weiner, 1972), the order of variables 2 and 3 (A-State and achievement) could be reversed. In the case of nonvanishing functional connections of the three variables, such a model would also be perfectly adaptable to observations.

Incomplete recursive systems are easier to interpret but involve problems of estimation. A simultaneous test of zero relationships and the estimation of those correlations that correspond to the regression coefficients set at zero represent such problems. Maximum-likelihood estimates exist, however generally require rather complicated iterative methods. Fundamentally they make it possible to test zero relationships (Jöreskog, 1973).

Wermuth (in press) suggests a solution that makes it possible to develop incomplete recursive systems under certain additional conditions by applying covariance selection models. In this case the maximum-likelihood estimates of all correlations are obtained by way of least square estimates of regression coefficients, so that an overall test may easily be specified for such models. For the zero relationships, implicit correlations r_{ij}^* can be calculated in the sequence $i = p - 1, \ldots, 1$:

$$r_{ij}^* = \begin{cases} r_{ij} & \text{(for existing paths from } j \text{ to } i \\ & \text{and for } i \text{ and } j \text{ exogenous)} \\ \sum_k \hat{a}_{ik} r_{kj}^* & \text{(for missing paths from } j \text{ to } i) \end{cases} \qquad (2)$$

with p as number of variables, and k as regressors on i. As overall test for the model, we can use the likelihood-ratio test,

$$\text{LR-Chi}^2 = n(\log \det \hat{\mathbf{P}} - \log \det \mathbf{R}) \qquad (3)$$

which for large n follows a chi square distribution. The degrees of freedom equal the number of zero relationships. $\mathbf{R}$ represents the original correlation matrix, $\hat{\mathbf{P}}$ the correlation matrix including implicit correlations. The specific advantage of this method is the fact that the model search procedure of the covariance selection makes it possible to examine the adaptability of the variables to an incomplete recursive system with or without specification of exogenous variables.

A Reanalysis of Data from Spielberger

The reanalysis of data from Spielberger et al. (1978) resulted in the covariance selection models presented earlier. The model for females may be transformed without difficulty into a recursive system, which fulfils the additional conditions stated by Wermuth (in press), so that the path coefficients may be calculated from the correlation matrix like regression coefficients. The equations of the model are

$$X_1 = 0 + a_{13}X_3 + a_{14}X_4 + \quad 0 \quad + \quad 0 \quad + U_1$$
$$X_2 = \quad 0 \quad + \quad 0 \quad + a_{25}X_5 + \quad 0 \quad + U_2 \qquad (4)$$
$$X_3 = \qquad \qquad a_{34}X_4 + a_{35}X_5 + \quad 0 \quad + U_3$$
$$X_4 = \qquad \qquad a_{45}X_5 + a_{46}X_6 + U_4$$

The additional conditions are given since the basic covariance selection model 134/25/345/456 represents a multiplicative model, and the coefficients a_{ij} $(i < j)$ put at zero fulfil

$$a_{hi}a_{hj} = 0 (h = 1, \ldots, i - 1). \qquad (5)$$

The order of the variables at the base of the recursive system is in accordance with the order of the variables following the theoretical background of the data. Achievement and A-State should be clearly recognized as dependent variables, in which case X_1 and X_2 may be interchanged readily. The decision to regard emotionality as dependent on worry can be derived from the results of Spiegler, Morris, and Liebert (1968), according to which the emotionality component increases considerably immediately before examinations. This proves the state-character of this variable in contrast to the individual constancy of the worry component. A-Trait and study skills represent the exogenous variables.

Figure 4 (females) shows the path diagram belonging to the model equations 4 with the calculated path coefficients. An observed marginal correlation may falsify the direct influence that a variable possesses over another variable because it is possible to split correlative relationships into direct and indirect ones (see Kerlinger & Pedhazur, 1973). The relationship between emotionality and achievement is a good example since it shows that despite the correlation of −.01 the influence of the emotionality component on achievement is definitely positive. A further result of theoretical significance is represented by the missing relationship between A-State and achievement, whereas the strong negative influence on achievement by the (cognitive) worry component was to be expected. The overall test of the model resulted in a chi square of 13.41 ($p = .06, df = 7$) in a good correspondence with the data.

The analysis of the data of males was more difficult. As already made clear in the path diagram (Figure 4, males), this model could not be simplified to the same extent. Model 134/234/245/246, found with the help of covariance selection, cannot be transformed into a recursive system without violating condition 5. Therefore we combined the variable groups 234, 245, and 246 so that the model 134/23456 could meet the required condition. As a result of this pooling, the variables study skills, A-Trait, emotionality, and worry are defined as exogenous variables whose correlations are used as a whole for the estimation of the path coefficients. It is no longer possible to determine the order of these variables. But the path coefficients calculated from this model result in—theoretically—interesting conclusions. A-State is again unrelated to achievement, which in turn is influenced to an even higher degree by worry and emotionality.

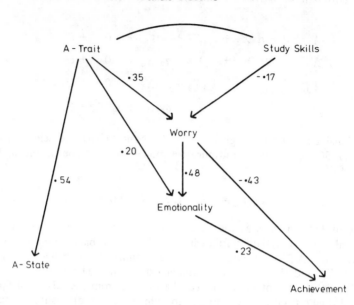

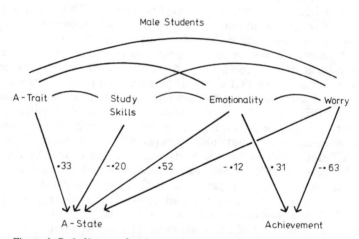

Figure 4 Path diagrams for the reanalyzed data of Spielberger.

Remarkable again is the positive relationship between emotionality and achievement, which in connection with the negative effect of worry points out the different significance of the two test-anxiety components. The facilitating effect upon achievement may be interpreted as the efficacy of drive-activating task characteristics or the energizing quality of an activation dimension whose influence on achievement is covered by the impairing attention to task-irrelevant, self-centered cognitions. The chi square of 3.36 ($p > .30$, $df = 3$) for this model also fits the data to a high degree.

The Testing of Hypotheses

Until now the hypothesis-generating character of the proposed causal analysis was stressed because of the application of the model search procedure, even though a clear decision for or against a certain model may be reached with the help of the statistical test. The statistical test and the possibility of testing a given model structure will be explained below. The following variables were collected from 134 pupils of the seventh grade, in addition to a written test in mathematics containing fraction problems: A-Trait, A-State,[1] test anxiety with worry and emotionality items, and an intelligence test, which covered the reasoning factor. We drew up the test in cooperation with the teachers, and only those classes participated that had used the same textbook and reached the same level. The pupils were told that the results of the test would be of consequence for their school reports (Weik, Note 1).

Then we formulated the model equations 6, allowing for the results of the reanalysis of the data collected by Spielberger et al. (1978).

$$X_1 = a_{13}X_3 + a_{14}X_4 + a_{16}X_6 + U_1$$
$$X_2 = a_{23}X_3 + a_{24}X_4 + a_{25}X_5 + U_2 \tag{6}$$
$$X_3 = a_{34}X_4 + a_{35}X_5 + a_{36}X_6 + U_3$$

However, a full comparison of the variable sets is impossible, since we used an intelligence variable instead of study skills. Achievement (X_1) was meant to be dependent on emotionality (X_3), worry (X_4), and intelligence (X_6); for A-State (X_2) we postulated a direct dependence on emotionality, worry, and A-Trait (X_5). A-Trait, worry, and intelligence were defined as exogenous variables.

Figure 5 shows the path diagram belonging to equation system 6 with the calculated path coefficients. While achievement is negatively influenced by the worry coefficient of test anxiety, the weak effect of emotionality on achieve-

[1] The A-State questionnaire was handed out after the test with the instruction to fill it out describing the feelings during the test.

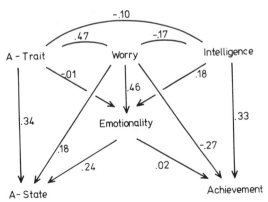

Figure 5 Path diagram for anxiety and achievement variables (134 seventh-grade pupils).

ment can be neglected. The relationship between intelligence and achievement is positive, as was to be expected. In contrast to the results of the reanalysis, there appears in our case a weak relationship between A-Trait and emotionality. A-Trait correlates, however, relatively highly with the worry component of test anxiety ($r = .47$). This result coincides with Kendall, Finch, Auerbach, Hooke, and Mikulka (1976), who interpret A-Trait as "cognitive anxiety." A-State seems to be influenced most by A-Trait.

The path coefficients calculated from our data are altogether lower than the corresponding coefficients of the data of Spielberger et al. (1978). However, it must be remembered, that the populations used in both studies were different. Furthermore, it needs to be tested whether the path diagram in Figure 5 as a complete model coincides with the data.

In order to test this we calculated according to equations 2 the implicit correlations for those relationships we set at zero a priori. The likelihood-ratio test resulted in a chi square of 9.56 ($p = .02$, $df = 3$). Because of the low level of significance we reject the total model for our data. We are now in a position to decide which of the implicit correlations deviate clearly from the observed correlations and thereby prove the insufficient adjustment of the total model to the data (see Table 2). The relationship between achievement and A-State differs most, and therefore putting this relationship at zero becomes questionable.

Since earlier studies led us to expect anxiety-intelligence interactions and sex-specific differences, the sample was separated according to the median of the intelligence scores. Furthermore, boys and girls were analyzed separately (see Table 3 for correlation coefficients). Afterwards path coefficients and the test statistics for verification of the models were again calculated. These path coefficients are shown in Table 4 together with the test statistics.

The given model structure fits well the data for the group of the more intelligent pupils. For the less intelligent the path coefficients leading to achievement are higher—not unexpectedly so. A comparison of the implicit and the observed correlations shows that the greatest deviation in the case of the less intelligent children occurs again in the A-State and achievement relationship.

Separated according to sex, one remarkable difference can be found in the influence of A-State. While for girls A-State seems to be dependent on emotionality, for boys the dependency is centered on worry. Furthermore, the analysis for girls results in a deviation from the given model structure. It is interesting to note that for the boys achievement depends only on intelligence and the worry component. Regarding the girls, there is a marked deviation of the

Table 2 Intercorrelations of Anxiety and Achievement Variables for 134 Seventh-Grade Pupils

	1	2	3	4	5	6
	Ach	A-St	Em	Wo	A-Tr	Int
1 Achievement	1.000	$-.124^a$			$-.157$	
2 A-State	-.313	1.000				$-.042$
3 Emotionality	-.062	.378	1.000			
4 Worry	-.318	.437	.426	1.000		
5 A-Trait	-.306	.468	.185	.468	1.000	
6 Intelligence	.376	-.064	.103	-.173	-.104	1.000

[a]The italicized correlations are the implicit ones.

Table 3 Intercorrelations of Anxiety and Achievement Variables for Seventh-Grade Boys and Girls

	1	2	3	4	5	6
	Ach	A-St	Em	Wo	A-Tr	Int
1 Achievement	1.000	−.288	−.122	−.390	−.289	.416
2 A-State	−.333	1.000	.340	.646	.605	−.122
3 Emotionality	.043	.379	1.000	.420	.242	.021
4 Worry	−.235	.200	.457	1.000	.562	−.109
5 A-Trait	−.317	.314	.066	.372	1.000	−.026
6 Intelligence	.339	−.017	.163	−.271	−.225	1.000

Note. Above the diagonal: boys ($n = 67$); below the diagonal: girls ($n = 67$).

implicit correlation of the A-State achievement relationship. This indicates the existence of a strong dependence that cannot be unraveled any further. It appears that an alternative model—including mutual influence—may be adequate here. Such models will be treated below.

SPECIAL PROBLEMS

Nonrecursive Models

Reciprocal Effects and Feedback-Loops in Anxiety Theories

So far we have dealt with recursive models, that is, models dealing only with influences defined in one direction, and where the variables of the system can be brought into a clear order according to their dependencies. No variable can influence another one higher up in the hierarchy. Such a model represents, of course, a restriction of the existing possibilities and entails a crude simplification for many analyses of psychological systems. A recursive system compatible with

Table 4 Path Coefficients and Test Statistics of Anxiety and Achievement Variables for Seventh-Grade Pupils

	Intelligence		Sex	
	Low[a]	High[b]	Boys[c]	Girls[c]
$\hat{a}_{13}$	.11	−.02	.02	.09
$\hat{a}_{14}$	−.39	−.24	−.36	−.20
$\hat{a}_{16}$	.28	.17	.38	.27
$\hat{a}_{23}$	.18	.27	.08	.41
$\hat{a}_{24}$	.27	.14	.41	−.11
$\hat{a}_{25}$	.26	.38	.35	.33
$\hat{a}_{34}$	.56	.44	.42	.57
$\hat{a}_{35}$	−.10	.03	.00	−.08
$\hat{a}_{36}$	.14	.17	.07	.30
LR-Chi²	9.95	3.32	1.67	11.36
$df = 3$	$p < .05$	$p > .30$	$p > .50$	$p < .01$

[a] $n = 62$
[b] $n = 61$
[c] $n = 67$

such a simple model structure is justified only within a particular theoretical framework.

Krohne (1976) points to a possible further development in anxiety research by employing models of anxiety control and processing that go beyond the assumptions of simple functional relationships. They include more complex connections such as reciprocal relationships and feedback loops. An example of a feedback loop is in the process of reappraisal described by Lazarus (Lazarus & Averill, 1972). Phillips et al. (1972) cite a further instance of a feedback loop by explaining a striking relationship between anxiety of pupils and their hostility toward classmates and the anxious pupils' tendencies for affiliation and dependence. Because of the anxious pupils' low group status, these tendencies lead more easily to frustrations, which in turn increase the anxiety level and hostility.

A basic idea of reciprocal causation lies in the conception of an inter-dependent relationship as a stabilized pattern of mutual variable influences in the past whereby the aim is to infer the processes or sequences that have led to the present pattern. Namboodiri, Carter, and Blalock (1975) emphasize the character-istics of such nonrecursive models and describe ways of estimating the parameters. In the following, two questions that arose in connection with the recursive models presented so far will be treated more extensively, and we will point out calculation methods that can easily be applied to simple nonrecursive models.

In order to calculate the coefficients of nonrecursive models, certain model structures, models with so-called identifiable equations, have to exist. This may be the case when two variables influence each other and each of these two variables in turn depends on different exogenous variables (see examples below). Basic problems are created by the assumption of uncorrelated residual variables within the feedback loop. In the two equations of these models a correlation between an independent and a residual variable is the consequence of the respective feedback loops. This difficulty, however, can be met by using instrumental variables (cf. Heise, 1975). In the case of the simpler models described below, with one exogenous variable respectively related to an endogenous one, the coefficients can be easily calculated by multiplication of the model equations with the exogenous (instrumental) variables. The case of two exogenous variables influencing an endogenous one leads to an overidentified system that can be solved by the two-stage least squares technique (for a detailed presentation of methods we refer to Duncan, 1975; Namboodiri et al., 1975, or textbooks on econometrics, e.g., Goldberger, 1964; Wonnacott & Wonnacott, 1970).

The Relationship between Worry and Emotionality

In the relationship of worry and emotionality, worry was defined as the predetermining variable. This is in agreement with a cognitive view emphasized in the test anxiety theory (Sarason, 1975; 1978; Wine, chapter 10 of this volume). Seen from other theoretical standpoints, a reversed order of these variables would be feasible. Finger and Galassi (1977) start with the stress model by Lazarus and confirm a mutual influence of cognitive and affective factors. The data of Morris and Liebert (1970) permit the assessment of nonrecursive relationships postulated in this way.

We executed a covariance selection to receive a first impression of the direct and indirect connections of variables in the study of Morris and Liebert (1970). The compatibility of the structure of the variable relationships with an identifiable model could be checked this way. Thus we can avoid wrong model specifications (cf. Duncan, 1975) that otherwise might arise from an unforeseen, but really existing, influence of an exogenous variable.

A direct connection between emotionality and worry appeared in studies I and II by Morris and Liebert (1970). In addition the heart rate item was directly connected with emotionality, and worry with expectancy. Moreover, in study II, achievement was connected with worry. The coefficients for the causal models were calculated according to the method of the instrumental variables (Figure 6).

At first sight the results seem surprising because of their contradictory appearance. Study I and study II, however, differ in that the order used in study I (i.e., pulse rate—questionnaire) was varied in study II. Therefore it may be assumed that in study I the individuals filling in the questionnaires were strongly influenced by the previous measuring of the pulse and by having to record the frequency in the protocol sheets. The causal relationship of the variables suggested above seems confirmed in study II. Although the correlation between emotionality and worry differs minimally in both studies (0.62 and 0.55), the relationship must be interpreted differently each time. The method of instrumental variables requires a number of restrictions regarding the exogenous variables, so that a further testing of this result will be necessary.

A-State and Achievement

Our models were not satisfactory for the relationship between A-State and achievement since a possible influence of achievement on A-State was not taken into account. Such an influence could be explained by the theory of attribution, according to which affective reactions are the results of attributional processes linked to action results (Weiner, 1972). According to our data, a direct relationship between A-State and achievement could not be excluded for the total group and for the females.

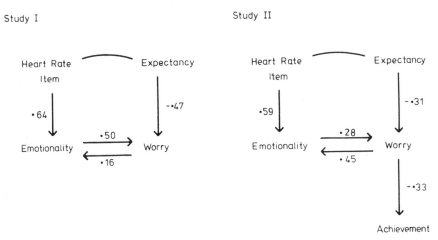

Figure 6 Causal models and coefficients for the data of Morris and Liebert (1970).

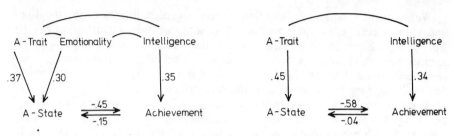

Figure 7 Reciprocal causal model for the relationship between A-State and achievement (134 seventh-grade pupils).

To avoid error specification, covariance selection models were computed. They revealed, only for the total group, variables suitable as instrumental variables. Figure 7 shows two nonrecursive models calculated with the methods mentioned above. The results prove clearly the sequence postulated in the Trait-State Anxiety Theory: Trait anxiety leads to an increment in A-State, which in turn has impairing effects on achievement in complex learning. This effect is even clearer when the less reliable emotionality variable is removed from the equations. These results may be mainly valid for girls since for this group covariance selection shows that achievement is influenced by A-State and emotionality; whereas for boys the detrimental effects of worry are characteristic.

Panel Analyses

Method

The quasi-experimental design of the cross-lagged panel correlation (Campbell & Stanley, 1963) is a frequently used means for finding the causal direction in correlation relationships. In the simplest case, measurements are available of two variables at two different times. The hypothesis of a causal relation is justified when the cross-lagged correlations, (i.e., the correlations of the two variables over the two measurement periods) are not equal (Marmor & Montemayor, 1977).

The advantage of a panel analysis lies in the fact that the direction of some correlative relationships is obvious, as it seems logically impossible that a variable of a later period should influence a variable measured earlier. This can be useful for approaches that formulate the variable relationships with the help of equation systems. Thus Goldberger (1971) points to the inadequate formalization of the cross-lagged panel correlation technique and instead suggests a regression analytical treatment of this approach (see also Duncan, 1969).

Kenny, attempting to formalize Campbell's technique more precisely, favors testing hypotheses rather than estimating parameters (Kenny, 1975). Special emphasis is placed on the condition of stationarity, but it remains uncertain how, for example, the stationarity assumption can be justified without estimation of parameters. Transferring the cross-lagged panel scheme into a complete recursive system, we assume that X causally influences Y within and between the measurement periods. In this case the two synchronous correlations $r_{X_1 Y_1}$ and $r_{X_2 Y_2}$ differ, even if the same path coefficients (and causal relationships) can be taken as a basis for these different correlations. Rozelle and Campbell (1969) are not right in their suggestion that equality of the synchronous correlations can be deduced from the stationarity assumption.

An Empirical Example

We expanded our study by testing the 134 seventh-grade pupils 6 weeks later. In addition to the anxiety measurements an achievement test was made in decimal arithmetic (Wüst, Note 2). If, for demonstrating the principal aims of panel analyses, we accept a significance level of $p = .10$, the total model shown in Figure 8 with $p = .49$ would be acceptable. Especially so since in the next model the relatively strong single relationship A-Trait (t_1), achievement (t_2) with a chi-square of 7.52 $(p < .01, df = 1)$ has disappeared. The anxiety measures and achievement at time 1 were defined as exogenous variables.

As condition 5 is not fulfilled, there is no possibility of transferring this covariance selection model into a recursive system within the framework of the presented methodology. Nevertheless there is evidence from this model that A-Trait influences achievement as well as A-State; a relationship between A-State and achievement cannot be proven here. As there exist no relationships between achievement and anxiety variables at t_2, a complete comparability of the two measurement times may be questioned. Testing effects and different motivation at time 1 and 2 cannot be ruled out. Our results, however, are in agreement with King et al. (1976), Heinrich (Note 3) and Schaffner and Laux (1979), who carried out panel analyses too, employing the FCPM-technique (Yee & Gage, 1968).

Although the relationships are weak and critical objections could be added in each case, the uniform results lead us to believe that achievement is being influenced by A-Trait and habitual test anxiety, which in turn influence A-State and task-irrelevant cognitions. The relationship between A-State and achievement remains doubtful. King et al. (1976) report an influence on achievement by the A-State; Schaffner and Laux (1979), in agreement with us, could not confirm this result. Heinrich (Note 3), who also found no influence, supposes a reciprocal relationship between A-State and achievement.

On the whole the studies manifest a unified impression that habitual anxiety

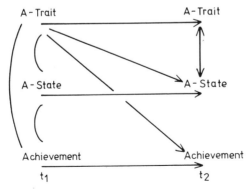

Figure 8 Covariance selection model of the panel
analysis data (seventh-grade pupils).

variables influence achievement. On the other hand an influence of achievement on habitual anxiety variables could not be proved. Since the problem of the "causal interval" was not considered, the existing studies do not permit a definite answer to the question of whether state anxiety variables can influence achievement. The causal interval is the period of time necessary for a change of one variable to have an effect on the second variable. Measurement periods should correspond with this interval (Pelz & Andrews, 1964). Trait and state measurements certainly require different intervals; this should be considered in the design.

DISCUSSION

As examples from anxiety research have repeatedly shown, correlations can give a wrong impression of a variable relationship when the remaining variables of the system are not taken into account. With the methods described here, it is possible to analyze more precisely directed and nondirected variable relationships and to represent separately the effects of single variables. Thus more valid conclusions of field experiments may be reached that go beyond the interpretation of correlative studies. It should be noted that the linear, additive model does not take into account nonlinear relationships and effects of interactions of the variables. However, textbooks on econometrics contain the description of models that treat this problem further (see also Hornung, 1977). An interesting perspective for dealing with the problem of measurement errors is opened by the development of models with latent variables (Jöreskog, 1973).

The examples analyzed here demonstrate that correlations can contain more information than may be believed at first sight. More subtle correlation analyses challenge the cognitive view that the anxiety-achievement relationship is characterized only by the negative effect of task-irrelevant, self-centered cognitions. Despite this dominating effect, which has been proved consistently, emotional components of test anxiety (emotionality and A-State) may show a direct relationship to achievement as well. The kind of task and degree of difficulty may influence the sign and the strength of this relationship. Though the causal sequence—trait anxiety influences achievement through A-State—could be established by our data to some extent, a clearer distinction between emotional and cognitive state anxiety measures would be useful and, possibly, could clarify further questions.

Some evidence speaks for the fact that especially in connection with the emotional component of test anxiety, sex-related answer patterns should be expected (Feld & Lewis, 1969; Morris, Finkelstein, & Fisher, 1976; Schwarzer, 1975, p. 52).

REFERENCES

Anderson, J. G., & Evans, F. B. Causal models in educational research: Recursive models. *American Educational Research Journal*, 1974, *11*, 29–39.

Blalock, H. M. (Ed.) *Causal models in the social sciences*. Chicago, New York: Aldine/Atherton, 1971.

Bunge, M. *Causality: The place of the causal principle in modern science*. Cambridge, MA: Harvard University Press, 1959.

Campbell, D. T., & Stanley, J. C. *Experimental and quasi-experimental designs for research*. Chicago: Rand McNally, 1963.

Dempster, A. P. Covariance selection. *Biometrics*, 1972, *28*, 157–175.

Dohrenwend, B. S. Social states and responsibility for stressful life events. In C. D. Spielberger & I. G. Sarason (Eds.), *Stress and anxiety* (Vol. 5). Washington, DC: Hemisphere, 1978.

Duncan, O. D. Some linear models for two-wave, two variable panel analysis. *Psychological Bulletin*, 1969, *72*, 177–182.

Duncan, O. D. *Introduction to structural equation models*. New York: Academic Press, 1975.

Feld, S. C., & Lewis, J. The assessment of achievement anxieties in children. In C. P. Smith (Ed.), *Achievement-related motives in children*. New York: Russel Sage Foundation, 1969.

Finger, R., Galassi, J. P. Effects of modifying cognitive versus emotionality responses in the treatment of test anxiety. *Journal of Consulting and Clinical Psychology*, 1977, *45*, 280–287.

Gaudry, E., & Spielberger, C. D. *Anxiety and educational achievement*. Sydney: Wiley, 1971.

Goldberger, A. S. *Econometric theory*, New York: Wiley, 1964.

Goldberger, A. S. Econometrics and psychometrics: A survey of communalities. *Psychometrika*, 1971, *36*, 83–107.

Heise, D. R. *Causal analysis*. New York: Wiley, 1975.

Hornung, C. A. Social status, status inconsistency and psychological stress. *American Sociological Review*, 1977, *42*, 623–638.

Jöreskog, K. G. A general method for estimating a linear structural equation system. In A. S. Goldberger & O. D. Duncan (Eds.), *Structural equation models in the social sciences*. New York: Seminar Press, 1973.

Kendall, P. C., Finch, A. J., Jr., Auerbach, S. M., Hooke, J. F., & Mikulka, P. J. The State-Trait Anxiety Inventory: A systematic evaluation. *Journal of Consulting and Clinical Psychology*, 1976, *44*, 406–412.

Kenny, D. A. Cross-lagged panel correlation: A test for spuriousness. *Psychological Bulletin*, 1975, *82*, 887–903.

Kerlinger, F. N., & Pedhazur, E. J. *Multiple regression in behavioral research*. New York: Holt, Rinehart and Winston, 1973.

King, F. J., Heinrich, D. L., Stephenson, R. S., & Spielberger, C. D. An investigation of the causal influence of trait and state anxiety on academic achievement. *Journal of Educational Psychology*, 1976, *68*, 330–334.

Krohne, H. W. *Theorien zur Angst*. Stuttgart: Kohlhammer, 1976.

Lazarus, R. S., & Averill, J. R. Emotion and cognition: With special reference to anxiety. In C. D. Spielberger (Ed.), *Anxiety: Current trends in theory and research* (Vol. 2). New York: Academic Press, 1972.

Marmor, G. S., & Montemayor, R. The cross-lagged panel design: A review. *Perceptual and Motor Skills*, 1977, *45*, 883–893.

Morris, L. W., Finkelstein, C. S., & Fisher, W. R. Components of school anxiety: Developmental trends and sex differences. *The Journal of Genetic Psychology*, 1976, *128*, 49–57.

Morris, L. W., & Liebert, R. M. Relationships of cognitive and emotional components of test anxiety to physiological arousal and academic performance. *Journal of Consulting and Clinical Psychology*, 1970, *35*, 332–337.

Namboodiri, N. K., Carter, L. F., & Blalock, H. M. *Applied multivariate analysis and experimental design*. New York: McGraw-Hill, 1975.

Pelz, D. C., & Andrews, F. M. Detecting causal priorities in panel study data. *American Sociological Review*, 1964, *29*, 836–848.

Phillips, B. N., Martin, R. P., & Meyers, J. Interventions in relation to anxiety in school. In C. D. Spielberger (Ed.), *Anxiety: Current trends in theory and research* (Vol. 2). New York: Academic Press, 1972.

Rozelle, R. M., & Campbell, D. T. More plausible rival hypothesis in the cross-lagged panel correlation technique. *Psychological Bulletin*, 1969, *71*, 74–80.

Ruebush, B. K. Anxiety. In H. W. Stevenson (Ed.), *Child psychology: The sixty-second yearbook of the National Society for the Study of Education* (Part 1). Chicago: University of Chicago Press, 1963.

Sarason, I. G. Anxiety and self-preoccupation. In I. G. Sarason & C. D. Spielberger (Eds.), *Stress and anxiety* (Vol. 2). Washington, DC: Hemisphere, 1975.

Sarason, I. G. The Test Anxiety Scale: Concept and research. In C. D. Spielberger & I. G. Sarason (Eds.), *Stress and anxiety* (Vol. 5). Washington, DC: Hemisphere, 1978.

Schaffner, P., & Laux, L. Der Einfluss der kognitiven und der emotionalen Angstkomponente auf die Prüfungsleistung bei Studenten. In L. H. Eckensberger (Ed.), *Bericht über den 31. Kongress der Deutschen Gesellschaft für Psychologie in Mannheim 1978.* Göttingen: Hogrefe, 1979.

Schwarzer, R. *Schulangst und Lernerfolg.* Düsseldorf: Schwann, 1975.

Spiegler, M. D., Morris, L. W., & Liebert, R. M. Cognitive and emotional components of test anxiety: Temporal factors. *Psychological Reports,* 1968, *22,* 451–456.

Spielberger, C. D., Gonzales, H. P., Taylor, C. J., Algaze, B., & Anton, W. D. Examination stress and test anxiety. In C. D. Spielberger & I. G. Sarason (Eds.), *Stress and anxiety* (Vol. 5). Washington, DC: Hemisphere, 1978.

Spielberger, C. D., O'Neil, H. F., & Hansen, D. N. Anxiety, drive theory and computer-assisted learning. In B. A. Maher (Ed.), *Progress in experimental personality research* (Vol. 6). New York: Academic Press, 1972.

Suppes, P. A probabilistic analysis of causality. In H. M. Blalock, A. Aganbegian, F. M. Borodkin, R. Boudon, & V. Capecchi (Eds.), *Quantitative sociology. International perspectives on mathematical and statistical modeling.* New York: Academic Press, 1975.

Weiner, B. *Theories of motivation: From mechanism to cognition.* Chicago: Markham, 1972.

Wermuth, N. Analogies between multiplicative models in contingency tables and covariance selection. *Biometrics,* 1976, *32,* 95–108. (a)

Wermuth, N. Model search among multiplicative models. *Biometrics,* 1976, *32,* 253–263. (b)

Wermuth, N. *Zusammenhangsanalysen medizinischer Daten.* Berlin: Springer, 1978.

Wermuth, N. Linear recursive equation, covariance selection, and path analysis. *Journal of the American Statistical Association,* in press.

Wermuth, N., Hodapp, V., & Weyer, G. Die Methode der Kovarianzselektion als Alternative zur Faktorenanalyse, untersucht an Persönlichkeitsmerkmalen. *Zeitschrift für experimentelle und angewandte Psychologie,* 1976, *23,* 320–338.

Werts, C. E., & Linn, R. L. Path analysis: Psychological examples. *Psychological Bulletin,* 1970, *74,* 193–212.

Weyer, G., & Hodapp, V. Job-stress and essential hypertension. In I. G. Sarason & C. D. Spielberger (Eds.), *Stress and anxiety* (Vol. 6), Washington, DC: Hemisphere, 1979.

Wonnacott, R. J., & Wonnacott, T. H. *Econometrics.* New York: Wiley, 1970.

Yee, D. H., & Gage, N. L. Techniques for estimating the source and direction of causal inference in panel data. *Psychological Bulletin,* 1968, *70,* 115–126.

REFERENCE NOTES

1. Weik, G. *Eine Untersuchung kausaler Beziehungen zwischen Angst und Rechenleistungen in 7. Hauptschulklassen mit Hilfe der Pfadanalyse.* Unpublished diploma thesis, University of Mainz, Germany, 1978.
2. Wüst, G. *Eine Panel-Studie zur kausalen Beziehung zwischen Angst und Rechenleistung bei Schülern 7. Hauptschulklassen.* Unpublished diploma thesis, University of Mainz, Germany, 1978.
3. Heinrich, D. L. *The causal influence of anxiety on academic achievement for students of differing intellectual ability.* Unpublished manuscript, Florida State University, 1977.

Author Index

Subject Index